ICCM - 2001

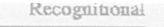

Proceedings of the 2001 Fourth International Conference on Cognitive Modeling

July 26 - 28, 2001
George Mason University
Fairfax, Virginia, USA

Erik M. Altmann, Axel Cleeremans,
Christian D. Schunn, & Wayne D. Gray

Sponsored by
Office of Naval Research
National Science Foundation
George Mason University College of Arts and Sciences
George Mason University Psychology Department
Air Force Research Laboratory Human Effectiveness Directorate
CHI Systems
BBN Technologies
George Mason University Human Factors and Applied Cognition

LAWRENCE ERLBAUM ASSOCIATES, PUBLISHERS

2001   **Mahwah, New Jersey**   **London**

Suggested format for citations taken from this volume:

Salvucci, D. D., & Macuga, K. L. (2001). Predicting the effects of cell-phone dialing on driver performance. In E. M. Altmann, A. Cleermans, C. D. Schunn, & W. D. Gray (Eds.), *Proceedings of the Fourth International Conference on Cognitive Modeling*. Mahwah, NJ: Lawrence Erlbaum Associates.

Distributed by Lawrence Erlbaum Associates, Inc.
10 Industrial Avenue
Mahwah, New Jersey, 07430

ISBN 0-8058-4042-7

Printed in the United States of America

Posters

Preface

ICCM - 2001 - Fourth International Conference on Cognitive Modeling.

Computational modeling has emerged as a central but complex and sometimes fractionated theme in research on cognition. ICCM provides a worldwide forum for cognitive scientists who build such computational cognitive models and test them against empirical cognitive data.

ICCM-2001 brought together researchers from diverse backgrounds to compare cognitive models, to evaluate models using human data, and to further the development, accumulation, and integration of cognitive theory. Attendees represented a wide variety of modeling approaches including symbolic production systems, connectionist, Bayesian, dynamic systems, and various hybrid approaches. As varied as the approaches to modeling were the systems that were modeled -- from taxi drivers' memory for street names, to automobile driving, to personality, to interhemispheric interaction, to the basal ganglia's role in learning and selecting motor behaviours

New features of ICCM-2001 included the Newell Award for best student paper and the Siegel-Wolf Award for the best applied research paper. The Newell Award was won by Michael D. Fleetwood for his paper with Michael Byrne, *Modeling Icon Search in ACT-R/PM*. The Siegel-Wolf award was won by Dario Salvucci and Kristan Macuga for their paper, *Predicting the effects of cell-phone dialing on driver performance*.

Another new feature of ICCM-2001 was the Doctoral Consortium. Seven doctoral students from universities around the world met with three faculty researchers the day before the rest of us began the Conference. The Doctoral Consortium provided an opportunity for the students to meet their peers and mentors and to explore their dissertation work in an intense but friendly, multi-approach environment. The work presented at the Doctoral Consortium was also presented during the ICCM-2001 poster session and is documented in this volume.

ICCM Committee

Conference Chair
Wayne D. Gray, George Mason University

Organizing Committee
Erik M. Altmann, Michigan State University
John R. Anderson, Carnegie Mellon
    University
Axel Cleeremans, Universite Libre de
    Bruxelles
Gary Cottrell, University of California, San
    Diego
John Hummel, University California, Los
    Angeles
Christian Lebiere, Carnegie Mellon
    University
Randy O'Reilly University of Colorado
Frank E. Ritter, The Pennsylvania State
    University
Christian D. Schunn, George Mason
    University
Gerhard Strube, University of Freiberg
Ron Sun, University of Missouri, Columbia
Niels Taatgen, University of Groningen
Richard M. Young, University of
    Hertfordshire

Local Arrangements
Christian D. Schunn, George Mason
    University
Deborah Krantz, George Mason University

Proceeding Editors
Erik M. Altmann, Michigan State University
Axel Cleeremans, Universite Libre de
    Bruxelles
Christian D. Schunn, George Mason
    University
Wayne D. Gray, George Mason University

Doctoral Consortium
Chair, Deborah A. Boehm-Davis, George
    Mason University
Stellan Ohlsson, University of Illinois,
    Chicago
Randy O'Reilly, University of Colorado

Awards Committee
Chair, Christian D. Schunn, George Mason
    University
Christian Lebiere, Carnegie Mellon
    University
Gregory Trafton, Naval Research
    Laboratory
Wayne Zachary, CHI Systems

Publications Committee
Deborah Krantz, George Mason University
Jeni Paluska, George Mason University
Frank E. Ritter, The Pennsylvania State
    University

Web Support
Anthony Harrison, George Mason
    University

Program Committee

Jans Aasman
KNP Research

Erik Altmann
Michigan State University

John Anderson
Carnegie Mellon University

Deborah Boehm-Davis
George Mason University

Bruce Burns
Michigan State University

Susan Chipman
Office of Naval Research

Axel Cleeremans
Université Libre de Bruxelles

Gary Cottrell
University of California, San Diego

Douglas Davidson
Michigan State University

Arnaud Destrebecqz
Université Libre de Bruxelles

Stephanie Doane
Mississippi State University

Dietrich Doerner
Universität Bamberg

Brian Ehret
Sun Microsystems

Michael Freed
NASA Ames Research Center

Danilo Fum
University of Trieste

Kevin GluckWilliams
Air Force Base

Fernand Gobet
Univerisity of Nottingham

Wayne Gray
George Mason University

Robert Holt
George Mason University

Anthony Hornof
University of Oregon

Andrew Howes
Cardiff University

Todd Johnson
University of Texas Houston

Irvin Katz
Educational Testing Service

Josef Krems
Technische Universität Chemnitz

Christian Lebiere
Carnegie Mellon University

Stephan Lewandowsky
The University of Western Australia

Richard Lewis
The University of Michigan

Marsha Lovett
Carnegie Mellon University

Michael Matessa
NASA Ames Research Center

Craig Miller
DePaul University

Fabio Missier
University of Trieste

Jessica Nowinski
NASA Ames Research Center

Randall O'Reilly
University of Colorado at Boulder

Stellan Ohlsson
The University of Illinois at Chicago

Alexander Petrov
Carnegie Mellon University

Richard Pew
BBN

Thad Polk
The University of Michigan

Matthias Rauterberg
Technische Universiteit Eindhoven

Robert Rist
University of Technology, Sydney

Frank Ritter
The Pennsylvania State University

Ardi Roelofs
Max Planck Institute for
Psycholinguistics

Dario Salvucci
Cambridge Basic Research

Michael Schoelles
George Mason University

Wolfgang Schoppek
Universität Bayreuth

Christian Schunn
George Mason University

Gerhard Strube
Universität Freiburg

Ron Sun
University of Missouri-Columbia

Niels Taatgen
University of Groningen

Gregory Trafton
Naval Research Laboratory

Maarten van Someren
University of Amsterdam

Alonso Vera
NASA Ames Research Center

Dieter Wallach
Universität Basel

Richard Young
University of Hertfordshire

Wayne Zachary
CHI Systems

Sponsors

Office of Naval Research

National Science Foundation

George Mason University College of Arts and Sciences

George Mason University Psychology Department

Air Force Research Laboratory Human Effectiveness Directorate

CHI Systems

BBN Technologies

George Mason University Human Factors and Applied Cognition

Invited Address

The Hidden Face of Representation in Modeling

Arthur B. Markman (markman@psy.utexas.edu)
Department of Psychology, University of Texas
Austin, TX 78712 USA

Representation

All computational models of cognition make some assumption about the nature of knowledge representation along with additional assumptions about the way those representations are processed. Indeed, part of the importance of developing cognitive models is that they make explicit a theory's assumptions about representation and process.

The importance of representation in cognitive modeling has led to a number of debates. For example, in the 1970s, considerable ink was spilled in a debate between proponents of analog and propositional representations for mental imagery. More recently, there has been significant discussion about whether cognitive science needs representation at all.

In this talk, I focus on three issues that have not taken center stage in debates over knowledge representation. First, there are two sources of meaning in mental representation, and proposals about representation differ in their reliance on these sources. Second, representations differ in what they are able to encode. Third, there is a mutual influence of representational assumptions and data collection that often goes unrecognized. I believe these issues lie at the heart of many discussions about representation.

Meaning and Mental Representation

There are two primary sources of meaning mental representation: *correspondence* and *functional role*. Briefly, correspondence means that a representational element stands in some relation to an item in a represented world. Functional role is the recognition that the meaning of some representation elements is dependent on its relationship to other representational elements.

Different proposals about representation rely on these sources of meaning to different degrees. For example, there has been much interest in dynamical systems as the basis for cognitive models, particularly in research on sensory and motor processes. Dynamical systems rely primarily on correspondence as a basis for meaning. In contrast, relational symbol systems of the sort that appear in production system models rely more heavily on functional role as a source of meaning. Both sources are important for explaining cognitive processing.

The Power of Representations

Representations also differ in what they are able to encode and in the operations they support. For example, spatial representations such as those derived from multidimensional scaling, many distributed connectionist systems, and high-dimensional semantic space models (like HAL and LSA) permit calculations of distance within a space, but do not support access to specific properties of a representation. Symbolic models may support access to specific properties at the expense of more laborious comparison processes. A failure to recognize the limitations of particular representational assumptions has led to many false starts in cognitive modeling. Because the same representational assumptions may be embedded in models that seem quite different on the surface (as in the three examples of spatial representations described above), it is possible to miss the way limitations of one system may signal limitations in other models that make the same representational assumptions.

Representation and Data Collection

An important part of cognitive modeling is the interplay between the model and data from human or animal subjects. Often a model is created to explain the data from a particular set of experiments. Then, new experiments are run to test the model. When cognitive science performs at its best, new studies lead to refinements in the model, which in turn lead to new studies.

A potential danger with this cycle is the possibility of creating data in the image of the model. For example, many mathematical models of classification tasks in psychology use arrays of independent dimensions. This assumption simplifies the mathematics, as it allows separate dimension weights to be calculated when fitting data and eases the creation of similarity metrics for determining the proximity among stimulus items. These assumptions are also incorporated into experimental materials. The stimuli in classification studies often involve items with an obvious set of independent dimensions. This parallel between the structure of the model and the design of the stimuli may inflate the degree to which subjects' performance fits a model's predictions. To combat this bias, experimenters must design studies that go beyond the representational assumptions of their models.

Allen Newell Award
for Student Paper

Introduction for Allen Newell Award for Student Paper

Everyone's cognitive science education should begin with a reading of Allen Newell's 1973 manifesto, "You can't play 20 questions with nature and win". Here he laid out the creed that guides us at this conference today. Beyond such tangibles, however, it was how Allen interacted with his students that makes it seem so apt to name the best student paper at ICCM in his honor.

For Allen, science was a democracy. Where other projects were hierarchical and local, the Soar project was egalitarian and distributed. All of us -- students, staff, faculty -- got our weekly time with him, no mean feat given that there may have been a score of us from time to time. The Soar leadership itself was distributed, across three sites each with its own principle investigator. And where sites in such projects typically communicated through PIs alone, Allen insisted that every nine months or so -- long enough for research to give birth to progress -- the entire Soar community congregate in one place to hear one another's reports. At these meetings, legendary for their staccato pace of short talks, everyone got a chance to speak. Characteristically, if Allen were caught in mid-stream when the buzzer sounded, he would stop dead, arm in mid-gesture, and break into a grin -- it was time for the next speaker. It mattered not whether it was a petrified first-year graduate student with five minutes to announce his or her intentions for the coming year, or a science writer playing participant-observer, or a programmer with a technical update, or a fellow PI with a daring new vision. This was Camelot, and we were all knights, because that's how science was done, and that's how science was fun.

Allen would like this conference. We have three days to think and talk about nothing but models and their role in understanding the mind. We have a healthy mix of integration, computation, and ideas from beyond the pale. We have students and project leaders presenting on the same stage. In short, now is not the time to relax -- we have all we need to keep us desperately busy.

Erik Altmann

Modeling Icon Search in ACT-R/PM

Michael D. Fleetwood and Michael D. Bryne
{fleet, byrne}@rice.edu)
Rice University, Department of Psychology
6100 Main Street MS-25, Houston, TX 77005 USA

Abstract

As the use of graphical user interfaces expands into new areas, icons are becoming an increasingly important aspect of GUIs. Oddly, little research has been done into the the costs and benefits associated with using icons. One aspect of icons, icon borders, has been proposed as a means of adding information to icons. An experiment was conducted in which the potential cost in response time of using simple icon borders was investigated. Two models were then constructed in ACT-R/PM to carry out the same icon search task as in the experiment. The results of the modeling effort indicated an area where the design of the experiment could be improved. A second, "improved" experiment was carried out, the results of which suggest areas for further improvement in the ACT-R/PM models.

Introduction

Graphical icons are a standard feature of most graphical user interfaces (GUIs), representing a range of commands and objects. Usage of icons is, if anything, on the rise as small, low-resolution displays (e.g. mobile phones, PDAs), which make display of large amounts of text difficult, proliferate. Unfortunately, there is strikingly little empirical and theoretical work on how users interact with icons. A clearer understanding of the ways in which users search iconic displays could be of great value to designers of such interfaces, possibly allowing the display of more information in less space. The studies in this paper are aimed at examining the visual search processes employed by users as they search displays of labeled icons, a task we call *icon search*.

One aim of this particular line of research is to better understand how iconic displays can convey more information without penalizing the user by increasing search time. This was done by exploring the impact of adding borders to icons. A second goal is to explore the use of computational modeling in this critical task domain. We would like, ultimately, to be able to predict search times of iconic displays on an *a priori* basis through the use of computational models. This is an iterative, symbiotic process (Gray & Altmann, 1999). That is, we use models to gain greater insights into an applied HCI problem, while at the same time using the applied problems to identify areas where the models and modeling architecture can be improved. In that spirit, the first experiment was aimed at understanding an applied issue, the impact of simple icon borders. We then constructed ACT-R/PM models of the experiment, which in turn drove us to revise the experiment. Results from that experiment indicate shortcomings in the

model and suggest places where our view of the strategies employed by users require revision.

1. Experiment 1

One aspect of icons that is ripe for improvement is the use of icon borders (Houde & Salomon, 1993). Currently icon borders are typically nothing more than a simple rectangle surrounding the graphical icon. Used in this manner, icon borders do little to convey additional information to the user. It may be that they only serve to add visual clutter to the display, and to provide another common element of targets and distractors, thereby potentially slowing down visual search (Mohr, 1984). It would be valuable to the graphical user interface (GUI) design community to have some understanding of the costs, if any, associated with using icon borders in this manner. It would also be valuable to gain some understanding of the relative efficiency or inefficiency of icon search in general. The following experiment was designed with these research goals in mind.

Figure 1. Some examples of the icons used in the experiments.

1.1 Method

1.1.1 Users

The users in the experiment were 20 undergraduate students at Rice University who were participating in order to meet a requirement for a psychology course.

1.1.2 Design

Three independent variables were manipulated, all of which were within-subjects factors. The first of these factors, set size, had four levels, 6, 12, 18, or 24 icons. A second within-subjects factor, target border, had three levels. The target icon to be searched for could be presented without a border (no-border condition), with a circle as a border (circle), or with a box as a border (square).

The final within-subjects factor, icon quality, had three levels. Icons were designed that varied in their level of distinctiveness. On one end of the spectrum were icons of "good" quality. These icons were designed to be easily distinguishable from other icons based on the basic visual ("pop-out") features of color and shape (specifically curvature). Icons in the good quality set were one of six colors (red, blue, green, yellow, brown, or black) and one of two shapes (circle or triangle). On the other end of the quality spectrum were icons that were not easily distinguishable (referred to as "poor" quality icons). They were designed to be distinguishable in a set of two icons, but quite indistinguishable in a large distractor set. These poor quality icons were all of the same basic shape and did not include color (other than white, black and shades of gray). The "fair" quality icons were designed to be representative of the area in between these two ends of the spectrum. They were generally of a distinct shape, although more complex than the simple circles and triangles in the good quality icons, and none of them contained any color outside of the spectrum of gray scale colors. Refer to Figure 1 for examples of borders and quality levels. Each block in the experiment consisted of 36 trials (4 set sizes x 3 borders x 3 qualities).

The dependent variable being measured was the response time of the users—specifically, the time from when they clicked on a "Ready" button to indicate that they were finished examining the target icon to when they clicked on the target icon among the set of distractor icons. When the "Ready" button was clicked, the button and the target icon were removed and the display containing the distractor icons was presented.

One potential independent variable that was held constant in this experiment was the number of icons matching the target in the search display. On each trial one-third of the icons in the search display had the same pictorial icon and matching border. Thus, ultimately the user was forced to differentiate among the icons by the filename.

The location of the target icon was randomly selected for each trial. Also randomly selected were the file names for the icons. The distractor file names and the target file names were randomly selected without replacement from a list of 750 names until the list was exhausted. At which time, the list was recycled.

Each user completed four blocks of trials in addition to the practice block for a total of 180 trials.

1.2 Results

In Figure 2, mean response times are presented as a function of set size and icon quality. Here, it is evident that as icon quality decreases (good to fair to poor), response times increase. This is confirmed by a significant main effect of quality, $F(2, 38) = 52.14$, $p < 0.001$. Also, not only are the three qualities significantly different, but the slopes of the lines appear to be different, as confirmed by a reliable quality by set size interaction, $F(6, 114) = 5.20$, $p < 0.01$.

Relevant to the hypothesis concerning borders, there was no effect of icon borders on search time, $F(2, 38) = 1.66$, $p = 0.20$, nor did borders interact with any other factors. This suggests that users can indeed ignore the icon borders, and

this may be an effective method for conveying additional information without increasing search costs.

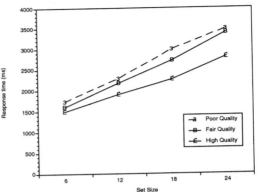

Figure 2. Mean response times by set size and icon quality, illustrating a main effect of icon quality.

2. Modeling the Experiment

We used ACT-R/PM (Byrne & Anderson, 1998) to model the experiment. Because the cognitive demands of the icon search task are minimal, modeling the perceptual-motor processes (e.g., shifting visual attention, pointing and clicking) with some fidelity is critical. The ACT-R/PM architecture combines ACT-R's theory of cognition (Anderson & Lebiére, 1998) with modal theories of visual attention (Anderson, Matessa, & Lebiére, 1997) and motor movement (Kieras & Meyer, 1997). ACT-R/PM explicitly specifies timing information for all three processes as well as parallelism between them.

2.1 The Task

The task performed by users seems simple: remember a target icon and filename, find it on a second display, and move the mouse to click on it. The first phase of this task, remembering the target icon and filename, is relatively straightforward to model in ACT-R/PM. The model attends the icon and selects a random element of the icon (e.g. "gray rectangle") to guide later search, which is noted in the goal chunk. The filename is also noted by storing it in the goal chunk. Searching for the target among the distractors in the second phase of each trial is more complex, and more than one strategy was implemented as described in the following section. Once the target icon was located, the model moved the mouse to the target and clicked on it.

2.2 The Models

Because our goal was to explore the space of strategies that users might employ, we constructed two models of the icon search task representing slightly different strategies. Both of the two strategies will be considered in some detail. Both of the models follow the same basic control structure but they differ slightly in strategy used to locate the target icon amongst distractors.

2.2.1 The "Double-Shift" (DS) Model

The double-shift model is so named because it requires two shifts of attention to examine each candidate icon. First, the model directs its visual attention to an icon that has at least one descriptive characteristic in common with the target icon (a red circle for example). This is done by finding a visual-location that contains the specific characteristic that was stored in the goal to "remember" the target icon. Then the model shifts attention to the filename directly below. This filename is compared with the target filename. If the filenames match, then visual attention is shifted back to the target icon so that it can be clicked on. If they do not match, then the process begins again by finding another icon on the distractor screen with the appropriate matching descriptive characteristic.

The quantitative predictions of this model are easy to compute in cases where there is no feature overlap between the target icon and the distractors, because the time parameters for all the operations are known and this model never re-visits icons on the display. For each icon examined, the model requires an additional 420 ms: one production to initiate the first shift to the icon (50 ms), time for the first shift (135 ms), one production to initiate the second shift to the filename (50 ms), time for the second shift (135 ms) and one production to do the comparison of the attended filename and the remembered filename (50 ms). Because there is no feature overlap in the "good" quality icons, and each set size adds two icons that match the target to the display (meaning on average one of them will be visited), the model clearly predicts a 420 ms slope for the RT by set size function for "good" icons. For other icon qualities, the slope depends on the degree of feature overlap between the target and the distractors. That is, if the target icon contained a gray square and the model selected that feature to guide search, then all icons on the display containing gray squares are candidates. The number of such icons will vary from trial to trial depending on the features in the target icon and the composition of the distractors, so Monte Carlo simulations are required to produce RT predictions.

2.2.2 The "Text-Look" (TL) Model

The text-look model is so named because attention is focused directly on the filename below the icon, and the actual icon is never actually attended. As in the double-shift model, an icon with a matching feature is located, but rather than shifting visual attention to the icon, it is shifted directly to the filename below the icon. This process is meant to simulate the process of preattentive search and the use of parafoveal vision by subjects. It is assumed in this model that under conditions where the target icon shares few features with the distractor icons—i.e. they are somewhat unique—then users do not need to examine the icon in detail, rather, they just look directly at the filename. The model does shift attention to the icon eventually, in order to move the mouse and click on it, but this attention shift only occurs after the target filename (and thus the target icon) has been identified.

Quantitative predictions from this model are not so easy to compute because this model may re-examine icons. This is because the icons themselves are never actually attended, and ACT-R/PM only "remembers" locations to which it has shifted attention. Because this revisitation is probabilistic, analytic predictions are difficult to derive and again Monte Carlo simulations are required.

2.3 Comparison of the Models

The two models represent slightly different strategies for the visual search. The DS model makes two shifts of attention per each additional icon examined, while the TL model makes only one, suggesting the TL model may be more efficient. However, the DS model does not revisit previously-seen items, which could make the DS model more efficient. We had no *a priori* predictions about which model would actually be faster.

The models have some key similarities as well. The production which selects the next icon to be examined selects randomly from all the candidates that match the remembered feature (e.g. "gray circle"). That is, there is no right-to-left or top-to-bottom pattern employed by the models. Because the location of the target was random, incorporating such a strategy would have made little difference in the ultimate predictions of the model in this experiment. Furthermore, the models employ the same strategy for all set sizes and icon qualities. These properties will be discussed further later in the paper.

Finally, both models depend on the representation of the icons themselves. Each icon is "seen" by ACT-R/PM's Vision Module as a list of features. For the "good" quality icons, this list is a singleton; that is, each icon is represented by a single feature (e.g. "red circle"). In contrast, more complex icons will have a number of features and colors associated with them, gray triangles, white circles, etc. What makes these more complex icons "poor" icons in the experiment is not the number of features the icon has per se, but rather the number of features the icon shares with other icons in the distractor set. For example, many of the icons in the poor quality set have gray triangles and white circles. As a result, the model will often examine icons that do not match the target icon exactly, but rather only share one particular feature with the target icon. It is this overlap of features, or "similarity," that makes such icons poor icons in context. In contrast, the good quality icons have no feature overlap with other good quality icons, and thus, only icons exactly matching the target icon are examined by the model. The exact nature and number of the features used to represent each icon in the "fair" and "poor" conditions are free parameters in the models; however, we used the same feature sets for both the DS and TL models.

2.4 Simulation Results

The model data was gathered by running the models for 80 blocks of trials, which approximates the number of real blocks of subject data involved.

It is clear from Figure 3 that the performance of the model is quite similar to that of real subjects. The model and the data show some divergence at the largest set size. This is

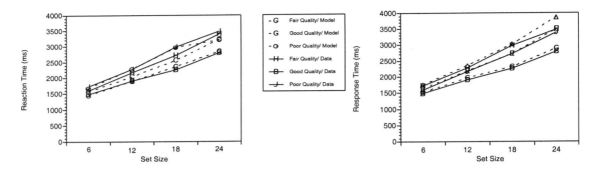

Figure 3. Mean response times by set size and icon quality for the TL model (left) and the DS model (right).

somewhat to be expected due to the greater amount of variability in reaction times at large set sizes. Most importantly, the model has retained each of the pronounced effects that were seen in the data—those of set size and iconquality. A final quantitative comparison of the two sets of data was obtained by examining the correlation and the percent mean deviation (root-mean-square) between the two sets of mean reaction times.

The R^2 between the data matrices for both the text-look and double-shift models is 0.98. The high correlation between the models and the data suggest that the models both do an excellent job of accounting for the major trends in the data. This provides some measure of validation for the models and the timing parameters incorporated into ACT-R/PM. However, these fits also depended on hand-tweaking of the basic visual features used to represent the icons, which will be discussed in the next section.

The root mean square error (RMSE) and percent average absolute error between the model and the data for the two charts shown previously are presented in Table 1. Note that the percent average absolute error in each of the above matrices of data remains in the remarkably low range of three percent—again indicating that the models were quite accurate in their performance in reference to the real subject data.

Table 1. Quantitative analysis of model data as compared to experiment data—root mean squared error and percent average absolute error.

	Double-Shift	Text-Look
RMSE	125.41ms	112.28 ms
Percent average absolute error	2.95%	3.19%

2.5 Discussion of Models

Based on the standard fit metrics, the fit of the models to the data is excellent for both models. The difference between the DS and TL models was very small, suggesting the increased number of attention shifts

generated by the DS model were, in effect, cancelled out by the revisitation of the TL model. Based on the fits, there is no strong argument for preferring one model over the other, suggesting that strategy variation among users may not play a large role in determining search times. This was highly encouraging. However, there are two caveats. The first is that the feature lists used to represent each icon were generated *post hoc* to provide good fits of model to data. Ideally, we would like to have a principled way of constructing the feature lists on an *a priori* basis to make the models predictive rather than simply explanatory. This is an involved subject for future research.

The second caveat is that the DS model makes an analytic point prediction about the slope of the RT vs. set size function of 420 ms. What was distressing about this is that the observed slope *as well as the slope generated by the model* were approximately 460 ms. This was a surprise for us, and caused us to carefully re-examine the behavior of the model because it did not match our own analytic prediction. This led us to the discovery of an interesting point in the programming of the experiments. When the experiments were designed and programmed, we originally expected icon borders to play some significant role in the search strategies of users. One factor that we wanted to keep consistent in our design was the number of icons identical to the target icon except with different filenames (one-third of the icons in the set). However, because we assumed that icons with different borders would be seen as different than the target icon, we allowed icons matching the target icon except for the border to be included in the distractor set. As this experiment (and others we have conducted) have shown, borders such as those used in the experiment do not play a role in icon search. Thus, icons with different borders but with the same base pictorial icon may be seen as functionally the same icon. Because the distractor icons were chosen randomly, the experiment software occasionally (and randomly) allowed one or more additional (beyond the predetermined one-third) icons matching the target icon but with a different border to be present in the distractor set. The inclusion of this additional icon drove up reaction times for both users and the model, and was a cause of the steeper than predicted slope.

While this was certainly a flaw in the design of the experiment, it speaks to a strength of the approach employed. The ACT-R/PM models interact with the same experimental software as human subjects, and thus are sensitive to the same factors. It was therefore encouraging to see that the model was affected by this flaw as well, and we certainly would not have noticed this flaw had it not been for the (mis)behavior of the DS model. As a result, in order to examine the model's predictions, and directly compare its results with those of users, we needed to remove this element of randomness from our design, and a follow-up experiment was conducted which did just that.

3. Experiment 2

By removing the aforementioned source of unpredictability in our program and, hence, a source of randomness or unexplained variance in our data, Experiment 2 was designed to get a "cleaner" picture of the data to allow for comparisons with a computational model.

3.1 Method

The design, procedures and apparatus of Experiment 2 were nearly identical to those of Experiment 1. The only factor that changed was the number of distractor icons in the distractor set that matched the target icon. In Experiment 2, distractor icons with the same base pictorial icon, but with a different border, were allowed to be randomly selected for the distractor set. In this experiment, icons with the same base pictorial icon as the target icon were excluded from the distractor set. The users in the experiment were 20 undergraduate students at Rice University who were participating in order to meet a requirement for a psychology course.

3.2 Results

In Figure 4, mean response times are presented as a function of set size and icon quality. Here again, as in Experiment 1, it is evident that as icon quality decreases (good to fair to poor), response times increase. This is confirmed by a significant main effect of quality, $F(2, 38) = 58.71$, $p < 0.001$. Also, not only are the three qualities significantly different, but the slopes of the lines appear to be different, as confirmed by a reliable quality by set size interaction, $F(6, 114) = 6.89$, $p < 0.01$. Additionally, as in the first experiment, there was no effect of icon borders on search time, $F(2, 38) = 1.10$, $p = 0.34$, nor did borders interact with any other factors.

3.3 Discussion of Experiment 2

Clearly, this experiment was able to produce the same general results from Experiment 1—effects of icon quality and set size and a lack of an effect of icon borders. Such replication allows us to draw our conclusions with even greater confidence.

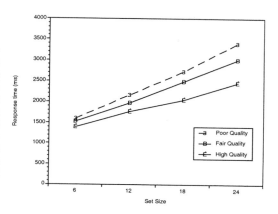

Figure 4. Mean response times by set size and icon of quality, illustrating a main effect of icon quality.

The particular aspect of this experiment that we were most interested in was not, however, these broader effects. We were interested in closely examining the effect of set size on the high quality icons. Specifically, we wanted to study the slope of the reaction time by set-size function for the good quality icons and determine if it approximated 420 ms, the value predicted by the DS model.

At first glance, the slope of the line appears to be shallower than 420 ms. The specific data points that make up the line are presented in Table 2 below. The average slope for the four data points was calculated as 355.08, quite a bit lower than 420 ms.

Table 2. Mean Reaction Times for Good Quality Icons across set size.

Set Size	6	12	18	24
RT (ms)	1385	1765	2042	2451

We computed the slope for each subject and generated the 95% confidence interval for the slope, which covered 311 ms/icon to 392 ms/icon. Thus, the model's analytic prediction of 420 ms is clearly an overestimation of the true slope. This is a significant misfit of the data by the model, and provides the impetus for a revision of the model.

Section 4: General Discussion

Our model, in fact, is too slow. Real subjects can find the icon faster than our model can under optimal conditions of zero feature overlap. The solution then is to change the model, but that is certainly easier said than done. There are numerous ways that the strategy of real subjects may differ from the strategy implemented by the model. It would make sense then to investigate what the real strategies of users are in the icon search task. In order to do this, one would have to actually study users' eye movements while engaged in the task, accomplished through the use of an eye tracker.

Our current research is therefore concentrated on eye tracking the icon search task. Initial data have been collected, and although they have yet to be quantitatively analyzed, two aspects of users' search strategies are apparent from a purely qualitative look at the data. For one, it seems that users employ different search strategies based on the quality of the icons. For example, one strategy employed in the good quality condition is a "global grouping effect." In this condition, it appears that users are able to identify clusters of icons preattentively. Having identified a group of icons that match the target icon, they begin their search in this group. In this manner, they do not follow a simple left to right or random strategy of examining icons that match the target icon. In contrast, in the poor quality condition, there is no apparent directed strategy to any group of icons or area of the screen. Some of the users' quicker response times, relative to the model response times, may be due to such a directed and superior strategy.

Another pattern that is suggested by the data is potentially that a strategy approximating the text-look strategy is more frequently employed by users than the double-shift strategy. It appears that users rarely look directly at the icon before looking at the filename below it. However, even the text-look strategy falls short of the behavior of users. Often, they do not have to even look at the filename in order to reject it as a possible candidate for the filename they are searching for. For example, users seem to be able to reject certain filenames based on the length of the word. If they are looking for a short filename they can reject a long filename without actually reading it and vice versa. In order to extract such information from the display without foveating the source of the information, users must be able to extract information parafoveally.

We would like to be able to incorporate these two findings into an improved version of the icon search model. ACT-R/PM currently assumes a direct correspondence between unobservable attention shifts and observable eye movements; that is, people fixate the target of attention. Such an assumption holds in some cases, but it is agreed upon in the research community that it does not hold in general (Henderson, 1992; Rayner, 1995). The experiments modeled here may provide an example of one such case where this does not hold. Therefore, in order to model the experiment accurately in ACT-R/PM, some of the underlying assumptions of the Vision Module need to be improved upon. Fortunately, there already exist computational models that serve as a bridge between observable eye movements and the unobservable cognitive processes and shifts of attention that produce them, such as EMMA (Eye Movements and Movements of Attention) developed by Salvucci (2000).

Such a recommendation for improving ACT-R/PM illustrates the symbiotic, iterative nature of empirical experimentation and computational modeling that was alluded to previously. We initially turned to modeling in order to get a better conception of an applied task and some experiments dealing with that task, icon search. Indeed, the modeling effort proved valuable in this respect, even pin-pointing where the conceptual design of our study needed to be improved. However, the implementation of these improvements in our experimental design has brought to our attention an aspect of the Vision Module in ACT-R/PM that might be improved. Our next step is to turn to creating a new model of the icon search task based on the information in the eye-tracking study.

References

Anderson, J. R., & Lebiere, C. (1998). *The Atomic Components of Thought*. Mahwah, NJ: Lawrence Erlbaum Associates.

Anderson, J. R., Matessa, M., & Lebiere, C. (1997). ACT-R: A theory of higher level cognition and its relation to visual attention. *Human-Computer Interacton*, 12, 439-462.

Byrne, M. D. & Anderson, J. R. (1998). Perception and Action. In J. R. Anderson & C. Lebiere (Eds.) *Atomic components of thought*. Hillsdale, NJ: Erlbaum.

Gray, W. D., & Altman, E. M. (1999) Cognitive modeling and human-computer interaction. In W. Karwowski (Ed.), *International encyclopedia of ergonomics and human factors*. New York: Taylor & Francis, Ltd.

Henderson, J. M. (1992). Visual attention and eye movement control during reading and picture viewing. In K. Rayner (Ed.), *Eye Movements and Visual cognition: Scene Perception and Reading*. New Your: Springer-Verlag.

Houde, S. and Salomon, G. (1993). Working towards rich and flexible file representations. *Proceedings of the CHI '94 conference companion on Human factors in computing systems*.

Kieras, D. E., & Meyer, D. E. (1997). A computational theory of executive cognitive processes and multiple-task performance: Part 1. Basic mechanisms. *Psychological Review*, 104, 3-65.

Mohr, W. (1984). Visuelle Wahrnehmung und Zeichenfunktion, (Roderer, Regensburg); cited in Scott, 1993.

Rayner, K. (1995). Eye movements and cognitive processes in reading, visual search, and scene perception. In J. M. Findlay, R. Walker, & R. W. Kentridge (Eds.) *Eye Movement Research: Mechanisms, Processes, and Applications*. New York: Elsevier Science Publishing.

Salvucci, D. D. (2000). *An integrated model of eye movements and visual encoding*. Submitted manuscript.

Scott, D. (1993). Visual search in modern human-computer interfaces, *Behaviour & Information Technology*, 12, 174-189.

Siegel-Wolf Award
for Best Applied Paper

The Siegel-Wolf Award for Best Applied Paper

The Siegel-Wolf award is named in recognition of the seminal work of Art Siegel and Jay Wolf, who worked together at Applied Psychological Services, Inc. in Wayne, PA in the late 1950s through the 70s. In a collaboration that spanned more than twenty years, Jay and Art developed a series of computer simulation models to predict and analyze human performance in complex systems such as submarines and nuclear power plants. At a time when both computers and modeling of human information processing were still very new ideas (their first models, which were published in 1958, were executed on very early computers), they already saw great potential for human performance simulations to be applied to practical problems. Their models incorporated representations of decision-making, psychomotor reaction times and accuracies, and even the effects of stress and fatigue, and developed the concepts and principles of hierarchical decomposition of tasks into finer-grained building blocks which could be modeled separately and then aggregated. This approach is still the fundamental notion in most varieties of tasks analysis, cognitive task analysis, and human performance modeling in use today.

The basic 'Siegel-Wolf' model, used a hierarchical network representation for the task structure and then provided various ways for assigning performance parameters to the lowest level task nodes and aggregating these elemental performance parameters to generate global performance predictions. Eventually, they expanded this individual human-operator modeling framework to represent performance of teams of multiple interacting operators.

Art and Jay never produced a general-purpose modeling shell, only a series of specific applications. As a result their models were never used very widely beyond the initial developers. The approach was very generally used, however. One notable general-purpose modeling tool that carried on the Siegel-Wolf concept was called SAINT (Systems Analysis through Integrated Networks of Tasks) that continues in wide use today in many academic and commercial derivatives.

Although Art was an experimental psychologist, Jay was a mathematician with no academic training in human behavior. He brought a fresh insight and formal way of thinking to develop modeling strategies and approaches that are used across the cognitive modeling field today. Art Siegel died in 1985, and Jay Wolf passed away in late 2000. Having worked in the private sector, they produced no students, but rather left an influential body of work and an example that even the most advanced thinking in human modeling can have direct and immediate application to the 'real world.'

Wayne Zachary and Floyd Glenn, III

Predicting the Effects of Cell-Phone Dialing on Driver Performance

Dario D. Salvucci (dario@cbr.com)
Kristen L. Macuga (kristen@cbr.com)
Nissan Cambridge Basic Research, Four Cambridge Center
Cambridge, MA 02142 USA

Abstract

Legislators, journalists, and researchers alike have recently directed a great deal of attention to the effects of cellular telephone ("cell phone") use on driver behavior and performance. This paper demonstrates how cognitive modeling can aid in understanding these effects by predicting the impact of cell-phone dialing in a naturalistic driving task. We developed models of four methods of cell-phone dialing and integrated these models with an existing driver model of steering and speed control. By running this integrated model, we generated *a priori* predictions for how each dialing method affects the accuracy of steering and speed control with respect to an accelerating and braking lead vehicle. The model predicted that the largest effects on driver performance arose for dialing methods with high visual demand rather than methods with long dialing times. We validated several of the model's predictions with an empirical study in a fixed-based driving simulator.

Introduction

Driving is a highly complex skill that requires the continual integration of interdependent perceptual, motor, and cognitive processes. Nevertheless, driving becomes routine enough to many of us that we can comfortably perform minor secondary tasks while driving — for instance, turning on headlights or adjusting the defogger. However, technological advances now enable the incorporation of increasingly sophisticated devices in the vehicle for both driver support (e.g., navigation aids) and "infotainment" (e.g., news and email). In particular, cellular telephones (or "cell phones") have received a great deal of attention related to the potentially distracting effects of cell-phone use while driving (e.g., Alm & Nilsson, 1995; McKnight & McKnight, 1993; Reed & Green, 1999; Serafin et al., 1993). While it may be convenient to have devices such as cell phones available for driver use, safety is clearly the primary concern, and thus it is essential that we understand the impact that in-car devices may have on driver behavior and performance.

This paper demonstrates how cognitive modeling can aid in this effort by predicting the effects of secondary devices on driver performance. In particular, we focus on the task of cell-phone dialing and the impact that dialing has on driving. To this end, we utilize an integrated modeling approach that centers on combining cognitive models of the primary and secondary tasks into a single integrated model (Salvucci, 2001; see also Aasman, 1995). We begin with a task analysis of cell-phone dialing for four distinct dialing methods and describe straightforward models for these methods implemented in the ACT-R cognitive architecture (Anderson & Lebiere, 1998). We then combine the dialing models with an existing ACT-R model of driver behavior (Salvucci, Boer, & Liu, in press), producing an integrated model that can interleave dialing and driving. Finally, we run the integrated model to generate behavioral protocols, which in turn embody *a priori* predictions about the effects of the dialing on driving (as well as vice-versa).

This study improves and extends an initial modeling study of cell-phone dialing and driving (Salvucci, 2001) in two important ways. First, the previous study used a simplified cell-phone interface with a non-functional phone keypad and examined four invented dialing methods based on this interface. In contrast, this study uses a commercially-available cell phone and examines four dialing methods built into this phone. Second, the previous study involved a simpler task in which drivers dialed the phone while steering down a single-lane straight road at a constant speed. In contrast, this study involves a more complex and naturalistic environment in which drivers dial while navigating down a curvy lane in a construction zone and following lead cars at highly varying speeds. These two aspects of the new study provide increased realism and allow us to predict and examine the effects of dialing not only on driver steering but also on driver speed control during car following in a naturalistic task. We should note that while conversation on cell phones may also impact driver behavior, this study focuses specifically on the dialing component of cell-phone use.

The Driving and Dialing Task

In studying the effects of cell-phone dialing on driving, we desired a task in which both the dialing and the driving would be as realistic and natural as possible. However, for the driving task, potential safety concerns as well as legal restrictions due to driver distraction precluded the use of an actual vehicle on real roadways. Thus, we chose a task in which drivers navigated a naturalistic roadway in our medium-fidelity driving

Figure 1. Driving task environment, shown as a sample scene from the driving simulator with construction cones, lead cars, and rear-view mirror.

simulator (Beusmans & Rensink, 1995). The simulated environment was a three-lane highway in a construction zone with driving restricted to the center lane, as shown in Figure 1. The road alternated between segments of straight roadway and segments of various curvatures, all of which could be negotiated comfortably at highway speeds without braking. The driver followed three cars and was tailed by another car, which was visible in the simulated rear-view mirror. The speed of lead car varied from 5-35 m/s (11-78 mph) according to a sum of three sinusoids that resulted in an apparently random pattern. The rear car followed at distance of 9-21 m (29-68 ft) also varying as the sum of three sinusoids. Cones on either side of the center lane prevented drivers from passing other cars and emphasized the need for maintaining a central lane position. Thus, the cell-phone dialing scenario could be thought of in terms of the driver being caught up in a construction zone and needing to call several people to notify them of a delay.

For the dialing task, we employed a commercially-available cell phone (Samsung SCH-3500 with Sprint PCS), shown in Figure 2. This phone (like many similar phones) allows for multiple methods of dialing. In order to examine differential effects of various dialing methods, we chose four of the phone's built-in methods, which can be described as follows:

- *Manual*: dial the phone number and press **Talk**

- *Speed*: dial the party's single-digit "speed number" and press **Talk**

- *Menu*: press the up arrow to access menu, scroll down to the desired party with the down arrow, and press **Talk**

- *Voice*: press and hold **Talk**, say the party's name when prompted, and wait for confirmation

Table 1 shows examples of using each of these dialing methods to make a call. Note that two of the methods, speed and menu dialing, require that numbers be added to an internal phone book and associated with a unique

Figure 2. Cell phone and keypad.

"speed number." The four methods thus serve well to illustrate our modeling approach for comparing effects of different dialing methods on driver performance.

The Integrated Dialing-Driving Model

The prediction of effects of dialing on driving centers on an integrated cognitive model that combines individual models for each task. To facilitate the development and integration of these models, we implemented the models in the ACT-R cognitive architecture (Anderson & Lebiere, 1998). ACT-R is a production-system architecture based on condition-action rules that execute the specified actions when the specified conditions are met. Like most cognitive architectures, ACT-R provides a rigorous framework for cognitive models as well as a set of built-in parameters and constraints on cognition and perceptual-motor behavior (when using ACT-R/PM: Byrne & Anderson, 1998); the parameters facilitate *a priori* predictions about behavior, while the constraints facilitate more psychologically (and neurally) plausible models. In addition, the architecture allows for straightforward integration of models of multiple tasks: generally speaking, the modeler can combine the models' rule sets and modify the rules to interleave the multiple tasks (see Salvucci, 2001). All these qualities of the architecture are essential to our ability to integrate models of dialing and driving to predict the effects of each task on the other.

Dialing Models

We first consider the development of the cognitive models for dialing the cell phone using each of the four methods. To this end we employed a straightforward task analysis and implemented a simple, minimal model for each method based on this analysis. The procedure required by the cell phone highly constrains the model in that it specifies the sequence of keypresses needed to dial. However, the model must also incorporate the cognitive and perceptual processes needed to execute the procedure.

Table 1. Cell-phone dialing methods with examples and task models. Sample calls are based on calling "Jenny" at the number 867-5309 with speed number 3. The model outlines include sequences of steps in which each step is implemented in the model as an ACT-R production rule. Steps marked with ↵ indicate that the model cedes control to the driving task after executing the step.

Method	Manual	Speed	Menu	Voice
Sample Call	Press 8, 6, 7, 5, 3, 0, 9 Press **Talk**	Press 3 Press **Talk**	Press ▲ (display menu with first item selected) Press ▼, ▼ (scroll down to third item) Press **Talk**	Press and hold **Talk** Hear prompt Say "Jenny" Hear "Jenny" Hear "Connecting…"
Model Outline	Recall phone number Move hand to phone ↵ Attend to phone Recall number block Press digit (repeat until last digit) Press last digit ↵ (repeat until last block) Attend to phone Press **Talk** ↵ Move hand to wheel ↵	Recall speed number Move hand to phone ↵ Attend to phone Press speed number ↵ Attend to phone Press **Talk** ↵ Move hand to wheel ↵	Recall speed number Move hand to phone ↵ Attend to phone Press ▲ ↵ Attend to phone Press ▼ (repeat until speed number is reached) ↵ Attend to phone Press **Talk** ↵ Move hand to wheel ↵	Move hand to phone ↵ Attend to phone Press **Talk** ↵ Move hand to wheel ↵ Confirm prompt Say name ↵ Confirm name ↵ Confirm connection ↵

Table 1 includes an outline of the dialing models for each method. We employed a few simple rules to augment the basic procedures with cognitive and perceptual processes. First, we assumed that drivers look at the phone to guide their keypresses and that they group these keypresses in small blocks to minimize the time during which the eyes are off the road. Second, we assumed that for the manual condition, drivers chunk their keying of the seven-digit number as a sequence of three, two, and two digits, for the purposes of keeping working memory load low in addition to minimize off-road gaze time. Third, we assume that drivers move their right hand to the phone just before the first keypress and move back to the steering wheel just after the final keypress. Of course, these assumptions may not hold for all drivers; for instance, drivers very familiar with dialing on this particular phone may be able to type by feel without looking. However, these models nicely represent drivers who are familiar with using cell phones but are beginners or intermediates at using the phone while driving.

Driving Model

To model driver behavior, we employed an existing ACT-R model that drives in naturalistic simulated highway environments, including multi-lane highways with other vehicle traffic (Salvucci, Boer, & Liu, in press). In essence, this model controls steering and speed based on two salient visual features of the roadway: the "near point" centered immediately in front of the vehicle, which guides lane positioning; and the

"far point" -- either a distant roadway point or a lead vehicle -- which guides prediction and response to the upcoming road. These features are encoded and control is updated through an augmented version of ACT-R's perceptual-motor mechanisms (ACT-R/PM: Byrne & Anderson, 1998). The model in the initial study (Salvucci, 2001) included and tested only the steering component of the model; this study includes and tests both the steering and speed control components of the model, allowing us to examine for similar and/or parallel effects across modalities.

Although space constraints here preclude a full description of the driver model, we should note two important aspects of the model that are critical to this study. First, because of its implementation in the ACT-R architecture, the model has very limited parallelism (in its perceptual-motor modules) and thus must encode the visual scene and update control in a sequential fashion. When the model performs secondary tasks, its processing for these tasks takes away from processing of the primary driving task, and thus the model cannot update control as frequently. Second, the model generates time-stamped behavioral protocols through its perceptual-motor modules, including both vehicle control and eye-movement data. This aspect facilitates straightforward comparison between model and human behavior for effects of cell-phone dialing on driving using the same standard metrics, as discussed in the next section.

Integrated Model

As mentioned earlier, the integration of the dialing and driver models is accomplished by combining the rule sets and modifying them slightly such that the integrated model interleaves both tasks. The integrated model in this study was formed in this straightforward manner, just as the integrated model in the initial study (Salvucci, 2001). Briefly, the driver model decides on each control cycle whether it can safely perform a secondary task for a short time; this decision depends on several aspects of the environment, such as stability of the near and far points, lane position, and time headway. If the model determines that the car is stable, it passes control to the dialing model. After some incremental processing (described below), the dialing model passes control back to driving and the driver model again handles the primary task.

The primary difficulty of integration arises in determining when the dialing model should cede control back to the driver model. As in the initial study, we determined these points through task analysis and a simple heuristic: any step that would block and wait for some process to complete — for instance, moving the hand to the phone or listening for a prompt — should cede control to the driver model. The exception to this rule arises in the perceptual processes: because the dialing models are required to look at the phone during keypresses (by assumption), they must wait for the eyes to reach the phone and then execute a short block of keypresses before ceding control. The determination of these blocks was performed by task analysis; for instance, for menu dialing, we assumed that drivers press the down arrow quickly in succession to scroll down to the desired party, and that they maintain their gaze on the phone for both keypresses and monitoring the phone display. The steps after which the dialing models cede control to driving are indicated in Table 1 with the symbol ✍.

One final concern for the integrated model is the setting of parameter values. Almost all parameter values in the integrated model were ported directly from the integrated model in the initial study (Salvucci, 2001). We changed the value of one parameter, the desired following time headway, from 1 to 2 seconds to better represent how drivers fall back from a lead car when they expect a high workload (i.e., dialing the phone). We also assumed a 1 second duration for the speech signal representing the dialed party's name for the voice dialing method.

Model Simulation and Validation

Given the integrated model, we generated behavioral protocols and examined the model's *a priori* predictions about the effects of dialing on driving. In addition, we collected analogous protocols from human drivers performing the dialing-driving task in a fixed-base driving simulator. This section describes the collection of these data and the comparison and validation of the model's predictions to the human data.

Model Simulations

The model was given the simulator driving task (see Figure 1) starting behind the lead car at a full stop. After one minute of driving to accelerate to highway speed, the model was made to dial the cell phone using one of the four methods. When dialing was completed, the model drove normally for 20 seconds until again made to dial the phone. This continued at 20-second intervals until the model had dialed 8 times using each of the four dialing methods for a total of 32 trials in a driving session. We ran a total of 8 model sessions. Separately, we ran another 8 sessions in which the model simply dialed the phone without driving, thus giving us baseline data on the model's dialing times.

Empirical Study

Seven licensed subjects between the ages of 18-40 with at least 2 years of driving experience participated in the experiment. Subjects each performed one session of the driving task in the Nissan CBR driving simulator (Beusmans & Rensink, 1995). The phone (with headset) was mounted on the center console positioned just to the right of the steering wheel, so that the subject could dial without holding the phone. Before driving, subjects listed four regularly-dialed phone numbers and practiced dialing these numbers with each of the four methods. Subjects then completed a driving session completely analogous to that for the model: after an initial one minute, the experimenter asked the subject to dial the phone using a particular method (in a blocked manner, such that all calls using one method occurred consecutively). The data thus comprised 32 dialing trials (8 trials per method) per subject. Collected data included vehicle control data as well as eye-movement data using an IScan (Burlington, MA) head-mounted eye tracker. In addition, prior to and following the driving session, baseline dialing time data were collected with subjects dialing without driving.

Results

Figure 3 shows the results for both the model simulation and the human drivers. The results include analysis along four measures: dialing time, or time to complete dialing either with driving or without driving ("baseline"); lateral deviation, or RMS error of the vehicle's lane position with respect to the lane center; speed deviation, or RMS error of the vehicle's speed with respect to the speed of the lead vehicle; and gazes to the phone.

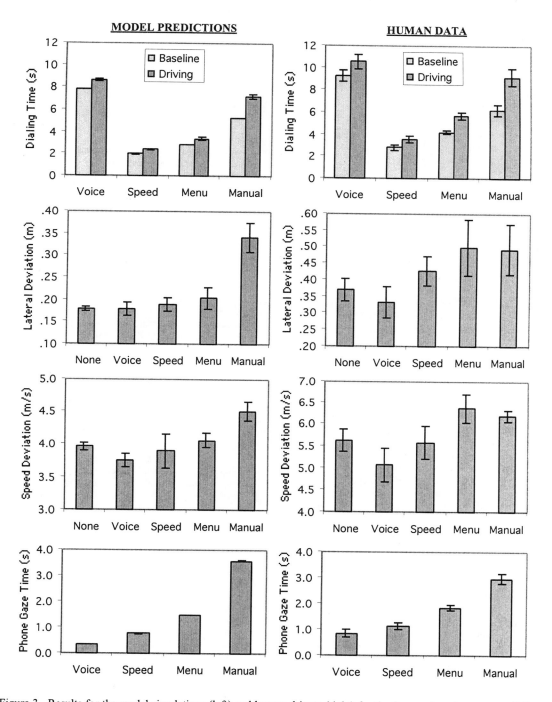

Figure 3. Results for the model simulations (left) and human drivers (right) for the four analyzed measures: dialing time, lateral (lane) deviation, speed deviation, and gaze time at phone per dialing trial. Error bars for the human data represent standard errors of subject means; bars for the model predictions represent standard errors over simulation run means. Note that some adjacent graphs are plotted on different scales to best display the overall patterns.

The model's predictions for dialing time indicate that voice and manual dialing require the most time while speed and menu dialing require the least. Dialing times increase approximately half a second to three seconds while driving. These predictions, which arise primarily from ACT-R's perceptual-motor parameters and the specification of the models from task analysis, correspond very well to the human data, $R > .99$.

The predictions for lateral deviation and speed deviation indicate the effects of dialing on driver performance. The model predicts increasing deviations for the methods in the order of voice, speed, menu, and manual dialing. For both measures, manual dialing results in deviations much greater than any of the other methods. Compared to the human data, we see a similar overall pattern with lower deviations for voice and speed dialing and higher deviations for manual dialing. However, human drivers exhibited similar deviations for menu and manual dialing. We suspect that the cognitive time needed for human drivers to retrieve the speed number as needed for menu and speed dialing was larger than the model predicted, and thus the model underpredicted the performance effects in these conditions. In addition, the magnitudes of the model predictions are approximately half those for the human drivers (note the different graph scales); however, it should be noted that effects in driving simulators are commonly larger than those in real-world field studies (Reed & Green, 1999). In any case, the model seems to capture the basic rank-order effects of the various dialing methods, $R = .65$ for lateral deviation, $R = .75$ for speed deviation.

The model also predicts the mean total time of gazes to the phone per dialing trial. While these predictions are related to our task analysis in determining the frequency of phone gazes, they do incorporate emergent predictions of gaze durations and illustrate how the dialing methods differ with respect to visual demands. The model and human data correspond well, $R > .99$.

Taken together, the model predictions suggest that total dialing time does not seem to be a good indicator of the effects of a given dialing method on driver performance (as measured by lateral and speed deviations): although voice dialing required the most time, it produced the smallest deviations, while two faster methods, speed and menu dialing, produced larger deviations. Instead, visual demand as measured by phone gazes *does* seem to be a good indicator of the effects of a method on driver performance: the methods with the least visual demand resulted in the smallest deviations and vice-versa. These predictions are confirmed by the empirical data. Of course, this does not mean that visual demand is the only contributor to driver distraction — for instance, conversation and conversation-like tasks seem also to affect driver behavior (see Serafin et al., 1993, for a review).

Conclusions

We have demonstrated that the integrated model approach helps to predict and evaluate the effects of cell-phone dialing on driver performance. However, the approach can be generalized to assess arbitrary on-board interfaces such as navigation devices, climate controls, and "infotainment" systems. Given an arbitrary interface, a straightforward task analysis can be performed to develop new models of behavior for the interface; as is common with modeling frameworks such as GOMS (Card, Moran, & Newell, 1983). By integrating these models with the driver model, developers can predict and compare the effects of different interfaces and narrow down the number of interfaces to analyze more rigorously through prototyping and field testing. We hope that the integrated model approach can thus facilitate the development and testing of safer, less distracting on-board systems and devices.

References

Aasman, J. (1995). Modelling driver behaviour in Soar. Leidschendam, The Netherlands: KPN Research.

Alm, H., & Nilsson, L. (1995). The effects of a mobile telephone task on driver behaviour in a car following situation. *Accident Analysis & Prev., 27*, 707-715.

Anderson, J. R., and Lebiere, C. (1998). *The atomic components of thought.* Hillsdale, NJ: Erlbaum.

Beusmans, J., & Rensink, R. (Eds.) (1995). Cambridge Basic Research 1995 Annual Report (Tech. Rep. No. CBR-TR-95-7). Cambridge, MA: Nissan CBR.

Byrne, M. D., & Anderson, J. R. (1998). Perception and action. In J. R. Anderson & C. Lebiere (Eds.), *The Atomic Components of Thought* (pp. 167-200). Hillsdale, NJ: Lawrence Erlbaum Associates.

Card, S., Moran, T., & Newell, A. (1983). *The psychology of human-computer interaction.* Hillsdale, NJ: Lawrence Erlbaum Associates.

McKnight, A. J., & McKnight, A. S. (1993). The effect of cellular phone use upon driver attention. *Accident Analysis & Prevention, 25*, 259-265.

Reed, M. P., & Green, P. A. (1999). Comparison of driving performance on-road and in a low-cost simulator using a concurrent telephone dialing task. *Ergonomics, 42*, 1015-1037.

Salvucci, D. D. (2001). Predicting the effects of in-car interfaces on driver behavior using a cognitive architecture. In *Human Factors in Computing Systems: CHI 2001 Conference Proceedings* (pp. 120-127). New York: ACM Press.

Salvucci, D. D., Boer, E. R., & Liu, A. (in press). Toward an integrated model of driver behavior in a cognitive architecture. *Transport. Research Record.*

Serafin, C., Wen, C., Paelke, G., & Green, P. (1993). Development and human factors tests of car phones (UMTRI-93-17). Ann Arbor, MI: UMTRI.

Symposium

Panel on Government Interests and Opportunities in Cognitive Modeling

Panel Organizer and Chair:

Kevin Gluck (kevin.gluck@williams.af.mil)
Research Psychologist, Warfighter Training Research Division
Air Force Research Laboratory (AFRL)

Panel Participants:

Terry Allard (tallard@mail.arc.nasa.gov)
Chief, Human Factors Research and Technology Division
NASA Ames Research Center

Laurel Allender (lallende@arl.army.mil)
Team Lead, Cognitive and Perceptual Modeling Team
Army Research Laboratory (ARL)

Susan Chipman (susan_chipman@onr.navy.mil)
Program Officer, Cognitive Science Base Program
Office of Naval Research (ONR)

Ephraim Glinert (eglinert@nsf.gov)
Deputy Division Director, Information and Intelligent Systems
National Science Foundation (NSF)

John Tangney (john.tangney@afosr.af.mil)
Program Manager, Perception and Cognition Program
Air Force Office of Scientific Research (AFOSR)

Rik Warren (richard.warren@wpafb.af.mil)
Associate to the Chief Scientist, Human Effectiveness Directorate
Air Force Research Laboratory (AFRL)

There are a variety of U.S. government research laboratories and funding agencies with interests and opportunities in cognitive modeling. Holding the 4th International Conference on Cognitive Modeling in the U.S., and especially in close proximity to Washington, D.C., provided an opportunity to gather a group of distinguished representatives from these various organizations and engage in an information sharing session regarding their specific cognitive modeling interests and opportunities.

The panel participants listed above each spoke briefly on one or more of the following topics, as applied to their respective organizations:

- specific cognitive modeling research areas of interest in the near-, mid-, and long-term
- programs that support collaborations between government researchers and university faculty
- programs that support international communication/collaboration with government researchers and their counterparts in other countries
- current and future job opportunities for cognitive modelers

Following these brief presentations, panel participants were available at the poster session for additional discussion regarding interests and opportunities in cognitive modeling.

Presented Papers

A Modular Neural-Network Model of the Basal Ganglia's Role in Learning and Selecting Motor Behaviours

Gianluca Baldassarre (gbalda@essex.ac.uk)
Department of Computer Science, University of Essex
CO4 3SQ Colchester, UK

Abstract

This work presents a modular neural-network model (based on reinforcement-learning actor-critic methods) that tries to capture some of the most-relevant known aspects of the role that basal ganglia play in learning and selecting motor behavior related to different goals. In particular some simulations with the model show that basal ganglia selects "chunks" of behaviour whose "details" are specified by direct sensory-motor pathways, and how emergent modularity can help to deal with multiple behavioral tasks. A "top-down" approach is adopted. The starting point is the adaptive interaction of a (simulated) organism with the environment, and its capacity to learn. Then an attempt is made to implement these functions with neural architectures and mechanisms that have a neuroanatomical and neurophysiological empirical foundation.

Introduction, Methodology, Empirical Evidence Addressed

What is the role that basal ganglia play in mammals' sensory-motor behaviour? When organisms have different needs/goals, sometimes they have to associate slightly different behaviours to the same perception patterns, some other times they have to associate completely different behaviours to them. This work presents some simulations that suggest that in the former case the differences are dealt with within the same sensory-motor pathway (implemented by a neural module) while in the later cases different sensory-motor pathways are selected. In fact if the behavioral response to associate to a given perception were different with different needs/goals, using the same neural synapses/ pathways would only cause interference. In this context basal ganglia could play a role in selecting different sensory-motor pathways when necessary.

This work follows a "top-down" approach, where the starting point is organisms' behaviour and learning processes (cf. Meyer & Guillot, 1990). On this purpose it presents a simulation of an organism that has different needs (signals coming from the body and indicating a physiological unbalance, cf. Rolls, 1999) or, alternatively, different goals (desired states of body-world) associated to different positions in the environment (for example we can assume that these different positions are occupied by resources that satisfy different needs). The organism learns through classical and instrumental learning (Lieberman, 1993; in Baldassarre & Parisi, 2000, these two learning mechanisms are integrated in a comprehensive actor-critic model. Cf. Barto, 1995, and Sutton & Barto, 1998, for this model) to navigate in the environment in order to reach those positions. Given this behaviour as a starting point, the work attempts to yield it by building a neural-network controller that satisfies (some of) the constraints coming from the known empirical evidence about basal ganglia. Since the starting point of this approach is to simulate sophisticated organisms' behaviours, sometimes there is no empirical data suggesting which mechanisms underlie them. In these cases some computational solutions are adopted that do not have a known empirical correspondent (they will be appealed as "arbitrary" in the rest of the paper). These solutions should be considered as a useful theoretical exercise, eventually suggesting interesting ideas to the empirical investigation, and should not be judged too severely on the basis of the neural evidence.

The anatomical and physiological evidence specifically addressed in this work is now illustrated. Chevalier & Deniau (1990) propose that a double-inhibition mechanism is the basic process of basal ganglia's functioning. They report that in some experiments where monkeys have to carry out a delayed saccade to a remembered target, some striatal cells (usually mute) are induced to fire with local injection of glutammate. The striatal discharge inhibits (via GABAergic connections) a group of cells in the substantia nigra pars reticulata (usually tonically active) that release from (GABAergic) inhibition a subset of cells of the superior colliculus responsible for the saccade. In the case of skeletal movements the double inhibition releasing mechanism is implemented by the striatum-globus pallidus-thalamus pathway. The authors report that while in rodents this mechanism is sufficient to trigger movements, in the reported experiments the execution of a saccade requires temporal coincidence of basal ganglia disinhibition with command signals from other sources. This aspect is present in the model: basal ganglia select a particular sensory-motor pathway that then yields the detailed behavioral output.

Graybiel (1998), addressing the role that the basal ganglia's neural modules play in human slow habit learning and animal stimulus response association, draws an abstract parallel between the striatum's anatomical organization in partly interconnected zones, called "matrisomes", and the modular architecture of the neural networks of Jacobs et al. (1991). As we shall see, the computational model presented here proposes a possible way to specify such parallel.

Houk, Adams, & Barto (1995) suggest a possible correspondence between the actor-critic models' architecture and functioning (Barto, 1995; Sutton & Barto, 1998) and the architecture of the basal ganglia. In particular they propose that the circumscribed regions called "striosomes" (differently from matrisomes, they are identifiable for their chemical make-up and output connectivity) may implement the function of the critic (predicting future rewards and yielding a step-by-step reward signal in cases of delayed rewards) and the surrounding "matrix" regions may implement the function of the actor (selecting actions or, as in the model presented here, sensory-motor pathways). As we shall see, the actor-critic model is at the base of the model presented here.

Lots of other aspects of these contributions have been incorporated in the model, and will be presented in detail in the next section. The numerous brain-imaging studies of basal ganglia's role in sequence learning are not directly addressed in this paper (see Graybiel, 1998, for some references).

Scenario and Model of Basal Ganglia

The environment used in the simulations is a square arena with sides measuring 1 unit (Figure 1). The organism cannot see the boundaries of the arena and cannot exit it. Inside the arena there are 5 circular landmarks/obstacles that the organism can see with a one-dimension horizontal retina covering 360 degrees with 50 contiguous sensor units. Each unit gets an activation of 1 if a landmark is in its scope, of 0 otherwise. The signals coming from the retina are aligned with the magnetic north through a compass. Before being sent to the controller, these signals are re-mapped into 100 binary units representing the image "contrasts". Two contiguous retinal units activate one contrast unit if they are respectively on and off, another contrast unit if they are respectively off and on, no contrast units if they are both on or both off (cf. Figure 1). At each cycle of the simulation the organism selects one of eight actions, each consisting in a 0.05 step in one of eight directions aligned with the magnetic north (north, northeast, east, etc.). The outcome of these actions is affected by a Gaussian noise (0 mean, 0.01 variance). The organism's task is to reach one of the three goal positions showed in Figure 1.

Figure 2 illustrates the main features of the organism's controller and the possible brain areas and nuclei corresponding to the model's components. Now a computational description of the controller is given, and its possible links to the mammal brain's neural

structures are illustrated (notice that the units used in the model sometimes represent whole neural assemblies and at other times single units).

The matcher is a (arbitrary) hand-designed network responsible for generating an internal reward signal r by detecting the similarity between the goal and the current input contrasts (a goal is the contrasts' pattern at that goal position). When these patterns have at least 94% of bits with same value, the matcher returns 1 otherwise it returns 0. It is assumed that some memory process, not simulated in the model, evokes the goal patterns (when a goal is reached, another goal is evoked that is randomly chosen between the three goals). In real brains, goal patterns may be generated within frontal areas (e.g. by the frontal eye fields in the case of saccades) and recognition could take place here or in the sensory areas themselves (cf. Kosslyn, 1999).

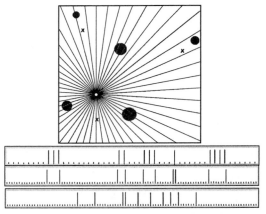

Figure 1: (Top) the scenario of the simulations containing three goals (marked with x), five landmarks (black circles), the scope of the organism's 50 visual sensors (delimited by the rays), and the organism (white circle at origin of rays). (Bottom) the activation of the visual sensors, its re-mapping into contrasts, and the bottom left goal (contrast pattern).

There is an alternative way to view this part of the model. Animals are endowed with innate neural structures that take input from the environment and map it into a "reward" or "punishment" internal signal. This usually happens when some states of the environment are achieved that are relevant for adaptation, for example some food is ingested or the body is hurt (primary reinforcements). Notice that these signals are produced only if a correspondent appetitive need (e.g. hunger) is present (Rolls, 1999). In the model the presence of a certain need could be thought of as corresponding to an arbitrary pattern (the "goal") coming from the body, while the signal relevant for adaptation is the signal coming from the sensors (e.g.

from the sensors in the mouth that detect the ingestion of food). In this case the matcher would yield a rewarding signal when a need and the corresponding satisfying input pattern are present together (in this case the matcher would correspond to limbic structures, cf. Rolls, 1999). In both cases the matcher's signal arrives to the substantia nigra pars compacta and ventral tegmental area, capable of generating a dopaminergic signal that triggers learning.

The actor, with the 6 "expert" networks (6 different input areas - thalamus - frontal areas pathways), implements the organism's "action-selection policy". Each expert is a two-layer feed-forward neural network that gets the goal and the visual contrasts as input, and has 8 sigmoidal output units that locally encode the actions (the experts may correspond to thalamus' neural assemblies: here the details of the model are quite arbitrary). To select one action, the activation m_k (interpretable as "action merit") of the output units is sent to the frontal areas where a stochastic winner-take-all competition takes place (cf. Hanes & Schall, 1996, on this possibility). The execution of one action has to be thought of involving the activation of a particular muscle template. The probability P[.] that a given action a_k becomes the winning action a_w (to execute) is given by: $P[a_k = a_w] = m_k / \Sigma_f m_f$. The role of the basal ganglia is to select an expert which, in its turn, has to select the actions to be executed through the mechanism of double inhibition illustrated previously involving the matrix of the striatum and the globus pallidus. This is done with another winner-take-all competition analogous to the previous one, but this time involving the experts instead of the actions (could this mechanism correspond to the bistable behaviour of the striatum spiny cells?). Notice that the basal ganglia can only release the proper expert from inhibition, but cannot trigger an action directly.

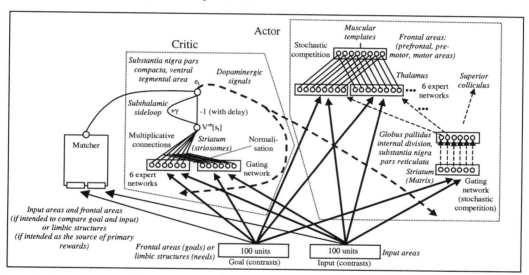

Figure 2: The components of the organism's controller. Labels in *Italic* indicate the possible brain areas and nuclei corresponding to the model's components. Thin arcs indicate one-to-one connections with weight +1 when not differently indicated. Dashed thin arrows indicated unit-to-unit/area inhibitory connections (strong enough to make the target units/areas silent). Bold arrows indicate connections updated on the basis of the dopaminergic signal. Dashed bold arrows indicate the dopaminergic signal.

The critic is a "mixture of experts network" (Jacobs et al., 1991) based on 6 expert networks. Each expert is a two-layer feed-forward neural network that gets the goal and the visual contrasts as input and has one linear output unit. The critic learns to yield the estimation $V'^{\pi}[s_t]$ of the "evaluation" $V^{\pi}[s_t]$ of the current contrast pattern s_t. $V^{\pi}[s_t]$ is defined as the expected discounted sum of all future reinforcements r, given the current action-selection policy π expressed by the actor: $V^{\pi}[s_t]$

$= E[\gamma^0 r_{t+1} + \gamma^1 r_{t+2} + \gamma^2 r_{t+3} + ...]$ where $\gamma \in (0, 1)$ is the discount factor, set to 0.95 in the simulations, and E[.] is the mean operator. In order to compute $V'^{\pi}[s_t]$ the output v_k of the experts is weighted and summed: $V'^{\pi}[s_t] = \Sigma_k[v_k \, g_k]$, and the weight g_k is computed as the softmax activation function of the output units o_k of the gating network: $g_k = \exp[o_k]/\Sigma_f \exp[o_f]$. This part of the model is arbitrary, but the modularity of the striosomes confers some plausibility to the model (the model is an implementation of what is suggested in Houk et al., 1995: different striosomes may be specialized in dealing with different behavioral tasks. As we shall see, this is obtained as an emergent feature of the model). The last component of the critic (subthalamic loop, substantia nigra pars compacta and ventral tegmental area) is a neural implementation of the computation of the "temporal-difference error" e defined as: $e_t = (r_{t+1} + \gamma\ V'^{\pi}[s_{t+1}]) - V'^{\pi}[s_t]$ (Houk et al., 1995). Each critic's expert has a specific error defined as: $e_{kt} = (r_{t+1} + \gamma\ V'^{\pi}[s_{t+1}]) - v_k[s_t]$. These error signals correspond to the dopaminergic signals and are at the base of the learning processes of the actor and critic.

Each critic's expert is trained on the basis of the expert's dopaminergic error signal that assumes the role of error in the estimation of $V'^{\pi}[s_t]$ in a supervised learning algorithm. The weights of the experts are updated so that their estimation $v_k[s_t]$ tends to be closer to the target value $(r_{t+1} + \gamma\ V'^{\pi}[s_{t+1}])$. This target is a more precise evaluation of s_t because it is expressed at time t+1 on the basis of the observed r_{t+1} and the new estimation $V'^{\pi}[s_{t+1}]$. The formula (a modified Widrow-Hoff rule, cf. Widrow & Hoff, 1960) to update the weights of each expert is: $\Delta w_{ki} = \eta\ e_{kt}\ y_i\ h_k$ where w_{ki} is a weight of the expert, η is a learning rate (set to 0.01 in the simulations) and y_i is the activation of the goal and contrast units. h_k (absent in the Widrow-Hoff rule) is the (updated) contribution of the expert k to the global answer $V'^{\pi}[s_t]$, and is defined as: $h_k = g_k\ c_k\ /\ \Sigma_f\ [g_f\ c_f]$, where c_k is a measure of the "correctness" of the expert k defined as: $c_k = \exp[-0.5\ e_{kt}^2]$. The gating network weights z_{ki} are updated to increase the weight in yielding $V'^{\pi}[s_t]$ of the experts who had low errors: $\Delta z_{ki} = \xi\ (h_k - g_k)\ y_i$ where ξ is a learning rate set to 0.1 in the simulations. This algorithm leads the experts to specialize in the different regions of the goal-contrast space. Notice that ξ is higher than η. This has been found to be a necessary condition for the controller to work. With $\xi = 0.01$ the experts did not specialize and interference between different goals prevented learning.

The actor is trained according to the dopaminergic signal e_t. In this case this signal is interpreted as the actor's capacity to select actions that bring the organism to new states with an evaluation higher than the average evaluation experienced previously departing from that same state. The updating of the action merits of the selected expert (and only this) is done by updating the weights of the neural unit corresponding to the selected action a_w (and only this) as follows: $\Delta w_{wi} = \zeta\ e_t\ (4\ m_w (1 - m_w))\ y_i$. ζ is a learning rate (0.01) and $(4\ m_w (1 - m_w))$ is the derivative of the sigmoid function multiplied by 4 to homogenize the size of the learning rates of the actor and the <u>linear</u> critic. The model's dopaminergic signal affecting the sensory-motor pathways may correspond to the real brain dopaminergic signal

targeting the frontal areas downstream the thalamus. For simplicity in the model these dopamine-sensitive areas have been designed upstream the thalamus. The weights of the winning gating network's unit are updated in the same way used for the experts' merits (learning rate 0.01).

The learning mechanism of the critic and the actor differ because in the later case it is not possible to have a teaching pattern to implement a supervised learning algorithm (as in the former case). The stochastic nature of the actor is necessary to produce new behaviours that are then strengthened or weakened according to their outcome in terms of rewards. At the beginning of the simulations the weights of the critic and actor (only those affected by the dopamine) are randomized in the interval [-0.001, +0.001]. This implies that the evaluations expressed by the linear critic are around 0, and the merits (probabilities) expressed by the "sigmoidal" actor (stochastic selector) are around 0.5 (0.125). This implies that initially, the organism's behaviour is a random walk. Then the critic and the actor are trained simultaneously (policy iteration): the evaluator learns to evaluate the states of the world on the basis of the actor's action-selection policy, and the actor improves the policy by increasing the probabilities of those actions that yield an evaluation higher than the expected one (cf. Sutton & Barto, 1998).

Simulations, Results, Interpretations

As mentioned, the task of the organism is to reach one of the three goal positions shown in Figure 1. When a goal is reached a new one (randomly chosen between the three goals) is assigned to the organism and this has to reach it from its current position. Figure 3 shows the organism's learning curve in terms of number of steps taken to reach a goal (mobile average for 100 successes, average for 10 random seeds). The performance improves from about 1000 to about 30 steps.

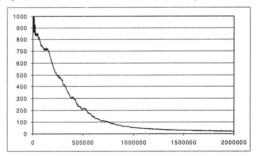

Figure 3: The learning curve of the organism. Y-axis: cycles per success. X-axis: cumulated cycles.

Figure 4 presents some data about how the neural-network controller of one of the 10 simulations has self-organized during learning (the other random seeds have produced results with analogous quality). Concerning the critic, we see that each goal is dealt with by a different expert (in each possible position of the arena the weight of this expert in determining the evaluation is over 0.99. The second column of Figure 4 shows the resulting gradient field of the evaluations for the three goals). This probably means that the positions in the arena need to receive a different evaluation for the three different goals, so that using the same weights (same

expert) would only cause negative interference. This also means that the connections from the (contrast) input pattern to the critic's gating network are redundant. The fact that different parts of the striosomes specialize for different goals as in the model, is an interesting hypothesis that has not yet been verified empirically. Notice that the controller is capable of <u>not</u> using some of the resources available (expert 1, 3, 4). These resources could be used for other goals.

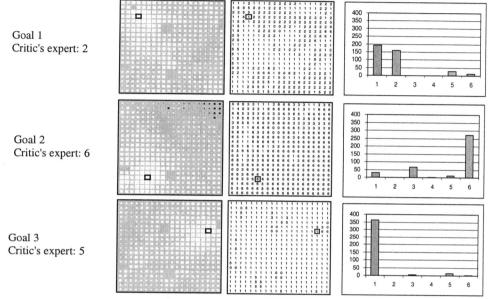

Goal 1
Critic's expert: 2

Goal 2
Critic's expert: 6

Goal 3
Critic's expert: 5

Figure 4: Data about the self-organization of the controller during learning (1 out of 10 random seeds). The three rows of graphs are relative to the three different goals. The first column reports the expert that is used by the critic for the particular goal (only 1 expert per goal). The second column of graphs reports the gradient field of evaluations $V'^{\pi}[s_t]$ yielded by the critic in 400 different positions (corresponding to the 20×20 cells of the grid). The area of the white (positive evaluations) and black (negative evaluations) cells is proportional to the evaluation yielded. The third column of graphs reports the order number of the actor's expert with highest probability of being selected (for the same 400 positions of the previous column). The last column of graphs reports the histograms that summarize the frequencies of the experts illustrated in the previous column.

With regard to the actor, Figure 4 shows that the specialization of the experts is much less pronounced. In particular the graphs of the third and fourth column of the Figure 4 show that while pursuing a goal the actor uses different experts in different position in the arena. The histograms report the frequency of use of the different experts for the different goals. Clearly the controller tends to use different experts when dealing with different goals, but now (differently from what is observed in the critic) the visual input plays an important role. An interesting fact coming out from the third and fourth column of Figure 4 is that the same experts are being used for different goals (e.g. expert 1

for goal 1 and 3). Further investigation should show if this different use of the experts in the critic and in the actor are due to the differences in the role they play or if it is due to the difference between the algorithms employed (supervised learning and stochastic unsupervised learning; cf. Calabretta et al., 1998, on the evolutionary emergence of modular networks' function through genetic algorithms). Notice that in the actor, as in the case of the critic, there is a partial use of the resources available (marginal role of expert 3, 4, and 5).

The exploration of some parameters and simulation conditions has shown some limits of the controller. Too high learning rates (especially for the critic) produce instability, while too low rates produce slow learning. The system is also quite sensitive to the "aliasing" problem (this is the problem that occurs when there are states of the world that appear to be the same or very similar, cf. Whitehead & Ballard, 1991). In particular if there are positions that are similar to the goal positions, the organism tends to waste time searching on them (this happens because they will tend to have a high evaluation). With more goals some problems also occur: with some random seeds the same critic's expert is used for more than one goal. This produces a gradient field with more than one peak. This causes the organism to pursue the positions corresponding to these peaks at the same time so that the behaviour results to be dithering.

Conclusion

This work has presented a computational model that attempts to summarize in a coherent picture some of the most relevant properties of basal ganglia regarding motor behaviour. An attempt has been made to design a model that on one side is capable of controlling an organism in a non-trivial behavioral task, and on the other side is based on architectures and mechanisms possibly grounded on the empirical evidence about the anatomy and physiology of basal ganglia. The model has shown that the role of the striosomes in the striatum might be that of producing an evaluation of the expected future rewards, and to build a dopaminergic signal corresponding to previously neutral input patterns on the basis of some primary reinforcers. The dopaminergic signal is used to learn to express the evaluations themselves on the basis of a supervised learning algorithm. The simulations have shown that the modularity of the striosomes is used to deal with different behavioral tasks the organism meets during its life. The model has also shown that the role of the matrix in the striatum might be that of learning to generate stochastic variants of behaviour, eventually consolidated on the basis of the dopaminergic signal. Here the role of the basal ganglia's double-inhibition mechanism is not that of directly triggering particular patterns of behaviour, but that of releasing from inhibition sensory-motor pathways that then yield a particular behaviour suitably related to the current goals and percepts.

Acknowledgments

The Department of Computer Science, University of Essex, funded the author's research. Special thanks are expressed to Prof. Jim Doran (University of Essex) and Domenico Parisi (Italian National Research Council) for their valuable contribution of ideas, and Anthony Pounds-Cornish for his precious help in the preparation of the article.

References

Baldassarre, G., & Parisi, D. (2000). Classical Conditioning in Adaptive Organisms. *From Animals to Animats 6: Proceedings of the 6th International Conference on the Simulation of Adaptive Behaviour - Supplement Volume* (pp. 131-139). Honolulu: International Society for Adaptive Behaviour.

Barto, A. G. (1995). Adaptive critics and the basal ganglia. In C. J. Houk, L. J. Davis & G. D. Beiser (Eds.), *Models of Information Processing in the Basal Ganglia*. Cambridge, Mass.: The MIT Press.

Calabretta, R., Nolfi, S., Parisi, D., & Wagner, G. P. (1998). Emergence of functional modularity in robots. *From Animals to Animats 5: Proceedings of the 5th International Conference on the Simulation of Adaptive Behaviour* (pp. 497-504). Cambridge, Mass.: The MIT Press.

Chevalier, G., & Deniau, M. (1990). Disinhibition as a basic process in the expression of striatal functions. *Trends in Neurosciences*, 13, 277-280.

Graybiel, A. M. (1998). The basal ganglia chunking of action repertoires. *Neurobiology of Learning and Memory*, 70, 119-136.

Hanes, D. P., Schall, J. D. (1996). Neural control of voluntary movement initiation. *Science*, 274, 227-230.

Houk, C. J., Adams, L. J., & Barto, G. A. (1995), A model of how the basal ganglia generate and use neural signals that predict reinforcement. In C. J. Houk, L. J. Davis & G. D. Beiser (Eds.), *Models of Information Processing in the Basal Ganglia*. Cambridge, Mass.: The MIT Press.

Jacobs, R.A., Jordan, M. I., Nowlan, S.J., & Hinton, G. E. (1991). Adaptive mixtures of local experts. *Neural Computation*, 3, 79-87.

Kosslyn, S. M. (1999). *Image and Brain*. Cambridge, Mass.: The MIT Press.

Lieberman, A. D. (1993). *Learning - Behaviour and Cognition*. Pacific Grove, Ca.: Brooks/Cole Publishing.

Meyer, J.-A., & Guillot, A. (1990). Simulation of Adaptive Behavior in Animats: Review and Prospect. *Proceedings of the First International Conference on Simulation of Adaptive Behavior* (pp. 2-14). Cambridge, Mass.: The MIT Press.

Rolls, E. (1999). *Brain and Emotion*. Oxford: Oxford University Press.

Sutton, R. S., & Barto, A. G. (1998). *Reinforcement Learning: An Introduction*. Cambridge, Mass.: The MIT Press.

Whitehead, S. D., & Ballard D. H. (1991). Learning to perceive and act by trial and error. *Machine Learning*, 7, 45-83.

Widrow, B., & Hoff, M. E. (1960). Adaptive switching circuits. *IRE WESCON Convention Record, Part IV* (pp. 96-104).

Inducing models of human control skills

Rui Camacho (rcamacho@fe.up.pt)
LIACC - Laboratório de Inteligência Artificial e Ciências da Computação,
Rua do Campo Alegre, 823, 4150 Porto, Portugal
FEUP - Faculdade de Engenharia da Universidade do Porto,
Rua Roberto Frias, 4050-123 Porto, Portugal

Abstract

We propose a model, called Incremental Correction (IC) model to address the problem of reverse engineering human control skills using the *Behavioural Cloning* methodology. The proposed model is based on the concept of closed loop or feedback control. The controllers are induced via Machine Learning tools from traces of human expert control performance.

Controllers using the IC model exhibit an increase in robustness and a reduction in encoding complexity when compared to previous models used in *behavioural cloning*.

Introduction

The problem addressed by the reported investigation concerns the automatic synthesis of human control skills models using behavioural traces, also known as *behavioural cloning* [Michie et al., 1990]. The problem is one of knowledge acquisition from expert performance. The behavioral cloning methodology uses the performance traces of a control expert together with Machine Learning (ML) algorithms to induce artificial controllers. We are particularly interested in being able to bring insight to human control skills. The objective of behaviour cloning is three fold. To construct controllers using ML algorithms that should replicate the robustness features of the human subject being modeled, be intelligible to human understanding and should be induced automatically. In this study we improve two aspects of the results of previous studies in *behavioural cloning*: robustness and encoding complexity of the artificial controllers. The results were achieved by means of using a model different from the one being used in previous studies and using a more expressive representation scheme to encode the artificial controllers.

Being able to reverse engineer human control skills offers a useful process of fast construction of controllers, specially in tasks where traditional Control Theory is not applicable. As pointed out by [Sammut et al., 1992] it is also a very useful tool for training student pilots, particularly with regard to determining the aptitude of a candidate at an early stage of training. Hamm (1992) refers that Westland Helicopters Ltd uses helicopter engineering simulations, controlled by pilot models, for rotor loads and performance prediction studies. Because a human pilot is not included in the control loop, it is not necessary for the helicopter simulation to run in real time — performance models may be run faster than real time for chart data production, and complex models may be run at less than real time, in cheap workstations, for applications such as rotor load prediction studies. Urbancic and Bratko (1994) describe the application of the *behavioural cloning* methodology to the control of a crane simulation in loading/unloading ships in a harbor.

From an Artificial Intelligence point of view, the problem is harder than traditional knowledge acquisition for Expert Systems due to the fact that control knowledge is tacit ([Anderson, 1988]) and can not be articulated by its owner. The model and its parameters must be conjectured and experimentally evaluated. Traditional knowledge acquisition methods for Expert Systems are therefore not applicable. The data that result from the behavioural traces have a set of features that make them "hard" for ML algorithms. The data has, usually, a considerable number of misclassified examples due to the fact that humans do not provide ideal control actions. There is also a natural unbalance in the situations represented in the behavioural traces. Most of the time the system being controlled is near an equilibrium state and therefore, most of the time the controls do not change and therefore less examples of corrective actions are collected.

The methodology of *behavioural cloning* has been applied using models other than the Incremental Correction (IC) model. However, the controllers synthesised (see [Sammut et al., 1992] and [Michie and Camacho, 1994]) have the following limitations. They were not robust. For example, the same controller was not adequate to fly different flight plans. Varying the training conditions is an important feature to obtain robust controllers [Sammut and Cribb, 1990]. The complexity of the model encoding was quite high, specially in complex manoeuvres.

Most of the shortcomes of the previous work are overcome by the use of the IC model. The new model has an underlying control strategy based on a sequence of adaptive control actions. Each control action, apart from the first of the sequence, corrects the previous action after its effects on the controlled system have been perceived. The corrective actions are done, in the IC model, by means of increments/decrements to the control variables. In previous models there was no concept of correcting a previously made control change. Always the magnitude of a control variable were determined as a function of the situation (not including that control variable previous values). The experimental results show that the new model produces a significant improvement in the controllers robustness and a significant reduction in the complexity of the controllers encoding. The "clean-up" effect [Michie et al., 1990] is also quite evident from the performance measurements made. The use of goals in the model and the computation of deviation measures from those goals allows the same controller to be used under quite different situations. The model becomes parametric with the goals being the parameters that can be set and changed dynamically.

The requirement for a comprehensible model precludes the use of Reinforcement earning algorithms or Neural Networks. Without extra post-processing they do not produce symbolic (non-numerical) representations of the models.

The structure of the rest of the paper is as follows. In Section "Methodology for *Behavioural Cloning*" we describe the methodology used. In Section "Models of Human Control Skills" we review previous models used in experiments of reverse engineering human control skills and the proposed IC model is presented. The experiments that evaluated the model are reported in Section "The Experiments". The last section presents the conclusions.

Methodology for *Behavioural Cloning*

The *Behavioural Cloning* methodology enables the extraction of control knowledge that cannot be verbalises by the human expert controller. Although control knowledge may not be verbalised, the expert may exemplify how he/she actually uses control by performing control tasks. *Behavioural cloning* uses the traces of human expert control to construct the clone (new controller). The objective is to construct robust and intelligible controllers. For doing so the methodology follows the sequence of steps we describe now.

System characterisation

The first step of the methodology consists in the characterisation of the controlled system. The controlled system is characterised by its state and control variables (actuators). These variables are going to be recorded periodically, during task execution, to constitute the behavioural traces. The values of these variables is all the information we have to reconstruct the model and therefore it is very important that they contain all the relevant information used by the original controller and sufficient for the reconstruction process[1]. One of the problems of applying the *behavioural cloning* methodology occurs in the very first step. It is difficult to know if the original controller used only the information recorded in the trace values or used extra information other that the system variables. If the extra information may be derivable from the recorded variables then it is necessary to improve the preprocessing of the data. Extra features that lie in this case are structured features composed using the system variables for example. If the original controller uses features that are not derivable from the state variables and are crucial for the control task then *behavioural cloning* is not the methodology to adopt. This later case occurs less often in control tasks.

Conceptualisation

In control tasks, more complex than the pole and cart, and needing more complex controllers the controller is composed and constructed by modules. In general each module is constructed separately after the pre-processing of the behavioural traces. It is current practice to divide complex task plans into a sequence of n_s smaller parts called stages and to treat separately the n_a actuators (control variables). With this decomposition in mind a controller has usually one module for each stage and actuator. The total number of modules is therefore n_s x n_a. Identification of basic control manoeuvres and definition of the corresponding set of goals associated with each of them is very relevant. When deciding on the task's plan and the definition of the stages it is advisable to make a task stage to correspond to a *basic control manoeuvre*.

Execution of the control task

In step three of the methodology the expert controller provides the behavioural traces. The expert performs the control task, according to the task plan, a pre-specified number of times. While executing the task the controlled system variables are recorded periodically. To increase robustness it is recommended that the data should contain a diversity of control situations. The task plan should be executed under as many different circumstances as possible providing a greater diversity of control situations for the induction algorithm. Using exact

---

[1]The task plan and the goals defined in the plan are also known.

repetitions of the task plan may cause the induction algorithm to pick up special circumstances in which the task plan has been executed and limiting thus the robustness of the final controller. The difficulty at this point of the methodology is to guarantee to cover the complete space of situations. The situations recorded during this step should be a super set of the situations in which the controller is going to be used. For complex systems and tasks there are quite a large number of situations to cover and would require a large number of traces to be learned. If the representation model allows for extrapolation then this situation may be ameliorated but care should be taken. The use of stratified sampling may also help matters.

Pre-processing

The pre-processing procedure prepares the raw data for the ML induction algorithm basically making a series of filtering operations. The trace data is first split into stages. A dataset is then created for each control variable and for each stage in a format required by the ML algorithm. The pre-processing takes into account the *perceive-act* delay δ_{pa}. δ_{pa} accounts for the human *perceive-act* delay. In each sample, the value of the control variable is associated with the state variables of a sample recorded exactly δ_{pa} time units before. The actuator (control variable) constitutes the data set class and the state, together with the other control variables are the attributes. A critical aspect is the choice of the attribute set. The human controller may use features that are not directly measurable (state and control variables). The attribute set for the ML algorithm may, however, be extended with plausible extra features constructed using the sampled ones.

Construction of the controller

As suggested by Sammut (1992) a controller should have a set of *basic control operators* one for each *basic task operation*[2]. Each *basic operator* is built out of a set of modules, one for each actuator. In most of the studies using *behavioural cloning* the *basic operators* have been built using decision[3] or regression trees. A controller's *basic operator* has a set of decision trees, one for each control variable.

Step five of the methodology uses the chosen ML algorithm to induce the controller. As said before, in general, the controller is composed by several modules. Each module is induced separately

---

[2]In the flight simulator domain a *basic task operation* is a *basic flight manoeuvre*.

[3]We will use the terms decision tree and classification tree interchangeably although some authors use the term decision tree to refer to both classification and regression trees.

by the ML algorithm. The main concern in this step is to tune the ML algorithm parameters to obtain a controller that is robust and encoded as a comprehensible theory. The representational schemes used to encode the controllers play a central role in achieving those properties. To assess that claim we compare the use of two different representations: univariate classification trees and multivariate classification and regression trees.

Assembly of the controller

The artificial controller is assembled in step six. All induced structures (e.g. decision trees) are converted into executable code. Apart from the induced code for determining the actuators value in each stage, it is necessary to guarantee that the *basic operators* are switched whenever there is a stage change in the task plan. In current studies of *behavioural cloning*, the part that is responsible for the stage sequencing is hand-coded and therefore not subject to inductive construction. When assembling the controller code should be generated to implement the human perceive-act time lag. Code should also be generated to implement a smooth change in control values as is characteristic of human control behaviour.

Evaluation of the controller

In the last step the controller is evaluated by using it in actual control tasks. When the artificial controller is executing, the state variables of the control system are provided to it and the actuator values are obtained at each moment by interpreting the induced structures (e.g. decision trees). One serious problem with *behavioural cloning* is that there is no guarantee that the behavioural traces contain examples of all the "state space". There may be regions of the space not visited during the task execution leading to a non full prove controller. To validate the clone it should be tested on all possible regions of the state space or at least on the regions where fault-free performance is mandatory.

Models of Human Control Skills

The model of the artificial controller used in the experiments of [Sammut et al., 1992] and [Michie and Camacho, 1994] has a two-level hierarchy of control: a high level module and a low-level one. The high-level module is hand coded and its only role, so far, is to sequence the stages of the task plan. The high-level module is also responsible for establishing the context for the low-level module. It switches the low-level components according to the stage of the task plan. The context is further specified by defining the goal values for the new stage. At each stage only the components constructed for that stage are active. The low-level module is the only one induced from the behavioural traces and will be referred as the "model" from now on.

Early models

The models used before IC model are characterised by the following equation

$$Ctrl_i(t) = \mathbf{f}(S(t-\delta), Ctrl_{*-i}(t-\delta)) \quad (1)$$

where Ctrl() is the vector of control variables and S() is the vector of the state variables. The equation reads as follows. The magnitude of each control variable is determined by the values of state and other control variables of the controlled system sampled δ time before. S(t-δ) and Ctrl$_{*-i}$(t-δ) characterise an undesirable situation, where a control change is required. The δ value accounts for the human *perceive-act* delay. The rationality being that if the human controller made a control change at instant t that corresponds to a reaction to the situation perceived at instant t-δ. In [Sammut et al., 1992], [Michie and Camacho, 1994] and the experiments reported here, the delay is empirically chosen from a set of plausible values. We recognise that there is no good method to estimate its value. The δ may vary with the control variable, the task stage or even with the context. In the experiments the δ is estimated in the pre-processing phase of the methodology and hard-wired in the controller code. The objective of learning is to acquire the correct definition of the function $\mathbf{f}$ from its instances recorded in the behavioural traces.

Within this framework, a controller is a mapping from a context to a control position. A context being characterised by the controlled system state and control variables. The model is induced only from the events in the behavioural traces. An event being signaled by a change in a control variable.

A controller induced within this model framework acts as a mapping from a situation (or range of situations) to the magnitude of a control variable. This model, therefore requires that the control device position has to be memorise for each situation or range of situations. We conjecture that human controllers do not use this approach.

The Incremental Correction model

The Incremental Correction model, that is proposed in this study, as the following underlying assumption about the human real-time control procedure. There is an acceptable situation in which the controlled system is most of the time. The acceptable situation is characterised by a very small or non existing deviation from the homeostatic goal values. An acceptable situation requires no control change. Action is taken whenever the goal variables values

deviate from the goal value. There is a reasonable "wild guess" to make the first correction, specially if the deviation is large. After the first change, a sequence of (re)evaluation, corrections and waiting for the effects of the correction to become perceivable takes place until the acceptability of the situation is restored. The amount of waiting time involved in real-time control is usually very small. The control strategy is adaptive, in the sense that the direction and magnitude of the correction is directly affected by the previous change. If the previous change produces a too small reduction in the deviation then the direction of the next change is maintained and the amount of change increased. On the other hand, if the deviation is reduced too much or an overshooting is expected, then the direction is changed in the next cycle.

The IC model has a module, that we call the Coarse Decision module, to determine if the situation requires a change in the controls. If a change in the controls is required (*sit. not ok*), then another module computes the values of the increment/decrement of the control variables, the Refined Decision module. Whenever a change in a control is made the controller uses a waiting time for the effects of control change to become perceivable. The IC model inherits the goals and the perceive-act delay from previous models.

Both modules, Coarse Decision and Refined Decision are ML induced from the behavioural traces of the human subject as explained in Section "The Experiments". The Coarse Decision module implements the *action/noaction* decision making. The Refined Decision module determines the increment control value to apply whenever a control value has to be changed. The model has two parameters. The "perceive-act" delay of previous models and a delay to account for the time lag after performing a corrective action and the perception of the effects of that action (the "wait for effects" delay).

Morey *et al.* (1986) demonstrate that the change of feedback control actions from a closed-loop to open-loop behaviour is noticed as operators become mode experienced at the set of tasks.

The Experiments

We have investigated the influence of the representation scheme in the complexity of the controller encoding. We have evaluated two representation schemes: univariate decision trees and multivariate decision trees.

Experimental setting

The control task chosen for the experimental evaluation of the models consists in the control of a simulation of an F-16 aircraft performing a levelled left turn manoeuvre. A levelled turn is a nontrivial manoeuvre requiring a close coordination among the controls. The experiments were carried out using

ACM 2.4 public domain flight simulator running on a HP Apollo *Series* 735 workstation. The author played the role of the human pilot necessary for this study. The data used in the experiments are traces of 90 levelled left turn missions performed by the author. The 90 missions are split into two halves, one for constructing the model and the other to estimate the predictive accuracy of the constructed model. A detailed description of the empirical setting and of the evaluation of the models can be found in [Camacho, 2000].

The experiments were done using the *behavioural cloning* methodology explained earlier. The turn manoeuvre was carried out using the ailerons and the elevators controls only. We compared the use of two representation schemes to encode the model: univariate decision trees and multivariate classification and regression trees. The attributes used in the construction of the controller's ailerons trees were: bank angle; bank angle derivative; bank angle acceleration; pitch and; pitch rate. The attributes used in the construction of the controller's elevators trees were: altitude deviation; climb rate; climb rate derivative; bank angle; bank angle derivative and; climb rate acceleration.

The target definitions to learn within the IC model are: "change the control or not" and if the previous decision is favorable to change the control then the next decision is "what is the increment/decrement value to use". The model is constructed in two stages. First the Coarse Decision module is constructed. The model is then used to filter the data for the Refined Decision module. In the second stage the Refined Decision module is constructed. The C4.5 (Quinlan 1987) system was used to induce univariate decision trees. The CART system (Breiman et al. 1984) induced the multivariate classification and regression trees.

Performance Evaluation

The predictive power of the induced trees was estimated by measuring the Error Rate and the Root Mean Square Error (RMSE) on an independent test set. The Error Rate measures the percentage of errors made on the test set giving equal weight to each individual error. The RMSE is defined as $RMSE = \sqrt{\frac{\sum_{i=1}^{N}(cls'_i - cls_i)^2}{N}}$ where cls_i is the actual class and cls'_i is the predicted value.

One of the most desirable features of the constructed model is its intelligibility. To estimate the complexity of the model we measure the tree size.

The *robustness* of the controllers was estimated by the number of successful missions within the total used. A mission is successful if there is no crash between the initial and final points.

The flight *smoothness* is evaluated using a deviation measure associated with each of the three homeostatic attributes. For each homeostatic attribute

	incomplete missions	altitude (ft)	climb rate (ft/min)	b ang (°)
previous	15	1970	1814	8
IC (C4.5)	0	34	94	0.5
IC (CART)	0	14	104	0.4
Human	0	21	194	0.70

Table 1: Deployment-time results. The values represent the MADs on test missions. *b ang* stands for bank angle

Model		tree size	Err Rate	RMSE
previous		255	74.7	4.8e-4
IC (C4.5)	Coarse Dec	83	38.6	-
	Refined Dec	663	-	4.0e-4
IC (CART)	Coarse Dec	47	37.3	-
	Refined Dec	75	-	1.8e-4

Table 2: Independent test set results for **ailerons**.

the Mean Absolute Deviation (MAD) is measured using the definition $MAD = \frac{\sum_{i=1}^{N}|att_i - goal|}{N}$

Results and discussion

The deployment-time performance of the controllers constructed are shown in Table 1. The table contains the results of the following controllers: previous model; IC model constructed with C4.5; IC model constructed using CART and; human subject performance. The entries for the altitude, climb rate and bank angle measurements in the table represent the average of the MADs. The average is computed using the successful missions and are weighted with the flying times. The deployment-time results for the previous model controller show a considerable lack in robustness since only 30 out of 45 missions were successful in the test set conditions. On the other hand, both IC model controllers successfully flew the missions exhibiting therefore a better degree of robustness. The smoothness measure (MAD) of the previous model controller indicate that most of the time the aircraft is considerably far from the acceptable situation. The smoothness results show that both IC model controllers largely outperform either the previous model controller and even the human subject. The results of Table 1 show that the IC model controller constructed with CART outperformed the human controller in all of the three measures whereas the C4.5 surpasses the human subject in two of the three measures (climb rate and bank angle). For example, the climb rate MAD of the controller constructed with CART is 54% the human subject. These results represent a significant evidence of the "clean-up effect"[Michie et al., 1990].

The evaluation of the trees that constitute the controllers was done on an independent test set, and the results are shown in Table 2 and Table 3

Model		tree size	Err Rate	RMSE
previous		3173	84.2	5.0e-3
IC (C4.5)	Coarse Dec	65	42.4	-
	Refined Dec	143	-	2.1e-3
IC (CART)	Coarse Dec	21	37.5	-
	Refined Dec	15	-	1.5e-3

Table 3: Independent test set results for **elevators**.

for both controls. The IC model controllers induced with CART show a much smaller tree size than the controllers using the previous model. With the exception of the ailerons of the Refined Decision module, the size of the trees of the IC model controller constructed with C4.5 are much smaller than the corresponding tree size of the previous model controller and even of previous experiments [Michie and Camacho, 1994]. The controllers constructed with CART have a smaller tree size than the ones constructed with C4.5. However the complexity of the nodes in the CART trees are bigger since CART trees have linear combination of attributes in the nodes. The error rates of the IC model controllers are nearly half the values found with the previous model trees and very close for both C4.5 and CART tools. The RMSE of the IC model trees are also smaller than the previous model ones. The RMSE of the CART trees are much smaller than the C4.5 ones, less than a half for the ailerons tree.

Conclusions

The main contribution of the IC model is a substantial increase in robustness of the new controllers. The deployment-time performance values outperform the human subject on the same missions. Both ML tools, C4.5 and CART, produce robust controllers although CART controllers exhibited better performances.

The trees constructed within the new model exhibit a smaller size than the ones from previous experiments in reverse engineering human control skills. Intelligibility of the models is an essential point in the success criteria and the small tree sizes are a good step towards their comprehensibility.

The new model avoids the "situation-control value" indexing mechanism underlying the previous models. The referred indexing mechanism would require a controller to have a memory of control positions for each situation(s), which is not realistic.

Acknowledgements

I thank my PhD supervisor, Pavel Brazdil, for all support and excellent comments on my work.
I thank "Programa de Financiamento Plurianual de Unidades de I&D" of Fundação para a Ciência e Tecnologia and to FEDER that contributed to the funding of the study.

References

[Anderson, 1988] Anderson, J. R. (1988). *Cognitive Psychology and Its Implications*. W.H. Freeman and Co.

[Breiman et al., 1984] Breiman, L., Friedman, J. H., Olshen, R. A., and Stone, C. J. (1984). *Classification and Regression Trees*. Chapman & Hall, New York • London.

[Camacho, 2000] Camacho, R. (2000). *Inducing Models of Human Control Skills using Machine Learning Algorithms*. PhD thesis, Universidade do Porto.

[Camacho and Michie, 1995] Camacho, R. and Michie, D. (1995). Behavioural cloning: a correction. *AI Magazine*, 16(2):92.

[Hamm, 1992] Hamm, J. C. (1992). The use of pilot models in dynamic performance and rotor load prediction studies. In *Proceedings of the Eighteenth European Rotorcraft Forum*, pages 15–18, Avignon, France. Association Aeronautique et Astronautique de France.

[Michie et al., 1990] Michie, D., Bain, M., and Hayes-Michie, J. (1990). Cognitive models from subcognitive skills. In J. McGhee, M. G. and Mowforth, P., editors, *Knowledge-Based Systems for Industrial Control*, pages 71–99. Peter Peregrinus for IEE, London, UK.

[Michie and Camacho, 1994] Michie, D. and Camacho, R. (1994). Building symbolic representations of intuitive real-time skills from performance data. In eds. K. Furukawa, D. M. and Muggleton, S., editors, *Machine Intelligence 13*, pages 385–418. Oxford University Press, Oxford, United Kingdom.

[Moray et al., 1986] Moray, N., Lootsteen, P., and Pajak, J. (1986). Aquisition of process control skills. *IEEE Transactions on Systems, Man ans Cybernetics*, SMC-16(4):497–504.

[Quinlan, 1987] Quinlan, J. (1987). Simplifying decision trees. *International Journal of Man-Machine Studies*, 27:221–234.

[Sammut and Cribb, 1990] Sammut, C. and Cribb, J. (1990). Is learning rate a good performance criterion for learning? In *Proceedings of the Seventh International Workshop of Machine Learning 90*, pages 170–178, Texas.

[Sammut et al., 1992] Sammut, C., Hurst, S., Kedzier, D., and Michie, D. (1992). Learning to fly. In *Proceedings of the Ninth International Workshop of Machine Learning 92*, pages 385–393, Aberdeen, U.K.

The Application of Mathematical Techniques for Modeling Decision-Making: Lessons Learned from a Preliminary Study

Gwendolyn E. Campbell (CampbellGE@navair.navy.mil)
Wendi L. Buff (BuffWL@navair.navy.mil)
Amy E. Bolton (BoltonAE@navair.navy.mil)
David O. Holness (HolnessDO@navair.navy.mil)
Naval Air Warfare Center Training Systems Division AIR-4961
12350 Research Parkway
Orlando, Florida 32826

Abstract

We are conducting a series of research studies to investigate the application of mathematical modeling for training decision-making. Along the way, we have learned many lessons in trying to apply math modeling to training such as choosing the right domain, including a sufficient number of observations, adding the right predictors to the mathematical equations, and selecting the right model on which to base training feedback. We hope these lessons learned will help other researchers who are interested in applying mathematical modeling techniques.

Introduction

Our first boss had a favorite way of responding to junior psychologists who would troop into his office on a weekly basis, proudly displaying the latest tests that they had devised to measure the effectiveness of some training manipulation. "Yes, yes, yes," he would say as someone rhapsodized about how cool or clever her new test was, "but is it diagnostic?" There is a lot of insight in that question. It's not enough, when you are designing or providing training, to know whether your student's answer was right or wrong. You need to know why the student gave that answer. Designing focused and adaptive training feedback and/or remediation requires that you understand what your students are thinking and how they are reasoning.

It wasn't long before we realized that the same question could be applied to mathematical modeling of human decision-making. There is plenty of evidence demonstrating that mathematical modeling techniques are capable of predicting what decision a person is likely to make under a particular set of circumstances. But that doesn't mean the math model necessarily tells you anything about why or how the person made that decision. Consider, for example, the task of modeling the tipping behavior of the first author's mother. If you

collected a number of different restaurant bills and the corresponding tips that she left, you could easily generate the mathematical model:

$$tip = 0.17(bill) \qquad [Eq.1]$$

You would find that this model was highly (although not perfectly) predictive of her tipping behavior. However, it does not reflect the actual mental strategy that she uses to calculate the appropriate tip. She does not multiply 0.17 by her bill – either mentally or with a calculator.

In fact, she uses the heuristic of tipping one dollar for every six dollars in the bill. More specifically, she uses her knowledge of the multiplication table to identify the multiple of 6 that comes closest to the bill without going over to determine the base tip. Then she estimates the proportion between the remainder and 6 to determine the approximate amount of change to add on to the base tip. For example, if the bill was $27, she would recognize that 6 x 4 is 24, making the base tip $4, and 27 – 24 is 3, which is half of 6, and so she would add half of a dollar to the base tip. The end results of her approach and Equation 1 are basically the same (predictive validity), however the cognitive processes associated with applying each approach are very different (diagnostic validity). Thus, a model can be predictive of human performance without being diagnostic.

Interestingly enough, there is a long tradition in psychological research (called "policy capturing") of assuming that math models are diagnostic, and, when models do not match self-reports of people's strategy, concluding that people are not aware of their own mental processes (Brehmer, 1994; Reilly & Doherty, 1989; Zedeck & Kafry, 1977). Recently, we have undertaken the project of finding a way to actually evaluate the diagnosticity of mathematical models, rather than just assuming it. Our basic premise is that, if a model is diagnostic of actual decision-making processes, then feedback based on a critique of that model should lead to improved performance. Conversely, if the model is not diagnostic of a person's actual decision-making strategy, then feedback based on that model is not likely to have much impact on performance. Our first study compared the performance improvements that followed three types of feedback: (a) feedback derived from critiquing a regression model of student performance, (b) feedback derived from critiquing a fuzzy model of student performance, and (c) feedback based on the student's percent accuracy (control condition.) The results of pilot data are presented elsewhere (Campbell, Buff, & Bolton, 2000), and the data from the full study are currently under analysis. In the process of conducting this study, we have learned many practical lessons about applying mathematical modeling to human decision-making data, and it is these lessons that are the focus of this paper.

Experimental Approach

We selected a low fidelity simulation of a Navy air defense warfare task that could be taught to undergraduate college students as our experimental testbed (Gay et al., 1997). The participant in this task is responsible for monitoring a radar screen and attempting to identify the type (helicopter, commercial airliner, etc.) and intent (friendly, hostile) of all the aircraft that appear. In addition, a series of "rules of engagement" dictate the conditions under which the participant may send warnings and fire upon those aircraft.

Each participant came in for three, 3-hour sessions. During the first session, participants received training on the air defense warfare task. During the second session, participants performed five, 30-minute scenarios and completed a subjective strategy questionnaire indicating which cues they believed were most useful for making decisions.

In between the second and third experimental sessions for each participant, we built mathematical models of that person's performance data and constructed tailored feedback. The qualitative feedback statements were built by comparing the mathematical model derived from the participant's data to the mathematical model derived from data generated by an expert completing the same set of scenarios. We took great care to ensure that the feedback messages derived from a comparison of linear regression models were as comparable as possible to feedback messages derived from a comparison of fuzzy models, in the amount and specificity of information that was provided. Please refer to Campbell, Buff, and Bolton (2000) for a more

in-depth discussion of the methods used to derive the feedback messages.

During the third session, participants received the performance feedback, performed four more 30-minute scenarios, and completed another subjective strategy questionnaire. We assessed participant performance both before and after receiving feedback by calculating the percent accuracy with which the participant correctly selected and identified each aircraft on the radar screen.

Modeling Approach

While participants completed five scenarios during the second session of the experiment, our pilot data indicated that we could capture more variance in their performance data if we only included observations from the last three of those five scenarios. This is not surprising when you consider that the task is moderately complex and they have only had three hours of training at this point in the experiment. We believe that their behavior was actually less systematic on those earlier scenarios, as they were probably still getting oriented to the task and developing their strategies.

We used Matlab© software to build all of the mathematical models. Traditionally, a subset of data is held back during the process of building a math model, and that data is later used to evaluate the fit of the model. This process, called cross-validation, is followed to check for the problem of overfitting the model to the data. The only potential concern with this approach is that it is difficult to ensure that the holdout sample is representative of the entire data set.

In order to avoid this potential problem, we used a variation of a bootstrapping procedure. First, we generated 100 different random splits of the data into $2/3^{rd}$ training and $1/3^{rd}$ testing subsets. For each of those 100 random splits, we used $2/3^{rd}$s of the data to build a model and then estimated the fit of that model by calculating the correlation between the model's predictions and the actual decisions on the $1/3^{rd}$ testing (or holdout) subset. Our final measure of the cross-validated fit of the modeling technique was the average of the 100 correlations between the models' predictions and the actual data in each of the 100 holdout samples. This procedure is analogous to actually building part of a sampling distribution by hand.

In addition, because Matlab's© fuzzy logic toolkit does not automatically evaluate the relative contribution of each predictor to the model's overall predictive validity, we used a jackknifing procedure to determine which cues from the environment were the significant predictors of performance. Specifically, using the bootstrapping procedure described above, we built models with all possible combinations of up to four predictors. While there were seven potential cues in the environment that a person could use to make the decision, due to time constraints, we were not able to collect enough observations (or decisions) from each person to justify building a single model with seven predictors. We selected four as the maximum number of predictors because the majority of participants made at least 70 decisions across the experimental scenarios, and this was enough observations to build a model with four predictors. (Participants who did not make enough decisions were not invited back to complete the final session of the experiment. We will elaborate on this issue later in the paper.) Finally, we compared the cross-validated correlations of these candidate models statistically, in order to select the final model of a participant's data.

To illustrate the procedure we followed, we had a set of seven cues (altitude, speed, point of origin, radar signal, response to query, distance away from and flight heading relative to own position) that could potentially be used to predict a participant's intent decisions (i.e., is an aircraft hostile or friendly?) in our experimental task. From that set of seven cues, there are seven unique subsets with one cue each, 21 unique subsets with two cues, 35 unique subsets with three cues and 35 unique subsets with four cues, producing a total of 98 different models to be evaluated via jackknifing. Using the bootstrapping variation described earlier, each of these 98 different models was built and evaluated (against randomly selected holdout data samples) 100 times. A single model was selected based on a statistical comparison of the cross-validated correlations for each of the 98 models.

To summarize, in order to select the best model for one participant's intent decisions, we built 9,800 mathematical models. We followed this same procedure when building both the regression models and the fuzzy models and when modeling different types of decisions made within the context of our experimental task (such as determining the type of aircraft or determining the best aircraft to attempt to identify at any given time).

Lessons Learned

Over the last couple of years, between running 24 participants through a predictive validity study (Campbell, Buff, & Rhodenizer, 1999), and 12 pilot (Campbell et al., 2000) and 48 study participants in the current experiment, we estimate that we have built between 19,600 and 53,400 models per participant and upwards of 3,000,000 mathematical models of human decision-making data in total. In the process of building all of these models, we have learned some

practical lessons, and we offer these now, with the hope that other researchers will find them useful.

Lesson #1: The Right Domain

Mathematical modeling is simply not practical for every domain. Your ability to build a robust math model of performance is limited by your ability to collect a large number of performance observations. Domains like air defense warfare, which can easily require dozens of identification decisions within a 30-minute scenario, are well suited to providing the quantity of data required for math modeling. Consider, on the other hand, the task of maneuvering a submarine in open waters. This slow-paced task is likely to only require, at most, half a dozen navigational decisions during a 30-minute scenario, and thus it would not be practical to collect enough observations in this domain (under realistic conditions) to build a math model.

In addition, even when the domain seems rich enough to elicit a sufficient amount data, that will not necessarily be the case for every single participant. As mentioned earlier, even within our air defense warfare domain, we were not able to build mathematical models for every participant, as some individuals did not make enough decisions (i.e., generate enough data) during our scenarios.

Lesson #2: The Right Number of Decisions

So, exactly how many observations do you need to build a math model? Most people are familiar with the rule of thumb that suggests approximately 15-20 observations per predictor variable or cue in your equation. What everyone may not realize is that this rule of thumb applies only when the relationships between the predictors and the decision are additive and linear.

This fact played out in an interesting way in our research. We followed this rule of thumb when modeling data from an expert and from a number of novices performing our task. Across three, 30-minute scenarios, our expert made more decisions than our novices did. In addition, we feel confident that our expert behaved more systematically than our novices did. Thus, we were reasonably surprised to discover that our models captured more variance in our novice data than in our expert data. In retrospect, we believe that this reflects the fact that the strategies that the expert used were more complex and less linear than the strategies the novices used. Thus, the number of decisions suggested by the heuristic was sufficient to abstract patterns from the novice data, but insufficient to abstract expert performance patterns. We found confirming evidence for this suspicion when we included expert performance data from two additional scenarios and the predictive validity of the models increased significantly.

Lesson #3: The Right Scenarios

We speak loosely of modeling a person's decision-making strategy, and so it's easy to slip into believing that decision-making strategies exist as independent entities. In fact, decision-making strategies are inseparably linked to decision-making contexts. The very best you can ever hope to do with a model is to capture *the decision-making strategy that the person used in response to a particular set of stimuli.* He may have used a completely different strategy if he had been responding to different stimuli. A good model will be able to generalize an existing strategy to similar stimuli appropriately. But no model in the world can magically divine a new strategy that a person might switch to out-of-the-blue under a different context.

This means that the tasks or scenarios that you ask your participants to respond to will both drive and bound the strategies that your participants will use, and thus will limit the generalizability of your model. We cannot overemphasize this point. There is no such thing as putting too much thought, planning, analysis and effort into designing or choosing the scenarios that you are going to use to collect data for your modeling effort.

We learned this lesson early on in the course of conducting this research. We ran our expert through our first set of air defense warfare scenarios and found that 2 (of 7) cues allowed us to accurately predict her behavior. Then we ran some pilot participants through those scenarios and found that the scenarios were too easy to be used in our training study (ceiling effect.) We modified the scenarios to make them more difficult. As you would expect, when the scenarios became more difficult, the expert was forced to use a more complicated decision-making strategy. Thus, we discovered that additional cues were now needed to predict the expert's performance. Our first model would have effectively predicted expert performance on a variety of easy scenarios similar to our first ones. However, harder scenarios forced the expert to use a different strategy, and there is no way that the original model could have reflected that new strategy without prior exposure to it.

Lesson #4: The Right Cues / Predictors

It would be nice to believe that, if you choose a mathematical modeling approach, you do not have to invest as much time into task and cognitive task analyses that are more typically associated with building a cognitive model. We have heard some people propose that math modeling will do much of the work of your traditional training analyses

automatically. However, our experience clearly indicates that, if you do not already have a very deep and rich understanding of the task and task environment, you will not be able to build predictive math models.

Consider, again, the seemingly simple situation of trying to build a model that predicts how much tip a person will leave in a restaurant. The obvious input data from the environment is the amount of the bill. But just a moment's reflection will lead you to realize that the size of a tip is also influenced by the quality of the service received. In addition, the number and denomination of coins that a person has available will influence the tip amount. (If the exact tip should be $1.22, the person with only 2 dimes will probably leave $1.20 and the person with only a quarter will probably leave $1.25.) Of course, there are any number of personality variables and experience variables (has the customer ever worked as a waitress or waiter?) that also influence this behavior.

If the only predictor you use in your model of tipping behavior is the size of the bill, there is likely to be variance that your model cannot explain. Is it because that portion of the behavior is random or unpredictable? No, it is because you did not include the predictors that are systematically related to that performance variance. But the only way to determine what predictors need to be included is from conducting an analysis of the domain up front.

Next, consider an example from our experience in the current study. One of the decisions we attempted to model was the decision of which one of the set of unidentified aircraft on the radar screen (at any given time) should be identified first. We started with the premise that you would try to identify the aircraft that was the most potentially threatening to your ship. We presumed a bit further, that the major factor associated with potential threat was the distance between the aircraft and your ship, and thus the most likely candidate for attention would be the closest aircraft. Our final presumption was that certain characteristics of the other aircraft (such as their speed or heading) might sometimes draw your attention away from the closest aircraft. For example, if the second closest aircraft was going a lot faster and flying right at your ship, you might try to identify that one before you identified the closest one. All of these presumptions led us to select a particular set of predictors to use in our modeling algorithms.

To our surprise, we were not able to capture a respectable amount of the variance in the expert data. After much thought and discussion with the expert, we finally were able to figure out why. Our expert actually had two goals as she was playing the game. On one hand, she did want to protect her ship and identify and respond to the aircraft that were potential threats. On the other hand, she also wanted to make sure that she identified every possible aircraft that ever appeared in the scenario, as this is analogous to racking up points in a video game. This meant that sometimes her highest priority for identification was an aircraft that was very far away from her ship and moving away from it, because she knew that that aircraft would only appear on her radar screen for a very short period of time. Our lack of understanding of this goal led us to select a set of predictors that were not able to account for a reasonable amount of variance in her data.

In other words, math modeling is not just as simple as "throw in all the predictors and the algorithms will do all the work for you". Including the right predictors requires a significant investment in front end analyses, just as would be required for building other types of models.

Lesson #5: The Right Model

When you are working with an artificial task in a psychology laboratory, you have the ability to design the perfect environment for a mathematical modeling algorithm. One component of that perfect environment would be a set of completely orthogonal cues. Unfortunately for modelers, (but fortunately for decision-makers), the real world often comes with correlated cues. Consider various types of aircraft (747s, F-15s, helicopters, etc.). They differ in their typical cruising altitudes and speeds. But there are regularities in the combinations of altitude and speed that you will find in the real world. We do not have vehicles capable of traveling at each of the possible combinations. The fact that our real world cues are sometimes correlated means that mathematical algorithms will not always be able to identify a single best model. If speed and altitude are correlated in the environment, then the algorithm cannot tell which cue the person is using when making a decision.

In our research experience, it was not uncommon for us to find upwards of a dozen different subsets of predictors (out of the 98 possible combinations described earlier) that could be used to build models with statistically equivalent predictive validity. Thus, we needed a method for selecting "the" model to use for generating feedback. We experimented with many different approaches, most focusing on some operationalization of model parsimony. In the end, we followed a simple, two step algorithm. First, we compared the predictor subsets appearing in the statistically equivalent math models to the participant's responses on the subjective strategy questionnaire. If one of those models had the same set of cues, then we selected that model. If none of the math models matched the participant's subjective report, then we simply used the math model with the highest cross-

validated correlation as the basis for deriving the training feedback. While this approach may not work for every application, researchers do need to be aware of the possibility that multiple models may be equally predictive of performance data, and some technique for selecting from among those models must be used.

Lesson #6: The Right Feedback

Our final lesson might seem more relevant to the training context that we are interested in than to mathematical modeling itself, but we believe that it may have broader applicability. In our current study, we delivered two types of model-based feedback (regression and fuzzy) on three different categories of decisions within our experimental task. [Those were: (1) which unknown aircraft should be selected for identification next, (2) is the aircraft hostile or friendly, and (3) is the aircraft military or commercial.] We were interested in comparing the ability of the two modeling approaches to produce effective training feedback. Unfortunately, our preliminary data analyses indicate that neither modeling approach yielded effective feedback for two of the three decision categories. In all cases, the feedback was partially based on the mathematical models of expert performance data, and the variable that was consistent with these results was the fit of the models to that expert data. For those two categories of decisions that were not facilitated by feedback, the models did not have a very good fit to the expert data. On the other hand, for the one category of decision where there is evidence that model-based feedback was effective, the model did have a good fit to the expert data.

While the reasons that the models did not fit the expert data were different across those two categories of decisions (one reason was not enough observations, see Lesson #2 and the other reason was poor selection of predictors, see Lesson #4), the bottom line appears to be this: if the model isn't predicting what the expert is doing, then giving feedback based on that model doesn't help improve participants' performance. Abstracting this lesson beyond our training context might yield the following conclusion: just because you have a predictive model doesn't mean you have a model that is reflecting cognitive processes, but if your model isn't even predictive, then you don't have much of anything.

Discussion

While the lessons presented above were derived from experience with mathematical modeling techniques, it is interesting to speculate how they may or may not apply to other modeling approaches, such as those that are more explicitly cognitive. Some of the issues we have raised are uniquely mathematical ones. For example, math models require a large number of observations because they take a bottom-up approach to abstracting patterns from the data. Models based on cognitive task analyses are often built from a detailed, top-down analysis of a few carefully selected cases.

Other lessons are probably also important for developers of cognitive models, but maybe for different reasons. Certainly it is important to select the "right domain" when building a cognitive model. For example, the domain should be at least moderately cognitively complex and interesting. Gary Klein tells a story of attempting to conduct a cognitive task analysis of laundry soap purchasing behavior and discovering that some people just buy the product that smells good to them (G. Klein, personal communication, March 13, 2001). However, as we described earlier, part of the criteria for a domain to be "right" for mathematical modeling is that it elicits a large number of decisions, and this is not a criteria for cognitive modeling domains.

Finally, some issues are important for the same reasons for all modeling endeavors. For example, no matter what type of model you are trying to develop, you need to use the right set of scenarios to elicit data and you need to demonstrate the predictive validity of your model.

As computing power continues to grow in leaps and bounds, more and more mathematical modeling approaches are readily available to psychologists interested in studying human decision-making and cognition. The extent to which any of these modeling techniques are able to abstract actual cognitive processes is still an open empirical question, as is the potential capability of any of these techniques to support practical endeavors such as training. We have begun a program of research investigating both of these questions, with a focus on fuzzy modeling. While we are still a long way from being able to answer these questions in any definitive way, we have presented here a number of lessons learned from our preliminary research. We hope that these lessons will help other researchers interested in investigating mathematical modeling.

Acknowledgements

We would like to thank Randy Astwood, Jr. for all of his hard work collecting the data necessary to support our model-building addiction. Our thanks also go to Dr. David Dorsey and three anonymous reviewers for their thoughtful comments on the first draft of this paper.

References

Brehmer, B. (1994). The psychology of linear judgement models. *Acta Psychologica, 87,* 137-154.

Campbell, G. E., Buff, W. L., & Bolton, A. E. (2000). The diagnostic utility of fuzzy system modeling for application in training systems. In *Proceedings of the XIVth Triennial Congress of the International Ergonomics Association and the 44th Annual Meeting of the Human Factors and Ergonomics Society.* (pp.2-370 – 2-373). Santa Monica, CA: Human Factors & Ergonomics Society.

Campbell, G. E., Buff, W. L., Rhodenizer, L. G., & Dorsey, D. W. (May 1999). Decision making in a tactical setting: crisp or fuzzy reasoning? In *Proceedings of the Third International Conference on Cognitive and Neural Systems* (pp. 23). Boston, MA: Department of Cognitive and Neural Systems, Boston University.

Gay, P., Phipps, D. A., Bisantz, A. M., Walker, N., Kirlik, A., & Fisk, A. D. (1997). Operator specific modeling of identification judgments in a complex dynamic task. In *Proceedings of the Human Factors and Ergonomics Society 41st Annual Meeting* (pp. 225-229). Santa Monica, CA: Human Factors & Ergonomics Society.

Reilly, B. A. & Doherty, M. E. (1989). A note on the assessment of self-insight in judgement research. *Organizational Behavior and Human Decision Processes, 44,* 123-131.

Zedeck, S. & Kafry, D. (1977). Capturing rater policies for processing evaluation data. *Organizational Behavior and Human Decision Processes, 18,* 269-294.

Modelling Children's Case-Marking Errors with MOSAIC

Steve Croker (sfc@psychology.nottingham.ac.uk)
Julian M. Pine (jp@psychology.nottingham.ac.uk)
Fernand Gobet (frg@psychology.nottingham.ac.uk)
ESRC Centre for Research in Development, Instruction and Training
School of Psychology, University of Nottingham,
University Park, Nottingham, NG7 2RD

Abstract

We present a computational model of early grammatical development which simulates case-marking errors in children's early multi-word speech as a function of the interaction between a performance-limited distributional analyser and the statistical properties of the input. The model is presented with a corpus of maternal speech from which it constructs a network consisting of nodes which represent words or sequences of words present in the input. It is sensitive to the distributional properties of items occurring in the input and is able to create 'generative' links between words which occur frequently in similar contexts, building pseudo-categories. The only information received by the model is that present in the input corpus. After training, the model is able to produce child-like utterances, including case-marking errors, of which a proportion are rote-learned, but the majority are not present in the maternal corpus. The latter are generated by traversing the generative links formed between items in the network.

Case-Marking Errors

Children in the early stages of language development are known to make case-marking errors. These errors are utterances in which a nominative pronoun (e.g. 'he') has been replaced with a non-nominative pronoun, such as the accusative (e.g. 'him'), resulting in utterances such as 'him does it' instead of 'he does it' and 'her get it' instead of 'she gets it'.

There are a number of possible explanations for this phenomenon. According to Schütze and Wexler's (1996) ATOM (Agreement/Tense Omission Model) (see also Wexler, 1998, for an overview of this model), pronoun case-marking errors occur because the child produces the accusative form of the pronoun as a default when the abstract features of agreement (which are necessary for correct case assignment) are absent from the child's underlying representation of the sentence.

The ATOM predicts that once children have the relevant nominative and accusative forms in their productive lexical inventories, they will produce nominative subjects when agreement is present in the underlying representation of the sentence, and non-nominative subjects when agreement is absent. Since

agreement can be present but hidden when tense is absent, nominative subjects are predicted to occur with both agreeing forms (e.g. 'he goes' and 'she's singing'), and non-agreeing forms (e.g. 'he go' and 'she singing'). In the latter, agreement is 'hidden' in the surface structure, but present in the underlying structure. However, since agreement assigns nominative case, non-nominative subjects are predicted to occur only with non-agreeing forms (e.g. 'him go' and 'her singing', and not 'him goes' and 'her is singing'). Since the ATOM makes no predictions about how often case and agreement will surface in children's speech, and allows for the occurrence of nominative subjects with agreement, and nominative and non-nominative subjects without agreement, the only real prediction that it makes is that one will never find children who make certain kinds of errors (i.e. 'him goes' and 'her is' type errors), or, more realistically, that one will never find children who make such errors at rates higher than would be consistent with the notion that they can be disregarded as noise (Schütze, 1999).

Rispoli (1999) shows that, in fact, accusative pronouns do occur with agreeing verbs. Another related phenomenon is presented by Rispoli (1998): overextension of 'her' for 'she' occurs with greater frequency than overextension of 'him' for 'he'. Rispoli explains this in terms of a 'double-cell' effect, whereby 'her' fills the 'slots' for both accusative and genitive pronouns. 'Her' is used in the same contexts as both 'him' and 'his', which could lead to 'her' appearing in more contexts than 'him'.

The model we present here is an attempt to simulate two basic effects found in child case-marking errors. First, a greater proportion of case-marking errors occur with feminine subjects than masculine subjects. Second, not only do agreeing verbs occur with case-marking errors, they occur more often in feminine contexts. Nina, a child presented by Schütze (1997), uses 'her' proportionally more often than 'him', both with and without an agreeing verb. However, she also produces 'she' less often than 'he'. As a result, the ratio of 'her' for 'she' is greater than that of 'him' for 'he' and any analysis in which masculine and feminine forms are analysed together will show a lower rate of case-marking errors than an analysis of just feminine forms.

A Distributional Account

The ATOM derives much of its power from the abstractness of the categories with which its proponents are prepared to credit the language-learning child — and hence to analyse the multi-word speech data. Thus, analysing the child's correct performance in terms of abstract features such as tense and agreement, as opposed to the lexical items which instantiate these features, means that any correct use of third singular present or past tense verb forms, whether these forms are copulas, auxiliaries or lexical verbs, can be used to support the notion that knowledge of tense and agreement is available to the child from the outset. On the other hand, analysing the child's incorrect performance in terms of tense optionality ignores the possibility that, in the early stages at least, many of the verbs used by children in untensed form may never occur in tensed form in their speech, or at least only as non-finite verb forms in combination with tensed auxiliaries (e.g. 'she will go').

An alternative explanation for the phenomena described by Schütze and Wexler is that the formation of syntactic relationships in children's speech can be explained in terms of the input the child receives from external sources, in particular parental input. In the account we propose here, the child's use of lexical forms is a result of the distribution of these forms in the input. Most of the predicted speech patterns have models in the speech of adults which act as the linguistic input to the child. For example, a child may produce the utterance 'her go' which is accounted for in the ATOM as the use of an untensed form in a position where tense is required. Obviously, a child should not hear her mother saying 'her go'. However, she will hear utterances such as 'did you see her go?'. Likewise, a child may hear 'where did she go?' and 'she goes out'. Thus, all three of the combinations predicted to occur by the ATOM can be rote-learned. Our main concern is to show the ability of a simple distributional analyser to produce utterances with errors of the same types as those made by children (see Croker, Pine & Gobet, 2000 for a preliminary analysis).

MOSAIC

MOSAIC (Model Of Syntax Acquisition In Children; Gobet & Pine, 1997) is a computational model based on the CHREST architecture (Gobet 1993, 1998; De Groot & Gobet, 1996). CHREST is, in turn, a member of the EPAM family (Feigenbaum & Simon, 1984). Variants of CHREST have been used to model a number of areas of human cognition including the acquisition of multiple representations in physics (Lane, Cheng & Gobet, 1999) and the acquisition of vocabulary (Jones,

Gobet & Pine, 2000). See also Gobet et al. (in press) for an overview.

Network Formation

Knowledge is modelled in CHREST as a discrimination network, which is a hierarchically structured network consisting of nodes and vertical links between layers of nodes. Each node has an 'image', which contains the information available at this node (in MOSAIC, it consists of information regarding the links traversed to arrive at that node). Nodes and links each consist of one or more words.

When an utterance is presented, each word in the utterance is considered in turn, which allows the utterance to be sorted to a given node. If the word currently considered has not previously been seen by the model, the process of discrimination is used to create a new node corresponding to that word. The new node is created at the first layer of the network, just below the root node. This first layer may be seen as the layer where the 'primitives' of the network (i.e., the individual words that have been seen by the model) are learned and stored.

In cases where nodes only consist of one word, the image of the node matches the test link (described below) immediately above it, as that is the only link to have been traversed. However, at deeper levels, the image will contain more information relating to the sequence of tests. As noted above, at their first presentation, all words are encoded as primitives at the first layer of the network; a particular word must be 'seen' again in order for it to occupy a second location in the network. Subsequent words in an utterance are represented as nodes below the primitive, as long as they are already encoded as primitives themselves. Test links above nodes refer to the 'test' (one word or a

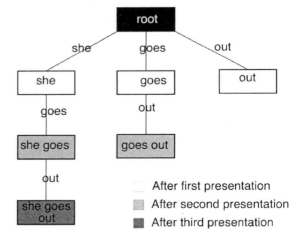

Figure 1: Network formed after the utterance 'she goes out' is presented 3 times to the model.

sequence of words) that has to be passed to travel down that link to the node, and are represented as the final element in the image of that node. These are created during discrimination, at the same time as a new node.

Figure 1 shows a small network created by presenting the utterance 'she goes out' to the model 3 times. On the first presentation, the primitives (white nodes) are created. When the model sees the utterance again, the network can be extended as the primitives have already been learnt (light grey nodes). The dark grey level 3 'she goes out' node is created on the third presentation.

When an utterance starts with a word already seen by the model, the *image* of the matching node is compared to the utterance. The utterance is then compared at the next level down to see if the second word of the utterance is already in the network below the primitive. The network is followed down as far as possible until one of two possibilities occurs: 1) The entire utterance is already accessible by traversing the network; 2) A point is reached where the utterance can not be traced down the network any further. In this case, discrimination takes place and a new node is created.

In contrast to earlier versions of the model (Croker, Pine & Gobet, 2000; Jones, Gobet & Pine, 2000), MOSAIC learns both from left to right and right to left. We feel this provides a more plausible account of learning as it allows sensitivity to the context of a word in terms of both the preceding and succeeding items (see Figure 2).

Generative Links

As well as learning utterances by rote, MOSAIC is able to generate novel utterances using generative links, an important feature of the model. Generative links are 'lateral' links between nodes which have contextual similarities. If two words occur frequently in similar contexts, then a generative link can be made between these items. These two nodes do not have be on the same level – a level 2 node can be linked to a level 3 node, for instance. The similarity measure is the degree of overlap between items that precede and succeed any two nodes. This is calculated by taking all the children of any two nodes and assessing whether the proportion of children shared by both nodes exceeds a certain threshold with respect to the total number of child nodes. For the purposes of this study, that parameter was set to 4% in each direction.

This, again, is in contrast to earlier versions of MOSAIC in which an absolute value was used in creating generative links (e.g. 15 succeeding items in common). It is our hope that this change, coupled with bidirectional learning, will enable the model to capture more subtle effects found in children's speech.

Production of Utterances

Once a network has been created, it can be used to produce utterances in two ways: by recognition and by generation. Utterances produced by recognition are essentially rote-learned (i.e. they are utterances or portions of utterances presented to the model in the

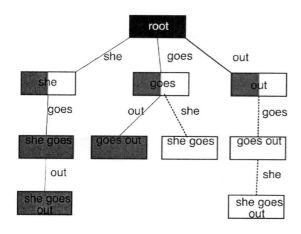

■ Nodes learnt from left to right

☐ Nodes learnt from right to left

Figure 2: Right to left learning.

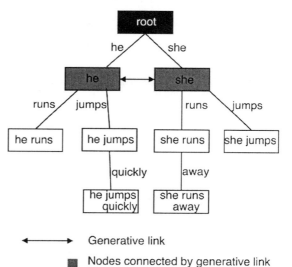

⟷ Generative link

■ Nodes connected by generative link

Figure 3: Generative link formation: 'he' and 'she' are linked by virtue of possessing child nodes in common. (Nodes learnt from right to left have been omitted in order to preserve clarity.)

input corpus). These are produced by starting at each node in turn, and following the left-to-right test links down the network. For example, from the fragment of a network shown in Figure 3, utterances such as 'she runs away' and 'he jumps' could be produced by recognition. Production by generation utilises the generative links to create utterances not seen in the input. This occurs in a similar way to production by recognition, the difference being that lateral generative links can be traversed as well as vertical test links, although only one generative link can be followed per generated utterance – this is simply to limit the number of generated utterances produced by the model. Thus, utterances such as 'he runs away' and 'she jumps quickly' could be produced by generation.

Methods

In this paper, we present data obtained from MOSAIC, trained on maternal input to one child between the ages of 1;10 and 2;9, which was taken from the Manchester corpus (Theakston, Lieven, Pine & Rowland, 2000) of the CHILDES database (MacWhinney & Snow, 1990). This corpus consists of transcripts of audio recordings made twice every three weeks for a period of 12 months. There are two half-hour recordings for each session, one made during free play and the other made during structured play. The model was trained on 15,000 utterances of maternal speech. We also present data from three children from this corpus, Anne, Becky and Gail.

There are two important points regarding data produced by MOSAIC. First, a word used as a verb is often used in other syntactic categories. An analysis was made of the frequencies with which words were used as verbs by the mother. A word was classified as a verb for the purpose of this research if it occurred as a verb in 90% or more of its instances in the mother's speech corpus. Second, the data used in analysing the performance of the model consists of types, not tokens. Much of the research in children's speech is based on analysis using tokens as the entire corpus is considered. MOSAIC, however, does not produce multiple instances of utterances in the same way that a child does. The model produces all the utterances it is capable of producing, whereas a child produces speech in response to the context in which the child is situated. We analysed only utterances which started with the pronouns 'he', 'him', 'she' and 'her' which contained a verb of which that pronoun was the subject. The restriction to third-person-singular forms is necessary as this is the only case in which agreement can be reliably distinguished in English. The same analysis was made of the utterances produced by the children.

Comparison With Human Data

Case-marking errors with an agreeing main verb are predicted not to occur within the ATOM. The literature

in the field (see Rispoli, 1998) provides evidence of these error types occurring in children's speech. As we shall see, MOSAIC can also produce these errors. Although the model embodies a very simple learning mechanism, it captures aspects of the data which, at best, the ATOM cannot explain and which at worst count directly against it.

Anne, Becky and Gail (Tables 1 - 3) all produce a number of case-marking errors with both masculine and feminine subjects. It is immediately apparent that the rate of overextension of 'her' for 'she' is greater than that of 'him' for 'he'. What these data also show is that there is no consistent error rate across children. As a result, we can not model 'typical' performance, as there is no typical error rate for children. The 'him' for

Table 1: Case-marking errors (Anne)

Case	Subject	
	He	She
Nominative	263	36
Accusative	3	7
% Accusative	1.13%	16.28%

Table 2: Case-marking errors (Becky)

Case	Subject	
	He	She
Nominative	398	95
Accusative	5	13
% Accusative	1.24%	12.04%

Table 3: Case-marking errors (Gail)

Case	Subject	
	He	She
Nominative	176	17
Accusative	10	19
% Accusative	5.38%	52.78%

Table 4: Case-marking errors (MOSAIC)

Case	Subject	
	He	She
Nominative	783	631
Accusative	34	52
% Accusative	4.16%	7.61%

$\chi^2 = 8.201$, p=0.004

Table 5: C/M errors with agreeing verbs (Anne)

Case	Subject	
	He	She
Nominative	183	17
Accusative	1	4
% Accusative	0.54%	19.05%

Table 6: C/M errors with agreeing verbs (Becky)

Case	Subject	
	He	She
Nominative	296	62
Accusative	3	13
% Accusative	1.00%	17.33%

Table 7: C/M errors with agreeing verbs (Gail)

Case	Subject	
	He	She
Nominative	124	14
Accusative	4	9
% Accusative	3.13%	39.13%

Table 8: C/M errors with agreeing verbs (MOSAIC)

Case	Subject	
	He	She
Nominative	523	409
Accusative	21	30
% Accusative	3.86%	6.83%

$\chi^2 = 4.367$, p=0.037

'he' error rate varies from 1.13% (Anne) to 5.38% (Gail) and the 'her' for 'she' error rate varies from 12.4% (Becky) to 52.78% (Gail). The results from MOSAIC (Table 4) are consistent with these findings – the masculine and feminine error rates are significantly different. In addition, it can be observed that case-marking errors often occur with verbs that carry agreement, in direct opposition to the predictions of the ATOM. Tables 5-8 show the error rates for utterances which contain an agreement-inflected verb-form. Once more, it is apparent that 'her' for 'she' overextensions outnumber 'him' for 'he' overextensions. Again, we make no attempt to model the absolute frequency of such errors, as they are variable across children (Tables 5-7). All that we can claim is that there is a 'gender bias' and that MOSAIC (Table 8) can capture this effect.

Discussion

This study utilises a computational model to present a distributional account of case-marking errors in children's speech. The output of the model was compared to phenomena found in child data. The results show that, after training, MOSAIC was able to produce case-marking errors with both masculine and feminine subjects, and with verb forms in which agreement can be present or absent. Some of these errors were produced by virtue of being present in the input corpus. For example 'did you see her sit?' gives the child the potential to produce 'her sit'. Others were produced by traversing generative links between lexical items linked by virtue of similarity. The reason that MOSAIC was able to reproduce the differences between masculine and feminine forms is due to the distributional difference between 'her' and 'him'. This difference can be explained in terms of a 'double-cell' effect in which 'her' is the feminine equivalent not only of 'him', but also of 'his', and therefore appears in more contexts than 'him'. The ability of MOSAIC to produce these errors suggests that an account of these phenomena in which the child is attributed with abstract categories such as 'tense' and 'agreement' as parts of underlying representation of an utterance is unnecessarily abstract. Once one abandons the assumption that children are operating with adult-like syntactic categories from the outset, their apparently sophisticated use of tense and agreement and the absence of particular kinds of errors in their speech can be explained in much more limited-scope terms.

The results presented here suggest that children's variable use of verb forms with respect to case-marking errors can be explained in terms of the learning of different verb forms from different positions in the surface structure in the mothers' speech from which they have been extracted. The implication is that children's early knowledge can be characterised as a vocabulary of unanalysed verb forms, or unanalysed sequences including verb forms, and a set of limited-scope formulae which specify how these verb forms pattern with respect to other items in their vocabularies (e.g. Braine, 1976, 1987).

Verbs with and without agreement marking are likely to come from different populations with the exception of high-frequency verbs, for which the child may have learned several morphological markers (Brown, 1973; Pine, Lieven & Rowland, 1998). As a result, errors which involve verbs with third-person-singular inflection (e.g. 'goes') are less likely to occur if the child has not learned many third-person-singular verb forms, not because children understand agreement. This explains why case-marking errors can occur with agreeing verb forms relatively infrequently. What is not considered in the ATOM is the likelihood of particular errors being made. An argument based on the low frequency of a particular error type needs to take into account the expected error rate (Lieven, Pine & Baldwin, 1997; Rubino & Pine, 1998). This means that the low error rates which are either dismissed as performance errors or predicted not to occur at all, as in the case of the accusative+agreement errors discussed in this paper, are not necessarily due to an understanding of the rules of grammar by the child, but more simply due to the low probability of two lexical items being used in conjunction, given the statistical distribution of such items in a language, in this case English.

It is clear that although MOSAIC is perfectly capable of capturing the phenomena found in child speech, it is not fully capturing the degree to which masculine and feminine forms behave differently. The children whose data we report show very sparing use of the word 'she', which results in a higher proportion of 'her' for 'she' errors than would be the case if 'she' were produced in similar quantities to 'he'. MOSAIC does show greater production of 'he' than 'she', but still produces 'she' and 'her' disproportionately, when compared with the frequencies at which children produce these items. We hope that by making MOSAIC sensitive to the frequency of individual words in future, we may be able to model the proportions in which children produce different pronouns, which should, in turn, bring our results in line with the child data.

References

Braine, M.D.S. (1976). Children's first word combinations. *Monographs of the Society for Research in Child Development, 41* (1, Serial No. 164).

Braine, M.D.S. (1987). What is learned in acquiring word classes - A step towards an acquisition theory. In B. MacWhinney (Ed.), *Mechanisms of language acquisition* (pp. 65-113). Hillsdale, NJ: Erlbaum.

Brown, R. (1973) *A first language*. Cambridge, MA: Harvard University Press.

Croker, S., Pine, J.M. & Gobet, F. (2000) Modelling optional infinitive phenomena. In *Proceedings of the Third International Conference on Cognitive Modeling* (pp.78-85). Veenendaal: Universal Press

De Groot, A. & Gobet, F. (1996) *Perception and memory in chess*. Assen: Van Gorcum.

Feigenbaum, E.A. & Simon, H.A. (1984) EPAM-like models of recognition and learning. *Cognitive Science, 8*, 305-336.

Gobet, F. (1993) A computer model of chess memory. *Proceedings of the 15th Annual Meeting of the Cognitive Science Society* (pp. 463-468). Hillsdale, NJ: Erlbaum.

Gobet, F. (1998) Memory for the meaningless: How chunks help. *Proceedings of the 20th Meeting of the Cognitive Science Society* (pp. 398-403). Mahwah, NJ: Erlbaum.

Gobet, F., Lane, P.C.R., Croker, S., Cheng, P.C-H., Jones, G., Oliver, I. & Pine, J.M. (in press) Chunking mechanisms in human learning. *Trends in Cognitive Science.*

Gobet, F. & Pine, J.M. (1997) Modelling the acquisition of syntactic categories. *Proceedings of the Nineteenth Annual Meeting of the Cognitive Science Society* (pp. 265-270). Hillsdale, NJ: Lawrence Erlbaum Associates.

Jones, G., Gobet, F., & Pine, J.M. (2000) Learning novel sound patterns. In *Proceedings of the Third International Conference on Cognitive Modeling* (pp. 169-176). Veenendaal: Universal Press.

Lane, P.C.R., Cheng, P.C-H., & Gobet, F. (1999). Learning perceptual schemas to avoid the utility problem. In M. Bramer, A. Macintosh and F. Coenen (Eds.) *Research and Development in Intelligent Systems XVI*, Cambridge, UK, pp. 72-82 (Springer-Verlag).

Lieven, E.V.M., Pine, J.M. & Baldwin, G. (1997) Lexically-based learning and early grammatical development. *Journal of Child Language*, 24, 187-219.

MacWhinney, B., & Snow, C. (1990) The child language data exchange system: An update. *Journal of Child Language,* 17, 457-472.

Pine, J., Lieven, E. & Rowland, C. (1998) Comparing different models of the development of the English verb category. *Linguistics,* 36, 807-830.

Rispoli, M. (1998) Patterns of pronoun case error. *Journal of Child Language,* 25, 533-554.

Rispoli, M. (1999) Case and agreement in English language development. *Journal of Child Language,* 26, 357-372.

Rubino, R.B. & Pine, J.M. (1998) Subject-verb agreement in Brazilian Portuguese: What low error rates hide. *Journal of Child Language,* 25, 35-59.

Schütze, C. (1997) INFL in child and adult language: Agreement, case and licensing. Ph.D. Thesis. MIT.

Schütze, C. (1999) Different rates of pronoun case error: Comments on Rispoli (1998). *Journal of Child Language,* 26, 749-755.

Schütze, C. & Wexler, K. (1996) Subject case licensing and English root infinitives. In A. Stringfellow, D. Cahma-Amitay, E. Hughes & A. Zukowski (Eds.) *Proceedings of the 20th Annual Boston University Conference on Language Development* (pp. 670-681). Somerville, MA: Cascadilla Press.

Theakston, A.L., Lieven, E.V.M., Pine, J.M., & Rowland, C.F. (2000) The role of performance limitations in the acquisition of 'mixed' verb-argument structure at stage 1. In M. Perkins & S. Howard (Eds.) *New directions in language development and disorders.* New York: Plenum

Wexler, K. (1998) Very early parameter setting and the unique checking constraint: A new explanation of the optional infinitive stage. *Lingua,* 106, 23-79.

Bootstrapping in Miniature Language Acquisition

Rutvik Desai (RUDESAI@Indiana.Edu)
Computer Science Department and The Cognitive Science Program,
Indiana University, Bloomington, IN 47405 USA

Abstract

Given the difficulties in learning meanings of words by observing the referent, it has been suggested that children use the syntactic context of the word to predict part of its meaning, a hypothesis known as syntactic bootstrapping. Semantic bootstrapping is the opposite theory that the knowledge of semantics helps in acquiring syntax. While there is evidence that children can apply their knowledge of correlations between syntax and semantics to perform bootstrapping, it is not clear how they come to know about these correlations in the first place. Here, a connectionist network is presented that learns to comprehend a miniature language by associating sentences with the corresponding scenes. In doing so, it learns the syntactic/semantic correlations and exhibits bootstrapping behavior. It is argued that such specialized phenomena can emerge when general mechanisms are applied to a specific task, and it is not always necessary to endow the learner with pre-existing specialized mechanisms.

Introduction

It is generally accepted that children aged 18 months to 6 years learn 5 to 10 new words every day. Assuming that children can hypothesize some appropriate set of concepts in a given situation, and they attempt to map speech segments onto those concepts, how do they determine which sound segment corresponds to which concept? A potential solution to this problem of assigning meanings to words is that word meanings are learned by observing the real-world contingencies of their use. The meaning of *rabbit* is learned by observing that it is uttered in the presence of rabbits. However, this simple explanation seems to be inadequate when trying to account for acquisition of all words. Gleitman (1990) lists some of the problems: (1) This theory fails to account for the fact that children with radically different exposure conditions (*e.g.*, the blind and the sighted) acquire much the same meanings, (2) many verbs are used for the same events and only provide a perspective on an event (*e.g.*, *chase* and *flee*), and (3) many verbs only differ in the level of specificity at which they describe single events (*e.g.*, *see*, *look*, *orient*). Furthermore, learning of verbs by observation of extralinguistic context seems to be especially problematic. Lederer, Gleitman, & Gleitman (1995) have shown that verb use by mothers aligns poorly with ongoing events. In this study, mothers of very young children usually uttered nouns just when the

corresponding objects were the focus of conversation or were being manipulated by the child. This was not the case with verbs. Verbs were not uttered in a tight time-lock with the events they describe. Verbs standardly encode relational concepts, and the meaning that the speaker has in mind is rarely accessible by observation alone (Gentner, 1982).

To overcome these difficulties in the learning of verb meaning by observation, it has been suggested that children use another important source of information: The systematic relationship between verb meaning and syntactic structure. This proposal is known as *syntactic bootstrapping* (Landau and Gleitman, 1985; Gleitman, 1990; Gleitman & Gleitman, 1992). The learner observes the real world situations and also observes the language structures in which various words appear. If there is a correlation between meanings and a range of syntactic structures, the meaning (or some components of the meaning) of an unknown word can be predicted when it appears in a familiar structure.

Semantic bootstrapping (Grimshaw, 1981; Pinker, 1984) is in some ways a mirror image of the syntactic bootstrapping proposal, where syntax is acquired with help from semantics. This is the hypothesis that children exploit mappings or linking rules from cognition to syntax to acquire grammatical categories. These linking rules are innately specified and are part of a special language-acquisition device. For example, a linking rule might specify that all names of objects are count nouns. Thus children might learn that *car* describes a solid object and infer that it is a count noun. When they learn that count nouns follow the determiner *a*, from phrases like *a car*, they can infer from a phrase like *a problem* that *problem* is a count noun.

Prerequisites for bootstrapping

For the syntactic and semantic bootstrapping proposals to work, several pieces need to be in place: (a) There must be stable syntactic/semantic correlations, (b) children must be able to parse the sentence so as to make the structural information available, (c) children must somehow know about the syntactic/semantic correlations, and (d) children must apply this knowledge of correlations to perform bootstrapping.

Significant amount of evidence has been accumulated for (a), (b), and (d) above. We do not discuss this evidence in detail here; see Naigles, Gleitman, and Gleitman (1993), for a summary. However, (c), the question of how children position themselves to use syntactic/semantic correlations, remains open. Naigles, Gleitman, and Gleitman (1993) state this clearly:

> "The weakest link in both the semantic bootstrapping and syntactic bootstrapping proposals has to do with where the appreciation of the presumed correspondence comes from. ... No one, to our knowledge, has stated how these rudimentary presuppositions about syntax/semantic correspondences might serve as a sufficient basis for setting in motion so powerful a bootstrapping procedure as we, and others, have proposed — either for acquiring the semantics "from" the syntax or for acquiring syntax "from" semantics." (pp. 136-137)

In this work, I address this question with aid of a connectionist simulation. A connectionist network attempts to learn a miniature language given some sentences of this language and the corresponding "scenes" which the sentences describe. A trained network is expected to produce the correct scene given a sentence. In doing this task, the network learns the correspondences between syntactic frames and semantics using statistical correlations.

In the following sections, first the network architecture is presented and its training on the basic comprehension task is described. Then some of the evidence relating to syntactic bootstrapping is reviewed and the network's ability to perform syntactic bootstrapping is demonstrated. Next, we deal with semantic bootstrapping and the network's ability to acquire new syntax with the help of semantics is shown. We end with discussion and conclusions.

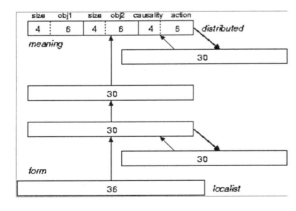

Figure 1. The network architecture. The numbers in the layers show the number of units. Downward connections are one-to-one fixed copyback weights.

The Network

The architecture of the network is shown in Figure 1. It contains recurrent connections in the hidden layer as in a Simple Recurrent Network or SRN (Elman, 1990) to handle temporal sequences of words. In addition to the standard SRN architecture, recurrent connections are added to the output layer. These connections take on the responsibility of remembering what has already been learned from the earlier portion of the sentence, reducing the burden of the hidden layers.

Input

Then input to the network consists of sentences or noun phrases (called "sentences" from here on) describing one or two objects and optionally an action, generated by the grammar shown in Figure 2.

```
S  → NP | NP1 | NP is IV | NP1 are IV |
     NP is TV NP
NP → DET N | DET SIZE N
NP1 → NP and NP
N  → boy | girl | dog | mouse
SIZE → large | small
IV → jumping | dancing | running | walking
TV → pushing | holding | hugging | kicking
DET → a
```

Figure 2. The grammar used to generate input sentences for the network.

One can divide the sentences generated by this grammar into five basic types:

(a) a boy (N)
(b) a boy and a girl (NN)
(c) a boy is jumping (NV)
(d) a boy and a girl are jumping (NNV)
(e) a boy is pushing a girl (NVN)

With optional adjectives describing the size, sentences such as *a girl and a big dog are jumping* or *a small dog and a big mouse* are obtained. These sentences are presented to the network sequentially, one word at each time step. Words are represented in a localist manner by turning on a single bit in the input layer. The simplifying assumption here is that the speech stream is segmented into words and other sources of information such as prosody are ignored. Also, *ing* is treated as a separate word, with the assumption that it can be discerned from the word stem as a separate unit. An end-of-sentence marker, STOP, is presented after the last word of each sentence, at which point all context units in the network (i.e., the units that receive the copyback connections) are reset.

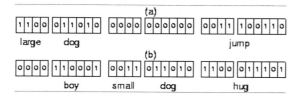

Figure 3. The representations of scenes corresponding two (a) *a large dog is jumping* and (b) *a boy is hugging a small dog*.

Output

On the output or the semantic end, the descriptions of "scenes" corresponding to the input sentence are presented as a 30-bit fixed-width vector. There are two slots for objects, and one for the action or the event taking place. Each object slot is divided into two slots of 4 and 6 units each, which represent the attribute large (1100) or small (0011) and type of object respectively. In the 10-bit event slot, the first 4 bits indicate whether the action is causal or non-causal (with activations 1100 and 0011 respectively), and the remaining 6 bits describe other features of the action.

A distributed representation for each individual object and event is generated by turning on 3 randomly chosen bits in its slot. If each bit is viewed as representing a feature, this creates representations with partially overlapping features. The slots for an attribute, object, or action not described in the scene are set to 0. Figure 3 shows the scene corresponding to two sample sentences.

Comprehension

We first test if the network is capable of performing the basic task of producing the correct scene corresponding to an input sentence. The set of all sentences generated by the grammar in Fig. 2 was probabilistically divided into two parts, one for training and the other for testing generalization. There is significant variability in the total number of different types of sentences generated by the above grammar: There are 12 sentences of type (a), 144 sentences of type (b), 48 sentences of type (c), and 576 sentences each of type (d) and (e). Hence, these sentences were included in the training set with differing probabilities: 1.0 for type (a), 0.4 for type (b), 0.7 for (c), and 0.2 for (d) and (e). Researchers have noted that when there are a small number of patterns of a certain type in the training set, other more frequent patterns can overwhelm the network causing it to ignore the former pattern type. To avoid this problem and give more representation to sentences that have a lower frequency, type (a) sentences were included thrice in the training set while type (c) sentences were included twice. These probabilities are simply meant to ensure that all sentence types have a significant representation in the training set; the exact values are not critical.

The network was trained using backpropagation on the sentences in the training set. The complete target was held constant for the duration of the entire sentence. This ensures that no words are given a special status and encourages the network to process the words as soon as they arrive. A learning rate of 0.0005 and no momentum were used. The weights can be updated after every pattern, at the end of each epoch, or at some intermediate point between the two. Somewhat better results were obtained when weights are updated after every epoch, when the entire training set is presented. Training was continued till there was no significant improvement in the error.

There are several ways to compare the output of the network with the desired output in order to assess the performance of the network. Here, if the activation of an output unit was less than 0.5, it was considered OFF and it was taken as being ON otherwise. A sentence was declared to be processed correctly if, at the end of the sentence, all output units had the desired ON or OFF activation. With this criterion, after 18000 epochs, 100% accuracy was achieved on a training set of 322 (different) sentences and 96.7% of sentences were processed correctly in the remaining 1034 sentences of the testing set, which the network had not seen during training. Similar results were obtained during different runs. The network was, then, largely successful in this task of producing semantics given a sentence, or comprehension.

Next we look at the experiments regarding bootstrapping behavior in the network.

Syntactic Bootstrapping

As noted earlier, syntactic bootstrapping is the hypothesis that children can use the knowledge of syntax to predict meanings of words. There is evidence that children use syntactic bootstrapping (*e.g.*, Brown, 1957; Katz, Baker, & Macnamara, 1974; Naigles, 1990; Fisher, Hall, Rakowitz, & Gleitman, 1994; Fisher, 1996). Some of the experiments regarding syntactic bootstrapping are briefly summarized below.

Brown (1957) presented preschoolers with a picture and syntactically contrasting sentences with a novel word. Three groups of subjects were presented with the picture depicting a novel action being done to a novel substance with a novel instrument. Children were asked to show *some blick*, *a blick* or *blicking*. The children's choices were the substance, the instrument, and the action, respectively.

Naigles (1990) used a preferential looking paradigm where the task of children (mean age 24 months) was to decide between two disjoint interpretations of a novel verb by looking at one of the two screens in front of them depicting different scenes. The children who heard sentences such as *the rabbit is glorping the duck* chose the causal action (*e.g.*, rabbit pushing the duck down). On the other hand, the children who heard

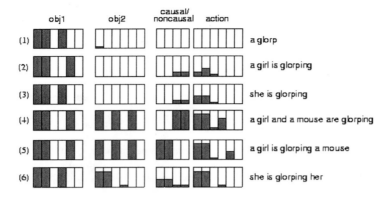

Figure 4. The activations of the output units at the end of various input sentences. The height of the bars indicates the approximate strength of the activations.

sentences such as *the rabbit and the duck are glorping* chose the intransitive interpretation (*e.g.*, rabbit and duck wheeling their arms).

Fisher (1996) carried out experiments similar to those by Naigles (1990), with ambiguous pronouns like *she* and *her* used to describe events. Again, children who heard sentences such as *She's glorping her over there* tended to choose the transitive or causal interpretation of the novel word, while those who heard *She's glorping over there* chose the intransitive interpretation.

Experiment

Here, the goal was to examine the network's "guess" about the meaning of a novel word when the word is presented in different syntactic contexts. Six different types of sentences were presented to the network, all containing the same unknown word: (1) *a glorp*, (2) *a girl is glorping*, (3) *she is glorping*, (4) *a girl and a mouse are glorping*, (5) *a girl is glorping a mouse*, and (6) *she is glorping her*.[1]

The results are shown in Figure 4 in terms of the activations of various output units. The two slots for the sizes of the two objects are omitted since they are not activated in any case. As can be seen from the figure, mainly the slot for the first object is activated for sentence (1), and the action slot is also activated for sentence (2). By and large, the network is able to predict the causality and non-causality of the unknown verb when embedded in a transitive and an intransitive frame respectively. Recall that in the four output units indicating the causality of the action, 1100 implies a causal meaning while 0011 stands for a non-causal meaning. A pattern of 0011 is obtained in the case of *a girl and a mouse are glorping*, while a 1100 pattern is

obtained indicating causality in the case of *a girl is glorping a mouse*. For sentences (2) and (3), the indication of non-causality is not very strong, but clearly the activation pattern is closer to 0011 than to 1100. For unknown words such as *she*, the network guesses the meaning from one of the words in its vocabulary. Similar results are obtained for sentences with four different unknown verbs and various known nouns. The network seems to have developed an ability to use the syntactic context to predict a component of the meaning of a novel word.

Semantic Bootstrapping

Semantic bootstrapping can be viewed as a proposal complementary to the semantic bootstrapping hypothesis. Originally developed by Grimshaw (1981) and Pinker (1984), in this procedure children first learn meanings of words by observing their real-world contingencies. Then innate linking or mapping rules are invoked which specify the structures that the word might be used in. Later on, the term "semantic bootstrapping" has also been used for the idea that the knowledge of semantics can be helpful in learning syntax, just as syntax is useful in acquiring word meanings. Here, I use it in this more general sense. Perhaps a different term such as "pragmatic bootstrapping" is more appropriate.

Unlike syntactic bootstrapping, there is relatively little direct empirical support for semantic bootstrapping, mainly due do methodological difficulties. Bowerman (1977, 1982) provides evidence that given the meaning of a verb, children can make predictions about the syntactic structures in which the verb will appear. If a child knows that a verb, indicating the motion of some entity can appear intransitively as well as transitively (*e.g.*, The ship sinks and The *pirate sinks the ship*, i.e., causes the ship to sink), she can

---

[1] It should be noted that *she* and *her* are just unknown words for the network, while they were familiar to the children in the experiments of Fisher (1996).

extend this relationship to new cases for verbs with similar meaning (*e.g.*, *The lion falls* and *The horse falls the lion*, i.e., causes the lion to fall). Similar overextension errors are well-known in literature.

Experiment

The aim of the experiment was to examine if the network benefits from the knowledge of semantics in learning new syntax or syntactic frames[2]. First, one must decide how to determine whether the network has learned a new syntactic frame, since assessing the knowledge of syntax is not as straightforward as assessing the knowledge of word meanings. One could rely on production for this determination: If the new frame is used only in appropriate ways in a variety of situations, one can consider it as having been learned. Since the current model does not involve production, an indirect measure is used. A new frame is considered to be learned at the point where it can be used to perform syntactic bootstrapping.

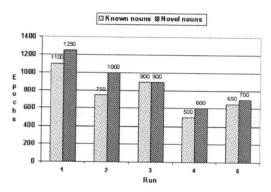

Figure 5. The number of epochs required to learn the transitive frame when known and unknown nouns are used in the frame.

With this criterion in mind, the network was trained in a way similar to one used in the comprehension task, except that no NVN sentences were used in training. In addition, no adjectives were used which allows for a training set of a smaller size and faster learning. Thus the network was only familiar with intransitive verbs after training. This network was then further trained in two different ways. In the first case, NVN sentences were added to the training set using three familiar nouns and three new transitive verbs. In the second case, three novel nouns were added to the vocabulary. The same number of NVN sentences were added to the

_____

[2]We do not attempt to model any specific experiments here, but explore the general idea behind semantic bootstrapping that knowledge of semantics can help in acquiring syntax.

training set, with the provision that only the novel nouns were used in the NVN frames.

Initially, the network classified the new verbs as intransitive, as those were the only type of verbs it had seen. Then the network was trained using the two training sets with the NVN frame, using identical parameters. The weights were updated after every pattern. During this training, network's knowledge of the new NVN frame was assessed periodically (every 50 epochs) by giving as input an NVN sentence where the two nouns and the verb were all unknown words (i.e., not included in either training set). The time, in terms of the number of epochs, for the network to learn to classify a verb in the NVN frame as transitive, was measured in both cases. The results of five different runs (each containing two runs mentioned above) carried out with this procedure are shown in Figure 5.

As is clear from the figure, learning the new frame was faster in most cases when known nouns were used in the frame. On average, the network was faster by 12.2% with familiar nouns. Although this is not "one-shot" learning, the knowledge of semantics of the nouns does seem to help in learning the new syntactic frame.

Discussion and Conclusions

A connectionist network was trained to comprehend a miniature language, or to produce scenes given sentences of that language. The trained network exhibited the ability to predict components of the meanings of novel words when they were presented in familiar syntactic frames. It is believed that children also possess this ability to perform syntactic bootstrapping. There is evidence that there are correlations between syntax and semantics, and that children can apply these correlations to learn word meanings. However, it is unclear how children come to know about this linkage. This simulation suggests that the this knowledge can be acquired by experience with linguistic and corresponding extralinguistic events. The network works with an environment where there is a prefect correlation between sentences and the corresponding scenes, which is clearly unrealistic. In spite of this, the simulation provides evidence that if such a (sufficiently strong) syntactic/semantic correlation exists then it may be learned without any prior knowledge of the specific nature of language. Infants have heard approximately 6 million words by 7 months of age, and they can use some of this rich experience to detect regularities within language as well as correlations between linguistic and extra-linguistic events.

We noted earlier that learning verbs by observation is especially difficult because the events that verbs describe are distributed in time. In the simulation, however, events are presented in the same way as objects, always available in the scene for mapping. This makes them easier to learn for the network "by observation," and it does not necessarily need to relay on syntactic information. The correlations between syntactic frames and meanings are discovered nonetheless. This suggests that the syntactic context of a word can useful in learning the meaning even when it is not strictly necessary. One might expect the network to show even stronger bootstrapping effects if the events are distributed in time.

The network also exhibits what might be described as semantic bootstrapping in a general sense, or pragmatic bootstrapping. The network's learning of new syntactic frames is aided by the knowledge of semantics.

In the experiments with the network, I have attempted to use sentences that are similar to the ones used in experiments with children. Use of a wider variety of sentence types and a larger vocabulary are desirable, and can be useful in showing bootstrapping effects more robustly. Bootstrapping behavior in the network is related to the well-established ability of connectionist networks to do pattern completion, so one might expect these effects to scale up to a larger domain as well. It should be noted, however, that the primary goal of this work is not to produce a general-purpose "natural language processing" system with adult-like capabilities such as story processing, but to show that certain linguistic phenomena in development can emerge in a simple network when performing association of syntax and semantics. Extensive comparisons with language processing systems is out of the scope here, but one might mention Elman's (1990) well-known network that is also able to pick up regularities in the input sentences. That network is trained on the artificial task of predicting the next word in the input. It has been said that this is like trying to learn language by listening to radio. The task here, that of mapping sentences to scenes, is relatively more natural and more suitable for showing bootstrapping effects.

To summarize, syntactic and semantic bootstrapping appear to be mechanisms designed specially for the purpose of acquiring language. However, there is nothing in the network specifically designed to perform bootstrapping. These behaviors emerge as a result of the network's attempts to associate sentences with scenes. Whenever one observes such specific behaviors, it may seem natural to assume that they were designed that way. I hope to have provided some evidence that such assumptions are not always necessary, and general mechanisms can give rise to specialized behaviors when applied to specific tasks.

Acknowledgments

I thank Michael Gasser and the members of the Grounding Lab at Indiana University for many enlightening discussions and suggestions. I also thank anonymous reviewers for their valuable comments.

References

Bowerman, M. (1977). The acquisition of rules governing "possible lexical items:" Evidence from spontaneous speech errors. *Proceedings of Research in Child Language Development, 13*, 148-156.

Bowerman, M. (1982). Starting to talk worse: Clues to language acquisition from children's late speech errors. In S. Strauss (Ed.), *U-shaped behavioral growth*. New York: Academic.

Brown, R. (1957). Linguistic determinism and the part of speech. *Journal of Abnormal and Social Psychology, 55*, 1-5.

Elman, J.L. (1990). Finding structure in time. *Cognitive Science*, 14, 179-211.

Fisher, C. (1996). Structural limits on verb mapping: The role of analogy in children's interpretations of sentences. *Cognitive Psychology, 31*, 41-81.

Fisher, C., Hall, D., Rakowitz, S., & Gleitman, L. (1994). When it is better to receive than to give: Syntactic and conceptual constraints on vocabulary growth. *Lingua, 92*, 333-375.

Gentner, D. (1982). Why nouns are learned before verbs: Linguistic relativity versus natural partitioning. In S.A. Kuczaj (Ed.), *Language Development, Volume 2: Language, Thought, and Culture*. Hillsdale, NJ: Erlbaum.

Gleitman, L. (1990). The structural sources of verb meanings. *Language Acquisition, 1*, 3-55.

Gleitman, L. & Gleitman, H. (1992). A picture is worth a thousand words, but that's the problem: The role of syntax in vocabulary acquisition. *Current Directions in Psychological Science, 1*, 31-35.

Grimshaw, J. (1981). Form, function, and the language acquisition device. In C.L. Baker and J.J. McCarthy (Eds.), *The Logical Problem of Language Acquisition*. Cambridge, MA: MIT Press.

Katz, N., Baker, E., & Macnamara, J. (1974). What's in a name? A study of how children learn common and proper names. *Child Development, 45*, 469-473.

Landau, B. & Gleitman, L. (1985). *Language and Experience: Evidence From the Blind Child*. Cambridge, MA: Harvard University Press.

Lederer, A., Gleitman, L., & Gleitman, H. (1995). Verbs of a feather flock together: Structural properties of maternal speech. In M. Tomasello & E. Merriam (Eds.), *Acquisition of the Verb Lexicon*. New York: Academic.

Naigles, L. (1990). Children use syntax to learn verb meanings. *Journal of Child Language, 117*, 357-374.

Naigles, L., Gleitman, H., & Gleitman, L. (1993). Children acquire word meaning components from syntactic evidence. In E. Dromi (Ed.), *Language and Cognition: A Developmental Perspective*. Norwood, NJ: Ablex.

Pinker, S. (1984). *Language Learnability and Language Development*. Cambridge, MA: Harvard University   Press.

A Self-Organizing Neural Network Model of the Acquisition of Word Meaning

Igor Farkaš (ifarkas@richmond.edu)
Ping Li (pli@richmond.edu)
Department of Psychology
University of Richmond
VA 23173, USA

Abstract

In this paper we present a self-organizing connectionist model of the acquisition of word meaning. Our model consists of two neural networks and builds on the basic concepts of Hebbian learning and self-organization. One network learns to approximate word transition probabilities, which are used for lexical representation, and the other network, a self-organizing map, is trained on these representations, projecting them onto a 2D space. The model relies on lexical co-occurrence information to represent word meanings in the lexicon. The results show that our model is able to acquire semantic representations from both artificial data and real corpus of language use. In addition, the model demonstrates the ability to develop rather accurate word representations even with a sparse training set.

Introduction

A central debate in the domain of language acquisition is how children acquire the meanings of words. Although numerous studies have addressed this question in the last few decades, researchers have not yet reached any consensus. One important line of disagreement is whether children can use contextual or structural knowledge from the sentence to bootstrap their learning of the semantic contents of words. Proponents of the *syntactic bootstrapping hypothesis* (e.g., Gleitman, 1990) argue that children can and do make use of the structural information to learn word meaning, whereas advocates of the *semantic bootstrapping hypothesis* (e.g., Pinker, 1994) are suspicious of such an approach that relies on the child's distributional analysis of the input.

In recent years, connectionism and computational analyses of large-scale corpora have revitalized the interest in structural relationships and distributional analyses of language. Independent of proposals like the syntactic bootstrapping hypothesis in child language, research has revealed the power of distributional information in deriving accurate representations of the meaning and function of linguistic components. In particular, it is argued that both grammatical and semantic categories can be acquired by connectionist networks or similar statistical machines through the computation of the statistical regularities inherent in the input data. For example, Elman (1990) showed that categories of nouns and verbs, and subcategories of animates versus inanimates (within nouns), and transitives versus intransitives (within verbs), can emerge from a simple recurrent network's analyses of the lexical co-occurrence properties in the input. Redington, Chater, and Finch (1998) demonstrated that the use of distributional properties in a large-scale speech corpus allows a statistical system to derive grammatical categories. Landauer and Dumais (1997) showed that it is also possible to accurately represent semantic relationships through a high-dimensional word-to-text matrix.

Burgess and Lund (1997, 1999) proposed a high-dimensional space model to represent the meaning of the lexicon. Their model, the Hyperspace Analogue to Language (HAL), attempts to capture meaning by reference to global lexical co-occurrences – how many words co-occur with the target word, and how often, in a large moving window that runs through the text. A co-occurrence matrix for any number of words in a given window is derived, and weighted by the frequency of co-occurrence among the words. The columns and rows in this matrix represent the co-occurrence values for words that follow and precede the target, respectively. The target word is then represented by concatenating the column and row values. Burgess and Lund claim that this method captures the global lexical constraints for words, and the constraints reflect the total contextual history of a word in a high-dimensional space of language use. In an attempt to apply this method to the acquisition of word meaning, Li, Burgess, and Lund (2000) analyzed the 3.8 million word tokens of parental speech in the CHILDES English database (MacWhinney, 2000) and found that it is possible to derive accurate semantic representations given a reasonable size of corpus such as the CHILDES adult speech (rather than a very large corpus such as the Usenet data for the original HAL model). The implication is that young children can acquire word meanings if they exploit the considerable amount of contextual information in the linguistic input. However, this study, like HAL, does not qualify as a true developmental model, because no learning was involved in arriving at the representations – only statistical analyses of the data were involved (e.g., window size, corpus size, and the constraint dimensions were manipulated at each stage). In short, HAL is a representation model and not a processing or learning model, as Burgess and Lund (1999) pointed out.

In this study, we present a self-organizing neural network model that can learn semantics from linguistic input. The basic idea is similar to HAL, but there are two major distinctive features to our model: (1) it is based on unsupervised neural networks that learn on line, (2) it incorporates a mechanism that leads to accurate word representations (and consequently meaningful lexical maps) even when the training data are sparse. Our model builds on the basic concepts of self-organization and Hebbian learning (Kohonen, 1990; Miikkulainen, 1993), and incorporates ideas from semantic categorization in feature maps (Ritter & Kohonen, 1989; Li, 1999, 2000). [1] Preliminary results show that our model is able to acquire rather accurate semantic representations from both artificial data and real corpus of language use.

Method

Our model consists of two neural networks that functionally interact with each other. Fig. 1 presents a diagrammatic sketch of the model. The lower part is a special recurrent neural network, the word co-occurrence detector (WCD), whose modifiable connections are trained to approximate word transitional probabilities. The upper part is a self-organizing map (SOM; Kohonen, 1990), which reads the words distributively represented in the modifiable connections and creates a two-dimensional layout of the lexicon.

An initial assumption of the model is that we have a pool of N localist word representations corresponding to the lexicon. Whenever the word w_i is read, the corresponding unit in layer A becomes activated, creating localist representation $\mathbf{o} = [o_1, ..., o_N]$. At the same time step, layer B holds the previous word w_j (context) represented by vector $\mathbf{c} = [c_1, ..., c_N]$, which was copied over there from layer A in previous time step.

The algorithm

The adaptable connections between layers A and B serve to approximate the transitional probabilities between successive words, and as such, they are trained by Hebbian learning with implicit normalization to become probabilities. Therefore, two co-occurrence matrices instead of one are used in this model. Assume that at time t, the current word is w_i, and is preceded by word w_j. At every time step, both $\mathbf{l}$ and $\mathbf{r}$ links are modified. Specifically,

---

[1] Lowe (1997) presented a similar model to simulate semantic priming. Developed independently of his research, our model differs from his in implementation details, and focuses on different theoretical issues.

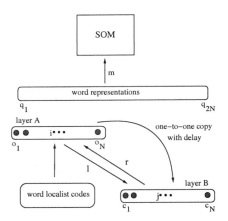

Figure 1: The architecture of the model. Layers A and B of the WCD (see the text) have full connectivity via modifiable $\mathbf{l}$ and $\mathbf{r}$ links of the WCD. Other, one-to-one links serve to feed the unit activity from A to B with (discrete single time-step) delay. The SOM is a self-organizing neural network trained on distributed word representations extracted from modifiable links.

the link l_{ij} is updated to approximate $P(w_j^{t-1}|w_i^t)$, i.e. the probability that the word w_j preceded the word w_i. At the same time, the link r_{ji} is updated to approximate $P(w_i^t|w_j^{t-1})$, i.e. the probability that the word w_i follows the word w_j. Each word is then characterized by a concatenation of vectors

$$\mathbf{l}_i = [l_{i1}, l_{i2}, ..., l_{iN}]$$
$$\mathbf{r}_i = [r_{1i}, r_{2i}, ..., r_{Ni}]$$

where $\mathbf{l}_i$ approximates the probability distribution of words preceding w_i (left context), and $\mathbf{r}_i$ the probability distribution of words following w_i (right context). Each word is thus represented by a real-valued vector $\mathbf{q}_i = [\mathbf{l}_i, \mathbf{r}_i]$ of dimensionality $2N$.

The learning rules used for updating the connections have the form

$$\Delta l_{ij}^t = \beta o_i^t (c_j^t - l_{ij}^t)$$
$$\Delta r_{ji}^t = \beta c_j^t (o_i^t - r_{ji}^t)$$

where $0 < \beta < 1$ is the learning rate. [2] Simultaneously with $\mathbf{q}_i$ update, the SOM is also trained on $\mathbf{q}_i$ as inputs. Every SOM unit k has an array of connections in the form of a codevector $\mathbf{m}_k = [m_{k1}, ..., m_{k,2N}]$ associated with it, which learns to approximate the inputs in such a manner that every SOM unit tends to become "specialized" for a concrete word $\mathbf{q}_i$, and that neighboring units will become specialists ("winners") to similar words.

---

[2] Basically, these learning rules work as counters, as in the HAL model, except that normalization is performed simultaneously with counting.

The SOM algorithm is standard (Kohonen, 1990). At every time step, the winner k^* is found to satisfy the condition $k^* = \arg\min_k\{\|\mathbf{q}_i(t) - \mathbf{m}_k(t)\|\}$, where $\|.\|$ denotes the Euclidean distance, and then all codevectors within winner's neighborhood are shifted towards the current input via

$$\Delta\mathbf{m}_k(t) = \alpha(t)\left[\mathbf{q}_i(t) - \mathbf{m}_k(t)\right],$$

for all k in the neighborhood of k^*. During learning, both neighborhood radius and learning rate $0 < \alpha < 1$ decrease in time.

It is reasonable to start training the SOM codevectors at a relatively later stage of the WCD network. The reason is that the SOM sees statistically accurate word representations only towards the end of training, so delayed update of codevectors facilitates their ordering and convergence.

Generalization

To extend the basic algorithm, we would like the model to have some generalization property for novel word transitions. So far the links would be updated only between adjacent words seen in the training data. For example, if the model has been trained on word strings like John sees and Mary loves we would like the model to have non-zero prediction probabilities (stored in SOM connections) when processing the word strings John loves or Mary sees, which have never occurred in the training data. It is well known that human learners are able to make this type of generalization (Fodor & Pylyshyn, 1988; Elman, 1998).

Our hypothesis is that words that occur in the same contexts will tend to have similar vectors, as our model represents words by distributed vectors $\mathbf{q}_i$ that incorporate context information. We can exploit these vector similarities to obtain generalization properties for novel word transitions.

We applied the following mechanism in the later phases of training when the SOM units are expected to have already established some global order. At each time step, the winner for the current word is found in the SOM. A few units j among its neighbors are also identified, which have the status of being the winner for any word. This requires a unit labeling procedure running on line (based on majority voting, so that every unit could have only one word label associated with it). Next, for each SOM unit k, the corresponding output units o_j in the WCD network are set to one, thus enabling the update of their connections. This strategy enables an extended update of connections from *previous-word neighborhood* to *current-word neighborhood*, instead of simply from previous word to current word. As a consequence, more accurate $\mathbf{q}_i$'s can be obtained even when the WCD network sees only a fraction of word transitions in the training data. [3]

---

[3]This method may be thought of as a kind of smooth-

Normalized negative log-likelihood   To evaluate the model's generalization ability, we measure how the model can generalize to previously unseen word strings. We use the normalized negative log-likelihood (NNL), a commonly used method for performance measure in symbol prediction tasks (Ron, Singer, & Tishby, 1996). This is done as follows. The parameters of the model are fixed after training and for every word in the vocabulary there is a corresponding winner among the SOM units. In a sequence of words $W = w_1 w_2 ... w_s$, every time the model sees the word $w(t)$, we find its winner k^* in the SOM, and the estimate of its next correct-word probability $\hat{P}(w^{t+1}|w^t) = m_{k^*,j+N}$ is read out (from the right-context part of connections' array), where j is an index of w^{t+1}. Hence, for every model $\mathcal{M}$ and the test sequence W_{test} we evaluate

$$NNL_{\mathcal{M}}(W_{test}) = \frac{-1}{s-1}\sum_{t=1}^{s-1}\log_N \hat{P}(w^{t+1}|w^t),$$

where the base of the logarithm equals the number of words in the lexicon. The higher the next correct-symbol probabilities are, the lower the *NNL* is, and vice versa. If $NNL = 0$, prediction accuracy is 100%; if $NNL = 1$, the distribution of probabilities is uniform.

Results

Artificial corpus

We tested our model on data created by a simple language generator (SLG, Rohde 1999). Compared to the well-known Elman 29-word data set (Elman, 1990), our data set was slightly more complex (with 45 words). We added plurals, optional adjectives and determiners to SV(O) sentences, which allowed us to generate more complex sentences such as the hungry lion chases boys, girls sit-in a bus, and a dog barks.

Out of the hundreds of sentences generated by SLG we used 435 unique sentences so that none of the sentences was repeated. All sentences had the end-of-sentence mark (EOS) as an additional symbol. Sentences were presented to the model in random order, one word at a time for each sentence. Learning started in the WCD network ($\beta = 0.005$), and during the second half of the training, learning also took place in the SOM network. Figure 2 shows the SOM for all 45 words. Clearly, word representations based on $\mathbf{q}$'s from our model provide a considerable amount of information, sufficient for the data to be correctly mapped onto a 2D topology preserving space according to syntactic as well as semantic categories.

---

ing the bigram probability estimates based on words with similar statistics, as used in statistical NLP (e.g., Manning & Schütze, 1999).

Figure 2: The SOM trained on artificial data. The network identified various grammatical as well as some semantic categories.

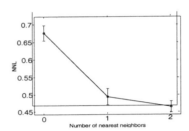

Figure 3: Prediction accuracy of the model during test on artificial data. Inclusion of neighbors in connections' update helps to derive more accurate word representations even with a small amount of training data.

Next, we investigated the generalization property of the model. We wanted to model the fact that human learners (children in particular) process a fraction of all possible (meaningful) word combinations and are able to produce and understand novel word combinations. To simulate this ability, the model should have non-zero next-word prediction probabilities so that new word associations can occur.

The model was trained on a very small portion of the data (81 sentences) and tested on the remaining data (354 sentences). The effect of neighborhood update becomes even more visible in this case. Random splitting was performed 10 times and the results were averaged. As shown in Fig. 3, *NNL* was smaller, if we included at least one nearest neighbor in adaptation. However, higher numbers of nearest neighbors did not improve accuracy, since they already tended to induce non-existing word transitions in word representations. Improvement in accuracy could also be observed in the corresponding maps.

Realistic corpus

To test whether our model can scale up to realistic data, we examined our model's performance on the parental/caregivers' speech in the CHILDES database (see Li, Burgess, & Lund, 2000 for a de-

scription of how the data were extracted). We took parental speech from the Wells corpus (Wells, 1981) and used the 300 most frequent words (roughly 150,000 word tokens) from the data. All other words were treated as a single unknown word w_x in the lexicon (hence $N = 301$). However, because of the relatively high frequency of the unknown words (33%) in the data, treating them all as one would induce a bias toward w_x. To correct this word imbalance, we imposed a probability restriction on w_x: whenever the word w_x was read, the update of connections occurred only in 1% of cases; in other cases reading was skipped to the next word (this might simulate the process of treating unknown words as noise).

Training on this large-scale data set was rather time-consuming. To speed up learning, we first trained the WCD network to develop word representations ($\beta = 0.01$) and then trained the SOM off-line on converged word representations.

Fig. 4 presents the SOM that was trained on the CHILDES Wells corpus for two epochs. Upon closer examination, one can observe various grammatical categories that were clustered in the map: proper nouns, verbs, auxiliary verbs, adjectives, pronouns, etc. Semantic similarities also emerged within the categories.

Discussion

An important premise behind the syntactic bootstrapping hypothesis is that children can acquire word meanings through their distributional analyses of the linguistic input. The distribution-analysis approach has a long tradition in linguistics and psycholinguistics. In fact, much of the pre-Chomsky linguistics is the so-called structuralism that examines the structural relationships between linguistic units (Bloomfield, 1935). Saussure (1916) proposed that the function of a given linguistic "entity" (e.g., a word) is defined entirely by reference to the relationships that hold between this entity and other entities, much like that the role of a chess piece is determined by its relationship with other pieces on the chessboard. For example, words of the same class tend to occupy the same slot in a sentence (*paradigmatically* similar) and have the same co-occurrence constraints with other words (*syntagmatically* similar). [4] Chomsky (1957), however, treating structuralism as purely associationist, threw out this approach in linguistics and replaced it with an emphasis on higher-order hierarchical relationships for linguistic structures. Thus, few linguists today believe that associationism or structuralism could work for language.

---

[4]In this context, we can claim that our model places paradigmatically similar words close to each other in the map, whereas syntagmatically similar words can be far from each other. However, the mutual associations between the latter are captured in the SOM codevectors in the form of prediction probabilities.

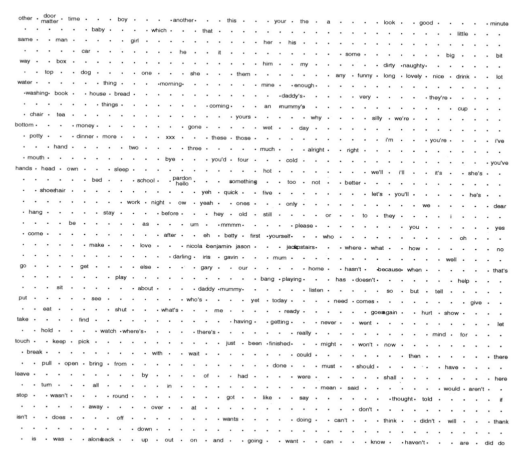

Figure 4: The SOM (40×40 units) of 300 most frequent words in a portion of the CHILDES parental data. Various grammatical categories are distributed across the map, showing considerable structure. For example, one cluster of nouns can be located in the top left part of the map, whereas a group of proper nouns can be found in the center. Adjectives are located in top right corner. Pronouns are mainly placed in top middle part. Verbs are spread mainly over the bottom half of the map space and within this category, one can identify auxiliary verbs in the bottom right part, etc. Also, semantically similar words are often positioned to neighboring units in the map. For example, mummy's, daddy's in top middle part, now, then and there, here bottom right, up, down bottom left, and so on.

Connectionist approaches represent a new way of looking at associations and structural relationships in language. Our model, along with many other similar statistical models of NLP, appears to fare well in capturing the higher-order relationships in language without recourse to strictly symbolic rules and hierarchies. The model we presented here shows that lexical semantics, traditionally considered a difficult part of language, can indeed emerge from the learning in connectionist systems, in particular, self-organizing neural networks (see also Li, 1999, 2000, in press). Some researchers may also view our model as a connectionist implementation of statistical NLP, because we examine many of the same issues there.

We have demonstrated in this paper that it is possible to learn meanings of words through the learning of co-occurrence statistics, in line with the syntactic bootstrapping hypothesis and the HAL model. Our model learns very simple co-occurrence constraints, and acquires syntactic and semantic categories, in both artificial and realistic linguistic corpora. Our model is also able to display generalization characteristics, that is, to learn novel combinations of word strings that are absent in the training data. The simulation results also indicate that the model does not require a very large amount of data to arrive at accurate semantic representations, contrary to what is commonly expected of statistical learning models.

Self-organizing maps provide an important tool for us to capture lexical relationships, as demonstrated in this study. There is a lot of information in the SOM connections (both lateral and input) which quantitatively describe how the words are associated with each other. Although our model does not directly incorporate lateral connections, these connections can replace the grid topology in the SOM and can be used to represent more complex semantic relationships. One future research direction is to implement lateral connections in our model.

Several other directions/limitations will also be considered in extending the current model. First, the dimension of the word representations grows with the number of words, which makes it difficult to scale up to a very large lexicon. It is a challenge to overcome the initial localist representation while preserving lexical identities. Second, in the current model, the information for SOM is extracted from WCD connections, thus making the model somewhat unusual in terms of information access and flow. Therefore, it would be useful to transform this information to unit activations which then feed to the SOM. Third, the current model is not designed to learn lexicon incrementally; that is, it is unable to take new words to the existing lexicon during learning. Finally, the model uses only the shortest window of context (immediately before and after the target word) to derive semantic representations. Experiments in the HAL model show that larger window sizes yield more accurate word representations (Li, Burgess, & Lund, 2000). In English, this parameter may appear less significant due to the strict word order; in other languages with relatively flexible word order (e.g., Chinese, Italian), the size of the context window may prove to be very important.

Acknowledgments

This research was supported by an NSF grant (#BCS-9975249) to P.L. We are grateful to Curt Burgess, Brian McWhinney, Risto Miikkulainen, and Peter Tiňo for comments and discussions at various stages of the project, and to three anonymous reviewers for final comments. I.F. is also with the Slovak Academy of Sciences, Bratislava, Slovakia.

References

Bloomfield, L. (1935). *Language*. London: Allen & Unwin.

Burgess, C. & Lund, K. (1997). Modelling parsing constraints with high-dimensional semantic space. *Language and Cognitive Processes*, 12, 1–34.

Burgess, C. & Lund, K. (1999). The dynamics of meaning in memory. In Dietrich, E. and Markman, A. (Eds.), *Cognitive Dynamics: Conceptual and Representational Change in Humans and Machines*, Lawrence Erlbaum, Hillsdale, NJ.

Chomsky, N. (1957). *Syntactic Structures*. The Hague: Mouton.

Elman, J. (1990). Finding structure in time. *Cognitive Science*, 14, 179–211.

Elman, J. (1998). Generalization, simple recurrent networks, and the emergence of structure. In Gernsbacher, M. & Derry, S. (Eds.), *Proceedings of the 20th*

Annual Conference of the Cognitive Science Society. Lawrence Erlbaum.

Fodor, J. & Pylyshyn, Z. (1988). Connectionism and cognitive architecture: A critical analysis. *Cognition*, 28, 3–71.

Gleitman, L. (1990). The structural sources of verb meaning. *Language Acquisition*, 1, 3–55.

Kohonen, T. (1990). The self-organizing map. *Proceedings of the IEEE*, 78, 1464–1480.

Landauer, T. & Dumais, S. (1997). A solution to Plato's problem: the latent semantic analysis theory of induction and representation of knowledge. *Psychological Review*, 104, 211–240.

Li, P. (1999). Generalization, representation and recovery in a self-organizing feature map model of language acquisition. In Hahn, M. & Stoness, S. (Eds.), *Proceedings of the 21st Annual Conference of the Cognitive Science Society* (pp. 308–313). Mahwah, NJ: Lawrence Erlbaum.

Li, P. (2000). The acquisition of lexical and grammatical aspect in a self-organizing feature map model. In Gleitman, L. & Jashi, A. (Eds.), *Proceedings of the 22nd Annual Conference of the Cognitive Science Society* (pp. 304-309). Mahwah, NJ: Lawrence Erlbaum.

Li, P. (in press). Language acquisition in a self-organizing neural network model. In Quinlan, P. (Ed.), *Connectionist Models of Development*. Psychology Press, Philadelphia and Briton.

Li, P., Burgess, C., & Lund, K. (2000). The acquisition of word meaning through global lexical co-occurrences. In Clark, E. (Ed.), *Proceedings of the 30th Child Language Research Forum.* (pp. 167–178). Stanford, CA: Center for the Study of Language and Information.

Lowe, W. (1997). Semantic representation and priming in a self-organizing lexicon. In *Proceedings of the 4th Neural Computation and Psychology Workshop* (pp. 227–239). Springer-Verlag.

MacWhinney, B. (2000). *The CHILDES project: Tools for analyzing talk*. Hillsdale, NJ: Lawrence Erlbaum.

Manning, C. D. & Schütze, H. (1999). *Foundations of Statistical Natural Language Processing*. MIT Press.

Miikkulainen, R. (1993). *Subsymbolic Natural Language Processing: An Integrated Model of Scripts, Lexicon and Memory*. MIT Press, Cambridge, MA.

Pinker, S. (1994). How could a child use a verb syntax to learn verb semantics? *Lingua*, 92, 377–410.

Redington, M., Chater, N., & Finch, S. (1998). Distributional information: A powerful cue for acquiring syntactic categories. *Cognitive Science*, 22, 425–470.

Ritter, H. & Kohonen, T. (1989). Self-organizing semantic maps. *Biological Cybernetics*, 61, 241–254.

Rohde, D. (1999). *The simple language generator: Encoding complex languages with simple grammars* (Tech. Rep. CMU-CS-99-123). Pittsburg, PA: Carnegie Mellon University.

Ron, D., Singer, E., & Tishby, N. (1996). The power of amnesia: learning probabilistic automata with variable memory length. *Machine Learning*, 25, 117–149.

Saussure, F. de (1916). *Cours de Linguistique Générale*. Paris: Payot.

Wells, C.G. (1981). *Learning Through Interaction: The Study of Language Development*. Cambridge: Cambridge University Press.

Modeling Task Performance Using the Queuing Network Model Human Processor (QNMHP)

Robert Feyen (rfeyen@umich.edu)
Department of Industrial and Operations Engineering, The University of Michigan
1205 Beal Ave., Ann Arbor, MI 48109-2117 USA

Yili Liu (yililiu@umich.edu)
Department of Industrial and Operations Engineering, The University of Michigan
1205 Beal Ave., Ann Arbor, MI 48109-2117 USA

Abstract

Human performance modeling approaches (HPMAs) that are comprehensive and computational are particularly useful for engineering design. Current approaches have strengths in modeling a person's actions, but lack underlying mathematical foundations on which to base predictions of time and capacity related performance measures. This paper presents a complementary approach that combines elements of the GOMS/Model Human Processor approach with the mathematical concepts and methods of queuing networks. Called the Queuing Network Model Human Processor (QNMHP), the approach provides quantitative predictions and theoretical insights regarding a person's performance. The general queuing network and the approach are discussed with respect to human performance and neuroscience findings. The QNMHP is used to model reaction time tasks and the results compare favorably to prior literature; these findings are discussed briefly along with current efforts to model a driving task.

Introduction

An oft-stated goal in human factors research is providing product and system designers access to human factors information early in a product's development cycle. One crucial element for reaching this goal is a set of engineering models that describe the various aspects of a user's behavior. To be used effectively in product development, human performance modeling approaches (HPMAs) should be both comprehensive and computational (e.g., Elkind, Card, Hochberg, & Huey, 1990). Comprehensive models are not restricted to a specific aspect of human performance (e.g., visual scanning), but attempt to model several aspects of human performance in a single, coherent structure as well as provide insight into the cognitive processes underlying human performance. Computational models are expressed using specific computational methods or languages to allow quantitative analyses of human performance.

Existing HPMAs that attempt to meet these criteria include GOMS/Model Human Processor (Card, Moran, and Newell, 1983), ACT-R and ACT-R/PM (Anderson & Lebiere, 1998), EPIC (Kieras and Meyer, 1997), Soar (Newell, 1990). One issue that has received attention

from these different modeling approaches is the prediction of human performance in systems that require two or more task components to be completed concurrently (e.g., Kieras and Meyer, 1997). The problem-solving tradition in which these approaches are rooted lends considerable strength to predictions of the actions that a person might choose when interacting with a product or system. However, they lack an underlying mathematical foundation capable of providing both the theoretical rationale for and accurate predictions of time- and capacity-based measures of performance, especially in a multiple task context. Some issues in multiple task performance that may be related to such measures include workload, scheduling and attention allocation between individual tasks, and interference between tasks (Damos, 1992).

This paper presents a complementary approach that combines elements of the GOMS/Model Human Processor approach with an underlying framework based on the mathematical concept of queuing networks. This combination, called the Queuing Network Model Human Processor (QNMHP), yields a computational and comprehensive HPM approach that has unique strengths for explaining and predicting time- and capacity-based performance measures in both single and multiple task performance. An overview for both GOMS and queuing networks is given below, followed by a brief description of the QNMHP. The paper concludes with a discussion of predictions made using the QNMHP for a set of reaction time tasks and the current modeling efforts.

Overview of GOMS

The family of GOMS/Model Human Processor models was developed and extensively validated in the area of human-computer interaction. In general, the majority of these models are procedural in nature. By assuming that people learn how to complete a task by generating rules for use, these models represent how a person interacts with any devices required to complete the task by defining those rules and sequencing through them one by one until the task is complete. The GOMS family of models is based on the concept that a person has one or more goals (G) to achieve and can do so by using methods (M). Methods, in turn, are a series of steps comprised of operators (O) representing elementary perceptual, cognitive, or motor activities. If more than one method can be used to accomplish a goal, then selection rules (S) can be applied to indicate the appropriate method for the current situation (Card, Moran, and Newell, 1983). However, these models are limited by assumptions that the user being modeled is an expert and that stimuli can only be processed serially, one at a time (Olson & Olson, 1990). By applying the critical path method (CPM) to the GOMS approach, John was able to relax the serial processing assumption and illustrate the critical path of information for tasks in which discrete steps occurred in parallel (John, 1990). CPM-GOMS has been used successfully in design applications to model tasks such as those performed by telephone operators (Gray, John, and Atwood, 1993). However, the step completion times in CPM-GOMS are assumed to be constants, yielding an average time with no indication of variance. This assumption may pose interpretation problems in situations where the individual steps have an element of randomness, which may cause the critical path to vary from cycle to cycle.

One crucial aspect of any cognitive modeling approach is a methodology by which specific tasks are represented in the model. An effective methodology provides consistency so that, even if different analysts model the same task, the descriptions of the cognitive elements required to accomplish the task are both sufficient and similar. Since predictions from the GOMS models depend on the skill and experience of the analyst in representing the task, the Natural GOMS Language (NGOMSL) was developed to address consistency issues. This approach uses computer programming-like language to represent the steps in a task and defines a recommended syntax for describing a task (Kieras, 1988). For example, modeling efforts using EPIC have used NGOMSL task descriptions as a basis for developing the production rules used in a given model (e.g., Kieras and Meyer, 1997).

Overview of Queuing Network Theory

Queuing theory, in essence, is the study of how waiting in line can impact the time to complete a task. In queuing theory, the two primary elements are called servers and customers. A server is a resource that provides a service or performs a function whereas a customer is anything that arrives at the server to obtain service. The customer arrives at the server, and, if the server is busy, waits in a queue (i.e., a waiting line). Once the server becomes available, the customer receives service and leaves. A queuing system is the collection of one or more servers and the one or more queues that may form in front of these servers. Because queuing theory was originally developed to explain the behavior of systems with randomly arising demands (e.g., communications networks), HPMAs that utilize

this theory are uniquely suited to estimating time- and capacity-based performance measures.

Early queuing-based approaches assume that human performance can be analyzed as a single server queuing system processing information in a serial fashion (e.g., Rouse, 1980). Although the resulting models are adequate for some applications, these models often poorly predict performance in multiple task situations. As mentioned above, one reason is that humans appear to be capable of processing stimuli in parallel. The concept of multiple resources addresses this concern by proposing that different types of tasks utilize different types of resources (Wickens, 1992). Although multiple resources theories provide convincing explanations for many multiple task situations, they are not quantitative.

Addressing this concern, Liu proposed queuing network models (QNMs) (Liu, 1994; Liu, 1996; Liu, 1997) which had the mathematical structure capable of integrating the considerations of single server queuing systems with those of the multiple resources theory in a quantitative manner. A queuing network is a network of servers and queues that allow two or more servers to act serially, in parallel, or in any network arrangement. Because these networks include queuing behavior, they are capable of addressing issues of task selection and processing bottlenecks; since they may include parallel servers, they are capable of addressing the issues of simultaneous task performance and task structure (e.g., the effect of manual versus vocal response on performance). In demonstrating that several disparate theories used to describe behavior in reaction time experiments could each be represented by queuing networks, Liu's research appears to support the use of queuing networks to represent the flow of information through the brain during task performance (Liu, 1996). Further work indicated that QNMs were especially applicable to predicting multiple task performance (Liu, 1997). Liu's models also suggested that the pattern of information flow and routing had a significant impact on performance measures in multiple task scenarios. However, to apply the queuing network approach for modeling tasks, two issues had to be resolved: one, finding a general queuing network from which specific task models representing information flow and routing could be generated and, two, linking task and environment descriptions to a specific model.

Building the QNMHP

Looking at other HPMAs, many adopt elements from the Model Human Processor (MHP) proposed by Card, Moran, and Newell (1983). Based on human information processing theory, the MHP utilizes three discrete processing stages: perception, cognition, and motor actions. The MHP draws on empirical evidence to assign parameters to memory storage and decay, capacity, cycle (processing) time, and type of stimuli. In the MHP, the time elapsed for a

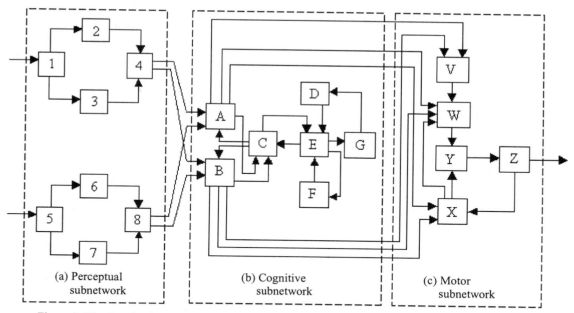

Figure 1: The Queuing Network Model Human Processor (QNMHP). (a) Perceptual: 1 = common visual processing; 2 = visual recognition; 3 = visual location; 4 = location and recognition integrator ; 5 = sound localization; 6 = linguistic processing; 7 = processing of other sounds; 8 = linguistic and other sounds integrator. (b) Cognitive: A = visuospatial sketchpad; B = phonological loop; C = central executor; D = goal procedures; E = performance monitoring; F = high-level cognitive operations; G = goal selection. (c) Motor: V = sensorimotor integration; W = motor element storage; X = movement tuning; Y = motor programming; Z = actuators

stimulus to traverse the three stages of the MHP model is the human's response time. This suggested that the MHP could be used as a general queuing network framework if the stages could be decomposed into a set of linked servers utilizing the various MHP parameters.

The theoretical basis for decomposing the MHP stages into individual servers is the cortical field and neuronal population activation theory described by Roland (1993). This theory states that activity in the brain is accomplished by the activation of functional elements in the cerebral cortex called "fields". Each field, comprised of millions of neurons, accomplishes a certain type of mental function with the specific function depending on the population of neurons in the field that are activated. Cognitive activities such as thought, perception, and action are the result of multiple fields working together to process entities of information. Associated with this theory is the interference principle: if different mental tasks utilize a similar neuronal population, the tasks cannot be performed simultaneously. Based on this theory, the QNMHP servers represent major cortical fields and, as inferred from the interference principle, information entities may form queues at servers already in use.

To select and link the individual servers in the network, neuroscience texts and functional imaging studies of the brain were reviewed to identify areas of

the brain that might represent common cortical fields activated during the performance of a given task and to determine the primary connections between these fields. In setting up the QNMHP, three assumptions of the original MHP were relaxed. First, information entities could be processed in parallel, following the multiple resources theory. Second, a given entity could trigger activity elsewhere in the model, even though it may not have been completely processed at its current stage. Third, when competing for processing resources at the same stage, an entity might impact the processing of other competing entities. The resulting network (Figure 1) is comprised of three subnetworks representing the perceptual, cognitive, and motor stages of the MHP. By default, an unlimited number of entities can be processed simultaneously at any given server except as noted in the following.

Perceptual subnetwork

The visual, auditory, and somatosensory systems are the typical sensory systems considered when modeling a person's perception of the surrounding environment. Of these, the MHP considers visual and auditory perception together as a single processing stage. However, sensory information enters a person's brain through different sensory systems. In support of the processing modality dimensions of multiple resources theory (Wickens, 1992), the visual system processes information separately from the auditory system. Further, the visual system routes information along two parallel paths to simultaneously recognize and locate an object of interest in the field of view (Courtney and Underleider, 1997). The auditory system first locates the source of a sound and then routes information associated with naming and identification of sounds (typically linguistic information) to a different cortical region than elements such as tonal quality (e.g., Mazziotta, Phelps, Carson, and Kuhl, 1982). Based on this, visual and auditory perception are represented in the QNMHP as separate subnetworks, each with four servers (Figure 1a). Because the servers in the perceptual system are assumed to have very high processing capacity, a single input shown entering a server (e.g., server 1 in Figure 1a) does not necessarily imply a processing bottleneck. Also, although investigated, the somatosensory system has been left for later implementation.

Cognitive subnetwork

Functional imaging studies show a number of specific areas in the brain associated with certain cognitive functions. For example, working memory appears to consist of a visuospatial sketchpad, a phonological loop, and a central executive (Baddeley, 1992), each of which has been shown to correspond with specific areas of the brain (Baddeley, 1998). The central executive coordinates attentional control to a task (de Fockert, Rees, Frith, and Lavie, 2001) and communicates with other sections of the brain to carry out various higher-level cognitive functions. These include complex task performance (e.g., search, mental rotation), goal planning, priority selection, and performance monitoring, each of which appears to activate distinctly separate regions of the brain (e.g., Roland, 1993; Frackowiak, Friston, Frith, and Mazziotta, 1997; Carter, 1998). Thus, the QNMHP represents these regions and their functions as separate servers (Figure 1b). Unlike most of the servers in the network, each working memory structure is limited to processing no more than three entities simultaneously.

Motor subnetwork

Once a motor response is initiated in the cognitive subnetwork, it is routed to the motor subnetwork via the working memory structures to gather any additional perceptual information necessary to carry out the response (e.g., target coordinates) (Roland, 1993). The motor subnetwork (Figure 1c) contains five servers to handle sensorimotor integration, motor element recall, motor programming, movement tuning, and execution (e.g., Gilman and Newman, 1992; Carter, 1998; Pritchard and Alloway, 1999). The actuators (hands and eyes) carry out response execution and are limited

to processing one entity at a time. Regression equations to determine hand and eye movement times are based on data from Methods-Time Measurement (MTM) tables for reaches, moves, and eye travel (Niebel, 1993) and depend on whether a movement is to a target with intrapersonal or extrapersonal coordinates.

Memory arrays

For tasks requiring long-term memory retrieval, functional imaging studies have shown that different regions of the brain are accessed depending on the nature of the memory (e.g., procedural, declarative, episodic) (e.g., Frackowiak et al, 1997). When initializing a task simulation in the QNMHP, task and environment specifications are copied into one of five general arrays: stimuli, targets, actions, goals, and actuators. As the task simulation is run, these arrays can be accessed by the various servers as needed and are continually updated to keep track of the status and location of elements required for task completion.

Cycle processing times

A server that simply routes information to another server is assumed to require no processing time. However, memory access by a server requires a cycle processing time that is assumed stochastic and exponential distributed with mean X and an axis shift of Y [written as e(X,Y)]. The axis shift ensures that a minimum time is obtained for each processing cycle.

Perceptual Subnetwork Two memory access cycles are assumed to occur during the perceptual processing of a simple reaction time task. To be consistent with the MHP, the QNMHP requires the minimum processing time to be equivalent to the Fast processing time and the average processing time equivalent to the Middle processing time. For example, due to the two memory access cycles,

$$Fast = 2*Y \text{ and } Y = 25 \text{ msec}$$
$$Middle = 2*(X+Y) \text{ and } X = 25 \text{ msec}$$

This yields an exponential distribution of e(0.025, 0.025) for one perceptual processing cycle.

Cognitive Subnetwork Three memory access cycles are assumed to occur during cognitive processing of a simple reaction time task. Using similar logic as before, the exponential distribution for one cognitive processing cycle is e(0.015, 0.008).

Motor Subnetwork Two memory access cycles are assumed to occur during the response in a simple reaction time task, yielding an exponential distribution for one motor processing cycle of e(0.020,0.015).

Model implementation

The QNMHP network is implemented in ProModel, a commercially available discrete event simulation program. The network is supplemented with a small set of subroutines, each of which accomplishes the function of an operator that may be specified in an NGOMSL task description. Once an individual task procedure is described using NGOMSL, the sequence and operators are translated by the analyst into a form that can be entered into the appropriate memory arrays, along with environmental specifications. As a simulation progresses, these arrays dictate the sequence and type of subroutines required to carry out a task.

Modeling reaction time tasks

Simple reaction time

To confirm that the exponential distributions are reasonable approximations of the MHP cycle time parameters, a simple reaction time task was entered into the model (i.e., move finger in response to a visual stimulus, assuming perfect detection). 500 stimuli were presented to the model and the overall processing times recorded. No processing delays other than the memory access cycles discussed above occurred in these simulation runs. As seen in Table 1, the distributions seem reasonable when compared to the MHP values. Because the upper limit of exponentially distributed values approaches infinity, the 95th percentiles of the resulting data are reported as the maximum times.

Choice reaction time

In the MHP literature, choice reaction time is compared to Hick's law for unequal probabilities (Card *et al*, 1983). By this law, a person confronted with N alternative stimuli that are associated one-to-one with N unique responses has a reaction time given by

$$RT = a + b \, Log_2 \, H \text{ where } H = \Sigma \, p_i \, log_2 \, (1/p_i)$$

(H) is a measure of the information contained by the given stimulus, (p_i) is the perceived probability that a stimulus will occur, (a) represents the simple reaction time, and (b) is the rate of information processing.

A choice reaction task in which the "subject" was to depress a button uniquely associated with one of eight visual stimuli was modeled in the QNMHP, assuming perfect detection and performance. A sensitivity analysis using different combinations of perceived stimulus probabilities (equal and unequal) and distribution values indicated that the QNMHP and Hick's law were correlated with r > 0.99. This fit appears to be a characteristic of the implicit fork-join network used in the QNMHP for task-dependent memory access, which is assumed to utilize simultaneous searches in parallel for a match to the requested task information. The number of forks is a

function of the subject's perceived probability that the requested match will be required during the task:

Number of forks, $M = (1/prob)^z$

The overall search time is the maximum time of all simultaneous searches. The hypothesis is that higher probabilities imply more certainty about where the subject must "look" in memory so that a person can search a smaller cortical field area (requiring fewer forks) to find the match. In support of this hypothesis, the sensitivity analysis indicated that the rate of information processing is a direct function of the search speed and the size of the cortical field accessed:

$b = (2/3)*y*z$ where y = average cognitive access time and z = exponent in "fork" equation

Current Efforts

Modeling a vehicle steering task

Current efforts are underway to use the QNMHP technique to predict performance for a specific multiple task environment: driving a car while pressing buttons on an instrument panel. Driving simulator experiments have provided the empirical data for comparison purposes to QNMHP predictions. In these studies, subjects ranging in age from 17 to 74 were prompted to depress buttons on instrument panels while controlling a simulated vehicle (e.g., Feyen and Liu, 2000).

The driving simulator environment has been modeled to present the QNMHP with the same driving scenarios, prompt sequences, and control locations as presented to the subjects in the driving experiments. By modeling steering as a discrete, repeated task, an NGOMSL-style task description provided the basis for entering the task elements required to control the task simulation. At the time this article was submitted, initial results from the QNMHP steering model were promising, although a detailed analysis comparing the model's data and the empirical data was not yet complete.

Modeling concurrent tasks

The next step, which is underway, involves combining a button pressing task (similar to the choice reaction task described above) and the steering task. A priority allocation scheme is being implemented for this scenario. In the QNMHP, task priorities are evaluated whenever a goal is completed or an entity reaches the goal selection server. In the driving experiments, the priority for the steering task is a function of the current time-to-lane-crossing (TLC), which represents the driver's estimate of the time in seconds before the vehicle's heading and speed results in the vehicle crossing one of the current lane's boundaries. The button task priority defaults to 2 seconds and interrupts the steering task when its priority is less than the TLC.

Table 1: Model and MHP processing times (in seconds) for simple reaction time task

Processing stage	Data "source"	Cycle time distribution	Minimum time (Fast)	Average time (Middle)	"Maximum" time (Slow)
Perceptual	Model	e(0.025, 0.025)	0.050	0.098	0.196
	MHP		0.050	0.100	0.200
Cognitive	Model	e(0.015, 0.008)	0.026	0.068	0.155
	MHP		0.025	0.070	0.170
Motor	Model	e(0.020, 0.015)	0.030	0.069	0.148
	MHP		0.030	0.070	0.100

References

Anderson, J.R. & Lebiere, C. (eds.) (1998). *Atomic components of thought.* Hillsdale, NJ: Erlbaum.

Baddeley, A. (1992). Working memory. *Science, 255,* 556-559.

Baddeley, A. (1998). Recent developments in working memory. *Current Opinion in Neurobiology, 8,* 234-238.

Card, S., Moran, T.P., & Newell, A. (1983). *The psychology of human-computer interaction.* Hillsdale, NJ: Lawrence Erlbaum Associates.

Carter, R. (1998). *Mapping the mind.* Berkeley, CA: The University of California Press.

Courtney, S. & Ungerleider, L. (1997). What fMRI has taught us about human vision. *Current Opinion in Neurobiology, 7,* 554-561.

de Fockert, J., Rees, G., Frith, C., and Lavie, N. (2001). The role of working memory in visual selective attention. *Science, 291,* 1803-1806.

Damos, D. (ed.) (1992). *Multiple task performance.* London: Taylor and Francis.

Elkind, J.I., Card, S.K., Hochberg, J., & Huey, B.M. (eds.) (1990). *Human performance models for computer-aided engineering.* San Diego: Academic Press, Inc.

Feyen, R. & Liu, Y. (2000). Age performance differences in a multiple task driving environment. *Proceedings of the 44th Annual Meeting of the Human Factors and Ergonomics Society.* Santa Monica, CA: Human Factors and Ergonomics Society.

Frackowiak, R.S., Friston, K.J., Frith, C.D., & Mazziotta, J.C. (eds.) (1997). *Human brain function.* London: Academic Press.

Gilman, S. & Newman, S. (1992). *Manter and Gatz's Essentials of Clinical Neuroanatomy and Neurophysiology (8th edition).* Philadelphia: F.A. Davis.

Gray, W., John, B., & Atwood, M. (1993). Project Ernestine: Validating a GOMS analysis for predicting and explaining real-world performance. *Human Computer Interaction, 8(3),* 237-309.

John, B.E. (1990). Extensions of GOMS analyses to expert performance requiring perception of dynamic visual and auditory information. *Proceedings of CHI '90* (pp. 107-115). Association for Computing Machinery.

Kieras, D.E. (1988). Towards a practical GOMS model methodology for user interface design. In M. Helander (Ed.), *The handbook of human-computer interaction.* Amsterdam: North-Holland Elsevier.

Kieras, D.E. & Meyer, D.E. (1997). An overview of the EPIC architecture for cognition and performance with application to human-computer interaction. *Human-Computer Interaction, 12(4),* 391-438.

Liu, Y. (1994). Queuing networks as models of human performance and human-computer systems. *Proceedings of the '94 Symposium on Human Interaction with Complex Systems* (pp. 256-270).

Liu, Y. (1996). Queuing network modeling of elementary mental processes. *Psychological Review, 103,* 116-136.

Liu, Y. (1997). Queuing network modeling of human performance of concurrent spatial or verbal tasks. *IEEE Transactions on Systems, Man, and Cybernetics, 27,* 195-207.

Mazziotta, J, Phelps, M., Carson, R., & Kuhl, D. (1982). Tomographic mapping of human cerebral metabolism: Auditory stimulation. *Neurology, 32,* 921-937.

Newell, A. (1990). *Unified theories of cognition.* Cambridge, MA: Harvard University Press.

Niebel, B. (1993). *Motion and Time Study* (9th ed.). Boston: Irwin.

Olson, J.R. & Olson, G.M. (1990). The growth of cognitive modeling in human-computer interaction since GOMS. *Human-Computer Interaction, 5,* 221-265.

Pritchard, T.C. & Alloway, K.D. (1999). *Medical neuroscience.* Madison, CT: Fence Creek Publishing.

Roland, P. (1993). *Brain activation.* New York: Wiley-Liss.

Rouse, W. (1980). *Systems engineering models of human-machine interaction.* New York: North Holland.

Wickens, C.D. (1992). *Engineering psychology and human performance* (2nd Ed.). New York: HarperCollins Publishers, Inc.

Modelling the optional infinitive stage in MOSAIC: A generalisation to Dutch

Daniel Freudenthal (DF@Psychology.Nottingham.Ac.Uk)
Julian M. Pine (JP@Psychology.Nottingham.Ac.Uk)
Fernand Gobet (FRG@Psychology.Nottingham.Ac.Uk)
Department of Psychology, University of Nottingham
University Park Nottingham, NG7 2RD, UK.

Abstract

This paper presents a model of a stage in children's language development known as the optional infinitive stage. The model was originally developed for English, where it was shown to provide a good account of several phenomena. The model, which uses a discrimination network, analyzes the distribution of words in the input, and derives word classes from them by linking words that are used in a similar context. While the earlier version of the model is sensitive only to characteristics of phrases that follow target words, the present version also takes preceding input into consideration. Also, the present version uses a probabilistic rather than a deterministic learning mechanism. Generalisation of the model to Dutch is considered a strong test of the model, since Dutch displays the optional infinitive phenomenon, while its syntax differs substantially from that of English. The model was presented with child-directed input from two Dutch mothers, and its output was compared to that of the respective children. Despite the fact that the model was developed for a different language, it captures the optional infinitive phenomenon in Dutch as it does in English, while showing sensitivity to Dutch syntax. These results suggest that a simple distributional analyzer can capture the regularities of different languages despite the apparent differences in their syntax.

Introduction

Theories of language acquisition can be roughly divided into *nativist* and *constructivist* theories. A central tenet of nativist theories is that children come into the world equipped with universal knowledge about grammars, and they then have to learn parameter settings for the specific language they are exposed to (Chomsky, 1981). One reason for assuming this innate knowledge is the fact that the input to the child is *underspecified*. That is, the number of legal utterances in a grammar is limitless, yet the child learns to produce legal utterances with exposure to only a limited set of utterances. Since children are able to generate new legal utterances, the reasoning is, they must have represented the rules that govern the legality of an utterance. It is furthermore assumed that these rules are too complex for a child to learn; therefore, they must be innate.

Constructivist theories, on the other hand, do not assume a large amount of knowledge being present at birth, but assume that most of the syntactic knowledge is acquired as a result of exposure to a specific language. A challenge to constructivist theories is to provide general-purpose learning mechanisms which can acquire the grammars of different languages despite their apparent differences.

This paper aims to show that MOSAIC, a constructivist model of syntax acquisition which was developed to model and explain certain phenomena in English, can do a good job of modelling similar phenomena in Dutch, despite the syntactic differences between these two languages. The model takes as its input child-directed speech from mothers, and builds a representation of the syntax of the language by analysing the distribution of instances of words in the language. After the model has processed the input, it can generate utterances which were not present in the original input. The output of the model is then compared to children's speech. This paper addresses the adequacy of the model in simulating the *optional infinitive* stage in Dutch.

The Optional Infinitive Stage

One phenomenon which has received a considerable amount of attention in the area of syntax acquisition is the so-called optional infinitive stage (Wexler, 1994, 1998). Children in the optional infinitive stage use a high proportion of (root) infinitives, that is, verbs which are not marked for tense or agreement. In English, root forms such as *go*, or *jump* are infinitive forms, whereas *goes* or *jumped* are marked for agreement and tense respectively. Verbs which are marked for agreement or tense are known as *finite* verbs. (Technically, infinitives are a subclass of the class of *non-finite* verbs forms, which also includes past participles and gerunds). The optional infinitive stage is furthermore characterized by the fact that the subject of the sentence is often dropped. That is, children will say things such as *throw ball*, deleting the subject (*I*). While the proportion of infinitives is (considerably) higher than for adult speech, children in the optional infinitive stage show competence regarding other syntactic attributes of the language. Typically, children will get the basic verb-object order right. English-speaking children, for instance, will say *throw ball*, but not *ball throw*. One puzzling feature of the optional infinitive stage is that children produce both the inflected and infinitive forms, in a context requiring the inflected form without substituting finite forms in infinitive contexts.

Wexler (1998) proposes a nativist account of why children in the optional infinitive stage produce a large number of non-finite forms. He theorizes that children in the optional infinitive stage actually know the full grammar of the language. The only thing they do not know is that inflections for agreement and tense are obligatory. This approach accounts for the fact that children produce both correct finite forms and the incorrect (optional) infinitive. It furthermore explains why children rarely produce other types of errors. An obvious alternative to Wexler's account is a learning theory. On this account, children learn the grammar of a language through exposure to this language. Wexler discounts learning-based approaches on the grounds that the optional infinitive stage lasts too long (years), the fact that children produce both the correct and the incorrect form, and the claim that when children do use finite forms, they use them correctly (Wexler, 1994).

The optional infinitive stage is an interesting phenomenon to model, since it exists in many languages which may differ considerably in terms of other syntactic attributes. A strong test of a model of the optional infinitive stage, is to see whether the model correctly predicts the occurence of the optional infinitive phenomenon in a language where the phenomenon occurs, but which differs in other syntactic attributes. Dutch is such a language where the optional infinitive stage occurs, but which differs considerably from English in its Object-Verb order. Dutch is what is known as an SOV/V2 language. This means that the verb in Dutch can take one of two positions, depending on its finiteness. A non-finite verb takes the sentence final position, whereas finite verbs take the second position. Therefore, in the sentence

Ik gooi een bal   (1)
(I throw a ball)

the verb *gooi (throw)* is finite and takes second position. In the construction

Ik wil een bal gooien   (2)
(I want a ball throw/ I want to throw a ball)

the verb *gooien* is a non-finite form, and takes sentence final position. (The auxiliary *wil* is finite and takes second position). In English, which is an SVO language, verb position is not dependent on the finiteness of the verb. Dutch furthermore differs from English in the fact that finite forms are far more numerous than they are in English. In English, in the present tense, only the third person singular can be

distinguished from the infinitive form. In Dutch, the first, second and third person singular are unambiguously finite. If, for instance, an English speaking child meant to say *I throw ball*, but dropped *I*, the resulting *Throw ball* would be counted as an infinitive in analysis. The Dutch equivalent *(ik) gooi bal* would be classified as a finite form, because *gooi* is different from the infinitive *gooien*. Thus, the number of unambiguously finite forms is larger in Dutch than it is in English. If a model is to learn from the distribution of naturalistic speech input, then the production of a large number of infinitives would appear easier in English than in Dutch.

Given these differences between the languages, generalisation of an optional infinitive model from English to Dutch provides a strong test of the generality of the mechanisms incorporated in the model. The remainder of this paper is devoted to a description of the model, and the results of the simulation of the optional infinitive stage in Dutch.

MOSAIC

MOSAIC (Model of Syntax Acquisition In Children) is an instance of the CHREST architecture, which in turn is a member of the EPAM (Feigenbaum & Simon, 1984) family. CHREST models have succesfully been used to model phenomena such as novice-expert differences in chess (Gobet & Simon, 2000) and computer programming as well as phenomena in diagrammatic reasoning (Lane, Cheng & Gobet 1999) and language acquisition (Jones, Gobet & Pine, 2000a, 2000b). The basis of the model is a discrimination net which can be seen as an index to Long-Term Memory. The network is a n-ary tree, headed by a root node. Training of the model takes place by feeding utterances to the network, and sorting these (see Figure 1). Utterances are processed word by word. When the network is empty, and the first utterance is fed to it, the root node contains no test links. When the model is presented with the utterance *He walked home*, it will create on its first pass three test links from the root. The test links hold a key (the test) and a node. The key holds the actual feature (word or phrase) being processed, while the node contains the sequence of all the keys from the root to the present node. Thus, on its first pass, the model just learns the words in the utterance. When the model is presented with the same sentence a second time, it will traverse the net, and find it has already seen the word *he*. When it encounters the word *walked* it will also recognize it has seen this word before, and will then create a new link under the *he* node. This link will have *walked* as its key, and *he walked* in the node. In a similar way, it will create a *walked home* node under the primitive *walked* node. On a third pass, the model will add a *he walked home* node under the *he walked* chain of nodes. The model thus needs three passes to encode a three-word phrase with all new words. Figure 1 shows the development of the net through the three presentations of the sentence.

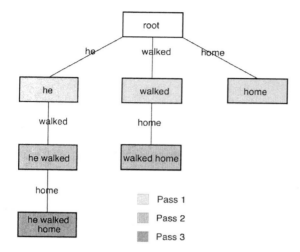

Figure 1: MOSAIC learning an input.

As the model sees more input, it will thus encode larger and larger phrases. Apart from the standard test links between words that have followed each other in utterances previously encountered, MOSAIC employs *generative* links that connect nodes that are similar. Generative links can be created on every cycle (after an utterance has been processed). Whether a generative link is created depends on the amount of overlap that exists between nodes. The overlap is calculated by assessing to what extent two nodes have the same nodes directly above and below them (two nodes need to share 10% of both the nodes below and above them in order to be linked). This is equivalent to assessing how likely it is that the two words are preceded and followed by the same words in an utterance. Since words that are followed and preceded by the same words are likely to be of the same word class (for instance Nouns or Verbs), the generative links that develop end up linking clusters of nodes that represent different word classes. The induction of word classes on the basis of their position in the sentence relative to other words is the only mechanism that MOSAIC uses for representing syntactic rules. Note that MOSAIC does not have access to any morphological information concerning words or phrases. All the morphological information it acquires is based on a simple distributional analysis of the input.

The main importance of generative links lies in the role they play when utterances are generated from the network. When the model generates utterances it will output all the utterances it can by traversing the network

until it encounters a terminal node. Once it encounters a terminal node, it will output the contents of the nodes it encountered, thus producing utterances. When the model traverses standard links only, it produces utterances or parts of utterances that were present in the input. In other words, it does *rote* generation. During generation, however, the model can also traverse generative links. When the model traverses a generative link, it can supplement the utterance up to that point with a phrase that follows the node that the current one is linked to. As a result, the model is able to generate utterances that were not present in the input. Typically, the output of a MOSAIC model will consist of more than 50% generated (non-rote) utterances. The model thus is highly generative. Figure 2 gives an example of the generation of an utterance using a generative link.

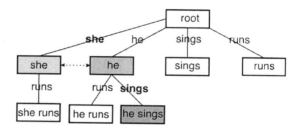

Figure 2: Generating an utterance. Because *she* and *he* have a generative link, the model can output the novel utterance *she sings*. (For simplicity, preceding nodes are ignored in this figure).

As was mentioned earlier, generativity is certainly a characteristic that children display. In fact, proponents of nativist theories of language acquisition have argued that since the number of grammatical utterances in a language is infinite, the child can never hear them all. Seeing that children are able to create utterances they have never heard is seen as evidence for the existence of a grammar-like representation in the child.

The Simulations

An earlier version of the model described above has been shown to provide a good account of optional infinitive phenomena in English (Croker, Pine & Gobet, 2000). The present model differs from the Croker et al. version in two ways. Firstly, when deciding whether two nodes should have a generative link, the previous version only assessed whether two words were likely to be *followed* by the same words. The present version is sensitive to both the words preceding and following the two words. Secondly, the present model calculates the overlap as a percentage of the nodes preceding and following the nodes that are considered. The previous model only considered the absolute number of nodes. These changes were not required to simulate the Dutch data, but constitute a refinement of the earlier model on theoretical grounds. Simulations have shown that the newer version of MOSAIC also provides a good account of the optional infinitive stage in English. Apart from the two newer preconditions for creating generative links, the version of MOSAIC used for these simulations is identical to the one used by Croker et al.

The data that were simulated were taken from Wijnen, Kempen & Gillis (in press). Wijnen et al. analysed two Dutch corpora of child and adult speech (The corpora of Matthijs and Peter and their mothers). The corpora consisted of transcribed tape recordings between mother and child. For Matthijs, the recordings were made between the ages 1;9 and 2;11. For Peter this was 1;7 and 2;3. Wijnen et al. analysed the children's and mothers' utterances with respect to the presence of the optional infinitive phenomena in both the mother's and the children's speech. Since the corpora that Wijnen et al. analysed are available in the CHILDES data base (MacWhinney & Snow, 1990), we had access to the same corpora analysed, and used these as input for the model.

It seems appropriate to point out at this juncture that the corpora used to train the model are just samples of the mother's speech, which are taken to be representative of the mother's speech towards the child. Obviously, the child is subject to other sources of speech as well, but the mother's speech is considered a fairly representative sample. Also, the sample from the child covers a period during which the child develops as well. In fact, between the ages one and three the child moves through four phases (one word, early two word, optional infinitive and end phase). By the time the child reaches the end phase, its speech is fairly similar to the mother's speech in terms of basic syntax. The present model is a model of the child's performance in the optional infinitive stage only. Thus, in the analyses performed, the model was trained on the entire corpus of maternal speech, and the model's output was compared to the speech of the child during the optional infinitive stage. Potential ways of extending the model to other stages are explored in the discussion.

The samples of the mother's speech are 14,000 utterances for Matthijs, and 12,500 utterances for Peter. Two separate analyses were run for the two corpora. For both analyses, the model was trained using all the mother's utterances. After the model was trained, all the utterances that the model could produce (both rote and generated) were collected. This resulted in a sample of 35,000 utterances for Matthijs, and 26,000 utterances for Peter. This relatively large difference in output given the small quantitative difference in input is caused by differences in lexical diversity and mean utterance length in the two corpora. The proportion of rote utterances was .30 for Matthijs and .37 for Peter.

Thus, the majority of the utterances that the model created was not present in the mother's speech.

As was mentioned earlier on, the optional infinitive stage is characterized by 3 phenomena:
1. The child produces a large number of non-finite verb forms.
2. The basic pattern of verb placement is correct.
3. The child drops the subject of the sentence relatively often.

Of the generated utterances, those which contained one or more verbs were collected, and divided into utterances with a finite and a non-finite verb form. Cases where the utterance contained a finite auxiliary verb plus non-finite form (e.g. *He wants to go*) were counted as non-finite forms. This same procedure was used by Wijnen et al.

Table 1 shows the proportions of non-finites that were present in the corpora of the children in the optional infinitive stage, the mothers, and the models of the two children. It is clear from table 1 that the proportion of non-finites for the children is higher than it is in the adult speech.

Table 1: Proportion of non-finites for mothers, children and simulations.

	Matthijs	Peter
Mother	.40	.35
Child	.73	.62
Model	.62	.47

Table 1 also shows that the scores for the model are higher than those for the mothers. From the mother's input, the model has generated output that looks more like the child's output. The model does underestimate the proportion of non-finites, though. Another way of assessing whether the model's output resembles the child's output is to look at the proportion of *root infinitives*. Formally, non-finite forms include all verb forms that are not marked for agreement or tense. This includes past participles, gerunds and auxiliary-plus-infinitive constructions. A special form of the infinitive is the root infinitive, where the infinitive (root) form of the verb is the only verb in the sentence. An example of a root infinitive in English is:

He build house   (3)

Root infinitives are relatively rare in adult speech, and only acceptable in special cases. In children's speech (during the optional infinitive stage), they are fairly common, though. In the speech of Mathijs' mother, root infinitives only occurred in 5% of the utterances containing a verb. For Peter's mother this figure was 10%. The simulation shows that the model of Matthijs produced 40% root infinitives, while Peter's model produced 22% root infinitives. Thus the models have learned constructions which are quite infrequent in adult speech, and resemble the children's data more closely (unfortunately, exact proportions for the children are not available).

An obvious question now is how the model has learnt to produce these utterances that were not so prominent in the mother's speech. A possible source of these utterances lies in the auxiliary + infinitive construction (which is used in around 30% of the mother's utterances). Suppose the model has seen an utterance like:

Wil je met de blokken spelen?   (4)
(*Want you with the blocks play?*)

Because the model can output partial utterances, it may well produce the last two words of the sentence, i.e. *blokken spelen*, which is a root infinitive. Needless to say, if the node for *blokken* has a generative link to another word, say, *trein* (*train*), the model could also produce *trein spelen*, a generated (new) root infinitive.

As was mentioned earlier, a second feature of the optional infinitive stage is that, while children produce a relatively large number of non-finites they do place them in the right position in the sentence. In order to check whether the model has done so, samples of the utterances containing finite and infinitive verbs were coded with respect to verb placement. Table 2 gives the relevant data for Mathijs' and Peter's model.

Table 2: Percentages of correct verb placement for Matthijs and Peter's model as a function of the verb's finiteness.

	Finite	Infinitives
Matthijs	.88	.89
Peter	.95	.87

Table 2 clearly shows that the model has learnt the basic rules of verb placement, and, coupled with the relatively large number of infinitives, the model thus conforms to the definition of the optional infinitive stage.

A third analysis performed by Wijnen et al. was to examine to what extent the children's placement of the object relative to the verb conformed to the mother's placement. Klein (1974) observed that for Dutch children in the optional infinitive stage the Object-Verb order was dominant over the Verb-Object ordering. In order to compare the model's output to that of Matthijs and Peter's, two samples of 1,500 utterances were examined for utterances containing a possible object and a verb. In these utterances, the order of object and

verb was assessed using the semantics of the verb and the potential object. This resulted in some 300 utterances per sample where we were fairly confident what constituted the object. (Note that not all utterances contain a phrase that could be considered an object, and some utterances are ambiguous with respect to object placement.) Table 3 gives the proportions Object-Verb orderings for the mothers, children and the model's samples.

Table 3: Proportion of Object-Verb orderings for mothers, children and simulations.

	Matthijs	Peter
Mother	.65	.60
Child	.90	.68
Model	.65	.57

Table 3 confirms Klein's observation that Dutch children in the optional infinitive stage use the OV order more than their mothers, though the effect is more pronounced for Mathijs than it is for Peter. The model does not conform to this prediction however, as it resembles the mother's data more than the children's data. In fact, it might be argued that the model looks too much like an adult. The general underestimation of the data analysed earlier also seems to point in this direction. One possible cause for this relative maturity of the data might be found in the fact that the model may learn too quickly. The fact that the model is learning too quickly is certainly true when comparing the amount of input for the model and the actual children. The input for the two models consist of 12,500 and 14,000 utterances respectively, which is to simulate the exposure to a language that a child has had in slightly over two years. The high speed of learning is also apparent in another measure; the mean length of an utterance (MLU). The MLUs for Matthijs and Peter are 2.0 and 2.3 respectively. For both models, the MLUs are around 3.1, roughly 50% too high. These relatively high MLUs may be a cause of the low incidence of object-verb orderings in the models' output since long sentences may contain subordinate clauses which have a verb-object ordering (e.g. *I know it, you want an ice cream*).

In order to assess whether short utterances conform more closely to the data, a sample of utterances containing three words or less was selected, and object placement was again coded. Though this is not equivalent to decreasing the learning rate, it does give some insight into properties of shorter sentences which would be more frequent in the output of a model with a lower learning rate. The resultant MLUs for the new sample were 2.44 and 2.45, still slightly higher than the data-MLU, but considerably lower than for the full output. Re-analysis of the sample showed the Object-

Verb order proportion to be .82 for Matthijs' model and .64 for Peter's model. These figures are actually quite close to the values of .90 and .68 in table 3. For Matthijs's model anyway, the figure is closer to Matthijs's data than to his mother's data. This suggests that the fit for Object placement would be better for a model with a lower learning rate. (Overall, changes to the proportions reported in earlier tables tended to be negligible, and/or in the direction of the children's data rather than the mother's data).

Conclusions

Results show that MOSAIC, which was developed as a model of English speaking children, gives a good account of the performance of Dutch speaking children. As such, it supports the contention that general purpose learning mechanisms can account for cross-linguistic variation. It also shows that phenomena in different languages can result from a simple distributional analysis of input from that language. Comparing this account to Wexler's (1998) approach, it clearly shows that a distributional analysis can be sensitive to the broader syntactic properties of a language and at the same time produce the correct inflected form as well as the incorrect infinitive form. Importantly, it does so without postulating innate knowledge about the grammar in the child.

A final note might be added regarding the speed of learning. At present, MOSAIC is seen as a model of a child in the optional infinitive stage. From the results presented here, it is apparent that the data it produces appear to be too adult. Limiting the output to shorter sentences results in a closer fit to the children's data. It was argued that decreasing the learning rate might improve the performance of the model. We have attempted to decrease the learning rate by increasing the number of times a word has to be seen before being encoded, but this did not have the desired effect. One other way in which the learning rate might be decreased is by increasing the number of times *sequences* must be seen before being encoded in the network. At present, a two-word sequence only has to be seen once before it is encoded (provided the two words have been seen in another context). Future work will address the issue of learning rates and the effect this has on the length and characteristics of generated utterances. Investigations into ways of decreasing learning rates (and manipulating the amount of input) may also allow us to examine more closely the developmental patterns that are evident in the model's output. That is, analyzing the model's performance after it has seen varying amounts of input may allow us to model developmental stages that precede and follow the optional infinitive stage.

Acknowledgements

This research was funded by the Leverhulme Trust under grant number F/114/BK.

References

Chomsky, N. (1981). *Lectures on government and binding*. Dordrecht: Foris.

Croker, S., Pine, J.M., & Gobet, F. (2000). Modelling optional infinitive phenomena: A computational account. In N. Taatgen & J. Aasman (Eds.), *Proceedings of the Third International Conference on Cognitive Modelling*. Veenendaal: Universal Press.

Feigenbaum, E.A. & Simon, H.A. (1984). EPAM-like models of recognition and learning. *Cognitive Science*, 8, 305-336

Gobet, F. & Simon, H.A. (2000). Five seconds or sixty: Presentation time in expert memory. *Cognitive Science*, 24, 651-682.

Jones, G., Gobet, F. & Pine, J.M. (2000a). A process model of children's early verb use. In L.R. Gleitman & A.K. Joshu (Eds.), *Proceedings of the 22nd Annual Meeting of the Cognitive Science Society*. pp. 723-728. Mahwa, N.J.: LEA.

Jones, G., Gobet, F. & Pine, J.M. (2000b). Learning novel sound patterns. In N. Taatgen & J. Aasman (Eds.), *Proceedings of the Third International Conference on Cognitive Modelling* (pp.169-176). Veenendaal: Universal Press.

Klein, R.M. (1974). Word order: Dutch children and their mothers. *Publications of the Institute of General Linguistics* 9. University of Amsterdam.

Lane, P.C.R., Cheng, P.C-H., & Gobet, F. (1999). Learning perceptual schemas to avoid the utility problem. In M.Bramer, A. Macintosh and F. Coenen (Eds.) *Research and Development in Intelligent Systems* XVI, (pp. 72-82) Cambridge, UK: Springer-Verlag.

MacWhinney, B. & Snow, C. (1990). The child language data exchange system: An update. *Journal of Child Language*, 17, 457-472.

Wexler, K. (1994). Optional infinitives, head movement and the economy of derivation in child grammar. In N. Hornstein & D. Lightfoot (Eds.), *Verb Movement*. Cambridge: Cambridge University Press.

Wexler, K. (1998). Very early parameter setting and the unique checking constraint: A new explanation of the optional infinitive stage. *Lingua*, 106, 23-79.

Wijnen, F. Kempen, M. & Gillis, S. (in press). Root infinitives in Dutch early child language. To appear in *Journal of Child Language*.

Modeling Counteroffer Behavior in Dyadic Distributive Negotiation

Danilo Fum[*] **(fum@univ.trieste.it)**
Department of Psychology; via S. Anastasio 12
Trieste, I-34134 Italy

Fabio Del Missier (delmisfa@univ.trieste.it)
Department of Psychology; via S. Anastasio 12
Trieste, I-34134 Italy

Abstract

An experiment on dyadic distributive negotiation is presented that analyzes the role of the market price as a credible reference point in a bargain between a human buyer and a computerized seller implementing a contingent negotiation strategy. The market price had strong effects on the initial reservation and aspiration prices, and indirectly affected the settlement price and the number of negotiation cycles, but not the agreement likelihood. An explicit frame-related manipulation, induced by the instructions, did not yield significant effects. Two simulative models of the offer formation process, grounded on the behavioral decision approach, were proposed and evaluated. The results support the view of the negotiator as a limited information-processing decision-maker, and suggest the possibility of contingent selection of reference points.

Introduction

Behavioral decision research on negotiation has highlighted various aspects of the bargaining process (Bazerman, Curhan, Moore, & Valley, 2000; Carnevale & Pruitt, 1992) identifying some of the factors that influence it (Neale & Bazerman, 1991). Significant attention, in particular, has been devoted to the reference points used by negotiators. Several researchers investigated the role of the initial offer and of the market price (Kristensen & Gärling, 1997a), of the negotiators' reservation (White, Valley, Bazerman, Neale & Peck, 1994; Kristensen & Gärling, 1997b) and aspiration price (White & Neale, 1994), and of the reservation price of the opponent (Kristensen & Gärling, 1997c). An anchoring and adjustment process has been proposed to explain the counteroffer behavior of the negotiators, and the effect of reference points (Kahneman, 1992; Kristensen & Gärling, 1997d).

According to the cognitive approach (Carroll, Bazerman & Maury, 1988; Carroll & Payne, 1991), the negotiator is considered as a decision-maker with limited processing resources. Under this perspective, it is therefore important to be able to specify what kind of information is processed, and what cognitive operations are performed in the various negotiation stages. This task is difficult, due to the relevant individual differences among negotiators (Rubin & Brown, 1975), and to the effects of different settings and negotiation strategies (Raiffa, 1982).

In the paper we present an experiment that analyzes the negotiation process at a fine grained level in a high self concern context (Carnevale & Pruitt, 1992). The experiment assessed the effect of the market price as a credible reference point, and collected the participants' judgments and estimates in various stages of the transaction. Experimental data were used to build and evaluate two simulative models of counteroffer formation and cognition updating, the first focused on the buyers' reservation price, the second on the their aspiration price. As far as we know, these are the first simulative models of the counteroffer formation process in dyadic bargaining directly derived from behavioral decision research.

The Experiment

In the experiment we investigated the role of market price in a dyadic distributive negotiation. To this purpose, we arranged a scenario involving a computer-mediated bargain between a buyer and a seller. Participants played the role of the buyer, and were led to believe that some other person was assigned the role of the seller. The seller was in fact a computer program implementing a contingent negotiation strategy.

We adopted a procedure similar to that used by De Dreu, Carnevale, Emans, & Van De Vliert (1994) who implemented a negotiation strategy in the computer opponent that resulted in a fixed pattern of offers. In our experiment, however, the programmed seller adopted a contingent negotiation strategy, and varied its pattern of concessions according to the behavior of the human buyer.

---

[*] The order of authorship is arbitrary; each author contributed equally to all phases of this project.

In an attempt to modify the effect of the implicit negative frame associated with the buyer role (Neale, Huber, & Northcraft, 1987), we manipulated the instructions given to the participants, and tried to arouse explicit gain, loss, and neutral frames.

Finally, in order to study the determinants of offer formation in the negotiation process, we collected the participants' statements about their own reservation and aspiration prices, and their estimates about the reservation and aspiration prices of the opponent.

Method

Participants Seventy undergraduates (46 females and 24 males) aged 18 to 28, enrolled in a General Psychology course participated in the experiment. None of them was suffering from any perceptual, cognitive or motor deficiency. All participants were familiar with computers and were able to use keyboard and mouse.

Procedure The experiment required participants to negotiate the purchase of some hypothetical out-of-print books that were necessary to complete a course assignment. Participants were informed about the current market price of used books as reported in the catalog of a credible and respectable nonprofit organization (a student union). They were told they had to negotiate with an interested seller connected to another computer. In addition to evaluating the seller's requests and making counteroffers, participants would be asked to rate their satisfaction with the seller's proposals, and to formulate some judgments during the deal[1]. It was highlighted that the experiment comprised several trials during which a different book had to be negotiated.

The instructions explained that a substantial reward (consisting in extra credits for the course) would be given to the 10% top scoring participants. Participants were informed that only their best performance would be taken into account for reward. Finally, they were taught that it was better to break a negotiation than to accept an unsatisfactory deal.

After reading the instructions, participants went through a warm-up trial to familiarize themselves with the apparatus and the procedure. The experiment required four negotiation trials to be performed, during which the market price of a different book was varied.

---

[1] The effects of judgments and estimations were tested in an experiment in which four versions of the program were used by different groups of participants. A version was identical to that adopted in the present study, while the others required only judgments about the buyer, only judgments about the seller, or no judgment at all. The results did not show any statistically significant difference related to the judgment procedure on the negotiation behavior and outcome.

Each negotiation trial comprised a variable number of cycles. At the beginning of each cycle the market price of the book was shown on the computer screen. After that, the seller's offer was displayed, and the participants had to rate it on a five-point scale (ranging from "very unsatisfied" to "very satisfied"). Then they were asked about their reservation price (i.e., "the maximum amount of money [they] were willing to spend") and aspiration price (i.e., "the best outcome [they] could reasonably expect from the negotiation"), and were requested to provide an estimate of the seller's reservation price (rephrased as "the minimum amount of money the seller will be willing to accept") and aspiration price. Finally, the participants had to reply to the sellers offer by (a) accepting it, (b) breaking the negotiation trial, or (c) making a counteroffer.

Participants had been informed that only their reply would be conveyed to the seller, while the satisfaction ratings and the price estimates were kept confidential. After an interval ranging from 10 to 30 s, a new seller's offer was presented, and another negotiation cycle started again by asking the buyer to rate it.

There were different ways to end a negotiation trial. The participant could accept the seller's last offer, or decide to break the negotiation. On the other hand, the computer seller could accept the buyer's offer or it could make a final, not negotiable proposal.

The experiment lasted 20 to 50 min. An informal debriefing session ensued with the participant requested to comment upon the negotiating strategy of the opponent. None of the participants revealed any doubt about the human nature of their opponent. A week after the conclusion of the experiment, during a class meeting, the rationale of the experiment was explained, and the identity of the seller was disclosed.

The Computer Negotiation Strategy An important aspect of the experiment is constituted by the strategy followed by the computer seller. The strategy had in fact to produce a pattern of concessions that looked sensible and natural to the human buyer. A second requirement was that the strategy should be robust and give reasonable results independently of any behavior shown by the opponent. A final requirement for the strategy was to be free from weak points that could be exploited by a keen (or malicious) negotiator.

The strategy is based on the following assumptions (Carnevale & Pruitt, 1992: Raiffa, 1982): (a) the seller's concessions progressively decrease; (b) the amount of the seller's concessions is related to that of the buyer's; (c) a contentious attitude of the buyer is reciprocated by the seller.

A critical part of the strategy is represented by the choice of the function to be used in formulating the seller's request during the "negotiation dance". Other issues the strategy had to take into account were the criteria to be followed in accepting a buyer's offer, and in proposing an ultimate deal.

The program follows three different policies to formulate its requests. The basic function used to compute the requested price is given by $R_n=IR \cdot e^{-n/k}$, where R_n is the amount of money requested by the seller, IR is the initial seller's request, n is the negotiation cycle within the trial, and k is a constant (set to 10 in the current implementation). The value of R_n is then incremented or decreased by a further 2% according to concessions made by the negotiating parts. More precisely, the concessions made by the buyer and the seller are given by the difference between the offers they made in the previous two cycles (i.e., $n-1$ and $n-2$). If the buyer's concession is greater, in absolute value, than the seller's, the value of R_n is reduced by 2%. The value of the request is augmented by the same percentage in case the seller made the bigger concession. In this way, a contingent negotiation pattern is implemented that softens the seller's position when the buyer is willing to concede, and tightens it when confronted with an uncooperative partner.

A different criterion is followed when the concession made by the seller in the last cycle outweighs that of the buyer (i.e., when the difference between the concessions exceeds a given threshold, currently set to 3,000 Italian lire). In this case, the program averages between its previous request (i.e., R_{n-1}) and the request it would have done by following the previous procedure, thus asking for a higher amount of money. In other words, when the difference between the concessions made by the parts is small, the behavior of the program is controlled by the $R_n \pm 2\%$ criterion, when the program notices that it concedes more than the opponent, it resorts to a more conservative policy.

A third criterion, implementing the third theoretical assumption, is used when the buyer makes the same offer in successive negotiation cycles, or withdraws a previous offer by proposing a smaller bid. In this case the program keeps its request fixed for two negotiation cycles. In the third cycle, to show its bona fide and its willingness to negotiate, it lowers the request according to the $R_n \pm 2\%$ criterion. In case the buyer does not cooperate, the program makes an ultimate request.

Finally, the program follows some simple rules to end a negotiation cycle. It is willing to accept a buyer's offer when it is equal or higher than the request it would have made in the following cycle. It makes an ultimate request in the case of sustained non-cooperation or, however, after six negotiation cycles.

The seller strategy was developed through a series of empirical tests, and its psychological plausibility was evaluated in a final pilot study.

Apparatus A Compaq Deskpro EP/SB PC with a Pentium II processor, 120 MB of RAM and Windows 98 as the operating system was used for the experiment. A

program implementing the human-machine interface and the seller negotiating strategy was written using the Java language. The program presented the seller's requests and recorded the satisfaction ratings, the price estimates, and the offers made by the participants. Participant gave estimates and offers by typing in text fields that were automatically on-focus, while ratings and final decisions (i.e., "accept" and "break") required pushing screen buttons. No other communication between the human and the computer was requested.

Experimental Design Two independent variables, one between-subjects (instruction type) and one within-subjects (market price of the used book), were manipulated in a 3x4 mixed design. Participants were randomly assigned to three experimental groups, and received instructions emphasizing the fact that they had to maximize their gain, minimize their expense, or make a good deal, respectively. During each negotiation trial, a different market price (95,000, 100,000, 110,000, and 115,000 Italian lire) was randomly assigned to the book to be purchased. The initial seller's offer was kept fixed for each trial and set to 105,000 lire. This was also the market price of the book used in the warm up trial.

Results

Initial Satisfaction At the beginning of the experiment, the participants had to rate on a five-point scale how much they were satisfied with the seller's initial offer. A main effect ($F(3,201)=22.21$, $MSE=5.26$, $p<.00001$) of the market price of the book on the ratings was found, with satisfaction increasing with the price. In evaluating this result it should be taken into account that, because the initial offer was kept fixed at 105,000 lire, in the first two conditions a sum higher than the market price was asked, while the opposite was true in the last two conditions. A post hoc analysis[2] showed that the only non significant difference was that between the 95,000 and 100,000 conditions. No main effect of the instructions was found nor any interaction between instruction type and market price.

Reference Points Judgments Table 1 reports the judgments given by the participants of their own initial reservation (B-RP) and aspiration (B-AP) prices, and of the reservation and aspiration price of the seller (S-RP and S-AP, respectively). For every potential reference point, a significant effect of the market price was found with values increasing with an increase in the price. The ANOVA yielded the following results: $F(3,201)=3.39$, $MSE=73791400$, $p<.05$ for the buyer's reservation price; $F(3,201)=41.94$, $MSE=29477000$, $p<.00001$ for the

---

[2] All post-hoc analyses were carried out with the Tukey HSD test adopting an alpha level of 0.05.

buyer's aspiration price; $F(3,201)=48.05$, $MSE=35537100$, $p<.00001$ for the seller's reservation price, and $F(3,201)=43.17$, $MSE=50987600$, $p<.00001$ for the seller's aspiration price. Only the main effect of the market price was significant, with the exception of a two-way interaction Price x Instruction ($F(6,201)=2.38$, $MSE=17601900$, $p<.05$) concerning the seller's reservation due to the fact that, with "neutral frame" instructions, the judgments for the 110,000 and 115,000 lire conditions did not differ.

Table 1: Mean initial values of the reservation and aspiration prices.

	95,000	100,000	110,000	115,000
B-RP	68.900	72,600	91,000	84,400
B-AP	62,900	65,300	72,700	77,000
S-RP	70,600	71,700	81,000	85,000
S-AP	88,600	92,900	103,700	106,500

Negotiation Cycles per Trial The market price (and only the market price) had also a significant effect ($F(3,201)=5.94$, $MSE=6.99$, $p<.001$) on the number of negotiation cycles per trial. The mean number of cycles in the different price conditions were 4.06, 4.10, 3.84, and 3.41, respectively. A higher market price brought forth a lower number of negotiation cycles per trial. A post hoc analysis showed significant differences between the 95,000 vs. 115,000, and between the 100,000 vs. 115,000 conditions. No difference in the number of cycles was found between trials ending with an agreement vs. trials in which the negotiation had been broken[3].

Final Buyer Offer The mean values of the buyer's final offer in the different market price conditions were 80,200, 81,400, 82,700, and 86,400 lire, respectively. Only a main effect ($F(3,201)=11.68$, $MSE=50104000$, $p<.00001$) of the market price was found, with the value of the final offer increasing with price. A post-hoc analysis showed significant differences between the 115,000 and the other conditions. Significant differences at the Mann-Whitney U test were found between trials ending with an agreed-upon price vs. a break in the 100,000 and in the 115,000 lire conditions ($U=175.50$, $z=-2.945$, $p<.01$, and $U=119$, $z=-2.381$, $p<.05$, respectively). In these conditions, the final offer was lower for agreements (the mean differences being 12,100 and 9,600 lire, respectively).

---

[3] A high proportion of negotiation cycles ended with an agreed-upon price. The percentages of agreements were as follows: 81% in the 95,000 and 100,000 conditions, 91% in the 110,000, and 89% in the 115,000 condition. The differences were not significant at the Cochran test. The instructions did not have any effect on the agreements, too.

Negotiation Strategies There is evidence for the use of different negotiation strategies by participants. The buyers followed generally a concessive strategy (70% of the trials), consisting of progressive increases in the offers. Two other strategies seem to be used: the Boulware (Raiffa, 1982) strategy i.e., keeping the counteroffer constant (9% of trials), and a "withdraw" strategy (21%) probably induced by the need to correct an ill-calibrated offer. It is also important to note that 63% of the participants adopted a single strategy in all the negotiation trials (81% concessive, 5% Boulware, and 14% withdraw). The concessive strategy was the predominant one, being used by 63% of the participants.

Cognition Updates The analysis of the negotiation traces with at least two cycles ($N=251$) showed a slight increase in the buyer's reservation price (Wilcoxon test, $T=7849.5$, $z=3.28$, $p<.01$, $M=1,200$), a major increase of the buyer's aspiration price ($T=4654$, $z=7.15$, $p<.001$, $M=4,400$), and a substantial decrease of the seller's estimated aspiration price ($T=2627$, $Z=9.68$, $p<.001$, $M=-12,300$). The seller's estimated reservation price remained constant ($M=-300$).

Discussion

In the experiment we manipulated two independent variables: (a) the instructions given to the participants, and (b) the market price of the book to be purchased. While the former had practically no influence on the participants behavior, the latter had a significant effect on all the dependent variables taken into account.

As previously remarked, the very fact of playing the buyer role elicits an implicit negative frame that was not substantially changed by the explicit instructions to "maximize the gain" or "make a good deal". It is known (e.g., Bazerman, Magliozzi, & Neale, 1985; Carnevale & Pruitt, 1992; De Drue, Carnevale, Emans & Van De Vliert, 1994) that people under a negative frame make lower concessions, and are less likely to come to an agreement. In our experiment, the negative frame associated with the buyer's role could be responsible for the very low satisfaction ratings given to the initial buyer's offer. A manipulation based exclusively on the instructions was unable to affect this implicit frame.

The most important outcome of the experiment is to provide another case for the role of the market price in dyadic negotiation. The findings support the statement that "External information, such as market prices, may be mostly useful in the prenegotiation stage when the parties determine their own aspirations and reservation prices." (White et al., 1994 p.438). We demonstrated that, when the market price is perceived as a reliable estimate, it could play a crucial role in the negotiation process through the definition of the initial reservation and aspiration prices, indirectly affecting the settlement price and the negotiation extent.

By focusing only on the experimental data, however, we cannot identify the determinants and the mechanisms of the offer participants make in each negotiation cycle. To clarify this issue, we ran a simulation in which different explanatory models were compared.

The Simulation

Two models of the buyer's counteroffer, encoded as ACT-R (Anderson & Lebiere, 1998) production sets, were used in the simulation. Both the models rely on the idea of the negotiator as a decision-maker with limited processing resources: "When juggling multiple pieces of information relevant to the negotiation, the negotiator streamlines and simplifies to focus primarily upon one performance reference point." (White et al., 1994, p 442). The models use therefore a simple Markovian mechanism for updating the negotiator's preferences and estimates, and generate the counteroffer by a process that combines the previous offer and a core reference point.

The first model (RP) is based on the idea that the buyers' offer in each cycle depends on their current reservation price, and on the offer they made in the previous cycle. The second (the AP model) considers the offer dependent on the buyers' current aspiration price, and on the previous offer. The reservation price and the aspiration price of the buyer are also considered as dynamic quantities that vary during the negotiation process. In each cycle they are computed by taking into account the previous offer, and the previous reservation and aspiration price, respectively.

Essentially, the models attribute a different importance to the variables they take into account, and combine them linearly. The model's parameters have therefore a clear symbolic meaning: they are interpreted as weights people use to scale the variables' values. They are similar to the weights used in decision-making strategies, such as the WADD (Payne, Bettman & Johnson, 1993). For this reason we decided to estimate the parameters from data, using a randomly selected subset of trials.

For each relationship among the models' variables we estimated a corresponding simple or multiple regression model (the intercept was set to zero). Then we used the regression parameters as simulation parameters. This estimation method has the advantage of avoiding any parameter tuning. Furthermore, it is analogous to the statistical modeling methods used in judgment tasks to identify relevant factors and quantify their weights (Dawes, Faust, & Meehl, 1989).

The AP model and the RP model consist essentially in the same productions with the exception of the empirically derived parameters ruling the estimation of the reservation and aspiration price, and the quantification of the counteroffer.

We constructed two variants for each model. The first one implements a perfect-retrieval memory process (PM), which is always able to correctly retrieve the previous offer and reference point. The second is a "real" ACT-R model (AM), using the default values for the ACT-R parameters, in which the retrieval from memory is guided by the activation-based mechanisms embedded in the memory architecture.

We considered in the simulation all the traces (N=85) with more than two cycles in which the last counteroffer was greater than the first one (i.e., those possibly associated with the predominant concessive strategy we wanted to model), and that had not been used for the parameter estimation. We executed 500 runs of the AM models on all the traces to obtain a reliable evaluation of their performance.

Results and Discussion

The results of the simulation of the buyer's counteroffer are presented in Table 2. The unit of analysis is the single negotiation trial: the r^2 and the mean absolute difference (MAD) between the model offer and the human offer were computed for each negotiation trial, and their means and the standard errors for each model are reported. It is important to underline that we performed a very strict test of the models, running them through a "generative" procedure. An alternative way to evaluate their performance, in a typical sequential task like a negotiation, is to adopt the model-tracing method. To investigate whether the use of this technique could affect the simulation results, we utilized it to evaluate the PM model and presented the results in Table 2 with the label PM-mt.

Table 2: Simulation results for the models. The dependent variable is the counteroffer.

Model	Type of Memory	R^2 M	R^2 SE	MAD M	MAD SE
RP	AM	.43	.001	4,500	17
	PM	.57	.026	18,800	1,197
	PM-mt	.46	.024	14,300	940
AP	AM	.47	.001	4,500	17
	PM	.62	.027	20,300	1,263
	PM-mt	.68	.022	11,900	906

The main finding is that the AP model obtains a better result than the RP model. The mean variance explained is quite satisfactorily, given the high variability usually associated with the negotiation tasks. The second basic result deals with the difference in the MAD between the PM and the AM models. The PM models have a higher mean absolute difference than the the corresponding AM models, whose values, in absolute terms, are quite low. The last finding is that the use of the model-tracing method did not produce different results.

These results support a model based on the buyer's aspiration price. They are in compliance with the studies that have highlighted the significance of the aspiration price in two-party bargaining (White & Neale, 1994). The difference between the AM models and the PM models on the MAD can be accounted by the specific nature of the human-computer interaction in our negotiation task. Over many negotiation cycles, it is reasonable to assume that proactive interference could have had some negative influence on the participants' capacity to retrieve from memory their previous offers and aspiration prices. Retrieving an older offer or reference point yields the formulation of a new offer that is lower than the one predicted by the perfect-memory model and closer to the experimental data. This hypothesis is supported by the empirical observation that the perfect-memory model overestimates the buyers' real offers. The cognitively grounded ACT-R (AM) models are able to capture this memory-related effect, thus obtaining a lower MAD.

Conclusions

The experimental results showed a strong effect of the market price in a high self-concern negotiation context. The market price had strong effects on the initial reservation and aspiration prices, and indirectly affected the settlement price and the number of negotiation cycles, but not the agreement likelihood. An explicit frame-related manipulation, induced by the instructions, did not yield significant effects. We described a simple cognitive ACT-R model of the counteroffer formation process that was able to obtain satisfying results in the simulation of the negotiation task. Further work should investigate whether models with these basic features could be generalized to other negotiation contexts, characterized by different scoring systems or opponent's strategies. Other important issues in the research agenda are to establish whether the reference points are selected in a contingent way, and to extend the research approach to modeling the seller's behavior.

References

Anderson, J. R. & Lebiere, C. (1998). The atomic components of thought. Hillsdale, NJ: Erlbaum.

Bazerman, M. H., Curhan, J. R., Moore, D. A. & Valley, K. L. (2000). Negotiation. Annual Review of psychology, 51, 279-314.

Bazerman, M.H., Magliozzi, T., & Neale, M.A. (1985). Integrative bargaining in a competitive market. Organizational Behavior and Human Decision Processes, 35, 294-313.

Bottom, W. P. & Paese, P. W. (1999). Judgment accuracy and the asymmetric cost of errors in distributive bargaining. Group Decision and Negotiation, 8, 349-364.

Carnevale, P. J. & Pruitt, D., G. (1992). Negotiation and mediation. Annual Review of Psychology, 43, 531-582.

Carroll, J. S. Bazerman, M. H. & Maury, R. (1988). Negotiator cognitions: A descriptive approach to negotiators' understanding of their opponents. Organizational Behavior and Human Decision Processes, 41, 352-370.

Carroll, J. S. & Payne, J. W. (1991). An information processing approach to two-party negotiations. In M. H. Bazerman, R. J. Lewicki & B. H. Sheppard (Eds.), Research on negotiation in organizations. Vol. 3. Greenwich, CT: JAI.

Dawes, R. M., Faust, D., & Meehl, P. E., (1989). Clinical versus actuarial judgement. Science, 243, 1668-1673.

De Dreu, C. K. W., Carnevale, P. J. D., Emans, B. J. M. & Van De Vliert, E. (1994). Effects of gain-loss frames in negotiation: Loss aversion, mismatching, and frame adoption. Organizational Behavior and Human Decision Processes, 60, 90-107.

Kahneman, D. (1992). Reference points, anchors, norms and mixed feelings. Organizational Behavior and Human Decision Processes, 51, 296-312.

Kristensen, H. & Gärling, T. (1997a). Adoption of cognitive reference points in negotiations. Acta Psychologica, 97, 277-288.

Kristensen, H. & Gärling, T. (1997b). The effect of anchor points and reference points on negotiation process and outcome. Organizational Behavior and Human Decision Processes, 71, 85-94.

Kristensen, H. & Gärling, T. (1997c). Determinants of buyers' aspiration and reservation price. Journal of Economic Psychology, 18, 487-503.

Kristensen, H. & Gärling, T. (1997d). Anchor points, reference points, and counteroffers in negotiations. Göteborg Psychological Reports, 27, 1-12.

Neale, M. A. & Bazerman, M. H. (1991). Cognition and rationality in negotiation. New York: Free Press.

Neale, M. A., Huber, V. L., & Northcraft, G. B. (1987). The framing of negotiations: contextual versus task frames. Organizational Behavior and Human Decision Processes, 39, 228-241.

Payne, J. W., Bettman, J. R., & Johnson, E. J. (1993). The adaptive decision maker. New York: Cambridge University Press.

Raiffa, H. (1982). The art and science of negotiation. Cambridge: Harvard University Press.

Rubin, J. Z. & Brown, B. (1975). The social psychology of bargaining and negotiation. New York: Academic Press.

White, S. B. & Neale, M. A. (1994). The role of negotiator aspirations and settlement expectancies on bargaining outcomes. Organizational Behavior and Human Decision Processes, 57, 91-108.

White, S. B., Valley, K. L., Bazerman, M. H., Neale, M. A. & Peck, S. R. (1994). Alternative models of price behavior in dyadic negotiations: Market prices, reservation prices, and negotiator aspirations. Organizational Behavior and Human Decision Processes, 57, 430-447.

Learning Relational Correlations

Michael Gasser (Gasser@Indiana.Edu)
Department of Computer Science; Indiana University
Bloomington, IN 47405 USA

Eliana Colunga (EColunga@Indiana.Edu)
Department of Computer Science; Indiana University
Bloomington, IN 47405 USA

Abstract

A conventional view of object categories is that they represent correlations among sets of object features. In this paper we present an analogous view of relational categories, the Micro-Relation Theory. On this view, relational categories such as ON and HIT are built up out of correlations among primitive relational features, which we call **micro-relations**. The process of learning relational categories involves three phases, the learning of the micro-relations within object dimensions, the learning of correlations between the micro-relations across dimensions, and the generalization from absolute to relative relations within dimensions. This paper focuses on the first two phases. We describe an experiment demonstrating the first phase of relational learning and a neural network simulation of the experiment. We conclude with a discussion of future work on the second and third phases of relational learning predicted by the theory.

Grounding Object Categories

For an animal, an object is a cognitive achievement, the outcome of a process that segments sensory/perceptual input into regions as it attends to the sensory/perceptual dimensions that have proven useful in making predictions, dimensions such as color, texture, size, and (the multiple dimensions that make up) shape. An object can be seen in part as the co-occurrence of a set of values on these dimensions, that is, as a feature vector.

Two sorts of generalizations about objects are possible. One singles out a range of values along a single object dimension, treating all objects with that feature as belonging to a one category for some purpose. Such generalizations are often realized in natural language as adjectives (Gasser & Smith, 1998). For example, the object category RED groups together all objects with a particular range of values on the COLOR dimension. The generalization is that there is a set of objects of this type. Typically more useful is a second type of generalization, based on the discovery that certain features co-occur regularly. Categories in this second sense are bundles of correlations of values along different object dimensions. We will refer to these as **object feature correlations**; they usually take the form of nouns in natural language. For example, the category APPLE is characterized by a particular shape, size, taste, smell, and texture. Categories of this type are valuable because of the inferences

(predictions) they permit; given a subset of the associated features, the system can predict values on the other, correlating dimensions.

This view of objects and object categories is straightforward to implement within a simple connectionist model. Each processing unit represents a range of values along a particular dimension. A pattern of activation across the units, that is, a vector of activation values, represents an object. That is, rather than being represented by an atomic symbol, an object is **distributed** across a set of **micro-features**. Categories can be learned through unsupervised Hebbian learning, which strengthens the weights on connections between units which are co-activated. The weights then represent correlations across dimensions, the basis of correlational categories such as APPLE. Thus the matrix of weights after learning encompasses all correlational categories, and each category can be seen as a subset of the units which are mutually excitatory. Activation of some of these units causes others to be activated or inhibited, representing inference or prediction.

Grounding Relational Categories

Now let's consider how we can similarly view relations in terms of co-occurring features and correlations. Starting again with object feature dimensions, a (binary) relation instance is the co-occurrence of **pairs** of feature values on the object dimensions. Note that some dimensions which may not be relevant for the identification of the objects because they tend not to be stable *are* relevant for relations, in particular, the location of the objects.

As with objects, there appear to be two sorts of relational categories. One type is defined over a single dimension. Analogous to RED for objects, a particular **pair** of values for two objects along a single dimension may characterize a class of relation instances in the world. For example, in some environment it may be the case that red and blue objects tend to occur together. The co-occurrence of red with blue objects is an example of a primitive **micro-relation**. Because a micro-relation is relational, it already involves a correlation, a correlation between values in two ranges along a single dimension such as COLOR or SIZE. Thus we will also refer to micro-relations as **simple relational correlations**. Note that unlike primitive object features, micro-relations are not normally labeled. There is no word in English, for example, for the situation in which a red and a blue object co-occur. Instead labels are often applied to an elaboration of a micro-relation, a **relative relational correlation**. For such a correlation, the object dimension in question must be ordinal (for example, SIZE or DARKNESS rather than COLOR or SHAPE), and the relation applies to multiple pairs of values across the dimension. Examples are DARKER and SAME SIZE.

Analogous to object feature correlations, we have a second type of relational category: correlations between relational features on different dimensions. Thus a LOCATION relational feature may co-occur with a SIZE relational feature, for example, if an object of a particular size is on top an object of another size. We refer to these as **complex relational correlations**. When such relational feature correlations remain specific to particular values or ranges of values on the two dimensions, they normally do not have associated linguistic labels. But when the relations along one or both dimensions become relative (HIGHER, SMALLER), we often do. Thus for the relation we call *sunset* in English several dimensions seem to be relevant, including the movement of the sun with respect to the horizon, the changing color and apparent shape of the sun, and the changing color of the western sky. An extremely important class of categories involving complex relational correlations consists of relational terms, such as the word *on*. These represent correlations between syntactic patterns, in particular the relative position of the noun phrase arguments of the relational term and semantic dimensions such as the relative position of the referents of the noun phrases. Thus the spatial relation ON correlates with the syntactic pattern associated with the English preposition *on*. Note that for complex relational correlations, it is necessary to specify which of the arguments in one relation corresponds to which of the arguments in the other relation. Thus it is the first of the two noun phrases in a phrase like *the book on the table* which refers to the upper object and the second which refers to the lower. (This is the main way in which *on* differs from *under*.)

The next section spells out our claims about the three phases in the learning of relations and describes a connectionist implementation of the model.

Micro-Relation Theory

Phases in Learning Relations

Our main claim is that relations are built up out of micro-relations, associations between specific features on two object dimensions, and that the most important and easy-to-learn relations involve complex relational correlations (between micro-relations). There are three phases on the way to full-blown relations.

1. The micro-relations themselves must be built up. In the neural network implementation of the model each is represented by a unit with initially weak weights from the units representing the two object features. These weights are strengthened if the unit is activated in response to input patterns containing the associated object values.

2. Once the micro-relation unit is sufficiently activated by object feature input, it can be associated with another micro-relation unit on another dimension, representing a complex relational correlation.

3. Once the system comes to explicitly represent ordering within an object feature dimension such as LENGTH, it becomes possible to learn relative relational correlations such as LONGER.

Phase 1 must precede phase 2 because complex relational correlations are formed micro-relations; hence the micro-relation units must be sufficiently activated for the weight that represent these correlations to be learned. Phase 1 should also precede phase 3 because there is nothing preventing relational learning from beginning even before the dimensions themselves have been figured out.

The Architecture of Relational Learning

Representing relation instances requires a way of distinguishing the different objects from one another, that is, a way of binding together the features associated with a given object. The **binding problem**, in one form or another, has surfaced in many forms in recent years, and a number of connectionist solutions have been proposed (Hummel & Biederman, 1992; Hummel & Holyoak, 1997; Shastri & Ajjanagadde, 1993). Most of these solutions, including the one we proposed in earlier versions of this model (Colunga & Gasser, 1998; Gasser & Colunga, 2000), make use of a dimension in addition to activation which characterizes network processing units, with synchronization along this dimension representing the binding of units. Here we propose a simpler solution, one that makes use of copies of dimensions. The idea is to treat relative position in space or time as a special dimension, one that maps directly onto hardware. This requires a relatively large number of units, but the visual system already utilizes a similar approach in deploying multiple feature detectors of a particular type (for example, motion in particular direction) that are specific to particular regions within the visual field.

Multiple copies of object feature units alone do not solve the problem of where relations come from, however. There is still the need for some sort of segmentation mechanism, a process which can "find" objects in sensory input. A full-blown account of how this happens is beyond the scope of our model. We assume that the process involves two sorts of **micro-relation units**, those that tend to respond to inputs from features of a single object (**sameness units**) and those that tend to respond to inputs from features of different objects (**difference units**). Each micro-relation unit multiplies, rather than adds, the inputs along the connections from the two objects features that it joins, similar to the "sigma-pi" units introduced by Rumelhart, Hinton, and Williams (1986).

Thus with respect to these inputs, it behaves like something like an AND unit. Micro-relation units also excite or inhibit each other to the extent that they represent consistent or inconsistent parsings of the scene.

Micro-relations (simple relational correlations) take the form of difference micro-relation units. The model begins with one of these for each combination of ranges of values on each dimension, but the connections to the relation object dimension units are initially weak, and all of the connections between micro-relation units begin with 0 weights. Each time a micro-relation is co-activated with its related object feature units, the weights on the multiplicative connections are strengthened. Each time two connected micro-relation units are co-activated, the connection between them is strengthened.

The details of our proposal, in particular how it implements the binding of relation roles in complex cases like the meanings of relational terms and how relative relational correlations are handled, are beyond the scope of this paper.

Learning

Units are connected to one another in an extension of a continuous Hopfield network. All connections are symmetric. The learning algorithm is an unsupervised variant of Contrastive Hebbian Learning (Movellan, 1990). There are two phases to learning for each pattern, a "positive" and a "negative" phase. In the positive phase, a training pattern is first clamped on a set of input units. Next the network is allowed to settle, and for each weight Hebbian learning is performed. That is, each weight is incremented by an amount which is proportional to the activations of the two connected units. Then, in the negative phase, the input units are unclamped, a small amount of noise is injected into the network, and the network is allowed to settle again. Next *anti-Hebbian* learning is performed for each weight; each weight is *decremented* by an amount proportional to the product of the two units' activations. The negative phase functions to eliminate spurious attractors in the network, providing a solution the problem of the lack of negative evidence: the network is punished for producing patterns that do not occur in the training set. When the positive and negative phase weight changes cancel each other out, learning has been successful. That is, for each pattern, the network settles to the same states when the input units are clamped and when they are then immediately unclamped.

Predictions

Micro-Relation Theory, as implemented in a network of the type described, predicts that people should be sensitive to relational correlations in input patterns. Presented with a set of training patterns embodying relational correlations, subjects should later accept patterns agreeing with the correlations and reject those violating them. In addition, the theory predicts that relational correlations should begin as absolute (between specific object features) rather than relative.

We developed the micro-relational architecture because of our interest in the learning of relational terms in natural language, perhaps the best example of relational correlations in human behavior. While it is clear that people do learn the meanings of relational terms, it is difficult to test the specific predictions of the theory in this complex domain. For this reason, we began with a much simpler task, described in the next section. While there has been research of this sort on unsupervised correlational learning (Billman & Knutson, 1996), to our knowledge it has not addressed the learning of relational correlations.

Experiment

The goal of this experiment is to explore to what extent people are sensitive to relational correlations. To do this we presented subjects with a simple unsupervised learning task. Subjects were shown instances of parent-child alien pairs from a fictitious planet. The members of these pairs represent the two arguments in a relation. The instances follow three "rules" realized as relational correlations between dimensions characterizing the parent and the child. We wanted to know (1) whether people could learn what made a pair of aliens a good example of a parent-child pair and if so, (2) what it was that they were actually learning.

Method

Subjects   10 undergraduates participated in this experiment.

Stimuli   The familiarization stimuli consisted of 128 computer-generated pictures of parent-child pairs. The stimuli included four "species" of aliens. The aliens within a species all had the same basic body shape but varied along the dimensions of size, darkness, body shape, body hue, and eye color. We used four values along each of these dimensions. The parent-child pairs followed the following "rules":

1. The child was always at least as big as the parent. This represents a relative simple relational correlation. Each specific combination of size values constitutes an (absolute) simple relational correlation.

2. The parent was always at least as dark as the child. This is also a relative relational correlation with a simple relational correlation for each combination of values.

3. The size of the child matched the darkness level of the parent. This takes the form of specific combinations of parent and child values along both dimensions. Each of these constitutes an (absolute) complex relational correlation. The rule itself would be a relative complex relational correlation.

For each of the first two rules, there were 10 possible specific combinations of size or darkness values. For the third rule, both size and darkness values were relevant, and there were 20 possible combinations of these.

The testing stimuli consisted of 72 computer-generated pictures of parent-child pairs. Half of the test pictures followed all of the above rules: half of these were completely familiar patterns ("valid"), and the other half were generalizations of the rules ("darkness-size") in which values on the distracter dimensions differed from those presented during training but the darkness and size values were combinations that had been presented. The other half violated the rules in one way or another:

1. All three rules were violated ("wrong").

2. The darkness rule was violated ("size").

3. The size rule was violated ("darkness").

4. The darkness-size complex relational correlations were violated ("darkness & size"); that is, for a given pair, the pair of darkness values and the pair of size values did occur during training, but the combination of the two pairs did not.

Procedure At the start of the experiment the subjects were told: "The following are scenes representing animals on Planet X. Each scene shows a parent-child pair of some species on Planet X. The child is always on the left. Study the scenes carefully, taking as much time as you need to look at each one. You will be tested on the pictures later." During this familiarization phase, the scenes were presented on a computer screen and the subject was allowed to look at a scene for as long as desired before going on to the next.

After the familiarization phase, subjects were told: "For each of the following pictures, hit 'y' if they represent a parent-child pair and 'n' if they don't." Again, they were allowed to look at each picture for as long as they wanted before judging it.

Results and Discussion

Figure 1 shows the mean proportion of each type of test item accepted as a parent-child pair by the subjects.

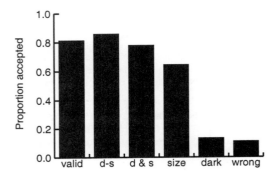

Figure 1: Results of experiment. Mean proportion of each type of test item accepted as a parent-child pair by the subjects.

Subjects accepted at significantly greater than chance frequency the valid ($p < .0001$) and darkness-size ($p =$

.007) patterns and rejected at significantly greater than chance frequency the darkness ($p = 03$) and wrong ($p = .004$) patterns. Subjects were also significantly more likely to accept the darkness-size patterns than either the size ($p < .0155$) or the darkness ($p < .0001$) patterns.

The answer to our first question, then, is that people can learn what it is that makes a good parent-child pair. The subjects generalized over the training patterns, readily accepting novel patterns (darkness-size) which differed from the training patterns on non-correlating dimensions. The answer to our second question is that people are sensitive at least to the simple relational correlations in the data. The advantage of the darkness & size patterns over the darkness, size, or wrong patterns shows that they have learned these correlations. That is, in terms of our account, they have reached the first phase of relational learning. The subjects also preferred patterns obeying the complex relational correlations (darkness-size) to patterns which matched the training patterns on *both* size and darkness but failed to obey the complex correlations (darkness & size), though this difference was not significant. Thus there is as yet no evidence that the subjects have achieved the second phase of relational learning.

Simulation

To simulate the results of the experiment, we trained a relational network on a simplified version of the subjects' task. Input layers were divided into CHILD and PARENT groups; that is, we assumed that segmentation of the input had already taken place. Within each of these groups there were separate layers of units for the two correlating dimensions (size and darkness) and one of the distracter dimensions (body hue). These layers had a single unit for each possible value on the relevant dimension.

For each input dimension there was an associated hidden layer of micro-relation units. Each of these units was joined by multiplicative connections to two object feature units, one each for the child and the parent. These units represent potential simple relational correlations. These weights were initialized at a constant, small value (0.04). All of the micro-relation units were also joined to each other by ordinary additive connections initialized with weights of 0.0. It is these connections that have the potential to represent complex relational correlations. The architecture of the network is shown in Figure 2.

On each training trial, one of the 56 combinations of child and parent darkness, size, and hue that the subjects were trained on was presented to the network. Input units representing the child and parent values on the three dimensions for the training pattern were clamped on, and all of the other input units were clamped off. Then the units in the relational layers were allowed to settle, and the weights were updated using Hebbian learning. Next the input units were unclamped, a small amount of noise was injected into the network, and the network was allowed to settle again. Finally the weights were updated using anti-Hebbian learning.

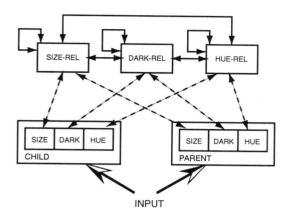

Figure 2: Architecture of simulation network. Rectangles indicate layers of units, arrows connections between layers. There are input layers for each of three dimensions, for both parent and child. Hidden layers consist of micro-relation units. Micro-relation units are connected locally to pairs of object feature units in a given dimension, one for child, one for parent. These connections are multiplicative (indicated by the dashed lines). Each micro-relation unit is also connected to all other relation units by conventional additive connections.

We tested the network and examined the weights following 1 and 10 epochs of training patterns. Following 1 epoch, the multiplicative weights into those relation units representing the simple relational correlations embodied in the training patterns had already clearly increased while the others were near zero. Following 10 epochs of training, we examined the weights connecting the relation units. For each of the (absolute) complex relational correlations between size and darkness in the training patterns, the network had learned a positive weight between the corresponding relation units. All of the other weights connecting relation units had become negative or very close to 0. Thus the network seems to have learned all of the absolute complex relational correlations and to have learned negative weights (during anti-Hebbian learning) which inhibit other combinations of values.

The network was tested on the same set of patterns as the subjects (except that since the network had only one distracter dimension, there were fewer patterns that generalized over the rules).

To measure the extent to which the network treated a pattern as acceptable, we followed a procedure similar to that followed during training. We first clamped the test pattern on the input units, just as during training, and allowed the relational layers to settle. We recorded the activations of all of the units in the network at this point. Next we unclamped the input units and allowed the network to settle again. We calculated the Euclidian distance between the final vector of activations of all units (input and hidden) and that recorded after the clamped phase. For patterns that the network accepts, there should be relatively little change in activation. For

patterns that the network treats as unfamiliar, activation should change during the unclamped phase as the network alters the input pattern in the direction of more familiar patterns. To make the network performance comparable to the subjects' data, we subtracted each activation change from an estimate of the maximum possible change in activation (the largest change observed over the test patterns before training). We will refer to this measure as "clamped-unclamped similarity".

Figure 3 shows the mean performance of two separate networks[1] We combined the valid and darkness-size patterns because there were not enough patterns in the darkness-size set to compare the two. We show darkness, but not size, since the two are completely analogous.

Like the subjects, the network "prefers" patterns that agree with both size and darkness simple relational correlations to those which agree on neither or on only one of the two dimensions. In fact, from the observed weights and the data in the graph, we see that these correlations, representing the first phase of relational learning, were learned with a single pass through the patterns. The main difference following additional training is in the significantly increased preference for patterns obeying the (absolute) complex relational correlations (darkness-size). As in our account of relational learning, the mastery of the simple relational correlations is followed by mastery of the complex relational correlations.

Of course it is not surprising that the network treats the patterns it was trained on as more familiar than patterns which differ from the training patterns. The main points of the simulation have been to show that the network exhibits two of the phases of learning that we posited and that it is not just the values on each dimension that matter but the combination of values.

Discussion

Both the subjects in our experiment and the relational network respond to absolute simple relational correlations in unsupervised learning. But note that the model predicts a stronger effect than we found among the subjects. The network preferred patterns obeying the complex relational correlations to those in which both of the dimension-specific rules were obeyed but the complex relational correlations were violated. We believe that this behavior will emerge in the subjects with more training; at least one of our subjects did exhibit this advantage for the patterns obeying the complex correlations.

A further prediction of the theory is that relational categories start out highly specific, that *relative* relational correlations come later. This prediction is not tested directly in the experiment we reported. To test this, we will need to work with dimensions that are less familiar to subjects, dimensions for which they have not already learned an ordering of the values.

The solution to the binding problem that we offer in

---

[1]Both networks started with the same weights, but because units are selected randomly during network settling, performance varied somewhat from one network to another.

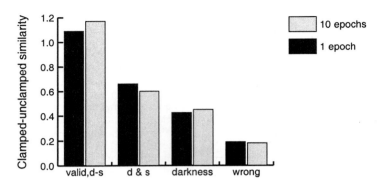

Figure 3: Results of simulation. Similarity between activations following clamping of test patterns and immediate unclamping at two points during training.

this paper also applies to another sort of binding, the binding of a variable with its value. While this may seem quite different from the binding of the features of an object with one another, the Micro-Relation Theory also offers an account of behavior that seems to require explicit variables. Like the roles in a relation, the variables in a rule on this view are implicit in the pattern of activation across a set of micro-relation units representing the primitive relations of sameness and difference in object features. Thus our theory may offer a unified account of a wide range of basic behaviors.

Conclusions

Human cognition is deeply relational, yet we lack a clear picture of how relations emerge in the first years of life and how we acquire new ones later on. Like object categories, relational categories are grounded in experience. Like object categories, they are presumably built up out of more basic stuff. In this paper, we have argued that basic relation stuff is quite similar to basic object stuff; it takes the form of distributed patterns across simple processing units. We have argued that a correlational, associationist account of the learning of relations is possible. We believe this is a first step towards an understanding of where relations come from.

References

Billman, D. & Knutson, J. (1996). Unsupervised concept learning and value systematicity: a complex whole aids learning the parts. *Journal of Experimental Psychology: Learning, Memory, and Cognition, 22*, 458–475.

Colunga, E. & Gasser, M. (1998). Linguistic relativity and word acquisition: a computational approach. *Annual Conference of the Cognitive Science Society, 20*, 244–249.

Gasser, M. & Colunga, E. (2000). Babies, variables, and relational correlations. *Annual Conference of the Cognitive Science Society, 22*, 160–165.

Gasser, M. & Smith, L. B. (1998). Learning nouns and adjectives: a connectionist account. *Language and Cognitive Processes, 13*, 269–306.

Hummel, J. E. & Biederman, I. (1992). Dynamic binding in a neural network for shape recognition. *Psychological Review, 99*, 480–517.

Hummel, J. E. & Holyoak, K. J. (1997). Distributed representation of structure: a theory of analogical access and mapping. *Psychological Review, 104*, 427–466.

Movellan, J. (1990). Contrastive Hebbian learning in the continuous Hopfield model. In Touretzky, D., Elman, J., Sejnowski, T., & Hinton, G. (Eds.), *Proceedings of the 1990 Connectionist Models Summer School*, pp. 10–17. Morgan Kaufmann, San Mateo, CA.

Rumelhart, D. E., Hinton, G., & Williams, R. (1986). Learning internal representations by error propagation. In Rumelhart, D. E. & McClelland, J. L. (Eds.), *Parallel Distributed Processing, Volume 1*, pp. 318–364. MIT Press, Cambridge, MA.

Shastri, L. & Ajjanagadde, V. (1993). From simple associations so systematic reasoning: a connectionist representation of rules, variables, and dynamic bindings using temporal synchrony. *Behavioral and Brain Sciences, 16*, 417–494.

In Search of Templates

Fernand Gobet (frg@psyc.nott.ac.uk)
Samuel Jackson (jacksonnumber5@hotmail.com)
School of Psychology
University of Nottingham
Nottingham NG7 2RD, UK

Abstract

This study reflects a recent shift towards the study of early stages of expert memory acquisition for chess positions. Over the course of fifteen sessions, two subjects who knew virtually nothing about the game of chess were trained to memorise positions. Increase in recall performance and chunk size was captured by power functions, confirming predictions made by the template theory (Gobet & Simon, 1996, 1998, 2000). The human data was compared to that of a computer simulation run on CHREST (Chunk Hierarchy and REtrieval STructures), an implementation of the template theory. The model accounts for the pattern of results in the human data, although it underestimates the size of the largest chunks and the rate of learning. Evidence for the presence of templates in human subjects was found.

Introduction

There has been widespread research into experts' remarkable memory for domain-specific material. Much interest stems from how experts apparently overcome normal cognitive limitations, such as limits in short-term memory (STM). Research has covered a wide variety of areas, including games, music, academic domains, mnemonics, and sports. In developing theories of expertise, focus has been almost entirely centred on comparing high performers, such as Grandmasters in chess, with intermediate individuals and novices. Relatively little is known, however, about the details of the very early stages of learning in complex domains. This study aims at helping to bridge this gap, both by collecting new empirical data and by carrying out computer simulations.

Chase and Simon's (1973) Chunking Theory

In studying strong and weak chessplayers in a problem-solving situation, De Groot (1965) found that there was no real difference in type of heuristics used, depth of search, or number of positions searched. However, in a recall task for briefly-exposed positions, he found a clear difference in performance. Masters and Grandmasters achieved near perfect recall, while performance dropped off dramatically below Master level. De Groot concluded that expertise is not dependant on superior information-processing skills, but on the acquisition, over years of dedicated practice, of a large amount of domain-specific information, which can be rapidly accessed during problem solving.

Chase and Simon (1973) gathered further experimental data and developed an influential theory of expertise, the chunking theory. A *chunk* is defined as long-term memory (LTM) information that has been grouped in some meaningful way, such that it is remembered as a single unit. Each chunk will only take up one slot in STM, in the form of a 'label' pointing to the chunk in LTM. Using Miller's (1956) estimate, Chase and Simon proposed that 7 ± 2 chunks can be stored in STM (this estimated has later been revised to four for visual material; Zhang & Simon, 1985, Gobet & Simon, 2000). In chess, a chunk may consist of up to 4-5 pieces, which are related to each other in any number of different ways, such as colour and proximity. Therefore, while a novice may only be able to recall around 7 single-piece chunks, a master can recall around 7 multi-piece chunks, more than 30 pieces. Even though recall performance of *random* positions is a great equaliser between Masters and weaker players, the former still maintain a small but reliable advantage over the latter. The chunking theory accounts for this superiority in terms of the small patterns that will appear by chance in random positions (Gobet & Simon, 1998).

Chase and Simon's (1973) study included a copy task of positions in full view, as well as a recall task of briefly-presented positions. Glances at the board being copied, and latencies greater than 2 seconds between the placements of pieces during recall, were used to analyse the size and nature of chunks. They found that the size of chunk increased as a function of skill level. Additional support for the chunking theory was found in several studies where the concept of chunk was studied in detail (see Gobet & Simon, 1998, for review).

Aspects of the chunking theory were implemented in a computer program by Simon and Gilmartin (1973), who proposed that LTM is accessed via a discrimination net. Identification of a chunk in LTM results in a pointer to that chunk being placed in a limited-capacity STM. Expertise requires the acquisition of a large database of chunks, with the appropriate discrimination net.

From Chunks to Templates

Although the chunking theory has explained many of the phenomena discovered in expertise research (Gobet, 1998), a few problems were later uncovered. One of its assumptions was that insufficient time is available during the brief presentation time of a position for any LTM encoding. Therefore, recall depends only on labels in STM pointing to LTM chunks. However, several experiments using interfering tasks have shown that LTM encoding does in fact happen (e.g., Charness, 1976; Gobet & Simon, 1996).

The template theory (Gobet & Simon, 1996), which is in part implemented in CHREST (Chunk Hierarchy and

REtrieval STructures, Gobet & Simon, 1998, 2000), was proposed to account for these data, while keeping the strengths of the original chunking theory. The most important improvement over the chunking theory is the presence of templates, which are larger and more sophisticated forms of retrieval structure than chunks. Like traditional schemas in cognitive science, templates have a *core* that remains unchanged, and a set of *slots*, perhaps with default values, whose value can be rapidly altered. CHREST incorporates mechanisms explaining how chunks evolve into templates through extensive experience, using frequent but variable information to create slots. The rapid encoding leaves the information safe from interference in STM, and so the template theory overcomes the problems created by the interference studies.

A Shift to Early Learning

The importance and influence of the chunking theory is clearly evident in the literature, and certainly not limited to the domain of chess. However, the research to date has been almost entirely focussed on the higher skill levels, as it naturally should in the study of *expertise*. But surely, when studying the acquisition of a skill, the first few hours of learning can be equally informing on the mechanisms involved. An important shift towards the early stages of expertise came from Fisk and Lloyd (1988), who studied novices' acquisition of skilled visual search in a chess-like game. They found that learning followed a negatively accelerating learning curve, in which improvement was very rapid at first but quickly became much slower. They could not, of course, have seen this so clearly by studying later stages of skill acquisition alone. The presence of this learning curve, which has also been found in other domains (Rosenbloom & Newell, 1987), could provide an explanation of why so many more years of practice are needed to become a Master than to become a good amateur.

In a similar study, Ericsson and Harris (1990) trained a novice chess player to the point when she could recall briefly-presented game positions to the standard of a Master player. However, performance on random positions did not reach that of Masters'. Saariluoma and Laine (2001), extending Ericsson and Harris' (1990) study, had two novices learn a set of 500 positions over the space of a few months. The participants were tested intermittently with a brief (5 s) presentation task. They had to recall 10 game and 10 random positions in each testing session. The results showed a clear improvement in percentage correct, from about 15% to 40-50% for game positions. The learning curve also looked like a power function, as found by Fisk and Lloyd for skilled visual search, with the greatest recall percentage increase within the first 100-150 positions learned. In addition, a slight increase was seen in percentage correct for random positions.

Saariluoma and Laine (2001) compared their human data to two computer models. Their aim was to differentiate between two possible methods for constructing chunks, both emphasising the flat (as opposed to hierarchical) organisation of chunks in LTM. From their simulations, they concluded that frequency-based associative models fit human data better than those based on spatial proximity of pieces. However, Gobet (2001) shows that CHREST, which uses a proximity-based heuristic for chunk construction, accounts for Saariluoma and Laine's human data equally well as their frequency-based heuristic. CHREST also accounts for the subtle effect found for random positions, which none of Saariluoma and Laine's models could do.

Preview of the Experiment

The present study differs from Saariluoma and Laine's in three important ways. First, while their participants had some experience with chess prior to the experiment, our participants were selected on the criteria that they knew as close to nothing about chess as possible. Second, the diagnostic power of Saariluoma and Laine's results is weakened by the lack of indication about how well the participants had learned the positions during the training sessions. In the present study, the participants are tested after every position in the learning phase. This helps keep motivation going, and keeps tabs on when concentration may have faltered. Third, presentation and reconstruction of positions was done on the computer, which allows precise and detailed data collection. In particular, our apparatus records latencies in piece placement, which can be used to infer chunks (Gobet & Simon, 1998).

With regard to the computer simulation, the present study is fundamentally different to Saariluoma and Laine's. While these authors were interested in comparing general learning algorithms, the present study aims at exploring how well a computational model that had already been well validated with experts' data could account for novices' data.

Human Data

Method

Subjects

There were 2 subjects, CE and JD, both female Psychology Undergraduates at the University of Nottingham, who had never taken any interest in chess and didn't know the rules. They were paid £6 per session and were told that they would be paid a bonus of between £5 - £15 at the end, depending on performance.

Materials and Stimuli

Positions, taken from a large database of Masters' games, were presented on a Macintosh 2cx, and subjects used the mouse to reconstruct positions. The software was the same as that used by Gobet and Simon (1998), to whom the reader is referred for additional detail.

Each session started with a *training* phase and ended with a *testing* phase. During training, 20 positions were presented for 1.5 minutes each. All positions were after the 20th move of Black. Of the 20 positions, 12 were game positions selected randomly from the database. The remaining 8 were pairs of game positions selected from 4 specific types (or 'families') of positions, which were used to help induce the putative learning of templates.

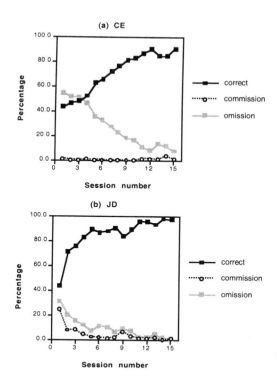

Figure 1. Training phase: Average percentage of correct placements, omissions and commissions for game positions against session number. Each position could be studied for 1.5 minutes.

Twenty positions were used in testing, with each presented for 5 seconds. Four were 'old' positions taken from the training phase, 2 of the game and 2 of the family positions. Four new game positions were selected randomly from the database. A new position was selected from each of the 4 family positions used in training. A position from each of 4 new families was also selected. The remaining 4 were random positions, created by shuffling the location of pieces from a game position. The order in which the positions were presented in both training and testing was randomised and different for each subject, as a control for any systematic effects of presentation order.

Procedure

At the start of both training and testing, the subjects were presented with an empty board on which they could familiarise, or re-familiarise, themselves with the placement/removal of pieces. This also gave them control over when the first position was to be presented, by clicking an "OK" button, as they did with each successive position after reconstruction. There was a pause between the training and testing phases for as long as the subjects wanted, which was never more than 5 minutes.

Table 1. Testing phase: Power functions ($y = ax^b$) computed for percentage correct against session number.

		CE			JD		
		a	b	r^2	a	b	r^2
Human data	Game	18.1	.24	.86‡	17.7	.32	.95‡
	Rand	13.0	.10	.16	12.2	.10	.13
Model	Game	19.4	.19	.71‡	28.5	.10	.66‡
	Rand	8.7	.18	.35	14.2	.00	.00

Note: ‡ p < .001

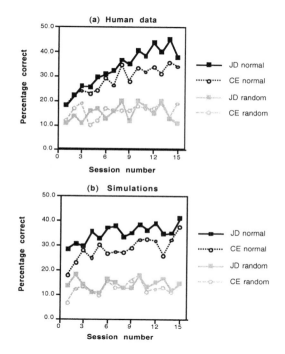

Figure 2. Testing phase: Average percentage correct for game and random positions as a function of session.

Results

To keep the data presentation short and highlight the contrast with random positions, we have grouped all the non-random positions into a single category called 'game' positions, both for the human data and the simulations, and both for training and testing.

The subjects varied greatly on the amount of time they spent on recall in both the training and testing phases, in

Table 2. Testing phase: Power functions ($y = ax^b$) computed for the size of the largest chunk against session.

		CE			JD		
		a	b	r^2	a	b	r^2
Human data	Game	4.2	.24	.84‡	5.6	.18	.77‡
	Rand	2.5	.23	.54*	4.4	.02	.01
Model	Game	3.5	.28	.86‡	5.0	.11	.54*
	Rand	2.4	.18	.53*	4.0	-.01	.01

Note: * p < .01   ‡ p < .001

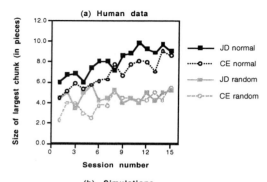

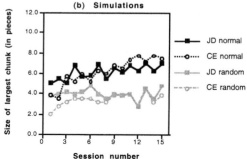

Figure 3. Testing phase: average largest chunk for game and random positions as a function of session number.

that JD spent consistently more time than CE. For example, during training, CE used consistently between 2500 s and 3000 s, while JD used between 3000s and 4000 s.

Performance with Training Positions

Figure 1 shows the relationship between the percentage of correctly placed pieces and that of errors of commission (pieces placed incorrectly) and omission (pieces not placed) in the training phase, over the fifteen sessions. For both participants, a power function accounts for the

percentage correct well (for CE: 39 * $N^{.31}$, r^2 = .93, p< .001, and for JD: 55 * $N^{.23}$, r^2 = .81, p<.001, where N stands for the session number). Both subjects were averaging above 90% correct towards the end, and JD was often recalling full positions, as shown by the higher average.

CE made a small percentage of commission errors across the sessions, especially at the start, leaving omissions as an almost direct reflection of the percentage correct. JD made more commission errors in the first sessions than CE. In both cases, omissions were more frequent.

Performance with Testing Positions

Figure 2a shows the percentage of pieces correctly replaced during testing for the two subjects, for game and random positions. The graph suggests the presence of power functions for performance against session number with game positions, but not with random positions. This impression is confirmed in Table 1. Figure 2a and Table 1 also show that there was a slight improvement for the recall of random positions, although this does not result in statistically significant power functions.

Size of Chunks

The average median size of chunk for each type of position was extracted from the data (counting single-piece placements as chunks). Pieces placed in succession with a latency of less than 2 seconds were classified as belonging to the same chunk (Chase & Simon, 1973; Gobet & Simon, 1998). Analysis showed that the average median size of chunk increased as a function of session number, often with a significant power function. However, the nature of the data, which was often highly skewed due to many single-piece chunks (particularly by JD), meant that the median was a particularly noisy and volatile measure of the average chunk size.

The average size of the largest chunk within a position was a more robust measurement of the increase in chunk size. The size of the largest chunk increased reliably during training, both for CE (7.42 * $N^{.21}$, r^2 = .77, p<.001) and JD (7.09 * $N^{.22}$, r^2 = .97, p<.001). Towards the end, the average largest chunk contained up to 10 pieces. A similar increase was observed for testing (Figure 3).

Table 2 shows the results of power functions computed on the average size of largest chunk against session number, for testing. Significant power functions are displayed across all types of position, except random for JD.

Number of Chunks Recalled

Two measures of the number of chunks recalled were used. One measure counted the average number of all chunks, including single-piece chunks. The other measure only took the average number of chunks that contained at least 2 or more pieces. The first measure tended to over-estimate the average number of chunks, as placements of single pieces may indicate guessing. The second measure tended to under-estimate the number of chunks recalled, as single-piece placements are just as likely as not to be valid chunks, particularly for beginners. Due to the large number of single chunks recalled by JD, as compared to

CE (probably as a result of guesswork), we only discuss the total number of chunks *excluding* single pieces.

During training, the two subjects showed an opposite pattern: CE recalled increasingly more chunks as a function of session number, while JD recalled increasingly fewer. By the end, however, both were recalling around 3 chunks. Given the long presentation time, however, the number of chunks reflects mostly subjects' strategies and their readiness to guess.

Testing, where positions are presented for only 5 seconds, offers a better way of measuring STM capacity, as there is little time to encode information into LTM. As predicted by the template theory, the number of chunks recalled during testing by CE and JD was consistently 3 or less, even when counting single pieces as chunks. Only occasionally did either subject exceed 3 chunks.

Computer Simulations

Methods

We essentially used the same version of CHREST as that described in Gobet and Simon (2000), to which the reader is referred for additional detail. There were two differences. The first was that eye-movement heuristics based on attack and defence were disabled. The second relates to how much CHREST knows about piece location. In previous simulations, it was assumed that players could readily encode the piece and its location as a single chunk (e.g., "Pawn on g4"). Here, given that we dealt with absolute beginners, we assumed that they had to construct such chunks. They would first learn a chunk for "Pawn", then one for the column "g", and finally one for the row "4". They would then combine these bits of information by chunking to learn the chunk "Pawn on g4".

For the simulations, CHREST was run twice, using the same order of positions and the same time per training session as each subject (see De Groot & Gobet, 1996, and Gobet & Simon, 2000, for details about the time parameters used in CHREST).

Results

We focus on the results from the testing phase, analysing in turn the percentage correct, the size and number of chunks, and the correspondence between humans' chunks and CHREST's templates. After 15 sessions, the model had acquired 4,772 chunks and 107 templates for the simulation of CE, and 5,811 chunks and 111 templates for the simulation of JD.

Percentage Correct

Figure 2b shows the results for the average percentage correct for the simulations, and Table 1 gives the power-function analysis. The overall percentage correct and the fluctuations of performance from session to session are reasonably similar to that of CE and JD, both for game and random positions. With both CHREST and the human subjects, power functions account for the recall of game positions, but not of random positions. However, learning was slower in CHREST in the simulation of JD,

although, in this case, performance after one training session started at a higher percentage correct than with JD. The correlation between model and human data is .80 for the estimated a, and .22 for the estimated b.

Size and Number of Chunks

Figure 3b shows the results for the size of the largest chunk for the model, and Table 2 gives the results of the power functions used to fit the data. The correspondence between human data and model is good for CE, and a bit less for JD. Interestingly, the model captures the differences in parameters between CE and JD—which is due either to the order of positions or to the difference on time spent on task by the two subjects. However, although the absolute values are not far off, the model underestimates the size of the larger chunks, in particular with JD. The correlation between model and human data is .99 for the estimated a, and .93 for the estimated b.

Given its limited-capacity STM and the relatively small number of templates it possesses, especially at the early stages of learning, CHREST predicts that the number of chunks should not exceed three. As we have seen, this prediction was beautifully borne out by the data.

Templates

The templates that were formed by CHREST in the course of the simulation were compared to the human data. A search was carried out to match these templates to the groups of pieces recalled by the subjects, as defined by latencies. Only groups containing 4 or more pieces were included in the search, and a match was made only when at least 4 pieces were the same in both the template and group. The types of position searched were those belonging to the 'position families' used during the training phase (see section 'Material and Stimuli').

For training, out of the total number of chunks recalled by the subjects containing 4 or more pieces, about half were explained by CHREST's templates. During testing, this drops to nearer 30% of the total number of chunks for both subjects. Of the pieces accounted for by the templates, most of these were in the core. This is particularly true of CE, who for the majority of templates, placed no pieces predicted to be in the slots. JD, however, placed about 25% of the template pieces in the slots.

Discussion

The testing phase showed an increase in recall performance across sessions, an increase that is captured by power functions for game positions. This replicates the negatively accelerating learning curve found by Ericsson and Harris (1990), Fisk and Lloyd (1988) and Saariluoma and Laine (2001), and confirms predictions made by the chunking and template theories. The slight, but not significant, improvement for random positions is also predicted by the theory.

Another phenomenon predicted by both theories is the stability in chunk number across testing sessions; the number of chunks recalled was consistently 3 or below, for both subjects. Because of the limits of STM, only a certain number of chunks can be stored for recall of briefly-presented positions. Even if a template is used in the later stages of the experiment, its contents would be output as a single sequence of rapid placements, which would not inflate the number of STM chunks.

The substantial size of the largest chunk was predicted by the template theory, but not by the original chunking theory. Towards the end of the testing sessions, the subjects were recalling chunks containing an average of 10 pieces, meaning that some individual chunks were much larger still. The chunking theory assumed chunks containing at most 4-5 pieces.

Overall, the simulations accounted for the human data reasonably well, especially when one considers the fact that no parameter of the model was varied to improve the fit of the simulation. The differences were that learning was somewhat slower and chunks smaller than with the human data. Power functions captured the same dependent variables in the humans and in the simulations, although the estimated parameters differed somewhat. Templates formed by the simulation matched a substantial number of piece groupings by the subjects. The matching method was rather simple, however, and better methods should be developed to assess the presence of templates.

The exact method of chunk construction could be an underlying factor towards explaining some of the differences between humans and the model. As noted above, CHREST first learns the piece (e.g. 'P'=white pawn), then the location horizontally (e.g. 'Pg'), and finally the exact position (e.g. 'Pg4'). The subjects in the present study did not show any sign of using such notation, and subjects did not have to know the name of the piece (and often did not), or the exact location. The subjects were probably more likely to recognise shapes and patterns of pieces, like chains of pawns, which they both mentioned during the course of the experiment. However, the fact that about 50% of subjects' placements in training were explained by CHREST's templates suggest that the two types of representation are not fundamentally different.

The data from training highlight marked differences between the two subjects, which are reflected to some degree in their performance during testing, and are worth some discussion. One difference is that JD made almost as many errors of commission as errors of omission near the beginning of the experiment. This suggests that she was guessing a lot more than CE, who made almost no errors of commission. Indeed, the number of chunks JD recalled decreased as a function of session (despite her increased performance), suggesting that she may have been guessing numerous, small chunks, possibly incorrectly. We speculate that the extra time spent on recall by JD is the result of time spent deliberating over whether she had recalled all that she knew. CE spent no such extra time before moving on to the next position, and so time spent simply increases as a function of the number of pieces being placed (hence the opposite trends between the two subjects). JD did appear to be especially highly motivated to perform to the best of her abilities (reflected in time spent and guesses).

In spite of these individual differences, the predictions of the template theory proved robust with regard to chunk size, STM capacity, and the shape of learning. As a first trial at comparing the simulation data to detailed human data for complete novices, the results are promising, and suggest that the same cognitive mechanisms operate with novices and experts.

Acknowledgements

This study was supported by the Economic and Social Research Council of the United Kingdom. We thank Daniel Freudenthal and Peter Lane for helpful comments.

References

Charness, N. (1976). Memory for chess positions: Resistance to interference. *Journal of Experimental Psychology: Human Learning and Memory, 2,* 641-653.

Chase, W. G., & Simon, H. A. (1973). Perception in chess. *Cognitive Psychology, 4,* 55-81.

De Groot, A. D. (1965). *Thought and choice in chess.* The Hague: Mouton.

De Groot, A. D., Gobet, F. (1996). *Perception and memory in chess.* Assen: Van Gorcum.

Ericsson, K. A., & Harris, M. S. (1990). Expert chess memory without chess knowledge. A training study. *Poster presentation at the 31st Annual Meeting of the Psychonomics Society, New Orleans.*

Fisk, A. W., & Lloyd, S. J. (1988). The role of stimulus to rule consistency in learning rapid application of spatial rules. *Human Factors, 30,* 35-49.

Gobet, F. (1998). Expert memory: A comparison of four theories. *Cognition, 66,* 115-152.

Gobet, F. (2001). Chunk hierarchies and retrieval structures: Comments on Saariluoma and Laine. *Scandinavian Journal of Psychology, 42,* 149-157.

Gobet, F., & Simon, H. A. (1996). Templates in chess memory: A mechanism for recalling several boards. *Cognitive Psychology, 31,* 1-40.

Gobet, F., & Simon, H. A. (1998). Expert chess memory: Revisiting the chunking hypothesis. *Memory, 6,* 225-255.

Gobet, F., & Simon, H. A. (2000). Five seconds or sixty? Presentation time in expert memory. *Cognitive Science, 24,* 651-682.

Miller, G. A. (1956). The magical number seven, plus or minus two: Some limits on our capacity for processing information. *Psychological Review, 63,* 81-97.

Rosenbloom, P., & Newell, A. (1987). Learning by chunking: A production system model of practice. In D. Klahr, P. Langley, & R. Neches (Eds.), *Production systems models of learning and development.* Cambridge, MA: The MIT Press.

Saariluoma, P., & Laine, T. (2001). Novice construction of chess memory. *Scandinavian Journal of Psychology, 42,* 137-147.

Simon, H. A., & Gilmartin, K. J. (1973). A simulation of memory for chess positions. *Cognitive Psychology, 5,* 29-46.

Zhang, G., & Simon, H. A. (1985). STM capacity for Chinese words and idioms: Chunking and acoustical loop hypothesis. *Memory and Cognition, 13,* 193-201.

The Influence of Resource Parameters on Incremental Conceptualization

Markus Guhe (guhe@informatik.uni-hamburg.de)
Research Group Knowledge and Language Processing (WSV),
Department for Informatics, University of Hamburg,
Vogt-Kölln-Straße 30, D-22527 Hamburg, Germany

Christopher Habel (habel@informatik.uni-hamburg.de)
Research Group Knowledge and Language Processing (WSV),
Department for Informatics, University of Hamburg,
Vogt-Kölln-Straße 30, D-22527 Hamburg, Germany

Abstract

INC (*incremental conceptualizer*) is a cognitively motivated model of the first component of the language production process, conceptualization. It produces preverbal output for the domain of giving on-line descriptions of events that has the same structure as verbalizations of humans given the same task. The architecture and processing mechanisms of INC are based on simple, cognitively motivated principles. Its behavior is controlled by parameters that are set according to the available resources. Thus, INC requires no explicit and complex instructions about how to perform a given verbalization task, e.g. with respect to the level of detail, because the level of detail is an effect that depends on resources.

Towards an Incremental Architecture for Conceptualization

An important goal in psycholinguistics is the development of a cognitively plausible architecture of language production. In contrast to language comprehension—cf. Lewis (to appear)—only few proposals for the architecture of the human language production faculty follow the methodological idea of computational architectures (cf. Anderson 1983, Newell 1990), viz. to combine empirical investigation and computational modeling. Levelt (1989) argues convincingly in his psycholinguistic approach that the language production component works incrementally, which means that a sequential information stream is processed in parallel. To achieve this, multiple processes, which are ordered in a fixed sequence, work simultaneously on an information stream, so that the output of one process is the input of the following one. In performing the task of describing of what happens in a permanently changing world, incrementality can improve the overall quality of the model substantially: (1) The dynamic nature of a continuous input stream can be handled faster, as only the most recent change has to be considered—in relation to the current state of affairs. This also optimizes the required storage capacity. (2) Incremental models can account for the fact that humans are capable of producing fluent speech, i.e. speech without artificial auditory gaps. (3) The parallelism that comes with incrementality optimizes the runtime, because the processes need not wait for each other, or only for short periods.

There are some incremental models for that part of the language production faculty that does the linguistic encoding, i.e. the one that solves the *how to say* problem, cf. Kempen & Hoenkamp (1987), De Smedt, Horacek & Zock (1996). This component, called the *formulator* by Levelt (1989), which contains the stages of *sentence planning* and *surface generation* in Reiter's (1994) analysis, gets the input from the *what-to-say* component—*content planning* according to Reiter, or the *conceptualizer* in Levelt's approach. From a cognitive point of view, an incremental formulator (e.g. Abb, Günther, Herweg, Lebeth, Maienborn & Schopp 1996; De Smedt 1990; Kempen & Hoenkamp 1987) is plausible only in combination with a conceptualizer that produces preverbal messages, which are the interface between conceptualizer and formulator, incrementally.

INC (*incremental conceptualizer*) models this first stage of the language production process. It is based on the considerations described in Habel & Tappe (1999) and Guhe, Habel & Tappe (2000) and is specialized on producing preverbal messages for the on-line description of events. In the present paper we report on simulations performed by the implementation of INC in the domain of on-line descriptions of drawing sketch maps.[1] For that purpose we recorded in a first study the drawing of sketch maps with a drawing tablet. These sequences of space-time coordinates are the fundamental data structures for the two lines of our research. First, the recorded drawing processes—not the resulting sketch maps—are presented to participants of a psycholinguistic verbalization study, who are instructed to 'describe what they see', cf. Tappe & Habel (1998) and

---

[1] INC is restricted to describing events but domain-independent otherwise. Domain specificity is due to the content of the *concept storage*, cf. Figure 3. Beyond the domain of drawing events we have, up to now, used it for the description of motion events, cf. Guhe, Habel & Tappe (2000).

Habel & Tappe (1999). Second, they are the input for the implementation of the computational model INC. The simulations described in the following show a high correspondence between these two lines of research.

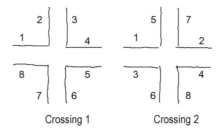

Crossing 1   Crossing 2

Figure 1: Example sketches

The two drawing processes symbolically depicted in Figure 1 serve as examples in the following. The two processes, i.e. their recordings, differ solely in the order in which their lines are drawn. This is indicated by the annotated numbers, which were not present in the recordings presented to the study participants. The different sequencing leads to different hierarchical event structures built up by the conceptualizer, e.g. the temporal ordering of the elements. The event structure of the genesis of Crossing1 is depicted in Figure 2. (The relation between dr-Parallel4 and dr-H-Line1 is left out for better readability.) There, dr-H-Line stands for 'drawing a horizontal line', dr-V-Line for 'drawing a vertical line'; hence, dr-H-Line2 stands for the event that created the fourth line. The left-to-right ordering in the event structure stands for temporal precedence on each of the three layers. The nodes of the intermediate layer each subsume two nodes of the basic layer; dr-Parallel means 'two parallel lines were drawn', dr-Corner 'two lines that touch each other at their endpoints were drawn' (regardless of their angle). [NB: events, not their results are the subject of verbalization task and modeling.]

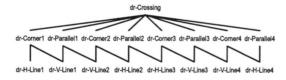

Figure 2: Event structure of the sketch map Crossing 1

An Overview of INC

Overall Architecture

INC starts with so-called *basic entities* as input. They are produced by a pre-processing unit that converts the input stream—consisting of coordinates of the drawing pen, which are read in a fixed time interval—into basic events and objects. This conversion is computed ac-

cording to the empirically founded cut-hypothesis of Avrahami & Kareev (1994, p. 239): "A sub-sequence of stimuli is cut out of a sequence to become a cognitive entity if it has been experienced many times in different contexts." These basic entities are used to build up a hierarchical event structure, from which elements are selected for verbalization. In this way INC forms preverbal messages out of basic entities. The basic events for our examples here are dr-H-Line and dr-V-Line. For each line-drawing one *basic object*, which represents the result (the line), and one *basic event*, containing information like drawing speed and duration. are generated.

The processes of incremental models are often depicted as a cascade of processes (Levelt 1989): like water in a water cascade splashes down from one level to the next, information splashes down from one process to the next. This symbolizes the simultaneous processing of information on subsequent stages. In INC four processes form this cascade: *construction, selection, linearization*, and *pvm-generation* (preverbal message generation), cf. Figure 3. The processes all operate on the *current conceptual representation* (CCR), which contains a representation of the current state of affairs, e.g. the event structure from Figure 2 enriched by object information. This representation is a network of inter-related concepts, where the concepts are represented as nodes and the relations between them as links. The *construction* process builds up the CCR. *Selection* chooses the to-be-verbalized events from it, i.e. it chooses a path through the network, which we call the *traverse*. *Linearization* brings these events into an appropriate order, and *pvm-generation* generates preverbal messages from the chosen events. Since linearization is not yet implemented, it plays only a minor role here.

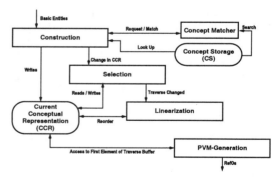

Figure 3: Architecture of INC

Construction

The construction process reads the basic entities that are provided by the pre-processing unit and builds up the CCR from them. To do so, it uses an additional process: the *concept matcher*: each time a new basic entity or a modification for an already existing one[2] is read from the pre-processing unit, construction calls the concept matcher to determine the best matching concept from the *concept storage* that subsumes this entity and some 'surrounding' ones, which are determined by a heuristic. The concept matcher then determines the *best match* by computing the *degree of agreement* (DoA) between these entities and the concepts stored in the concept storage. The best match is the concept with the highest DoA. A pair consisting of best match and DoA is given back to construction. The best match need not be complete; that is, even if parts of this concept are missing—up to this point—it can nevertheless be introduced into the CCR, with the missing parts marked as 'expected'. Finally, construction compares the DoA with the *degree of agreement threshold* (DoAT). If DoA is greater than DoAT, construction carries out one of three available operations:

Generate introduces a new concept into the CCR. This operation is needed when (1) a new basic entity comes in from the pre-processing unit or (2) DoA > DoAT for the best match, and the best match is not yet contained in the CCR. In the latter case the matched entities are subsumed under the concept.

Modify is used when (1) the observed events demand an adaptation of an already existing basic entity or (2) an element of the CCR marked 'expected' is actually recognized. Then its status is changed to 'regular'.

Discard is called when expectations in the CCR no longer correspond to the best match. It removes all elements marked 'expected'. After *discard* is finished, the operation *generate* is usually called to introduce (an expectation for) the new best match into the CCR. Basic entities cannot be discarded.

Varying DoAT influences the behavior of INC. By this principle INC's behavior is determined: there is a set of parameters, whose values are set when INC is initialized and which are the reason for different outputs.

Selection

As already mentioned, selection assembles the traverse. To be more precise, it operates on the *traverse buffer*, viz. the last part of the traverse. Its variable length is determined by the parameter *length of traverse buffer* (LoTB). This part of the traverse can be modified, because its elements are not yet handed on to the subsequent unit of the language generation system, the formulator. This buffering is necessary for two main reasons; first, linearization needs some time to take place, and a part of the traverse where it can exchange the order of the elements. Second, selection needs a possibility for revising its choices, especially with the selection method we are using here. It is based on what we call *Extended Wundt's Principle*. Levelt (1989) formulates

Wundt's Principle: an incremental process starts computing as soon as it obtains some characteristic input. Our extension consists in not only starting to process input as soon as possible but to produce output as quickly as possible, as well. The disadvantage of this method is that quite a lot of choices need to be revised. However, the advantage is that linearization has the maximum amount of time to operate on the elements in the traverse buffer, before they are taken out by pvm-generation. Additionally, this method results in an *anytime* capability of INC: pvm-generation is capable of producing a preverbal message at any point in time.

Selection has available two operations for modifying the traverse buffer: *append* and *replace*. The selection algorithm is applied to each new or modified node and consists of three parts:

1. *Append* the node if 2 and 3 are not the case (default case).
2. If there is already a more complex node in the traverse buffer that contains this one, do *not* select it.
3. If there are nodes in the traverse buffer that are contained by the node *replace* these nodes with it.

In the cases 1 and 3 the time of insertion—a time stamp—is also saved with the element.

PVM-Generation

Pvm-generation has access to the first element of the traverse buffer. It takes out this first element to produce a preverbal message based thereon if the specified *latency time* (LT), computed as the difference between the current point of time and the time stamp, has passed. The element is then no longer part of the traverse buffer (but, of course, still a part of the traverse).

For the present purpose, viz. producing preverbal structures that can be compared to our recorded human verbalizations, the output of pvm-generation consists simply of the unique number with which this element is internally labeled. This, obviously, is no complete preverbal message that can be used by a formulator to produce an utterance, but it will suffice here.

Three Resource Parameters that Determine the Behavior of INC

The behavior of INC is highly dependent on resource parameters, of which we discuss here:

1. *degree of agreement threshold* (DoAT)
2. *length of traverse buffer* (LoTB)
3. *latency time* (LT)

In the present section we describe these parameters, their function and their effects in processing in more detail. To test their functioning and effects in detail, we studied INC's behavior by varying them systematically; these simulations are described in the next section.

Degree of Agreement Threshold (DoAT)

Function DoAT is instantiated with a value between 0 and 1. It determines whether the *degree of agreement*

---

[2] A basic event needs to be modified if, for example, the drawing of a line has been interrupted (the basic event is generated) but then has been continued (modification).

(DoA) of a *best match* determined by the concept matcher is high enough, i.e. whether the match is good enough, to cause construction to work on the CCR.

Motivation DoAT can be regarded as a technical necessity as well as being cognitively adequate. The crucial question is, whether humans do not generate expectations if the DoA is not high enough (in our terms: introduce expected nodes into the CCR) or whether they generate any expectation they are capable of creating but do not select these expectations from the CCR for verbalization. Since generating expectations is costly (in the sense that it requires time and other resources), the solution we have used in INC seems to be the plausible one, cognitively as well as technically.

Expected Effects By varying the value for DoAT the amount of expectations the construction process generates is increased or decreased. The effect of DoAT = 0 is that construction uses any best match to work on the CCR. For our two example sketches this means that the drawing of only one line already leads to the expectation that this is the drawing of a rectangle, because this is the simplest concept in the concept storage containing a line. DoAT = 1 means that no expectations are generated at all; only after the drawing is finished, the completely perceived crossing is verbalized. (Basic events can, of course, be verbalized before that.)

Comments Both borderline cases are untypical in our recorded verbalizations, because (1) almost no participant keeps silent or talks only of lines until the sketch is complete (DoAT = 1)—it looks like they cannot resist speculating about what the final result will be—, (2) no participant utters expectations permanently (DoAT = 0), and (3) no participant jumps to such 'unjustified' conclusions that the drawing of a line will result in the drawing of a rectangle (DoAT = 0). The typical case is that they use lines and their interrelations until they find the DoAT is high enough, whereupon they produce an utterance about what they expect the final result will be.

Length of Traverse Buffer (LoTB)

Function LoTB specifies the number of elements that can be stored in the traverse buffer.

Motivation LoTB models the capacity of the working memory of the verbalizer that is available for conceptualization. Thus, the maximum value of LoTB is determined by the individual's current storage capacities.

Expected Effects If the value for LoTB is too small, elements get lost (are forgotten), because pvm-generation does not use them in time to produce a preverbal message. Thus, by increasing its value the chance is decreased that elements get lost and vice versa.

Comments LoTB = 0 is not possible: INC would not work, because elements must be put in the traverse buffer to be accessible for pvm-generation; this would be like a working memory with no storage capacity, thus LoTB $\geq$ 1. There is no technical reason to limit length of the traverse buffer, because of processing limitations of INC. Thus, this value is purely motivated by cognitive considerations. In Guhe, Habel & Tappe (2000) we showed that there are technical settings in which this capacity limitation is not desirable.

Latency Time (LT)

Function LT is the span of time that an element is kept in the traverse buffer, before it is taken by pvm-generation so as to produce a preverbal message for it.

Motivation This value is necessary for selection to be able to change its choices and for linearization to be able to perform its operations.

Expected Effects A lower value for LT has the effect that utterances are temporally closer to the genesis of the sketch map. A higher value means that the produced output is better and more reliable, because (1) selection and linearization have had more time to improve their output, and (2) more input from the pre-processing unit is available, which means that the CCR contains more reliable information about what is happening.

Comments The latency time models the time pressure on the verbalization task. If the traverse buffer is permanently filled or if elements are even lost, the latency time can be reduced to compensate this—the participant 'talks faster'. This can be especially important when the value for LoTB is comparatively small.

Fixing the Resource Parameters

The experimental design

The two sketches of our simulations are shown in Figure 1. We obtained corresponding human verbalizations by presenting sketches to 12 participants, 10 of which used the following pattern for Crossing 1:
- first segment (dr-H-Line)
- intermediary complexes (dr-Corner[3], dr-Parallel, dr-Corner)
- crossing expected
- intermediary complexes (dr-Corner, dr-Parallel, dr-Corner)
- crossing complete

One of the other two kept silent until the sketch was complete and only then uttered: 'A crossing or a cross.' The twelfth uttered no expectations but only described the emerging lines, before naming the result. The other 10 differed only slightly in how much of the crossing

---

[3] When pvm-generation produces an intermediary complex concept like 'dr-Parallel', this stands for utterances like 'A line parallel to the previous one is drawn.'

was visible when they produced the expectation; but all named it before it was fully visible. The verbalizations of Crossing 2 stick to a similar standard pattern:

- the first two segments (dr-H-Line, dr-H-Line)
- intermediary complexes (dr-Parallel, dr-Parallel, dr-Corner)
- crossing expected
- intermediary complexes (dr-Parallel / dr-Corner[4], Parallel / dr-Corner)
- crossing complete

Example Output of a Simulation

The output of the simulation for Crossing 1 with DoA = 0.5, LoTB = 6, and LT = 125ms yields this output:

```
hline1
hline1      vline1
gen(hline1)
corner1
corner1
corner1      vline2
gen(corner1, sum(vline1, hline1))
parallel1
parallel1
parallel1      hline2
parallel1      corner2
gen(parallel1, sum(vline2, vline1))
corner2
corner2      hline3
gen(corner2, sum(hline2, vline2))
parallel2
crossingE
crossingE      vline3
gen(crossingE, sum(vline1, hline1, hline4,
  vline4, vline3, hline3, hline2, vline2))
corner3
corner3
gen(corner3, sum(vline3, hline3))
vline4
parallel3
parallel3
parallel3      hline4
gen(parallel3, sum(vline4, vline3))
corner4
corner4
gen(corner4, sum(hline4, vline4))
parallel4
crossingR
crossingR
gen(crossingR, sum(vline1, hline1, hline4,
  vline4, vline3, hline3, hline2, vline2))
```

Here, we adopt the following notation: names of nodes like `hline1` stand for the node dr-H-Line1. `cross-`

`ingE` stands for an expected crossing, `crossingR` for a complete one. The lines containing only node names show the content of the traverse buffer at that point of time; lines starting with `gen` (generate) mean that pvm-generation generates a preverbal message for this element. For example, `gen(hline1)` can be understood as the core of a preverbal message that leads to an utterance like 'A horizontal line has been drawn.' If a complex node is generated its parts are given as well to verify the internal relations produced during the simulation. A comparison with Figure 2 shows that INC produces the desired structures in the CCR, the only difference (due to a peculiarity of the implementation) being that the parts of `crossing` are traced back to the level of basic events. Two consecutive lines with the same content, e.g. `corner3`, are typed out by the system, when something in the CCR is modified, but the traverse buffer does not change.

Results and Discussion

Overall Results With the simulations we come close to the observed verbalizations of humans (Tappe & Habel 1998; Habel & Tappe 1999) for both examples. This means that the sequences of preverbal messages (`gen` lines) in the output correspond structurally to the sequences of utterances of the observed human verbalizations. The values for LT and the runtime of the program in the following are machine dependent and possess only limited cognitive adequacy, because the implementation of INC reads prefabricated input files. This is faster than simulations that run in real-time[5] but directly proportional to it. The values for DoAT and LoTB certainly come closer to the goal of being psychologically real, but are merely proportional to the actual measures.

For DoAT we used two values: 0.5 and 0.9, for LoTB values between 2 and 6, and we varied LT between 50ms and 2000ms. The runtime of one execution of the program is split into two phases: 1400ms for the initialization of program and concept storage, and the runtime of the conceptualization. The second value, which is the important one here, is 2700ms to 3000ms for Crossing 1 and 2500ms to 2800ms for Crossing 2. (We used several pre-processing file per sketch, all of which yield equivalent results but take different runtimes.)

The values for both crossings that result in the simulation of the human verbalizations sketched above are: DoAT = 0.5, LoTB > 1, LT = 125ms. When varying these values, which we regard as our standard settings, we obtain the expected effects.

Degree of Agreement Threshold (DoAT) The maximum DoA for the crossings before they are complete is 0.81. Therefore, the maximum value of DoAT that has the effect that an expected crossing is introduced into

---

[4] Here, dr-Parallel and dr-Corner are generated at the same time. Since there is no temporal criterion for selecting one of the two, the choice is made randomly.

[5] Real-time means that the input for the pre-processing unit reads coordinates in the time interval with which they were recorded and produces basic entities for INC accordingly.

the CCR is 0.8. Thus, using DoAT = 0.9 instead of 0.5 means that no expectation is inserted into the CCR.

Latency Time (LT) When increasing the value for LT, more preverbal messages are produced, decreasing LT leads to the production of less. From a LT ≥ 800ms on no simple elements and no intermediary complexes are verbalized but only the expected and the complete crossing. The maximum value that still leads to the production of a preverbal message for the expected crossing is ca. 500ms for Crossing 1 and ca. 1000ms for Crossing 2. (These values should be—more or less—identical. This gap is an artifact that arises, because we use pre-processed files as input.) With LT < 125ms more basic events and some intermediary complexes—which are otherwise 'swallowed' by condition 3 of the selection strategy—are verbalized. With LT = 0ms each selected node is verbalized.

Length of Traverse Buffer (LoTB) We never need a value for LoTB > 5. LoTB = 5 is required for LT ≥ 800ms, if no elements of the traverse buffer shall get lost. LoTB = 3 suffices for most settings; only with LT < 125ms a value of 2 suffices. Other settings (LoTB < 3 with 125ms < LoTB < 800ms or LoTB < 5 for LT ≥ 800ms) have the effect that elements are lost. A value of LoTB = 1 means that elements are lost, and in almost all cases only the complete crossing is verbalized.

Conclusion and future work

With INC we present a cognitively motivated model of the first part of the language production process, the conceptualizer. By using simple design principles we get a model that exhibits behavior very similar to that observed in verbalizations of humans when they give on-line descriptions of events. By varying three resource parameters we were able to identify those parameter settings that lead to the typical verbalizations. Furthermore, INC produced all types of verbalizations we found in the verbalization corpus, e.g. even the rare case of participants uttering nothing until it is plain that the final result is or will be the drawing of a crossing.

Thus, INC does not need explicit instructions about what degree of detail or what level in the event hierarchy is used for the verbalization. This accounts for that it is very unlikely that humans deliberately choose one level. Instead, we use three parameters, motivated by cognitive considerations (DoAT, LoTB, LT), that determine INC's resources. By assigning different combinations of values we obtain our results.

A more elaborate model should be capable of adapting the values to the current demands of processing and to the currently available resources. For example, LoTB is a measure of what amount of the working memory is available for utterance planning. If, however, a participant has to perform additional tasks, LoTB needs to be reduced in accordance with the other cognitive subsystems that make use of this resource.

Acknowledgements
The research reported in this paper was conducted in the project ConcEv (Conceptualizing Events), which is supported by the DFG (Deutsche Forschungsgemeinschaft) in the priority program 'Language Production' under grant Ha-1237/10 to Christopher Habel.

References
Abb, B.; Günther, C.; Herweg, M.; Lebeth, K.; Maienborn, M. & Schopp, A. (1996) Incremental grammatical encoding—an outline of the SYNPHONICS formulator. In G. Adorni & M. Zock, eds., *Trends in natural language generation: An artificial intelligence perspective*, Berlin: Springer.

Anderson, J. R. (1983). *The Architecture of Cognition*. Cambridge, MA: Harvard UP.

Avrahami, J. & Kareev, Y. (1994) The emergence of events. *Cognition*, 53, 239–261.

De Smedt, K. (1990) IPF: An Incremental Parallel Formulator. In R. Dale, C. Mellish & M. Zock, eds., *Current Research in Natural Language Generation*, London: Academic Press.

De Smedt, K.; Horacek, H. & Zock, M. (1996) Architectures for natural language generation. In G. Adorni & M. Zock, eds., *Trends in natural language generation*, Berlin: Springer.

Guhe, M., Habel, C. & Tappe, H. (2000) Incremental Event Conceptualization and Natural Language Generation in Monitoring Environments. *INLG 2000*.

Habel, C. & Tappe, H. (1999) Processes of segmentation and linearization in describing events. In R. Klabunde & C. von Stutterheim, eds., *Representations and Processes in Language Production*, 117–153, Wiesbaden: Deutscher Universitäts-Verlag.

Kempen, G. & Hoenkamp, E. (1987) An Incremental Procedural Grammar for Sentence Formulation. *Cognitive Science*, 11:2, 201–258.

Levelt, W.J.M. (1989) *Speaking: From intention to articulation*. Cambridge, MA: MIT Press.

Lewis, R.L. (to appear). Specifying architectures of language processing: Process, control, and memory in parsing and interpretation. In. M. Crocker, M. Pickering & C. Clifton, eds., *Architectures and mechanisms for language processing*. Cambridge: CUP.

Newell, A. (1990). *Unified theories of cognition*. Cambridge, MA: Harvard UP.

Reiter E. (1994) Has a consensus NL generation architecture appeared, and is it psycholinguistically plausible? *IWNLG-1994*, 163–170, Kennebunkport, ME.

Tappe, H., Habel, C. (1998) Verbalization of Dynamic Sketch Maps: Layers of Representation and their Interaction. [full version of one page abstract / poster at CogSci 1998.] http://www.informatik.uni-hamburg.de/WSV/sprachproduktion/CogSci98.ps.gz

An ACT-R Model of the Evolution of Strategy Use and Problem Difficulty

Glenn Gunzelmann (glenng@andrew.cmu.edu)
John R. Anderson (ja+@cmu.edu)
Department of Psychology, Carnegie Mellon University
Pittsburgh, PA 15213

Abstract

Research has shown the importance of strategies in guiding problem solving behavior. The experiment and model presented here provide further specification of how more optimal strategies come to be adopted with experience. Isomorphs of the Tower of Hanoi were used to allow participants to develop a degree of expertise with a novel task. In the solutions, evidence for at least two strategies is apparent. The results suggest that when strategies are not successful in achieving the goal, other strategies may emerge and eventually come to dominate performance in a task. The ACT-R model of this task captures participant performance by using the same strategies to solve the problems and by gradually switching to more effective ones as simple strategies fail in solving the problems.

Introduction

Strategies are ubiquitous in problem solving. Even in novel tasks, participants bring general strategies to bare while searching for the correct solution. As experience is gained with a problem, these strategies often are abandoned in favor of strategies that are more particular to the task (Anzai & Simon, 1979). As the new strategies are discovered and practiced, solving problems within the task becomes easier and solutions become more efficient. Eventually, a strategy or set of strategies may be developed that can produce a correct solution to any problem for a particular task.

Strategic Influences on Problem Solving

Research on strategies in problem solving has taken two general forms. First, some researchers have focussed on the impact of particular strategies on solution times and accuracy (e.g. Altman and Trafton, 1999; Anderson, Kushmerick, and Lebiere, 1993). These researchers accurately model the particulars of strategy execution in participants. They do not, however, track the shifts in strategy use that typically occur as experience is gained with a particular task. Others have looked at the use of different strategies as individuals learn to solve problems (Lovett and Schunn, 1999; Reder & Schunn, 1999; Siegler, 1987). These researchers look at how multiple strategies for a task may coexist. The experiment presented here looks at the evolution of strategy use in solving the Tower of Hanoi problem. In addition, an ACT-R model of the task captures overall participant performance while closely matching the strategies they use and the transitions among them.

The Tower of Hanoi has served as a useful task in problem solving research for a number of years (e.g.

Anderson, et. al., 1993; Anzai and Simon, 1979). The task itself consists of three pegs upon which are placed any number of disks. Figure 1 illustrates the elements of the Tower of Hanoi task and the two isomorphs that we will be studying in our experiments. The goal is to change the disk arrangement from some start state into some particular goal state. There are three rules to guide movement through the problem space for the Tower of Hanoi. The first rule states that only one disk may be moved at a time. The second rule indicates that if more than one disk is on a particular peg, then only the smallest of these disks may be moved. The final rule says that a larger disk may not be moved to a peg where there is a smaller disk. This results in the necessity that the disks form a tower structure at all times, with larger disks always being underneath smaller disks.

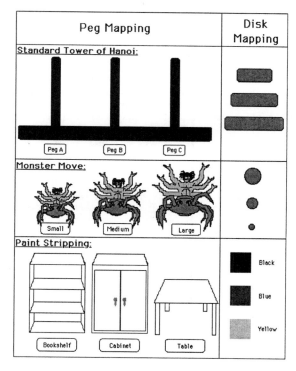

Figure 1: Mapping of the elements of the isomorphs used in this study to the standard Tower of Hanoi.

Research on the Tower of Hanoi indicates the importance of some variant of a disk subgoaling strategy (Anzai & Simon, 1979). In this strategy, subgoals are created to deal with the largest disk out of place. When the largest disk is placed into its goal state, focus is shifted to the next largest disk. This process is repeated until the smallest disk is placed. This strategy is quite effective, usually producing an optimal solution, regardless of the particular problem presented. While disk subgoaling may come to dominate participant solutions in the end, it is not usually the case that participants initially use this strategy. Rather, it tends to emerge as familiarity with the task increasese (Anzai & Simon, 1979). This is particularly the case with isomorphs (Kotovsky, Hayes, & Simon, 1985) where participants tend to start out with some sort of random search or simple hill-climbing strategy and only gradually evolve a preference for subgoaling. Also, subgoaling is not initially as predominant if participants are presented with flat-to-flat problems (problems with start and goal states where one disk is on each peg) rather than with classic tower-to-tower problems. Our research will use isomorphs and flat-to-flat problems, where other strategies often predominate early. However, these are not as effective as subgoaling. We want to study and model the process by which participants come to prefer the disk subgoaling strategy.

Experiment

In the three-disk Tower of Hanoi, there is a particular class of problem states in which there is one disk on each of the three pegs (flat states). There are a total of six of these states, and for each there are exactly two other flat states that are 5 moves away (minimum number of moves). Based on the disk subgoaling strategy, getting to one of these other flat states involves deeper subgoaling (hard) than getting to the other (easy). The breakdown of the subgoal structure of these problem types is illustrated in Figure 2. It shows that two subgoals need to be formed in the hard problems before making the first move, while a single subgoal is sufficient in the easy problems. An important feature of these two problem types is that they are otherwise quite similar. They both require 5 moves to solve, utilize the same set of start and goal states, and can be solved optimally using a similar sequence of moves. Because of these interesting characteristics, it is these problems that are used in the current study.

Since the superficial features of a task (cover story) can exert a strong impact on difficulty (Kotovsky, et. al., 1985), two different isomorphs of the Tower of Hanoi are. This is to help insure that any differences found are not simply an artifact of the cover story, but rather involve something more directly related to the task's structure. The Tower of Hanoi isomorphs used in this study are the Monster Move isomorph (Kotovsky, et. al., 1985) and the Paint Stripping isomorph (Gunzelmann & Blessing, 2000). In terms of the isomorphs, the pegs in the Tower of Hanoi are synonymous

with monsters in the Monster Move isomorph and with pieces of furniture in the Paint Stripping isomorph. The disks are represented by globes held by the monsters and by layers of paint on the furniture. The relationships among these three isomorphs are illustrated in Figure 1. The relationships among elements are a bit easier to describe in terms of the standard Tower of Hanoi, so the results will be discussed in terms of "disks" and "pegs".

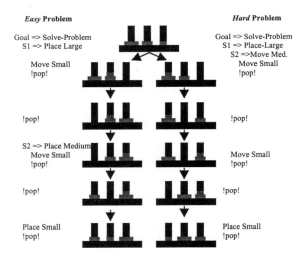

Figure 2. Breakdown of the easy and hard problem types used in this study.

Since these problems all begin and end with flat states they tend to encourage a particular kind of problem solving strategy in which participants simply transform flat state into flat state, looking for the goal state. One flat state can be transformed into another flat state using a three-move sequence of moving one disk onto a second disk, moving the other disk to where the first disk had been, and then moving the first disk to where the third disk had been. In effect, this switches the location of the first and third disk. At best, such a flat-to-flat strategy will solve the problems in 6 moves (two disk switches each taking 3 moves) rather than the optimal 5. We were interested in seeing how this flat-to-flat strategy would evolve in competition with a disk subgoaling strategy.

Method

The participants were 24 undergraduate students from Carnegie Mellon University. Participants received either course credit (n=7) or were paid (n=17) for their participation in the one-hour experiment.

The entire experiment was completed on a computer. Each participant was given a sequence of three tasks, with the first and third being the same Tower of Hanoi isomorph. The second task was given as a filler task. Before they began solving the problems for each task, participants were presented with a problem statement (cover story), a set of three rules, and an explanation of how to use the interface. Participants were instructed to solve each problem for each task by reaching the goal state that was presented on the screen. If an error was made while solving any of the problems, a message box appeared restating the rule that had been violated. After each problem, a message box appeared indicating that they had solved it correctly. The same procedure was followed for each of the three tasks.

Participants were randomly assigned to groups based upon, (1) The cover story for the Tower of Hanoi isomorph, (2) The type of problems they completed in the first set of problems (*easy* vs. *hard*), and (3) the type of problems for the second set. Each participant completed 6 problems in each isomorph set. Since the pattern of results was the same for both isomorphs, the data presented here is combined across them.

Results and Discussion

Evidence for the use of a strategy like disk subgoaling comes from problem solutions and the corresponding move latencies. Of all problems, 42% were solved optimally, and an additional 30% had solutions that incorporated an optimal 5-move final path. The move latencies for these solutions support the conclusion that participants were planning and executing 2-moves in sequence, similar to the data reported by Kotovsky, et. al. (1985). That is, move latencies were longer for the first and third moves than for the other three (7.2 versus 2.0 seconds on average), suggesting that more planning occurs before those moves are made. While this does not necessarily mean that participants were using the disk subgoaling strategy specifically, it is reasonable to conclude that they were using a strategy at least quite similar to it.

The evidence also suggest that flat states were particularly attractive to participants as they tried to find a solution. If moves were made entirely at random, it would be expected that participants would arrive at flat states every 4.5 moves (6 of 27 states are flat states). However, the rate was actually every 3.33 moves for participants (ignoring flat-to-flat 5-move final paths), with the minimum distance between flat states being 3 moves (see above). In addition, of the problems that were not solved using a 5-move final path, half had a final path that incorporated only a single additional move, which involved moving through an intermediate flat state en route to the correct solution. The data indicating a preference for flat states is further enhanced by the latency data collected. For *every* participant, move latencies were greater for flat states than for other states. This provides persuasive evidence that more planning occurred in flat states than in other states and that participants were implementing a flat-to-flat strategy. That is, participants seemed to be planning and executing sequences of 3 moves that transformed the problem state from one flat state into another.

There are two explanations for why participants may have learned such a strategy. First, as stated above, both the start state and the goal state were flat states, immediately drawing participants attention to them as somehow important in the task. Second, in flat states, rule 2 does not apply (if there is more than one disk on a peg, only the smallest may be moved), simplifying the evaluation needed to plan a move. This would reduce the memory load for planning a move, and perhaps allow participants to look further ahead in the problem to plan multiple moves. As such, these states become a "home base" of sorts where participants can regroup and consider alternatives.

It is important to recall that the participants in this study were not given training on strategies for solving any of the problems. Thus, the solution strategies were developed by the participants as they worked through the problems. Still, the *hard* problems took, on average, 1.1 additional moves to solve than the *easy* problems. Though this effect did not reach statistical significance in this experiment, it was fairly robust. It was constant across isomorphs and remained fairly stable across problem number. The fact that this difference did appear, and in the expected direction, lends insight into participants' representations of the problems and how they sought to solve them. Combined with the evidence for disk-subgoaling, these findings suggest that the added level of subgoaling made it more difficult for participants to successfully plan and execute the moves to solve the hard problems optimally.

There is ample evidence for both a disk-subgoaling and a flat-to-flat strategy in participants' data. In the next section on the model, we will provide further analysis of these results. Also there is evidence for a shift in these strategies. During the first 6 problems, subjects solved 64% of the problems in the 5 moves dictated by the disk subgoaling and 24% of the problems by going through a pair of flat to flat transformations. For the second 6 problems these percentages were 83% disk-subgoaling and 14% flat-to-flat.

Model

An ACT-R model (Anderson, 1976; Anderson & Lebiere, 1998) of participant performance was developed with the goal of capturing the overall performance of participants while simultaneously matching their strategy use. Based on the data presented above, the model was constructed to use three different strategies as it went about solving the problems presented. These were the disk subgoaling strategy, the flat-to-flat strategy, and a random strategy. The random strategy allows for the unfocussed meandering about the problem space that is particularly characteristic of the early stages of problem solving in a novel task (Kotovsky, et. al., 1985).

Model Design and Mechanisms

The ACT-R model evaluates the success of a strategy by noting whether or not each use of the strategy leads to a solution to the problem. If the evaluation of one strategy becomes increasingly negative, there will be a tendency to switch to other, potentially more effective, strategies. Over time, the model will come to settle on the strategies that are generally more effective. To accomplish this, the model goes through a series of iterations of (1) choosing a strategy, (2) executing the strategy, (3) evaluating the result (i.e. has the problem been solved). The critical stage in this process within the model is strategy selection. At the point in the problem where a strategy needs to be chosen, there are three productions that may fire (one for each of the strategies). The choice of which production fires in ACT-R is governed by the calculation of the "expected gain" (E) for each production. In this process, a quantity is calculated for each production to represent how quickly its use is expected to result in satisfying the goal. The production producing the highest value for this quantity is selected and fires. The equation for expected gain (E) in ACT-R is:

$$E = PG - C$$

where P is the probability that both the production will succeed and the goal eventually will be achieved, C is the anticipated cost (in seconds) of achieving the goal using the production, and G is a global variable representing the value (in seconds) of achieving the goal (i.e. how much time is the model willing to spend to solve the problem). The value of G was set at 50. While this value is traditionally set at 20 in ACT-R, these problems take longer than that for participants (and the model) to solve. So, this value was raised to accommodate the greater amount of time needed to solve them. For this model, the initial values of C were equal for all the strategies. But, as the model performs the task, it adds the cost incurred in executing each strategy to the value of C in the strategy-choice production. In contrast, the P values were estimated for each production. The equation for P is:

$$P = Successes/(Successes + Failures)$$

where "successes" and "failures" refer to the number of eventual successes and eventual failures that occurred when this production was used. That is, how often has the goal been achieved and how often has the goal not been achieved when this production has been used? The initial values for the "successes" and "failures" for each of the three strategy choice productions were parameters estimated in fitting the model. While all these values were set, it is really the relative difference in this ratio among the three productions that matters most in the model. In addition, the sum of successes and failures was made to equal 50 for all three. This quantity controls the stability of E by influencing how much a single success or failure will affect the calculation of

P. As the model performs the task, it gains experiences and adds to these values. Each time a strategy is executed either a success (if the problem is solved during the execution of the strategy) or a failure (if the problem is not solved) is added to the calculation of P. Thus, as the model gains experience, the rapidity of change and the impact of any single attempt at using a strategy diminishes. That is, the model slowly begins to settle on the most successful strategies. The initial values and the values after learning for the variables (for a single run of the model in one condition of Experiment 1) are presented in Table 2.

Table 1: Initial parameter settings for model and their values after learning.

	Successes	Failures	P	E
Initial				
Disk-subgoal	25	25	.50	23.95
Flat-toFlat	26	24	.52	24.95
Random	28	22	.56	26.95
12 *hard* trials				
Disk-subgoal	34	29	.54	22.16
Flat-toFlat	29	31	.49	21.35
Random	28	36	.44	20.13
100 *hard* trials				
Disk-subgoal	121	37	.77	24.89
Flat-toFlat	30	42	.42	16.62
Random	28	46	.38	16.76

The values of P are not perfectly correlated with the values in E is because E includes the costs incurred for executing each strategy (C). Although disk-subgoaling is more successful at solving the problems, it is more costly (in terms of time) because it involves more planning and more moves per attempt than the others. These offsetting influences maintain the mixture of strategies over the course of the experiment. With more problems, the degree of separation increases, leaving the disk-subgoaling strategy as the preferred strategy. The values for the variables after the model solves 100 *hard* problems are presented at the bottom of Table 2.

The final parameter of importance is a noise parameter that is added to the calculation of E. A noise value is produced separately for each production on each cycle of the model. In this model, the value is randomly selected from a distribution with a mean of 0 and a standard deviation of about 1.8. The strategy-choice production selected to fire is the one that has the highest value of E after noise has been added to the calculation described above for each.

A major assumption of the model is that most participants would begin the experiment without a clear idea of how to solve the problems. In the model, this is instantiated in the initial values of E for the three strategy-choice productions. In particular, the "successes" and "failures" were set such that the random strategy was initially preferred. This was followed by the flat-to-flat strategy, with the disk-subgoaling strategy least preferred. The reason for this ordering is that the disk-subgoaling strategy is the most sophisticated strategy in the model. Thus, the model tends to begin with the simplest strategy (i.e. make a move and evaluate the result) and moves toward more efficient, though more complicated ones.

There is one additional mechanism that is critical for the fit of the model to the data presented. It is largely responsible for the difference in difficulty found between the *easy* and *hard* training problems and operates similarly to the strategy-choice mechanism described above. At the point in the disk-subgoaling strategy where a second subgoal needs to be formed, there are two productions that may fire. One accurately forms the second subgoal and the problem is ultimately solved correctly from that point. The other gives up on the strategy and goes on to try a different approach (perhaps returning to try disk subgoaling at a later point). The critical parameter for this mechanism is once again the initial difference in the expected gain value for the two productions. For the sake of simplicity, the same sum of successes and failures (50) was used for these productions as for the strategy-choice productions. The estimated "successes" and "failures" for the production to give up were 40 and 10 respectively (P=.80, E=38). For the production that successfully pushed the second subgoal, the values were 38 and 12 respectively (P=.76, E=36). These impact the value of E for these productions similarly to the strategy choice productions presented in Table 2. This means that the model tends to give up initially. However, since this inevitably means that the strategy will fail to achieve the goal (adding a failure to the production that gives up), it learns rather quickly to press on, execute the additional level of subgoaling, and solve the problem successfully (adding a success to the "push-on" production). All of these parameters were estimated to fit the aggregate move data (Figures 3 and 4; averaged into quartiles). The more detailed data on strategy use is examined next.

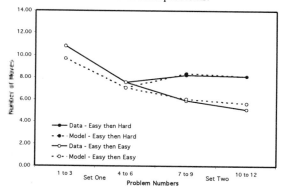

Figure 3: Model fit to moves to solve data where the first set consisted of *hard* problems.

Figure 4: Model fit to moves to solve data where the first set of problems was *easy* problems.

Fit to the Strategy Data (Final Paths)

The rather good fit to the average move data (r^2=.91, mean-deviation=.798) suggests that the model is capturing human performance and learning in the task. However, a more compelling argument for the model comes from the fit of the model to more detailed accounts of the participants' solutions. The best way to examine strategies that participants were using is to look at how they actually solved the problems they were given. From Kotovsky, et. al. (1985) comes the idea of a 2-stage solution process, an initial exploratory phase where no progress is made toward the goal followed by the final path, where generally a rapid and efficient solution is produced. The final path begins when the person is the same number of moves from the goal as he or she was at the start of the problem. For the *hard* and *easy* problems, this means that the final path begins the last time the participant is 5 moves from the goal (via the shortest path) before actually solving it.

Previous research has found that the exploratory moves relate more closely to problem difficulty than length of the final path (e.g. Kotovsky, et. al., 1985). In concert with this finding, the difference in final path behavior between the *easy* and *hard* problems is not large. On the other hand, final path length is informative about the strategies being used by participants as they solve problems. In particular, the final path length of the problems used here can help to differentiate among problems solved using a disk-subgoaling strategy, solutions using a flat-to-flat strategy, and solutions involving a more random sequence of moves. As stated above, the disk subgoaling strategy, if executed correctly, will give rise to perfect solutions and optimal final paths. On the other hand, the flat-to-flat strategy will produce solutions that are slightly less than optimal. For the 5-move problems used here, a flat-to-flat solution would take 6 moves (2 consecutive flat-to-flat transformations).

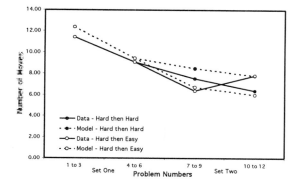

To examine the fit of the model to the solutions produced by participants, the length of the final path was determined for each problem solution in both the model and the data. In Table 2, the percentage of problems solved with final paths suggestive of each strategy is indicated by condition. The remaining problems involved longer final paths that did not follow a readily identified pattern.

Table 2: Percentage (%) of problems supporting the disk subgoaling and flat-to-flat strategies by condition.

	Data	Model
Set One		
Easy		
Disk Subgoal	63	68
Flat-to-Flat	25	22
Hard		
Disk Subgoal	67	68
Flat-to-Flat	24	15
Set Two		
Hard (from Hard)		
Disk Subgoal	86	78
Flat-to-Flat	6	13
Hard (from Easy)		
Disk Subgoal	77	82
Flat-to-Flat	19	15
Easy (from Hard)		
Disk Subgoal	83	81
Flat-to-Flat	14	12
Easy (from Easy)		
Disk Subgoal	83	87
Flat-to-Flat	17	12

From the data presented in Table 2, it is clear that the model reproduces much of the strategic richness of participant performance. To test this assertion, a Chi-square test was performed on the participant versus model data. This statistic provides a rough indication of the similarity of the predicted model data to the obtained empirical data. For the data in Table 2, $X^2(11)=7.59$, P>.05. This suggests that the model is doing a very good job of modeling the strategies used by participants while solving the problems.

Conclusion

The data and model presented here provide evidence that the failure of simple strategies to reach the goal can lead individuals to switch to the use of more sophisticated strategies for achieving that end. As strategies are attempted, they are evaluated in terms of their success in achieving the goal, but also in terms of the costs associated with executing them. While sophisticated strategies may initially fare poorly, due to a greater cost, in the end they are likely to emerge as the preferred strategy due to their greater likelihood of successfully solving the problem.

The participants in this study were given no instruction on how to solve the problems they were given. Initially, they were unsure of how to maneuver through the problem space, as suggested by the many apparently random moves that

were made. But, as they gained experience with the isomorphs, their solutions became increasingly organized, and clear evidence of the two strategies described here emerged. The model accurately captures this aspect of participant solutions, showing a gradual and noisy shift from completely undirected random moves to optimal solutions using a sophisticated strategy. This kind of transition in strategies is certain to appear in other tasks, as it has already been noted in children solving addition problems (Siegler, 1987). The richness of strategy use in participants is an important aspect of problem solving behavior, and one that warrants careful consideration in problem solving research.

References

Altman, E. M., & Trafton, J. G. (1999). *Memory for goals: An architectural perspective.* Proceedings of the Cognitive Science Society (pp. 19-24).

Anderson, J. R. (1976). *The Adaptive Character of Thought.* Hillsdale, NJ: Lawrence Erlbaum Associates.

Anderson, J. R. (1998). *Atomic components of thought.* Hillsdale, NJ: Lawrence Erlbaum Associates.

Anderson, J. R., Kushmerick, N., & Lebiere, C. (1993). The Tower of Hanoi and Goal Structures. In Anderson, J. R., *Rules of the Mind* (p. 121-142). Hillsdale, NJ: Lawrence Erlbaum Associates.

Gunzelmann, G., & Blessing, S. B. (2000). *Why are some problems easy? New insights into the Tower of Hanoi.* In Proceedings of the Cognitive Science Society (p. 1029).

Kotovsky, K., Hayes, J. R., & Simon, H. A. (1985) Why are some problems hard? *Cognitive Psychology, 17,* 248-294.

Lovett, M. C., & Schunn, C. D. (1999). Task representations, strategy variability, and base-rate neglect. *Journal of Experimental Psychology, General, 128,* 107-130.

Reder, L. M., & Schunn, C. D. (1999). Bringing Together the Psychometric and Strategy Worlds: Predicting in a Dynamic Task. In Gopher, D. & Koriat, A. (Eds). *Cognitive regulation of performance: Interaction of theory and application. Attention and Performance XVII* (pp. 315-342). Cambridge, MA: MIT Press.

Siegler, R. S. (1987). The perils of averaging data over strategies: An example from children's addition. *Journal of Experimental Psychology, General, 116,* 250-264.

Spitz, H. H., Minsky, S. K., & Bessellieu, C. L. (1984). Subgoal length versus full solution length in predicting Tower of Hanoi problem-solving performance. *Bulletin of the Psychonomic Society, 22,* 301-304.

The role of abstract patterns in implicit learning

Volodymyr V. Ivanchenko (vlad@cogs.nbu.acad.bg)
Central and Eastern European Center for Cognitive Science
Department of Cognitive Science and Psychology,
New Bulgarian University,
21 Montevideo Street, Sofia 1635, Bulgaria

Abstract

Implicit learning is thought to underlie language acquisition, acquisition of reading and writing abilities and many other phenomena central to cognition. The main finding in this field is that humans exposed to the stimulus material, which comprises some regularities, unintentionally acquire an ability to discriminate between stimuli with and without these regularities. Moreover, when these regularities are instantiated with a symbol set different from the training one participants still succeed in the task (so-called transfer effect, Reber, 1967). I hypothesized an existence of one general mechanism capable of explaining both the discrimination and the transfer phenomenon. This mechanism is sensitive to the existence of a symbol repetition pattern in a stimulus string. I called such a repetition an abstract pattern (AP) since a fact of symbol repetition is instantiation independent. Two experiments were conducted in order to check whether participants base their grammaticality judgment on the fact of presence of AP in the test material during implicit learning of artificial grammar (AG). I found a tendency to recognize as grammatical, items with an arbitrary AP rather than those without any AP and items with an AP seen during training rather then those with an unseen AP. A computer simulation in the form of a three layer autoassociator was run and found useful for explaining participants' overall performance as well as their responses to the particular stimuli.

Introduction

The term implicit learning "…characterizes those situations where a person learns about the structure of a fairly complex stimulus environment, without necessarily intending to do so, and in such a way that the resulting knowledge is difficult to express" (Berry & Dienes 1993). One of the experimental paradigms used in this field is learning of an artificial grammar (AG). Reber (1967) conducted one of the pioneering works in implicit learning of AGs. The main finding was that people become sensitive to the structure of an AG just after memorizing some exemplar strings. A typical schematic diagram of AG is shown in Fig 1. Strings that can be generated by a particular grammar are called grammatical (consequently those strings that cannot be generated by the same AG are called ungrammatical). An experiment with an AG generally consists of two stages. In the first stage participants are

told to memorize the set of grammatical strings. They are not informed about the existence of any grammar. In the second stage participants are told about the existence of rules and given an unexpected classification test. The task is to judge every new string as being grammatical or ungrammatical. Reber (1967) found that participants performed significantly above chance though they could not explain which rules might be imposed on these strings.

There are several competing theories explaining these results. The fragmentary theory (Perruchet & Pacteau 1990; St. John & Shanks, 1997; Servan-Schreiber and Anderson, 1990) claims that humans encode short fragments (chunks) of strings. The exemplar based account (Brooks and Vokey, 1991) advocates encoding whole exemplars of strings. Grammaticality judgment in both theories typically involves a kind of similarity estimate between memorized strings/fragments and a test string.

While all above-mentioned theories are symbolic, there is a number of researchers who claim that the phenomenon of implicit learning may be fully explained with the help of the connectionist approach (Elman, 1990; Cleeremans, 1997). This approach emphasizes a unique framework that may account for both implicit and explicit learning.

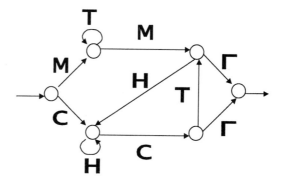

Figure 1: The AG used in experiment 1. It was instantiated by 3 different letter sets: ПВХЛК, МСНТГ, ФЗЖРЪ.

All theories described so far, however, have a problem with explaining a transfer phenomenon, namely when participants are exposed to stimuli based on one letter set and are tested with the stimuli based on a different letter set (while rules remain constant). Reber (1969) showed that even in this case participants were able to manage the task, though their performance dropped compared to that in the discrimination task. Moreover, Altmann, Dienes, & Goode (1995) demonstrated a small but significant transfer between letters and musical tones.

To be fair though, there were some attempts to model transfer. Druhan & Mathews (1989) proposed a model (THIYOS) that takes as input verbal instructions. THIYOS is a kind of production system, which among other things encodes repetitions of adjacent symbols in every stimulus. However, as Altmann et al. (1995) showed, transfer occurs even for those test strings in which every element is different. Thus repetition of adjacent symbols in a string is not necessary for successful performance. Still another attempt to model transfer was done by Dienes, Altmann & Gao (1995) who modified SRN in such a way that it could transfer knowledge across different domains. Despite the model's good fit to experimental data, it requires learning even during a test phase and consequently cannot perform well at the beginning of the test.

In my work I tried to answer the question about the role that non-adjacent symbol repetitions may play in implicit learning, particularly during transfer. I considered strings generated by an AG with repetitions separated by up to two elements (e.g. GABG). I called letter independent representation of such repetition an abstract pattern (AP). For example, both strings AKKA and RTTR have one and the same abstract pattern (1001). In experiment 1 I will explore whether APs may be encoded and used as clues for grammaticality. In experiment 2, I will consider participants' ability to discern strings with seen (during training) APs from those with unseen APs. And finally, I will report on the results of computer simulation meant to suggest a mechanism for AP encoding and processing.

Experiment 1. Do participants encode abstract patterns?

In experiment 1 I intended to show that chunking is not the only way to encode data during implicit learning of an AG. For that purpose I manipulated the form in which strings were learned, biasing participants to encode either chunks or APs. In this case a difference in performance may indicate difference in encoding of learning material. It was also planned to check whether or not participants would be able to discriminate between seen and unseen (during training) APs separately within grammatical and ungrammatical groups of strings.

Method

The experiment consisted of three parts: learning, testing (which included discrimination and transfer tasks) and a follow-up interview. There were two groups of factors, which served as independent variables. The first group, between-subject factors, defined the appearance of the training material and the second group, within-subject factors, related to different groups of the test stimuli. The dependent variable was participants' level of performance in discrimination and transfer tasks, calculated as d prime.

Procedure

Training phase In the training phase all participants were randomly and equally placed in one of four groups, according to the 2 by 2 between-subject design (where one factor was presence/absence of chunking as in ПЛЛЛПК/ П ЛЛЛ ПК in the training material and the other factor was the use of one or two letter sets). The chunking form was supposed to stimulate chunk encoding, while a two-letter set was supposed to bias participants to encode APs (and inhibit chunking because the frequency of chunks was reduced by half). After each of 17 grammatical strings was presented on the computer screen for 5 sec. in the fixed order. The participants had to reproduce it on a piece of paper and give it to the experimenter. The procedure repeats until the criterion of two correct reproductions in a row was reached. This task was presented in the instructions as a simple memory task.

Test phase After a short period of rest (1-2 min) existence of the rules was revealed and participants were given new strings, half of which were grammatical (fit the rules) and half were not. Participants judged the strings as grammatical/ungrammatical by pressing corresponding buttons. For the transfer task there was an additional instruction concerning the change of a letter set but not a change of the rules. Participants saw strings one by one, self paced, without feedback, and in a random order. 17 grammatical and 17 ungrammatical strings were presented twice in the discrimination test. Participants trained with two letter sets had to classify two 34-item sequences instantiated with each of the original letter sets. The test phase also included a transfer task (with a new letter set) consisting of 17 grammatical and 17 ungrammatical strings presented just once. Letter sets and the testing orders (transfer/discrimination) were counterbalanced across all participants in a group.

Stimulus Material

All grammatical stimuli were generated by an AG shown in Fig. 1. This AG produces 34 different grammatical strings (6-8 letters long) and half of them were used in the training phase while the other half was reserved for the test session. Ungrammatical strings were formed in such a way that they have only one letter and chunk violation and there were no violations of marginal chunks. Actual chunk configuration was adopted from Servan-Schreiber and Anderson (1990).

Participants

Fifty-five university students served as participants. Their participation was a part of requirements for the course in experimental psychology or was rewarded with a flat fee.

Results and discussion

All data were normally distributed within all groups. There were no significant main effects of the counterbalanced and controlled variables so all the data were collapsed across these variables. Performance of participants as a whole in both discrimination and transfer tasks was above chance level, which was confirmed by a 95% confidence interval (see Table 1).

As may be seen from Table 1, participants were unable to discriminate between seen and unseen (in training session) APs (95% confidence interval includes zero). The experiment also failed to find main effects of or interactions between two factors concerning the appearance of training material (two-way ANOVA, all $F(1,51) < 3.1$, all $p > 0.08$). Thus the hypothesis about the difference in performance for various appearances of training stimuli and participants' ability to discriminate between seen and unseen APs should be rejected for now. But then at least one question remains unanswered: how did participants manage to cope with the transfer task if they ignored APs? It happened that since almost all (more than 80%) training strings contained an AP, participants discriminated between whether the stimulus had some (seen or unseen) AP or not. Participants classified items in such a way for both

Table 1: Mean d' s and their confidence intervals in discrimination and transfer tasks. Abbreviations: Gram/ungram means d' of discrimination between grammatical and ungrammatical strings; Seen/unseen - d' in discrimination between seen and unseen (in training session) AP in grammatical strings; AP/without - d' for discrimination between ungrammatical strings with AP and without any AP.

Task	Group of strings	Mean d'	Confidence int. -95%	+95%
Discrim.	Gram/ungram.	.39	.25	.53
	Seen/unseen	-.09	-.56	.38
	AP/without	.41	.003	.81
Transfer	Gram/ungram.	.21	.09	.34
	Seen/unseen	-.14	-.77	.49
	AP/without	.68	.16	1.21

discrimination and transfer tasks (see table 1: d' AP/without = 0.41, for discrimination and d' AP/without =0.68 for transfer, both significant). In fact, picking up the items with an arbitrary AP would guarantee (because of the structure of test stimuli) a very high performance (d' >3.00). However, the fact that the average performance of participants was somewhat 10 times lower indicates unconscious behavior. Follow-up interviews showed that only about 1/3 of participants noticed and intentionally used symbol repetitions.

APs as clues for grammaticality regardless of their presence in the training material has little to do with actual learning. It is, nevertheless, an important behavioral characteristic that deserves further consideration. That is why a percent of grammatical replies for every item with an AP averaged across all participants was calculated. The more detailed analysis as to which features of APs participants are sensitive to, showed a preference (correlation between % of grammatical replies and value of a pattern feature) for longer patterns and for the less probable patterns[1] (see table 2). Interestingly, for all test items with an AP there was a very strong correlation (Rs=0.8-0.9) between grammatical replies and a Compression Parameter (CP). The meaning of this parameter is to what extent an AP may be compressed (see Equation 1). Dependence of grammaticality judgment on the CP was further confirmed by four linear regression analyses for 4 groups of strings from table 2. All regressions were significant (all Ps<0.002). The high percentage (up to 87%) of variance explained by the CP suggests subjects' strong preferences for compact APs.

In sum, there is some evidence that during implicit learning participants became sensitive not only to chunk structure of stimuli but also to the presence of APs. Specifically, participants prefer to reply grammatically to items that comprise an AP and to the extent to which

Table 2: Correlation between percentage of replying grammatical and values of features of APs for different groups of strings. Empty cells mean non-significant correlation.

AP' characteristic	Discrimination Gram.	ungram.	Transfer gram.	ungram.
Probability	-.60	-.61	-.80	-
Length	.72	.80	.85	-
CP	.94	.92	.86	.80

[1] Probability of occurrence was computed as if any repetition of a symbol in a string was an event with a chance of occurrence equal to 1/5 (because there are five different symbols in the letter set).

$$CP = Log \frac{Length \_ of \_ pattern}{Amount \_ of \_ different \_ letters}$$

Equation 1: The definition of compression parameter. For example, for the string <u>ABAB</u>KLM Length_of_pattern is 4 and Amount_of_different_letters is 2 ('A' and 'B'), thus CP=log 4/2.

these APs might be effectively compressed. This finding supports an assumption that implicit processing of strings involves compression of data rather than extraction of complex rules. Chunking, by the way, may be regarded as another example of compression. However, the lack of evidence for actual learning of APs suggests the need for further investigation.

Experiment 2. Can AP be learned?

The main hypothesis in experiment 2 was that participants would prefer to classify as grammatical items with a seen AP rather than those with an unseen AP. Their failure to do so in experiment 1 may be partially attributed to the prevalence of APs in the stimulus material (thus participants might use presence of an arbitrary AP as a clue for grammaticality in the test).

Method

The method was similar to experiment 1. The main difference was that the independent variables were groups of test strings (ungrammatical strings with seen or unseen AP, and grammatical strings with any AP or without AP).

Procedure

The procedure was similar to experiment 1. During the training session 20 strings were presented twice in a fixed order.

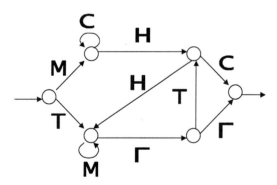

Figure 2: The AG used in experiment 2. It was instantiated by 2 different letter sets: МСНТГ, ПВХЛК.

The learning criterion was relaxed to just one correct reproduction. In a test session 14 grammatical and 14 ungrammatical strings were presented twice in a random order. The test consisted of transfer only.

Stimulus Material

The AG chosen had the same wiring as the AG in experiment 1 but produced less symbol repetitions in a string (see Fig. 2). As a result there was less stimuli with AP which could be balanced with those having no AP. This AG produces 34 different grammatical strings of length 6-8. 10 of them with an AP and 10 without an AP were used in the training session. The remaining 14 strings were reserved for the test.

Participants

Twenty-four university students served as participants in experiment 2. Otherwise, details regarding participants were identical to experiment 1.

Results and discussion

The first general result was that average transfer performance was above chance and greater by 50% than in experiment 1 (see Table 3). Value of d' =.31 is actually very close to the results obtained by other researchers who worked with this type of AG (see Reber & Manza, 1997). The most exciting result was that participants preferred to classify as grammatical items with a seen (during training) AP rather than those with an unseen AP (d' =1.11). Both groups of strings were ungrammatical. Similar to the first experiment, participants preferred to interpret as grammatical those strings that had an arbitrary AP rather than strings without an AP (though both groups of strings were grammatical). They do it despite equal number of strings with and without an AP in the training session.

Finally, I want to draw attention to the magnitude of d'≈0.3 for grammaticality judgment versus d'≈1.0 for seen/unseen or AP/without groups of strings (see Table 3). This huge difference in favor of issues connected with AP rather than with grammaticality status may indicate that the mechanism of AG learning possesses some intrinsic biases.

Table 3: Mean d's and their confidence intervals for the transfer task. Abbreviations are the same as in table 1.

Group of strings	Mean d'	Confidence int.	
		-95%	+95%
Gram/ungram.	.31	.11	.52
Seen/unseen	1.11	.60	1.61
AP/without	1.13	.68	1.57

Computer Simulation

In order to suggest a possible algorithm for AP processing I used a connectionist simulation in the form of a three- layer autoassociator. The reasons for this were that this architecture corresponds well to the experimental task. It has a parallel input and analysis of strings reproduced during the training session showed that they were often processed in parallel fashion (written backwards or starting from easy chunks in the middle). Like the participants on the training session, the autoassociator is required to reproduce the input string in the output. And finally a hidden layer with relatively small number of units seems to support a compression hypothesis.

The basic modules of the model are depicted in Fig. 3. The input representation was crucial for the work of the model and consisted of two parts (each corresponding to a particular type of compression: chunking and AP extraction). The first part of input was local representations of letters in a string with additional start and end bits. This type of representation was given some position invariant properties (to correspond to chunks) by encoding only part of a string located in the current moving window (6 letters wide). Local encoding was then re-represented with an abstract representation system (see Fig. 4) to form a repetition pattern. For example, strings AKKA and KAAK will result in one and the same systems output pattern.

In order to assess model performance different moves of a window on the output were again assembled into whole strings by averaging corresponding bits. The actual measure of similarity was calculated as the cosine of the angle between the input and output vectors (see Dienes, 1992). While the measure of item grammaticality in the experiment might be the "easy-to-reproduce" criterion, in the simulation a cosine reflects the accuracy of such reproduction (see Equation2).

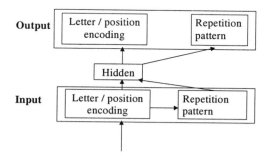

Figure 3: The slab diagram of the three-layer autoassociator with two types of input. All connections were trained by back propagation.

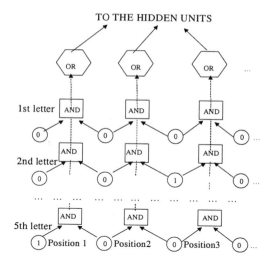

Figure 4: The simplified version of the abstract representation system. Circles with numbers are the original local representations of letters. The square units perform the AND function (they are detectors of the 11 pattern, in the real simulation there were also detectors for the 1.1 and 1..1 patterns). Finally OR units are excited whenever any of the corresponding AND units is activated. Every AND layer corresponds to the particular letter. The single OR layer gathers information from every layer of letters and thus is letter independent.

The model was trained on the same number of trials and with the same stimulus material as in experiment 1 (there were 20 hidden units, learning rate=2, momentum=0). The model was run on 40 artificial subjects constructed from 10 pairs of training/test files and 4 different random seeds. The model's performance for discrimination and transfer tasks were d'=0.41; 0.29 (corresponding to d'=0.39; 0.21 in experiment 1).

$$P(gram\ .) = \frac{1}{1 + e^{-k(\cos\ \alpha - \overline{\cos\ \alpha})}}$$

Equation 2: Probability of the reply being grammatical depending on the cosine ($\cos\alpha$) of an angle between input and output vectors. $\overline{\cos\alpha}$ is an average $\cos\alpha$ for the last 10 trials that is used as a dynamic threshold (initial threshold was set to 0.8). k is a constant set to 10;.

I also looked on the model replies with regard to every particular test string. Correlation with experimental replies was R=0.60, p=0.006 for discrimination and R=0.40, p=0.019 for the transfer tasks. A categorized histogram for the discrimination task is shown in Fig. 5.

Conclusions

The aim of this experimental study was to take a closer look at the potential ways of information encoding during implicit learning. I proposed a mechanism based on using both chunks and APs, which makes both discrimination and transfer possible. Fragmentary and exemplar theories are mostly concerned with the question of how accurate participants' knowledge may reflect AG rules. I stressed another question, namely, what participants are typically looking for and what abilities they acquire irrespectively whether these abilities are relevant to the AG rules or not. For example, in experiment 2, participants' discrimination ability between seen and unseen (in training session) APs was several times greater than actual grammaticality performance in the transfer task. Such observation may give important clues as to how participants behave when learning "natural grammars" and what these grammars are. To summarize, participants' sensitivity to the presence of APs as a clue for a rule in general and their ability to discriminate between seen and unseen APs in particular indicate an important behavioral constraint in studying implicit learning. The computer simulation demonstrated that using a repetition pattern as an input to a three-layer autoassociator along with chunk encoding might produce results similar to the experimental ones in both discrimination and transfer tasks. It is important to note that the network did not process APs in an explicit symbolic way. Thus an AP per se may be treated as a behavioral characteristic rather than a form of knowledge representation.

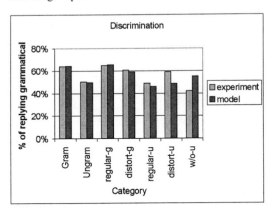

Figure 5. The comparison of the model and participants' performance on the discrimination task. (Abbreviations for groups of strings: g or Gram - grammatical; u or Ungram. - ungrammatical; distort - items with unseen, and regular - with seen AP; w/o - without AP).

Acknowledgments

The experimental part of this work was carried out in the Laboratory for Experimental Psychology at NBU. I would like to thank my scientific supervisor Prof. Boicho Kokinov for the valuable ideas and help in designing experiments and writing the paper.

References

Altmann, G.T., Dienes, Z., & Goode, A. (1995). On the modality independence of implicitly learned grammatical knowledge. *Journal of Experimental Psychology: Learning, Memory, and Cognition, 21*, 899-912.

Berry, D. C., & Dienes, Z. (1993). *Implicit learning: Theoretical and empirical issues*. Hillsdale, NJ: Lawrence Erlbaum Associates.

Brooks, L.R., & Vokey, J.R. (1991). Abstract analogies and abstracted grammars: A comment on Reber, and Mathews et al. *Journal of Experimental Psychology: General, 120*, 316-323.

Cleeremans A. (1997). Principles of implicit learning. In D. C. Berry (Ed.), *How implicit is implicit learning?* Oxford University Press.

Dienes, Z. (1992). Connectionist and memory-array models of artificial grammar learning. *Cognitive Science, 16*, 41-80.

Dienes, Z, Altmann, J. T. & Gao, S. (1994). Mapping across domains without feedback: A neural network model of transfer of implicit knowledge. *Proceeding of the 3rd Neural computation and Psychology Workshop*, Stirling, Scotland.

Druhan, B. B. & Mathews, R. C. (1989). THIYOS: A classifier system model of implicit knowledge of artificial grammars. *Proceedings of the Eleventh Annual Conference of the Cognitive Science Society*. Hillsdale, NJ: Lawrence Erlbaum Associates.

Elman, J. L (1990). Finding structure in time. *Cognitive Science, 14*, 179-211.

Perruchet, P. & Pacteau, C. (1990). Synthetic grammar learning: Implicit rule abstraction or explicit fragmentary knowledge? *Journal of Experimental Psychology: General, 119*, 264-275.

Reber, A., S. (1967). Implicit learning of artificial grammars. *Journals of Verbal Learning and Verbal Behavior, 5*, 855-63.

Reber, A., S. (1969). Transfer of syntactic in synthetic languages. *Journal of Experimental Psychology, 81*, 115-119.

Servan-Schreiber, E. & Anderson, J. R., (1990). Learning Artificial Grammar with Competitive Chunking. *Journal of Experimental Psychology: Learning, Memory, and Cognition, 16*, 592-608.

St. John, M.F. & Shanks, D.R., (1997). Implicit learning from an information processing standpoint In D. C. Berry (Ed.), *How implicit is implicit learning?* Oxford University Press.

An Attractor Network Model of Serial Recall

Matt Jones (mattj@umich.edu) and Thad A. Polk (tpolk@umich.edu)
Department of Psychology, 525 E. University
Ann Arbor, MI 48109 USA

Abstract

We present a neural network model of verbal working memory which attempts to illustrate how a few simple assumptions about neural computation can shed light on cognitive phenomena associated with the serial recall of verbal material. We assume that neural representations are distributed, that neural connectivity is massively recurrent, and that synaptic efficiency is modified based on the correlation between pre- and post-synaptic activity (Hebbian learning). Together these assumptions give rise to emergent computational properties that are relevant to working memory, including short-term maintenance of information, time-based decay, and similarity-based interference. We instantiate these principles in a specific model of serial recall and show how it can both simulate and explain a number of standard cognitive phenomena associated with the task, including the effects of serial position, word length, articulatory suppression (and its interaction with word length), and phonological similarity.

Introduction

Working memory is among the most intensively studied cognitive processes in both cognitive psychology and neuroscience, and yet results from the two fields have not made as much contact with each other as one might hope. For example, cognitive psychology has discovered a host of robust empirical phenomena associated with verbal working memory and has developed elegant theoretical models, such as Baddeley's phonological loop, that can explain the empirical results (Baddeley, 1986). Nevertheless, the details of how these psychological hypotheses are instantiated in the brain is an open question (but see Burgess & Hitch, 1999, for one recent proposal). Similarly, there is a substantial body of neuroscientific research investigating the neural substrates of working memory in both animals (Fuster, 1973; Funahashi, Bruce, & Goldman-Rakic, 1989) and humans (Smith & Jonides, 1999), but this work has typically only addressed a small subset of the rich behavioral data and theories available in cognitive psychology.

In this paper, we attempt to illustrate that a simple and independently motivated model of neural computation can make contact with, and even shed light on, the cognitive psychology of verbal working memory. We begin by describing a few widely accepted assumptions about neural computation. Next, we discuss some of the emergent computational properties of these assumptions that are relevant to verbal working memory (e.g., maintenance, decay, interference). We then illustrate how these assumptions can be instantiated in a specific computational model that simulates and explains many of the major psychological phenomena associated with the serial recall task.

A Simple Model of Neural Computation

We begin with three simple and widely accepted assumptions about neural computation. The first is that representations in the cortex are generally distributed across a population of neurons, rather than being localized to individual cells. The second is that there is massive connectivity among neurons within local areas of cortex and that this connectivity is recurrent rather than unidirectional. The third assumption is that synaptic efficiency is modified based on the correlation between pre- and post-synaptic activity (Hebbian learning; 'cells that fire together wire together').

Taken together, these assumptions give rise to networks with interesting emergent properties, many of which are relevant to working memory. For example, such networks are known to be capable of maintaining an activation pattern via internal reverberatory activity even after the input to the network has been removed (Hopfield, 1982). Those patterns which the network can maintain in this way are termed attractors, and under the Hebbian learning rule they tend to become those patterns to which the network is repeatedly exposed. Furthermore, when presented with a noisy or incomplete version of a previously trained pattern, the activity of the network will tend to converge upon that attractor state which is most similar to the input, thereby retrieving the original pattern.

Another property of attractor networks that is relevant to working memory is that they naturally exhibit similarity-based interference. Attractor networks are capable of storing multiple patterns as attractor states, but if those patterns are similar to each other (overlap substantially) then there is a greater likelihood of error. In particular, we have found that these networks often retrieve a pattern that in some sense represents a group of similar patterns, but from which it is not possible to recover a single specific pattern unambiguously.

Finally, we have also found that attractor networks can be easily extended to exhibit time-based decay. In the original formulation of attractor networks, each unit was binary (either ON or OFF) and activation patterns could be maintained for indefinite periods of time (Hopfield, 1982). Hopfield (1984) subsequently showed that networks using more realistic continuous-valued units could also exhibit similar computational properties. We have found that such continuous-valued attractor networks are also capable of exhibiting time-based decay once external input is removed.

The Serial Recall Task

In the standard serial recall task, a subject is presented, either visually or auditorially, with a sequence of items, most often words, letters, or digits. Once presentation of the list has been completed, the task of the subject is to repeat back the list in its original order, either by speaking or by writing.

This task has been intensively studied and a large number of robust behavioral phenomena have been identified. Below are some of the major phenomena which we will address in this paper. For a more thorough review of the literature see Gathercole (1997).

Serial Position The effects of an item's position within the presented list are generally described as two separate phenomena (see, e.g., Crowder, 1972). *Primacy:* Items from the start of the list tend to have a higher probability of recall than those from the middle of the list. *Recency:* Items from the end of the list tend to be recalled better than those from the middle.

Word Length Lists composed of items which take a longer time to articulate tend to be associated with poorer recall (Baddeley, Thompson, & Buchanan, 1975).

Articulatory Suppression Requiring subjects to overtly articulate irrelevant verbal material during presentation of a list tends to impair their performance (Murray, 1968).

Word Length x Articulatory Suppression The effect of word length is significantly reduced under conditions of articulatory suppression, provided that suppression continues throughout recall (Baddeley et. al., 1984).

Phonological Similarity Recall of a list tends to be decreased when the items of the list are phonologically similar to or confusable with each other (Conrad & Hull, 1964). Furthermore, when phonological similarity is limited to a subset of the items, e.g. those in the even positions, then performance on that set is selectively impaired as compared to the non-confusable items (Baddeley, 1968).

An Attractor-Based Model of Serial Recall

The goal of the present model is to demonstrate that the basic assumptions about neural computation outlined

previously are relevant to our understanding of some of the behavioral phenomena associated with serial recall. To do so, we show how these computational principles can be instantiated in a specific model of serial recall that exhibits many of these phenomena.

The model is composed of a number of separate yet interconnected attractor networks of the type described previously (Figure 1).

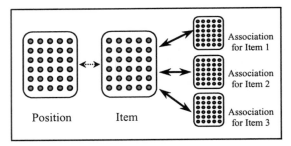

Figure 1. The architecture of the model. Circles represent individual units, rectangles represent individual attractor networks, arrows represent connections between units in different networks. Units within each network are all interconnected (not shown). Both these connections and connections between the Item and Association networks (thick arrows) are assumed to reflect long-term memory and do not change in the simulation. Connections between Position and Item (dashed arrow) reflect short-term position-item associations and are modified according to a Hebbian learning rule as each item is presented or rehearsed.

Position Network

This network encodes position within an arbitrary list of items. As currently modeled, each position corresponds to an activity pattern in which 10 out of 100 units are active. Patterns for different positions are pairwise disjoint, although this assumption could be changed to model more detailed data on positional confusions. Although the network itself does not draw a distinction, we interpret these patterns as encoding relative, rather than absolute, position in the list. Note that the Position network itself encodes no information about item identity; this knowledge will be stored in connection weights, learned during list presentation and rehearsal, between the Position and Item networks.

Item Network

The Item network is where the actual elements of the list are represented, again as distributed patterns comprising 10 active units each. Individual units are meant to correspond to various phonological or otherwise acoustic properties of the stimulus (a word or letter), and the network is presumed to have learned these patterns via Hebbian learning over repeated exposure to each of them. Thus units which are active in the same pattern(s) have mutual excitatory connections between them while units which are active in different patterns tend to inhibit each other. The result is that the network, when given external input, e.g. from the Position network, and then allowed to evolve its activity over time, will settle into the learned pattern that most closely matches the pattern of the input.

Association Networks

One crucial aspect of the Item network is that it is competitive. This means that whenever one item is represented by the network, representations of all other items are wiped out, so that as far as the Item network is concerned, all information about which items have been recently encountered is lost. This property allows the network to select a response. However the fact that competitive dynamics wipe out past information also implies that there must be some other source of item information in the system. This other source of item information is provided by the Association networks associated with each item.

Each Association network has a single attractor whose constituent units share permanent excitatory connections with those comprising the corresponding attractor in the Item network. Crucially though, the Association networks don't interact with each other, allowing multiple Association networks to be active at the same time. Consequently the item information in these networks is not erased by the representation of later items, but rather it remains and slowly decays. This residual activity provides another source of (non-position-specific) information to the system to be used at the time of recall.

The assumption then is that when a new item is represented, it partially overwrites the activation associated with other items, but that it does not do so completely. For example, if presented with the list "K B", the assumption is that presentation of "B" partially overwrites the representation of "K", but that some aspects of the representation of "K" are preserved. In the model, this distinction is captured by the distinction between the Item network (in which previous activity is overwritten) and the Association networks (in which it is not).

Model Operation

Simulation of the serial recall task in the model consists of three phases: list presentation, rehearsal (which is interleaved with presentation), and recall. During presentation of each item, the Item, Association, and Position networks are put into the attractor patterns corresponding to the present item and list position. The

source of the input that generates these patterns is not modeled but is presumed to be early sensory processing, as well as perhaps some executive input in the case of the Position network. Co-activation of units in the Position and Item networks now leads to formation of excitatory connections via a Hebbian learning rule, so that later activation of the same pattern in the Position network will under suitably favorable conditions lead to the corresponding pattern appearing in the Item network.

Between presentations of each successive list item, the model rehearses already presented items in order to further strengthen the Position to Item connections that have been learned. This is accomplished by putting the Position network into the attractor pattern corresponding to a given position, and allowing the connections from there to the Item network, along with inputs coming from the Association networks, to generate a pattern in Item. After allowing activity to evolve for a short period of time (reflecting the time constraints during this portion of the task), the system uses the resultant pattern of activity to rehearse. Rehearsal is presumably accomplished via covert articulation generating a sensory-level input to the Item network of the same type as it receives at presentation, after which the same Hebbian learning rule as was used during presentation is applied to update the Position to Item connections.

Because rehearsal is restricted to items that have already been presented, we have by the termination of presentation a gradient in number of rehearsals across serial positions which favors the earlier items. This gradient translates into an advantage for the earlier positions in two ways. First, the extra learning of associations between early position patterns and their corresponding item patterns leads to stronger connections and thus a stronger memory trace. Second, the additional learning has a significant effect on proactive interference: leftover connections from position patterns to item patterns from previous lists get attenuated with each application of the learning rule (because those old item patterns are not active when the rule is applied), thus leaving less potential for interference during recall.

Also worth noting at this point is another positional gradient in the state of the system at the conclusion of presentation, this time in the level of activity in the Association networks. Because each Association network is activated at the time of presentation of its corresponding item and then decays after that, the networls for items most recently presented, i.e. those at the end of the list, will be most active at the start of recall.

The process of recall is quite similar to the retrieval processes that operate in rehearsal. For each list position starting with the first, the Position network is placed into the attractor pattern corresponding to that position (presumably by some executive process). Activity in the Item network is then allowed to evolve until it stabilizes, with inputs from both the Position and Association networks tending (in ideal conditions) to drive that activity towards the pattern for the correct response. Once the network has stabilized the system probabilistically chooses an item for response based on the similarity of all known patterns to the actual pattern.

Experiment 1: Simulation of Standard Phenomena

The following set of simulations provides a demonstration of the model's ability to predict many of the standard phenomena associated with the serial recall task. The data we attempted to simulate were taken from Baddeley et. al. (1984; Experiment 5), which explores the effects of serial position, word length, and articulatory suppression.

Experimental Design

As in the design of Baddeley et. al. (1984), we ran the model on lists of both short and long words, both with articulatory suppression and without. The short and long word lengths used allowed for 5 and 9 item rehearsals per presentation, respectively (note Baddeley's presentation rate was 1.5 sec/word). Proportion of correct responses (or rather mean probability of responding correctly) were recorded for each serial position in each condition.

Results

The results of 150 runs on each condition are presented in Figure 2, along with the empirical data. Both empirical and simulated data exhibit the initial increase in error percentage over the first few serial positions (primacy effect), as well as a decrease on the final position (recency effect). In both cases performance is impaired for longer words and in conditions of articulatory suppression, with an interaction between these two effects indicated by a smaller effect of word length under the suppression conditions.

Discussion

Closer inspection of the model's performance and inner workings during the task reveal the following explanations for the phenomena:

Primacy Effect As described previously, increased rehearsals for earlier position-item pairs, and thus more applications of the Hebbian learning rule, lead to better quality of information encoded in the connections from the earlier position patterns to the Item network. This in turn lead to higher rates of correct recall for earlier items in the list.

Recency Effect In keeping with the other positional gradient described previously, the Association networks for the final items on the list were more active at the time of recall. As a result the additional information encoded by their inputs to the Item network acted to increase rates of correct recall at the end of the list.

Word Length Rehearsal was assumed to take place via covert articulation (which provides the source of the simulated sensory input to the Item network), and thus the time to rehearse should be dependent on the articulation time of the items in question. Lists of longer words were therefore allowed fewer rehearsals, and so were given less opportunity for learning associations between positions and items, thus leading to lower overall performance.

Articulatory Suppression Articulatory suppression was modeled as reducing the probability that each attempt at rehearsal was successful, rather than being interrupted by the process of overt articulation. As with the word length effect, this reduction in rehearsals led to less learning and in turn lower performance.

Word Length x Articulatory Suppression Under suppression rehearsals were less likely to be successful, and thus reducing the number of attempts at rehearsal by increasing word length had less of an effect on learning. Conversely, with longer words there were fewer rehearsals than with shorter ones, and thus interfering with them by imposing articulatory suppression made less of a difference.

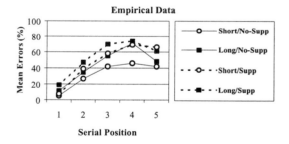

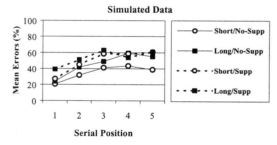

Figure 2: Mean percent error on the serial recall task in both empirical (Baddeley, et. al., 1968) and simulated studies. Data in each graph are divided into condition according to word length and articulatory suppression.

Experiment 2: Phonological Similarity

The last effect we attempted to model was that of phonological similarity between list items.

Experimental Design

The experiment followed the design of Experiment V of Baddeley (1968). In that experiment, lists of length 6 were taken from a pool of 12 letters, 6 of which were acoustically similar to each other (B,C,D,P,T,V) while the other 6 were all dissimilar (J,K,L,R,W,Y). In one condition only the even positions had confusable letters, and in another only the odd positions did. In both cases the resultant serial position curves had a characteristic sawtooth shape, with greater percentages of errors on confusion positions than on non-confusion positions.

Our approach in modeling phonological similarity was to assume that it is reflected by increased similarity between representations in the Item network. Our hypothesis was that similarity-based interference would lead to conditions in which the network failed to retrieve a single item but rather retrieved a pattern that was a combination or superposition of multiple items. The main change made to the model in order to capture this idea was to include a set of units in the Item network that were shared by the representations of all 6 acoustically similar items. Other changes included reducing the level of inhibition in the network in order to facilitate superpositional patterns.

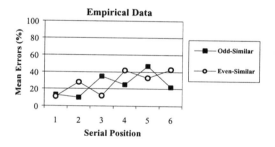

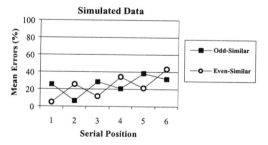

Figure 3: Mean error rates in the phonlogical similarity experiment in both empirical (Baddeley, et. al., 1968) and simulated studies. Data in each graph are divided into condition according to which list positions (evens or odds) contain the phonologically similar items.

Results

The model was run for 100 lists in both the Odd-Similar and Even-Similar conditions. Mean probability of a correct response was calculated for each serial position in each condition and is shown in Figure 3 along with the empirical data from Baddeley (1968). Both graphs clearly show the effects of phonological similarity, with greater error rates on the acoustically confusable items.

Discussion

As hypothesized, the model produced phonological similarity effects by often falling into spurious attractor states representing the combination of two or more similar items. When this happened, the system was left with only partial information about the identity of the correct item, and had to guess based on similarity between the actual and idealized patterns. This explanation differs from classical theories about acoustic confusion among items, but may be better seen as a theory of redintegration (Schweickert, 1993).

General Discussion

Psychological theories of verbal working memory, such as Baddeley's (1986) phonological loop model, have had great success in explaining serial recall at a cognitive level. These models have identified a core set of cognitive constructs (e.g., similarity-based interference, information maintenance with time-based decay, reactivation by articulatory rehearsal, etc.) that have proven extremely useful in explaining human behavior in this task. Nevertheless, these models do not typically address how those cognitive constructs are realized computationally in the brain. Conversely, research on neural computation has shown how many of these same cognitive constructs can arise as emergent properties in neural networks inspired by properties of the brain. However, these findings have not previously been exploited to explain detailed behavioral data regarding verbal working memory. In this paper, we have tried to show that ideas from cognitive psychology and neural computation can be fruitfully combined to produce an integrated model of verbal working memory that begins to bridge the gap between the cognitive and neural levels.

Most of the assumptions incorporated in the model are already well supported and widely accepted. For example, in keeping with many other models of verbal working memory, we assume that participants rehearse the items in an effort to keep their representations active (and that early items are rehearsed more), that rehearsal is related to covert articulation, that articulation suppresses the ability to rehearse, that similar-sounding items interfere with each other, etc. Similarly, the simple assumptions about neural computation that are incorporated in the model are well established and their emergent computational properties are well known.

Incorporating assumptions from both psychology and neural computation in a single, integrated model has a number of benefits. For example, most psychological theories have little to say about some fundamental issues regarding the mechanisms underlying verbal working memory. For example, how is information actually maintained, why does it decay over time if not rehearsed (and how does rehearsal refresh it), and how do similar items interfere with other? Indeed, even computational models of verbal working memory often build in these assumptions rather than simulating them (e.g., by explicitly weakening memory traces as a function of time or by assuming that similar-sounding items are occasionally confused with each other). By exploiting a few independently motivated assumptions about neural computation, the current model is able to provide computationally explicit answers to these kinds of questions.

Considering constraints from both fields also led to a model with a number of novel theoretical features. For example, assuming that the neural representation of a stimulus/concept corresponds to a specific distributed activity pattern suggests that different instances of the same item involve the same units. This contrasts with model such as the Phonological Loop which allow for multiple independent instances of a repeated item.

Learning also plays a much more important role in the attractor model than it does in the phonological loop model and its variants. With each presentation of the item, the attractor model learns an association between a position representation and an item representation. These associations interfere with the learning of new position-item associations and therefore allow the model to predict intrusion errors from similar positions on previous lists and, more generally, substantial proactive interference (learning previous lists impairs the model's ability to learn subsequent lists). Furthermore, Hebbian learning within the Item network can provide a natural account of long-term learning of new vocabulary.

There are a number of aspects of serial recall that the model has not yet accounted for. Among some of the most important of these are the effects of visual presentation (articulatory suppression reduces the phonological similarity effect with visual presentation, unlike with auditory presentation) lexicality (memory for words is better than nonwords), temporal grouping (presenting items in groups that can be chunked improves performance), and positional similarity (errors often involve transposing items that are nearby in the list). The lack of coverage for these phenomena is among the most important limitations of the current model and work is underway investigating whether it

can be extended to address them.

References

Baddeley, A. D. (1968). How does acoustic similarity influence short-term memory. *Quarterly Journal of Experimental Psychology: Human Experimental Psychology*, *20A*, 249-264.

Baddeley, A. D. (1986). *Working memory*. Oxford: Clarendon Press.

Baddeley, A. D., Lewis, V., & Vallar, G. (1984). Exploring the articulatory loop. *Quarterly Journal of Experimental Psychology*, *36A*, 233-252.

Baddeley, A. D., Thompson, N., & Buchanan, M. (1975). Word length and the structure of short-term memory. *Journal of Verbal Learning and Verbal Behavior*, *14*, 575-589.

Burgess, N. & Hitch, G. J. (1999). Memory for serial order: A network model of the phonological loop and its timing. *Psychological Review, 106,* 551-581.

Conrad, R. & Hull, A. J. (1964) Information, acoustic confusion and memory span. *British Journal of Psychology*, *55*, 429-432.

Crowder, R. G. (1972). Visual and auditory memory. In J. F. Kavanaugh & I. G. Mattingly (Eds.), *Language by ear and by eye*. New York: McGraw-Hill.

Funahashi, S., Bruce, C. J., & Goldman-Rakic, P. S. (1989). Mnemonic coding of visual space in the monkey's dorsolateral prefrontal cortex. *Journal of Neurophysiology, 61,* 331-349.

Fuster, J. M. (1973). Unit-activity in prefrontal cortex during delayed-response performance: Neuronal correlates of transient memory. *Journal of Neurophysiology, 36,* 61-78.

Gathercole, S. E. (1997). Models of verbal short-term memory. In M. A. Conway (Ed.), *Cognitive models of memory*. Cambridge, MA: The MIT Press.

Hopfield, J. J. (1982). Neural networks and physical systems with emergent collective computational abilities. *Proceedings of the National Academy of Sciences, 79,* 2554-2558.

Hopfield, J. J. (1984). Neurons with graded response have collective computational properties like those of 2-state neurons. *Proceedings of the National Academy of Sciences, 81,* 3088-3092.

Murray, D. J. (1968). Articulation and acoustic confusability in short-term memory. *Journal of Experimental Psychology*, *78*, 679-684.

Schweickert, R. (1993). A multinomial processing tree model for degradation and redintegatration in immediate recall. *Memory and Cognition, 21(2),* 168-175.

Smith, E. E. & Jonides, J. (1999). Storage and executive processes in the frontal lobes. *Science, 283,* 1657-1661.

Factorial Modeling: A Method for Enhancing the Explanatory and Predictive Power of Cognitive Models

Rita Kovordányi (ritko@ida.liu.se)
Department of Computer and Information Science
Linköpings Universitet, SE-581 83 Linköping, Sweden

Abstract

The construction and evaluation of cognitive models can, and often do, lead to *novel* insights into what might constitute a valid account for an empirical phenomenon. These insights constrain the space of viable models, and could be useful also on a theoretical plane, by promoting a deeper understanding of the studied phenomenon. We propose the factorial method for deriving novel, that is, not theory–based constraints *in a principled way* during model development. The method is based on a systematic comparison of alternative models, realized through a cross–combination of model components in a generic cognitive model. We illustrate the method by describing an application in the area of mental imagery. We conclude by discussing ways to increase the generalizability of results that can be obtained using the factorial method.

Introduction

From a modeling perspective, cognitive theories are presumed to guide and constrain model construction. Often however, there is a considerable gap between what has been theoretically established and what can be consistently modeled and simulated. This gap may not only concern an inherent difference in levels of description, but could additionally reflect a genuine lack of knowledge about the studied phenomenon. Bridging this gap is thus a nontrivial task: It often requires numerous iterations between tentative model construction and evaluation.

In this process, new insights may emerge regarding how cognitive models ought to be constructed in order to fit the empirical data. From the modeler's perspective, these insights constrain the space of viable models, further narrowing down the envelope allowed by the underlying cognitive theory. The theoretical value of these constraints will in part be determined by their original motivation: whether they are motivated by implementational considerations or have a logical basis (cf., e.g., Cooper et al, 1996).

Additionally, the theoretical value of newly discovered constraints may also depend on whether they were accidentally found, and thus cannot be guaranteed to hold in all cases, or if they were systematically uncovered. Note that the intrinsic requirement for internal consistency and computational tractability that computational models must comply with, and the stringency that these requirements impose on model development, would provide a firm basis for deriving non-theory-

based constraints—as long as alternative models are evaluated and compared in a principled way.

As an example of *systematic* exploration of alternative model solutions, Kieras and Meyer (1995) describe an investigation where dual–task performance was modeled using EPIC, a symbolic unified cognitive architecture. Various resource–sharing strategies were explored and the corresponding reaction times simulated. Simulated reaction time for alternative strategies were compared to empirical data on dual–task performance. On the basis of an extensive search for alternative strategies which would reproduce the empirical data, the authors draw the conclusion that human subjects must be using a near–optimal task strategy, pipelining their visual input for one task, while executing the other task. This conclusion is based on the fact that the authors were not able to fit model performance to the empirical data using any other strategy, given the framework of EPIC.

The question of whether and how a search for feasible model properties should be conducted is common for many modeling projects. Model development and validation often involves a more or less systematic search for model properties (parameter values) that make the model behave in the desired way and reproduce the empirical data. What is important to realize in this context however, is that individual model properties may be dependent on each other. In other words, one model property may affect model validity in a certain way only when other model components are present, or are implemented in a certain way. In this situation, the model may only reproduce empirical data if a particular *combination of model properties* is present.

We propose a formal (and automatic) method for mapping out the intrinsic dependencies between model properties, while also estimating their individual contribution to model performance. This method relies on a systematic exchange of model components and/or alternative implementations of model components, and an evaluation of their effect on model validity or some other measure of model performance.

In a broader perspective, the proposed method entails a shift of focus from simply demonstrating *that* a specific model is valid, to characterizing *under which conditions* the model—or rather a generic model framework—could account for empirical data. In this sense, our proposal could be seen as a first step towards a more principled way of theory testing (cf. Roberts and Pashler, 2000).

In the following sections, we will shortly describe the factorial method, and illustrate its use by accounting for an example application in the area of mental imagery (Kovordányi, 1999, 2000a). Finally, we will discuss limitations in the generalizability of results obtained with the method, and propose an extension of the method as a way of dealing with these limitations.

The two-level factorial design

Systematic exploration of alternative model instances can be organized according to a full two-level factorial design (Law and Kelton, 1991; Box et al, 1978). This design emphasizes that the question of which model parameters are *causally* involved in a particular type of simulated behavior can be answered only if all parameters have been fully cross-combined. In order to keep down the computational cost of exploring all parameters, parameter values are varied between a predetermined min- and max-value, in what is called a two-level factorial design.

Note that, for the above reasons, if some model parameters were to be fixed at some "reasonable value" in order to keep down simulation complexity, the power of the simulation design would decrease. Simply expressed, parameters may have been fixed at a value where they strongly modulate the effect of central model parameters.

In practice, a minimal set of model properties will inevitably be determined a priori on the basis of the underlying cognitive theory. This generic model framework could still leave unconstrained a large number of model design decisions. How should the final simulations be designed if the corresponding number of model parameters turn out to be unmanageably large?

Ideally, for a problem with k degrees of freedom, the minimal number of simulations which needs to be run in order to detect causal dependencies between model parameters is 2^k. However, if the number of simulations turn out to be unmanageably large, a fractal two-level factorial design may be used instead of a full design (cf. Law and Kelton, 1991; Box et al, 1978). Note that in these designs, peripheral parameters are not fixed at an ad hoc value, but are instead defined dynamically as a function of those parameters which are varied.

In addition to providing a minimally sufficient basis for detecting causal relationships in the simulation results, using a two-level factorial design renders the analysis of simulation results conceptually simple. A simulation where k parameters are varied is captured in a design matrix of size 2^k x k containing +s and –s representing low and high parameter values (cf. Law and Kelton, 1991; Box et al, 1978). The way the matrix is set up, each row will represent a unique combination of parameter values, which in turn corresponds to a particular simulation run (cf. figure 1). As the design matrix is regular, it is easy to set up. In addition, once it is computed, the same matrix can be used to control the simulations and to conduct data analysis.

To illustrate the data analysis procedure, let us assume that the possible interaction between parameters p_1, p_3, and p_7 are inquired. In this case, columns 1, 3, and 7 of the design matrix are multiplied with each other entry-by-entry, and then multiplied, again entry-by-entry, with the corresponding simulation results. The effect of these multiplications is that the correct signs will be added to the results–column. A final summation of all the signed entries in the results–column, divided by 2^{k-1}, where k denotes the number of model parameters varied, yields the desired mean interaction of the parameters involved.

run	par 1	par 2	sim. result
1	–	–	R_1
2	–	+	R_2
3	+	–	R_3
4	+	+	R_4

Figure 1: A two-level factorial design matrix for two parameters. Each row in the matrix denotes a unique combination of parameter values. The last column in the design matrix designates the outcome of simulating a model instance for that particular parameter combination.

Application of the method

In the following sections, we will briefly describe an investigation of mental imagery where a full two-level factorial design was used (Kovordányi, 1999, 2000b). Although the effect of several possible factors, such as mental image fading, were taken into account, the analysis of simulation results was centered on revealing the effect of focusing early versus late selective attention on part of a mental image in a mental image reinterpretation task. As the empirical results of Finke and colleagues (Finke et al, 1989) and Peterson and colleagues (Peterson et al, 1992), which were used for model validation, were qualitative, no attempt was made to optimize the models towards these data. Model validity was instead defined qualitatively, and served as a means for evaluating the feasibility of alternative models.

Identifying variable model components

The model framework used in our project drew its main architectural components from the comprehensive model of mental imagery developed by Kosslyn (1994; Kosslyn et al, 1979; Kosslyn et al, 1990). Within this framework, lower–level model components remained partially unconstrained. For instance, should attentional selection be implemented as an early or late selectional mechanism? Is selective attention involved (focused) at all during mental image reinterpretation? These choices were expressed as variable model components that were systematically exchanged between simulation runs to allow for a comparison of various model instances. As a result, half of all simulation runs would be based on models containing a late selectional model component, a quarter of all simulations run would be based on models containing a late selectional component *and* also implementing an inhibitory fringe around the selectional 'spotlight', etcetera.

We chose to implement our model framework as an interactive activation model (cf. McClelland, 1979; McClelland and Rumelhart, 1981, 1994/1988;). In these models, the localist nodes are arranged into reciprocally connected layers of processing, thereby increasing the structure and penetrability of the model. Units within the same processing layer are assumed to have the same inhibitory and excitatory connection weights.

Within our interactive activation model framework, variable model components were expressed in terms of connection weights, activation thresholds, resting levels, and/or "control flags". Control flags were also used to control whether processing was to be initiated top-down or bottom-up. These two modes of processing corresponded to mental imagery vs. visual perception in human subjects.

Variable model components could equally well be delineated in symbolic models, as alternative (sets of) production rules, or simply alternative definitions (fnc1 – fnc2) of a cognitive mechanism together with a means for activating them at run-time. Hence, the factorial method can be applied to any modularly constructed computational model with a minimal overhead cost.

Simulations

Our model framework for mental imagery encompassed three mutually interacting layers of processing (figure 2). At the lowest level, the visual buffer contained detectors for oriented line segments. At the next stage, these feature detectors would evoke (and receive feedback from) simple geometric patterns, such as composite lines and triangles. These patterns were stored in visual long-term memory. At the highest level of processing, the low–level geometric patterns were combined into concepts stored in associative long-term memory. In addition to the between-layer connections, we assumed lateral that is, within-processing-level inhibition, between mutually inconsistent groups of computational units. Image interpretation in this cascading system was based on the establishment of a correspondence between lower-level and higher-level representations across the processing layers.

We simulated mentally- and perceptually based reinterpretation of two composite line drawings adopted from Finke and colleagues (1989, exp. 1). Possible interpretations of these figures were limited to a small set of predefined geometric forms and abstract concepts. For example, possible interpretations of the first figure,

formed from an upper case 'H' superimposed on an upper case 'X', were limited to "four small equilateral triangles", "two large isosceles triangles", "a butterfly", "a tilted hourglass" and "a bow-tie".

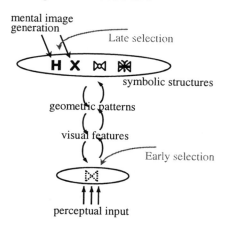

Figure 2: An outline of the interactive activation model used in our simulations of mental and perceptual image reinterpretation. Processing is based on three bi–directionally connected layers of localist units. Processing in cascade allows focus of attention to be propagated with a negligible time delay to both earlier and later stages of processing. In spite of this, the point of initiation of attentional focus turns out to influence model validity.

As processing layers were reciprocally connected, simulations could be initiated either top-down or bottom-up. This made it possible to compare reinterpretation performance in visual perception and in mental imagery. When simulations were run in mental mode, a chosen symbolic concept was activated in associative long-term memory, and this activation was projected into the visual buffer, where an activation pattern emerged, which represented a visual mental image. When simulation was run in perceptual mode, visual input entered the system at the visual buffer, and was forwarded through consecutive stages of processing, and matched to geometric patterns and abstract concepts. One of these patterns or concepts was selected for verbal report.

Simulations were run through four phases: Mental image generation, followed by mental image reinterpretation, continued with perceptual stabilization of the same line-figure, concluded by perceptually based reinterpretation. Each simulation was run for 10 simulated seconds in discrete steps of 50 ms.

Two instances of the model framework were scrutinized: One where attentional selection affected processing at a late stage, at the level of associative long-term memory, and one where selection was initiated early, at the level of the visual buffer. For these models, the effect of focusing attention (versus not focusing attention) was investigated, taking into account that interaction might arise between these central and other peripheral model components.

Data analysis

In this example project, data analysis began with semi-automatic preparation of the raw simulation data (see below). The prepared data were then visualized. The aim was to facilitate the discovery of significant parameter interactions, and in addition provide a basis for estimating model validity for the different parameter combinations. Below we briefly describe the key stages of this process.

Identification of interacting model components

For simplicity, we will denote model components as *simulation parameters* in the sections on data analysis. Activation levels of all response units in the interactive activation network were measured for each simulation run that is, for each parameter combination. From these activation values the probability for reinterpretation was calculated. Reinterpretation rates were classified as valid if they qualitatively matched the reinterpretation rates obtained by Finke and colleagues (1989, exp. 1), and Peterson and colleagues (1992).

These empirical data posed the following constraints on the simulation results: First, reinterpretation rates were required to be less for symbolic than for geometric interpretations (cf. Finke et al, 1989). In addition, interpretations obtained during mental imagery had to be below those obtained during the perceptual phases of the simulations.

Second, reinterpretation rates were required to be qualitatively consistent with the findings of Peterson and colleagues (1992). These findings are interpreted as an indication that reinterpretation rates should increase after a de- and refocus of attention.

Calculation of model component effects

The calculation of individual component effects and interactions was based on a design matrix of –s and +s, representing high- and low simulation parameter values (cf. figure 1). In this matrix each column denoted a model parameter and each row represented a specific parameter combination. Two measures of model performance: simulated mental reinterpretation probability and model validity, were associated with each row in the design matrix. In general, in order to obtain a parameter's average effect on overall model performance, those rows in one of the results–column which corresponded to a low parameter value were summed and subtracted from those rows which corresponded to high values. Higher-order interaction effects were obtained in a similar manner (Law and Kelton, 1991; Box and Hunter, 1978). Given the simulation design matrix, these calculations could be expressed as a sequence of simple matrix operations.

Visualizations of interactions

Those groups of interacting parameters whose modulating effect exceeded 20% of the central parameter's effect (in our case this parameter denoted the focusing of attention) were prepared for visualization.

The type of visualizations obtained (illustrated in figure 3) can be conceived of as a high-dimensional cube of changes in model performance, each dimension representing changes caused by one of the interacting parameters. This cube can be sliced and stacked recursively onto a two-dimensional plot (cf. Bosan and Harris, 1996; Harris et al, 1994).

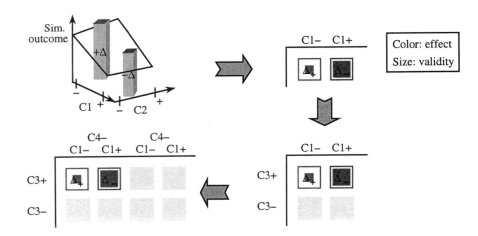

Figure 3: Visualization of the simulation results is achieved through recursive slicing of the high–dimensional volume of simulation data. Simulation results are color-coded to facilitate the perception of interaction patterns. The relative area of the square markers reflects mean model validity for the underlying parameter combinations.

Each x-y coordinate in these plots denotes a specific combination of interacting parameters. In our project, the direction of change in model performance was coded along two different color scales, and the magnitude of change was indicated by variations in hue within these scales, with darker, more saturated colors depicting a bigger change.

In addition, we made the relative area of each colored square reflect the *average* validity of models corresponding to the central parameter's high value. In our case, this amounted to selective attention being focused during image reinterpretation. As a result of including model validity in the visualizations, simulation data contributed to the visual appearance of the plot only to the extent to which they were valid.

Results obtained in the example project

We focused our simulation and data analysis on the question of early vs. late attentional selection, our hypothesis being that late selection would account for the empirical data, while early selection would not. This hypothesis seems to be supported by our simulation results: In short, models were valid when selective attention was focused during image reinterpretation—as compared to simulations when attention was not focused. In addition, when comparing models containing an early vs. late selectional component, the latter models turned out to produce valid behavior, while the former did not. Although these results can be interpreted an indication of an overall pattern, the generalizability of these results need to be further examined.

Extension of the method

By its systematicity, the factorial method enhances the reliability of any constraints discovered during model development and simulation. However, we would like to point to one limitation of this method. The factorial method, in the form presented above, is aimed at characterizing the space of alternative models. The underlying assumption is that transitions in this space are smooth that is, slow, and monotonic, and hence can be characterized on the basis of the two data points per dimension used to calculate parameter effects.

We see two problems with this assumption. First, model validity, or model performance in general, could vary between the sampled points. Second, model performance is characterized on the basis of a limited subspace of the complete model space. For example, connection weights in a connectionist model might have been varied within a narrow range, which may not cover the complete interval allowed for that particular type of connection. Hence, component effects and interactions might look different both within and outside the subspace, or *segment*, which has been sampled. Both of these limitations affect the generalizability of results obtained using the factorial method

Hypothesis testing by searching for counterexamples in model space

We would like to propose one way of approaching this problem. For practical reasons, we cannot ensure in the general case that any effects found will hold throughout model space. However, researchers are frequently interested in finding support for or refuting one particular hypothesis. For example, it would be interesting to know if an assumption of late attentional selection is *the only way* to account for empirical data. This amounts to the question of 'Would early attentional selection account for empirical data if a different segment of model space was examined?'

In this limited setting, a search of model space becomes tractable. The objective is to examine various segments in model space, in order to ensure that any results found in one segment are general enough to also hold in other segments of the model space. This extension of the method relies on *random* sampling of segments using, for example, genetic algorithms.

Note that while genetic search can be used to delimit various segments in model space, characterization of each of these segments must be based on the factorial method. The reason for this is that in order to be able to attribute model validity to a specific model component that is, exclude the possibility of some peripheral aspect of the model affecting model validity, all variable components must be cross–combined. In essence, we want to detect *causal relationships* between model component(s) and model validity.

Hence, for example, the objective in the example project would be to ensure that late selection *causes* models to be valid in all segments in model space. In other words, we want to ensure that model validity can be attributed to late selection, and not some fortunate interaction of other model components.

In the empirical sciences, a favorite hypothesis is supported by evidence, when the scientist has done everything to prove its negation, the null hypothesis, and failed. In the same manner, the objective in the example project could be to search for segments in model space where model validity can be attributed to, not late, but *early* selection.

There can be two outcomes of such a search. The first possibility is that early selection models turn out to be invalid throughout model space. This result could be used as a basis for making general statements about the necessity of a late selectional mechanism in models of mental imagery. The second possibility is that early selection turns out to result in valid models in some segments of model space. In this latter case, one might attempt to detect common features in those segments where early selection turned out to result in valid models. Again, this would produce generalizable *new* knowledge about the studied phenomenon.

Summary

As is often pointed out in the modeling methodology literature (cf., e.g., Cooper et al, 1996), there is an inherent gap between cognitive theories and their realizations as computable cognitive models. Novel, that is, not theory–based constraints on what could constitute a viable account for an empirical phenomenon are thus often discovered during the development and testing of cognitive models. These constraints could turn out to be *theoretically* useful, provided that they were uncovered in a systematic fashion.

We propose the factorial method for deriving novel that is, not theory–based, constraints in a principled way. The method relies on a systematic validation and comparison of alternative models, and in practice, entails a shift of focus from simply demonstrating *that* a specific model is valid, to characterizing *under which conditions* the model can account for empirical data.

The method provides a formal basis for stating that, given a set of fundamental, theory–based assumptions, the studied phenomenon can be modeled successfully only if certain additional assumptions are made. These assumptions can be about subjects' choice of task strategy when performing dual–tasks, or concern the necessity of a particular cognitive mechanism in models of mental imagery.

The reliability of model constraints is increased if the causal relationship between the inclusion of a specific model component and resulting model validity can be demonstrated to hold irrespective of which part of model space is examined. As model space cannot, in general, be searched in its entirety, we suggest a more focused approach of hypothesis testing: Given an initial hypothesis, model space is searched for sub–segments in which a designated alternative model solution leads to valid models. Depending on the outcome, the initial hypothesis can be reliably refuted or supported.

Acknowledgments

We would like to thank three anonymous reviewers for valuable comments. This work was supported by the Swedish Council for Research in the Humanities and Social Sciences.

References

Bosan, S. & Harris, T. R. (1996). A visualization-based analysis method for multiparameter models of capillary tissue-exchange. *Annals of Biomedical Engineering, 24,* 124-138.

Box, G. E. P., Hunter, W. G., & J. S. (1978). *Statistics for experimenters: An introduction design, data analysis, and model building.* New York: Wiley.

Cooper, R., Fox, J., Farringdon, J., & Shallice, T. (1996). A systematic approach for cognitive modeling. Artificial Intelligence, 85, 3-44.

Finke, R. A., Pinker, S. & Farah, M. J. (1989). Reinterpreting visual patterns in mental imagery. *Cognitive Science, 13,* 51-78.

Harris, P. A., Sorel, B., Harris, T. R., Laughlin, H. & Overholser, K. A. (1994). Parameter identification in coronary pressure flow models: A graphical approach. *Annals of Biomedical Engineering, 22,* 622-637.

Kieras, D. E., & Meyer, D. E. (1995). Predicting performance in dual-task tracking and decision making with EPIC computational models. In *Proceedings of the First International Symposium on Command and Control Research and Technology.*

Kosslyn, S. M. (1980). *Image and mind.* Cambridge, MA: Harvard University Press.

Kosslyn, S. M. (1994). *Image and Brain: The resolution of the imagery debate.* Cambridge, MA: MIT Press.

Kosslyn, S. M., Pinker, S., Smith, G. E. & Swartz, S. P. (1979). On the demystification of mental imagery. *The Behavioral and Brain Sciences, 2,* 535-581.

Kosslyn, S. M., Flynn, R. A., Amsterdam, J. B., Wang, G. (1990). Components of high-level vision: A cognitive neuroscience analysis and accounts of neurological syndromes. *Cognition, 34,* 203-277.

Kovordányi, R. (1999). Mental image reinterpretation in the intersection of conceptual and visual constraints. In Paton, R. & Neilson, I. (eds): *Visual representations and interpretation.* London: Springer Verlag.

Kovordányi, R. (2000a). Full factorial simulation modeling of selective attention in mental imagery. Presented at *the Twenty Seventh International Congress on Psychology,* Stockholm.

Kovordányi, R. (2000b). Controlled exploration of alternative mechanisms in cognitive modeling. In *Proceedings of the Twenty Second Annual Meeting of the Cognitive Science Society.*

Law, A. M. & Kelton, W. D. (1991). *Simulation modeling and analysis.* New York: McGraw-Hill.

McClelland, J. L. (1979). On the time relations of mental processes: An examination of systems of processes in cascade. *Psychological Review, 86,* 4, 287-330.

McClelland, J. L. & Rumelhart. D. E. (1981). An interactive activation model of context effects in letter perception: Part 1. An account of basic findings. *Psychological Review, 88,* 5, 375-407.

McClelland, J. L. & Rumelhart. D. E. (1994/1988*).* *Explorations in parallel distributed processing: A handbook of models, programs and exercises.* Cambridge, MA: MIT Press.

Peterson, M. A., Kihlstrom, J. F., Rose, P. M. & Glisky M. L. (1992). Mental images can be ambiguous: Reconstruals and reference-frame reversals. *Memory and Cognition, 20,* 107-123.

Roberts, S. & Pashler, H. (2000). How persuasive is a good fit? A comment on theory testing. *Psychological Review, 107,* 2, 358-367.

Modelling Taxi Drivers' Learning and Exceptional Memory of Street Names

Tei Laine (telaine@cs.indiana.edu)
Indiana University
Computer Science Department and the Cognitive Science Program
150 S. Woodlawn Ave.
Bloomington, IN 47405-7104 USA

Virpi Kalakoski (virpi.kalakoski@helsinki.fi)
University of Helsinki: Department of Psychology
P.O. BOX 13, FIN-00014 Helsinki Finland

Abstract

A computer simulation was designed to model taxi drivers' learning and memory performance, and predict experimental results in a memory test in which the stimuli are lists of street names ordered with varying degrees of meaningfulness. The objectives of the study are, firstly, to explicate the quantitative and qualitative differences between performance outcomes observed in expert and novice drivers in memory tests, and secondly, to formalise the behavioural traits assumed to constitute the essence of expertise. Finally, we test the adequacy of these assumptions with a computer simulation.

Introduction

Domain specific skills often result in superior memory for skill-related meaningful material. In a standard memory recall task an expert subject can utilise his or her knowledge in constructing efficient retrieval structures if the stimulus material is related to subject's domain of expertise. The skill effect cannot be transferred to other expertise domains. A novice without adequate knowledge about the domain heavily relies on short-term memory when trying to memorise the study items. This exceptional memory performance appears in several areas of expertise, such as in memory of chess positions, digits, dinner orders, and figure skating choreographies (Ericsson & Kintsch, 1995).

This study is based on the distinction, made by Vicent & Wang (1996), between process theories and product theories. Process theories try to describe the psychological mechanisms and knowledge structures underlying the exceptional memory recall. Vicente & Wang suggest that the process theories are able to explain expertise effects only in the domains in which memory recall is an intrinsic task (i.e., the memory performance is a definitive feature of the domain of expertise). However, expert reasoning processes are usually studied in domains in which memorising is a contrived task, i.e., memory performance is a by-product of the skill. To overcome the difficulties of explaining expertise effects in contrived tasks, Vicente and Wang (1998) introduce a product theory that does not commit to a particular psychological mechanism but tries first predict the exact

expertise effects. Vicente and Wang's (1998) constraint attunement hypothesis suggests that the expertise advantage in memory performance is affected by the number of goal-relevant constraints available, which experts are attuned to. The distinction between product and process theories is an active, current research topic (Ericsson, Patel & Kintsch, 2000; Simon & Gobet, 2000; Vicente, 2000).

The aim of this study is to model expertise in memory recall using a new domain in which memory recall is a contrived task. The phenomenon is expert taxi drivers' superior memory compared to novice drivers in recalling lists of street names (Kalakoski & Saariluoma, in press). Taxi drivers' memory recall is a contrived task since the serial recall of briefly presented street names is not a definitive feature of expertise in taxi driving. Therefore, it is a suitable domain to study skilled memory as a by-product of the specific skill.

Our approach is to unite two levels of analysis. First, the product theory is adopted in order to define the constraints that the environment places on expert taxi drivers. Then we take a step further, and model the skill acquisition — emphasising the account of what domain specific knowledge is acquired instead of mechanisms behind how it is acquired. Finally, a memory task is conducted on the model, and we study whether the same expertise effects are observable as in the original empirical data.

Experimental Study

The experimental results modelled in this paper are from unpublished data, provided by Kalakoski & Saariluoma. In the original experiments, the role of pre-learnt knowledge in recalling street names is investigated by comparing expert taxi drivers' and control subjects' recall of Helsinki city street names.

In order to study the nature of the retrieval structures, three types of street name lists are used. Firstly, street names are presented in route order, so that successive streets in the list form a physically driveable route in the city (one-way streets are not taken into account). Secondly, fully randomised lists are constructed, in which street names are in an order that does not form a driveable route. Thirdly, block-randomised lists are created with randomly ordered blocks of five continuous streets each. We hypothesise that, if route-like organisation of knowledge is crucial for taxi drivers, organised lists should be recalled better than block-randomised ones which are recalled better than fully randomised lists. In control group no difference in recall is expected between the list types.

Furthermore, to specify the limits of experts' skilled memory span, lists consisting of 5 to 25 names are used. The participants of the original experiment are eight taxi drivers with at least three years of experience in full-time taxi driving in the Helsinki city area, and eight students from Helsinki University. The subjects are asked to retrieve the auditorily presented lists in the presentation order. The results are analysed as the number of correctly recalled items from the beginning of the list. The outcome shows a clear effect of skill level and degree of list randomness. Expert taxi drivers' recall of random lists is less successful than their recall of block-randomised or ordered lists. They also tend to retrieve more names when presented with longer lists. In the control group there is not a statistically significant difference in recall between presentation orders or different list lengths. The experimental results are depicted in the Figures 1 and 2 (in figures ra = random order, b = block-randomised, ro = route order).

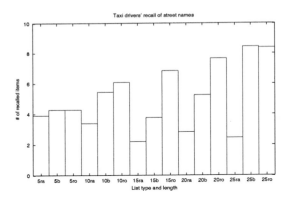

Figure 1: Average number of street names recalled by taxi drivers for list lengths of 5, 10, 15, 20 and 25.

Background of the Model: the Product Theory

Based on the empirical results, it is assumed that taxi drivers' superior memory for street names is based on spatial and route knowledge acquired through navigation (Kalakoski & Saariluoma, in press). Applying the constraint attunement hypoth-

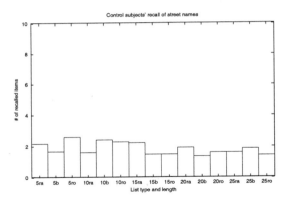

Figure 2: Average number of street names recalled by novice drivers for list lengths of 5, 10, 15, 20 and 25.

esis (Vicente & Wang, 1998), a possible abstraction hierarchy for taxi driving could be the following. At the lowest level, there are streets, their spatial organisation in the city and the successive order of the streets is represented. At the second level, there are rules of driving, e.g. one-way streets, which define drivable street combinations. At the level of tactics, it is possible for example to choose the shortest or the fastest route between two addresses. The strategies level, for instance can define that, if there are traffic jams, a longer route may be faster. In taxi driving, the general purpose of the business is to take the customer from point A to point B. In order to achieve this goal, the taxi driver has to recognise the current location in the city, the given destination street name, as well as to associate the street name to its physical location. Furthermore, the driver has to find a route between these two streets.

Despite surpassing novices in generating routes and naming streets, there is no difference between expert and novice drivers in drawing a map, drawing streets, recalling neighbourhoods, placing neighbourhoods on a map and estimating distances. These principles seem to explain the experimental findings that expert taxi drivers' mental representation of routes and streets in a city is hierarchical. (Chase, 1983; Peruch, Giraudo, Gärling, 1989)

Based on the need to understand earlier experimental findings and the task constraints, the taxi driver's learning of a large-scale environment is first modelled. In order to do this, the memory structure and knowledge representation (what to learn) has to be explicitly defined. Then, the learning process (how to learn) is modelled.

The Model

The experimental results imply that taxi drivers' qualitative and quantitative superiority in recall is based on mental navigation through the environment, whereas the inexperienced drivers cannot relate the test items to spatial images or mental representation of the physical environment. Their memory performance is dictated by the limited short-term memory capacity.

We assume that the skill effect arises from the aspects of the environment that are relevant for taxi drivers in their profession and makes them especially attuned to these constraints. Therefore, all the presumed differences between different skill levels of drivers are built into the learning material while the memory architecture and processes — memorising, forgetting and retrieving — are implemented in a uniform fashion, independent of skill level.

Memory Architecture and Knowledge Representation

The model's knowledge is stored in an associative network with two kinds of components: *memory elements* and *associations*. The elements represent either language-based or spatial knowledge; the former kind of knowledge refers to street names and the latter kind refers to physical street scenes or blocks. *Block* is chosen to present a unit of meaningful spatial knowledge that is useful in navigating the environment. It is taken here to mean the portion of a street that does not intersect with another street and it is inherently directional, having several numerical attributes presented as real numbers.

Memory elements are connected by associations, which are memory elements themselves, so that different kinds of elements are connected with different kinds of associations. The associations between street names are based on language, and the associations between block elements are based on physical adjacency. Thus, the basic components of the semantic network are:

1. **Elements**

    Block: The block has a *weight* attribute that measures the strength of the memory trace for that element, and an *activation* attribute that reflects the element's status as a focus of attention. Other attributes are: *size*, corresponding to the physical width or capacity of the street, and *recency*, that tells how often the driver has passed the street recently.

    Street name: This is the real-life name of the street, along with weight and activation attributes.

2. **Associations**

    An association from a block to a block, depicting the image of the same portion of the street going in the opposite direction (if any): The model captures the images of real-life blocks viewed in different directions as two separate blocks. The *weight*

attribute measures how familiar the driver is with the fact that two blocks represent the portions of the street between the same pair of crossings.

An association from a block to the next block ahead: This connects together the blocks that follow each other without a turn; in most cases these blocks are parts of the same street. This association has an *existence weight* attribute, which measures how strongly the association is made between blocks belonging to the same street. *Drive weight* measures how frequently the transition is made from one block to another when driving. *Orientation angle* gives the turning angle from one block to the next; i.e., how much and the direction one has to turn in order to make the proper transition.

An association from a block to a block that requires a turn: This represents transitions between blocks belonging to intersecting streets. The attributes are identical to the previous one.

An association from a block to a street name: The *weight* attribute measures how strongly the connection is made.

An association from a street name to a block: The *weight* attribute gives the strength of the association.

An association from a street name to another street name: Here again, the *weight* attribute gives the strength of the association.

All associations are directed; it is possible that the model learns an association between consecutive blocks only to one direction if it only "travels" it in one direction (e.g., in one-way streets).

Learning

The model learns new long-term memory elements. The knowledge about blocks, street names and the associations between them accumulates with experience. All the elements are first stored in limited-capacity short-term memory before they are transferred into long-term memory. If an element cannot gain enough activation while in short-term memory, it is never consolidated.

Learning process The primary learning occurs via *activation spreading*, since it is the factor that influences the strength of the memory traces (by updating the weight values) and thus reflects experience. The spreading activation (ρ_i) that element i sends to element j is determined by the current activation of the sending element (a_i), the weight of the association between the sending and receiving element (w_{ij}) and the distance between the elements, calculated as the number of intermediate elements

(n). The magnitude of spreading activation is calculated according to the equation:

$$\rho_i = \alpha w a_i e^{-\beta n}$$

where $\alpha \in [0,1]$ and $\beta \in [0,1]$ are constants.

There are two situations when an element gets activated: when it receives activation from its neighbouring element, and when it is the focus of attention (it is the street block the taxi driver model is currently driving on). The former kind of update is a function of the element's current activation (a_t), and the one it receives via the association from neighbouring units. The latter update depends on the current activation and the recency value of the element. The activation update happens according to the following equation:

$$a_{t+1} = 1 - \frac{1}{\rho + \frac{1}{1-a_t}}$$

where t is time and ρ is the incoming activation from neighbouring units or the recency value of the element that is updated, depending on the activation update scenario discussed above.

Both element and association weights are updated uniformly as a function of the current weight and the element's or association's activation. Forgetting is implemented as decreasing the weights periodically, proportional to the current weight and the recency value of the element or association.

Training material For the model the training material is formalised as routes from a presentation of the city map of Helsinki, excluding the suburban areas. The presentation consists of crossings, names of the streets, directions, one-way streets and forbidden turnings. The generation of the routes is automatised so that the above mentioned constraints are given as parameters to the search algorithm.

Five different skill levels of taxi drivers are modelled. Each level has a different method of finding a route between places so that routes become closer to optimal as the experience of the driver accumulates. Distance and travelling time are used as the criteria for optimality. At the first skill-level of taxi drivers, the training set consists of routes following the largest streets of the city. The routes tend to follow the same street as long as possible, even if this lengthens the journey. The second level only adds some smaller streets to the routes. Routes at the third level minimise travelling time by taking into account the size of the street. At the fourth level routes are generated by minimising the amount of travelled blocks or turns. The fifth level is created so that a very experienced taxi driver would also becomes familiar with the smallest streets. Routes at this level tend to follow the smallest streets of the city. Before entering the higher levels, the model

is given training sets from lower levels. This progressive change of the quality of the travelled routes follows the idea of base and secondary networks of a hierarchical representation of the city (Chase, 1983).

The novices are simulated as well. There are three different training sets for the novices, so that two of them consist of rather well known streets and streets belonging to the novices' assumed neighbourhood. One set consists only of streets that do not cross each other, so that the novice model is not able to learn any route-like representations.

Recall and Retrieval Structure

The retrieval structure is only covered here briefly. The retrieval structure is rooted in a short-term memory with a limited capacity, which in the current simulations can hold at most four elements. The implementation is motivated by the fact that the typical score in recalling senseless words from a list is about four items (Ericsson & Kintsch, 1995); the subject is incapable of maintaining more in the first level of working memory unless interconnecting their contents associatively. However, the subject can perform the recall task significantly better by using further levels of memory structure through chunking related material into meaningful wholes.

In recall tasks like the one in this study, where the order of recalled items is stressed, one possible way to maintain sequential order is to link the test elements into a tree structure in pre-order. The hierarchy of the retrieval structure is constructed one subtree at a time (compared to the strategy adopted by Ericsson & Kintsch (1995) in which the retrieval structure is constructed one level at a time). Here, a new item in the memory list is inserted as a child of the last element added, if the weight between the elements exceed some threshold. If the weight remains below the threshold, the item is attached to the next available slot in the first level. The weight is calculated as a function of the weight between the corresponding street name elements learnt earlier into the associative network and the weight between the associated block elements in long-term memory. A newly inserted element gains some activation, which depends on the above mentioned weights and the element's depth level in the retrieval structure. The closer to the leaf it is inserted, the weaker the activation.

The activation in turn influences the probability of retrieval. Once inserted to the retrieval structure, the element's activation gradually decreases. The average of the weight and the activity is chosen as an estimate to the probability of retrieval. If the retrieval of the element fails, the associated element in the retrieval structure with the highest activation is selected and the corresponding street name element is retrieved from long-term memory.

Simulation

Subjects The tests are run for a total of 20 different models of taxi drivers and 12 different models of control subjects. There are four models for each of the five taxi drivers' skill levels. All taxi drivers, despite similar skill levels, are trained with different training sets. Novices, on the other hand, have three different training sets that are tailored by hand to match the very limited knowledge of the city.

Procedure Three different test materials are constructed. Each taxi driver and novice model is tested on all of them. One individual material consists of 24 series of street names, with 5, 10, 15 or 20 streets and six series of each list length. Every alternate street presented in one series is a name of an intersecting street. Together they form a connected route through the city.

A condition equivalent to that of Kalakoski & Saariluoma's unpublished study is used. Lists are presented in three conditions, in route order, in random order and in block-randomised order, so that there are two series of each condition for every list length. The order of presentation of each condition is randomised.

Lists are given to the model one street name at a time. After each list, the model returns a series of street names that it recalls from the original list.

The results The scoring method used is the number of correct items returned in perfect order, starting from the beginning of the list. A street name has to be retrieved in its exact form in order to be counted as a correct response. The results of the experiment are presented in Figures 3 and 4 as numbers of correctly recalled street names averaged over all of the taxi driver models and all of the control subject models, respectively (in figures ra = random order, b = block-randomised, ro = route order).

Compared to the Kalakoski & Saariluoma's experimental results, especially with the longer lists, the skill effect can be readily observed. The absolute number of street names recalled for each list length by the taxi driver model is somewhat lower than those of the real subjects, but the number slightly increases with the list length. Particularly, the scores with the longest lists remain remarkably low deviating from Kalakoski & Saariluoma's empirical results. On the other hand, the taxi driver model produces the skill effect also for the shortest lists, which was not observed in the original study.

The recall scores of the novice models are comparable to the original study. No correlation, positive or negative, can be observed between the recall scores on the one side, and list length and organisation on the other.

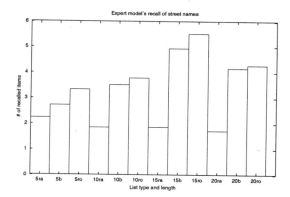

Figure 3: Average number of street names recalled by the taxi driver models for list lengths of 5, 10, 15 and 20.

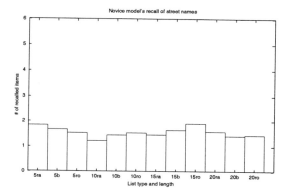

Figure 4: Average number of street names recalled by the novice models for list lengths of 5, 10, 15 and 20.

Discussion and Conclusion

A computer simulation was designed to model taxi drivers' learning and memory performance and predict experimental results in a test situation when stimuli were lists of street names organised into spatially meaningful entities. The objective was to study what kind of knowledge produces experienced taxi drivers' qualitatively unique performance when compared to novice drivers: whether taxi drivers' knowledge inherently consists of distinct routes or more abstract relations between spatially connected places. In order to study the differences in knowledge of expert and novice drivers, we first explicated the task relevant constraints with respect to the taxi driving enterprise and novices' acquaintance with the city.

Our hypothesis was that the differences between taxi drivers' and ordinary drivers' memory of street names arises from the quality of learning, i.e., the task specific constraints that professional driving poses to the taxi drivers, instead of a specific memory architecture or processes. We built this factor into the learning material taking into account what kind routes experienced professional drivers frequently use when navigating in the city of Helsinki.

Besides the explication of the task relevant constraints, another aim of our simulation study was to predict various phenomena observed in expert taxi drivers' performance in a serial recall task. We were especially interested in the phenomena which were assumed to be based on the organisation of environmental knowledge, not on an enhanced rote learning of street names. The taxi driver simulation can account for both qualitative and quantitative results of the memory test. Firstly, differences between the taxi driver model recall scores compared to the novice model are evident in all experimental settings. The taxi driver model retrieves more street names than the novices, and exceed the theoretical short-term memory capacity.

Secondly, the effect of word list order in recall scores was significant only for the taxi driver model: route ordered lists were retrieved better than block-randomised, which in turn were remembered better than random lists. Even in experimental conditions when the list length goes beyond the short-term working memory capacity, the meaningful list organisation facilitated recall. The order of word lists had no influence in the memory performance of novices. They recalled names from lists of length five as poorly as names from lists of length 20, independent of order.

Finally, what are the implications of this study? The aspect that distinguishes our model from previous attempts to simulate expert memory, for instance, EPAM IV (Richman, Staszewski, Simon, 1995) in the chess memory, is that our model learns all its knowledge in the field , i.e., by "driving" in a city. The model is not explicitly trained to memorise lists of street names. By navigating in the modelled city it constructs a complex representation of spatial relations from which it can derive various facts to improve its memory performance.

This is an important distinction because it allows more specific conclusions with respect to the accounts of process and product theories of memory recall. It especially facilitates the analysis of the expert effects which have the potential of improving memory performance in task domains where recall is a contrived task. Particularly, training the model as if memory recall were an intrinsic task leads to better performance because the model is trained with the same material it is expected to remember in the experiment. On the contrary, training the model by task practise, although in a simplified environment, does not bias the memory performance, because the model is not learning to memorise but only accom-

plish the task.

Acknowledgments

We are grateful for Virpi Kalakoski and Pertti Saariluoma, who allowed us to use their unpublished data for the simulation. We want to thank our excellent students for contributing in the implementation of the model, Saara Huhmarniemi, Mikko Koivisto, Janne Korhonen, Mikko Määttä and Mikko Nikkanen, and Kai Laine for helping to construct the Helsinki City map representation.

References

Chase, W.G. (1983). Spatial representations of taxi drivers. In D.A. Rogers & J.A. Sloboda (Eds.), *The acquisition of symbolic skills* (pp. 391-405). New York: Plenum Press.

Ericsson, K. A., & Kintsch, W. (1995). Long-term working memory. *Psychological Review, 102*, 211-245.

Ericsson, K. A., Patel, V., & Kintsch, W. (2000). How experts adaptations to representative task demands account for the expertise effect in memory recall: Comments on Vicente and Wang (1998). *Psychological Review, 107(3)*, 578-592.

Kalakoski, V. & Saariluoma, P. (in press). Taxi drivers' exceptional memory of street names. *Memory & Cognition.*

Peruch, P., Giraudo, M-D., Gärling, T. (1989). Distance cognition by taxi drivers and the general public. *Journal of Experimental Psychology, 9*, 233-239.

Richman, H.B., Staszewski, J.J., Simon, H.A. (1995). Simulation of expert memory using EPAM IV. *Psychological Review*, Vol. 102, No. 2, 305-330.

Simon, H. A., & Gobet, F. (2000). Expertise effects in memory recall: Comments on Vicente and Wang 1998. *Psychological Review, 107(3)*, 593-600.

Vicente, K. J. & Wang, J. H. (1998). An ecological theory of expertise effects in memory recall. *Psychological Review*, Vol. 105, 33-57.

Vicente, K. J. (2000). Revisiting the constraint attunement hypothesis: A reply to Ericsson, Patel, & Kintsch (2000) and Simon & Gobet (2000). *Psychological Review, 107(3)*, 601-608.

Intention superiority effect: A context-sensitivity account

Christian Lebiere (cl@cmu.edu)
Human Computer Interaction Institute; Carnegie Mellon University
Pittsburgh, PA 15213 USA

Frank J. Lee (fjl@cmu.edu)
Department of Psychology; Carnegie Mellon University
Pittsburgh, PA 15213 USA

Abstract

Intention superiority effect (Goschke & Kuhl, 1993; Marsh, Hicks, & Bink, 1998) is the finding that the times to retrieve memory items related to uncompleted or partially completed intentions are faster than for those with no associated intentions. However, this relationship reverses when the intended tasks are completed (Marsh, Hicks, & Bink, 1998; Marsh, Hicks, & Bryan, 1999). That is, the times to retrieve memory items related to completed intentions are slower than for those with no associated intentions. In this paper, we present a computational account of the intention superiority effect using the ACT-R (Anderson & Lebiere, 1998) cognitive architecture. Our modeling approach is based on the idea that uncompleted or partially completed intentions are available as context in the current goal, and they prime related memory items while inhibiting unrelated memory items. However, once the intended tasks are completed, they are removed from the current goal, which produces an inhibitory effect on memory items associated with them. We describe an ACT-R model that is able to reproduce all of the effects reported in Marsh, Hicks, and Bink (1998).

Keywords: Prospective memory, Intention superiority effect, ACT-R.

Introduction

Prospective memory has recently been receiving a lot of attention among psychologists (Brandimonte, Einstein, & McDaniel, 1996). The interest in prospective memory reflects a trend in psychology to investigate more "real-world" phenomena. For the ACT-R theory (Anderson & Lebiere, 1998), the importance of prospective memory research is clear. First, as a unified theory of cognition, especially with its roots in human memory, the ACT-R theory must endeavor to account for the results from this body of research. Second, as the ACT-R theory is pushed towards more complex and dynamic tasks, an account of prospective memory will be critical, because it is central to planning and multitasking in dynamic task environments.

To begin our task of understanding prospective memory from the ACT-R theoretical framework, we decided to focus on a particular phenomenon in prospective memory called the *intention superiority effect* (Goschke & Kuhl, 1993; Marsh, Hicks, and Bink, 1998; Marsh, Hicks, and Bryan, 1999).

Intention Superiority Effect

Intention superiority effect is the finding that the times to retrieve memory items related to uncompleted or partially completed intentions are faster than for those with no associated intentions (Goschke & Kuhl, 1993; Marsh, Hicks, & Bink, 1998). However, this relationship reverses when the intentions have been completed. That is, the times to retrieve memory items related to completed intentions are slower than for those with no associated intentions (Marsh, Hicks, & Bink, 1998; Marsh, Hicks, and Bryan, 1999). The data reported by Marsh, Hicks, and Bink (1998) provide a good overview of this phenomenon, and we review them here.

Marsh, Hicks, and Bink (1998)

Marsh, Hicks, and Bink (1998) reported results from four experiments, using slight variants of the procedure detailed in Goschke and Kuhl (1993). For each of their experiment, Marsh et al. prepared two pairs of scripts. Each script consisted of a title (e.g. *Setting Table*) and five action propositions (e.g. *set the tablecloth*, *place the candles*, etc.). The scripts were carefully made so that they were semantically distinct from one another and were counterbalanced. To measure the activation levels of the memory items associated with the scripts, they used response times on lexical decision tasks (LDTs) on the words from the scripts. The main manipulation between the four experiments in Marsh et al. was when the LDTs were given.

In Experiment 1, they had participants memorize a pair of scripts during each block of the two-block experiment. In one of the blocks, participants were told that they would *perform* the tasks specified in one of the scripts, and in the other block, they were told that they would *observe* the experimenter carrying out the tasks specified in one of the scripts to verify that it was performed correctly. Of the two scripts in each block of this experiment, the script that they were told to perform or observe was considered to be the *prospective* script, and the remaining script was considered to be the *neutral* script. The LDTs were given before they performed or observed the prospective script.

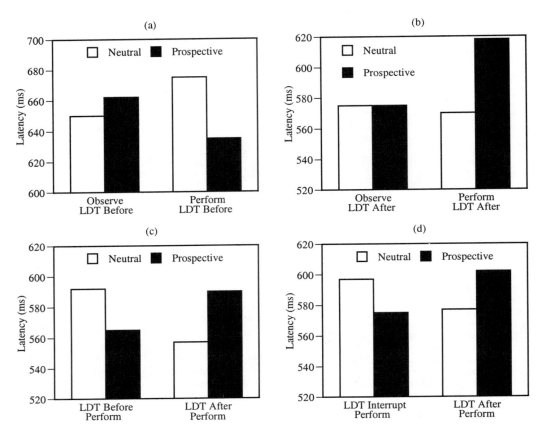

Figure 1: Reproduction of Figures 1 – 4 from Marsh, Hicks, and Binks (1998).

It is important to note that participants were told which script was the prospective script only after they memorized both scripts to criterion. This prevented them from privileged access (e.g., through additional rehearsals) to the prospective script over the neutral script during the initial study phase. After they were told which script was the prospective script, they were immediately given the LDTs.

In Figure 1a, we replot Marsh et al.'s data from Experiment 1. As can be seen, participants were faster in accessing the memory items related to the prospective script compared to their access to the items related to the neutral script. However, note that this difference did not exist for the prospective script that people were told to observe.

Marsh et al.'s Experiment 2 was identical to their Experiment 1, with the exception that the LDTs were given after people performed or observed the prospective script. In Figure 1b, we replot their data from Experiment 2. As can be seen, there is a striking reversal in people's response times to the memory items related to the prospective script after they perform the task. That is, their access to the memory items related to the prospective script was slower after they performed the task compared to their access to the items related to the neutral script in the *perform* condition. However, they found no such difference between the prospective and the neutral script in the *observe* condition.

Since Marsh et al. found no significant differences between the prospective and the neutral script in the *observe* condition in their first two experiments, they decided to focus on the *perform* condition in Experiments 3 and 4. In Experiment 3, the participants were told to perform the prospective script in both blocks of the experiment. In one of the blocks of the experiment, the LDTs were collected before they performed the script, and in the other, the LDTs were collected after they performed the script. In Figure 1c, we replot Marsh et al.'s data from their Experiment 3. As can be seen, they replicated the basic results from their previous two experiments in a within-subjects design. Namely, people were quicker to access the memory items of the prospective script compared to those of the neutral script before they performed the intended task, but after they completed the intended task, they were slower to access the memories items of the prospective script compared to those of the neutral script.

In Experiment 4, Marsh et al. Basically followed the procedure outlined in their previous three experiments, but in one of the blocks of this experiment, they interrupted the participants while they were performing the intended task and gave the LDTs, and in the other block, the LDTs were given after they completed the intended task. The main idea they were testing was the Zeigarnik effect (Butterfield, 1964;

Goschke & Kuhl, 1993). The Zeigarnik effect is the finding that people's access to the memory of the task after it is completed is poorer compared to their access to the memory of the task while they are performing it. As Marsh et al. noted, Zeigarnik effect seemed very close in spirit to the intention superiority effect, and hence they decided to investigate it using their experimental paradigm. In Figure 1d, we replot their data from their Experiment 4. As can be seen, the results mirrored those from Experiment 3 and added support for the Zeigarnik effect. Namely, people were quicker to access the memory items related to the prospective script compared to the neutral script during the execution of the intended task, but their access to the memory items related to the prospective script were slower compared to the neutral script after they completed the intended task. This would seem to suggest that the same mechanism underlies both phenomena.

In the next section, we describe an ACT-R (Anderson & Lebiere, 1998) model of the four experiments that we have reviewed above from Marsh et al. (1998).

Model

Symbolic Level

At the symbolic level, the ACT-R model of intention superiority effect, or more specifically of the Lexical Decision Task, is straightforward. There is only one type of declarative knowledge, contained in chunks of type *lexicon*. Those chunks contain three slots: *word*, which holds a word, *spelling*, which holds its spelling, and *context*, which hold the context in which this word occurred. The goal to perform the LDT is also of type *lexicon*. When a goal is completed, it becomes a new memory chunk or reinforces an existing one if an identical chunk already exists in long-term memory. Thus past goals to perform lexical decision tasks become long-term memory structures used in performing future ones.

Table 1: Production rules for Lexical Decision Task.

Name	Production Rules
Map	IF the goal is to perform lexical access on *spelling* and there is a chunk mapping *spelling* to *word* THEN note in the goal that the desired word is *word*
None	IF the goal is to perform lexical access on *spelling* THEN note that no word can be found
Output	IF the goal is to perform lexical access and the word is *word* THEN output *word* and focus on a new goal

Procedural knowledge consists of three production rules. The most important production, **map**, implements lexical access. Given a word's spelling that was encoded from the environment and is present in the current goal, **map** retrieves from declarative memory the lexicon chunk associating that spelling to a word and adds the word to the goal. If the retrieval fails, then the production, **none**, notes in the goal that no word can be found associated to that spelling. After either of these two productions fires, the production,

output, outputs the word then focuses on a new goal. The English form of these three production rules is given in Table 1. As is the case for the declarative knowledge, these productions are quite simple and are potentially learnable, an important constraint on any model.

Subsymbolic Level

While at the symbolic level the model is appealingly simple and straightforward, it wouldn't generate the prospective memory effects described previously. The symbolic level of productions and chunks merely provides the structure of the model on which the statistical learning mechanisms of the ACT-R architecture operate to tune its performance to the structure of the environment by determining the optimal subsymbolic parameters that control the availability of symbolic structures. The probability and time to retrieve a chunk from declarative memory is a function of its activation, which is given by the activation equation:

$$A_i = B_i + \sum_j W_j \cdot S_{ji} \qquad \text{Activation Equation}$$

A_i is the total activation of chunk i, B_i is its base-level activation, W_j is the attentional level of activation source j and S_{ji} is the strength of association between source j and chunk i. The base-level activation is learned to reflect the context-free history of use of the chunk, with chunks that were used more frequently or recently having higher base-level activation. The activation sources j are the components of the goal, which in the case of the LDT are the context and spelling chunks, evenly dividing between them a total attentional level, W. Therefore the strengths of association are learned to reflect the history of use of a chunk given the composition of the goal. The more a chunk is retrieved when an activation source is present, the larger the strength of association between the two. Formally, the strengths of association between activation sources and chunks reflect the log likelihood ratio of retrieving a chunk given a source over their past history. In addition, activations are stochastic through the addition of zero-mean gaussian noise. We will not describe in detail the equations that control the learning of base-level activations and strengths of associations other than to point out that the parameters controlling that learning as well as the magnitude of the noise were left at the default values used in many other models (Anderson & Lebiere, 1998) and were not optimized to fit the data.

Performance in the retrieval of a chunk is a function of its activation. In this model, we assume that retrieval is assured.[1] We are particularly interested in the latency of retrieval, which is given by the latency equation:

---

[1] This makes the **none** production unnecessary. However, in the experiment the lexical decision task included some non-words for which no corresponding lexicon chunk would exist. Thus while we did not model that part of the experiment we included here for completeness sake the production to deal with that case.

$$T_i = F \cdot e^{-A_i}$$ **Latency Equation**

T_i is the latency to retrieve chunk i and F is a time scaling factor. Thus, the higher the activation of a chunk, the faster its retrieval latency, and vice versa.

Assumptions and Results

The basic assumption of this model lies in the composition of the current goal, which determines the identity of the sources of activation. As previously described, in addition to the essential components of the lexical decision task, namely the spelling and the word to be accessed, the goal also includes a slot that encodes the current context or task to be accomplished. Because one expects the task to be strongly predictive of the words that need to be accessed, as is the case here where each script is associated to a limited number of words, including the task in the goal as a source of activation is a reasonable assumption in trying to maximize the activation of the chunks to be retrieved.

This provides a useful inhibition mechanism.[2] The chunks that were retrieved for a given task will be more active when the task is over, because the base-level learning mechanism has boosted their activation to reflect their recent use. To prevent these chunks from intruding on the following task because of this temporary boost in activation, changing the context to a new task not only boosts the activation of the words most likely to be encountered in that task, but also lowers the activation of the words that are not related to that task, including the words that are temporarily more active due to rehearsal in the previous task.

By boosting performance through the strategic use of basic architectural learning mechanisms, this assumption is therefore compatible with the spirit of the rational analysis underlying the ACT-R architecture (Anderson, 1990). Including in the goal an additional component that generally reflects the current context is similar to the key assumption of an ACT-R model of sequence learning (Lebiere & Wallach, 1998; 2000). In that model, the additional goal component is the previous stimuli in the sequence, but it serves the similar purpose of providing a discriminating source of activation in addition to the primary one, i.e. the current stimuli. This assumption is also compatible with the view of the current goal as ACT-R's working memory (Lovett, Reder & Lebiere, 1999), which makes it a natural place to keep the task(s) to be completed active as a reminder of their impending execution.

The one thing left to specify is which context is active in the goal given the various experimental conditions. The general rule is that if a task is expected to be performed in the near future (and no other pressing one is currently being

performed) then the context is set to that task to facilitate the retrieval of related information. When a task has been performed, the context is changed to some other task, even if it is not expected to be performed soon, to prevent the information associated with the task that was just performed from generating excessive interference.

The model worked as follows. Both prospective and neutral scripts were first studied. This means setting the goal context to the title of the script and performing lexical access (through the same productions as used in the lexical decision task) on all the words present in the script (10 for each script). For each word, this typically meant firing the **map** and **output** productions. The retrieval of the lexicon chunk for the word in the **map** production led to the increasing of the strength of association between the current context and that lexicon chunk. The rest of the operations would vary with each experimental condition. None of the model parameters were optimized to fit the data. The important aspect of the model is how simply it can capture the effects in the data, not the maximization of a quantitative measure of fit.

In Experiment 1, participants engaged in the Lexical Decision Task (LDT) before observing or performing the script, but after having been instructed which script they would have to observe (Observe condition) or perform (Perform condition). In the Perform condition, the context was set to the script to perform, because subjects would have to actively generate the script. In the less demanding Observe condition, the context was randomly set to either script with equal probability, on the assumption that subjects did not care to set the right context because they would merely have to observe the experimenter perform the script, which the externally provided components of the script providing enough spreading activation without needing to make the script itself a source of activation. This reflects the fact that maintaining a context in the goal exacts some costs, including the additional splitting of the total attentional level W. Alternatively, the context could be left empty or set to some other task than those of the experiment, which would yield comparable results.

Figure 2a presents the model results in terms of the average latency to perform the task in each condition. Comparing it to Figure 1a, all the significant effects in the subject data are reproduced. In the Observe condition, neutral and prospective scripts produce similar latencies because the context is equally likely to be set to one or the other, and the experimental conditions prevented one to be studied more than the other. In the Perform condition, the prospective script is recalled faster than in the Observe condition because the context is set to that script, leading through the strengths of association to an activation boost to lexical items present in that script, resulting in lower latency. The neutral script, on the other hand, is slower than both the prospective script and the Observe condition because the context is always set to the other script, leading to a lower activation through negative strengths of associations from the prospective script to neutral script items, and a longer latency.

---

[2] Since formally strengths of associations are log likelihood ratios, unless there is a strong association between a source and a chunk the corresponding probability ratio is often smaller than 1, resulting through the log in negative, i.e. inhibitory, strengths of association. However, there is no fundamental distinction in ACT-R between positive and negative strengths of association.

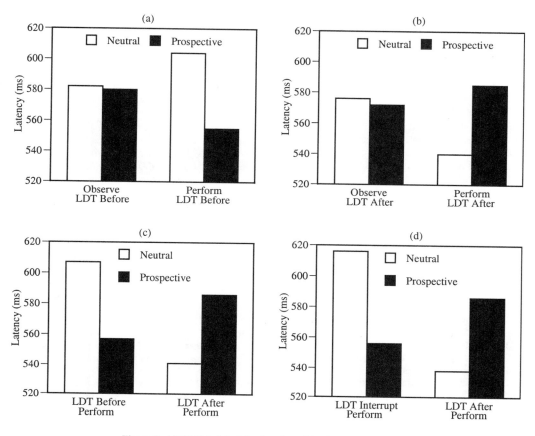

Figure 2: ACT-R Model of the data from Marsh, Hicks, and Binks (1998).

In Experiment 2, the same procedure was followed but the LDT was administered after the subjects observed or performed the prospective script. The observation or performance of the prospective script was modeled as an additional study phase identical to the original one.[3] In accordance with the model setup of Experiment 1, the context in the Observe condition is randomly set to either script while the context in the Perform condition is set to the neutral script to prevent interference from the prospective script. As in the subject data, the model generates roughly equal latency for both scripts in the Observe condition, as shown in Figure 2b, which can be compared to Figure 1b. The reason is that the additional rehearsals of the words in the prospective script have also strengthened the associations to those words from the prospective script. Since half the time the context in the LDT is the neutral script, the advantage of the rehearsal is lessened and access to lexical items associated with the prospective script is only slightly faster. In the Perform condition, the neutral script has much lower latency because the context has always been set to that script, whereas the pro-

spective script, despite its additional rehearsal, has higher latency because of consistent inhibition from the neutral script.

In Experiment 3, only the Perform condition was used, with the LDT administered either before or after the performance of the prospective script. The setting of the context was the same as in the previous experiments, namely the context was set to the prospective script before (and during) performance and to the neutral script afterwards. Figure 2c displays the results, which are consistent with those of the previous experiments, and can be compared to Figure 1c. When the LDT is given before performance, latency is lower for the prospective script because the context is set in its favor. When the LDT is given after the performance, latency is lower for the neutral script, because the context is then set in its favor, and higher for the prospective script. The overall latency is however lower than before the performance thanks to the additional rehearsal.

In Experiment 4, the procedure was similar except that the performance phase was interrupted halfway through and the LDT task administered both during the interruption and after the performance phase had been completed. Again, the context was set according the usual rule, meaning to the prospective script during the performance phase (including the interruption) and to the neutral script afterwards. Figure 2d displays the model results, which again reproduce the effects

---

[3] It might have been reasonable to assume that performance resulted in stronger rehearsal than observation, but there seemed to be no good a priori way of estimating that difference in the model. Thus the model provided equal rehearsal in both conditions.

of the subject data given in Figure 1d. During the interruption, words associated with the prospective script benefits both from the (partial) rehearsal and from the script being in the context. After the performance phase, the switch of the context to the neutral script then favors words associated with that script.

Discussion

Goschke and Kuhl (1993) and Marsh, Hicks and Bink (1998) interpreted their findings in terms of the ACT* cognitive theory (Anderson, 1983), a predecessor of the ACT-R theory, and found their results entirely consistent with the theory. They suggested that intentions were represented as goal nodes, which conferred them additional activation, which was quickly dissipated when the goal was popped off the stack and replaced by another. Marsh, Hicks and Bink (1998) moreover suggested that after completing a task people naturally directed their attention toward making a decision of which task to complete next, providing a rationale for our rule of switching the context to the neutral task after completing the prospective task. They also noted the inhibitory nature of such a switch, which we also observed. While many details have changed between ACT* and ACT-R (most important in this case is that change in activation as a result of goal switching is due to a change in spreading activation rather than a decay in goal activation) the basic account of the data in terms of the ACT theory remains valid.

Another advantage of the model is its compatibility with existing models of language (Anderson, Budiu, & Reder, in press; Lebiere, 1995). As such, this model of the lexical decision task provides a bridge between the written form of words, i.e. their spelling, and their internal representation, in terms of symbolic chunks. An isomorphic model could easily be written for the mapping between auditory input of word components, i.e. phonemes, and the words themselves. In either case, after the mapping between external presentations to internal representations is performed words can be manipulated irrespective of their presentation modality, providing a very desirable abstraction in the form of symbolic chunks. Such abstraction might be one of the fundamental purposes of language.

Conclusion

The main contribution of this paper is to present a simple yet precise model of the intention superiority effect. The model hinges on the fundamental assumption that a task that is or will be accomplished in the near future is kept in the goal as a source of activation, leading to faster access to related lexical items and inhibition of items related to other, competing contexts. However, once the task is completed, it is removed from the goal and attention is switched to a different context, thereby providing inhibition of the just completed task. Additional empirical and modeling work is clearly needed to determine the limits and circumstances of context maintenance. But the fact that such a simple model could provide a precise account of this complex and somewhat surprising phenomenon is an indication of the power of cognitive modeling to illuminate empirical data.

Acknowledgments

The research reported in this paper was supported by the Office of Naval Research, Cognitive Science Program, under Contract Number N00014-95-10223. All correspondences should be addressed to Christian Lebiere at the Human Computer Interaction Institute, Carnegie Mellon University, Pittsburgh, PA 15213.

References

Anderson, J. R. (1983). *The architecture of cognition.* Cambridge, MA: Harvard University Press.

Anderson, J. R. (1990). *The adaptive character of thought.* Hillsdale, NJ: Lawrence Erlbaum Associates.

Anderson, J.R., Budiu, R., & Reder, L.M. (in press). A theory of sentence memory as part of a general theory of memory. *Journal of Memory and Language.*

Anderson, J.R., & Lebiere, C. (1998). *Atomic components of thought.* Mahwah, NJ: Lawrence Erlbaum Associates.

Brandimonte, M., Einstein, G.O., & McDaniel, M.A. (Eds.) (1996). *Prospective memory: Theory and applications.* Mahwah, NJ: Lawrence Erlbaum Associates.

Butterfield, E.C. (1964). The interruption of task: Methodological, factual, and theoretical issues. *Psychological Bulletin, 62,* 309-322.

Goschke, T., & Kuhl, J. (1993). Representation of intentions: Persisting activation in memory. *Journal of Experimental Psychology: Learning Memory and Cognition, 19,* 1211-1226.

Lebiere, C. (1995). Individual differences in an ACT-R model of sentence reading. Presented at the joint session of the *CAPS Workshop* and the *Second ACT-R Workshop* at Carnegie Mellon University, Pittsburgh, PA.

Lebiere, C. & Wallach, D. (1998). Implicit does not imply procedural: A declarative theory of sequence learning. Paper presented at the *41st Conference of the German Psychological Association,* Dresden, Germany.

Lebiere, C., & Wallach, D. (2000). Sequence learning in the ACT-R cognitive architecture: Empirical analysis of a hybrid model. In Sun, R. & Giles, L. (Eds.) *Sequence Learning: Paradigms, Algorithms, and Applications.* Springer LNCS/LNAI, Germany.

Lovett, M. C., Reder, L. M., & Lebiere, C. (1999). Modeling working memory in a unified architecture: An ACT-R perspective. In Miyake, A. & Shah, P. (Eds.) *Models of Working Memory: Mechanisms of Active Maintenance and Executive Control.* New York: Cambridge University Press.

Marsh, R.L., Hicks, J.L., & Bink, M.L. (1998). Activation of completed, uncompleted, and partially completed intentions. *Journal of Experimental Psychology: Learning Memory and Cognition, 24,* 350-361.

Marsh, R.L., Hicks, J.L., & Bryan, E.S. (1999). The activation of unrelated and canceled intentions. *Memory & Cognition, 27,* 320-327.

Infinite RAAM: A Principled Connectionist Substrate for Cognitive Modeling

Simon Levy and Jordan Pollack
levy, pollack@cs.brandeis.edu
Dynamical and Evolutionary Machine Organization
Volen Center for Complex Systems,
Brandeis University, Waltham, MA 02454, USA
March 1, 2001

Abstract

Unification-based approaches have come to play an important role in both theoretical and applied modeling of cognitive processes, most notably natural language. Attempts to model such processes using neural networks have met with some success, but have faced serious hurdles caused by the limitations of standard connectionist coding schemes. As a contribution to this effort, this paper presents recent work in Infinite RAAM (IRAAM), a new connectionist unification model. Based on a fusion of recurrent neural networks with fractal geometry, IRAAM allows us to understand the behavior of these networks as dynamical systems. Using a logical programming language as our modeling domain, we show how this dynamical-systems approach solves many of the problems faced by earlier connectionist models, supporting unification over arbitrarily large sets of recursive expressions. We conclude that IRAAM can provide a principled connectionist substrate for unification in a variety of cognitive modeling domains.

Language and Connectionism: Three Approaches

Language, to a cognitive scientist, can be held to include natural language and the "language of thought" (Fodor 1975), as well as symbolic programming languages developed to simulate these, like LISP and Prolog. Attempts to build connectionist models of such systems have generally followed one of three approaches.

The first of these, exemplified by (Rumelhart and McClelland 1986), dispenses entirely with traditional representations (data structures) and rules (algorithms on those structures), in favor of letting the network "learn" the patterns in the data being modeled, via the well-known back-propagation algorithm (Rumelhart, Hinton, and Williams 1986) or a similar training method. This approach became the subject harsh criticism from members of the traditional "symbols-and-rules" school of cognitive science, based on the disparity between the strength of the claims made and the actual results reported (Pinker and Prince 1988), as well as the apparent inability of such systems to handle the systematic, compositional aspects of linguistic meaning (Fodor and Pylyshyn 1988).

The second sort of connectionist approach goes beyond the rules-and-representations view and directly to the heart of what computing actually means, by showing how a recurrent neural network can perform all the operations of a Turing machine, or more (Siegelmann 1995). Though such proofs may hold a good deal of theoretical interest, they do not address the degree to which a particular computational paradigm (connectionism) is suited to a particular real-world task (language). They are therefore not of much use in arguing for or against the merits of connectionism as a model of any particular domain of interest (Melnik 2000), any more than knowing about Turing equivalence will help you in choosing between a Macintosh and a Pentium-based PC.

The third approach, which some of its proponents have described as "Representations without Rules" (Horgan and Tienson 1989), is the one that we wish to take here. This approach acknowledges the need for systematic, compositional structure, but rejects traditional, exceptionless linguistic rules in favor of the flexible computation afforded by connectionist representations. Proponents of such a view are of course responsible for showing how these representations can support the kinds of processes traditionally viewed as rules. In the remainder of this paper we show how the behavior of neural network called an Infinite RAAM corresponds directly to one such process, unification, thereby supporting a systematic, compositional model of linguistic structure.

Unification

Unification, an algorithm popularized by Robinson (1965) as a basis for automated theorem-proving, has come to play a central role in both computer science and cognitive science. In computer science, unification is at the core of logical programming languages like Prolog (Clocksin and Mellish 1994); in cognitive science, it is the foundation of a number of category-based approaches to the analysis of natural language (Shieber 1986). The basic unification algorithm can be found in many introductory AI textbooks (e.g., Rich and Knight 1991 p. 152), and can be summarized recursively as follows: (1) A variable can be unified with a literal. (2) Two literals can be unified if their initial predicate symbols are the same and their arguments can be unified.

If, for example, we have a Prolog database containing the assertion male(albert),[1] meaning "Albert is male", and we perform the query male(Who), asking "Who is male?" the unification algorithm will first attempt to unify male(albert) with male(Who), and will succeed in matching on the predicate symbol male, by rule (2). The algorithm will then recur, attempting to unify the variable Who with the atomic literal albert, and will succeed by rule (1) and terminate, with the result that Who will be bound to albert, answering the query.

---

[1] Prolog examples are taken from the tutorial introduction in (Clocksin and Mellish 1994).

Of course, real programming-language and natural-language applications require unification algorithms more complicated than the one illustrated in this simple example, but the example suffices for our goals here.

RAAM

Before describing how the Infinite RAAM model is suited to performing unification, some historical background on this model is necessary.

Recursive Auto-Associative Memory or RAAM (Pollack 1990) is a method for storing tree structures in fixed-width vectors by repeated compression. Its architecture consists of two separate networks: an encoder network, which can construct a fixed-dimensional code by compressively combining the nodes of a symbolic tree from the bottom up, and a decoder network which decompresses this code into its two or more components. The decoder is applied recursively until it terminates in symbols, reconstructing the tree. These two networks are simultaneously trained as an autoassociator (Ackley, Hinton, and Sejnowski 1985) with time-varying inputs. If the training is successful, the result of bottom up encoding will coincide with top-down decoding. Figure 1 shows an example of a RAAM for storing binary trees using two bits of representation for each input and output.[2]

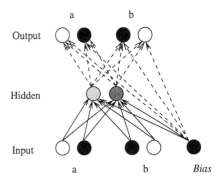

Figure 1: RAAM encoding and decoding the tree (a b), using two bits per symbol: a = 01, b = 10. Solid lines depict encoder weights, dashed lines decoder weights. Note the real-valued representation of the tree (a b) on the hidden layer, which would be fed back into the encoder to build a representation of the trees (a(a b)), (b(a b)), ((a b)a), etc.

Following the publication of (Pollack 1990), RAAM gained widespread popularity as a model of linguistic structure. Some researchers (Blank, Meeden, and Marshall 1991) found it an attractive way of "closing the gap" between the symbolic and sub-symbolic paradigms in cognitive science. Others (Van Gelder 1990) saw in RAAM a direct and simple refutation of the traditional cognitive scientists' backlash

against connectionism, or went as far as to show how traditional syntactic operations like transformations could be performed directly on RAAM representations (Chalmers 1990).

RAAM as an Iterated Function System

Consider the RAAM decoder shown in Figure 2. It consists of four neurons that each receive the same (X, Y) input. The output portion of the network is divided into a right and a left pair of neurons. In the operation of the decoder the output from each pair of neurons is recursively reapplied to the network. Using the RAAM interpretation, each such recursion implies a branching of a node of the binary tree represented by the decoder and initial starting point. However, this same network recurrence can also be evaluated in the context of dynamical systems. This network is a form of *iterated function system* (IFS) consisting of two *transforms*, which are iteratively applied to points in a two-dimensional space.

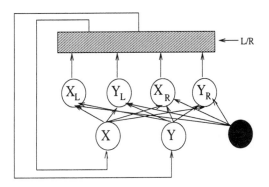

Figure 2: Detail of the decoder from the RAAM of Figure 1. Bar at top of figure is a "gate" that feeds the left or right output of the decoder back onto the hidden layer.

In a typical IFS (Barnsley 1993), the transforms are linear equations of the form $T_i(x) = A_i x + b_i$, where x and b are vectors and A is a matrix. The *Iterated* part of the term IFS comes from the fact that, starting with some initial x, each of the transforms is applied iteratively to its own output, or the output of one of the other transforms. The choice of which transform to apply is made either deterministically or by nondeterministic probabilities associated with each transform. If the transforms T_i are *contractive*, meaning that they always decrease the distance between any two input vectors x and y, then the limit of this process as the number of iterations N approaches infinity yields an *attractor* (stable fixed-point set) for the IFS. Most IFS research has focussed on systems whose attractor is a *fractal*, meaning that it exhibits self-similarity at all scales.[3]

The transforms of the RAAM decoder have the form $T_i(x) = f(A_i x + b_i)$, where f is the familiar logistic-sigmoid "squashing" function $f(x) = 1/(1 + e^{-x})$. Typical of connectionist models, the matrix A ranges over the entire set of

---

[2]Restricting the network to only two bits per symbol allows straightforward visualization of its hidden-layer dynamics as an X/Y plot. RAAMs for real-world tasks would use many more bits per symbol.

[3]A famous example of a fractal attractor is the beautiful Mandelbrot set, in which tiny copies of the entire set seem to appear as if by magic when you zoom in on certain regions.

146

real numbers, so it is not necessarily contractive. Nevertheless, the squashing function provides a "pseudo-contractive" property that yields an attractor for the decoder. In the context of RAAMs, however, the main interesting property of (pseudo-)contractive IFSes lies in the trajectories of points in the space. For such IFSes the space is divided into two sets of points. The first set consists of points located on the underlying fractal attractor of the IFS. The second set is the complement of the first, points that are not on the attractor. The trajectories of points in this second set are characterized by a gravitation towards the attractor, as follows: Each iteration produces a set of left and right copies of the points from the previous iteration. Finite, multiple iterations of the transforms have the effect of bringing the set of copies arbitrarily close to the attractor.

Taking the terminal test of the decoder network to be "on the attractor" solves a number of technical problems that limited the scalability of the RAAM model, and allows the model to represent extremely large sets of trees in small fixed-dimensional neural codes. The attractor, being a fractal, can be generated at arbitrary pixel resolution. In this interpretation, each possible tree, instead of being described by a single point, is now an *equivalence class* of initial points sharing the same tree-shaped trajectories to the fractal attractor.

Using the attractor as a terminal test also allows a natural formulation of assigning labels to terminals. Barnsley (1993) noted that each point on the attractor is associated with an address which is simply the sequence of indices of the transforms used to arrive on that point from other points on the attractor. The address is essentially an infinite sequence of digits. Therefore to achieve a labeling for a specific alphabet we need only consider a sufficient number of significant digits from this address.

These ideas are encapsulated in Figure 3, which shows a "Galaxy" attractor obtained by iterative Blind Watchmaker selection (Dawkins 1986) to a visually appealing shape,[4] along with sample derivations of the trees (a b) and (a (a b)).

Infinite RAAM

Using the "on-the-attractor" terminal test, we were able to use hill-climbing to train a RAAM decoder to generate all and only the strings in the set $a^n b^n \cup a^n b^{n+1}, n \leq 5$. As the simplest example of a non-regular, context-free formal language, $a^n b^n$ has been used as a target set by a number of recurrent-network research projects (Rodriguez, Wiles, and Elman 1999; Williams and Zipser 1989), so it serves as a benchmark for the formal power of a model such as RAAM.

Analysis of the decoder weights of our $a^n b^n$ RAAM revealed a pattern that we were able to generalize into a formal constructive proof for deriving a set of weights to generate this language for arbitrarily large values of n, as a function of the pixel resolution ϵ (Melnik, Levy, and Pollack 2000).

With this proof in hand, we felt justified in using the term *Infinite RAAM* (IRAAM) to refer to our decoder networks. Against a traditional approach in which grammars are the only sufficient competence models and neural networks are

---

[4]A gallery of several such attractor images can be viewed at **http://demo.cs.brandeis.edu/pr/mindeye/bwifs.html**

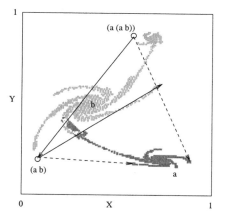

Figure 3: The Galaxy attractor, showing derivation of the tree (a (a b)) and its daughter tree (a b). Attractor points with addresss a, reachable from the attractor on the left transform, are colored dark gray; points with address b, reachable on the right transform, are light gray. The left transients to the attractor are shown as dashed lines, and the right transients as solid lines.

merely implementations (Fodor and Pylyshyn 1988) or performance models, the formally proven existence of a set of "pure" $a^n b^n$ weights provided evidence that a neural network can serve as both a competence model and a performance model, under a dynamical-systems interpretation of the network's behavior.

Unification-based IRAAM

Nevertheless, a fundamental problem exists in the general case when investigating the capacity of a given IRAAM decoder via discrete sampling of the space of tree equivalence classes. Transients to the attractor can potentially meander around the entire unit space before coming to rest on the attractor, so the potential depth of the trees encoded using even a low-resolution sampling is quite large. Because the number of possible trees grows factorially with the depth of the trees, the discrete sampling method is therefore doomed to find only an infinitesimal portion of the trees that a given IRAAM could be encoding. Solving this problem requires knowing precisely how many trees to search for, and where to find them.

To limit the number of trees, it is sufficient to limit the number of IFS iterations. Like sampling, limiting the iterations produces only an approximation to the actual, infinite attractor. For zero iterations, the entire space is the attractor approximate, and the only tree encoded is a terminal, which we may refer to generically as X. For one iteration, each point not on the attractor goes to the attractor on one iteration, and the only tree encoded is (X X). For two iterations, the trees encoded are (X (X X)), ((X X) X), and ((X X) (X X)), and so on for more iterations. This solves the first part of the problem.

Solving the second part of the problem – locating the trees in space – requires switching from a "top-down" approach to a "bottom up" approach. We no longer start at a point off the attractor and decode the tree as this point's path to the attractor. Instead, we start at a point (or set of points) on the attractor, and ask what other point(s) that point can be unified with, using the *en*coder: hence the term *unification-based* IRAAM.[5]

To perform this unification, we first compute the attractor, then take its image under the left and right *inverses* of the transforms. Unifications (trees) are located precisely within the intersections of these inverses. Under this interpretation, asking whether two constituents can be unified means asking whether their inverses have a non-empty intersection.

For example, to determine the locations of the binary trees of depth two or less, we iterate the IFS twice, producing four attractor pieces, each of which is an image of the unit square under the composition of two transforms (left/left, left/right, right/left, and right/right). The union of these is the attractor approximate A_2, which encodes the abstract terminal tree X. This process is shown in Figure 4.

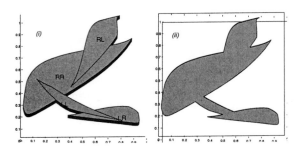

Figure 4: The Galaxy attractor approximated at two IFS iterations: individual overlapping images (*i*) and union of these images (*ii*). The union represents the outer boundary of the sampled attractor shown in Figure 3.

Taking the left and right inverse transforms of the attractor in Figure 4 gives us the regions shown in Figure 5. Intersecting these regions gives us the region encoding the trees X and (X X). As depicted in Figure 6, "subtracting out" the attractor (tree X) gives us the region encoding only the tree (X X).

At this point we have everything we need to encode the remaining trees of depth two. To encode the tree (X (X X)), we take the left inverse of the attractor and intersect this inverse with the right inverse of the region encoding the tree (X X). This right inverse is the entire unit square [6], so this intersection is effectively a no-op, giving us the same left inverse that we started with. Subtracting out the trees (X X) and X, which are contained in this inverse, gives us the region encoding only the tree (X (X X)). Swapping "left" for "right", the same operations can be done to obtain the tree ((X X) X); neither of these is shown, to save space.

---

[5]We find a compelling parallel in the historical switch from "top-down" Chomskyan rules (Chomsky 1957) to the "bottom-up" combinatorial categories of unification-based grammars (Shieber 1986)

[6]because we have performed the operation $R^{-1}(R^{-1}(R(R(\square))))$

Finally, the tree ((X X) (X X)) is encoded by the region not encoding any of the other trees.

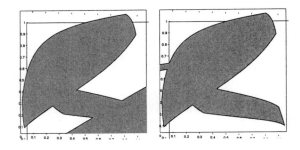

Figure 5: Left and right inverses of the attractor of Figure 4. These inverses encode the trees (X (X X)) and ((X X) X); see text.

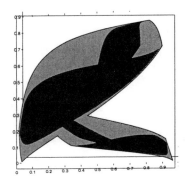

Figure 6: Intersection of inverse regions from Figure 5, which encodes the tree (X X). Black region is the attractor, which is "subtracted out" from the intersection.

Labeling the Terminals

The discussion of the hill-climbing $a^n b^n$ decoder described a scheme for labeling the points of the attractor terminal set by means of their fractal addresses. The method involved approximating the attractor at some pixel resolution, then labeling each attractor point by the transform(s) on which that point was reachable from any points on the attractor. This scheme cannot be implemented in a model in which the attractor is approximated by iteration, because the only points reachable from the current attractor approximate A_N lie on the approximates $A_{N+k}, k > 1$. Since these points themselves are not on the part of A_N reachable from outside A_N, this scheme cannot be used to label the terminals of trees, which by definition are transients the to attractor from points outside it.

For the current stage of the project, we are working around this problem by simply hand-labeling regions in the attractor, as illustrated in the simple database example below.

Bringing it All Together

By this point we hope to have persuaded the reader that IRAAM provides a plausible connectionist substrate for unification-based models. To make this point more concrete, we can consider how one would implement a simple logical database language, like first-order predicate calculus (FOPC), or Prolog, using an IRAAM.

Labeled attractor regions correspond to *atoms*: `albert`, `victoria`, `female`. *Facts* about atoms, like `female(victoria)` and `parents(edward, victoria, albert)`, are built recursively as intersections of the inverses of the labeled attractor regions, and intersections of the inverses of those intersections. Whether or not two constituents (atom, propositions) can be unified depends on the size and shape of their encoding regions, and on the connection weights of the IRAAM network.

Rules relating facts to each other and generalizing them using variables, correspond to intersections or unions of the recursively constructed facts. For example, the rule `woman(X) :- human(X), female(X), adult(X)` would be implemented by taking the intersection of the inverses of the attractor regions for the atoms `human`, `female`, and `adult`; this intersection would be the "definition" of the term `woman` in the model.

We can illustrate this process using our toy database, presented below in its entirety:

```
male(albert).
male(edward).
female(alice).
female(victoria).
parents(edward, victoria, albert).
parents(alice, victoria, albert).
```

Encoding these propositions in a format that a binary-branching IRAAM could represent requires some slight modifications: all propositions are first put in prefix form; e.g., `male(albert)` is re-coded as `(male albert)`. The three-place predicate `parents` is then re-coded ("curried") into a one-place predicate `parent`, with `((parent C) P)` meaning that the parent of C is P; this also requires that each parent be specified by a separate rule, resulting in four `parent` rules instead of two.

Figure 7 illustrates the derivation of a few propositional trees from this set, using another attractor from our image gallery. The figure shows a portion of the unit square which contains the attractor `(tree X)`, as well as the regions encoding the trees `(X X)` and `((X X) X)`. Sample encodings for the trees `(male edward)` and `((parent edward) victoria)` are also shown. The figure was generated as follows: First, we computed the depth-two attractor and tree-regions using the method shown in Figures 4 - 6. Then we hand-traced a closed curve in the region encoding the tree `((X X) X)`. Using a program which plots the left and right copies of the point at the current cursor position, this trace produced a left copy of this closed curve in the region encoding `(X X)`, and a right copy in the attractor region, encoding a terminal. We labeled this terminal attractor piece `victoria`. Hand tracing over the closed curve for `(X X)` resulted in a left and right copy of that curve on the attractor; we labeled these terminals `parent` and `edward` respectively.

These labelings yielded a set of attractor regions that unified to the tree `((parent edward) victoria)`.

To encoded the tree `(male edward)`, we hand-traced a close curve in the region encoding `(X X)`, producing a left and right copy on the attractor. We labeled the left copy `male` and the right copy `edward'`. By taking the encoding of `edward` to be a region including both this `edward'` and the encoding of `edward` from the other tree, we obtained a set of labels unifying to both propositions. Though this is a long way from a real solution to the tree-labeling problem, it is a first step toward adding "meaning" to the abstract structural configurations we have been presenting so far.

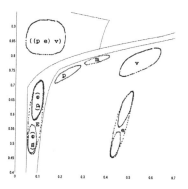

Figure 7: Encoding a few propositions using an IRAAM by hand-labeling of attractor regions. Funnel-shaped region at left side of figure encodes trees of the form `((X X) X)`. Thin diagonal band encodes trees `(X X)`. Lower-right area is the attractor. Abbreviations: `v` = `victoria`, `e` = `edward`, `p` = `parent`, `m` = `male`. Region E represents the set of facts about Edward: that he is male, that someone is his parent.

Conclusions and Future Work

This paper presented recent work on Infinite RAAM (IRAAM), a new connectionist architecture that fuses recurrent neural networks with fractal geometry, allowing us to understand the behavior of these networks as iterated function systems (IFSes). We have shown how limiting the number of IFS iterations allows us to use IRAAM as a connectionist substrate for unification, an algorithm that has come to play a central role in a variety of cognitive science disciplines. Fractal representation of language is a relatively new field, and we have yet to test the model on empirical data. We are however encouraged by the success of related work in fractal encoding of grammars (Tabor 2000), and see our work as contributing to this effort. We hope that such work will serve as a foundation for a principled "unification" of connectionist approaches with more traditional symbolic models, perhaps as an alternative to hybrid methods.

We see several possible research directions for our model. First, we need to apply unification-based IRAAM to something grander than a simple six-sentence database like the one used in the example. The obvious next step would be to find a non-trivial database of dozens or hundreds of propositions to test the model.

Such an effort would require a learning algorithm for IRAAM, which, given a set of propositions or other hierarchical structures, would use gradient descent or a similar method to learn a set of weights encoding just those propositions. Such an algorithm would have an error function assigning a penalty for both missing encodings and for encodings inconsistent with the examples from the training set (e.g., the proposition `female(albert)` in our example data set). An intriguing possibility would be to co-evolve both the network weights and a separate labeling program, using the paradigm described in (Hillis 1992) and (Juillé and Pollack 1996).

Finally, we suspect that inherent limitations in using a single set of network weights may hinder our attempts to use IRAAM as a model of unification in natural language, where the combinatorial possibilities are much richer than those of artificial languages like FOPC and Prolog. Research in image compression (Barnsley and Jacquin 1988) has shown the usefulness of combining several different IFSes to encode a single real-world image. We hope that a similar approach will allow IRAAM to scale up to the larger, more complicated phrases and sentences of natural language.

References

Ackley, D. H., G. Hinton, and T. Sejnowski (1985). A learning algorithm for boltzmann machines. *Cognitive Science 9*, 147–169.

Barnsley, M. F. (1993). *Fractals everywhere*. New York: Academic Press.

Barnsley, M. F. and A. Jacquin (1988). Application of recurrent iterated function systems to images. In *Proc. SPIE*, Volume 1001, pp. 122–131.

Blank, D., L. Meeden, and J. Marshall (1991). Exploring the symbolic/subsymbolic continuum: A case study of raam. Technical Report TR332, Computer Science Department, University of Indiana.

Chalmers, D. (1990). Syntactic transformations on distributed represenations. *Connection Science 2*, 53–62.

Chomsky, N. (1957). *Syntactic Structures*. The Hague: Mouton.

Clocksin, W. and C. Mellish (1994). *Programming in Prolog*. Berlin: Springer Verlag.

Dawkins, R. (1986). *The Blind Watchmaker: Why the Evidence of Evolution Reveals a Universe Without Design*. New York: W.W. Norton and Co.

Fodor, J. (1975). *The Language of Thought*. New York: Crowell.

Fodor, J. and Z. Pylyshyn (1988). Connectionism and cognitive architecture: A critical analysis. *Cognition 28*, 3–71.

Hillis, W. (1992). Co-evolving parasites improves simulated evolution as an optimization procedure. In C. Langton, C. Taylor, and J. Farmer (Eds.), *Artificial Life II*, pp. 313–324. Addison Wesley.

Horgan, T. and J. Tienson (1989). Representations without rules. *Philosophical Topics XVII(1)*, 147–175.

Juillé, H. and J. Pollack (1996). Co-evolving intertwined spirals. In *Proceedings of the Fifth Annual Conference on Evolutionary Programming*. MIT Press.

Melnik, O. (2000). *Representation of Information in Neural Networks*. Ph. D. thesis, Brandeis University.

Melnik, O., S. Levy, and J. Pollack (2000). Raam for an infinite context-free language. In *IJCNN 2000*. International Joint Conference on Neural Networks: IEEE.

Pinker, S. and A. Prince (1988). On language and connectionism: Analysis of a parallel distributed processing model of language acquisition. *Cognition 28*, 73–193.

Pollack, J. (1990). Recursive distributed representations. *Artifical Intelligence 36*, 77–105.

Rich, E. and K. Knight (1991). *Artificial Intelligence*. New York: McGraw-Hill.

Robinson, J. (1965). A machine-oriented logic based on the resolution principle. *Journal of the ACM 12(1)*, 23–41.

Rodriguez, P., J. Wiles, and J. Elman (1999). A recurrent neural network that learns to count. *Connection Science 11*, 5–40.

Rumelhart, D., G. Hinton, and R. Williams (1986). Learning internal representation by error propagation. In D. Rumelhart and J. McClelland (Eds.), *Parallel Distributed Processing: Explorations in the Microstructure of Cognition*, Volume 1. MIT.

Rumelhart, D. and J. McClelland (1986). On learning the past tenses of english verbs. In D. Rumelhart and J. McClelland (Eds.), *op. cit.*, Volume 2.

Shieber, S. (1986). *An Introduction to Unification Based Approaches to Grammar*. Number 4 in CSLI Lecture Notes. University of Chicago Press.

Siegelmann, H. (1995). Computation beyond the turing limit. *Science 268*, 545–548.

Tabor, W. (2000). Fractal encoding of context-free grammars in connectionist networks. *Expert Systems: The International Journal of Knowledge Engineering and Neural Networks*, *17(1)*, 41–56.

Van Gelder, T. (1990). Compositionality: a connectionist variation on a classical theme. *Cognitive Science 14*, 355–384.

Williams, R. and D. Zipser (1989). A learning algorithm for continually running fully recurrent neural networks. *Neural Computation 1*, 270–280.

Modeling Selective Attention: Not Just Another Model of Stroop (NJAMOS)

Marsha C. Lovett (Lovett@CMU.EDU)
Department of Psychology, Carnegie Mellon University
Pittsburgh, PA 15213 USA

Abstract

The Stroop effect has been studied for more than sixty years, and yet it still defies a complete theoretical account. The model NJAMOS offers a new theoretical account that integrates several explanations of the Stroop phenomenon into a hybrid model. NJAMOS is built within the ACT-R cognitive architecture (Anderson & Lebiere, 1998). Besides fitting a variety of experimental results, NJAMOS offers the potential to capture strategic variation in what is typically considered a low-level attentional phenomenon.

Introduction

The Stroop effect has been studied for more than sixty years (Stroop, 1935), and yet it still defies a complete theoretical account. One explanation for the apparent lack of progress is that so much empirical research has been conducted using this basic paradigm that what we now call the "Stroop effect" is actually a compendium of results derived from a multitude of manipulations applied to a family of Stroop-like tasks! The current article focuses on a select set of Stroop results in order to introduce the model NJAMOS. NJAMOS offers a new theoretical account that integrates several explanations of the Stroop phenomenon into a hybrid model. Specifically, NJAMOS performs competitive, parallel retrieval of information within a goal-based, sequential cognitive processor. NJAMOS is built within the ACT-R cognitive architecture (Anderson & Lebiere, 1998), so it applies a general, pre-specified set of learning and performance mechanisms to the particulars of the Stroop paradigm. Moreover, NJAMOS is unique among models of ("low level") attentional phenomena in that it allows for ("high level") strategic variability.

The organization of the paper is as follows. First a description of the Stroop phenomenon is presented. Then, major theoretical features of other computational models are reviewed. Next, the NJAMOS model is described and fit to a selection of relevant data.

The Basic Phenomenon

The Stroop effect offers a window onto the processes of selective attention in that stimuli with two prominent dimensions are presented in a task where one dimension must be processed and the other ignored. Typically, the stimuli are words, and the two dimensions are the form of the word and the color of the ink in which it is written. The task, then, is either to name the ink color or to read the word. The basic Stroop manipulation varies the relationship between the meaning of the word and the color of the ink to be *congruent* (e.g., the word "red" printed in red ink), *conflicting* (e.g., the word "blue" printed in red ink), or *neutral* (e.g., the word "dog" or a string of "X"s printed in red ink). A robust result emerges: for color naming, there is interference in the conflicting case and (usually) facilitation in the congruent case, but for word reading, there is no (or very little) effect of the congruency of this relationship.

Figure 1 shows a typical data set (along with the NJAMOS predictions to be discussed later). The interference and facilitation in color naming can be seen by the shifts in the color-naming curve as a function of congruency. The lack of such effects for word reading are shown by the relatively flat line for this condition. These results suggest an asymmetry in selective attention, namely, that subjects are strongly influenced by the word when naming the ink color but that they can ignore the ink color when reading.

Theoretical Accounts of the Stroop Effect

Two different views of the Stroop effect cover much of the theoretical work in this area. The "horse-race" view highlights the overall difference in speed of processing for words versus colors (See Figure 1, separation of the two curves) and assumes a response bottleneck. This view implies that the pattern of interference depends on the relative arrival of word versus color information to the response stage: whichever kind of information arrives first will produce interference for the other. Because word reading is, on average, faster than color naming, this view predicts the asymmetry of words interfering with colors but not vice versa.

The other view of the Stroop effect highlights the different levels of automaticity people have acquired for processing the two stimulus dimensions. Because word reading is so highly practiced among typical Stroop experiment subjects, it is more automatic than color naming. This greater automaticity implies that reading requires fewer attentional resources and hence interferes more easily with color naming.

The key similarity between the two views is that they both emphasize parallel processing of the two stimulus dimensions. Not surprisingly, then, the dominant computational accounts of Stroop phenomena have been implemented within connectionist models. The key difference between the two views is whether relative speed or automaticity is considered the main

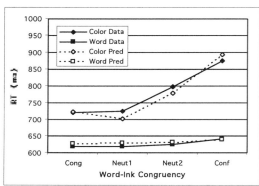

Figure 1. Reaction times for standard Stroop experiment. "Neut1" refers to a string of "X"s in colored ink for color naming and a word printed in black ink for word reading; "neut2" refers to a non-color word in colored ink for color naming.

determiner of interference effects. Note that manipulations of stimulus-onset-asynchrony (SOA) alter the timing of processing predicted to be important under the horse-race view, and manipulations of practice can alter the automaticity of processing that is predicted to be important under the automaticity view. Thus, experiments that employ these manipulations are crucial for evaluating specific theoretical and computational accounts of Stroop phenomena.

Existing Computational Models

Three existing computational models will be discussed. Two of these are connectionist models (Cohen, Dunbar, & McClelland, 1990; Phaf, van der Heijden, & Hudson, 1990), and the other is built as a production system (Roelofs, 2000). The Cohen et al. (1990) model was designed to capture an automaticity account of Stroop. It has input nodes that connect to hidden-layer nodes which connect to response nodes via either a word-reading or color-naming pathway. To represent the greater automaticity of reading, stronger weights are given along the word-reading pathway, making reading less sensitive to the congruency relationship between feature inputs. The Phaf et al. (1990) model was built as the Stroop extension to a general model of selective visual attention. This model's network architecture differs for word reading and color naming in that there are direct input-output connections for word reading only. This removes intermediate (hidden layer) processing for word reading which reduces the potential for semantically based interference in that task.

The Roelofs (2000) model of Stroop phenomena is built as an extension to the WEAVER++ model of word production (Levelt, Roelofs, & Meyer, 1999). As such, this Stroop model specifies separate processing stages for lemma retrieval, word-form encoding, etc. Like the Phaf et al. model, it builds in a word-reading advantage by requiring fewer processing steps, hence enabling different sized congruency effects across the two tasks.

These Models' Fits to Data

These three models all account for the basic results in Figure 1, but how do they fare in predicting other important Stroop results? As mentioned above, one critical Stroop manipulation varies SOA. Glaser and Glaser's (1982) Experiment 1 did this by presenting the two stimulus dimensions spatially separated so that the onset of word and color information could be lagged. SOAs were varied from –400ms to +400ms, where negative SOA means preexposure of the irrelevant information. Figure 2a presents these data.

All three models have simulated these data to varying degrees of success. They all predict the standard Stroop result at 0 SOA, and they all show a reduced Stroop effect for color naming at positive SOAs that is consistent with the data. There are several areas of misfit, however. Both PDP models show a small but notable congruency effect for word reading at negative SOAs, even though this is not present in the data. In addition, the Cohen et al. model predicts that, in color naming, the congruency effect will be largest at negative SOAs, when it is actually reduced here relative to 0 SOA. The Roelofs model has neither of these problems but fails to capture the gradual increase in interference for color naming from –400 to 0 SOA.

The other critical manipulation mentioned above is degree of practice. MacLeod and Dunbar (1988) devised a clever variant of the Stroop task in which they presented stimuli with dimensions shape and color and asked participants to either name the shape or the color. So that congruency of the shape-color relationship could be varied, the shapes came from a fixed set of unfamiliar shapes, and participants were trained to name each shape with a specific color word (e.g., the irregular hexagon is named "red"). Manipulating practice involved giving participants 20 sessions of shape training and measuring their Stroop performance along the way. Figure 3a presents these data.

The Cohen et al. model captures the early (training session 1) pattern of colors interfering with shape naming and not vice versa as well as the late (session 20) pattern of shapes interfering with color naming and hardly vice versa. This reversal is accomplished by the model's weight-learning mechanism that gradually strengthens the shape-naming pathway. An interesting transition point in the data (session 5) shows considerable interference for both tasks. However, the model makes its transition by predicting no interference in either task at this point.

Regarding practice effects, the Phaf et al. and Roelofs models are essentially silent. In both, the word-reading advantage is implemented as an qualitative change (a "short cut" for word-reading), and there is no specific learning mechanism presented.

Summary of Existing Models

To be competitive, any computational model of Stroop effects must demonstrate some added value.

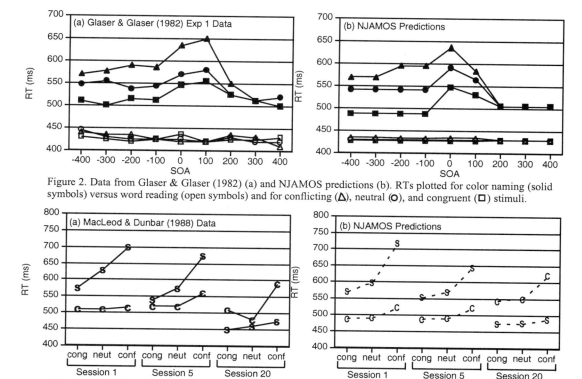

Figure 2. Data from Glaser & Glaser (1982) (a) and NJAMOS predictions (b). RTs plotted for color naming (solid symbols) versus word reading (open symbols) and for conflicting (△), neutral (○), and congruent (□) stimuli.

Figure 3. Data from MacLeod & Dunbar (1988) (panel a) and NJAMOS predictions (panel b). In each panel, RTs for shape naming (S) and color naming (C) are plotted separately across congruency and training manipulations.

What do each of these models offer? The Cohen et al. model offers the best coverage of Stroop-related data at present and does so with very simple, natural connectionist mechanisms for strengthening connections and gating activation along the two pathways. This trades off against the model's acknowledged exclusion of other processes (e.g., habituation, strategy choice, etc) that could help address its known areas of misfit.

The Phaf et al. model and the Roelofs model both offer an account of Stroop phenomena within a more general model of a related task. These models demonstrate how processes that play a central role in another task can help explain certain Stroop effects. However, this breadth tends to dilute the models' coverage of the Stroop literature per se.

A Hybrid Model, NJAMOS

There are several sources of added value in NJAMOS. First, it is built within the ACT-R cognitive architecture (Anderson & Lebiere, 1998), so it applies a general, pre-specified set of learning and performance mechanisms to the particulars of the Stroop paradigm. As such, it has many of the benefits of a general approach in that the mechanisms that drive its

predictions have been shown to produce accurate predictions for a variety of other tasks. This general-mechanisms approach also offers guidance and constraint in developing the specific task model beyond what the empirical data on that task can provide, i.e., the model must be built to fit the relevant data *within* a given, pre-specified structure (cf. Newell, 1990).

Second, building a specific task model within a cognitive architecture such as ACT-R still allows (and arguably facilitates) a focus on capturing as many experimental results associated with that particular task as possible. Indeed, with the architecture taken as given, model development involves specifying the knowledge used in performing the current task, some of which may come from prior experience and some of which may come from exposure to the task itself. Third, NJAMOS is unique among models of ("low level") attentional phenomena in that it allows for ("high level") strategic variability. Evidence suggests that participants can (and do) apply different strategies when performing the Stroop task (Chen & Johnson, 1991; Logan, Zbrodoff, & Williamson, 1984). This strategic variation may be considered a source of qualitative differences. Note that NJAMOS can also produce quantitative differences in performance by varying the ACT-R parameter associated with individual differences in working memory capacity (Lovett, Daily, & Reder, 2000).

NJAMOS Model Overview

NJAMOS specifies the knowledge relevant for performing Stroop-like tasks. In ACT-R, this is comprised by a set of production rules and a network of declarative chunks. Each production rule takes the form "IF <conditions> THEN <actions>" and has an associated measure of utility. A production rule's utility is learned through past experiences; it provides an index of how effective the production rule has been. In ACT-R, when more than one production rule's conditions are met, these rules compete on the basis of their utility values. The production rule with the highest utility (after some noise is added) is applied, and its actions are executed. In practice, this means that the system can learn to choose (and prefer) more effective strategies.

A declarative chunk is represented as a template with slots for related information. At the sub-symbolic level, each chunk has a base-level activation representing its overall accessibility. A network of chunks is specified by directed, pairwise connections, each with a strength of association. These strengths influence how strongly one chunk (in the current focus of attention) cues the availability of another chunk. The ACT-R equation for total activation of chunk i is

$$A_i = B_i + SW_jS_{ji}$$

where B_i is the base-level activation of chunk i, W_j is the amount of attention focused on chunk j, and S_{ji} is the strength of association from chunk j to i. This quantity then translates into the chunk's likelihood of being retrieved and latency to retrieval. The latency measure is more relevant in NJAMOS; it follows the function $L_i = Fe^{-A_i}$ where F is a latency-scale factor.

Some specific examples of the knowledge units specified in NJAMOS (and presented in English for readability) are as follows:

IF the goal involves a color-naming task, and the stimulus color has been encoded, THEN retrieve the associated color concept.

IF the goal involves processing a stimulus [generic goal] and the stimulus has word-like qualities, THEN retrieve the associated word concept.

Color-association-chunk1
  Stimulus: ∕
  Feature: color
  Concept: black

Current-goal
  Stimulus-word: "green"
  Stimulus-color: ∕
  Task: color

The first two examples above are production rules that would initiate processing of the color and word dimensions of the stimulus, respectively. The third example is a declarative chunk representing information about the color black. The last example is a specification of a goal chunk for the color-naming task after the stimulus has been perceived but before any color concept has been retrieved (either by processing the word or the color). In ACT-R, processing is in large part driven by the current goal. The goal is represented like other declarative chunks but it is considered to be the current focus of attention. A fixed, limited amount of source activation (W in ACT-R) is shared among the different slots of the current goal (W_j for each slot). This share of source activation is spread to connected chunks (proportionally to the strength of the connection) and added to the receiving chunk's base-level activation to comprise that chunk's total activation.

Given this specification of knowledge and ACT-R's fixed mechanisms, two important features of NJAMOS's performance follow. First, production rule choice favors word reading (even when the task is color naming). This is because the word-processing production (see above) is general enough that it applies whenever there is a word-like stimulus and because its utility value is taken to be much higher than that for color naming. (The former feature is taken to represent the extensive practice of reading such that words are processed regardless of the current goal; the latter comes from ACT-R's utility-learning mechanism given this extensive practice.[1]) Production-rule choice provides NJAMOS with a degree of sequentiality as each production rule in this model tends to focus on a single dimension (word or color). This also provides NJAMOS with strategic variability: processing of the word may either precede or follow processing of the color. Either way, a "check" production works to verify that the correct dimension was processed before enabling a response.

Parallel processing plays a role in producing the second important feature of NJAMOS performance, namely, that both dimensions of the stimulus influence the retrieval of declarative chunks. This is because all of the slots in the current goal provide contextual cues to influence the total activation of to-be-retrieved chunks (see total activation equation). Some of these slots represent the stimulus features (word *and* color); others may represent a concept retrieved during previous processing (e.g., if the word were partially processed when the word-processing production won over a color-processing production, then the concept of the word would provide another cue when retrieving the color of the ink). Recall that these contextual effects are proportional to the strengths of association between the relevant chunks. In NJAMOS, pairs of chunks that involve the same color concept (e.g., a color-association

---

[1] Note that the model's performance does not require that color naming be constrained by a specific goal. As long as word reading has a higher utility, both word-reading and color-naming productions could fire under a generic goal.

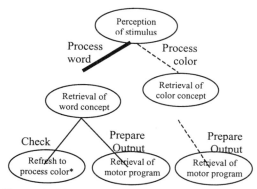

Figure 4. Flow of control in NJAMOS for color naming with standard stimuli. Lines represent production rules (note choices), and ovals represent parallel retrievals that modify the current focus of attention. From the bottom left oval (*), flow continues along the dashed path.

chunk for blue and a word-association chunk for blue) are given positive strengths of association, and chunks that involve different color concepts have negative strengths of association. These positive and negative strengths contribute to the facilitation and interference effects. NJAMOS produces larger facilitation and interference effects in color naming (see Figure 1) predominantly because (a) color-association chunks are given a lower base-level activation which, in the nonlinear latency equation (see above), makes them not only slower overall but more sensitive to contextual cueing and (b) the concept of the word will often have been retrieved into the goal before retrieving the color (but not vice versa), magnifying the contextual effect of the word dimension of the stimulus. Figure 4 presents a sketch of the flow of control in NJAMOS, summarizing these relationships and indicating other examples of production-rule choice and parallel chunk retrievals.

Fitting NJAMOS to the Data

This section describes how NJAMOS was fit to five separate experiments comprising a total of 92 data points (including Figure 1). For ease in estimating a set of best-fitting parameters, a mathematical description of NJAMOS was used. The same parameter settings were used to predict performance across all five experiments[2] with the following exceptions. For each experiment two parameters were varied. One of these is the latency-scale factor F (see latency equation above), and the

---

[2] Parameters taken as fixed but whose values departed from default include base-level activation for word-association chunks (set at 2) and for color-association chunks (set at 0), S_{ji}'s between same-color chunks (set at 1.5), between different-color chunks (set at −1.5), between same-task chunks (set at 0.6), & between different-task chunks (set at 0).

other was a latency intercept. These parameters appeared necessary to capture the experiment-to-experiment variation in latencies that appear even under very similar manipulations and experimental designs (e.g., compare RTs in Figures 1 and 5). In a couple cases, an additional single parameter was varied when relevant to a particular experiment, and those cases will be discussed below. To preview the quality of the NJAMOS fit, all 92 data points were fit by varying a total of 12 parameters for a R^2 of .95 and MSE of 1114. In essence, the goal was to test whether NJAMOS can produce reasonable accounts of these experiments without very much parameter varying.

Dunbar & MacLeod (1984)

Figure 5 shows the data and NJAMOS predictions for Dunbar and MacLeod's experiment (1984, p. 62). The design is similar to that presented in Figure 1, with the neutral condition corresponding to "Neut1." Both the data and model show the standard Stroop results.

Glaser & Glaser (1982)

Figure 2b shows the predictions of NJAMOS for the Glaser and Glaser (1982) experiment described above. Unlike previous models, NJAMOS appears to capture (at least qualitatively) three effects in the data: (1) no congruency effect for word reading at any SOA, (2) increase in overall latency for color naming as SOA goes from −400 to 0, and (3) increase and then decrease in interference effects from −400 to 0 to + 400 SOA. Much of this match to the data is driven by the model's tendency to choose word reading first, even on color naming trials. Note, however, that the size of the interference effect is not monotonically increasing from −400 to 0 as it is in the data and the facilitation effect in color naming is overpredicted. Under the parameter-fitting constraints applied here, this is not too surprising. The fit can be improved by allowing more parameters to vary (e.g., modifying one or two S_{ji} values has an impact).

MacLeod & Dunbar (1988)

Figure 3b presents the NJAMOS predictions for Dunbar and MacLeod's (1988) experiment. Note that this is a case where an additional parameter was required by the design of the experiment, namely, the initial base-level activation for the shape-name-association chunks. From there, ACT-R's learning mechanism naturally increased this base-level activation as the model underwent training by getting additional practice retrievals of the shape-name-association chunks. This makes the shape chunks less susceptible to context effects. Also, NJAMOS can learn to adjust its strategy of trying to name the color first (regardless of task) as the two competing (shape and color-processing) productions adjust their utilities. This changes the degree to which color information is present in the goal to add to the

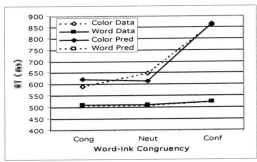

Figure 5. Dunbar & MacLeod (1984) data and model.

facilitating/interfering effect. In this model fit, procedural learning played a relatively small role.

NJAMOS shows three main results in this experiment: (1) at session 1, there is more interference and facilitation in shape naming than in color naming, (2) at session 5, there is some facilitation and interference in both tasks, and at session 20, there is more facilitation and interference in color naming than shape naming. Yet, the data show an increase in the interference effect for color naming between sessions 1 and 5 that is hardly present in the predictions. Also, the data show almost no interference of shapes on color naming in session 1 (5ms), whereas the model shows more (30ms). It is possible that adjusting the production parameters would address both of these issues, but for current purposes the goal was to find a reasonable model fit with a small number of free parameters.

Cohen et al. (1992)

Table 1 presents Stroop data from schizophrenic patients and matched controls along with NJAMOS predictions. The main result is a larger interference effect (for color naming) among the patients. While schizophrenia is a very complex condition, it is associated with a deficit in working memory. To capture this NJAMOS simply uses an adjusted W parameter. This was the extra parameter varied to fit these data. As the table shows, reducing W produces the effect as well as raising RTs among the patients.

Table 1. Data and model fit to schizophrenic data

	Neut-Word	Neut-Color	Conf-Color
Patient data	530	797	1467
Control data	420	603	1037
Patient pred	456	764	1345
Control pred	440	661	1137

Conclusions

The above model fits demonstrate that NJAMOS can fit a variety of Stroop results, when constrained by the ACT-R architecture and by limited free parameters. What does this mean for the value of the model? In the case of Stroop, the proof of a model comes from many sources: parsimony, generality, and coverage of many

results. NJAMOS aspires for all these. Because of the breadth of Stroop results, however, any model will likely focus on a subset. MacLeod's (1991) review lists 18 key results that may serve as a core, but even then, models can differ in how directly they address these various results. The best course may be to use Stroop models as a theoretical tool for understanding not only how well but *why* a certain result is or is not captured.

References

Anderson, J. R., & Lebiere, C. (1998). *The Atomic Components of Thought.* Mahwah, NJ: Erlbaum.

Chen, J., & Johnson, M. (1991). The Stroop congruency effect is more observable under a speed strategy than an accuracy strategy. *Perc. & Motor Skills, 73,* 67-76.

Cohen, J. D., Dunbar, K., & McClelland, J. L. (1990). On the control of automatic processes: A parallel distributed processing account of the Stroop effect. *Psychological Review, 97,* 332-361.

Cohen, J. D., Servan-Schreiber, D., & McClelland, J. (1992). A parallel distributed processing approach to automaticity. *Am J of Psych,* 239-269.

Dunbar, K., & MacLeod, C. M. (1984). A horse race of a different color: Stroop interference patterns with transformed words. *JEP: HPP, 10,* 622-639.

Glaser, M. O., & Glaser, W. R. (1982). Time course analysis of the Stroop phenomenon. *JEP:HPP, 8,* 875-894.

Levelt, W. J. M., Roelofs, A., Meyer, A. S. (1999). A theory of lexical access in speech production. *Behavioral & Brain Science, 22,* 1-75.

Logan, G. D., Zbrodoff, N. J., Williamson, J. (1984). Strategies in the color-word Stroop task. *Bulletin of the Psychonomic Society , 22,* 135-138.

Lovett, M. C., Daily, L. Z., & Reder, L. M. (2000). A source activation theory of working memory. *Cognitive Systems Research, 1,* 99-118.

MacLeod, C. M. (1991). Half a century of research on the Stroop effect: An integrative review. *Psychological Bulletin, 109,* 163-203.

MacLeod, C. M., & Dunbar, K. (1988). Training and Stroop-like interference: Evidence for a continuum of automaticity. *Journal of Experimental Psychology: Learning, Memory, and Cognition, 14,* 126-135.

Newell, A. (1990). *Unified Theories of Cognition.* Cambridge, MA: Harvard University Press.

Phaf, R. H., van der Heijden, A. H. C., & Hudson, P. T. W. (1990). SLAM: A connectionist model for attention in visual selection tasks. *Cognitive Psychology, 22,* 273-341.

Roelofs, A. (2000). Control of language: A computational account of the Stroop asymmetry. *Proc. of the Third Int'l Conf on Cognitive Modeling.* Veenendaal, The Netherlands: Universal Press.

Stroop, J. R. (1935). Studies of interference in serial verbal reactions. *Journal of Experimental Psychology, 18,* 643-662.

Learning of Joint Visual Attention by Reinforcement Learning

Goh Matsuda

Graduate School of Arts and Sciences, The University of Tokyo
3-8-1 Komaba, Meguro-ku, Tokyo, 153-8902 Japan

Takashi Omori

Graduate School of Engineering, Hokkaido University
Kita-ku, Kita 13 Jou Nishi 8 Cho, Sapporo, 060-8628 Japan

Abstract

In this paper, we propose a neural network model of joint visual attention learning that plays an important role in infant development, and we discuss previous studies of experimental psychology on joint visual attention based on simulation results using the model. We assumed an imaginary experiment to develop the model. A mother and an infant are sitting face to face with a table between them. Some objects familiar to the infant are placed on the table, and toys operated by remote control are put outside of the infant's view. The infant is given a reward of seeing something interesting only when the infant follows the mother's gaze after eye contact. We constructed the model of this experiment with a reinforcement learning algorithm, and simulated the experiment on a computer. As a result, it was revealed that the infant could learn a series of joint-visual-attention-like actions by receiving rewards from an environment, although it initially has little knowledge of the environment. This result suggests that infants can acquire joint visual attention without comprehension of the nature of joint attention, i.e., "I'm looking at the same thing that others are looking at."

Introduction

Modeling the development of infant intelligence is one of the strategies for understanding human intelligence. We focus on development in infancy from the viewpoint of engineering. Neonatal babies have little knowledge of the environment, nevertheless they acquire new knowledge and behavior suitable for the environment step by step in their developmental stage. Although the whole brain system of adults is very complicated, we believe that we can create a model of intelligence relatively easily by pursuing those developmental steps one by one. In this study, we focus on joint visual attention as one of those developmental processes.

In an engineering sense, joint attention can be defined as the sharing of attention with others, and joint visual attention is defined as looking at what others are looking at. Although this definition may cause some objections, we adopt it in this paper.

The detailed study of joint visual attention began with Scaife and Bruner's work (1975). They observed that a child in early and middle infancy follows an adult's gaze, and stated that this behavior is an important factor in early development. However, it is not yet clear how we acquire joint visual attention. There are two theories, nature and nurture, at present (Baron-Cohen, 1995; Butterworth & Jarrett, 1991; Corkum & Moore, 1995).

In this paper, we propose an engineering model of joint visual attention learning by conditioning with signals from the environment, and examine this behavior by computer simulation. Based on the results, we discuss the requirements of fundamental parts that are necessary for such learning.

Behavior Acquisition by Reinforcement Learning

Imaginary Experiment

We contrived the following imaginary experiment for our study based on the behavioral experiment of Corkum and Moore (1995). A mother and an infant are sitting face to face with a table between them. Some objects familiar to the infant are placed on the table. In the early stage of learning, the infant randomly directs its attention to the objects including the mother's face. The mother, however, is always gazing at the infant's eyes. Toys are set outside of the infant's view, and the observer can operate them by remote control (Figure 1). When the infant looks at the mother's face and they make eye contact, the mother moves her eyes to gaze toward any one of the toys. Furthermore, when the infant follows the direction of her gaze, the observer operates the toy, arousing pleasure in the infant's mind. In other words, the infant can obtain a reward of seeing something interesting only when it perform the two consecutive actions of looking at the mother's face and following her gaze.

Temporal Difference Learning

In this study, we used the temporal difference (TD) method (Sutton & Barto, 1998) for the learning of joint visual attention. TD learning is an algorithm that learns the value function $V(s_t)$ of each state s_t based on a reward r that is given later from the environment. An agent learns behavior strategy so that the value function may increase ($0 < \gamma < 1$).

Infant's view

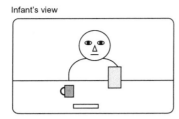

Bird's-eye view

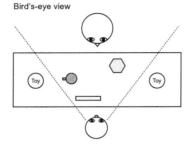

Figure 1: Imaginary experiment on infants

$$V(s_t) = E[r_t + \gamma r_{t+1} + \gamma^2 r_{t+2} + \gamma^3 r_{t+3} + \cdots] \quad (1)$$

The actor-critic architecture is a learning model that consists of two units called the critic and the actor (Sutton & Barto, 1998). The critic learns the value function, and the actor learns the behavior strategy. These two units are mutually related and learn simultaneously with the same criterion .

In the early stages of learning, an action of the agent is chosen at random. The critic learns the expected rewards that are obtained as a consequence of performing the action. TD error ϵ_{TD} generated at the moment is also used for the learning of the behavior strategy.

$$\epsilon_{TD}(s_t) = r_t + \gamma V(s_{t+1}) - V(s_t) \quad (2)$$

Setting of State Space

In the experiment, we designed three environmental states, s_1, s_2, and s_{goal}, that the infant must recognize in the reinforcement learning process (Figure 2). In state s_1, the infant decides which of the objects in its view to look at, and in s_2, it perceives the mother's gaze direction and then moves its gaze. If the infant looks in the same direction as its mother, the state changes to s_{goal} where the infant obtains a reward of seeing something interesting. In short, only when the infant performs a sequence of actions that causes the state transitions of $s_1 \to s_2 \to s_{goal}$, it can obtain a reward.

However, this state transition is ideal. Preparing the necessary states for learning in the agent before-

hand means ingraining an innate behavior strategy to the infant. The infant must acquire the states other than the goal through experience. What is given innately to the infant should be the ability to learn but not the result of learning. From this concept, we designed the following experiment.

Initially, an infant is given only the two states of s_{goal} and s_0. The latter includes states s_1 and s_2 in the ideal case. In the learning process, the infant must recognize that it cannot acquire correct actions with the behavior strategy using only s_0, and must find a new state transition by dividing s_0 into s_1 and s_2.

A computer simulation is conducted to evaluate the effect of the state dividing strategy on the acquisition of joint visual attention. We applied the adaptive basis function division (ABD) algorithm for the state space division (Samejima & Omori, 1999).

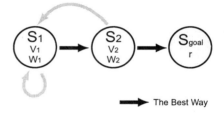

Figure 2: The ideal state transition

State and Behavior Acquisition by State Division

Distinction of State

The current number of states is represented as k. The agent recognizes a current state s_t based on input x_t from the environment. We use a Gaussian radial basis function (GRBF) $a_i(i = 1, \cdots, k)$ which has a center c_i and a variance matrix M_i.

$$a_i(x_t) = exp(-\frac{1}{2}(x_t - c_i)M_i(x_t - c_i)^T) \quad (3)$$

The GRBF represents the distribution probability within the input signal space. One GRBF corresponds to one state in our model. The state which has the largest value among a_i is determined to be the current state.

$$max = argmax_i(a_i) \quad (4)$$
$$s_t = s_{max} \quad (5)$$

Choice of Action

Each state s_i has a value $V(s_i)$ and a connection weight $W(s_i)$ that governs the action choice probability. The action choice probability p_t in the current state s_t is calculated by the following equation.

$$\hat{p}_t = exp(W_t x_t{}^T) \qquad (6)$$

$$p_t = \frac{\hat{p}_t}{\sum_n \hat{p}_t} \qquad (7)$$

Each element of p_t represents a choice probability of the corresponding action. The final output action y_t is decided by p_t.

Neural Network for Action Choice

The neural network to choose an action in the actor consists of input and output layers. Both have 8 cells, and a connection weight $W_i (i = 1, ..., k)$ connects them (Figure 3). Each cell takes the value of 0 and 1. In the initial state of learning, we prepare two states, s_0 and s_{goal}. Therefore, all the action is governed by the single connection W_0 in s_0.

In the input layer, objects that the infant is perceiving in its view are assigned to the upper 4 bits, and the direction to which the mother changes her gaze is assigned to the lower 4 bits. However, the upper and lower 4 bits do not fire simultaneously. When a signal is input to the upper 4 bits, all of the lower 4 bits become zero, since the infant cannot percieve the direction of the mother's gaze when it is looking at objects other than her face. Only when the infant gazes at its mother's face, the direction of the mother's gaze is input to the lower 4 bits the next time; then, all of the upper 4 bits become zero. If the infant performs other actions, objects in its view are input to the upper 4 bits.

In the output layer, the objects that the infant will gaze at are output from the upper 4 bits, and the direction to which the infant will shift its gaze is output from the lower 4 bits. In order to acquire a sequence of joint visual attention correctly, the infant must recognize that the situation for which the signal is input to the upper 4 bits and that for which the signal is input to the lower 4 bits are different states. Then the infant must divide the initial state s_0 into two states corresponding to s_1 and s_2 in Figure 2, and prepare behavior strategies W_1 and W_2 for each state.

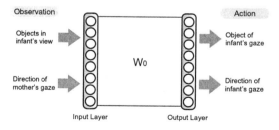

Figure 3: Neural network for action choice

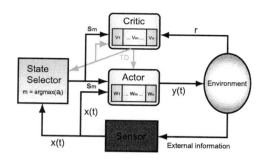

Figure 4: Modified ABD for the computer simulation

Learning Equations

$\Delta V(s_t)$ and $\Delta W(s_t)$ represent update differences of $V(s_t)$ and $W(s_t)$, respectively, and are defined by the following equations.

$$\Delta V(s_t) = \alpha \ \epsilon_{TD}(s_t) \qquad (8)$$

$$\Delta W(s_t) = \beta \ \epsilon_{TD}(s_t) \ y_t{}^T x_t \qquad (9)$$

Both α and β are learning coefficients. Figure 4 illustrates signal flow in the ABD algorithm.

State Division: When to Divide

For the decision of division, a criterion is calculated in each basis function. The basic idea of the division criterion is as follows. After the value function is updated and the action probability function is converged, and when there remains large TD error ϵ_{TD} in an area of input space, the basis function in that area should be divided to form a finer state space; that is, when the average TD error of each function is close to zero and its variance remains large, the basis function is divided. The agent evaluates the following equations in each basis function a_i, and divide the basis function when the criterion for division L_i is larger than the constant threshold θ. $\gamma_c \ (\gamma_c < 1)$ is the rate of decrease.

$$f_i(t+1) = \gamma_c f_i(t) + (1 - \gamma_c)\epsilon_{TD} \qquad (10)$$

$$g_i(t+1) = \gamma_c g_i(t) + (1 - \gamma_c)\epsilon_{TD}^2 \qquad (11)$$

$$L_i(t) = g_i(t)/f_i(t) \qquad (12)$$

Way of Division: How to Divide

The agent decides the direction of division by evaluating the distribution direction of the error-occurring locations from the center of the basis function (Figure 5). The mean of vector e_i toward the error-occurring direction is calculated in each basis function a_i.

$$e_i(t+1) = \gamma_c e_i(t) + (1 - \gamma_c)\frac{x(t) - c_i}{|x(t) - c_i|}\epsilon_{TD} \qquad (13)$$

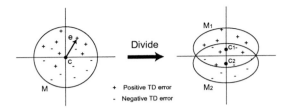
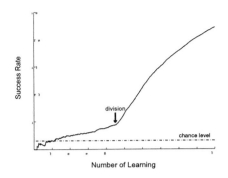

Figure 5: State division using ABD algorithm

The variance matrix M_i is divided according to the e_i direction. The equation for division is

$$M_{new} = P^{-1}\hat{Q}P \qquad (14)$$

$$P = \left[\begin{array}{cccc} \chi_1 & \chi_2 & \cdots & \chi_n \end{array}\right] \qquad (15)$$

$$\hat{Q} = \{q_{mn}\} = \left\{ \begin{array}{ll} \lambda_m + \eta \frac{e_i \chi_m}{|e_i||\chi_m|} & (m = n) \\ 0 & (m \neq n) \end{array} \right. \qquad (16)$$

$$c_{new} = c_i \pm \rho \frac{e}{|e|}. \qquad (17)$$

λ_j and $\chi_j (j = 1, \cdots, n)$ are the eigenvalue and eigenvector of matrix M_i, respectively. Both η and ρ are constants. We used the values $\eta = 1.0, \rho = 0.5$, and $V_{new} = V_{old}, W_{new} = W_{old}$.

Computer Simulation Results

Figure 6 shows the success rate of the joint-visual-attention-like behavior (the number of reward acquisitions / the number of actions). The success rate begins to increase immediately after the division. Figure 7 shows the changes of probabilities P_1 and P_2. P_1 indicates the probability that the infant looks at the mother's face selectively among the visible objects, and P_2 shows the probability that the infant follows the mother's gaze after making eye contact.

Before the state division, only the learning of gaze following progresses. After division, however, the probability of looking preferentially at the mother's face also increases, and the learning of gaze following progresses more rapidly. As a result, the infant could learn a series of joint-visual-attention-like behaviors, i.e., following the mother's gaze after looking at her face.

This result indicates that an infant who does not have sufficient behavior strategy can learn joint-visual-attention-like behavior by using input signals and receiving a small reward from the environment.

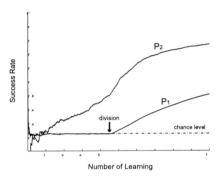

Figure 6: Success rate of joint-visual-attention-like behavior P_{goal}

Figure 7: Analysis of success rates P_1 and P_2

Discussion: What is Really Necessary?

Because the age at which the learning of joint visual attention become possible is at least 8 months (Corkum & Moore, 1995), we discuss the validity of our imaginary experiment for infants at this age.

Face Recognition

During the stage of looking at the mother's face selectively among the other objects, the minimum necessary cognitive ability is merely recognizing the mother's face. In our imaginary experiment, we assumed that the infant can recognize all objects in its view. However, even if the infant cannot recognize any object other than the mother's face, there is the possibility that it recognizes the significance of looking at her face as long as it can identify her face.

Can an infant really recognize its mother's face? Sherrod (1979) reported that infants of at least six months old tend to prefer real faces to those in pictures, and familiar faces over unfamiliar ones. That is, infants can distinguish human faces from other objects before six months of age. It is not revealed, however, whether infants' tendency to look at human faces preferentially is innate. Although it might be a reasonable result of evolution that young infants can distinguish the faces of humans who take care of them among the other objects, there still remains the possibility that rewards, such as the satisfaction of physical desire, cause the tendency to prefer human faces. Based on this discussion, although we cannot conclude whether face recognition is innate or acquired and there would remain a time lag to the actual manifestation of this ability, we can regard the learning of looking at the mother's face as an appropriate step of development in infancy.

At this point, one may object that we interpreted looking at the mother's face as meeting her gaze. Actually, the infant must gaze at her eyes to make eye contact, and they might have to learn this behavior. Our method for state space formation, however, can divide states into the required number even if the number of state transitions to the final reward is different from our initial design. For this reason, the difference in the number of states in each task does not affect the essence of this study.

Gaze Following

In the stage of following the mother's gaze, the infant needs the ability to perceive any direction vector from the mother's eye or head movements. Hood et al. (1998) revealed experimentally that an infant of 3 months old can perceive eye direction from digitized images of adult faces and shifts its attention. They proposed the existence of an eye direction detector (EDD) module (Baron-Cohen, 1995). Corkum & Moore (1995), in contrast, suggested that eye direction does not affect infant orienting until about 18 months of age. The former seems more plausible because Hood et al. used a briefly displayed digitized face to exclude unintentional information that may attracts the infant's attention.

On the other hand, Itakura (2000) concluded, from an experiment on human adults, infants (6 to 18 months), and chimpanzees, that all of them shift their attention most frequently when they see arrows. This result suggests that the ability to recognize direction vector depends upon a more primitive visual mechanism than EDD, for example, perception of an asymmetric figure.

In any case, it is certain that infants older than 6 months can extract direction vectors from visual cues. According to Itakura and Hood et al., it is difficult to conceive that the infant acquires this ability after birth. We therefore conclude here that this ability is innate, or at least acquired before joint visual attention learning.

Reward

In our imaginary experiment, we regarded the infant seeing a toy moving as a reward because infants tend to prefer looking at something novel. The infant was not given a reward when it looked at its mother's face in our experiment. However, if the infant has an innate rewarding system of feeling pleasure in looking at its mother's face, the learning of looking selectively at its mother's face would be accelerated. Such an innate rewarding system based on some kind of stimulus is necessary to enable reinforcement learning.

Conclusion

We suggested that an infant can learn early joint visual attention only if it has some primary cognitive abilities. In other words, infants can learn joint visual attention by a simple reward mechanism without comprehension of the nature of joint attention, i.e., "I am looking at what others are looking at." From this point of view, the learning of joint visual attention can be different from the joint attention that leads to the theory of mind afterward.

As for joint visual attention, this result suggests that three abilities, the detection of gaze direction as a visual sensor, reward system as an instinctive value system, and an algorithm such as the ABD method must be built into the brain as a basic learning mechanism before the learning can take place.

This model simulates one of the possible ideas on the system of human behavior development. Our experiment is insufficient to justify these mechanisms more definitively. The reinforcement learning we adopted in this study is a general learning model of acquiring the correct action for each state by trial and error. Moreover, our model can acquire the state needed according to the task requirement. Therefore this model can be applied to actual signals in the infant brain, although we used artificial signals in our simulation.

Finally, the fact that this model could acquire joint-visual-attention-like behavior indicates that joint-attention-like behavior in another modality can be acquired via a learning strategy in the same way of this model. Further study to examine this issue is needed.

References

Baron-Cohen, S. (1995). *Mindblindness: An Essay on Autism and Theory of Mind.* Cambridge, MA: MIT Press.

Butterworth, G. E. & Jarrett, N. L. M. (1991). What minds have in common space: Spatial mechanisms serving joint visual attention in infancy. *British Journal of Developmental Psychology, 9,* 55–72

Corkum, V. & Moore, C. (1995). Development of joint visual attention in infants. In C. Moore & P.

Dunham (Eds.), *Joint attention: Its origins and role in development.* (pp.61–83). Hillsdale, NJ: Erlbaum.

Hood, B. M., Willen, J. D., & Driver, J. (1998). Adult's eyes trigger shifts of visual attention in human infants. *Psychological Science, Vol.9, No.2,* 131–134.

Itakura, S. (2000). Mindreading: From the perspective of comparative cognitive development. *Intelligence and Complex System SIG, 122-5, Information Processing Society of Japan.* (pp. 25–30).

Samejima K. & Omori T. (1999). Adaptive internal state space formation by reinforcement learning for real-world agent. *Neural Networks, Vol.12, No.7-8,* 1143–1156.

Schaffer, M. & Bruner, J. S. (1975). The capacity for joint visual attention in the infant. *Nature, 253,* 265–266.

Sutton, R. S. & Barto, A, G. (1998). *Reinforcement Learning: An Introduction.* Cambridge, MA: MIT Press.

Validating a Tool for Simulating User Interaction

Jan Misker (jan@misker.nl)
Artificial Intelligence, University of Groningen,
Grote Kruisstraat 2/1, 9712 TS Groningen, The Netherlands
KPN Research,
Sint Paulusstraat 4, 2264 XZ Leidschendam, The Netherlands

Niels A. Taatgen (niels@ai.rug.nl)
Artificial Intelligence, University of Groningen
Grote Kruisstraat 2/1, 9712 TS Groningen, The Netherlands

Jans Aasman (J.Aasman@kpn.com)
KPN Research,
Sint Paulusstraat 4, 2264 XZ Leidschendam, The Netherlands
Industrial Design Engineering, University of Delft,
Jaffalaan 9, 2628 BX, Delft

Abstract

In this paper a tool will be presented that simulates human perception and motor behavior in interaction with graphical user interfaces in the Microsoft Windows environment. The simulated hand and eye tool can be used in combination with any cognitive architecture. In order to validate the simulated hand and eye an experiment has been conducted in which human subjects showed simple, low-level interaction behavior. Eye movements and finger presses were measured and recorded. This allowed for basic validation of the simulated hand and eye. Furthermore, based on the collected data, an adjustment of the EMMA theory is suggested. To demonstrate the full usage if the tool, ACT-R has been used to model basic skill acquisition in instructed interaction behavior.

Introduction

Much research has been done to describe human interaction with computer applications (HCI), as well as interaction with devices. Only recently this research has produced theories with a level of quantitative detail that allows for software implementations of these theories. These advances are also of interest to KPN Research[1], because one of the possible future results could be a tool that automatically tests user interfaces.

Requirements In order to research these possibilities, I did my M.Sc. research project at KPN Research. I was asked to design and implement a software tool that was required to (1) interact with any graphical user interface in the Microsoft Windows environment and (2) be usable in conjunction with common cognitive architectures. Furthermore; the tool should (3) produce realistic timing and accuracy information regarding the interaction.

For KPN Research, the main focus is on user interfaces of devices and appliances, for example, (mobile) telephones. Thus the user interfaces were regarded as interfaces of devices simulated or prototyped as MS Windows applications, not of computer applications. This means that humans would interact with them using their hands and fingers instead of a mouse, which should be reflected in the behavior of the tool.

Because the tool will simulate the hand and eye of humans, it is called the Simulated Hand and Eye, which is shortened to SHE.

Testing the tool To test the usefulness of this approach and give a proof-of-concept, another goal of the project was to build cognitive models in ACT-R that in combination with SHE interact with user interfaces based on explicit instructions.

Existing work In the literature several theories on human interaction with user interfaces can be identified, as well as some implementations of these theories. Of these, work done by Ritter et al. (2000) and Byrne (Byrne, in press) most closely resembles SHE.

Ritter already developed a simhand and simeye, although this tool currently does not interact with MS Windows. The general architecture of SHE has been adopted from his work (Ritter, Baxter, Jones & Young, 2000).

ACT-R/PM (Byrne, 2000; Byrne & Anderson, 1998) is also able to interact with user interfaces, however currently only to interfaces written in two Lisp variants[2]. The latter aims at simulating human computer

---

[1] KPN Research is the research department of the largest Dutch telecom company.

[2] It should be noted, that ACT-R/PM is designed to be usable with other interfaces as well, but because ACT-R/PM

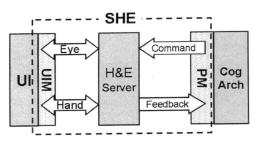

Figure 1: Overview of SHE.

interaction using a mouse, instead of human machine interaction using hands and fingers. Furthermore ACT-R/PM can only be used in conjunction with ACT-R, so users of Soar cannot benefit from this work.

Both of the efforts described above were very valuable in the design of SHE, but the requirements of the project demanded a more generally applicable tool.

Other valuable sources of information for this project were the Model Human Processor (Card, Moran & Newell, 1983), the EPIC architecture (Kieras & Meyer, 1997), the EMMA theory (Salvucci, 2000), the Driver model (Aasman, 1995), work done by Gray et al. (Gray, 2000; Gray & Altmann, in press) and the VisMap project (St. Amant & O. Riedl, in press).

The design of SHE

SHE will be a tool in between the user interface (UI) and the cognitive architecture. Figure 1 gives an overview of the overall design of the tool. This figure is an adapted version from the figure describing the Cognitive Modeling Interface Management System in Ritter et al. (2000). In the following paragraphs I will describe the technical issues and solutions in the design of SHE.

Knowledge Representation Level In the design of SHE, the level of knowledge representation is chosen at a high level. Visual information from the user interface is translated into objects like buttons, windows and textfields[3]. Each of these objects has a fixed set of attributes: id, type, text, position (absolute and relative to the current point of attention) and size.

---

primarily models human interaction with computer applications instead of devices, and time constraints did not permit to further investigate technical details of ACT-R/PM, it is not integrated with SHE.

[3] Actually, the type of the objects is the type it has in the MS Windows environment. As a result of this, a button in an application created with Visual Basic has another type than a button in an application created with Visual C++. It is of course conceivable to make a mapping from MS Windows types to some set of SHE types, but in the current version this is not done.

This relatively high level of knowledge representation was chosen because this was expected to be most useful for modeling interaction behavior. Also, this fits nicely with the level of representation available in the MS Windows environment.

An assumption underlying this level of knowledge representation is that the recognition of the user interface objects is easy and uniform for human subjects. This means that SHE cannot be used to model the problems in recognizing user interface objects, only humans that can easily identify buttons, labels, text and so forth can be modeled. This is not a major restriction, because most individuals that use devices can do this: people know what a button is.

Hand and eye The current implementation of SHE only has one hand with one finger, but SHE is designed to be easily extendible to two hands with five fingers each. SHE has one field of vision, divided into a point of gaze and a point of attention. The hand and eye are controlled through commands, discussed below.

All motor actions are assumed to first go through a preparation phase, which can be interrupted, before entering execution, which can not be interrupted. The duration of the various preparations and executions is extracted from various sources. The EMMA theory is used for eye movements (Salvucci, 2000). For the timing of the hand movements and actions, parameters were taken from EPIC and ACT-R/PM. However, these parameters did not suffice, mainly because ACT-R/PM is targeted to using a mouse for pointing, which is different from using hands and fingers for pointing. For these parameters, the experiment has also contributed, as described later.

Communication SHE communicates with the cognitive architecture through TCP/IP sockets. All modern programming languages have means to communicate using sockets, so using sockets for communication will allow for easy communication with any current and future cognitive architectures. Another advantage is that communication through sockets allows the cognitive architecture to run on a different machine in a network, which is an advantage in unstable situations or when the cognitive architecture is not implemented for the MS Windows platform.

Commands SHE responds to a set of commands that are used to set the point of attention and control the hand. Position arguments can be provided using absolute coordinates as well as relative coordinates. See Table 2 below for the most important commands.

There are also commands that control the simulated time and synchronization.

Table 2: Important SHE commands.

Command	Arguments	Usage
attend	a position or an id	Directs the point of attention (this may induce eye movements)
motorhand	move, moveto, click, press or release; and a position or id	Performs the specified action
motoreye	move, moveto; with a position or id	Moves the eyes directly, instead of using attention shifts

Table 3: Types of responses from SHE.

Type	Contents
visibles	The currently visible objects with their id, size, absolute position and position relative to the point of attention
object	Information on an object to which attention was directed: as above, but including type and text.
poa	The status of the point of attention: free, prep or busy.
hand	The status of the hand: free, prep or busy.

Feedback SHE gives feedback on various processes. This feedback is sent over the socket in a Lisp-like list structure. The most important types of feedback are listed in Table 3.

Simulated time SHE maintains an internal queue of events. Whenever a command is issued, SHE puts this command on the queue as an event. A set of processes reacts on the events on the queue with appropriate behavior.

For example, when a command is issued to move the hand, this is translated to a motor-hand-move-begin event, which when processed puts a motor-hand-move-prep-begin event on the queue. In turn this event will result in a motor-hand-move-prep-end event on the queue, with its time set to the time of the begin-event plus the duration of the preparation. Then a motor-hand-move-exec-begin event is put on the stack, and so forth. Of course events also trigger appropriate behavior (e.g. updating the point of attention or sending mouse-clicks to Microsoft Windows).

The progress of time is controlled by commands from the cognitive architecture. The reason for this, is that in most cases the common cognitive models need an amount of time for calculations that is several orders of magnitude greater than the time the processes they simulate are assumed to last in real time. However, SHE itself is quite fast and can operate user interfaces in real time.

It should be noted that SHE explicitly restricts the cognitive models in their control over the hand and eye. SHE controls the duration and accuracy of visual encoding, movements and other actions.

Programming language The final implementation of SHE was written in Microsoft Visual C++. This enables easy access to user interface elements in MS Windows. Also, C++ is an object-oriented programming language, which implies that it will be easy to reuse parts of the tool in new versions of the tool.

Because cognitive architectures communicate with SHE using sockets, the cognitive architecture can be written in any programming language on any platform, as long as it supports TCP/IP sockets.

Future enhancements

Currently, interaction works satisfactory for interfaces created in Visual Basic, Visual C++ and Java AWT, for other integrated development environments (IDE's) we experienced some limitations. These IDE's include Delphi (partially) and Java Swing. This issue could be resolved by implementing special interfaces with these interfaces or by using the VisMap tool (St. Amant & O. Riedl, in press). SHE is designed to be extensible regarding this aspect.

Another enhancement could be to add other modalities of interaction like audition, speech and tactile feedback.

The experiment

An experiment aimed at gathering human data has been conducted for two reasons. First of all, not all parameters of SHE could be extracted from the literature. So I used this experiment to collect basic eye movement and motor control data for simple interaction tasks. This data will be used to fine-tune the parameter settings of SHE.

A second reason to conduct the experiment was to collect data on tasks that included interactive behavior based on explicit instructions. In this case I was especially interested in the higher level dynamics between low-level interaction behavior and cognition at a higher level.

The experiment was conducted using 15 subjects who were asked to perform a series of tasks. All subjects were students of the Industrial Design Engineering Faculty of the Technical University of Delft, aged 19 through 24. During the experiment, the movements and fixations of both of their eyes were recorded, as well as their finger presses. With one of the subjects no measurements could be performed. In another case the touch-screen software stopped responding, resulting in a partially failed trial, the first two tasks could be measured completely, so only the third task was discarded.

Experimental setup

The equipment used in the experiment was a touch-screen display, a simulation of a programmable thermostat (see Figure 4) and an eye tracker consisting of two small cameras to measure the pupils, a set of infrared transmitters and an infrared detector to measure the position of the head and software to analyze and log the measurements.

The programmable thermostat was simulated and presented to the subjects on the touch-screen display. It was operated by pushing the buttons on the screen. In its standard way of operation, it showed the current day of the week, time, temperature and program mode[4].

The eye cameras and infrared detector were mounted on a helmet. Subjects reported that this did not bother them in their movements, at least for the duration of the experiment, which was 15 to 20 minutes.

This entire setup was located at the faculty of Industrial Design Engineering at the Technical University of Delft.

The tasks

Three different tasks were given to the subjects, each of them repeated 10 times in a row.

The first task required the subjects to push all buttons in the middle row, from left to right. The reason for presenting this very simple task was to gather measurements on low-level interaction behavior.

The second task was to adjust the target temperature of the thermostat. This required the subjects to push a few buttons and to look at the display to wait for feedback. It was expected that subjects would show some learning effects, observable in their timing.

The third task included an instruction on how to adjust the clock of the thermostat. In contrast to the other tasks, in the 10 trials of the third tasks there was a slight variation. Each trial the clock of the thermostat was set to a different day and time, and the subjects were instructed to set the clock to a different day and time on each trial. The procedure to set the clock did not change, of course. This task was expected to provide the most interesting data regarding learning of instructions.

Preliminary results

Data format The following data was collected in the experiment (1) position, time and duration of eye saccades and fixations, sampled at 250 Hz (i.e. 4 ms/sample) and (2) time and duration of button presses,

---

[4] The program mode is however not relevant for the experiment and no further reference to it will be made.

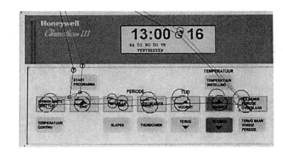

Figure 4: Sample of recorded eye movements.

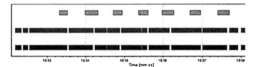

Figure 5: Sample of the combined measurements.

in milliseconds. For an example of the recorded eye movements, see Figure 4. Both sets of recordings are synchronized, thus the eye movements can be linked to the hand movements. This is shown in Figure 5, where the blocks in the upper row represent button presses and the blocks in the lower rows represent saccades of the left and right eye. The data still needs to be fully analyzed. Some preliminary results can, however, be addressed.

Possible EMMA enhancements A major result that might be derived from the collected data is a changed accuracy regarding the landing point of eye-saccades. In the EMMA theory used in SHE, the landing point of a saccade is assumed to follow a Gaussian distribution centered at the target of the saccade. However preliminary analysis of the data suggests a different distribution.

By examining the data, it becomes clear that indeed some saccades do not land at the intended position. Some saccades are very quickly followed by another saccade, which lands at a point nearby. This is predicted by the EMMA theory. However, the saccades that follow the inaccurate saccades are very rarely directed towards the previous origin of the saccade. This seems to indicate that undershoot happens more frequently than overshoot. One possible explanation could be that eyes do not "stop and return", they "pause and continue". This (micro)behavior seems reasonable, since it is conceivable that less energy is lost when "pausing" then when "stopping" the eyes, assuming that the eyes can fixate and process input when still moving with a (small) velocity.

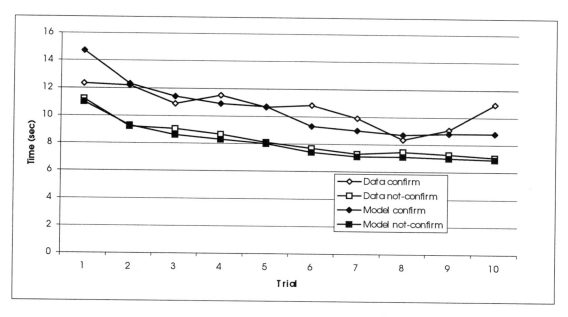

Figure 6: Data and model times for the first task.

In order to support this claim, further analysis is required. This analysis will be done by (1) selecting appropriate triplets of eye fixations in which the eye fixation in the middle has a small duration and the last fixation is spatially close to the middle fixation. Then calculate (2) the distance to the last fixation point and (3) the angle between the lines that (a) connect the first fixation-point and the second (inaccurate) fixation-point and (b) connect the second fixation-point and the final fixation-point. When it is indeed the case that undershoot happens more frequently than overshoot, this will be reflected in a higher frequency of angles in the range (-90°, 90°), possibly distributed following a Gaussian distribution with 0 at its center[5].

Models of interaction

To further test the tool, I have built various models of interaction in ACT-R, most of them to test certain specific details of SHE. The model of the first task fits the data, discussed below. The third task of the experiment is also partially modeled. Although not yet fully finished the models do show that it is relatively easy to make cognitive models that perform non-trivial tasks in interaction with fairly complex interfaces by using SHE.

---

[5] For this analysis it is necessary to assume that the last fixation is a correction to the short middle fixation. Therefore the middle fixation should have a very small duration, in order to assume that only the amount of visual input is processed that is needed to determine that the saccade was inaccurate.

One basic model All models were built on top of a basic ACT-R model. This basic model incorporates the use of instructions, based on the abstractions as introduced by Taatgen (1999, in press). This basic model contains all chunk-types, feedback-chunks and production rules necessary for interactive behavior.

The production rules operate on a set of standard instruction chunks that can be used to perform various basic interaction subtasks.

A model of the first task

The first task, in which subjects had to press the buttons in the center row, has been modeled successfully. The subjects showed two types of behavior and were divided in two groups accordingly. Subjects in the 'not-confirm' group (n = 10) pushed a button, looked at the next and pushed that one, repeated for all buttons. The subject in the 'confirm' group (n = 4) pushed a button and then looked at the display to look for a change, giving them feedback on whether the button was successfully pushed, after which they looked at the next button and continued.

Both groups were modeled using the same model that differed only in the way they handled confirmation of a button push.

Figure 6 shows the results. The time required for one trial was used as the measurement to fit.

Conclusions

The current implementation of SHE meets most of the requirements. It can be used to interact with most of the standard user interfaces in MS Windows, it can be operated in conjunction with common cognitive architectures and it simulates behavior comparable to human subjects interacting with user interfaces of devices. The latter can be further improved by further analyzing the data from the experiment and by using SHE for modeling more tasks.

Acknowledgements

The research presented here was made possible by support from KPN Research. The experiment was conducted in the laboratory for informational ergonomics at the faculty of Industrial Design Engineering at the University of Delft, with help from Theo Boersema, Kees Jorens and Arend Harteveld.

References

Aasman, J. (1995). *Modelling Driver Behaviour in Soar*. Doctoral Dissertation, Leidschendam, The Netherlands: KPN Research.

Anderson, J. R. & Lebiere, C. (1998). *The atomic components of thought*. Mahwah, NJ: Lawrence Erlbaum Associates.

Byrne, M. D., (in press). ACT-R/PM and menu selection: Applying a cognitive architecture to HCI. *International Journal of Human-Computer Studies*.

Byrne, M. D. (2000). The ACT-R/PM Project. *Simulating Human agents: Papers from the 2000 AAAI Fall Symposium* (pp. 1-3). Menlo Park, CA: AAAI Press.

Byrne, M. D. & Anderson, J. R. (1998). Perception and action. In J. R. Anderson & C. Lebiere (Eds.), *The Atomic Components of Thought*. Mahwah, NJ: Lawrence Erlbaum Associates.

Card, S. K., Moran, P. T. & Newell, A. (1983). *The Psychology of Human-Computer Interaction*. Hillsdale, NJ: Lawrence Erlbaum Associates.

Gray, W. D. (2000). The nature and processing of errors in interactive behavior. *Cognitive Science, 24*(2), 205-248.

Gray, W. D., & Altmann, E. M. (in press). Cognitive modeling and human-computer interaction. In W. Karwowski (Ed.), *International encyclopedia of ergonomics and human factors*. New York: Taylor & Francis, Ltd.

Kieras, D. E. & Meyer, D.E. (1997). An overview of the EPIC architecture for cognition and performance with application to human-computer interaction. *Human-Computer Interaction, 12*.

Ritter, F. E., Baxter, G. D., Jones, G., & Young, R. M. (2000). Cognitive models as users. *ACM Transactions on Computer-Human Interaction 7*(2).

Salvucci, D. D. (in press). An Integrated Model of Eye Movements and Visual Encoding. *Cognitive Systems Research*.

Salvucci, D. D. (2000). A model of eye movements and visual attention. In *Proceedings of the Third International Conference on Cognitive Modeling* (pp. 252-259). Veenendaal, The Netherlands: Universal Press.

St. Amant, R. & O. Riedl, M. (in press). A perception/action substrate for cognitive modeling in HCI. *International Journal of Human-Computer Studies*.

Taatgen, N. A. (1999). *Learning without limits: from problem solving toward a unified theory of learning*. Ph.D. Thesis, Department of Psychology, University of Groningen, The Netherlands.

Taatgen, N. A. (in press). A Model of Individual Differences in Learning Air Traffic Control. *Proceedings of the fourth International Conference on Cognitive Modeling*.

Extending Task Analytic Models of Graph-based Reasoning: A Cognitive Model of Problem Solving with Cartesian Graphs in ACT-R/PM

David Peebles (djp@psychology.nottingham.ac.uk)
Peter C.-H. Cheng (pcc@psychology.nottingham.ac.uk)
ESRC Centre for Research in Development, Instruction and Training,
Department of Psychology, University of Nottingham, Nottingham, NG7 2RD, U.K.

Abstract

Models of graph-based reasoning have typically accounted for the variation in problem solving performance with different graph types in terms of a task analysis of the problem relative to the particular visual properties of each graph type (e.g. Lohse, 1993; Peebles, Cheng & Shadbolt 1999, submitted). This approach has been used to explain response time and accuracy differences in experimental situations where data are averaged over experimental conditions. An experiment is reported in which participants' eye movements were recorded while they were solving various problems with different graph types. The eye movement data revealed fine grained fixation patterns that are not captured by current analyses based on optimal fixation sequences. It is argued that these patterns reveal the effects of working memory limitations during the time course of problem solving. An ACT-R/PM model of the experiment is described in which a similar pattern of eye fixations is produced as a natural consequence of the decay in activation of perceptual chunks over time.

Introduction

A recent development in the field of cognitive modelling is the proposal of frameworks to understand interactive behaviour with external representations and artifacts. Gray (2000; Gray & Altmann, 2000), for example, has proposed the *Cognition-Task-Artifact triad* within which to characterise behaviour in human-computer interaction tasks in terms of the complex interaction of three primary elements: the cognitive abilities of the user, the representational and physical properties of the artifact, and the specific requirements of the task. This framework has recently been developed by Byrne (in press) to encompass the perceptual and motor capabilities of the user. Similarly, in the area of graph-based reasoning, Peebles, Cheng and Shadbolt (1999, submitted) have proposed the *Graph-Based Reasoning* (GBR) model incorporating these three elements to account for the ability of users to retrieve and reason about information in different types of Cartesian co-ordinate (x–y) graph.

The primary purpose of these frameworks is to inform the development of detailed cognitive models of the cognitive, perceptual and motor processes involved in the tasks under study. In contrast with *cognitive task analysis* (Gray & Altmann, 2000) which simply specifies the cognitive steps required to perform the task, the construction of cognitive process models that are grounded in cognitive theory allows the incorporation and testing not only

of relevant cognitive factors such as the required declarative and procedural knowledge, the strategies adopted, and the limitations of working memory but also perceptual/motor factors such as mouse movements and shifts in visual attention.

One such model in the area of graph-based reasoning is UCIE (Lohse, 1993). By adding cognitive parameters to the GOMS class of task analysis techniques (Card, Moran, & Newell, 1983; Olson & Olson, 1990; John & Kieras, 1994), Lohse produced a model which simulated certain question answering procedures using line graphs, bar graphs and tables and predicted question answering times by assuming an optimal sequence of eye movements to scan the graphical representation that minimised the number of saccades and fixations to reach the target location.

More recently, the GBR model (Peebles et al., 1999, submitted), employed a similar set of assumptions to account for data from experiments investigating the various interacting factors affecting reasoning with different types of *informationally equivalent* (Larkin & Simon, 1987) Cartesian graph. Figure 1 shows examples of the types of graph used. Both graphs encode the same two functions between time and the variables A and B. The *Function* graph in Figure 1a represents time on the *x* axis and the A and B variables on the *y* axis whereas the *Parametric* graph in Figure 1b represents the A and B variables on the *x* and *y* axes respectively while time is plotted as a parameterising variable along the curve.

Our experiments have revealed significant differences in both response time and error rates between users of the two graph types for a wide range of questions (Peebles et al., 1999, submitted). The GBR model has been successful in explaining why such differences occur with these graph types despite their numerous visual and conceptual similarities. Using the graphs in Figure 1 as an example, we found that when participants were asked to retrieve the value of A when B equals 1, parametric graph users' responses were significantly more rapid and accurate than those of function graph users. The GBR model accounts for these differences in terms of the optimal visual scan path the users follow through the graph. The variability in responses is apparent from the sequence of hypothesised saccades in the two graphs. In Figure 1a, the sequence of saccades is *m, n, o*, whereas in Figure 1b the process requires just two saccades, as shown by the line sequence *a*, *b*. The higher probability of an erroneous response using the function graph was explained by the additional number of possible incorrect saccades that the function graph users may make.

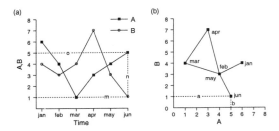

Figure 1: Informationally equivalent function and parametric graphs

The optimality assumptions incorporated into the U-CIE and GBR models are useful as they allow the prediction of response times and provide an explanation of variations in mean RT and error data for different graph types. It is clear, however, that such assumptions do not take important cognitive factors such as working memory limitations or strategic decisions into account. For example, it is likely that, during the time course of a complex graph-based reasoning problem, certain information may be forgotten and have to be rescanned. In addition, given that graph users are aware that information is available for rescanning at all times, it is possible that they may trade off additional saccades for a reduction in working memory load. If this is the case, then the current analyses may miss out an important level of detail which sheds light on the cognitive load that these tasks are imposing and the strategies by which graph users optimise their retrieval procedures. Furthermore, if the goal is to produce detailed cognitive models of these tasks, then information at this level of detail will provide valuable constraints on such models.

In this article we report the results of a graph-based reasoning experiment designed to address these issues. In the experiment, participants were asked to solve simple tasks using function and parametric graphs which, based on the optimality assumptions described above, would be predicted to produce varying response patterns by requiring different optimal fixation sequences. To determine whether these optimality assumptions are justified, some of the participants' eye movements were recorded as they solved the problems. We show that, although the RT and error data are in line with the GBR model's predictions, certain patterns in the eye movement data do not follow the optimal sequence predicted by the model which may be interpreted as indicating the effects of working memory limitations. We then describe an ACT-R/PM model of the experiment in which a similar pattern of eye fixations is produced as a natural consequence of the decay in activation of perceptual chunks over time.

Experiment

One of the most common tasks carried out when using a graph is to elicit the value of one variable corresponding to a given value of another. This task was chosen for the experiment as it is so widely performed and because the procedures involved are relatively simple. The knowledge required to carry out these tasks is primarily the sequence of fixations required to reach the *given location* in the graph representing the given value of the given variable and then from there to the *target location* representing the corresponding value of the required variable. In previous research, however, we have discovered that the effectiveness of a particular graphical representation for retrieving the required information depends on the details of the task, i.e. which variable is given and which is sought (Peebles et al., 1999, submitted).

Method

Participants and materials Forty-nine undergraduate and postgraduate psychology students from the University of Nottingham were paid £3 to take part in the experiment. Of these, four were paid an additional £2 to have their eye movements recorded while they carried out the experiment. The experiment was carried out using PC computers with 17 in displays. The eye tracker employed in the experiment was an SMI iView system using a RED II desktop pupil/corneal reflectance tracker with a 50 Hz sampling rate recording eye movements at 20 ms intervals remotely from a position in front of the computer display. In addition to the system's own automatic head movement compensation mechanism, participant's heads were restrained in a frame fixed to the table to reduce recording error due to head movement,

The stimuli used in the experiment were four graphs, shown in Figure 2, depicting the amount of UK offshore oil and gas production between two decades. Participants were seated approximately 80 cm from the 72 ppi computer display. The graphs were 15.5 cm square (including axis labels), corresponding to approximately 11.1° of visual angle. The characters representing variable values were 0.4 cm high (approximately .21° of visual angle) while those for the axis labels and questions were 0.4 cm and 0.5 cm high (approximately .29° and .36° of visual angle) respectively. Axis ticks were spaced 1.5 cm (approximately 1.1° of visual angle) apart.

The graphs and data sets were designed so that the independent variable (IV—year) and the two dependent variables (DVs—oil and gas) all had ten values ranging from 0 to 9 and that the full range of these values was represented by the data points for oil and gas in both decades. A set of 120 questions was produced using all of the values for the three variables in both decades. The questions had the same basic structure, giving a variable's value and requiring a corresponding variable value.

Design and Procedure The experiment was a mixed design with one between-subjects variable, (graph type) and two within-subjects variables (question type and

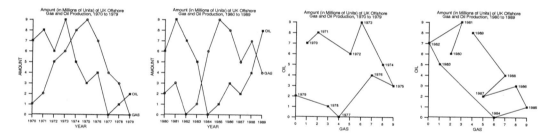

Figure 2: Function and Parametric Graphs Used in the Experiment

graph number). Participants were randomly allocated to one of the two graph type conditions. On each trial, a graph would be presented with a question above it. For example, the question GAS = 2, OIL = ? required the value of oil when gas is equal to 2 to be found. Participants were instructed to enter only the final number of the target year when a year value was required. Each element of the question was centered on a co-ordinate point which remained invariant throughout the experiment with approximately 3.5 cm (approximately 2.5° of visual angle) between the centres of adjacent text items. Together with the graph and question, a button labelled *Answer* appeared in the top right corner of the window. Participants were instructed to click on this answer button as soon as they had obtained the answer to the question. Response times were recorded from the onset of a question to the mouse click on the answer button. When this button was clicked upon, the button, graph and question were removed from the screen and a circle of buttons labelled clockwise from 0 to 9 appeared centered on the answer button. Participants entered their answers by clicking the appropriate number button. When the number button was clicked, the next graph, question, and answer button appeared on the screen. This method was devised so that participants in the eye movement study would not have to take their eyes away from the screen to enter answers, as would be the case if using the keyboard. Before starting the experiment, participants were asked to answer the questions as rapidly and as accurately as possible and were given time to become familiar with the graphs and practice entering numbers using the circle of number buttons and mouse.

Results

Response accuracy and latency data   The proportions of correct responses and mean response times (RTs) for each of the question types for the two graphs in each condition are presented in Table . The data reveal high levels of accuracy for all three question types in both graph conditions. An ANOVA on the response accuracy data, however, revealed a significant effect of question type $F(2, 239) = 28.187$, p < 0.01, $MSE = 0.123$. Although there is little variability in response accuracy between conditions, RTs vary significantly both between condi-

tions and within each condition according to the type of question being attempted. An ANOVA on the RT data revealed significant effects of question type $F(2, 239) = 18.447$, p < 0.01, $MSE = 4974038$, and graph number $F(1, 239) = 5.76$, p < 0.05, $MSE = 1223302$ and significant interactions between graph type and question type $F(2, 239) = 36.314$, p < 0.01, $MSE = 9791754$ and between graph type, question type and graph number $F(2, 239) = 3.913$, p < 0.05, $MSE = 466423$.

The results of this experiment are in line with predictions of the GBR model which explains these differences in terms of a detailed task analysis and the assumption of different optimal scan paths through the graphs to the target location. However, as the main focus of this article is the eye movement data and the ACT-R/PM model, no analysis of these data will be provided here. A full description of the GBR model, its predictions and analyses of these and similar tasks can be found in previous articles (Peebles et al., 1999, submitted).

Eye movement data   To analyse the eye movement data, the display was divided into three regions in a manner similar to that employed by Carpenter and Shah (1998). The regions, shown in Figure 3, were the same for all four graphs and define the relevant units of the display for the fixation analysis: *question, graph pattern,* and *answer* buttons. Dividing the display in this manner allows an analysis of the frequency and duration of fixations on the question and the graph and also the pattern of transitions between these regions during the time course of an individual trial. For the analysis, we adopt Carpenter and Shah's (1998) term *gaze* to refer to a sequence of consecutive fixations on a display region that is unbroken by fixations in other regions. The raw x and y coordinate data from the eye tracker were aggregated into gazes, the minimum duration of which, based on a preliminary study of the data, was defined as 100 ms. This value was sufficiently large to eliminate most saccades, short fixations and noise in the data while still capturing all the relevant fixations. The data from each participant were analysed so that fixations of 100 ms or more in each region were recorded and a scan path consisting of the sequence of gazes from question to graph to answer button regions for each trial was produced. From a total

Table 1: Correct response proportions and mean RTs for each question type in Function and Parametric conditions

Question Type	Correct Response				Response Time (s)			
	Function		Parametric		Function		Parametric	
	Graph 1	Graph 2	Graph 1	Graph 2	Graph 1	Graph 2	Graph 1	Graph 2
DV–DV	.911	.898	.925	.891	5.93	6.18	4.89	4.83
IV–DV	.971	.982	.993	.989	5.01	5.07	4.88	5.17
DV–IV	.943	.930	.939	.925	5.51	5.80	4.38	4.41

of 480 trials in the eye movement study, 28 were removed due to the analysis producing an unusable scan path (e.g. containing only one gaze recorded before reaching the answer region). The rest of the trials were placed into four categories according to the number of transitions from question to graph regions. Of these trials, 37.1% involved only one transition from the question to the graph, 48% involved two such transitions, 11.9% involved three transitions and 2.8% involved four or more transitions. An analysis of the data showed that these categories were not related to specific graph type or question type conditions. Figure 4 shows the average gaze duration on the question and graph regions for the first three categories, (the fourth was removed from the analysis due to its relative rarity).

Figure 4 shows that participants took on average just over 400 ms to read the three elements of the question. The fact that this time is consistent across all three transition groups is strong evidence that the categories do not indicate different problem solving strategies. If the transition categories simply reflected the use of different strategies, (e.g. to switch between the question and graph, reading individual question elements and then identifying their locations in turn), then it is likely that the first gaze duration on the question would be different for each category. In the 1 transition trials, participants took approximately 2.28 s to scan the graph before entering an answer whereas in the other trials, participants looked at the graph for a shorter time before looking again at the question for approximately 300 ms. In the 2 and 3 transition trials, participants then looked at the graph again for over a second before entering an answer or looking for a third time at the question, respectively. Participants in the 3 transition trials then scanned the graph for a third time before entering an answer.

These gaze patterns become clearer when interpreted in the light of the GBR model task analysis of the problem solving procedure. After reading the three items of information in the question, (the *given* variable, *given* value and *required* variable), in order to answer the questions, the user must carry out several graph location tasks in a specific order: (1) find the *start location* determined by the given variable, (2) find the *given location* representing the given value, (3) find the *required location* representing the required variable, (4) read off the *required value* which is the answer to the question. These four steps require the three items of information

in the question to be utilised at different stages of the problem solving process. It is likely therefore, that once the question has been read, the probability that each item can be recalled when required decreases as processing proceeds and that the item most likely to be forgotten is at the final stage of the process.

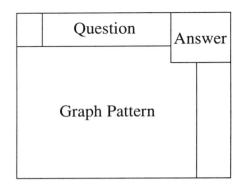

Figure 3: Three regions of the display defined for the fixation analysis

According to this analysis, therefore, the 37.1% of trials requiring only 1 transition suggests that participants were able to retain all three question items while solving the problem in these trials, whereas in the 48% of trials requiring 2 transitions and the 11.9% of trials requiring 3 transitions, participants had failed to retrieve one and two question items respectively. A detailed analysis of the raw eye movement data for individual trials and the duration of the first gaze on the graph for each transition group in Figure 4 support this account. In the 2 transition trials, participants took 1.71 s to identify the start location, find the given location before having to look again at the required variable in the question to find the required location and solve the problem. In the 3 transition trials, however, participants were looking at the graph for only 860 ms in order to identify the start location before having to look again at the given value in the question to find the given location and then having to look again at the required variable in the question to find the required location and solve the problem. It follows from this analysis that the probability of recalling each question item can be computed from the data. The probability of recalling the given variable is .972, that for the given value is .852 while that for the required variable falls sharply to .372.

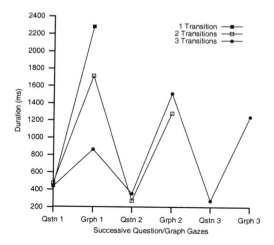

Figure 4: Mean gaze duration on Question (Qstn) and Graph (Grph) regions as a function of the number of transitions required to answer the question

The ACT-R/PM Model

One of the main aims of this research is to construct models of graph-based reasoning that are grounded in cognitive theory and incorporate cognitive factors such as memory decay and interference together with perceptual/motor components that provide realistic interactive behaviour. With these additional factors, it is expected that the optimal analyses provided by the GBR model may be extended to account for detailed experimental data such as eye movements and gaze durations. ACT-R/PM has the required cognitive and perceptual mechanisms with which to develop such models. More specifically, ACT-R's declarative memory has an activation-based retrieval process and includes a mechanism by which the base-level activation of a chunk decreases over time. In addition, the vision module of ACT-R/PM allows the activation of a chunk to be increased when visual attention is refocused upon the visual object that it represents. Space limitations preclude further elaboration of these mechanisms here but detailed discussions can be found in Anderson & Lebiére (1998) and Byrne & Anderson (1998).

An ACT-R/PM model of the experiment was constructed which was able to interact with an exact replica of the software used to run the experiment. The model consists of productions to read the three question components and a set of productions to locate the given variable, given value and required variable in the correct order. A further set of productions was created to allow the model to enter an answer using the mouse and answer buttons once the required value had been obtained.

Given a top level goal to do a trial of the experiment, the model sets a subgoal to read the question. When each question component has been read, a chunk representing that component is created in declarative memory. When all three elements of the question have been read, the model carries out a sequence of three main operations: (1) to identify the starting location (x axis, y axis, or plot region) corresponding to the given variable, (2) to find the given location (x axis tick label, y axis tick label, or plot symbol label) corresponding to the given value, (3) to find the required location (x axis tick label, y axis tick label, or plot symbol label) representing the required variable's value. The sequence of these operations is determined by the state of the problem represented by the current location of visual attention in the graph which is a slot in the top level goal. At each of these main steps in the problem solving procedure, the production initiating the step must retrieve the declarative chunk representing the relevant question element created when the question was read. As the base-level activation of these chunks is decreasing over time, however, the probability that the chunk will be retrieved reduces as problem solving proceeds. If the production fails to retrieve the chunk, a second production fires which stores the current location of attention, sets a subgoal to reread the appropriate question element, thereby increasing the activation of the associated chunk, and then returns the focus of attention to its previous location. With this chunk now sufficiently active, the first production is able to fire and the problem solving process continue. When the model locates the required value, a subgoal is set to enter the answer using the mouse and the answer buttons. When the answer has been entered, the next trial begins.

Simulation An initial test of the model in the parametric graph condition has been conducted. In this test, the model was run through the entire experiment five times and the number of times the question elements were reread was recorded for each run. Of the total of 600 trials, the given variable was never reread as the activation of the given variable chunk was always highly active at the start of a trial, while the given value had to be reread 59 times and the required variable 314 times. As with the eye movement data, the probability of recalling each question item can be computed from these scores. The probability of recalling the given variable is 1, whereas that for the given value is .9 while that for the required variable is .48. Table 2 shows these probabilities against those computed from the data and reveals a close similarity between the patterns of recall probabilities.

An analysis of the model's behaviour revealed that the large decrease in the recall probability between the given value and the required variable is due not only to the time interval between the recall of the two question elements, but also because when the given value was not recalled, the additional time required to reread the question element ensured that the required variable was also not recalled.

Table 2: Probability of recall for the three question elements computed from the eye movement data and the ACT-R/PM model

Question Element	Data	Model
Given Variable	.972	1.00
Given Value	.852	.902
Required Variable	.372	.477

Discussion

Reasoning with Cartesian graphs involves a complex interaction between the perceptual and cognitive abilities of the reasoner, the visual properties of the graph, and specific task requirements. Models of graph-based reasoning have largely focussed on providing detailed task analyses in relation to the the visual properties of the graph and explaining differences in performance in terms of the interaction of these two elements. By incorporating cognitive factors as the user's knowledge, strategies and working memory capacity and perceptual/motor components into graph-based reasoning models, the explanatory and predictive power of these models can be increased and greater insights into the processes and factors affecting these complex interactions can be obtained.

In such a visual domain as graph-based reasoning, eye movements are an important source of information regarding how people acquire and process graphical information during problem solving. The experiment and the eye movement study reported here show how eye movement data can be used to make hypotheses about effects of working memory limitations on problem solving with graphs. The scan paths revealed by the eye movement study show that the optimality assumptions of current models serve as an approximation that obscures the complex sequences of saccades made by individuals.

In contrast, the ACT-R/PM model of the experiment provides a detailed explanation of these scan paths in terms of the decay of base-level activation of perceptual chunks during the time course of problem solving. According to the model, participants initially encode all three elements of the question but are required to re-encode parts of it as the problem progresses, with the probability of re-encoding increasing over time.

This research shows that eye movement data can provide important information concerning the cognitive factors underlying reasoning with external representations that were commonly overlooked by optimal task analytic models and also how a cognitive model such as ACT-R/PM can account for these data.

Acknowledgements

This research is funded by the UK Economic and Social Research Council through the Centre for Research in Development, Instruction and Training.

References

Anderson, J. R., & Lebiére C. (Eds.) (1998) *The Atomic components of thought.* Hillsdale, NJ: Lawrence Erlbaum Associates.

Byrne, M. D., (in press). ACT-R/PM and menu selection: Applying a cognitive architecture to HCI. *International Journal of Human-Computer Studies.*

Byrne, M. D., & Anderson, J. R. (1998). Perception and action. In J. R. Anderson & C. Lebiére (Eds.) *The Atomic components of thought.* Hillsdale, NJ: Lawrence Erlbaum Associates.

Card, S. K., Moran, T. P., & Newell, A., (1983). *The psychology of human-computer interaction.* Hillsdale, NJ: Lawrence Erlbaum Associates.

Carpenter, P. A., & Shah, P. (1998). A model of the perceptual and conceptual processes in graph comprehension. *Journal of Experimental Psychology: Applied, 4,* 75–100.

Gattis, M., & Holyoak, K. (1996). Mapping conceptual to spatial relations in visual reasoning. *Journal of Experimental Psychology: Learning, Memory, and Cognition, 22,* 231–239,

Gray, W. D. (2000). The nature and processing of errors in interactive behaviour. *Cognitive Science, 11,* 205–248.

Gray, W. D., & Altmann, E. M. (2000). Cognitive modeling and human-computer interaction. In W. Karwowski, (Ed.), *International encyclopedia of ergonomics and human factors.* New York: Taylor & Francis, Ltd.

John, B. E., & Kieras, D. E., (1994). *The GOMS family of analysis techniques: Tools for design and evaluation.* (Tech. Rep. CMU-HCII-94-106). Pittsburgh, PA: Carnegie Mellon University, Human-Computer Interaction Institute.

Larkin, J. H., & Simon, H. A. (1987). Why a diagram is (sometimes) worth ten thousand words. *Cognitive Science, 11,* 65–100.

Lohse, G. L. (1993). A cognitive model for understanding graphical perception. *Human-Computer Interaction, 8,* 353–388.

Olson, J. R., & Olson, G. M., (1990). The growth of cognitive modeling in human-computer interaction since GOMS. *Human-Computer Interaction, 5,* 221–265.

Peebles, D., Cheng, P. C.-H., & Shadbolt, N. (1999). Multiple processes in graph-based reasoning. In *Proceedings of the Twenty First Annual Conference of the Cognitive Science Society.* Mahwah, NJ: Lawrence Erlbaum.

Peebles, D., Cheng, P. C.-H., & Shadbolt, N. (submitted). A model of graph-based reasoning: Integrating the role of visual features, knowledge and search.

Shah, P., & Carpenter, P. A. (1995). Conceptual limitations in comprehending line graphs. *Journal of Experimental Psychology: General, 124,* 43–62.

Fitting the ANCHOR Model to Individual Data:
A Case Study in Bayesian Methodology

Alexander A. Petrov (apetrov@andrew.cmu.edu)
Department of Psychology; Carnegie Mellon University
Pittsburgh, PA 15213 USA

Abstract

This paper presents a memory-based model of direct psychophysical scaling. The model is based on an extension of the cognitive architecture ACT-R and uses *anchors* that serve as prototypes for the stimuli classified within each response category. Using the ANCHOR model as a specific example, a general Bayesian framework is introduced. It provides principled methods for making data-based inferences about models of this kind. The internal representations in the model are analyzed as hidden variables that are constructed from the stimuli according to probabilistic representation rules. In turn, the hidden representations produce overt responses via probabilistic performance rules. Incremental learning rules transform the model into a dynamic system. A parameter-fitting algorithm is formulated and tested on experimental data.

Introduction

Parameter search is usually relegated to an appendix in the modeling literature, if it is discussed at all. And this is understandable: the emphasis usually is, as it should be, on describing the particular model and discussing its implications for the phenomena under study. Moreover, the search for suitable parameter values is often done by trial and error or by brute-force methods. This, however, need not necessarily be the case. There are principled ways of making data-based inferences about quantities used in a model, including parameter values. The immediate benefit of such methods is to speed up the model design cycle and expand the power, scope, and detail of the simulations. In addition, they can improve the conceptual understanding of the model by exposing relationships that would otherwise remain buried inside the black box.

This paper outlines a general Bayesian framework for probabilistic models involving internal representations modifiable by learning mechanisms. One such model—ANCHOR (Petrov & Anderson, 2000)—serves as a concrete example. First, the model is described in its own terms and is related to empirical data. It is then analyzed from a Bayesian perspective and a method for making data-based inferences is formulated. Next, the terms are generalized so that the resulting framework can be applied to a wide class of models. Finally, the algorithms are illustrated on experimental data.

The ANCHOR Model

ANCHOR is a memory-based model of psychophysical scaling tasks. It is based on the cognitive architecture ACT-R (Anderson & Lebière, 1998) extended with mechanisms for dealing with continuous (or analog) internal representations called *magnitudes*.

Empirical Phenomena

The model deals with unidimensional sensory continua such as loudness of tones or length of lines. The participants in direct scaling studies are shown stimuli of various physical intensities and are asked to report the corresponding subjective magnitudes. The reports are verbal and typically use some numerical scale. There are several variations of this basic paradigm, only one of which is chosen for the purposes of this paper. The responses in *category rating* are restricted to a fixed set of categories—for example, the numbers from 1 to 9. The participants are instructed to rate the least intense stimuli with 1, the most intense ones with 9, and to space the remaining categories evenly in between.

A number of robust empirical phenomena are well documented in the direct-scaling literature (e.g., see Gescheider, 1988, for review). Only the most salient ones are mentioned here—enough to provide some psychological substance to the abstract considerations in the following sections. Human performance is stochastic and a whole distribution of responses is observed for each stimulus level. The means of these response distributions are described by the so-called *Stevens' law* and their standard deviations by *Ekman's law*. The former states that the mean ratings tend to be a power function of the stimulus: $R = kS^n$ (Stevens, 1957). The latter states that the standard deviation of each response distribution is approximately proportional to its mean (Ekman, 1959).

The immediate stimulus on each trial is the major determinant of the corresponding response but other factors exert robust and measurable effects as well. These include the overall distribution of the stimuli used in the experiment (*context effects*, e.g., Parducci & Wedell, 1986), previous stimuli and responses (*sequential effects*, e.g., Jesteadt, Luce, & Green 1977), and various memory-related factors (*memory effects* and *practice effects*, e.g., Siegel, 1972). The ANCHOR model offers a unified explanation of these phenomena.

ANCHOR: Mechanisms and Equations

The ANCHOR model stands at the intersection of two broad theories—Thurstonian psychophysics (Thurstone, 1927) and the memory theory incorporated in ACT-R (Anderson & Lebière, 1998). From the former it adopts the notion of a subjective continuum of magnitudes. A stimulus with physical intensity S is represented by a magnitude M. Due to the intrinsic stochasticity of the perceptual mechanisms, a whole distribution of magnitudes is associated with each stimulus. It is assumed that these distributions are Gaussian, with mean and variance dependent on S. In keeping with Stevens law ANCHOR postulates that the mean of each distribution is a power function of the corresponding stimulus. Furthermore, in keeping with Ekman's law it assumes that each standard deviation is proportional to the corresponding mean. These are not the only choices that are theoretically possible and consistent with the available empirical data (Norwich & Wong, 1997). Still they are the most straightforward pair and are adopted for this reason. Note also that they imply Weber's law.

The data set used in this paper deals with a particularly convenient sensory modality—physical length. The Stevens exponent for length is very nearly one (Stevens, 1957; Petrov & Anderson, 2000) and hence the power function becomes a simple linear function. This leads to Equation 1, which defines the perceptual transformation of the ANCHOR model. The magnitude M is roughly proportional to the stimulus S but there is also some multiplicative noise. This "perceptual noise" ε_p is a normally distributed random variable with zero mean and standard deviation σ_p, which is a free parameter of the model and does not depend on S.

$$M = k S (1 + \varepsilon_p) \qquad [1]$$

The task of the participant is to translate the subjective sensation M into an overt response. Three classes of factors constrain the mapping between magnitudes and responses. First, there is an arbitrary component chosen by the experimenter and established by the instructions. This includes the number of response categories and their particular labels. Second, there is a constraint for homomorphism—a pressure to align the intrinsic ordering of the magnitude continuum with the ordering of the response scale. For instance, if M_1 is more intense than M_2, the corresponding responses should also be ordered appropriately. Finally, there is a tacit constraint for consistency—a pressure to use the same response for repeated presentations of the same stimulus throughout the experimental session.

The first and third of these constraints strongly suggest that memory plays an important role in the direct scaling tasks. The same hypothesis is supported by many empirical phenomena and in particular the sequential, memory, and practice effects mentioned earlier (Siegel, 1972; Petrov & Anderson, 2000). This leads to the centerpiece of the model—the *anchor*.

An anchor is an association between a magnitude and a response. There is one anchor for each response category. The anchor magnitude represents the prototypical member of this category. The collection of all anchors thus defines a mapping between the magnitude continuum and the response scale. When a stimulus is presented for rating, its corresponding magnitude M serves as a memory cue. The anchors then compete to match that target and one of them is retrieved. An alternative but equivalent conceptualization is that a pattern completion process fills in the response label given the magnitude. Either way, the final outcome is described by Equations 2 and 3.

$$G_i = -\left|M - \overline{A}_i\right| + h B_i \qquad [2]$$

$$P(A_i) = \frac{\exp(G_i / T)}{\sum_j \exp(G_j / T)} \qquad [3]$$

Anchor retrieval is a stochastic process, just as any act of memory retrieval in the ACT-R architecture. The probability $P(A_i)$ of selecting an anchor depends on two factors: (*i*) the similarity between the anchor magnitude $\overline{A}_i$ and the target magnitude M and (*ii*) the current availability of the anchor measured by its *base-level activation* B_i. The two factors are combined into a "goodness score" G_i (Eq. 2; h is a scaling parameter). The anchors then compete on the basis of their scores through the "softmax" Equation 3. The "temperature" T is a free parameter that controls the degree of non-determinism of the selection process.

Memory retrieval is noisy and is prone to biases B_i. Therefore it is not guaranteed to provide on each trial the anchor that best matches the target magnitude. The verbal protocols of human participants suggest that they are aware of the unreliability of their memory and seem to adopt a correction strategy. A typical report is, "This length looks like a *7*... No, it's too short for a *7*. I'll give it a *6*."

The ANCHOR model implements these corrections in the following way. The magnitude A_i of the anchor retrieved from memory is compared against the target magnitude M. If the discrepancy $\Delta = (M - A_i)$ is less than some cutoff value c (a free parameter of the model), the response associated with the anchor is chosen as the final response on the trial. Otherwise the anchor response is corrected by $+/-1$ or occasionally even $+/-2$ depending on the algebraic difference Δ (cutoffs $+/-c$ and $+/-3c$, respectively). The anchor magnitude is degraded by "memory noise" ε_a (Eq. 4) analogous to the "perceptual noise" in the target magnitude (Eq. 1). Due to this noise in the inputs, the correction mechanism is stochastic and error-prone too. Nevertheless, it plays a useful and important role in the model. Among other things, it promotes the homomorphism between magnitudes and responses.

$$A_i = \overline{A}_i (1 + \varepsilon_a)$$ [4]

So, the stimulus has been encoded, matched against anchors, and a response has been produced. Is this the end of the trial? According to the ANCHOR model and the broader memory theory, the answer is no. The cognitive system is plastic (within limits) and each experience seems to leave a mark on it. There are obligatory *learning mechanisms* that update the anchor magnitudes (Eq. 5) and their base-level activations (Eq. 6). Consider the magnitudes first. On each trial, only one of the anchors is updated—the one that corresponds to the actual response. The new magnitude $\overline{A}^{(t+1)}$ of this anchor is pulled slightly toward the target magnitude M (Eq. 5). The parameter α controls the learning rate. In the long run, each anchor magnitude becomes a weighted average of the magnitudes of all stimuli classified in the corresponding response category. Thus the anchors are true prototypes. However, recent stimuli weigh more than earlier ones. This introduces various sequential, transfer, and context effects (Petrov & Anderson, 2000).

$$\overline{A}^{(t+1)} = (1 - \alpha)\overline{A}^{(t)} + \alpha M^{(t)}$$ [5]

In contrast to the selective update of magnitudes, the base-level learning Equation 6 affects the availability of all anchors. The formula is not transparent and need be discussed only briefly here. It is an approximate and parameter-free version of the base-level learning equation in ACT-R (Anderson & Lebière, 1998, p. 124). The availability B of each anchor reflects the frequency and recency of use of the corresponding response. The formula disregards the detailed history of the anchor; it retains only three critical pieces of information: the lag since the most recent use t_{last}, the total time since the beginning of the experiment t_{life}, and the total number of uses n.

$$B = \ln\left[t_{last}^{-0.5} + \frac{2(n-1)}{\sqrt{t_{last}} + \sqrt{t_{life}}} \right]$$ [6]

Qualitatively, Equation 6 captures three important aspects of memory dynamics: sharp transient boost immediately after use, gradual buildup of strength with frequent use, and gradual decay in the absence of use. In terms of observable behavior, the rapid transient manifests itself in sequential assimilation and the gradual strengthening/decay in non-uniform response distributions (Petrov & Anderson, 2000).

General Framework

ANCHOR is just a specific instance of a whole class of models. It is useful to introduce a general framework for analyzing such models. Such broader view sharpens the understanding of the particular model and makes the discussion relevant to other modeling efforts as well.

It is assumed that time progresses in discrete steps or "trials". The *stimuli* $S^{(t)}$ and *responses* $R^{(t)}$ are the only observable quantities. The model builds and manipulates some *internal representations* $H^{(t)}$ to mediate between the two: $S \rightarrow H \rightarrow R$. These representations are hidden variables (or "hypotheses" in Bayesian terms).

The inner structure of the model specifies two kinds of rules: *representation rules* governing the transition $S \rightarrow H$ and *performance rules* governing the transition $H \rightarrow R$. Both kinds of rules are probabilistic. Thus on each trial the representation rules define a whole probability distribution over the space of possible representations conditional on the current stimulus $S^{(t)}$. Some sequence of chance events selects one specific realization $H^{(t)}$, which then drives the performance. The performance rules specify a probability distribution over the possible responses. Another chance event determines the final response $R^{(t)}$. Then the next stimulus is presented and the whole cycle repeats.

Each step of the process described so far depends on two kinds of parameters. The *global parameters* θ are relatively few in number, apply throughout the model, and remain fixed during the whole session. There are also *local parameters* $\lambda^{(t)}$ associated with the individual representational and/or processing units. Importantly, these local parameters are not static but may be updated on each step according to *learning rules*. This paper deals with the class of models whose learning rules are deterministic and incremental. That is, the updated values $\lambda^{(t)}$ depend only on their previous values $\lambda^{(t-1)}$, the current representations $H^{(t)}$, and on global parameters such as learning rates. In symbols:

$$\lambda^{(t)} = F_L(\lambda^{(t-1)}, H^{(t)}, \theta)$$ [7]

The learning mechanisms make the model a dynamic system. The performance on a given trial depends not only on the current stimulus but also on the whole history of the computation. In the class of models discussed here, this history is condensed solely in the most recent update of the local parameters $\lambda^{(t-1)}$. In other words the following *Markov property* is assumed: the operation at time t depends only on $S^{(t)}$, $H^{(t)}$, θ, and the most recent values $\lambda^{(t-1)}$. The representation rules can be written as Eq. 8 and the performance rules as Eq. 9. (Eq. 8 can be extended to include residual representations $H^{(t-1)}$ but this possibility is not pursued here.)

$$P(H^{(t)}) = F_R(S^{(t)}, \lambda^{(t-1)}, \theta)$$ [8]

$$P(R^{(t)}) = F_P(H^{(t)}, \lambda^{(t-1)}, \theta)$$ [9]

All these abstract notions can be illustrated on the ANCHOR model. It has six global parameters: perceptual noise σ_p, weight h, softmax temperature T, anchor noise σ_a, correction cutoff c, and magnitude learning rate α. This set of six values is collectively denoted Θ. There are two kinds[1] of internal representations: magnitudes M and anchors A. (In this case the symbol A denotes not an anchor magnitude but a discrete value indicating which of the several anchors is retrieved on the particular trial.) Thus, the hidden states (or hypotheses) in the model can be conceptualized as pairs $H=<M,A>$. They are constructed in two steps with probabilities given by two separate representation rules. First, Equation 1 produces a magnitude $M^{(t)}$ given the stimulus $S^{(t)}$. Based on this magnitude, Equations 2 and 3 then select an anchor $A^{(t)}$. This illustrates an important point about the formalism. The hidden variables $H^{(t)}$ (and, for that matter, $S^{(t)}$ and $R^{(t)}$) need not be unitary or constructed in a single step. Various intermediate stages can be involved. Still, it is always possible in principle to consider the Cartesian product of all the components and think in terms of a (joint) distribution conditional on the stimulus (Eq. 8). Two local parameters $\lambda^{(t-1)}$ are associated with each anchor: its magnitude $\overline{A}_i$ and availability[2] B_i. The corresponding update rules are given by Equations 5 and 6, respectively.

Model Tracing and Parameter Search

The stage is now set to confront the issue of estimating unobservable quantities from experimental data. For concreteness, consider the problem of finding suitable values of the global parameters Θ. One approach is to treat the model as a black box and use Monte Carlo simulations to evaluate its performance under different parameter settings. Based on these estimates, a search algorithm such as gradient descent can be used to optimize some goal function of interest. For example, if the empirical accuracy is 80%, the optimization goal would be to bring the model accuracy as close as possible to this target value. This approach requires little thought and is easy to implement but has serious drawbacks both on technical and conceptual grounds. Monte Carlo methods are computer-intensive and their estimates are blurred by sample fluctuations. This slows down the search and derails all optimization algorithms that depend on comparisons between close choices for Θ. Moreover, there is danger of overfitting because the validity of the model is measured by the same criterion that guides the search (e.g., overall accuracy).

This paper advocates another approach. It is to open the black box and work out in detail the various probability distributions underlying the overt behavior. This approach requires careful analytical derivations and a separate computer implementation. The returns on this

intellectual investment, however, can be considerable. The main leverage comes from the following idea: the probabilities are calculated directly from the structural equations of the model instead of being estimated by sampling. This information can then be used for various purposes as discussed below.

The calculations are done on a trial-by-trial basis. Assume the process has been carried up to trial $t-1$ and estimates of the local parameters $\lambda^{(t-1)}$ are available. The whole calculation is conditional on some global parameter set Θ. Under these circumstances, when the next stimulus $S^{(t)}$ arrives the representation rules (Eq. 8) allow to calculate the conditional distribution:

$$P(H^{(t)} \mid S^{(t)}, \lambda^{(t-1)}, \Theta) \qquad [10]$$

In Bayesian terms, this is the prior distribution over the hypotheses. To implement that, one follows the logic of the model but at any point in which the original program would do a probabilistic choice and commit to a particular alternative, the modified version keeps all branches open and maintains a table of their respective probabilities.

To illustrate, the first step in the "primary" ANCHOR implementation is to generate a random number ε_p and use it to compute the internal magnitude $M^{(t)}$ according to Equation 1. In contrast, the model-tracing version has to represent the whole distribution of potential magnitudes. The implementation (which is written in MATLAB) approximates the Gaussian distribution with an array of 15 discrete bins centered on $kS^{(t)}$ (Eq. 1) and spread out to cover 99% of the density. Thus, the modified program considers 15 alternative values in parallel instead of the single commitment $M^{(t)}$. Each of these values can occur in conjunction with any of the nine possible anchors. This creates a space of 135 hypotheses $H_{ij}=<M_i,A_j>$. The program represents it as a matrix and calculates the probability of each pair from Equations 2 and 3. Note that this requires knowledge of the current anchor magnitudes $\overline{A}_j$ and base-level activations B_j (that is, the local parameters $\lambda^{(t-1)}$).

Back to general terms, once the prior probabilities of all hypotheses have been calculated (Eq. 10), a straightforward application of the performance rules (Eq. 9) gives the joint distribution of hypotheses and responses:

$$P(R^{(t)} \times H^{(t)} \mid S^{(t)}, \lambda^{(t-1)}, \Theta) = \qquad [11]$$
$$= P(R^{(t)} \mid H^{(t)}, \lambda^{(t-1)}, \Theta) \cdot P(H^{(t)} \mid S^{(t)}, \lambda^{(t-1)}, \Theta)$$

This distribution contains a wealth of information. From that point on, the hidden variables introduced at earlier stages begin to be averaged out. This elimination can be engineered in various ways depending on the goals of the modeler. The following subsections outline some of the potential applications.

---

[1] Strictly speaking, the final response must also be represented internally. Due to the one-to-one correspondence with the overt response, however, this representation need not be considered among the hidden variables.
[2] Actually, three values must be maintained for each B_i but they stay hidden behind Equation 6.

Predicting the Responses and Fitting Parameters

The obvious way to proceed from Equation 11 is to average out the unknown internal representations $H^{(t)}$. This produces the (marginal) probabilities of all possible responses $R^{(t)}$:

$$P(R^{(t)} \mid S^{(t)}, \mathcal{X}^{(t-1)}, \Theta) \qquad [12]$$

If the model is a good approximation to the actual process generating the observations, Equation 12 should predict the actual response $R^{(t)} = r_k$ with high probability on most trials. The log-likelihood L (Eq. 13) measures the overall goodness of fit on all available data D (the full sequence of stimuli and responses). This quantity can be used to guide the parameter search. Notice that L is a deterministic function of the parameters Θ and $\mathcal{X}^{(0)}$ (given that the data are fixed). Thus, unlike in Monte Carlo methods, gradient algorithms can track the optimum much faster and with high precision.

$$L = \log P(D \mid \Theta, \mathcal{X}^{(0)}) = \sum_{t=1}^{N} \log P(R^{(t)} \mid S^{(t)}, \mathcal{X}^{(t-1)}, \Theta) \qquad [13]$$

It is worth pointing out that under this scheme the parameters are fitted using one criterion (L) while the final evaluation of the model is done by separate criteria (e.g., accuracy, response variability, sequential dependencies, and so forth) This reduces overfitting and discourages "fishing" for results.

Model Tracing. The internal representations that people use are of particular interest in applications such as intelligent tutoring (Corbett, Anderson, & O'Brien, 1995) or cognitive assessment (Martin & VanLehn, 1995). When a cognitive model is available for some task domain, the Bayesian framework advocated here can be used to trace the probable path that a student is following. In such applications, it is of little utility to eliminate the hidden variables in order to predict the next response. On the contrary, one wants to treat the observed response as an additional piece of information and obtain from Equations 11 and 12 posterior estimates about $H^{(t)}$ via Bayes rule:

$$P(H^{(t)} \mid R^{(t)}, S^{(t)}, \mathcal{X}^{(t-1)}, \Theta) \qquad [14]$$

Updating the Local Parameters. In addition to being useful in their own right, these posterior estimates (Eq. 14) are necessary to close the tracing cycle. The local parameters $\mathcal{X}^{(t-1)}$ must be updated at the end of trial t, so that the new values $\mathcal{X}^{(t)}$ are available on trial $t+1$. The learning rules of the model (Eq. 7) define this transition but they involve the specific internal representation H_i. It is impossible to know which of the many potential structures $H^{(t)}$ has actually been realized on that particular trial. The most that can be calculated are the posterior probabilities (Eq. 14). The cleanest option at this point would be to consider all possible updates $\mathcal{X}_i$

and propagate them in parallel through all subsequent trials keeping track of the respective probabilities. Unfortunately, this scheme is computationally intractable. Some approximation must be used instead.

There are several possibilities. One is to sample the posterior—to single out one value H_i at random according to Equation 14 and use it in $\mathcal{X}^{(t)}$. This approach, however, introduces randomness into the estimation process. The log-likelihoods calculated on this basis (Eq. 13) are no longer deterministic.

Another possibility is to single out the maximum *a posteriori* (MAP) hypothesis and use it in the update rule (Eq. 7). This approach restores the determinism of the estimation process and has certain intuitive appeal. It, however, systematically overestimates the coupling between the internal representations $H^{(t)}$ and the overt responses $R^{(t)}$ (cf. Eq. 9).

There is an important and widespread special case in which it is meaningful to combine alternative parameter estimates $\mathcal{X}_i$ into weighted linear combinations. In such cases, a "mean field" approximation is available. The idea is to take all alternative H_i, calculate the corresponding updates $\mathcal{X}_i$, and combine them into a single aggregate $\mathcal{X}^{(t)}$ that is passed on to the next trial. The posterior probabilities (Eq. 14) serve as weighting coefficients. (A related strategy using the prior probabilities (Eq. 10) can be preferable in some cases. The priors factor in the stimulus $S^{(t)}$ but not the response $R^{(t)}$.)

The ANCHOR model has two learning rules and thus illustrates the problem. The update of the base-level activations B presents little difficulty because no hidden variables are involved (Eq. 6). It is clear which anchor is strengthened on each trial—the one corresponding to the overt response. In contrast, the update of the anchor magnitudes is more problematic because Equation 5 involves the unobservable target magnitude M. As the magnitudes are additive, the mean field approximation is applicable. Recall that the hypotheses in the ANCHOR case are pairs $H_{ij} = \langle M_i, A_j \rangle$. To produce the posterior distribution of the magnitudes M_i alone, the anchor indicator variables must be averaged out from the joint posterior (Eq. 14). This leaves 15 probabilities $P(M_i)$ corresponding to the 15 target magnitude bins. The mean-field version of Equation 5 thus becomes:

$$\overline{A}^{(t+1)} = (1 - \alpha) \overline{A}^{(t)} + \alpha \sum M_i^{(t)} P(M_i^{(t)}) \qquad [15]$$

Empirical Test

This final section applies the global parameter search algorithm to data from a category rating experiment (Petrov & Anderson, 2000). The original paper reports group-level fits of the ANCHOR model. The present framework allows us to extend the analysis to the level of individual participants.

The stimuli for the experiment were pairs of dots presented on a monitor. The task of the 24 participants was to rate the distance between the two dots using the numbers from 1 to 9. Each session involved 450 trials.

The results replicated all classical category-rating phenomena that fell within the scope of the experiment, including sequential effects of various kinds and the linearity of the psychophysical scale for length. A battery of statistical measures designed to quantify these effects were calculated from the data of each participant. The ANCHOR model was then run on the same 24 stimulus sequences and the same statistics were calculated. The fits were very good on all dimensions (Petrov & Anderson, 2000, Table 1). The mean of each statistic calculated from the model data fell very close to the corresponding empirical mean. The variability in the empirical sample, however, was somewhat greater (by 40% on average) than that of the model.

The latter result is not surprising. The empirical data contain both within- and between-subject variability. All ANCHOR runs, on the other hand, used the same set of global parameters. Thus, the model data reflected only the inherent stochasticity of the mechanisms.

A better way to confront the model with the empirical data is to have an individual parameter set $\boldsymbol{\theta}_p$ for each participant p. The algorithms described in this paper make this easy to do. Each stimulus-response sequence D_p generates a log-likelihood "landscape" (Eq. 13) over the space of global parameters $\boldsymbol{\theta}$. A general-purpose optimizer (the *fmincon* function in MATLAB) can then be used to find the maximum-likelihood estimator $\boldsymbol{\theta}_p$.

We are now ready to derive individualized predictions. For concreteness, suppose we are interested in the overall accuracy (measured by the stimulus-response correlation R^2) and the shape of the response distribution (measured by its standard deviation SD). We fix a parameter set $\boldsymbol{\theta}_p$, run the model 10 times to generate 10 response sequences, and calculate R^2 and SD for each. After averaging over the 10 runs, we obtain a single prediction for R^2_p and one for SD_p.

This procedure yields a distribution of 24 predicted R^2 values—one for each participant—and similarly for the SDs. On the other hand, the corresponding empirical distributions are also available. The model is successful to the extent in which the predicted distributions are indistinguishable from their observed counterparts.

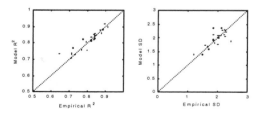

Figure 1: Correlations between model data and empirical data. Left panel: stimulus-response correlations. Right panel: response standard deviations.

Figure 1 illustrates the distribution overlap for our data. The correlation between the 24 empirical R^2 and the corresponding predicted R^2 is 0.93. The correlation among the standard deviations is 0.74. These results clearly indicate that the ANCHOR model is able to reproduce the data well and that the Bayesian algorithms are able to find appropriate parameter sets.

Acknowledgments

Special thanks are due to John Anderson for numerous stimulating discussions and his invaluable intellectual guidance. This research is supported by grant AFOSR F49620-99-10086 awarded to John R. Anderson. Three anonymous reviewers provided constructive criticism.

References

Anderson, J. R. & Lebière, C. (1998). *The atomic components of thought*. Mahwah, NJ: Lawrence Erlbaum Associates.

Corbett, A., Anderson, J. R., & O'Brien, A. (1995). Student modeling in the ACT programming tutor. In P. Nichols, S. Chipman, & R. Brennan (Eds.), *Cognitively Diagnostic Assessment*. Hillsdale, NJ: Lawrence Erlbaum Associates.

Ekman, G. (1959). Weber's law and related functions. *The Journal of Psychology, 47*, 343-352.

Gescheider, G. A. (1988). Psychophysical scaling. *Annual Review of Psychology, 39*, 169-200.

Jesteadt, W., Luce, R. D., & Green, D. M. (1977). Sequential effects in judgments of loudness. *Journal of Experimental Psychology: Human Perception and Performance, 3* (1), 92-104.

Martin, J. & VanLehn, K. (1995). A Bayesian approach to cognitive assessment. In P. Nichols, S. Chipman, & R. Brennan (Eds.), *Cognitively Diagnostic Assessment*. Hillsdale, NJ: Lawrence Erlbaum Associates.

Norwich, K. H. & Wong, W. (1997). Unification of psychophysical phenomena: The complete form of Fechner's law. *Perception & Psychophysics, 59* (6), 929-940.

Parducci, A. & Wedell, D. H. (1986). Category effects with rating scales: Number of categories, number of stimuli, and method of presentation. *Journal of Experimental Psychology: Human Perception and Performance, 12* (4), 496-516.

Petrov, A. & Anderson, J. R. (2000). ANCHOR: A memory-based model of category rating. *Proceedings of the Twenty-Second Annual Conference of the Cognitive Science Society* (pp. 369-374). Hillsdale, NJ: Lawrence Erlbaum Associates.

Siegel, W. (1972). Memory effects in the method of absolute judgment. *Journal of Experimental Psychology, 94* (2), 121-131.

Stevens, S. S. (1957). On the psychophysical law. *Psychological Review, 64* (3), 153-181.

Thurstone, L. L. (1927). A law of comparative judgment. *Psychological Review, 34*, 273-286.

The Role of Computational Modeling in Understanding Hemispheric Interactions and Specialization

James A. Reggia & Reiner Schulz

Dept. of Computer Science and UMIACS, A.V. Williams Bldg.
University of Maryland, College Park MD 20742 USA
{reggia/rschulz}@cs.umd.edu

Abstract

We describe results from three models of paired left and right cerebral regions communicating via a simulated corpus callosum. Conditions are identified under which lateralization emerges during learning, and under which an intact hemispheric region contributes to recovery when the contralateral one is damaged. It proved easy to demonstrate hemispheric specialization in the context of a variety of underlying cortical asymmetries, consistent with past arguments that lateralization of cognitive functions is a multi-factorial process. However, no single assumption about transcallosal influences could account for existing experimental data. Possible solutions to this "callosal dilemma" are suggested.

Introduction

Current understanding of lateralization and of how the cerebral hemispheres interact is surprisingly limited. For example, in spite of a century of experimental research, it remains unclear today which recognized underlying cortical asymmetries (regional size, connectivity, neurotransmitter levels, etc.) actually lead to cerebral specialization, whether the overall influence of one hemisphere on the other is excitatory or inhibitory, and the extent to which the intact contralateral hemisphere contributes to recovery following cortical damage (Hellige, 1993; Davidson & Hagdahl, 1995).

In recent years several neural models of interacting left and right cortical regions have provided evidence that modeling is a promising framework in which to explore implications of hypotheses concerning cerebral interactions and specialization, and ultimately to interpret/guide experiments. Early models demonstrated that oscillatory activity in one hemisphere could be transferred to the other via interhemispheric connections (Anninos et al, 1988), that inhibitory callosal connections produced slower convergence and different activity patterns in two simulated hemispheres (Cook & Beech, 1990), and that slow interhemispheric connections are not critical for short output times (Ringo et al, 1994). A recent mixture-of-experts backpropagation model examined how unequal visual receptive field sizes in two networks could lead to their specialization for learning spatial relations (Jacobs & Kosslyn, 1994),

and a symbol processing model showed how assuming partial lateralization of one function can lead to lateralization of others (Kosslyn et al, 1989).

Our research group over the last few years has systematically studied several neural models of paired cortical regions connected by a simulated corpus callosum. The left and right model cortical regions typically differed from each other in a single way (region size, excitability, synaptic plasticity, etc.), and these asymmetries sometimes led to "hemispheric specialization" as the model learned a behavioral task. These models have examined: 1. which individual hemispheric asymmetries consistently produce lateralization; 2. the implications of assuming that each hemisphere exerts predominantly an inhibitory versus an excitatory influence on the opposite hemisphere; 3. conditions under which transcallosal diaschisis (contralateral cortical impairment) can be readily produced; and 4. conditions under which the undamaged hemisphere makes a substantial contribution to post-damage recovery. In the following we briefly review some relevant information on hemispheric interactions and specialization, summarize some of our recent modeling work, and describe its implications for understanding cerebral specialization and corpus callosum functioning.

Cerebral Functional Asymmetries

A number of functional cerebral asymmetries are recognized to exist in humans (Hellige, 1993; Davidson & Hugdahl, 1995). These cognitive/ behavioral lateralizations include language, handedness, visuospatial processing, emotion and its facial expression, olfaction, and attention. The underlying causes of such hemispheric functional specializations are not well understood and have been the subject of investigation for many years. Established anatomic, cytoarchitectonic, biochemical and physiological asymmetries include a larger left temporal plane in 65% of subjects, differing intrinsic microcircuitry in left and right language areas, more gray matter relative to white matter in the left hemisphere, different distributions of important neurotransmitters between the hemispheres, and a lower left hemisphere threshold for motor evoked potentials.

Besides hemispheric differences, another potential factor in function lateralization is hemispheric interactions via pathways such as the corpus callosum. Callosal fibers are largely homotopic, i.e., each hemisphere projects in a topographic fashion so that roughly mirror-symmetric points are connected to each other (Mountcastle, 1998). However, interhemispheric connection density is variable, and some heterotopic connections exist. Most neurons sending axons through the corpus callosum are pyramidal cells, and these end mainly on contralateral spiny cells. Such apparently excitatory connections, as well as transcallosal diaschisis and split-brain experiments, suggest that transcallosal hemispheric interactions are mainly excitatory in nature (Berlucchi, 1983), but this hypothesis has long been controversial (Denenberg, 1983). Transcallosal monosynaptic excitatory postsynaptic potentials are subthreshold, of low amplitude, and followed by stronger, more prolonged inhibition, suggesting to some that transcallosal inhibitory interactions are much more important (Cook, 1986). Inhibitory transcallosal influences are hypothesized to explain hemispheric competition/rivalry and specialization. The case for transcallosal inhibition has been strengthened recently by transcranial magnetic stimulation studies indicating that activation of one motor cortex inhibits the contralateral one (Ferbert et al, 1992).

At present, it is not clear what physiological mechanisms are responsible for individual lateralization of functions. It is often suggested that anatomic asymmetries underlie functional asymmetries such as language lateralization to the (usually) left hemisphere, but it is difficult to see how such asymmetries alone, present in roughly 65% of the population, could account for left hemisphere dominance for language in over 90% of the population, and recent studies have challenged their nature and significance. Computational models provide a way to investigate such issues that complements traditional experimental studies.

Modeling Hemispheric Specialization

We recently developed and studied three different neural models of cortical regions interacting via a simulated corpus callosum (see Table 1). With each model we systematically determined conditions under which lateralization arose and the effects of simulating acute focal damage. Multiple independent models were studied because we wanted our results to be reasonably general, i.e., not tied to the specific choices of task, architecture, learning method, etc. that are necessarily made for any single neural model. Below we briefly describe the lateralization and lesioning results in each of these three models.

Phoneme Sequence Generation

The phoneme sequence generation model was our first attempt to investigate computationally the fac-

Table 1: Models of Hemispheric Specialization.

Task	Learning	Source
1. Word Naming	supervised	[21, 18, 25]
2. Map Formation	unsupervised	[13, 14]
3. Letter Identification	both	[23, 24]

tors influencing lateralization (Reggia et al, 1998). Its recurrently connected network is trained using supervised learning to take three-letter words (CAD, MOP, etc.) as input and to produce the correct temporal sequence of phonemes for the pronunciation of each word as output. Fig. 1 schematically summarizes the network architecture, where input elements (I) are fully connected to two sets of neural elements representing corresponding regions of the left (LH) and right (RH) hemisphere cortex. These regions are connected to each other via a simulated corpus callosum (CC), and are also fully connected to output elements (O) representing individual phonemes. State elements provide delayed feedback to the hemispheric regions via recurrent connections. Learning occurs on all connections in Fig. 1 except callosal connections. The supervised learning rule used to train the model is a variant of recurrent error backpropagation (Jordan, 1986).

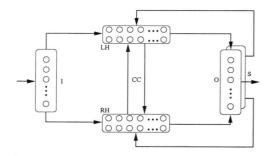

Figure 1: Network architecture for phoneme sequence generation. I = input elements, LH (RH) = left (right) hemisphere cortex region, CC = corpus callosum, O = output elements, S = state elements.

Over a thousand simulations were done with different versions of this model. The effects of different hemispheric asymmetries (relative size, maximum activation level, sensitivity to input stimuli, learning rate parameter, amount of feedback, etc.) were examined one at a time in isolation so that their individual effects could be assessed. For each hemispheric asymmetry and a symmetric control version of the model, the uniform value of callosal connection influences was varied over 17 values from -3.0 to +3.0. Lateralization was measured as the difference between the output error when the left hemispheric region alone controlled the output versus when the right hemispheric region alone did. These simulations showed that, within the limitations of the model, it is easy to produce lateralization. For example, lateralization occurred toward the side with higher excitability, higher learning rate parameter, or larger size depending on callosal strength (e.g., Fig. 2). Lateralization tended to occur most readily and intensely when callosal connections exerted predominantly an inhibitory influence, i.e., Fig. 2 was a commonly occurring pattern of lateralization. This supports past arguments that hemispheric regions exert primarily a net inhibitory influence on each other. However, with some asymmetries significant lateralization occurred for all callosal strengths or for weak callosal strengths of any nature.

In this specific model, the results could be interpreted as a "race-to-learn" involving the two hemispheric regions, with the "winner" (dominant side) determined when the model as a whole acquired the input-output mapping and learning largely ceased. Among other things, the results suggest that lateralization to a cerebral region can in some cases be associated with increased synaptic plasticity in that region relative to its mirror-image region in the opposite hemisphere, a testable prediction. This hypothesis seems particularly interesting in the context of evidence that synaptogenesis peaks during the first three years of life and may be an important correlate of language acquisition.

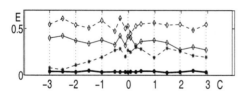

Figure 2: Error E vs. callosal strength C for model versions where the left hemisphere is more excitable. The upper dashed curve shows pre-training error and the lowest (thick solid) curve shows post-training error for the full intact model. The two middle curves show post-training output error when the left hemisphere alone (dashed line) or the right hemisphere alone (solid line) controls output.

For lesioning studies (a lesion is a region of damage), 10 versions of the intact model were used (callosal influence excitatory in 5, inhibitory in 5), representing a range of prelesion lateralization from none to essentially complete (Reggia, et al, 2000). Each lesion was introduced into an intact model by

clamping a randomly selected subset of elements in one hemispheric region to be non-functional. Performance errors of the full model and each hemisphere alone were measured immediately after the lesion (acute error measures) and then after further training until the model's performance returned to normal (post-recovery error measures). Lesion sizes were varied systematically from 0% to 100%. Not surprisingly, the results showed that acutely, the larger the lesion and the more dominant the lesioned hemispheric region, the greater was the performance impairment of the full model. The lesioned hemispheric region had a drop in mean activation levels, and exhibited impaired performance when assessed in isolation. In addition, when excitatory callosal influences existed, the intact, non-lesioned hemispheric region also often had a drop in mean activation, and exhibited impaired performance, representing the model's analog of transcallosal diaschisis (Meyer et al, 1993). When callosal influences were inhibitory, mean activation increased in the intact hemisphere. Experimentally, regional cerebral blood flow and glucose metabolism are found to decrease bilaterally following a unilateral stroke (Meyer et al, 1993). Thus, to the extent that coupling exists between neuronal activity and blood flow/oxidative metabolism, the mean activation shifts seen with excitatory callosal influences in this model are most consistent with those observed experimentally following unilateral brain lesions.

When the lesioned model was allowed to undergo continued training, recovery occurred with performance eventually returning to prelesion levels. The non-lesioned hemisphere very often participated in and contributed to recovery, more so as lesion size increased. This is consistent with a great deal of experimental evidence; see (Reggia et al, 2000) for discussion. Our results thus support the hypothesis of a right hemisphere role in recovery from aphasia due to some left hemisphere lesions. They also indicate that one possible cause for apparent discrepancies in past studies may be inadequate control for the effects of lesion size, a factor that should be carefully analyzed in future experimental studies.

Finally, a second phoneme sequence generation model was studied where the hemispheric regions were modeled as two-dimensional sheets of spatially-organized neural elements having more realistic intracortical connections and homotopic callosal connections. All of the experiments described above concerning conditions under which lateralization occurs and the interhemispheric effects of cortical lesions were repeated with this second model (Shkuro et al, 2000). Although quantitative differences occurred in the results, qualitatively the results were essentially the same.

Self-Organizing Topographic Maps

While lateralization and functional asymmetries have been most prominently associated with cognitive functions, it has also been demonstrated electrophysiologically that topographic maps in mirror image regions of sensory/motor cortex exhibit a rich range of patterns of asymmetries and lateralization (e.g., Nudo et al, 1992; Bianki 1993). Our second model consists of two mirror image hemispheric regions receiving input from a "sensory surface" (Fig. 3) or two surfaces (Levitan & Reggia, 2000). The model hemispheric regions have a spatial organization, intracortical activation mechanisms support a Mexican Hat pattern of lateral interactions (nearby excitation, more distant inhibition), and callosal connections are homotopic. Unlike our model for phoneme sequence generation, purely unsupervised learning is used: a variant of Hebb's Rule, competitive learning. We examined how map formation was affected by underlying cortical region asymmetries and the assumed excitatory/inhibitory nature of callosal connections, and by the interhemispheric effects of different size focal lesions.

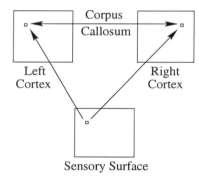

Figure 3: A network for self-organizing maps. Other model versions have two input sensory surfaces.

In all simulations, cortical maps were initially highly disorganized due to randomly assigned initial synaptic strengths. For excitatory, absent, or weakly inhibitory callosal interactions, complete and symmetric mirror-image maps appeared in both hemispheric regions. In contrast, with stronger inhibitory callosal interactions, map lateralization tended to occur (Fig. 4, top) or the maps became complementary (Fig. 4, bottom) similar to "mosaic patterns" described experimentally (Bianki, 1993). Lateralization occurred readily toward the side having higher excitability or a larger cortical region. Unlike with the phoneme sequence generation model, asymmetric plasticity had only a transitory effect on lateralization, indicating that the effects of this factor may differ substantially depending on whether supervised or unsupervised learning is used. We showed mathematically that in this model, a "phase transition" in

model behavior was to be expected with a callosal strength of around -1.3 to -1.4 (Levitan and Reggia, 1999). Above this value, bilateral symmetric maps are expected; below this value, lateralization and complementary maps are expected. This prediction was always found to be true in simulations.

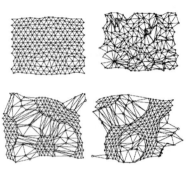

Figure 4: Pairs of cortical maps where map organization is shown using the method of Kohonen. Each pair of pictures plots the centers of receptive fields of the cortical elements in the space of the sensory surface (i.e., these are not pictures of the cortical regions). **Top:** Left map more organized than right. **Bottom:** Complementary mosaic maps.

As with the phoneme sequence generation model, we systematically examined the effects of unilateral focal cortical lesions of varying sizes in a representative subset of versions of our map model (Levitan & Reggia, 1999). As expected, more profound effects occurred with increasing lesion size. Activation changes in the intact hemispheric region were most consistent with experimental data when excitatory callosal influences were present. With excitatory or weak inhibitory callosal influences where pre-lesion maps were full and symmetric, no change or a small amount of post-lesion decreased organization occurred in contralateral unlesioned maps. With stronger inhibitory callosal influences where pre-lesion maps were complementary/lateralized, a substantial post-lesion increase of organization of the contralateral intact map often occurred. These testable predictions about effects of lesions on corresponding map regions in the intact contralateral hemispheric region have not been simulated computationally in the past, nor have they yet been measured experimentally to our knowledge.

Letter Identification

Our third model uses a combination of unsupervised and supervised training to learn to classify a small set of letters presented as pixel patterns in the left (LVF), midline, and right (RVF) visual fields (Shevtsova & Reggia, 1999). The network consists of interconnected two-dimensional arrays of cortical elements (Fig. 5). Each visual field projects to the contralateral primary visual cortex, which extracts only one important type of visual features: orientation of local edges. The primary cortex layers project onto ipsilateral visual association cortex layers. For simplicity and because biological primary visual cortex is largely lacking callosal connections, only the association layers in the model are homotopically connected via a simulated corpus callosum. Association layers project to an output layer where ideally only one output element is activated, representing the correct identity of the input element. Primary-to-association connection strengths are modified using a competitive unsupervised Hebbian rule, while associative-to-output weights are learned using a supervised error correction rule. Model performance is measured using root mean square error of output activation patterns; lateralization is measured as the difference in contribution of the two hemispheres to performance.

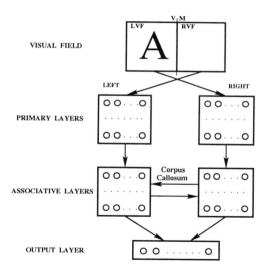

Figure 5: Network for visual character recognition task. VM = vertical meridian, LVF = left visual field, RVF = right visual field.

In this model, persistent lateralization occurred toward the side having larger size, higher excitability, or higher unsupervised/supervised learning rate. Lateralization tended to be more pronounced when callosal connections were inhibitory and to decrease when they were excitatory. Associative layer lesioning produced results similar to those with the other models: greater performance deficit with larger or dominant side lesions, acute post-lesion fall in activation in the intact hemispheric region as well as the lesioned hemisphere with excitatory but not inhibitory callosal influences, and frequent participa

tion of the non-lesioned hemisphere in recovery regardless of callosal influences, especially with larger lesions (Shevtsova & Reggia, 2000). While unilateral lesions generally produced the expected contralateral visual field impairment, an unexpected finding was that mild impairment also occurred in the visual field on the *same* side as the lesion. This occurred with excitatory but not inhibitory callosal influences. It is of interest because such surprising ipsilateral visual field impairment has been found in recent clinical studies with unilateral visual cortex lesions.

Discussion

In summary, we have used modeling to systematically investigate whether underlying asymmetries can lead to lateralization, how assumptions about callosal influences affect lateralization, and the interhemispheric effects of focal cortical lesions. We studied three models of cortical regions interacting via callosal connections that differ in their task, network architecture, learning method, etc. Use of three different models insures that the overall results obtained are reasonably general, i.e., they are not tied to a specific task, architecture, or learning method. Our models have been limited in size and scope, have each involved lateralization of only a single task, and have generally had only a single underlying asymmetry. While they are greatly simplified from neurobiological and behavioral reality, they are still based on some basic principles of biological neural elements, circuits and synaptic plasticity.

All three models exhibit certain results in common: 1. Each of a variety of underlying hemispheric asymmetries in isolation can lead to lateralization, including asymmetric size, excitability, and synaptic plasticity. This is consistent with past arguments that more than one underlying cerebral asymmetries may be contributing to lateralization (Hellige, 1993). 2. In the intact models, lateralization generally appeared most intensely with inhibitory interhemispheric interactions (although in some cases it also appeared with excitatory or absent callosal connections), lending support to past arguments that whatever the actual neurophysiological nature of callosal synapses, callosal influences are effectively inhibitory/suppressive in nature. 3. However, following focal lesions, an acute decrease was generally observed in activation and sometimes performance in the contralateral intact hemispheric region with excitatory but not inhibitory callosal interactions. These latter changes resemble those seen experimentally in acute stroke patients, lending support to past arguments that callosal influences are predominantly excitatory. 4. After a post-lesion recovery period, the intact, non-lesioned hemisphere was often partially responsible for recovery, supporting the controversial hypothesis that the right hemisphere plays a role in recovery from some types of aphasia due to left hemisphere lesions. This effect increased with increasing lesion size, suggesting that future experimental studies of this issue should carefully consider lesion size in interpreting data.

Perhaps the most intriguing result from these simulations is the finding that, in general, using inhibitory callosal connections in the model produces results most consistent with past theories of hemispheric rivalry, while using excitatory callosal influences produces results most consistent with lesioning data. This reflects the long-standing controversy about the overall excitatory/inhibitory role of callosal connections summarized earlier. We refer to this phenomenon as the "callosal dilemma". This dilemma might be resolved in a number of ways. For example, callosal effects might be a mixture in time and space of excitatory and inhibitory influences, similar to what has sometimes been observed with cortical sensory afferents (Stemmler et al, 1995). Another possibility is that callosal excitatory influences might be combined with subcortical cross-midline inhibition in afferent pathways. We have obtained encouraging initial results in examining this latter hypothesis in some of our models (Reggia et al, 2001a, b). The subcortical inhibition leads to cortical functional asymmetries, while excitatory callosal connections lead to post-lesion activity changes similar to those observed biologically.

Acknowledgments

Supported by NINDS award NS 35460. We thank the reviewers for helpful comments.

References

[1] Anninos P & Cook N. Neural Net Simulation of the Corpus Callosum, *Intl. J. Neurosci*, 38, 1988, 381-391.

[2] Berlucchi G. Two Hemispheres But One Brain, *Behav. Brain Sci.*, 6, 1983, 171-173.

[3] Bianki V. *The Mechanism of Brain Lateralization*, Gordon & Breach, 1993.

[4] Cook N. *The Brain Code*, Methuen, 1986.

[5] Cook N & Beech A. The Cerebral Hemispheres and Bilateral Neural Nets, *Int. J. Neurosci.*, 52, 1990, 201-210.

[6] Davidson R & Hugdahl K (eds.), *Brain Asymmetry*, MIT Press, 1995.

[7] Denenberg V. Micro and Macro Theories of the Brain, *Behav. Brain Sci.*, 6, 1983, 174-178.

[8] Ferbert A, Priori A, Rothwell J, Day B, et al. Interhemispheric Inhibition of the Human Motor Cortex, *J. Physiol.*, 453, 1992, 525-546.

[9] Hellige J. *Hemispheric Asymmetry*, Harvard Univ. Press, 1993.

[10] Jacobs R. & Kosslyn S. Encoding Shape and Spatial Relations, *Cognitive Sci*, 18, 1994, 361-386.

[11] Jordon M. Attractor Dynamics and Parallelism in a Connectionist Sequential Machine, *Proc 8th Ann Conf Cog Sci Soc*, 1986, 531-546.

[12] Kosslyn S, Sokolov M & Chen J. The Lateralization of BRIAN, in *Complex Information Processing*, D. Klahr & K. Kotovsky (eds.), Erlbaum, 1989, 3-29.

[13] Levitan S & Reggia J. Interhemispheric Effects on Map Organization Following Simulated Cortical Lesions, *Artificial Intelligence in Medicine*, 1999, 17, 59-85.

[14] Levitan S & Reggia J. A Computational Model of Lateralization and Asymmetries in Cortical Maps, *Neural Comp*, 12, 2000, 2037-2062.

[15] Meyer J, Obara K & Muramatsu K. Diaschisis, *Neurol. Res.*, 15, 1993, 362-366.

[16] Mountcastle V. *Perceptual Neuroscience: The Cerebral Cortex*, Harvard Univ. Press, 1998.

[17] Nudo R, Jenkins W, Merzenich M, et al (1992) Neurophysiological correlates of hand preference in primary motor cortex of adult monkeys, *J Neurosci*, 12, 2918-2947.

[18] Reggia J, Gittens S, & Chhabra J. Post-Lesion Lateralization Shifts in a Computational Model of Single-Word Reading, *Laterality*, 5, 2000, 133-154.

[19] Reggia J, Goodall S & Levitan S. Cortical Map Asymmetries with Transcallosal Excitatory Influences. *NeuroReport*, 2001a, in press.

[20] Reggia J, Goodall S, Shkuro Y & Glezer M. The Callosal Dilemma, *Neurological Research*, 2001b, in press.

[21] Reggia J, Goodall S, & Shkuro Y. Computational Studies of Lateralization of Phoneme Sequence Generation, *Neural Computation*, 10, 1998, 1277-1297.

[22] Ringo J, Doty R, Demeter S & Simard P. Time Is of the Essence: A Conjecture that Hemispheric Specialization Arises from Interhemispheric Conduction Delay, *Cerebral Cortex*, 4, 1994, 331-343.

[23] Shevtsova N & Reggia J. A Neural Network Model of Lateralization During Letter Identification, *J. Cog. Neurosci.*, 11, 1999, 167-181.

[24] Shevtsova N. & Reggia J. Interhemispheric Effects of Simulated Lesions in a Neural Model of Letter Identification, *Brain and Cognition*, 44, 2000, 577-603.

[25] Shkuro Y, Glezer M. and Reggia J. Interhemispheric Effects of Simulated Lesions in a Neural Model of Single-Word Reading, *Brain and Language*, 72, 2000, 343-374.

[26] Stemmler M, Usher M & Niebur E. Lateral Interactions in Primary Visual Cortex, *Science*, 269, 1995, 1877-1880.

Modeling How and When Learning Happens in a Simple Fault-Finding Task

Frank E. Ritter (ritter@ist.psu.edu)
School of IST, 504 Rider, 120 Burrowes St.,
The Pennsylvania State University
State College, PA 16801 USA

Peter Bibby (peter.bibby@nottingham.ac.uk)
School of Psychology,
The University of Nottingham
Nottingham, NG7 2RD UK

Abstract

We have developed a process model that learns in multiple ways using the Soar chunking mechanism while finding faults in a simple control panel device. The model accounts very well for measures such as problem solving strategy, the relative difficulty of faults, average fault-finding time, and, because the model learns as well, the speed up due to learning when examined across subjects, faults, and even series of trials for individuals. However, subjects tended to take longer than predicted to find a fault the second time they completed a task. To examine this effect, we compared the model's sequential predictions—the order and relative speed that it examined interface objects—with a subject's performance. We found that (a) the model's operators and subject's actions were applied in basically the same order; (b) during the initial learning phase there was greater variation in the time taken to apply operators than the model predicted; (c) the subject appeared to spend time checking their work after completing the task (which the model did not). The failure to match times on the second time seeing a fault may be accounted for by the subject spent checking their work whilst they learn to solve the fault-finding problems. The sequential analysis reminds us that though aggregate measures can be well matched by a model, the underlying processes that generate these predictions can differ.

Introduction

There is a speedup effect in the time taken to solve problems that is nearly universal across tasks and subjects (Rosenbloom & Newell, 1987). A major question has been understanding how people this learning occurs. Cognitive models have used several mechanisms to account for learning, such as knowledge compilation and strengthening in the ACT family of models (Anderson, Matessa, & Lebiere, 1998), connection strengthening in PDP models (Rumelhart, McClelland, & group, 1986), rule creation from impasses using analogical reasoning (VanLehn & Jones, 1993), and chunking mechanisms (Feigenbaum & Simon, 1984; Larkin, 1981; Rosenbloom & Newell, 1987). In order to study how multiple learning mechanisms can influence learning, and show how procedural learning may be composed of multiple mechanisms, we explored how to model behavior in a task familiar to us.

There are a number of problems that arise in testing the different approaches to modeling learning. First, the actual path of what is learned and when by an individual learning a

task, to a certain extent, remains predicted but untested. Secondly, there is the problem of the grain size of the measures of subject's performance that have been compared with computational models. Some modelers have focused at the level of problem solving strategy, but detailed comparisons remain rare. Thirdly, some models have automatic learning but few been compared with the time-course of behavior. Doing so would help understand when learning occurs.

These problems make it difficult to compare models of the learning process and have led to a proliferation of different, though equally plausible, accounts of how the time taken to solve problems reduces as cognitive skills develop. This paper will report the results of comparing a process model against subjects' behavior and will address these problems by:

(a) comparing subjects' behavior individually with the model as they both complete 20 problem solving tasks. Both of their answer times decrease by nearly an order of magnitude across these tasks.

(b) comparing subject's behavior with the model using several different kinds of measurements.

(c) using a computational architecture that has an automatic learning mechanism.

We will first explain the task that both subjects and the model completed, and then the model. A comparison between aggregate and individual measures of the model's and subjects' performance follows, which provides support for the model. Because the quality of this match is so high it provides few cues where to improve the model. We then turn to comparing the model's sequential predictions with an individual subject. We conclude by examining the implications of this work on problem solving, multiple learning mechanisms, post-event learning, and the role of aggregate and individual data.

The Fault-Finding Task

The task that subjects and the model solved consisted of trouble-shooting a control panel device using a memorized schematic. Previous research with a similar task (Kieras & Bovair, 1984; Kieras, 1988) has shown that instructions need to convey to subjects (a) knowledge of the structure of the system, (b) knowledge about the underlying principles that control the behavior of the system, and (c) knowledge about how to perform tasks using the topological and principle information. Previous work in this area has resulted in summaries of behavior in a series of related tasks such as the role of representations (Kieras & Bovair, 1984), operation of non-faulted circuits (Bibby & Payne, 1993; 1996), and process models that perform multiple tasks but do not learn (Bibby & Reichgelt, 1993).

Ten subjects, all university undergraduates aged 19 to 21 years, were given: (a) a general introduction to the task that included information about power flow through the system and that component indicators light up when the component is receiving power; (b) a picture of the interface that they studied (see Figure 1); and (c) a schematic of the underlying circuit (see Figure 1) showing how the components of the system were connected together by a series of switches, which they were asked to memorize. Subjects were also told that a fault existed when a component indicator light was not lit when it was receiving power. Taken together this information was sufficient to identify faults in the system.

On the interface display and later in the text and figures of this paper, straightforward abbreviations are used to refer to components in the schematic, such as PS standing for power supply and EB1 for energy booster 1.

Once subjects had learned the schematic they were introduced to a computer based version of the system and asked to complete a series of fault finding tasks. Subjects were told that one component in the circuit was faulty and were asked to indicate which component by clicking on it with the mouse. Their reaction times and choices were recorded and analyzed for latency, correct number of choices, and so on.

The Diag Model

Diag is implemented in the Soar cognitive architecture. The model's behavior is organized around search in problem spaces, and it learns while doing the task. We take these up in turn.

Soar represents problem solving as search through and in problem spaces using operators. When there is a lack of knowledge about how to proceed, an impasse is declared. Soar models will typically end up with a stack of problem spaces, as problem solving on one impasse may lead to further impasses. The stack will change as the impasses get resolved through problem solving. When knowledge about how to resolve an impasse becomes available from problem solving in an impasse, a chunk (a new production rule) is created. This chunk will contain as its condition the knowledge in the higher context that has been used in problem solving in the impasse to recognize the same situation, and it will contain the changes from the problem solving as its action. This simple chunking mechanism, by varying the type of impasse and type of knowledge, has been used to create over 20 complex mechanisms including search control, EBL, and declarative learning, in addition to the mechanisms presented here. Further information on Soar is available at ritter.ist.psu.edu/soar-faq/ , including online references, pointers to online tutorials, and an extensive bibliography.

Diag has to interact with the task, and there appear to be at least two control mechanisms for interaction that can be used in Soar that support learning. One way is to notice the

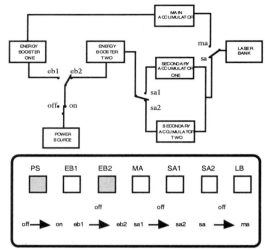

Figure 1. Schematic of the laser-bank device (top), and the laser-bank interface (bottom). Boxes (the lights) below the abbreviations and above the switches (arrows) are grayed out to indicate components are working. This diagram illustrates a faulty component (SA2).

multiple actions as they are proposed and learn to sequence them (Chong & Laird, 1997). Another way is to collapse the goal stack on output to enforce seriality whilst learning what component to attend to, and then to rebuild the stack. This is what Diag does.

Rebuilding the goal stack as an approach to learning interaction makes a testable prediction, that there will be a loss of problem-solving context when initiating an interaction with the environment. This is consistent with the results and review of Irwin and Carlon-Radvansky (1996), who showed that eye movements (which is analogous to the model's interactions) suppress mental rotation and other types of processing, including mental arithmetic and working memory search.

How the Model Finds Faults

The model begins at the level of minimum competence—the point at which subjects have just memorized the schematic. The model therefore assumes an understanding of power flow through the device, how to recognize a faulty component, and a basic strategy for diagnosing a fault. The combination of schematic and interface knowledge implements a common strategy in this task (strategy #1 in Bibby & Payne, 1996). The present version of the model consists of 186 initial production rules organized in 20 operators in 7 hierarchical problem spaces.

The model does not have immediate access to the entire world state. Rather than view the entire world at once, Diag continually decides where to look (as CHOOSE-COMPONENT), looking there (ATTEND), checking the part it saw (COMPREHEND), and then deciding where to look next (if necessary, again with ATTEND). The organization of components on the (memorized) interface schematic and the use of these operators moving across the interface representation causes the components to be checked in a basically left to right sequence.

If a subgoal requires an external action to be performed, this external action is passed up as an augmentation to the top state. Knowledge in the top problem space proposes a high priority operator to execute the action. The selection of this high priority operator removes the goal stack, which was in service of some other problem, typically trying to find the fault based on the current information. After the external information is obtained and comprehended, the goal stack is then re-built. The same goal stack may not be rebuilt if the input from the outside world gives rise to a different situation requiring a different response.

Figure 2 shows illustrates the model's performance, showing the operators and their order in solving a fault for the first time. The path illustrates the behavior of the model, particularly the cyclical behavior of choosing a component to check and then checking it. The horizontal lines represent levels in the hierarchical problem spaces.

No attempt to model subject's mistakes was made—incorrect responses were removed from the data used for comparisons with the model. Subjects who scored less than 80% correct were also excluded—this group would be very difficult to model as the assumptions concerning subjects' initial knowledge are harder to justify.

How and What the Model Learns

Diag learns how to perform actions more directly without internal search and learns which objects to attend to in the interface without internal deliberation. The number of rules learned varies according to the order and number of tasks. On average, the model learns around 200 new rules (chunks) over 20 problems (maximum 222). What Diag learns on each trial depends on the problem and what was learned from previous problems.

What is learned, when it is learned, and how it is learned arises from the architecture, the knowledge and its organization, and the model's problem solving experience. In Diag, these create three types of learning. (a) Operator implementation, where specific knowledge about how to apply an operator is learned through search in a sub problem space. This represents a type of procedural learning.

(b) Operator creation, where an operator is created in one problem space for use in another. The ATTEND operator is elaborated in this way. With practice, the model learns which objects to attend to. These new rules serve as a kind of episodic memory noting the results of problem solving. It is their transfer and application across faults that give the largest improvements.

(c) State augmentation rules, which augment the state with derivable knowledge that act as a type of declarative learning. For example, the model can learn that if EB1 has been checked (and was working) and the current light you are looking at (the main accumulator) is not lit, then the component MA is broken. Each of these types of learning can be seen individually in other architectures and models.

During the course of solving fault-finding tasks newly learned rules can transfer across trials. There is no transfer of newly learned rules within a trial because Diag does not backtrack in its problem solving.

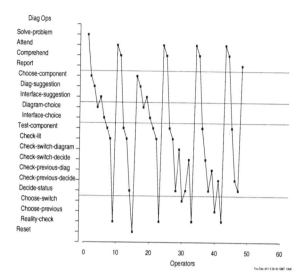

Figure 2. The order of Diag's operator applications the first time it solves the Energy Booster 1 fault.

When the Model Learns: Comparison with Aggregate Data

Diag accounts for numerous regularities in the data in both the fault-finding task (which we examine here) and the switching task. By matching the transfer between tasks over trials and tasks, we will show that the model matches when subjects learn.

A hierarchical linear regression was used to examine what best predicted problem solving time. The number of components examined predicts 11% of the variability in solution times. Model cycles (with learning off) predicts a further 4%. Diag's decision cycles with learning switched on accounts for an additional 60% of the variability. If the entry of terms is reversed, model cycles of the learning model accounts for all the variance accounted for (75%). The regression and figures to follow suggest that Diag accounts for the subject's behavior because it matches their problem solving *and* their learning.

There is a strong relationship between the time the model and the subjects took to solve the problems ($R^2 = 0.98$, $p < 0.0001$) over task order (Figure 3). As this model suggests, variation in problem solving time is not just due to noise, but much of it can be accounted for by variable amounts of transfer dependent on the current and previous faults. A learning curve is usually a monotonically decreasing curve (Newell & Rosenbloom, 1981) unless task difficulty substantially differs between tasks (Nerb, Ritter, & Krems, 1999); this data is not monotonically decreasing. A post-experiment analysis of the series of faults indicated that our software did not randomly assign faults. Fault 3 was, on average, later in the circuit than the first two faults. To obtain a smooth curve, the average difficulty of faults must remain uniform across the series.

The average variability in problem solving time per subject accounted for by model cycles is 79%. However, the regression was not significant for two of the subjects. When these subjects are removed from the analysis the average variability accounted for increased to 95%. The B coefficient represents the number of seconds per model cycle. S5 has a rate of 10 ms and S7 has a rate of 50 ms. Both these values are significantly lower than the average B coefficient. These subjects do not show the variation in time across tasks like other subjects, and that their performance does not correlate with practice or task type.

Finally, we also examined how the fit varied across trials for the eight subjects for whom Diag's model cycles provided a good fit to their total problem solving times. A typical (but not the best) match between subject and model is shown in Figure 4.

Where Soar problem solving models have been compared with subjects, the model cycle rate is generally longer than 100 ms (Nerb, Ritter, & Krems, 1999; Peck & John, 1992 analyzed in Ritter, 1992), indicating that models are too intelligent, performing the task more efficiently than subjects (taking less cycles because of a more efficient strategy) or not performing as much of the task as the subjects (e.g., not modeling moving the mouse). This is arguably better than being too short, which indicates the model is doing too much (Kieras, Wood, & Meyer, 1997). Models of simple tasks often come quite close to matching data with a 100 ms cycle without adjustments such as reading rate and disambiguating regions of text (Lewis, 1993, p. 201), simple reaction times (Newell, 1990), and covert visual attention (Wiesmeyer, 1991).

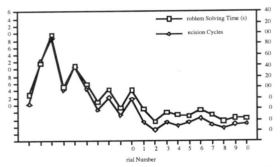

Figure 3. Problem solving time and model decision cycles across trials averaged over all subjects.

Comparison with Sequential Data

Subjects tended to take longer than predicted to find a fault the second time they completed a task, 32 times out of 47 opportunities. To examine this on a more detailed level, we compared the model's sequential predictions—the order and relative speed that Diag examined interface objects—with an additional subject's verbal and non-verbal protocol while solving five problems. The outcome of this comparison highlighted several places to improve the model and allowed us to identify a new way that the subject learned.

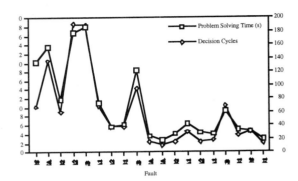

Figure 4. Problem solving time and model decision cycles for individual trials for the fifth best matched subject.

The subject performed the task correctly four times, with performance times comparable with other subjects. While this data may not seem extensive, it represents about 1% of the entire set of verbal protocol data compared with sequential model predictions through 1994 (Ritter & Larkin, 1994).

The model could be aligned with 32 of the 36 codable verbal utterances, and 21 of the 30 codable mouse moves and mouse clicks. The correspondence between subject and model was 91 ms/cycle on average.

Figure 5 shows the time course of how the model's sequential predictions matched the subject's behavior. Overt mouse behaviors are those that can be matched to overt task actions. Implicit mouse behaviors are those movements that can only be compared to internal actions of the model. For example, shifting attention in the model to a component can be aligned to a mouse movement over the same component.

If the model and the subject were solving the task at the same rate, a straight line with unary slope would appear. Deviations from this line indicate that the model and the subject are performing parts of the task at different relative rates, with some typical differences having diagnostic patterns (Ritter & Larkin, 1994). For example, when the slope is greater than 1, the model is performing relatively more work than the subject is.

In Trial 1, top, the subject and the model do not match so well. The relatively horizontal line indicates that interface objects in the subject's early verbal utterances could be matched to objects the model used late in the process, and that the subject spent a considerable time with the solution in mind. The negatively sloped segment around 6 s on the subject's axis indicates that the model and the subject performed two actions in different orders. Trial 2 (2nd from top), shows a slightly better correspondence, and this match improves through Trial 3 (third from top), until in Trial 4 (bottom) the subject and model now perform the task in roughly the same way, at a relatively constant rate.

While the correspondence is good enough to provide additional support for the model, the mismatches are now large enough and systematic enough to suggest that this subject was speeding up in additional ways, through step dropping perhaps.

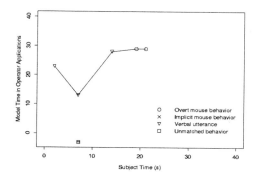

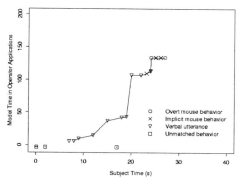

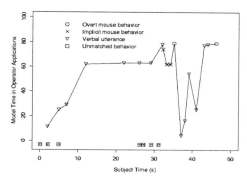

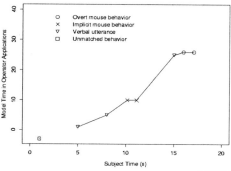

Figure 5. The relative processing rate plots for Trial 1, 2, 3, and 5 (top to bottom), for the protocol subject.

A tentative explanation can also be put forward for the effect where the subject takes a relatively longer time than the model on the second repetition of a task. While the protocol subject did not see a task three times, it appears that the model is learning in a more linear way than subjects, who may be taking time at the end of the second trial to learn in a different way, perhaps reflecting on the problem solving steps.

Discussion and Conclusions

Diag includes several types of learning. The procedural, declarative and episodic learning all contribute to the speed up on this task and appear to be necessary to predict transfer of learning between tasks. Thus, even though this task takes on average less than twelve seconds to complete, the model predicts that procedural, declarative and episodic learning all play an important part in the speed up in performance of this task. No single kind of learning is responsible for the high level of fit between the model and the subjects' performance. Rather, it is the combination of the different kinds of learning that leads to such a high degree of fit between the model and the data.

Given the high degree of fit between the model and the subjects' behavior failing to implement any of these types of learning would have detrimental effects on the modeling. Diag also interacts with its task, and this too seems essential. These two effects allow Diag to match the strategies that subjects use, the order and components that are examined, the problem solving time, the learning rate, and transfer effects. Overall, while Diag is not perfect, it would be difficult to argue that this model was not a good representation of what subjects do, learn, and transfer in this task.

The close fit of Diag to the learning data also sheds light on the power law of learning. Diag makes a stronger prediction than the power law about learning. Performance does not speed up according to a power law, but according to how much of previous learning transfers to the new task. If the tasks become harder in the course of a series of trials, as shown in Figure 4, then the power law is not obtained. If the amount of transfer truly varies, then the variation in performance, as shown repeatedly in Figure 4, is not noise, but is differential transfer. The power law appears when these details are averaged together, however.

It is quite possible that models in other architectures may be able to duplicate these results. In order to do so, they would have to include the ability to interact with a model of the task. This requires a variety of knowledge, including where to look, how to choose what to believe (internal or external representations), and how to learn through interaction. They must also include learning that leads to the power law in general and support a theory of transfer based on the individual tasks performed.

It looks like Diag leaves out at least two important learning mechanisms (which we can only see by having a learning mechanism in place already), that of decreasing amounts of retracing at the end of a trial, and faster motor output, and perhaps that of faster perceptual recognition (which is likely to exist in this as well as other tasks). These effects are either negligible or are mimicked by and highly correlated with the existing learning mechanisms. The sequential analysis reminds us that though aggregate measures can be well matched by a model, the underlying processes that generate these predictions can differ.

Acknowledgments

We thank Ellen Bass, Gordon Baxter, Peter Delaney, Fernand Gobet, Bonnie John, Clayton Lewis, Emma Norling, Mark Steedman, Richard Young and anonymous reviewers for comments and discussions. Sam Marshall provided extensive comments and programmed the model; Shara Lochun assisted with the analysis. Support was provided by the Joint Council Initiative in HCI and Cognitive Science, grant SPG 9018736.

References

Anderson, J. R., Matessa, M., & Lebiere, C. (1998). ACT-R: A theory of higher level cognition and its relation to visual attention. *Human-Computer Interaction, 12*, 439-462.

Bibby, P. A., & Payne, S. J. (1993). Internalisation and the use specificity of device knowledge. *Human-Computer Interaction, 8*, 25-56.

Bibby, P. A., & Payne, S. J. (1996). Instruction and practice in learning to use a device. *Cognitive Science, 20*(4), 539-578.

Bibby, P. A., & Reichgelt, H. (1993). Modelling multiple uses of the same representation in Soar. In A. Sloman et al. (Eds.), *Prospects for Artificial Intelligence*. 271-280. Amsterdam: IOS Press.

Chong, R. S., & Laird, J. E. (1997). Identifying dual-task executive process knowledge using EPIC-Soar. In *Proceedings of the 19th Annual Conference of the Cognitive Science Society*. 107-112. Mahwah, NJ: Lawrence Erlbaum.

Feigenbaum, E. A., & Simon, H. A. (1984). EPAM-like models of recognition and learning. *Cognitive Science, 8*, 305-336.

Irwin, D. E., & Carlson-Radvansky, L. A. (1996). Cognitive suppression during saccadic eye movements. *Psychological Science, 7*(2), 83-87.

Kieras, D., & Bovair, S. (1984). The role of a mental model in learning how to operator a device. *Cognitive Science, 8*, 255-273.

Kieras, D. E. (1988). Towards a practical GOMS model methodology for user interface design. In M. Helander (Ed.), *Handbook of Human-Computer Interaction*. North-Holland: Elsevier Science.

Kieras, D. E., Wood, S. D., & Meyer, D. E. (1997). Predictive engineering models based on the EPIC architecture for a multimodal high-performance human-computer interaction task. *Transactions on Computer-Human Interaction, 4*(3), 230-275.

Nerb, J., Ritter, F. E., & Krems, J. (1999). Knowledge level learning and the power law: A Soar model of skill acquisition in scheduling. *Kognitionswissenschaft [Journal of the German Cognitive Science Society]*. 20-29.

Newell, A., & Rosenbloom, P. S. (1981). Mechanisms of skill acquisition and the law of practice. In J. R. Anderson (Ed.), *Cognitive skills and their acquisition*. 1-51. Hillsdale, NJ: LEA.

Ritter, F. E., & Larkin, J. H. (1994). Using process models to summarize sequences of human actions. *Human-Computer Interaction, 9*(3), 345-383.

Rosenbloom, P. S., & Newell, A. (1987). Learning by chunking, a production system model of practice. In D. Klahr, P. Langley, & R. Neches (Eds.), *Production system models of learning and development*. 221-286. Cambridge, MA: MIT Press.

Rumelhart, D. E., McClelland, J. L., & group, PDP. (1986). *Parallel distributed processing: Explorations in the microstructure of cognition. Volume 1: Foundations*. Cambridge, MA: The MIT Press.

VanLehn, K., & Jones, R. M. (1993). Learning by explaining examples to oneself: A computational model. In S. Chipman & A. L. Meyrowitz (Eds.), *Foundations of knowledge acquisition: Cognitive models of complex learning*. 25-82. Boston, MA: Kluwer.

Hippocampal Cognitive Maps: An Alternative View

Alexei Samsonovich (asamsono@gmu.edu)
Krasnow Institute for Advanced Study at George Mason University
2A1 Rockfish Creek Lane, Fairfax, VA 22030-4444 USA

Giorgio A. Ascoli (ascoli@gmu.edu)
Krasnow Institute for Advanced Study and Department of Psychology, George Mason University
2A1 Rockfish Creek Lane, Fairfax, VA 22030-4444 USA

Abstract

Hippocampal place cells in rodents each selectively fire at a high rate when the animal is in a particular location of an environment; however, the firing rate never reaches zero. The present work is based on a hypothesis that the gradient of a firing rate distribution of each place cell encodes directions to an arbitrarily selected potential goal, located at the maximum of the firing rate. It is found that in a simple connectionist model this property of place cells can result from associative learning. After extensive, random exploration of a complicated maze, a simulated virtual robot finds quasi-optimal paths to/from any given locations in the maze and exploits shortcuts when new doorways are opened. The model's place cell dynamics are compatible with hippocampal multiunit data recorded from freely behaving rats. Interestingly, the same model can also solve non-spatial tasks.

Introduction

Rodent hippocampus is known to represent spatial maps of environments. Hippocampal pyramidal cells called place cells each fire when the animal is located in a particular spatial domain, called a place field of the place cell. The system of place fields forms a cognitive map of an environment. Although cognitive maps are believed to play a critical role in navigation and in formation of episodic memories, many questions about place fields remain unanswered. What are the general principles of place field formation? Why do they come in various shapes and sizes and typically have broad tails? How can a cognitive map be used for navigation, if its activity (e.g., during maze running) only provides information about the current location? Alternatively, what exactly do place fields encode? Previously proposed theoretical frameworks, including local view models (O'Keefe & Burgess, 1996), path integration models (Redish & Touretzky, 1997), trajectory learning models (Bloom & Abbott, 1996) and combinations of the above, do not suggest unambiguous and general answers.

In order to develop an understanding of these issues, we introduce an alternative view on hippocampal cognitive maps, according to which place fields (more exactly, the gradients of their firing rate distributions) encode directions to potential goals. In a spatial task, these potential goals are arbitrarily selected locations. In a general cognitive task, potential goals are situations, or states, randomly selected among all states discovered during exploration. Based on this concept, we propose a general learning mechanism that, given sufficient resources, finds efficient solutions for any cognitive task that is reducible to a navigation problem in a finite state space. This class of tasks includes finding a short path from one location to another in a maze, the Hanoi towers, the 15 puzzle, Rubik's cube, etc. Two particular cases, a maze and Rubik's cube, are studied here.

Assumptions of the Model

We assume that the graph of all possible states (the "environment") is not known initially; however, each of the states ("locations") has a unique representation in the system, meaning that it is associated with a particular model unit referred to as "a place cell". During exploration, the environment is navigated randomly, but extensively. Each visit to each particular location results in a strong activation of the corresponding place cell[1]. At various arbitrarily selected moments of time during exploration, the current location is taken as a potential goal. At this point the system pauses, and the activity mode changes from a regular place cell firing to reactivation of recently active place cells (one at a time) with a firing rate proportional to the recency of their last strong activation. In addition, the cell representing the current location (the potential goal cell) remains active. As a result, place cells become associated with the selected potential goal cell via Hebbian-like learning. The strength of the associations in our model is proportional to the recency of a place cell firing during exploration:

$$W_{ij}^{new} = \max\left\{W_{ij}^{old}, \frac{1}{t - s_i}\right\}, \qquad (1)$$

---

[1] In contrast, activation of place cells via recurrent connections is considered "weak" in this model.

where W_{ij} is the efficacy of the synaptic connection from unit i to unit j (unit j is the selected potential goal unit representing the current location: G in Figure 1), t is the current moment of time, and s_i is the time stamp of the last visit to the location associated with the unit i. The exact functional dependence (1) of W on t-s is not essential for the results of simulations, as long as the function remains strictly monotonic.

After an association process is over, the system continues random exploration of the environment, until another potential goal is randomly selected, and the associative process repeats. This exploration phase continues until all place cells come to represent potential goals and therefore acquire broad place fields. As shown below, at this point the network of place cells actually provides a capacity for finding a short path to any arbitrarily assigned goal, starting from any given location within the environment. This is accomplished by a simple algorithm: at each location, all possible local moves are tried, and the move that produces the strongest excitation of the place cell associated with the given goal is selected and performed. This process is repeated until the goal is reached. In practice, this algorithm results in a path that avoids dead ends and does not include loops (e.g., a path represented in Figure 3).

Implementation of the Model

In order to investigate the potential of this scheme, we implement a hybrid (connectionist and algorithmic) model of a virtual robot. This virtual robot can be formally described as consisting of five modules (Figure 2): the sensory, or state detection module (SM), the motor module (MM), the goal module (GM), the control module (CM), and the hippocampal module (HM). The core of the virtual robot is HM: an artificial neural network of place cells with all-to-all intrinsic excitatory connections. Associations between place

Figure 1: A random walk trajectory (thin solid line) in a randomly generated 41x30 maze covers almost the entire available area before it reaches by chance a given location G, at which time the trajectory is terminated. S: the starting point. Plaques crisscrossed with dotted lines are not available. The length of the represented random path is 83,058 steps.

cells are created with a simple Hebbian-like rule (1). SM sends output to HM, exciting one unit for each location. MM executes moves, which results in alteration of the sensory information received by SM. GM can remember a given goal and can track activity of the HM unit associated with the goal. CM monitors GM, effects mode switching in HM, and controls move selection and execution by MM.

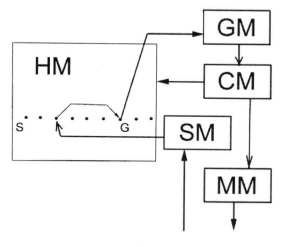

Figure 2: Block-diagram of the virtual robot. SM: sensory, or state detection module; MM: motor module; GM: goal module; CM: control module; HM: hippocampal module. HM is implemented as a neural network: an array of place units with all-to-all plastic excitatory connections. S: unit representing the starting location; G: unit representing the goal location. Only the unit representing the current location is strongly excited by SM. Modules CM, GM, SM and MM are implemented algorithmically. Arrows show input-output relations among the modules.

Simulation Results

Virtual Maze Navigation

The model was tested in several randomly generated 41x30 mazes of complicated topology. A typical maze is represented in Figure 1. The trajectory of random exploration of the maze by the virtual robot is shown by thin solid line. In this case, after exploration, the virtual robot was able to find an arbitrarily given goal from a random starting position in 78 steps (Figure 3).

In simulations performed with randomly generated virtual mazes of this sort the goal is typically reached from an arbitrarily given location in less than 100 steps after learning, which is about a thousand times shorter

than a typical length of a random walk between the same end points in the same maze. Typically, the result achieved in the first trial after learning is a remarkably short path that is of the same order as the shortest possible path, and, frequently, is one of the shortest possible paths (as in Figure 3).

The model performs very well in a stationary environment and can also be efficient in some non-stationary environments: e.g., it takes shortcuts, if new doorways are opened (not shown in Figure 3), and in principle can avoid new obstacles, such as doors that are no longer available, when the corresponding locations are represented internally as "negative goals".

Rubik's Cube

The model presented here does not utilize the planarity of the maze, nor does it rely on the spatial coordinates of particular locations. Moreover, the virtual robot does not explicitly remember the topology of the maze (e.g., availability of the doorways): this allows it to instantly exploit a new shortcut when a new doorway becomes available. All information about the environment gathered by the virtual robot amounts to individual familiarity with each visited location and a memory of the recency of the last visit to that location (a sort of "episodic memory"). Therefore, it seems logical that the model should work in many similar non-spatial tasks: Hanoi towers, Rubik's cube, the 15 puzzle, and the like.

In order to test this intuitive prediction, we studied the ability of the model to learn and navigate in the space of states of Rubik's cube. In a real computer simulation, this space of states cannot be explored exhaustively by random walk because of its enormous size (4×10^{19}). Nevertheless, Rubik's cube can be solved by the virtual robot, if at each step of exploration, instead of selecting a random move without any bias, the virtual robot preferentially moves to familiar states. In fact, we found numerically that when the probability of accepting a randomly drawn move leading to a novel state (the "curiosity parameter" of the model) is less then 0.005, the virtual robot persistently returns to the origin during exploration of the state space of Rubik's cube, at least during the first 300,000 moves.

In our final set of simulations the curiosity parameter was set to 0.001, and in addition, the exploration phase switched to the origin-search phase each time when the robot reached a novel state (see Discussion for motivations of our choice of the exploration strategy). After returning to the origin the robot continued exploration, and so on, until a total of 5,000 different states were stored in its memory. Every time upon reaching the origin the association procedure described above was applied.

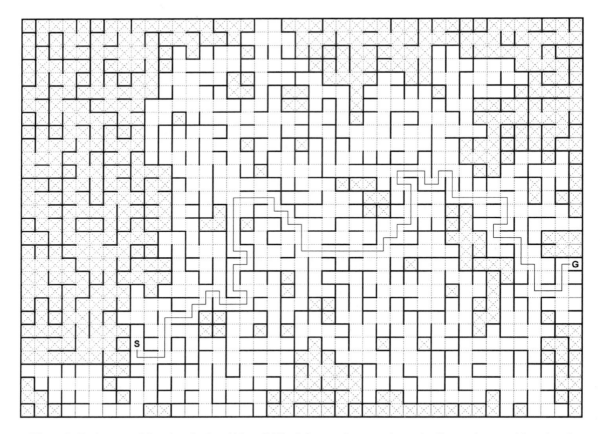

Figure 3: Trajectory of the virtual robot (thin solid line) from a given starting point S to a given goal location G in the same maze as in Figure 1. After random exploration of the maze (the learning cycle associated with the potential goal G is represented in Figure 1) this trajectory is found immediately and is reproduced in all subsequent trials, given the same locations S and G. The length of the path found by the virtual robot is 78 steps, which is the minimal possible length in this case.

After the exploration phase, the virtual robot was "given" a Rubik's cube in its initial state again and allowed to perform 2,500 random twists with it, with the only restriction that after each twist the state of the cube must be a familiar state. Otherwise the move was reversed. By the end of this process, the cube was in a state quite remote from the initial state and looked fairly random. In this condition, the virtual robot was assigned the goal to return the cube to its initial state. This was done by exactly the same procedure as in maze navigation. Typically the initial state was reached after no more than 8 steps. As in the maze navigation case, this constitutes a remarkably short path that is of the same order as the shortest possible path (for comparison, a shortest path connecting any two states of the Rubik's cube can be up to 22 twists long). In our case, the return path is about 300 times shorter than the preceding forward walk from the origin.

Discussion

In our simulations of maze navigation we assumed that SM provides a unique identifier for each given location. This assumption is consistent with single-unit recordings showing that granule cells in the rodent dentate gyrus are sharply tuned to particular locations of the animal in an environment. The activity of place cells in this model is also consistent with (and can potentially explain the emergence of) other experimentally observed phenomena related to place cells. For example, the phase precession of place cell activity (O'Keefe & Recce, 1993) would result from "trying" available moves in imagination (rather than physically moving back an forth).

Another strong assumption of our model is the learning rule (1). Our choice of the inverse law is not critical for the simulation results and could be replaced with an arbitrary monotonically decreasing function, giving the same quantitative results of simulations. In support of our general choice of this learning rule are observations of the skewness of rodent hippocampal place fields on a linear track that gradually develops over time, if the animal runs in one direction only (Mehta et al., 2000). Moreover, the related phenomenon of place field smearing (Mehta et al., 1997, 2000) naturally results from our model learning rules.

In addition, it is known from behavioral rodent experiments that rats exploring a maze do not run continuously. Rather, they intermittently pause, with a transient change in the hippocampal activity mode from Wonderwolf type I (theta mode) to large-amplitude irregular activity (LIA), during which sharp waves and "ripples" are observed. There are experimental evidence suggesting that time-compressed replay of the recent trajectory happens during sharp waves in sleep and wake states (Nadasdy et al.; 1999; Louie & Wilson, 2001). This phenomenon resembles the associative learning phase in our model, when recently active place cells become associated with the currently selected "potential goal" cell. The assumed monotonic relation between the recency of place cell activity during maze running and the frequency of its reactivation during LIA could be due to short-term potentiation effects.

From the point of view of artificial intelligence, the ideas of the learning rule of our model are not new: they are known in theory of reinforcement learning and Markov decision processes as Q-learning, TD-update, etc. (e.g., Russel & Norvig, 1995; Sutton & Barto, 1998). On the other hand, our model does not formally fall into the category of reinforcement learning models, because at each learning cycle the "potential goal" is selected by the robot arbitrarily a posteriori, rather than being given externally a priori.

Our selection of the exploration strategy of the Rubik's cube is motivated by rodent behavioral data. When positioned in the center of a novel environment, such as an office crowded with tables, computers, chairs, stacks of paper, etc., a rat does not run around. Instead, it makes a short exploratory walk in a randomly chosen direction, and then immediately returns to the original location. This exploratory pattern repeats many times (B. L. McNaughton, personal communication, 1996). As to our choice of a purely random exploration strategy in maze simulations, it was selected as the simplest possible rule. This particular choice does not invalidate applicability of our model to more intelligent strategies of exploration of a novel environment.

Similarly, the model is also robust with respect to various constraints: e.g., it works on directional graphs. We based our consideration on a novel assumption about the semantics of place cell firing, specifically, that the gradient of the firing rate distribution encodes "common sense directions": i.e., it points to the first step along a reasonably short path leading to the potential goal, rather than the direction of the radius-vector pointing to the potential goal.

We should stress that place cell firing in our model is omnidirectional (i.e., not sensitive to the direction of motion or the orientation of the head) and depends on the animal's location only. The experimentally observed directionality of place fields may have different origin. Usually in the case of one-dimensional motion the hippocampus develops separate maps for the two opposite directions; however, some cells show activity on both maps. In this case it is likely that the (initial) centers of these place fields will coincide. For this case our model predicts that these place fields will develop tails in opposite directions and eventually become adjacent to each other, with a small overlap: they will "tile". According to our model, the point of overlap, which is also initially the point of the maximal firing rate, is likely to be a place where the rat stops. All these features can be actually seen in the data of Markus et al. (1995, Fig. 10 G-H).

In summary, the model gives nontrivial predictions for place field shapes, including the following. (a) Skewness of place fields in the case of a unidirectional motion. (b) Stronger correlation of a firing rate distribution with the explored shortest path distance than with the Euclidean distance to the center of the place field. In particular, (c) Discontinuity of a place field at a barrier that partitions the environment, in contrast with predictions of the continuous two-dimensional map hypothesis. This discontinuity has been observed experimentally (B. L. McNaughton, personal communication). (d) "Tiling property" of the two place fields of a bi-directional place cell on a linear track.

The results of our study pose new open questions. For example, it is known that the hippocampal function in humans is far from being limited to the spatial domain. If the abilities found in the virtual robot are actually available in the hippocampus, then what might be their use besides spatial navigation? Although the model may not be efficient in situations that require deep reasoning or good heuristics, as in the case with Rubik's cube, we have shown that it can work in non-spatial tasks as well.

The modified Rubik's cube paradigm can be also considered as a metaphor for the exploration of the space of episodic memories. A view of the hippocampus as a context / mental state indexing device is currently discussed in the literature (Wheeler et al., 1997). According to this view, episodic memories are labeled by their contexts, and therefore remembering a reference to a particular episode implies (or amounts to) the ability to relate the context of that episode to contexts of other remembered episodes, as well as of currently ongoing events. In order to achieve this, one needs to find a "path" from one context to another. Individual steps of this path involve dropping or accepting various assumptions, beliefs, rules, conditions, etc. that apply to the entire world (or a state of mind) of a given episode. These parameters, that together constitute a "generalized context" of an episode, include among other things the time and the spatial location of the event, as well as the source (the subject) of the experience. It has been suggested many times in the literature that all parameters of a generalized context, rather than merely a spatial location, are represented in the hippocampus. If we accept that the hippocampus is a system that represents, remembers and later relates generalized contexts of episodic memories, then the problem of memory retrieval appears to be intimately related to the problem of finding a shortest path in a graph of all previously experienced contexts. The topology of this graph can be complicated, and this entire problem belongs to the class of problems considered above.

The view that the main hippocampal function consists of finding a short path from one generalized context to another is substantially different from other proposals made in the literature. In particular, a number of general as well as specific models have been proposed in order to account for hippocampal role in spatial navigation. One such model in a particular detail was similar to the model of the present work (Trullier & Meyer, 2000); however, none of these models explicitly utilizes the concept of hippocampal place fields encoding instructions of "how to get there" rather than merely spatial locations or neighborhoods *per se*. This is a distinguishing feature of the proposed framework that guarantees, e.g., equal applicability to directional and non-directional graphs, using asymmetric connections.

In conclusion, results of our model study suggest that the hippocampus could be used for spatial navigation in such a way that place cell activity would actually provide directions towards goals rather than mere self-localization. The model gives several testable predictions for place field shapes in complex mazes, e.g., discontinuity at barriers and elongation along corridors. The model allows for at least several generalizations: (i) hierarchically organized maps could cover large distances and combine independently acquired knowledge, and (ii) the same principles and the same neural network implementation can be used to solve a variety of tasks that are not specifically spatial in nature, ranging from logical reasoning to retrieval of episodic memories.

References

Bloom, K. I., & Abbott, L. F., (1996) A model of spatial map formation in the hippocampus of the rat. *Neural Computation 8*, 85-93.

Louie, K., and Wilson, M. A. (2001) Temporally structured replay of awake hippocampal ensemble activity during rapid eye movement sleep. *Neuron 29*, 145-156.

Markus, E. J., Qin, Y.-L., Leonard, B., Skaggs, W. E., McNaughton, B. L., and Barnes, C. A. (1995) Interactions between location and task affect the spatial and directional firing of hippocampal neurons. *J. Neuroscience 15 (11)*, 7079-7094.

Mehta, M., Barnes, C. A., & McNaughton, B. L. (1997) Experience-dependent, asymmetric expansion of hippocampal place fields. *Proc. Natl. Acad. Sci. 94 (16)*, 8918-8921.

Mehta, M. R., Quirk, M. C., and Wilson, M. A. (2000) Experience-dependent asymmetric shape of hippocampal receptive fields. *Neuron 25*, 707-715.

Nadasdy, Z., Hirase, H., Czurko, A., Csicsvari, J., and Buzsaki, G. (1999) Replay and time compression of recurring spike sequences in the hippocampus. *J. Neuroscience 19 (21)*, 9497-9507.

O'Keefe, J., & Burgess, N. (1996) Geometric determinants of the place fields of hippocampal neurons. *Nature 381*, 425.

O'Keefe, J., & Recce, M. L. (1993) Phase relationship between hippocampal place units and the EEG theta rhythm. *Hippocampus 3*, 317-330.

Redish, A. D., & Touretzky, D. S. (1997) Cognitive maps beyond the hippocampus. *Hippocampus 7*, 15-35.

Russel, S., and Norvig, P. (1995) *Artificial intelligence: A modern approach*. Upper Saddle River, NJ: Prentice Hall.

Sutton, R. S., and Barto, A. G. (1998) *Reinforcement learning: An introduction*. Cambridge, MA: MIT Press.

Trullier, O., & Meyer, J.-A. (2000) Animat navigation using a cognitive graph. *Biological Cybernetics, 83*, 271-285.

Wheeler, M. A., Stuss, D. T., & Tulving, E. (1997) Toward a theory of episodic memory: The frontal lobes and autonoetic consciousness. *Psychological Bulletin, 121*, 331-354.

The Anatomy of Human Personality: A Computational Implementation

Harald Schaub (harald.schaub@ppp.uni-bamberg.de)
Institute of Theoretical Psychology, Otto-Friedrich-University Bamberg
D-96045 Bamberg, Germany

Abstract

This work focuses on modeling of personality-specific behavior in complex situations. For that purpose we describe the basic assumptions of the underlying PSI - theory and point out which cognitive, motivational and emotional parameters seem to be suitable for modeling characteristics of different personality types. The modulation of parameter settings in the PSI-model generates different personalities patterns, which differ in the way of coping with specific situations. We will show the accordance of behavior pattern produced by the computer model with empirical data from human subjects.

Modeling Personality

Studies on human behavior in complex situations (Schaub, 1997a) show that strategies and failure of performance have a wide range of variation, depending on characteristics of the situation and on attributes of the person (Dörner & Schaub, 1994).

Obviously human behavior is adapted according to specific requirements of the particular circumstances. How a person is adapting to a concrete situation is regulated by aspects of knowledge, experience, skill etc. altogether factors building up personality. Cognitive modeling (Anderson & Lebière, 1998; Schaub & Schiepek, 1992; Schaub, 1997b) therefore has to achieve two goals: it has to simulate general aspects of information processing as well as the personality-specific modulation of these processes. In the following section, basic aspects of the PSI-theory will be introduced with emphasis on parameters, which allow to explain individual differences in behavior.

Aspects of the PSI-Theory as the Basis of Modeling Personality-Specific Behavior

The PSI-theory was developed to explain and to model how people act in situations, which are complex and require problem-solving behavior (Dörner, Schaub, Stäudel, & Strohschneider, 1988; Schaub, 1993; Schaub, 1997, Dörner, 1999). The theory explains processes of cognition, emotion, motivation and personality and their interaction.

In the following, we will discuss the theoretical background of the PSI-theory. These theoretical assumptions are implemented as a hybrid system of symbolic processes (which run the intention management system) and as neuronal, sub-symbolic processes (which run the perception and memory tasks).

The leading idea of the theory is the concept of *intention*. Intentions are based on needs. From our point of view needs indicate set-point-deviations of certain important variables of a system, which should be kept in homeostasis, such as the amount of glucose in the blood or intra-cellular water pressure. Besides needs concerning the survival of a system, it seems necessary to introduce „informational" needs, e.g. needs for the exploration of the environment. As soon as the set-point-deviation reaches a critical point, intentions are generated. An intention is a data structure comprising besides the respective need one or more goals, which appear to be suitable to satisfy the current need.

Intentions are stored in a special data structure (*MemInt*, Memory for Intention). Each intention includes a number of elements, particularly „start-situation", „goal-situation", „plan", „importance", „urgency" and „success-probability" and the corresponding „need". Imagine for instance the goal, to write an article for a workshop just a few hours before the deadline. It is necessary to get a laptop, to think about the contents and the structure while cooking a big pot of strong coffee. The importance of the work is high, the urgency even higher and the success-probability depends on your work in advance or our capability of improvisation.

The central process of the PSI-theory of action regulation is the intention-management-system, build up by four sub-processes: *GenInt, SelectInt, RunInt* and *Percept*. These processes manipulate intentions in the following way:

GenInt (Generate Intention) is the unit, which constructs intentions by retrieving the knowledge elements, which are necessary for completing the structure of an intention: the need, the desired goal states, and the plan or action sequence to reach it and its importance and urgency. GenInt files this information in the memory for intentions (*MemInt*).

SelectInt (Select Intention) performs the task of selecting the current intention that will govern action for the next period of time. The selection is taken according to an enlarged expectation × value-principle, using the importance and the estimated probabilities of success of the single intentions in MemInt. *SelectInt* is a kind of a conflict resolution mechanism by which the model can choose between alternative intentions. The intention with the highest value of expectation × value will be send to *RunInt*, to be executed.

RunInt (<u>Run</u> <u>Int</u>ention) takes up the active intention and executes the operations necessary to reach the goal.

Percept has the job of generating sequences of images of the environmental situation by a hypothesis-conducted process. Concurrently with RunInt, Percept produces a protocol memory, which stores actions and situations of the near past. Furthermore, the two instances produce an *expectation horizon*, which anticipates the near future.

The PSI-theory includes starting parameters that can describe the way of adapting individual behavior to situation-specific requirements. These parameters refer to the way a) individuals get information from the environment and b) how current intentions are generated, selected and elaborated.

The variation of these parameter leads to a modulation of cognitive processes, which considered as the core of personality for medium-term situations (and as emotions for the current situation). Personality is in the conception of the PSI-theory no process or structure of its own but the distinct form into which cognitive processes are cast under certain conditions. The kernel of personality is therefore a certain modulation of the processes preparing and controlling behavior. For instance: in terms of modulation of cognitive processes a certain personality could be described as characterized by:

- High *activation*, which means a high speed of information processing;
- a high *dominance of the actual intention*, i.e. a high tendency to concentrate on the actual intention and a low sensitivity for stimuli not concerning the current motivation and finally
- a low *resolution level*, standing for a rather rough way of looking on the environment and of planning

The parameters *activation*, *dominance* and *resolution level* determine whether behavior is fast or slow, preserving or not, concentrated on the task or on the environment and rough or fine. The variations of these parameters allow adapting actions to specific situational conditions.

Parameters as a Basis of Personality

In the first section we pointed out that the way a person adapts him/herself to a concrete situation is regulated by aspects of personality. Thus, personality factors can rely on individual differences in the range of possible variation of motivational, cognitive and emotional parameters.

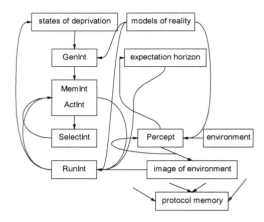

Figure 1: Main structures of the PSI-theory (compare Schaub, 1997b).

The idea, to implement personality as a system of attributes of a cognitive system, is also described by Kuhl (1998). He assumes in his personality-system-interaction theory, that personality is a pattern of interaction of cognitive functions. Even an older approach by Allport (1959, 1937) introduced the idea, that high-level traits may be based in low-level traits. He pointed out, that a high-level trait 'honesty' is generated by a set of low-level traits, like anxiety, ambition of power, and so on.

In the PSI-theory, the superior aspect of personality is considered as modulation of well-definite cognitive processes. Therefore, they have a central position with respect to modeling differences between individuals. The *mean* value of parameters as well as the *range* can be regarded as factors of personality. Interesting aspects for modeling individual differences in behavior are for that reason the current data, the variance and other aspects of the distribution of the parameters.

As we know, behavior is generated by an interaction between personality and the behavioral environment. This interaction with the environment will probably still occur and might be much stronger for personality defined as systematic cognitive biasing as in PSI theory as for traditional personality concepts. In the following section, we assume constant behavioral environment.

To illustrate, the table 1 shows different types of behavior depending on extreme values of same of the PSI-parameters.

Activation

When the activation is high, information processing will have a high speed. The Percept process will update the image of the environment within short sequences of time. The resolution level of perceiving will decrease as well as the resolution level of planning and decision-making. As a result, the Percept process works inaccurate. In extreme situations, individuals with a extreme high activation level tend to have delusions or hallucinations.

Table 1: Different types of behavior, depending on variations of the PSI-parameter.

	High	*Low*
Activation	high speed of information processing	easy-going, slow reactions
Dominance	dominance of the actual intention	high diversibility
Resolution-level	elaborate/ precise planning and acting	a rather rough way of looking on the environment, planning and acting

A low level of activation results in phlegmatic behavior. Cognitive processing will be slow. Persons with a low activation level seem good-natured, hearty and comfortable.

Activation, like the other parameters, has also a preferred range of values. Every person could have high or low activation, depending to the special circumstance of the situation. Nevertheless, high or low has a certain meaning for the individual person. People differ in the values and in the range of the parameters.

Dominance
Individuals who generally have a high level of concentration do not notice stimuli in their environment. The Percept process will run less frequently, so that the rate of updating the images of the environmental situation will be lower. As a result, individuals with a high dominance of the actual intention often experience surprise. The capability to anticipate events by constructing an expectation horizon is less successful. They foresee neither dangers nor opportunities. As the competence-level is decreasing when something unexpected happens, the individual will look for secure environments in which they can stabilize their feeling of competence. People with a high level of concentration will be successful in „chess-like-realities". The game is completely transparent and a strong need of control is suitable for effective playing.

On the other hand, individuals with a low level of dominance show motivational flexibility. They take any opportunity, though without durability. Quick success is important; otherwise, they tend to abandon their actual intention and pick up the next one. Individuals with a

low rate of dominance succeed in realities in which a quick „crisis-management" is favored. They have the ability to make quick decisions and to work hard as long as they anticipate a reward in the near future. In stock exchange they would profit from their capability of managing crises, in intellectual work however they will be less successful, as they are unable to work at a task with high tenacity.

Resolution level
Running a high-resolution level the way of looking to the world and the modes of planning and decision-making are quite elaborate. However elaborate planning and acting needs much time. Persons who have a generally high-resolution level tend to withdraw in critical situations and to brood a long time. If they are able to bring planning to an end, their plans will be elaborate but rather conservative ideas.

Individuals with a rather low-resolution level have a rather rough way of looking to the environment as well as of planning and decision-making. They do not take into account conditions for actions and side effects and long-term effects in detail. A low level of resolution results thus in „unconditional" behavior and „over inclusive" planning. However, their decisions can be quite unconventional. Creativity in problem solving could be a result of a low-resolution level coupled with intelligence.

The combination of these „personality" factors allows the grouping of several different types according to the values of the parameters illustrated above.

One type of personality could be represented by a person, who generally sticks to its current intention in a rigid way and at the same time has a high activation level and therefore the desire to do great things. Moreover, this person is planning and acting with a high-resolution level. His/her plans will be highly elaborated. Such a person will obviously be successful – as long as the situational conditions do not change. Another example for a personality-specific behavior simulated by the variations of PSI-parameter is the combination of low activity, low dominance of the current intention and high-resolution level. The behavior resulting from this combination of parameters would resemble the character.

Evaluation of the Model

In this passage, we will investigate the question relating to the aspects of the model's behavior that are similar to the subjects' behavior and those components, which do not fit the empirical data.

The basis of a group-statistical comparison will be the development of different behavior variables. Both, simulated model and human subjects, had to deal with a computer based complex task (compare Schaub, 1997b). Through chance-variation of the starting parameters (for each parameter activation, dominance, resolution-level a random uniform value is take from a range zero (minimum) to one (maximum)), 80 simulation-runs were produced which differed from each other as a consequence of their different outset parameters. These 80 'model subjects' in the following will be compared to 80 live subjects (first-year students, most of them from psychology, 40 male, 40 female, age 20-28 years).

The Task

The human subjects as well as the simulation model were confronted with the complex, dynamic computer-scenario 'garden'. In this situation, the task of the subject lies in being the gardener of a market garden. It is the objective of the subject to earn as much money as possible by growing, harvesting and selling the crop. Data were recorded in log files (the same format for model and live subjects), with videotape and with different tests and questionnaires. Each of the subjects played the game for 15 simulated year-cycles (with 365 days, which makes 5475 tiny cycles in total), which takes about 75 minutes to play. Human subjects as well as the model had to run these 5475 tiny cycles.

The subject can grow different plants, he/she has to irrigate and fertilize the fields and take steps against detrimental insects. Plants can be harvested and sold at the end of a year. The subject has his own laboratory where he or she can experiment in biological pest control. The laboratory offers means for changing the genetic code of the insects in a way that they are no longer harmful to the crop. Furthermore, it is possible to improve the fertilizers.

The variables of the system 'garden' can be separated into two different realms. The first of them is the realm of gardening, includes all the actions and variables that are directly connected to caring for the crop, such as fertilizing, harvesting and so forth. The second realm is that of the laboratory, including all the actions and variables concerning gene-manipulation of the insects and the quality of the fertilizer.

The goal subjects are asked to achieve is that of 'capital increase'. This goal can only be reached by selling the crop. Every operation however reduces capital. This fact determines two sub-goals:

- Increase of the produce (profit from the fields)
- Low measure-taking operation activity

These sub-goals however are not quite compatible, as the increase of produce requires a lot of activity from the gardener, such as fertilizing, irrigating, sowing and insect removal.

Medium term attainment of these sub-goals is only possible by operating in the laboratory. Work in the laboratory however is rather problematic since, in the beginning, it leads away from the two sub-goals. Occupation in the lab draws attention and activity away from

the garden and, at the same time, it is associated with the application of many measures. In medium term however, it allows reaching the two sub-goals 'produce increase' and 'measure minimization'. This means, optimizing the two sub-goals requires allowing for first moving further away from them.

If a subject avoids using the lab, capital can only be increased by intense activity in the garden, which therefore is not an optimal solution. The lab should not become an ulterior motive since a capital increase in the end is only possible through crop sales.

The first requirement of the 'garden' is a regulation problem, meaning that subjects have to apply the right means at the right time, taking into account the system's own dynamics. They have to find out when to sow which plant, how to proceed in fertilizing and irrigating and so forth. The requirement therefore is to find measures producing the intended effects, while bearing time, dosage and system-dynamics in mind.

The second requirement is handling insects and laboratory. „Interpolation-problems" are what subjects are supposed to solve in the lab, meaning that from a known genetic code of an insect, they have to get to a known optimum „goal-genetic-code". For this purpose, different means are at the subject's disposal. However, these means do have different application-conditions, which have to be taken into account. The requirement is characterized by the fact that subjects by planning as well as trial and error have to find the optimum sequence leading to the goal, choosing it from a huge variety of other sequences.

The co-ordination of operating on both of these problems in itself is a third requirement since an enormous number of combination possibilities for the first two requirements exist.

Comparison

One parameter (in figure 2) to compare subjects and simulation runs was behavior-activity, which was calculated from current operations in proportion to possible interventions in the give task (which gives a range from zero to one in the vertical variable in figure 2, 3 and 4). Several tests were carried out. In the following we describes the pearson correlation between mean time series of behavior produced by the live subjects and by the model.

Even though simulated subjects are working on a markedly higher activity level (intervening twice as often), both are very similar. Following a minor level of activity in the first section, both curves reach a plateau of activity with a slightly ascending tendency. During the first couple of sections, an orientation takes place; operations are tried out and practiced. The similarity between the two time series of behavior is represented by a correlation coefficient of r=0.87 (all presented correlation are statistical significant at a level of 5% or better). One reason for the higher activity level of the model might be, that the human subjects have changes in motivation, attention, or a tired in using the mouse. These factors don't vary in the model.

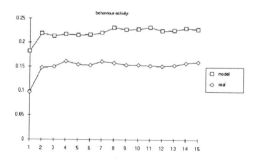

Figure 2: Behavior-activity. Compared PSI-*modeled* subjects and *real/live* subjects. Vertical variable is *activity* (maximum is 1); horizontal variable is *time periods*.

Further, the model showed a noticeable increase from trials 8-15 compared to trials 2-7, which is not significant.

Interesting in the context of personality is figure 3 and 4, presenting activity for different behavior types.

The vertical axis represents a special type of activity: The amount of input the subjects had in the gardens laboratory. Consider that there are three classes of action: Garden (to manure, to crop, and so on), laboratory (raising insects), and doing nothing. We picked one kind of this, the lab activity, and made a similarity analysis of the 80 human subjects regarding the run of the curve of the lab activity. We found four clear types of behavior (figure 3). These types were defined by a clear calculate criterion: The distribution of the lab activity compared to the gardening activity and doing nothing. The scissor-type e.g. started with a high amount of activity in the lab (low activity in gardening) and finished with high activity in the garden section (low lab activity). A value of 0.6 means 60% of all possible activity was in the laboratory in that cycle. We found a distribution of 20 subjects in the scissor-type, 19 in the tuning-type, and 15 in the delay-action-type and 26 in the mixed-type.

The sample of modeled subjects, created through a random uniform chance-variation of the starting parameters (activation, dominance, resolution-level), should also show the features of the four types founded in human subjects and the statistical distribution (measured with the same formal criterions).

If the 80 model subjects are partitioned according to the criterion for their organization of activity (lab vs. garden vs. doing noting), an interesting image arises.

Four different behavior types, similar to the four patterns founded in the human subjects, can again be encountered with a similar distribution of the types (figure 4).

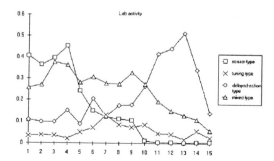

Figure 3: Activity (human subjects) of the four different behavior patterns. Vertical variable is *lab activity* (maximum is 1); horizontal variable is *time periods*.

Activity-development is rather similar for both samples. The 'types' of the modeled subjects however do show the behavior patterns in a more typical, more pronounced way. Thus ascend of activity (in the laboratory) is steeper for the (so called) „delayed action type" at the end of session. In the (so called) „scissors-type" activity is more pronounced right from the beginning, while activity of the (so called) „tuning type" is lower. Overall, the simulation model has produced the same types; they are however sharpened. The reason for this is a lack variation in factors of motivation, attention and so on in the model. Correlation between the time series of behavior of the corresponding types of simulation and human subjects (scissors-type with scissors-type; tuning-type with tuning-type; etc.) are between 0.44 and 0.88. Whereas in the human subjects the „mixed type" dominates, the simulation model seems to have specialized on the „tuning type".

Finally, the comparison of the real and simulated subjects was also being conducted at a more detailed, trial-by-trial level. The simulated and real subjects show a similar kind of changes in behavior from trial to trial. The current analysis focused on the Lab activity only, but the Garden activity and other behavioral data showed a similar pattern of transitions.

Discussion

In the basic behavior patterns, significant similarities show between the model and reality; especially distributions and tendencies have been correctly modeled. The absolute values of the model developments do however sometimes deviate considerably from those of the live subjects. Of great interest to us is how the model in fact replicates the basic behavior patterns of human subjects, which could serve as a basis of personality.

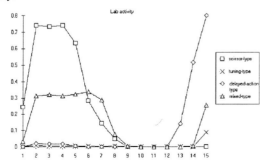

Figure 4: Activity (model) of the four different behavior patterns. Vertical variable is *lab activity* (maximum is 1); horizontal variable is *time periods*.

A complicated simulation system like the presented one, which is designed to model a large theory of action regulation and problem solving, is probably subject to several lines of criticism. So far, we have described the functions of the PSI-theory working with a complex task and compared its behavior with the behavior of human subjects. What we found was, on the focused level, similarities of the behavioral patters.

Summarizing these reflections, variations of parameter settings in the PSI-model can generate a framework for different personalities, which differ in the way of tackling specific situations. By varying the range of parameters, the PSI-theory can „build" different types of personalities.

We showed how the impact of a small number of parameters could adapt the behavior to situation-specific requirements and emerged behavior patterns, which could be stable over situations. This behavior pattern (and the underlying set of parameters) could be called „Personality". We have demonstrated the dependence of behavior patterns from specific parameters with different simulation models and their coincidence with empirical data.

Our approach has relations to cognitive styles research (c. Sternberg, 1997). However, cognitive styles have had a lot of past research, but there is no research basing the styles on a cognitive architecture like PSI and we think this is the advantage of our approach, to formulate a theoretical basis for behavior styles, our better: for personality.

It is an interesting way to go, to look at variations in models of general psychology and cognitive modeling not as a point of error or „white noise", but as a basis of a functional implementation of personality.

Acknowledgments

The work was funded by the German Research Community (DFG).

References

Allport, G.W. (1959²). *Persönlichkeit: Struktur, Entwicklung und Erfassung der menschlichen Eigenart* (Personality: A Psychological Interpretation, 1937). Meisenheim: Hain.

Anderson, J.R. & Lebière, C. (1998). *The Atomic Components of Thought*. Mahwah, NJ: Erlbaum.

Dörner, D. (1999). *Bauplan für eine Seele* (Blueprint of a Soul). Reinbek bei Hamburg: Rowohlt.

Dörner, D.& Schaub ,H, (1994). Errors in Planning and Decision-making and the Nature of Human Information Processing. *Applied Psychology: An International Review*, 43,4,433-453.

Dörner, D., Schaub, H., Stäudel, T. & Strohschneider, S. (1988). Ein System zur Handlungsorganisation oder: Die Interaktion von Emotion, Kognition und Motivation (A System for Action Regulation or the Interaction of Emotion, Cognition and Motivation). *Sprache und Kognition*, 4, 217-232.

Hille, K. (1997). *Die künstliche Seele. Analyse einer Theorie* (The Artificial Soul. The Analysis of a Theory). Wiesbaden: Deutscher Universitäts Verlag.

Kuhl, J. (1998). *Wille und Persönlichkeit: Funktionsanalyse der Selbststeuerung* (Will and Personality: Functional analysis of Self Regulation). Psychologische Rundschau, 49, (2), 61-77.

Rosenbloom, P.S., Laird, J.E., Newell, A. (Eds.) (1993). *The Soar Papers, Research on Integrated Intelligence*. Massachusetts: The MIT Press.

Schaub, H. (1993). *Modellierung der Handlungsorganisation* (Modeling Action Regulation). Bern: Huber.

Schaub, H. (1997a). Decision making in complex situations: Cognitive and Motivational Limitations. In: Flin, R., Salas ,E., Strub, M.E. & Martin ,L., *Decision Making Under Stress: Emerging Themes and Applications*. Aldershot: Ashgate.

Schaub, H. (1997b). Modeling Action Regulation. *Poznan Studies in the Philosophy of the Sciences and the Humanities*, 56, 97-136.

Schaub, H. & Schiepek, G. (1992). Simulation of Psychological Processes: Basic Issues and an Illustration Within the Etiology of a Depressive Disorder. In: Tschacher, W., Schiepek, G. & Brunner, E.H.: *Self-Organization and Clinical Psychology*. Berlin: Springer.

Sternberg, R. J. (1997). *Thinking styles*. Cambridge: University Press.

A Bayesian Model for the Time Course of Lexical Processing

Mark Steyvers
(msteyver@psych.stanford.edu)
Department of Psychology, Stanford University
Stanford, CA 94305-2130

Eric-Jan Wagenmakers
(pn_wagenmakers@macmail.psy.uva.nl)
Department of Psychology, University of Amsterdam
Amsterdam, The Netherlands.

Richard Shiffrin
(shiffrin@indiana.edu)
Department of Psychology
Indiana University, Bloomington, IN 47405-7007

René Zeelenberg
(pn_zeelenberg@macmail.psy.uva.nl)

Jeroen Raaijmakers
(raaijmakers@psy.uva.nl)

Department of Psychology, University of Amsterdam
Amsterdam, The Netherlands.

Abstract

A Bayesian-based model for lexical decision, REM-LD, is fit to data from a novel version of a signal-to-respond paradigm. REM-LD calculates the odds that a test item is a word, by accumulating likelihood ratios for each lexical entry in a small neighborhood of similar words. The new model predicts the time course of observed effects of nonword lexicality, word frequency and repetition priming. It can also make qualitative predictions for the response time distributions in tasks with subject paced responding.

Introduction

It is generally assumed that the understanding of the skill of reading should be based in part on an understanding of the storage and retrieval of words. These processes are often studied through the use of the lexical decision task, requiring participants to distinguish words (e.g., CHAIR and FUME) from nonwords (e.g., GREACH and ANSU). In tasks in which accuracy is near ceiling, three critical findings are seen in the response times: (1) The *word frequency effect*. Words that occur regularly in natural language (high frequency or HF words such as CHAIR) are classified correctly faster than words that occur relatively rarely (low frequency or LF words such as FUME). (2) The *repetition priming effect*. Prior exposure to a word leads to faster correct classifications for that word on a second presentation. This increase in performance is particularly pronounced for LF words (e.g., FUME benefits more from prior exposure than CHAIR). (3) The *nonword lexicality effect*. Nonwords that look like words (e.g. GREACH) take longer to be classified correctly than nonwords that are relatively dissimilar to words (e.g. ANSU). In this article[1], we use a new variant of a signal-to-respond procedure that produces findings in the accuracy domain that mimic those listed above for response times. We will fit a new Bayesian model, REM-LD, to the data. The advantage

of the signal-to-respond technique is that it allows one to track the time course of processing, obtaining multiple data points for each stimulus category while reducing concerns about higher order task strategies and speed-accuracy trade-off's. We will also present some preliminary work on predicting response time distributions in the lexical decision task with subject paced responding.

Experimental Data

The signal-to-respond paradigm has occasionally been applied to lexical decision (Antos, 1979; Hintzman & Curran, 1997). We used our new version of the signal-to-respond paradigm to replicate and extend Experiment 2 from Hintzman and Curran (1997).

Method

We used four types of stimuli: (1) 168 HF words, each occurring more than 30 times per million according to the CELEX lexical database (Burnage, 1998) (2) 168 LF words, each occurring 1 or 2 times per million (3) 168 pronounceable nonwords created by replacing one letter of an existing word (e.g., GREACH created from PREACH) (4) 168 pronounceable nonwords differing by at least two letters from any word (e.g., ANSU; this condition was absent in the Hintzman and Curran study). The first three stimulus categories were matched on neighborhood structure (i.e., a neighbor is a word differing from another word in one letter, so TIED is a neighbor of LIED); These categories had the same summed logarithmic word frequency of the neighbors. Stimuli were presented twice to study how prior exposure affects performance. To control for practice effects and shifts in response criteria, we presented stimuli in blocks of 48 trials, half of which were stimuli that were encountered in the previous block, half of which were new. For the first block, half of the items were filler items and half were stimuli that would be repeated in the next block. Each block contained 24 words and 24 nonwords. Subjects were required to respond at six different lags: 350, 400, 450, 500, 550, and 600 ms. The appropriate lag was indicated to the

---

[1] More details and related research can be found in Wagenmakers (2001).

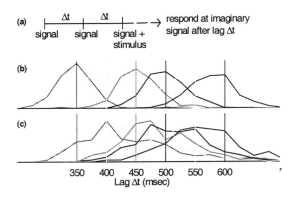

Figure 1. (a) the signal-to-respond procedure. (b) response time distributions for a participant with good timing and (c) for a participant with bad timing. Matching line-colors indicate correspondence between lag (vertical line) and response distribution.

subject by means of three tones (see Figure 1a). The tones were equidistant in time, and the onset of the third and last tone coincided with the onset of the stimulus. The subject had to respond at the fourth *imaginary* tone. We adopted this procedure in the hope that it would produce less interference than the presentation of a tone during processing. After each trial, subjects received feedback concerning the accuracy and latency of their response relative to the desired latency.

Results and Discussion

Forty-three students at Indiana University participated. we excluded 14 participants from the analyses because of extremely bad performance or bad timing. More specifically, subjects were excluded when their overall logarithmic d' was less than 1.0 and/or their average response latency was off by more than 50 ms from the required response latency. Figure 1b and 1c show the distribution of response times for a subject with good and bad timing, respectively. All response latencies were grouped into six bins for each subjects separately, the first bin containing the 16.7% slowest responses, and so forth. Next, the accuracy data from each bin were averaged over subjects. Other analyses such as binning by actual response latency or analyzing accuracy data by lag yielded similar results. The results can be seen in Figure 2. Performance for HF words is better than for LF words, and performance for nonwords that differ from any word in two letters (i.e., NW2) is better than for nonwords that differ from a word in one letter (i.e., NW1). Repeated stimuli (indicated by open symbols) are more likely to be classified as 'word' than new stimuli (indicated by filled symbols), an effect larger for LF words than for

HF words. As expected, performance increases dramatically with processing time, except perhaps for new LF words. This lack of increase could either be due to a very slow retrieval process for LF words, or to the possibility that some subjects might be uncertain concerning the lexicality of some LF words. One might argue that the gain in performance for repeated LF words reflects a retrieval of the feedback given on the earlier presentation ('I remember this stimulus is supposed to be a word'). However such a memory process would lead to improved performance for repeated nonwords ('I remember this stimulus is a nonword'), whereas the data show a *decrease* in performance for repeated nonwords. The hypothesis that repetition priming involves two distinct processes (i.e., familiarity and recollection) will be elaborated upon in the Discussion. Overall, the data consistently show effects of processing time, nonword lexicality, word frequency and repetition priming.

The REM-LD Model

The REM-LD model is similar to the REM model for episodic recognition (Shiffrin & Steyvers, 1997). In episodic recognition, participants have to distinguish 'old' words (i.e., words that were presented in a previous study list) from 'new' words. The REM-LD model is an application of the REM model to the lexical decision task. In the REM-LD model, we will make the following assumptions.

(1) Words and nonwords can be represented by vectors of feature values. We assume that these features arbitrarily represent attributes such as orthography and

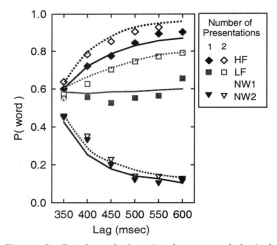

Figure 2. Results of the signal-to-respond lexical decision experiment. The observed data is indicated by the symbols while the REM-LD model fit is indicated by the solid lines (stimuli presented once) and dashed lines (stimuli presented twice).

phonology. Here we represent each word by a collection of 30 features with values 1 to 10 randomly drawn from a uniform distribution.

(2) Words have lexical entries (i.e., representations) in memory whereas nonwords do not. The presentation of the probe (i.e., the stimulus) leads to activation of n lexical entries that are orthographically *similar* to the probe (see Figure 3a). In a more complete model the value of n would probably be smaller for tests of dissimilar nonwords (i.e., nonwords that differ in two letters from any word), but for simplicity we set $n=10$ for all test items and instead vary the feature similarity for dissimilar nonwords. In case the probe is a word, one of the activated lexical entries is the probe (denoted s-entry for 'same', e.g. BEG in Figure 3a). The other activated entries are similar but different from the probe (denoted d-entries for 'different'). Note that a nonword can only activate lexical entries that are *similar* to it, since nonwords do not have lexical representations.

The degree of similarity between the probe and the entries is determined by the probability that the same feature value is present in probe features as in features from the lexical entries. Stored s-entry features will match the probe features with probability β_1; stored d-entry features will match the probe features with probability β_2, where $\beta_2 < \beta_1$. With probability $1-\beta$, feature values in the entries can differ from those in the probe. These feature values are obtained by sampling randomly from the uniform feature distribution, enabling matches to occur by chance. In the experiment, the similarity between the probe and the lexical neighbors was equated for NW1, LF and HF stimuli. However, the NW2 stimuli were more dissimilar from their lexical neighbors because they differed from any word in at least two letters. Therefore, we set $\beta_2(NW2) < \beta_2(NW1) = \beta_2(LF) = \beta_2(HF)$.

In REM-LD we assume that word frequency is represented by parameter β_1; the probability of a probe feature matching a trace feature is assumed to be higher for HF word probes than for LF word probes. The increased matching probability for HF words might involve various mechanisms such better matching context features because HF words occur in many different contexts. Therefore, we set $\beta_1(LF) < \beta_1(HF)$. In sum, the β_1 parameters determine the similarity or degree of overlap between a word probe and its corresponding lexical entry whereas the β_2 parameters determine the amount of overlap between the probe and lexical entries that are most similar to it.

(3) Mistakes in this task are made because the features in the lexical entries become only gradually available over time. The function $\alpha(t)$ gives the probability that a feature from a lexical entry is available at time t, in order to be compared with a probe

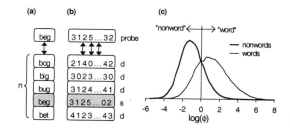

Figure 3. (a) a presented letter string activates n orthographically similar lexical entries. (b) letter strings and lexical traces are represented by vectors. (c) the distribution of $\log(\phi)$ for two conditions.

feature. To account for the improvement in the lexical decision task as a result of more processing time, we assume that the function $\alpha(t)$ is monotonically increasing over time according to:

$$\alpha(t) = 1 - e^{-b(t-t_o)} \qquad (1)$$

where b and t_0 are parameters of rate and starting point. Based on Equation (1), the probability that r features are available in the comparison process at time t is given by a binomial distribution:

$$P(r) = \binom{k}{r} \alpha(t)^r (1-\alpha(t))^{k-r} \qquad (2)$$

where k is the total number of features in each trace (always 30 here).

(4) The decision to respond 'word' or 'nonword' is based on an assessment of the evidence that the activated set of lexical entries contains an s-entry. An optimal decision is based on the odds ϕ that the probe is a word rather than a nonword, given the available data D: $\phi = P(w|D) / P(nw|D)$ where the data consists of the number of matches and mismatches between the probe features and the features of all activated lexical entries. Figure 3c illustrates typical log ϕ distributions generated by word and nonword probes, also illustrating the fact that log $\phi = 0$ is the optimal response criterion. By Bayes' rule, $\phi = [P(D|w)P(w)] / [P(D|nw)P(nw)]$. Because in our experiment the prior probability of the probe being a word, $P(w)$, equaled the probability of the probe being a nonword, $P(nw)$, we have:

$$\varphi = \frac{P(D \mid w)}{P(D \mid nw)} \qquad (3)$$

When the probe is a word, there is an equal probability that any activated lexical entry is a s-entry. This can be used in a simple derivation (Shiffrin & Steyvers, 1997) that leads to:

207

$$\frac{P(D \mid w)}{P(D \mid nw)} = \frac{1}{n}\sum_{j=1}^{n}\frac{P(m_j, q_j \mid s_j)}{P(m_j, q_j \mid d_j)} \qquad (4)$$

where m_j and q_j are the number of matching and mismatching features respectively in the comparison of the lexical entry j to the probe. Note that the total number of features that participate in the comparison process is given by Equation (2). The terms s_j and d_j represent the assumptions that the lexical entry j is a s-entry and d-entry respectively. Therefore, the odds for *word* is an average of the likelihood ratios for each of the lexical entries in the activated set. We can calculate each likelihood ratio in the following way:

$$\frac{P(m_j, q_j \mid s_j)}{P(m_j, q_j \mid d_j)} = \left(\frac{\hat{\beta}_1 + (1 - \hat{\beta}_1)\tfrac{1}{v}}{\hat{\beta}_2 + (1 - \hat{\beta}_2)\tfrac{1}{v}}\right)^{m_j} \left(\frac{1 - \hat{\beta}_1}{1 - \hat{\beta}_2}\right)^{q_j} \qquad (5)$$

In this equation, v is the number of distinct values from the uniform feature distribution (always 10 here).. The calculations of the system also involves the estimates $\hat{\beta}_1$ and $\hat{\beta}_2$. These system estimates are based on an arithmetic average of the different values that β_1 and β_2 can take on in the different experimental conditions.

(5) Prior exposure to a word primes the corresponding lexical entry. Therefore, the features of a repeated word probe will better match the features in the corresponding lexical entry. We model this by assuming that β_1 is increased by a small amount $\Delta\beta$ for repeated word probes. Similarly, prior exposure to a nonword primes the lexical entry of the word that is most similar to it. Therefore, the second occurrence of the nonword string will lead to more matching features in the comparison of the repeated nonword probe and the most similar lexical neighbor. We model this by increasing β_2 for one lexical entry by the amount $\Delta\beta$ for repeated nonword probes.

Simulation results

Figure 2 shows the results of a quantitative model fit of the REM-LD model to the observed data involving seven free parameters. The mean squared error (MSE) of the fit is 1.02e-003. The values of the seven parameters values found to produce the predictions were: $\beta_1(LF)$=.66, $\beta_1(HF)$=.77, $\beta_2(NW1)$=.44, $\beta_2(NW2)$=.40, $\Delta\beta$=.070, t_0=339, b=0.0050. The qualitative predictions were found to be relatively robust against variations in these parameter values. Because accuracy for HF words is higher than for LF words, $\beta_1(HF)$ was set higher than $\beta_1(LF)$ so that lexical probes would match their lexical entries better for HF words than LF words. Because NW1 nonwords are more often mistakenly judged to be words than NW2 nonwords, $\beta_2(NW1)$ was set higher than $\beta_2(NW2)$ so that a NW1 probe would activate its similar lexical neighbors to a greater extend than a NW2 probe. For both word and nonword conditions, probes that are

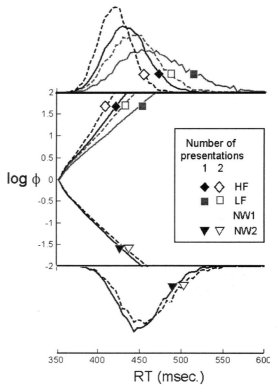

Figure 4. Predicted response time distributions for the lexical decision experiment. A word response is generated by the model at time t when the log odds (log ϕ: the current likelihood of responding "word" vs. "nonword") reaches the upper boundary set arbitrarily at 2. Similarly, a nonword response is generated when log ϕ reaches the lower boundary set at –2. The middle plot shows the mean log φ as a function of time; it displays the growth of evidence over time. The upper and lower plots show the response time distributions for correct responses in the eight conditions of the experiment. Note that the response time results mirror the accuracy results: repetitions speed up word responses but slow down nonword responses.

repeated are classified as 'word' more often then probes encountered for the first time. The model predicts this because a repeated word probe primes the corresponding lexical entry while a repeated nonword probe leads primes the lexical entry of the word that it is most similar to. The model also predicts that the repetition priming effect is more pronounced for LF words than for HF words. This is because the average value of log ϕ is closer to zero for the LF words than for the HF words. Hence, an identical increase in log ϕ due to priming of a lexical entry will have a greater impact on performance for LF words than for HF words.

Predicting Response Time Distributions

There are various ways to derive predictions for the response time distributions in the REM-LD model. Because the main aim of the model was to fit the accuracy results in the signal to respond task, we will only show some qualitative predictions for the response time distributions in the lexical decision task. We explored a method here that is based on diffusion models for response time distributions (e.g., Ratcliff, 1978; Ratcliff, Van Zandt, & McKoon, 1999). Instead of forcing the model to respond at specified lags, the model is simulated at a fine grained time scale. As time progresses, more and more features in the lexicon are activated and participate in the comparison process. For words, the calculated log odds (log ϕ) increases on average to larger positive values. For nonwords, the calculated log ϕ will increase to larger negative values. We predict response times by recording the times at which the log ϕ reaches an upper boundary a (for a word response), or a lower boundary $-b$ (for a nonword response). The boundaries a and b were arbitrarily set at 2. In Figure 4, the predicted response time distributions are shown using the same parameters as in the previous simulation. Only the distributions for correct responses are shown. The results mirror the accuracy results: the conditions that lead to more accurate responses are also the conditions that lead to faster responses. For example, words that are repeated are responded to more accurately and faster than non-repeated words. Similarly, nonwords that are repeated are responded to less accurately and slower than non-repeated nonwords. The model also predicts that the response time distributions are more skewed for the slower conditions. Such results have been observed several times in the literature (e.g. Balota & Spieler 1999).

Discussion

We have shown that a Bayesian-based model, REM-LD, can predict lexical decision effects such as word frequency, repetition priming, and nonword lexicality. This model takes into account the similarity of nonwords to words, thereby keeping the system 'centered' around the optimal criterion of log ϕ of zero. REM-LD can also handle the observed improvement in performance with processing time. In contrast to most extant models and empirical work in lexical decision, we focused on changes in accuracy over time, as seen in a variant of a signal-to-respond procedure. A Bayesian model is particularly suited toward explaining data from the signal-to-respond paradigm, since the system bases it decisions on the diagnosticity of the evidence, simultaneously considering the evidence for and against the 'word' response. When, early in processing, the evidence is noisy and supports neither the 'word' response nor the 'nonword' response, performance is at chance. Empirically, the most interesting finding is the decrease in performance for repeated nonwords. The current model assumes prior exposure of a nonword primes the most similar activated lexical entry, predicting the observed decrement in performance. However, Logan (1988) observed an *increase* in performance for repeated nonwords with subject-paced responding. This result might be attributed to the very short lag between repetitions in Logan's experiment. Therefore, it is possible that the net result of repetition priming for nonwords is the sum of two opposing effects: (1) An *implicit priming* component such as modeled by REM-LD, leading subjects to give the *erroneous* 'word' response, and (2) A *recollection* component that leads subjects to remember the *correct* 'nonword' response. This recollection process might be operative when subjects are under less pressure to give speeded responses, such as in experiments in which responding is subject-paced (e.g., Wagenmakers, 2001).

References

Antos, S. J. (1979). Processing facilitation in a lexical decision task. *Journal of Experimental Psychology: Human perception and performance*, 5, 527-545.

Balota, D.A., & Spieler, D.H. (1999). Word frequency effects, repetition, and lexicality effects in word recognition tasks: beyond measures of central tendency. *Journal of Experimental Psychology: General, 128*, 32-55.

Burnage, D. (1998). *CELEX: a guide for users*. Nijmegen: Centre for Lexical Information.

Hintzman, D. L., & Curran, T. (1997). Comparing retrieval dynamics in recognition memory and lexical decision. *Journal of Experimental Psychology: General*, 126, 228-247.

Logan, G. D. (1988). Toward an instance theory of automatization. *Psychological Review*, 95, 492-527.

Ratcliff, R. (1978). A theory of memory retrieval. *Psychological Review, 85*, 59-108.

Ratcliff, R., Van Zandt, T., & McKoon, G. (1999). Connectionist and diffusion models of reaction time. *Psychological Review, 106*, 261-300.

Shiffrin, R. M., & Steyvers, M. (1997). A model for recognition memory: REM—retrieving effectively from memory. *Psychonomic Bulletin & Review*, 4, 145-166.

Wagenmakers, E.J. (2001). *Priming in Visual Word Recognition: Empirical Studies and Computational Models*. Unpublished doctoral dissertation.

A Model of Individual Differences in Learning Air Traffic Control

Niels A. Taatgen (niels@ai.rug.nl)
Artificial Intelligence, University of Groningen
Grote Kruisstraat 2/1, 9712 TS Groningen, the Netherlands

Abstract

Individual differences in skill acquisition are influenced by several architectural factors. According to Ackerman's theory, general intelligence, speed of proceduralization and psychomotor speed influence different stages of skill acquisition. Ackerman tested this theory by correlating performance on an Air Traffic Controller (ATC) task with tests on specific abilities. The present study discusses an ACT-R model of the ATC task in which the relevant abilities can be manipulated directly, providing additional support for the theory.
Keywords: Skill acquisition, Air Traffic Control, Individual differences, ACT-R

Introduction

Skill acquisition is usually characterized as going through three stages: a cognitive stage, an associative stage and an autonomous stage (Fitts, 1964). The three stages can be characterized by moving from conscious, slow and error-prone to unconscious, fast and error-free. Anderson (1982) explains these three stages in terms of a transition from declarative knowledge to procedural knowledge. In the cognitive stage knowledge is declarative and needs to be interpreted. Interpreting knowledge is slow, and may lead to errors if the relevant knowledge cannot be retrieved at the right time. Procedural knowledge on the other hand is compiled and therefore fast and free of errors, and can be associated with the autonomous stage. The associate stage is an in-between stage, during which part of the knowledge is declarative and another part compiled.

A problem in the study of complex problem solving, especially in a learning context, is the vastness of individual differences. In order to study the acquisition of complex skills, it is a good research strategy to have a theory of individual differences. From the perspective of the cognitive architecture, there are two sources of individual differences: *architectural differences* and *knowledge differences* (Taatgen, 1999a). Architectural differences are differences in the cognitive architecture itself. In terms of an architecture like ACT-R, architectural differences can be tied to global parameters. For example, working-memory capacity is tied to the *W*-parameter in ACT-R, the parameter that controls the amount of spreading activation. Individual differences in working-memory capacity can be explained by estimating a different value of *W* for each individual (Lovett, Reder & Lebiere, 1997). Differences in knowledge are based on the

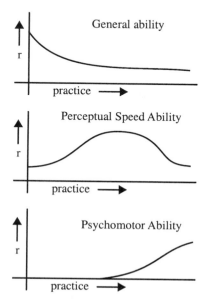

Figure 1: Predicted ability-performance correlations according to Ackerman. (adapted from Ackerman, 1988).

idea that people have different problem solving strategies. In terms of a cognitive model, this means individualized models have different initial contents of declarative and procedural memory.

In this paper I will focus on architectural differences. Ackerman (1988, 1990) identified three sources: general intelligence, perceptual speed, and psychomotor abilities. According to Ackerman, each of these three abilities correlates with a different stage of skill acquisition. In the cognitive stage, general intelligence is the most important aspect, as an adequate representation of the task needs to be formed. In the associative stage, the knowledge compilation process (which Ackerman associates with perceptual speed) will dominate performance, so individual differences in that aspect will become important. In the final autonomous stage, all knowledge is proceduralized, and differences in psychomotor abilities will be the most important factor. Figure 1 illustrates the general predictions of the theory.

Ackerman (1998; 1990) gathered evidence for this theory by correlating learning behavior on a complex task (the Kanfer-Ackerman Air Traffic Controller task[1], KA-ATC) with

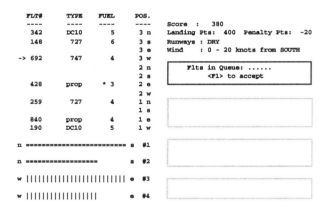

Figure 2: The KA-Air Traffic Controller task

performance on simpler tasks that explicitly test the three abilities Ackerman thought to be relevant in the three stages of skill acquisition. It turned out that measures of general intelligence correlate well with the first blocks of ATC performance, measures of perceptual speed with the middle blocks, and measures of psychomotor abilities with the later blocks.

Cognitive modeling offers a different approach to finding support for Ackerman's theory. Instead of correlating performance on different tasks, a model can be made of the complex task, and architectural parameters can be varied that correspond to the relevant dimensions of individual differences. This the approach we will examine in this paper.

A Model of the ATC Task

The ATC Task

Although the ATC task is a simplified version of real Air Traffic Control, it is still a complicated task. Figure 2 shows the interface of the task. The goal is to score as many points as possible by landing planes and making no errors. The planes that have to be landed are represented at the top-left part of the screen, and are organized in three hold levels (indicated in the POS. column). Planes can be moved between hold levels, and can be landed from hold level 1 (the bottom four slots). There are four runways in the bottom-left of the screen on which planes can be landed. The choice of runway is constrained by a number of rules concerning runway length (long or short), plane type (prop, 727, dc10 or 747), runway direction (north-south or east-west), runway condition (dry, wet or icy), wind direction (north, south, east or west) and wind speed (0-20, 25-35 or over 40-50 knots). The main rules of interest in the context of the model are the

---

1. Kanfer-Ackerman Air Traffic Controller Task© program is copyrighted software by Ruth Kanfer, Philip L. Ackerman, and Kim A. Pearson, University of Minnesota.

rules about whether a plane may land on the short runway (planes may always land on the long runway):

747's may never land on the short runway
727's may land on the short runway when the runway is dry or the wind speed is 0-20 knots
DC10's may land on the short runway when the runway is not icy and the wind is not 40-50 knots.
Prop's may always land on the short runway

Once a plane has successfully been assigned to a runway, it occupies the runway for some time. The runway has to be clear again before other planes may be assigned to it. Planes have a limited amount of fuel: the fuel column indicates the number of minutes the plane has left. When a plane runs out of fuel, it crashes. Except for the planes in the three hold levels, there is a queue of waiting planes. A waiting plane can be entered into an empty slot.

The interface is operated by the keyboard, mainly by using the up and down keys to move the arrow in the display up and down, and the return key to select planes and runways. Subjects receive 50 points for successfully landing a plane, 10 penalty points for violating a rule (the interface gives feedback on these violations), and 100 penalty points for each plane that crashes. Trials take 10 minutes each, after which the total amount of points is calculated.

The Model

The model presented here uses the ACT-R architecture (Anderson & Lebiere, 1998). As the ATC task is a complicated task, modeling all aspects is a major effort. As the model focuses on the learning aspects of the task, other aspects will be ignored or simplified. The model does not model the perceptual-motor parts of the task in detail, but rather uses an ad-hoc lisp-interface to do this. For example, a lisp function perceives all planes in hold level 1 and adds descriptions of them to declarative memory.

Another aspect the model simplifies are the more strategic aspects of the task. The main exploratory learning aspect is learning what planes under what conditions may land on the short runway. Other strategic aspects are not modeled. As a consequence, the model's peak performance (around 2000 points) is not as good as human peak performance (around 3500 points).

The basis for the model is the idea that the instructions are represented in declarative memory, and need to be retrieved and interpreted (Taatgen, 1999b; Anderson, 2000). The production rules that interpret the declarative instructions are not task-specific, and can be used for other tasks as well. The declarative representation that is used is a mixture of ideas expressed by Taatgen (1999b) and by Anderson (2000).

Declarative rules are organized in lists of instructions that are usually executed in order. Each rule has an action, and at most two arguments. An argument can be a constant, a variable or a reference. A constant is used as it is. A variable is something that needs a value, for example by retrieving something from declarative memory or by perceiving something in the outside world. Instantiating a variable creates a chunk of type binding, that holds the relation between the variable, its value and the current context. An argument of type reference later retrieves a binding.

The following example of a declarative instruction used in the model is part of the instruction to land a plane:

```
land1                              land2
    isa instruction                    isa instruction
    action perceive-a-plane            action perceive-weather
    arg1 plane                         arg1 wind-speed
    type1 variable                     type1 variable
    arg2 plane-type                    arg2 runway-condition
    type2 variable                     type2 variable
    prev land                          prev land1

land3                              land4
    isa instruction                    isa instruction
    action retrieve-experience         action decide-no
    arg1 plane-type                    arg1 take-long-runway
    type1 reference                    type1 constant
    arg2 wind-speed                    prev land3
    type2 reference
    prev land2
```

The first instruction is to perceive an arbitrary plane in hold level 1, and to store it and its type in two variables (which are added to declarative memory as binding-chunks). The second step is to check the weather, and to store the wind-speed and runway-condition. The third step tries to retrieve a past experience concerning the plane-type and the wind-speed. If this past experience is unfavorable, the fourth step decides to take the long runway.

The interpretation process of an instruction involves at least two steps (=production rule firings): the instruction has to be retrieved from memory, and the instruction has to be carried out. Additional steps are necessary if variables and references have to be instantiated, or if the instruction is complicated.

The current model is provided with a declarative instruction to do the ATC task. This instruction is not a literal interpretation of the instructions given to the participants, but reasonable first approximation of a strategy. Another assumption in this strategy is that the model has not memorized all the rules about when a certain plane may land on the short runway, but instead relies on trial-and-error to rediscover these rules. The instructions can be summarized as follows:

Main goal

1. If there are any planes in hold level 1, land one of them
2. Else, move an arbitrary plane from hold level 2 or 3 to hold level 2 or 1.
3. If there are no planes anymore, get between 1 and 6 new planes from the queue.

Landing a plane

1. Select an arbitrary plane in hold level one.
2. Look at the current weather conditions
3. Try to retrieve a past experience with the current plane type and the current wind-speed
4. If the past experience is unfavorable, select the long runway and move the plane there.
5. Try to retrieve a past experience with the current plane and the current runway condition
6. If the past experience is unfavorable, select the long runway and move the plane there
7. If both experiences were favorable, or not present, select the short runway and move the plane there

To move something from A to B

1. Press up or down keys until the arrow is at A
2. Press enter
3. Press up or down keys until the arrow is at B
4. Press enter

Learning in the Model

Four learning mechanisms play a role in the behavior of the model: declarative symbolic, declarative subsymbolic and procedural learning (symbolic and subsymbolic).

Declarative Symbolic Learning

ACT-R keeps past experiences in declarative memory. The current model uses these experiences to decide on whether to land a plane on the short or the long runway. The representation used for examples is restricted to two arguments, the plane type and either the runway condition and the wind speed. As a consequence, the model has no problems learning that 747's can never be landed on the short runway, and prop's always, but it has trouble with the DC10's and 727's, as these planes have complicated rules.

Declarative Subsymbolic Learning

Due to practise, the activation of the instruction chunks and the past experiences chunks steadily increases. As a consequence, retrieval times of these chunks decreases.

Procedural Learning

New productions are learned using a combination of specialization and compilation. Specialization involves substituting variables by constants, more in particular variables that occur in the retrieved chunk. As a consequence, retrieving the chunk is on longer necessary. Compilation involves making one rule out of two rules. In order to make sure the new rule has at most one retrieval, the first rule is specialized first.

This mechanism is not part of the current ACT-R 4.0, but part of the proposal for ACT-R 5.0 (Taatgen, 2000). The main function in the model that it compiles declarative instructions into production rules. Recall that interpreting instructions takes two steps: retrieving the instruction and carrying out the instruction. Production compilation specializes the retrieval of the instruction, and concatenates the result with the rule that carries out the instruction. The following rules gives an example of pushing enter (rules have been abbreviated for clarity):

```
(p retrieve-instruction          (p press-enter
  =goal>                            =goal>
    isa gen-goal                      isa gen-goal
    current =prev                     action press-enter
    action nil                      ==>
  =instr>                           =goal>
    isa instruction                   action nil
    prev =prev                      !eval! (press-enter))
    action =action
  ==>
  =goal>
    current =instr
    action =action)
```

These rules can interpret instructions like:

  mvhold3 isa instruction action press-enter prev mvhold2

Proceduralization produces the following rule given these ingredients:

```
(p compiled-rule
  =goal>
    isa gen-goal
    current mvhold2
    action nil
  ==>
  =goal>
    current mvhold3
    action nil
  !eval! (press-enter))
```

In order to promote a gradual introduction of new rules, their parameters are set to the parameter values derived from the parent rules, plus a penalty on the cost (b) parameter. So a new rule starts out at a slight disadvantage, and is slowly integrated into the system as parameters learning establishes the true values of the production parameters.

Modeling Individual Differences

The three abilities identified by Ackerman are modeled by varying three parameters. General ability is modeled by varying the *W*-parameter. The *W*-parameter controls the amount of spreading activation, and is associated with working-memory capacity (Lovett, Reder & Lebiere, 1997). Working-memory capacity itself is strongly correlated with general ability (Kyllonen & Christal, 1990). The simulation uses values 0.8, 1.0 and 1.4 as *W*-values. Speed of knowledge compilation, measured by Ackerman through perceptual speed, is modeled by varying a parameter that controls proceduralization speed. The parameter determines the probability that, given an opportunity to learn a new rule, the rule

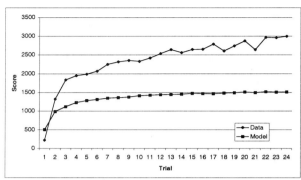

Figure 3: Points scored by the model and subjects in Ackerman (1990).

is actually learned. Values used are: 0.1%, 0.2%, 0.5%, 5%

Psychomotor speed is modeled by varying the time needed for a key-press. Values used for this parameter are: 150 ms, 200 ms and 250 ms

Results of the Model

In order to assess results of the model, I will compare the model outcomes to the data from Ackerman (1990).

A single run of the model consists of going through 24 trials of 10 minutes each. For each combination of individual difference parameters the model was run twice, producing 4x3x3x2 = 72 runs.

The model's performance in terms of the number of points scored is shown in Figure 3. As the model is only outfitted with a very basic strategy, and no means to improve it, it is no surprise the subjects outperform the model. The shapes of the curves are however similar.

Figure 4 shows correlations between abilities and performance on the ATC-task found by Ackerman, and the correlations between parameter settings and performance of the model. According to Ackerman's theory, these outcomes should resemble the graphs in Figure 1.

Figure 4a and d show the impact of general intelligence. Ackerman measured intelligence by administering a battery of tests for general intelligence (Letter sets, Raven progressive matrices, figure classification and analogies). The model simulates this ability by varying *W*. A higher value of *W* facilitates the retrieval process by increasing spreading activation. Initially this factor is very important, as both instructions and task information are represented declaratively. As more and more instructions are proceduralized, the stress on declarative memory lessens, so the impact of *W* on performance decreases.

Figure 4b and e show the impact of speed of proceduralization. Ackerman assessed this ability and psychomotor speed by administering a set of choice-reaction tests (9CRT, 4CRT, 2CRT and a simple reaction test) in 12 blocks. These tests span the range of perceptual speed ability (more choices and less practice) to psychomotor speed (less choices and

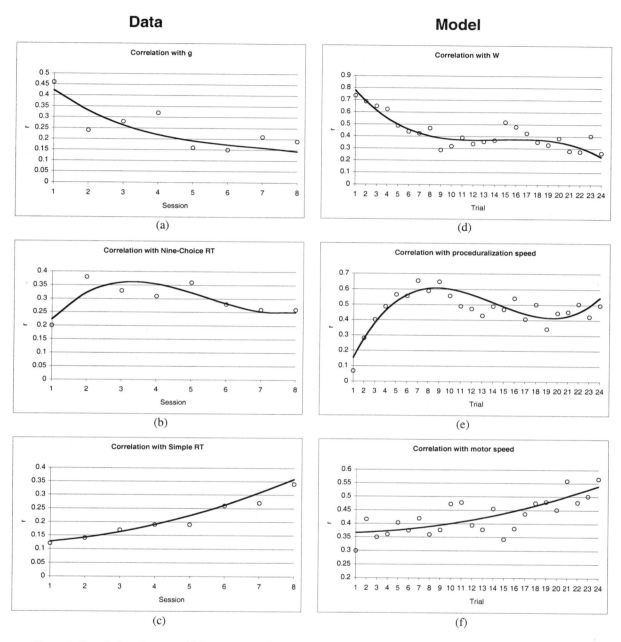

Figure 4: Correlations between Ability scores and performance on the ATC task. (a)-(c) Data from Ackerman (1990) (d)-(f) Outcomes of the model. Solid lines indicate the regression of the ability on practice (cubic polynomial). Each session in the data (a)-(c) consists of three trials.

more practice). Figure 4b uses the results of the first block of the 9CRT, the test at the perceptual-speed extreme of the range, while Figure 4c uses simple-reaction time results in block 12 at psychomotor-speed extreme of the spectrum.

In the model the speed of proceduralization has its main effect in the middle blocks of trials. As proceduralization

prerequires some experience with the knowledge it uses to construct new rules, it plays only a small role in the first few trials. Although proceduralization remains an important factor until the end of the experience, its impact trails off slightly, as productions that have the largest impact on performance are learned relatively early.

Figure 4c and f depict the impact of psychomotor speed. In the model this factor becomes more important as experience grows. Although the influence of the effort parameter that models psychomotor speed remains the same, the variance due to other factors decreases, increasing the impact of this psychomotor speed.

Note that for all three abilities, the correlations for the model are larger than the correlations for the data. This should be no surprise, as the parameter manipulations in the model have a direct impact on performance, while assessing these abilities through tests, as is done in the data, is only indirect. Another reason why the correlations in the model are higher is that the model ignores knowledge differences, thereby amplifying the architectural differences.

Discussion

Despite the limitations of the model, it succeeds in going through the three stages of skill acquisition, as demonstrated by the correlations with abilities that characterize these stages. As such it supports the ideas about skill acquisition put forth here and in earlier models based on the same principles (e.g., Taatgen 1999b).

The model also exhibits an example of an ACT-R model where all learning mechanisms are used, instead of a subset of mechanisms for a small task. As such it supports the notion of ACT-R as an architecture of cognition.

One might ask what the added value of a cognitive model is to Ackerman's theory. It can be observed that the outcomes of the model are much closer to the data than Ackerman's more qualitative predictions in Figure 1. The model allows the study of what the exact impact of an individual difference related parameter is, and may also help understand other experiments where Ackerman's theory does not seem to hold. Some issues need further exploration: for example, it is not clear what the exact relationship between perceptual speed and speed of proceduralization is. Ackerman doesn't have a clear explanation for this. A model of the 9CRT using proceduralization might clarify this issue.

The strategy of the model is still its main limitation: it cannot improve the simple initial strategy very much. The retrieval of examples to guide behavior is something that can be extended, and general strategies to improve on plans can be added. The declarative representation is very flexible, so allows easy modification (as opposed to productions). Work by Lee, Anderson and Matessa (1995) and John and Lallement (1997) may be useful for this purpose.

Finally, the perceptual-motor aspects of the model can be extended to improve is credibility and scope of modeling learning, possibly based on Lee and Anderson (in press).

Acknowledgements

I would like to thank Frank Lee and John Anderson for their help, and providing me with a Lisp implementation of the ATC task.

References

Ackerman, P. L. (1988). Determinants of individual differences during skill acquisition: Cognitive abilities and information processing. *Journal of experimental psychology: General, 117(3)*, 288-318.

Ackerman, P. L. (1990). A correlational analysis of skill specificity: learning, abilities, and individual differences. *Journal of experimental psychologie: learning, memory, and cognition, 16(5)*, 883-901.

Anderson, J. R. (1982). Acquisition of cognitive skill. *Psychological Review, 89*, 369-406.

Anderson, J. R. (2000). Learning from instructions. Proceedings of the seventh annual ACT-R workshop.

Anderson, J. R. & Lebiere, C. (1998). The atomic components of thought. Mahwah, NJ: Erlbaum.

Fitts, P. M. (1964). Perceptual-motor skill learning. In A. W. Melton (Eds.), *Categories of human learning*. New York: Academic Press.

John, B. E. & Lallement, Y. (1997). Strategy use while learning to perform the Kanfer-Ackerman air traffic controller task. In M. G. Shafto & P. Langley (Eds.), *Proceedings of the Nineteenth Annual Conference of the Cognitive Science Society* (pp. 337-342). Mahwah, NJ: Erlbaum.

Kyllonen, P. C. & Christal, R. E. (1990). Reasoning ability is (little more than) working-memory capacity. *Intelligence, 14(4)*, 389-433.

Lee, F. J., Anderson, J. R., & Matessa, M. P. (1995). Components of dynamic skill acquisition. In *Proceedings of the 17th annual conference of the cognitive science society* (pp. 506-511). Hillsdale, NJ: Erlbaum.

Lee, F.J. & Anderson J.R. (in press). Does learning a complex task have to be complex? A study in learning decomposition. *Cognitive Psychology*.

Lovett, M. C., Reder, L. M., & Lebiere, C. (1997). Modeling individual differences in a digit working memory task. In M. G. Shafto & P. Langley (Eds.), *Proceedings of the Nineteenth Annual Conference of the Cognitive Science Society* (pp. 460-465). Mahwah, NJ: Erlbaum.

Taatgen, N. A. (1999a). Cognitief Modelleren: Een nieuwe kijk op individuele verschillen. *Nederlands tijdschrift voor de psychologie*, 54(4), 167-176.

Taatgen, N. A. (1999b). A model of learning task-specific knowledge for a new task. In M. Hahn & S. C. Stoness (Eds.), *Proceedings of the 21th annual conference of the cognitive science society* (pp. 730-735). Mahwah, NJ: Erlbaum.

Taatgen, N. A. (2000). Learning new production rules in ACT-R. Online document: http://www.ai.rug.nl/~niels/proceduralization.html. University of Groningen, Netherlands.

An Explanation of the Length Effect for Rotated Words

Carol Whitney (cwhitney@cs.umd.edu)
Neural and Cognitive Sciences Program
Philosophy Department
University of Maryland
College Park, MD 20742

Abstract

We review a model of letter-position encoding, wherein position is tagged by timing of firing relative to an underlying oscillatory cycle. We show how this model can account for data concerning reaction times for lexical decision on rotated letter strings.

Introduction

Little is known of the representations used by the brain for cognitive processing. We suggest that the problem of how letter position within a string is neurally encoded provides a tractable area of investigation into this realm. This problem is circumscribed, yet involves important higher level processes such as the composition of a representation from constituent entities, and the formation of a representation that is independent of absolute location in visual space.

It is commonly assumed that a string's letters are processed in parallel. In contrast, we propose that letters are activated serially. This interpretation is based on the SERIOL framework for letter-position representation (Sequential Encoding Regulated by Inputs to Oscillating Letter units). The serial activation provides a natural way to encode letter order, and accounts for a variety of experimental results (Whitney & Berndt, 1999; Whitney, 2001a; Whitney 2001b).

Here we show how the model can explain the interaction of word length and angle of rotation on reaction time for a lexical decision experiment involving rotated letter strings (Koriat & Norman, 1985). First we recount those experimental results. Next, we review the SERIOL model. We then show, via computational modeling, how the SERIOL framework can account for the experimental data.

Letter string rotation experiment

Subjects were to determine whether or not a letter string was a word. The strings varied in length from two to five letters, and were presented rotated at various angles (in multiples of 20°) from normal horizontal presentation. Each string was rotated as a whole. The researchers found an interesting interaction between string length and rotation angle on reaction times (Koriat & Norman, 1985). The following results are for the word condition. (Non-words evoked a similar pattern.) See Figure 1. For

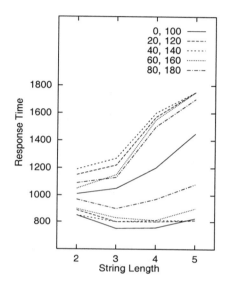

Figure 1: Experimental response times (in milliseconds) for the rotated string lexical decision task. Each line represents one angle of rotation, where the lower lines correspond to 0° through 80°, and the upper lines correspond to 100° to 180°.

angles of 60° or less, reaction time did not increase with string length. For 80°, reaction times were similar for words of two to four letters, while five-letter words incurred an increased reaction time. For 100°, two- and three-letter words had similar reaction times, with reaction times increasing for four- and five-letter words. For angles of 120° to 180°, reaction time varied approximately linearly with word length, with each additional letter adding 200ms.

Because of this non-uniform pattern of interaction between string length and rotation angle, the authors conclude that the results cannot be explained solely in terms of processing time related to mentally rotating the string to the horizontal position. Nor can the data be explained by supposing that processing switches from parallel to serial at some rotation angle, due to the intermediate region (80° and 100°) where reaction times are neither constant nor linear. In fact the authors state, "it is difficult to propose an interpretation of the results in terms of one unitary principle" (Koriat & Norman, 1985, p. 504). However, the SERIOL framework does offer such an interpretation based on how letter-position is encoded, as discussed below,

The SERIOL model

The SERIOL model is theoretical framework for letter-position coding. It unifies and accounts for a wide range of experimental data on reading, including positional perceptability of letters in strings, visual field differences in letter perceptability, the location of the optimal viewing position and its relationship to reading direction, hemispheric modes of processing, and positional patterns of letter priming within a string (Whitney & Berndt, 1999; Whitney, 2001a; Whitney, 2001b).

The theoretical framework consists of five layers, ranging from the retinal level to the word level. For this discussion, we concentrate on the letter level. The letter level is comprised of computational units (nodes) that represent individual letters. We assume that a feature level (nodes representing letter features) provides input to the letter level. This input is such that the features of the first letter are more highly activated than the features of the second letter; the features of the second letter are more highly activated than those of the third, and so on. That is, feature level activation decreases from left to right across the string. We denote this pattern of activation the *locational gradient*. The proposed mechanisms underlying formation of the locational gradient and experimental evidence for its existence are given in Whitney (2001a) and are not important for this discussion.

We propose that the locational gradient induces a temporal firing pattern across letter nodes wherein position is represented by the precise timing of firing relative to other letter nodes. That is, the first letter fires, then the second letter, then the third, etc. Thus, the temporal sequence of firing encodes the spatial order of the letters. See Figure 2.

This idea is consistent with current neurobiological models of information encoding. Hopfield has proposed that quantities are represented by the explicit timing of action potentials, rather than by their firing rate (Hopfield, 1995). In that model, encoding neurons undergo internal, sub-threshold1 oscillations of excitability. The magnitude of an input to such a neuron determines when threshold is exceeded. For a small input, threshold is not exceeded until late in the cycle when the cell's oscillation brings its potential near threshold. For a larger input, threshold is exceeded earlier in the cycle. Thus, the size of an input is represented by spike timing relative to the oscillatory cycle. See Figure 3.

It has been suggested that oscillatory activity in the 40 Hz range is related to cognitive processing (Tiitinen, Sinkkonen, Rainikainen, Alho, Lavi-Kainen, & Naatenen, 1993) and that short-term memories are encoded on 40 Hz sub-cycles of a low-frequency (5 Hz) oscillation (Lisman & Idiart, 1995). We propose that a simi-

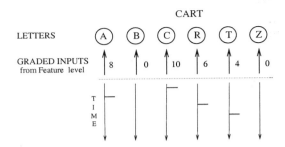

Figure 2: Proposed encoding of letter position; example for the word "cart". A subset of the letter nodes is shown with input levels (in abstract units). The simultaneous graded inputs, via interaction with the dynamics of the letter nodes, create the temporal firing pattern shown in the lower portion of the figure.

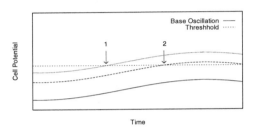

Figure 3: When a relatively large input is added to the base sub-threshold oscillation (top curving line), the cell potential crosses threshold at time 1 (action potential not illustrated). If instead, a smaller input is added, the cell potential crosses threshold later in the cycle, at time 2.

lar scheme underlies letter-position coding, wherein each letter position corresponds to a successive 40 Hz sub-cycle (i.e., lasting 25ms) within a 5 Hz oscillation (i.e., lasting 200ms).

In our model, all letter nodes are assumed to undergo synchronous, periodic oscillations of excitability. Due to the locational gradient, the letter node representing the letter in the first position receives the highest level of excitatory input and fires first, the second receives the next highest amount and fires next, and so on. Suitable input levels and lateral inhibition assure that only one letter node fires at a time. Once a letter node has received lateral inhibition following firing, its input from the feature level is inhibited, so it does not start firing again in the same oscillatory cycle. This coding scheme does not employ position-specific letter detectors; all nodes at the feature level provide input to all letter nodes. Any letter node can represent any position, depending on the level of input that it receives, and the resulting timing of firing. A precise description and simulation of this temporal encoding process is given in (Whitney & Berndt, 1999).

At the next level of the framework, this serial encoding is converted to a non-temporal, contextual encoding (bigrams). A bigram node is tuned to the ordered firing of letter pairs within an oscillatory cycle. For example, the sequence of letters C, A, R, T would activate bigram nodes CA, AR, RT, CR, AT, CT. At the final level of processing, bigram nodes activate word nodes.

Because reaction times for lexical decision for three- to six-letter words do not vary with word length (Fredriksen & Kroll, 1976), it has been assumed that letters are processed in parallel. How then can the SERIOL model be reconciled with this result? We have suggested that a minimal reaction time occurs, based on completion of the oscillatory cycle. That is, all words that can represented within a single cycle have similar reaction times (Whitney, 2001a). A similar suggestion has been made regarding reaction times in the Sternberg task. In that task, a subject is given a list of items, followed by a probe. The reaction times for 'yes' responses to the probe are the same as for 'no' responses, suggesting that subjects always perform an exhaustive search of the mental representation of the list. However, this explanation seems implausible, as it would be more efficient to initiate a 'yes' response as soon as the probed item is encountered in memory. Jensen and Lisman (1998) have proposed that the list of items is encoded serially within an oscillatory cycle, and that the search does indeed stop if the probe item is encountered, but that a motor response can only be initiated at the trough of the oscillatory cycle. This explains why there is no positional effect for the Sternberg task, which seems to require serial checking of the list members. Similarly, we propose that under normal presentation conditions, there is no length effect on lexical decision for words that can be represented in a single oscillatory cycle (i.e. words of seven or fewer letters).

However, we suggest that length effects can arise under conditions of degraded presentation, when input levels to letter nodes are reduced such that it takes multiple oscillatory cycles to represent a sequence of letters that is normally represented in a single cycle. We suggest that such a phenomenon underlies the reaction time results from the rotated word experiment. This analysis implies that such length effects should on the time scale of the oscillatory cycle. Recall that for the largest rotation angles, each additional letter increased reaction times by 200ms, exactly the length of the proposed oscillatory cycle. [1] Thus we propose that the unitary principle which can explain this data is that letter position is encoded temporally. When the input is degraded (by rotating the letter strings) the underlying temporal nature of the encoding is exposed. In the following section, we give the details of this analysis in terms of the SERIOL model.

---

[1] We do not address how words that are too long to be represented in a single cycle are normally represented. For horizontal presentation, there is no evidence for a sharp jump in reaction times as word length increases past seven or eight letters, as might be expected for going from one cycle to two cycles. Presumably a mechanism exists for smoothly integrating information across cycles under normal conditions. That mechanism is beyond the scope of this paper.

A SERIOL account of the rotated word data

In performing the experimental task, we assume that subjects mentally rotated the string to the canonical horizontal orientation, and processed the string as usual. This assumption is consistent with the fact that reaction times for two-letter words were smoothly increasing with rotation angle. We also assume that the act of mental rotation decreases the amount of input reaching the letter nodes, and that this degradation increases with the amount of rotation. These assumptions, in conjuction with the SERIOL model, provide a natural explanation for the experimental data. As the level of input to letter nodes declines, the number of oscillatory cycles required to represent the word increases. Up to a certain amount of rotation, there is still sufficient input to activate all the letters within a single oscillatory cycle (i.e., up to 60°). After that point, there is sufficient input to activate all of the letter in shorter words, while longer strings require an additional cycle (i.e., for 80° and 100°). This accounts for the intermediate region where reaction times are neither constant nor linear. With further degradation, only two-letter words can be represented in a single cycle; each additional letter incurs an additional cycle (i.e., 120° to 180°).

In the SERIOL framework, the serial encoding of letter order is converted to a non-temporal, bigram encoding at the next level of processing. Bigram activation depends on the ordered firing of letter nodes within a single oscillatory cycle. If, as we propose, severely degraded input causes each letter node to fire on a separate cycle, how then could the bigram nodes become activated? We propose that letters which have previously fired can refire again in succeeding cycles. However, this refiring can't be triggered by the feature-level input, since we assume that external input is inhibited once it activates a letter node (so that the letter node will not continually refire.) How then could a previously activated letter node refire?

It has been proposed that an afterdepolarization (ADP) can maintain short-term memory across oscillatory cycles (Lisman & Idiart, 1995). We suggest that this mechanism could maintain the order of letter nodes that have been previously activated when there is insufficient input to activate all the letter nodes within a single cycle. The ADP has been observed in cortical pyramidal cells, and is a slowly increasing excitability that peaks at approximately 200ms after spiking. As such, it could cause refiring on successive oscillatory cycles without external input. The slowly increasing ramp of the ADP can maintain the firing order of elements across oscillatory cycles, as demonstrated by a mathematical model (Lisman and Idiart, 1995).

We have implemented a mathematical model of the reaction time for the rotated word experiment based on these ideas. We modeled the interaction between the underlying oscillatory cycle, the input levels, the lateral inhibition, and the ADP to arrive at an initial firing time for the final letter of the string. This firing time, combined with other quantities, gives the modeled reaction time. The results of the simulation fit to the experimental data

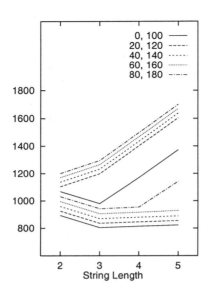

Figure 4: Simulated response times (in milliseconds) for the rotated string lexical decision task. Notation is the same as in Figure 1.

are shown in Figure 4.

Next we present the details of the computational model. Instantiating the theoretical framework in a simulation entails the specification of quite a few parameters. Most of these parameters are related to the neuronal dynamics (ADP, oscillations, and inhibition) and are set to physiologically plausible values, similar to those used by Lisman and Idiart (1995). In fitting the computational model to the experimental data, the primary focus of optimization was the function specifying the inputs from the feature level. This function was hand tuned.

The modeled reaction time, R, is given by:

$$R(\theta, l) = BR + H(\theta) + L(l) + W(\theta, l)$$

where θ denotes the angle of rotation and l denotes the string length.

BR denotes a base reaction time set to 730ms. H denotes the time required to mentally rotate the string; it is a linearly increasing function of θ. Fitting to the reaction times for two-letter words gives:

$$H(\theta) = \theta/20° * 30\text{ms}$$

L reflects a length effect that is not explicitly modeled. The experimental data indicate that two-letter words suffer a processing disadvantage. The SERIOL model does not account for this particular length effect. However, assuming constant, extra processing time for two-letter words on top of the explicitly modeled effects gives a good fit to the data. We have chosen to include this increment in the modeled results, in order to facilitate compar-

ison between the simulation and the experimental data. $L(l)$ is 100ms for $l = 2$ and 0 otherwise.

W denotes the time required to activate all the letter nodes corresponding to the string; that is, W is the first time at which the final letter node fires. The functions which determine W are the instantiation of the SERIOL framework. These functions specify the activation of the letter nodes.

Following Lisman and Idiart (1995), letter nodes are modeled as units that undergo a sub-threshold oscillatory drive, exhibit an increase in excitability after firing (ADP), and send lateral inhibitory inputs to each other. We use i to denote the letter node representing the ith letter of the word. The membrane potential, V, of a letter node is given by:

$$V(\theta, i, t) = O(t) + A(i, t) - I(t) + E(\theta, i, t)$$

where O denotes the oscillatory drive, A denotes ADP, I denotes inhibitory input, and E denotes excitatory external input (originating from the feature level). A node fires when V exceeds a threshold, TH. TH is specified relative to resting potential, and set to 10mV. Firing causes the node's ADP component to be reset, and inhibition to be sent to the other nodes.

The oscillatory function O has a cycle length of 200ms, and linearly increases from -5mV to 5mV during the first half of the cycle, and decreases back to -5mV during the second half.

The ADP and inhibition are modeled by functions of the form:

$$F(t; M, T) = M * (t/T)^{1.5} * \exp(1 - t/T)$$

which increases to a maximal value (controlled by M) and then decreases (on a time scale controlled by T). The ADP is given by:

$$A(i, t) = F(t - t_i; M_A, T_A)$$

where t_i denotes the time at which the ith node last fired. ($A(i, t)$ is 0 if the node has not yet fired.) The inhibition is given by:

$$I(i, t) = \sum_{j=1}^{l} F(t - t_j; M_I, T_I).$$

The following values were used: $T_A = 200\text{ms}$, $M_A = 11\text{mV}$, $T_I = 3\text{ms}$, $M_I = 3\text{mV}$. These quantities were hand tuned within a narrow range of values, in conjunction with specification of the external input functions, to give the desired firing pattern.

The external input E is a decreasing function of position i; this corresponds to the locational gradient in the SERIOL framework. The following function was used:

$$E(0°, i, 0\text{ms}) = 10.6\text{mV} - i * 0.5\text{mV}$$

We assume that mental rotation degrades the external input, so E decreases as θ increases. The following function was used:

$$E(\theta, i, 0\text{ms}) = E(\theta - 20°, i, 0\text{ms}) - 0.65\text{mV} * \sin(\theta)$$

Firing inhibits the external input, so $E(\theta, i, t) = 0$ if node i has fired prior to time t. We also assume that the external input builds up over time; if node i has not yet fired, $E(\theta, i)$ increases by 0.2Mv after each oscillatory cycle.

A simulation for each combination of l and θ was run, starting at time $t = 0$ and using a time step of 1ms. At each time step, the potential of each letter node was calculated using the equation for V. The value of $W(\theta, l)$ was taken to be the first t at which $V(\theta, l, t)$ exceeded threshold. The total reaction time was then calculated using the equation for R. For all rotation angles and string lengths, all active letters of the string fired in the correct sequence on each cycle.

For example, for $\theta = 0°$ and $l = 4$, nodes 1, 2, 3, and 4 fired at 49, 63, 74, and 84 milliseconds, respectively, giving $W(0°, 4) = 84$ms. For $\theta = 180°$ and $l = 4$, nodes 1 and 2 fired at 86 and 100 milliseconds. In the second cycle, nodes 1, 2, and 3 fired at 52, 65, and 94 milliseconds (relative to the start of that cycle.) In the third cycle, nodes 1, 2, 3, and 4 fired at 43, 55, 66, and 97 milliseconds, giving $W(180°, 4) = 2 * 200 + 97 = 497$ms. Each node refired earlier in successive cycles due to the ADP. This earlier firing, in conjunction with increasing external input, allowed more letters to fire on each cycle. The slowly increasing ramp of the ADP, along with lateral inhibition, maintained the proper firing sequence across cycles.

Conclusion

Koriat and Norman (1985) were unable to explain their data purely in terms mental rotation. By taking into consideration a possible scheme for the coding of letter position, we have accounted for this data. We propose that the rotation of the stimuli reveals the underlying temporal nature of the encoding. Although the computational model of this experimental data may seem complex, it is keyed on two basic assumptions: letter order is encoded temporally within an oscillatory cycle, and input levels to letter units are reduced for rotated input. The theoretical framework specifying the mechanism that induces this temporal encoding was developed previously; it accounts for a wide range experimental data on the interactions of string position, reading direction, and presentation duration on letter perceptability (Whitney & Berndt, 1999; Whitney, 2000a; Whitney, 2000b). Applying the SERIOL model to the experimental data of Koriat and Norman (1985) yields a natural explanation of those data. It accounts for the finding that there is an intermediate region of rotation angles where processing seems neither fully parallel nor fully serial, and predicts the finding that the increase in reaction time per letter for large rotation angles is 200ms (the proposed length of the oscillatory cycle).

Acknowledgements

The author would like to thank Corey Washington and anonymous reviewers for their helpful comments.

References

Frederiksen, J.R., & Kroll, J.F. (1976). Spelling and sound: Approaches to the internal lexicon. *Journal of Experimental Psychology: Human Perception and Performance, 2*: 361-379.

Hopfield, J.J. (1995). Pattern recognition computation using action potential timing for stimulus representation. *Nature, 376*: 33-36.

Koriat, A., & Norman, J. (1985). Reading Rotated Words. *Journal of Experimental Psychology: Human Perception and Performance, 11*: 490-508.

Jensen, O., & Lisman, J.E. (1998). An oscillatory short-term memory buffer can account for data on the Sternberg task. *Journal of Neuroscience, 18*: 10686-10699.

Lisman, J.E., & Idiart, M.A.P. (1995). Storage of 7 +- 2 short-term memories in oscillatory subcycles. *Science, 267*: 1512-1515.

Tiitinen, H., Sinkkonen, J., Rainikainen, K., Alho, K., Lavi-kainen, J., & Naatanen, R. (1993). Selective attention enhances the 40-hz response in humans. *Nature, 364*: 59-60.

Whitney, C., & Berndt, R.S. (1999). A new model of letter string encoding: Simulating right neglect dyslexia. *Progress in Brain Research, 121*: 143-163.

Whitney, C. (2001a). How the brain encodes the order of letters in a printed word: The SERIOL model and selective literature review. To appear in *Psychonomic Bulletin & Review.*

Whitney, C. (2001b) Position-specific effects within the SERIOL framework of letter-position encoding. Submitted.

Towards a Technology for Computational Experimentation

Peter Yule (p.yule@bbk.ac.uk)
School of Psychology, Birkbeck College, University of London, Malet St.,
London, WC1E 7HX

Richard Cooper (r.cooper@bbk.ac.uk)
School of Psychology, Birkbeck College, University of London, Malet St.,
London, WC1E 7HX

Abstract

The evaluation of cognitive models is sometimes compromised by inadequate comparison of model behaviour with human behaviour. Inadequacies may arise through unconstrained setting of model parameters to yield the target behaviours and/or through incomplete replication of the human participant's environment when running the model. This paper reviews methodologies for the evaluation of cognitive models that address (to varying extents) these difficulties. It is proposed that standard empirical psychology provides the basis for an adequate methodology, in which within-model variations are treated as between-subjects variables. The control of large-scale between-subjects designs requires substantial computational infrastructure, and the second half of the paper presents details of a general web-based client-server system that embodies this infrastructure. The system may be used to support the execution of computational experiments, human experiments, and computational parameter studies. Three case studies illustrate these different uses.

Introduction

The general aim of computational modelling — to develop implemented models that elucidate the cognitive processes that underlie human behaviour — brings together four qualitatively different domains: those of cognitive theory, empirical data, implemented systems, and model behaviour. The relation between model behaviour and human behaviour is clearly of central importance to the general aim, but the modelling community has not as yet converged on a widely accepted, sound methodology for model evaluation.

The necessity for a sound methodology for model evaluation stems from the relation between the four domains cited above: models typically include implementation details that are claimed to be of little theoretical significance and/or numerical parameters that affect the model's performance. Such aspects may impact upon model behaviour. In such cases, unconstrained parameter fitting and tuning of "implementation details" may undermine the direct comparison of model behaviour with empirical data.

A second factor that impinges upon the direct comparison of model and human behaviour concerns the equivalence or otherwise of the tasks performed by human participants and their counterpart computational models. While there have been moves in some circles to ensure task equivalence (by hooking up models and human participants to the same experiment generation software: cf. Anderson & Lebiere, 1998), such approaches are the exception rather than the norm. In general, there are few guarantees that comparisons of human and model behaviour are made on formally equivalent tasks.

The picture is complicated further by the range of measures available from empirical studies and natural variation in human behaviour. Empirical data may be based on any one of a number of measurement scales (e.g., categorical, ordinal scale, and interval scale), it may relate to a range of quantities or qualities (reaction times, error scores, confidence judgements, category choices), and it may include significant within and between subject variation. Each of these factors may impact upon model evaluation (e.g., by requiring that model output be interpreted in terms of reaction times, or through the inclusion of stochastic processes governed by numerical parameters).

One consequence of the above factors is that considerable methodological sophistication is required when evaluating cognitive models. In previous work we have suggested two approaches to the model evaluation problem: sensitivity/criticality studies (Cooper, Fox, Farringdon, & Shallice, 1996) and the tight coupling of empirical and computational research programmes (Cooper & Yule, 1999). This paper reviews these and other approaches to modelling methodology. It is argued that the methods of empirical psychology provide a sound basis for a range of model evaluation techniques, but that the practical application of such techniques requires substantial computational infrastructure. One suitable (implemented) infrastructure is described, and its use is illustrated via case studies.

Methodologies for Model Evaluation

A range of model evaluation methodologies are in use. Least adequate for the purposes of cognitive modelling is the engineering requirement that the model do no more than perform a specified task (e.g., that the model can solve the Tower of Hanoi task). This section reviews a number of more adequate model evaluation methodologies, and highlights one common feature: they all require models to be run many times within a constrained experimental environment.

Monte Carlo Simulations

One common approach to the evaluation of models that contain stochastic elements and whose behaviour may be characterised by one or more dependent measures (e.g., error score, category choice, etc.) is to employ a *Monte Carlo* simulation.

Such a simulation involves running the model multiple times, while the dependent measures are collected and collated, and then comparing the resulting distributions of those parameters with equivalent distributions obtained from human participants completing an equivalent task.

In its basic form the *Monte Carlo* technique may allow relations between model parameters and dependent variables to be established. However, the approach is open to criticism if such relations are then used merely to select parameters that yield a good fit between model behaviour and human behaviour, especially if the number of dependent measures on which the fit is based is fewer than the number of parameters in the model. In this sense, the simple *Monte Carlo* approach fails to address difficulties associated with the evaluation of parameterised models or with models containing implementational details.

A variation of the *Monte Carlo* approach, especially popular in the evaluation of models that include learning mechanisms (e.g., many connectionist models and some ACT-R models), consists of dividing the empirical data into two sets, training the model on one set, and testing it on the other. This technique is primarily intended to evaluate a model's generalisation. For it to be effective the empirical data must take the form of ⟨input, output⟩ pairs, and the key dependent variable is the degree of generalisation from the training set to the testing set. While this may yield an effective measure of generalisation, the task is far removed from that experienced by a human participant in most psychological experiments. Degree of generalisation is therefore difficult to interpret with respect to the domain of human behaviour. The variation also fails to address issues of the effects of model parameters and implementation details on model behaviour.

Variation of Implementation Assumptions

A methodologically superior approach is apparent in the work of Plaut & Shallice (1993) on deep dyslexia. They began by developing a basic (recurrent connectionist) model of the task, and demonstrated that 1) after training the model produced accurate orthography to phonology mappings (corresponding to a reading task); and 2) after subsequent lesioning the model produced errors in the orthography to phonology mapping similar in type and distribution to those of several deep dyslexic patients. They then demonstrated that a range of related models behaved in a similar fashion, showing that the phenomenon was independent of the precise structure of the connectionist architecture, elements of the learning mechanism, the approach to lesioning, and so on. The conclusion was that four key elements were critical for modelling deep dyslexia (e.g., the development of an attractor structure, the use of richer representations for content words than function words, etc.).

The evaluation methodology of Plaut & Shallice (1993) effectively addresses the issues arising from the possible effects of implementation details on model behaviour. Issues of model parameterisation were addressed (to a lesser extent) through a second aspect of the methodology: the requirement

that the model produce errors of different types in the same proportions as shown by deep dyslexic patients. The various models yielded multiple dependent measures, and all dependent measures were taken into account in the comparison between human and model behaviour.

Parameter Studies

Many cognitive models have one or more free parameters (e.g., governing learning, memory decay, etc.) which might have any of a range of values. The precise choice of values for these parameters is likely to affect the behaviour of the model. It is frequently important to understand the changes in behaviour of a model as these values change. For this, it is useful to run the model one or more times at each level of the parameter, or in the case of multiple free parameters, at each combination of possible levels of each free parameter, and record the model's behaviour at each point in this parameter space. From a model evaluation perspective, there are two uses of parameter studies: for parameter fitting (which is methodologically suspect), or, as described below, for model calibration within the context of coupled empirical/computational studies.

The number of cases to be examined in a parameter study is the product of the number of values for each parameter. It can therefore easily get quite large. The total number of runs will be increased further if multiple runs of the model are required at each combination of parameter values (which is likely if the model includes stochastic elements). Parameter studies can therefore involve large amounts of computation, and so they can be very lengthy and time consuming, sometimes extending to weeks or even months of CPU time on a typical PC or workstation.

In practice, parameter studies are highly amenable to parallelisation, since the separate runs with different parameters are independent of each other. Merely running the same model on different machines, with different sets of parameters, can therefore improve the overall completion time. However, the need to coordinate the separate machines, and to collate the data produced by the separate processes 'by hand', can still limit the feasibility of such an approach.

Sensitivity/Criticality Analyses

Cooper *et al.* (1996) proposed a model evaluation methodology that is closely related to that employed by Plaut & Shallice (1993) and described above. Central to the approach is the declaration of those aspects of a model that are held to be theoretically motivated (the core assumptions: Lakatos, 1970) and those that are purely implementational (Lakatosian peripheral assumptions), and the subsequent execution of studies on the criticality of core assumptions and the sensitivity of model performance to peripheral assumptions. If the division between theoretical and implementational assumptions is correct, model behaviour will be dependent on core assumptions and independent of peripheral assumptions.

This methodology may be coupled with an empirical research programme designed to provide critical data against

which alternate implementation assumptions may be distinguished, allowing the implementation assumptions to be refined and integrated into the core of theory in the spirit of a Lakatosian research programme (Lakatos, 1970).

Coupled Empirical/Computational Studies

The coupling of empirical and computational research programmes may be motivated by other concerns. Cooper & Yule (1999) demonstrate a technique for evaluating models containing free parameters that involves four steps: designing empirical studies which yield data that over-constrain the free parameters, performing those empirical studies, using data from nominated dependent variables to calibrate all free parameters within the model, and then using the calibrated model to predict the remaining dependent variables. In essence the technique depends upon ensuring that there are more degrees of freedom in the data than in the model. This in turn requires that the empirical work is designed specifically to provide sufficient data to over-constrain model parameters (and hence forbids the unconstrained modelling of existing data).

Common Requirements of the Methodologies

The various model evaluation methodologies surveyed above may be unified by the perspective brought by empirical psychology. Each of the methodologies can be viewed as involving a computational experiment akin to a standard laboratory experiment, in which the computational model plays the role of the human participant.

In the case of *Monte Carlo* simulations, a model might be run on a task 100 times. This is equivalent to running 100 participants on the task. Here, the methodological inadequacies of the simple *Monte Carlo* approach become apparent: it resembles an experiment with no within subject variables and no between subject variables — effectively a control condition without an experimental condition.

Methodologies that assess possible alternate implementation assumptions may be viewed as treating such assumptions as between-subjects variables. Consider a model in which some aspect may be implemented in three different ways. This aspect defines a variable with three levels. Assessing the sensitivity of the model to the implementation assumption involves running the model multiple times with each level of the independent variable — a standard between-groups experiment. Multiple implementation aspects will yield multiple between-subjects factors.

Parameters similarly amount to between-subjects factors, with each combination of parameter levels defining one type or group of model/participant. Parameter studies are thus equivalent to large between-subject experimental designs.

The coordination of between-subject experimental designs with large numbers of groups (either many factors or many levels per factor) and with many participants in each group (whether they be virtual or real) presents unique computational problems. Participants must be assigned to groups in order to balance group sizes and dependent variables must be appropriately collated and analysed. This is relatively simple to achieve if only one participant is run at a time, but this sequential approach results in model evaluation exercises that may run over days or weeks (and if a bug is later found the whole time-consuming process will have to be repeated). An alternative approach is to employ the parallelism made possible by the independence of each (virtual) participant, and to run different participants on different CPUs. The difficulty with this approach is that of coordination. The remainder of this paper describes a technology that we have developed in order to solve the coordination problems.

The Client-Server Model

The essence of our approach is to treat the model as a client, which communicates across the internet with a server. The server's role is to coordinate clients and collate their results. When the client is run, it begins by querying the server for a set of parameters (typically values of the experiment's independent variables). It then operates on these parameters to produce a set of dependent measures (i.e., values for the experiment's dependent variables). These measures are then returned to the server, which stores them for analysis. The client may then seek further parameters from the server, or terminate.

The use of a web-based client-server system has two major beneficial consequences for cognitive modelling methodology:

1. it makes large-scale parameter studies, with many parameters and/or levels, more practicable than they might otherwise be, since it can use distributed parallel execution to avoid the typically long execution times on single-processor systems, and

2. it allows both models and human subjects to interact with the same experimenter system, ensuring the maximum possible comparability between human and model datasets.

The second of these is not unique to the web-based client-server model, but it is an important advantage of the system described below when applied to model evaluation, because it ensures formal equivalence between the environments in which humans and models complete an experimental task.

The Server

Our server is derived from one originally written to support web-based human experiments. It is the product of four years' intermittent development, and it has been used to present a variety of experiments, often to groups of up to 25 students working simultaneously but independently. Therefore it has been forced to handle parallelism, in the form of multiple simultaneous requests.

The server is implemented as a CGI (Common Gateway Interface) program, running under a standard web server daemon (in our case Apache). The web server daemon receives input in the form of an encoded list of ⟨*Var* = *Val*⟩ pairs, such as is produced by an HTTP FORM submission, starts the experiment server program, and sends the input to it via one

of several well-known methods. The experiment server outputs plain text, possibly containing HTML via included files, but with another list of $\langle Var = Val \rangle$ pairs embedded in it, and then it exits. The outputs are sent to the client, which may be either a web browser window (if presentation is to a human participant), or a model.

Broadly, server inputs represent dependent variable values, while output $\langle Var = Val \rangle$ lists represent independent variable values, although we also make use of server inputs and outputs for control purposes, to coordinate the behaviour of client and server. This arrangement makes the server simple to use with web-based human experiments, either in the form of a series of independent pages, or as a more complex client written in a scripting language such as JavaScript.

But cognitive models are not usually web-based (unless they are implemented as Java applets or similar). Typically models are implemented either in cognitive modelling systems which lack server interaction facilities (Soar, ACT-R, PDP++), or they are stand-alone systems written in some standard programming language such as Lisp or Prolog, again without web functionality. Therefore, if a model is to interact with the server, then it, or the modelling system in which it is implemented, will have to be augmented with appropriate facilities.

Our own models are typically implemented in COGENT (Cooper & Fox, 1998; Cooper, Yule, Fox, & Sutton, 1998), which we have recently augmented with appropriate server interaction functionality. This took the form of a pair of simple routines, one to encode a list of $\langle Var = Val \rangle$ pairs, representing the values of independent and dependent variables in the model's state, and then send the resulting coded string to the server using HTTP, and the other to parse the server's output, returning another list of $\langle Var = Val \rangle$ pairs, specifying new values for the independent variables. These routines were implemented as additional commands within COGENT's scripting language, making the experiment server usable in principle by all COGENT models.

The addition of similar functionality to other modelling systems, or to stand-alone models, is straightforward, and a prototype API for models written in C (which takes the form of a library of interface functions for declaring dependent and independent variables, and for server interactions within a task and between tasks) has also been developed.

Server Functions

The experiment server currently supports the following functions:

- assignment of unique identifiers (IDs) to client instances (subjects) for tracking and collation purposes

- assignment of subjects in a balanced fashion to between-subjects groups

- sending of stimuli sequentially to clients, taking account of assignment to groups, and current position in the sequence

- recording and collating data from clients using IDs

- notification of clients when experiment is completed

- experiment monitoring and individual participant exclusion via a web-based experiment administration interface

- full design editing using the web-based administration interface

- display of data tabulations and calculation of statistics via the web-based administration interface

- exporting of data in a widely-used tab-delimited format suitable for external statistical/graphical analysis packages

These are described in more detail below.

ID assignment and access control   A client can originate a request for a new ID, typically at the beginning of an experiment. The server responds with a unique ID code, and a sequence of $\langle Var = Val \rangle$ pairs specifying levels of between and within subjects variables, allowing the client to begin the experiment.

Alternatively, a client can begin a session by providing an ID of its own, typically obtained from a human participant via a text input field. This facility can be used to restrict access only to those participants holding valid ID codes, and is most useful for human experiments.

Between-subjects balancing   If there are between-subjects variables, the server assigns IDs to each combination of levels of these variables (between-subjects category) in a balanced way. A new ID is assigned to the category which currently has fewest IDs assigned to it.

Sequencing   When the client initiates the experiment, or submits data (as at the end of a trial or block), the server must provide the next set of variable assignments to the client. Sequences of stimuli are specified in the server's design file (see below). If desired, different sequences can be associated with different between-variable combinations, allowing counterbalancing using hidden between-subjects variables.

Data collation   When the client submits data, the server saves it as a data record, using the ID to ensure data records from the same subject are appropriately tagged. The primary mechanism saves the values of declared dependent variables; these data can be used by the built-in tabulation and statistics facilities. There is also a secondary mechanism, for saving arbitrary 'raw' or uninterpreted data.

Administration   The online experiment administration system currently allows real-time monitoring of the progress of each participant and of summaries and analyses of relevant variables. Summaries may include tables of means, standard deviations, and numbers of records, and may use multiple independent and dependent variables. Data tables can be displayed in the form of HTML tables, for human inspection, or tab-formatted plain text, for export to commonly used statistical packages and spreadsheets. Some inferential statistics are also supported (only χ^2 at present). Tables and statistics are recalculated on request, allowing monitoring of results as the experiment progresses.

Server configuration   The server's behaviour is governed by a set of design parameters, which can be edited via the web-based administration interface. This provides an integrated set of visual editors for:

- declaration of independent (between-subjects and within-subjects) and dependent variables
- declaration of levels for all variable types, for use in assignment (between-subjects variables) and in tabulations and statistics
- option specification of the number of replications in each between-subjects category
- specification of materials sequences, depending on sequence number and (optionally) on between-subjects category
- specification of 'include' files (e.g., containing HTML, for use in human web-based experiments)
- specification of tabulations and statistics, using declared variables

Parallelism, Speed and Robustness

We have seen that the server can handle multiple sessions with human subjects, interacting with web-based client systems, in parallel. Model clients have the same relation with the server as do web-based, human experimental clients, which of course run on separate machines, and therefore we can also run models in parallel, on separate machines.

This ability is of particular importance for parameter studies and other evaluation methodologies involving multiple runs of a model, owing to the long completion times on single machines typically associated with them; if we run lots of parallel processes, cooperating on a single task, we can drastically reduce overall completion time. There is no requirement of synchrony between the multiple processes, so they can be run on a set of machines of widely varying power (even different operating systems): they all add together to effectively constitute a distributed supercomputer, which can be extended as required by simply adding more clients, on their own machines. Moreover, automated job assignment means that clients need not lie idle when they have finished a job, waiting for a human operator's attention; instead, they can immediately be assigned a new job and continue running until the whole parameter space has been exhausted.

The management of parallel arrays of clients presents peculiar problems, however. With a large array of machines working together for a long period, it is not unlikely that one or two will fail to complete their assigned jobs due to accidental power loss, operating system failure or some other unforeseen event. In such cases the rest of the array will continue to work despite the failure of one client, and the server will keep assigning new jobs on demand, but since the server assigns jobs on the basis that they have not been assigned before, such failures will result in 'holes' in the final dataset, as these jobs would never return their data. To fill in these holes, the server possesses a mechanism to reassign unfinished jobs once there are no more fresh jobs to be assigned (if

the number of replications is specified). So the server automatically repairs holes in its data coverage without human intervention, provided that at least one client continues running. If all the clients die, owing to a wide-spread power cut or a slow memory leak in the client, for example, the human operator merely needs to restart one or more clients, whereupon they will be assigned new jobs by the server, and the whole ensemble will continue until the dataset is complete.

A potentially more serious issue is that, since clients run in asynchronous parallel, occasionally two clients may attempt to communicate with the server at the same time. If a program is not designed to handle this scenario, as in some earlier versions of our server, data losses, ranging in severity from the minor (e.g., replication of ID assignment) to the catastrophic (e.g., overwriting of data files), may result. To solve this problem, all data storage and retrieval procedures are now designed to ensure that data can never be overwritten. ID assignment procedures also guarantee uniqueness of assigned identity under parallel conditions. In general, all the server's client-interaction procedures are now believed to be parallel-safe.

Case Studies

Case study 1: An empirical program   Over the last few years we have run a series of standard laboratory experiments using a categorisation and information seeking task based on medical diagnosis (e.g. Yule, Cooper, & Fox, 1998; Cooper & Yule, 1999). These experiments have all been presented using a web browser based interface (client), written in JavaScript and HTML. The function of the client is to present a randomised series of trials, comprising a single block. The server specifies the type of block and the number of trials in each block. Each human participant receives a unique ID, and produces one data record per block, giving mean diagnostic accuracy and overall time for that block, and preferred symptom queries given each presenting symptom. (These are the variables declared in the relevant design file for the server.)

Early experiments used a simple structure of four blocks of the same type, containing 20 trials each, in two between-subjects categories. Later experiments controlled not only the type of block (what types of querying and diagnosing options are open to the participant), but also the sequence of trials in the block, using between-subjects variables. The most recent studies have investigated different within-subjects block-type sequences and materials, and between-subjects manipulations of disease base-rate.

Case Study 2: A coupled study with COGENT   A different mode of interaction is illustrated by a parallel parameter study of a model developed within the COGENT modelling environment. The model used was a version of one of our categorisation and information-seeking models, using the experimental design investigated by (Cooper & Yule, 1999). In this study, the COGENT client was designed to run a complete experiment, comprising a full complement of 128 virtual subjects for each combination of free parameters, with server interaction only at the start and end of the experiment. The client used the COGENT scripting language to structure the internal details of the experiment, overcoming the current server's limited sequencing abilities.

The model included two free parameters: *Learning rate* and *Memory Decay*. These were treated as between-subjects variables (or more accurately, "between-ID variables"), each with 41 levels. Thus the parameter space was defined by a pair of between-subjects variables declared, with their 41 possible values, in the design file. For each experiment run, the server provided a unique ID and a pair of parameter values at the beginning, allowing the client to run the experiment with those values. When the client-side processing was complete, the client returned its ID and a set of dependent variables (diagnostic accuracy in each of the six blocks, and a measure of distance between that learning curve and the one derived from the human experiment) to the server for collation.

Once the dataset was complete, the system was used to tabulate the distance measures, which were then exported to a spreadsheet. This allowed the data to be display as a surface, minima of the surface to be determined, and hence determination of optimum 'humanoid' parameter values for model calibration. The calibrated model was then used to generate predictions about a further set of dependent measures (query preferences given presenting symptoms), which were then compared with human query preference data collected in a standard laboratory-based experiment (which was also supported by the server: cf. case study 1).

Case Study 3: A parameter study in C   Only one machine was available when case study 2 was performed. Parallel server operation was examined in a further case study that used a prototype API written in C to allow a model of routine action selection (also written in C) to interface with the server. The study involved exploration of a four-dimensional parameter space, with five levels of each parameter and ten replications at each point in the space. The client ran simultaneously on four machines (under LINUX, Solaris and IRIX). The server proved to be robust, though a memory leak in the client code led to individual clients crashing when their machine's swap space was exhausted (generally after more than 12 hours of processing). Nevertheless, data were not lost, and the parameter study was successfully completed by periodically restarting each client.

Conclusion

We have raised the issue of model evaluation as critical to the methodology of cognitive modelling, and emphasised the importance of between-subject variables in a number of model-evaluation paradigms. Furthermore, we have presented a system which automatically manages between-subject variable assignment for both human and computational experiments. As a 'free' additional benefit, the server makes the parallel execution of computational experiments as easy as serial execution, largely overcoming the practical limitations traditionally associated with intensive model-evaluation techniques.

We believe that the server can provide these benefits to virtually any computational model in the cognitive sciences, with appropriate interface modification, and additionally that it is possible to interface the server with widely-used experiment presentation systems (e.g., MEL, SuperLab, etc.), which often omit to provide support for between-subject designs, since they are designed with single-machine operation in mind.

The features provided by the software in its present state are sufficient to allow control and monitoring of a range of experimental designs. However, a number of extensions are planned, including:

- improved sequencing, allowing hierarchically structured, fully randomised stimulus sequences to be generated and served, on the basis of independent variable declarations and design principles;
- improved statistics, including ANOVA, correlations, t-tests, and non-parametric alternatives;
- publication of the API to allow other modelling and experiment presentation systems to interface with the server.

Acknowledgement
This research was supported by EPSRC grant GR/M89621.

References

Anderson, J. R., & Lebiere, C. (1998). *The Atomic Components of Thought*. LEA, Mahwah, NJ.

Cooper, R., & Fox, J. (1998). COGENT: A visual design environment for cognitive modelling. *Behavior Research Methods, Instruments, & Computers*, 30(4), 553–564.

Cooper, R., Fox, J., Farringdon, J., & Shallice, T. (1996). A systematic methodology for cognitive modelling. *Artificial Intelligence*, 85, 3–44.

Cooper, R., & Yule, P. (1999). Comparative modelling of learning in a decision making task. In Hahn, M., & Stoness, S. C. (Eds.), *Proceedings of the 21st Annual Conference of the Cognitive Science Society*, pp. 120–125. Vancouver, Canada. LEA.

Cooper, R., Yule, P., Fox, J., & Sutton, D. (1998). COGENT: An environment for the development of cognitive models. In Schmid, U., Krems, J. F., & Wysotzki, F. (Eds.), *Mind Modelling: A Cognitive Science Approach to Reasoning, Learning and Discovery*, pp. 55–82. Pabst Science Publishers, Lengerich, Germany.

Lakatos, I. (1970). Falsification and the methodology of scientific research programmes. In Lakatos, I., & Musgrave, A. (Eds.), *Criticism and the Growth of Knowledge*, pp. 91–196. CUP, Cambridge, UK.

Plaut, D. C., & Shallice, T. (1993). Deep dyslexia: A case study of connectionist neuropsychology. *Cognitive Neuropsychology*, 10, 377–500.

Yule, P., Cooper, R., & Fox, J. (1998). Normative and information processing accounts of medical diagnosis. In Gernsbacher, M. A., & Derry, S. J. (Eds.), *Proceedings of the 20th Annual Conference of the Cognitive Science Society*, pp. 1176–1181. Madison, WI. LEA.

Generating Subjective Workload Self-Assessment from a Cognitive Model

Wayne W. Zachary (Wayne_Zachary@chiinc.com)
Jean-Christophe Le Mentec (j-c_le_mentec@chiinc.com)
Vassil Iordonav (vassil_iordanov@chiinc.com)
CHI Systems, Inc. 716 N. Bethlehem Pike
Lower Gwynedd, PA 19002 USA

Abstract

Cognitive modeling has paid little attention to workload assessment, particularly subjective self-assessment. This paper demonstrates an approach by which a computational cognitive model can make self-assessments of its subjective workload. Comparisons with human subject data show a good degree of correspondence. The methods used are generalizable to modeling other introspective and self-assessment processes.

Introduction

Workload is an important cognitive construct in engineering psychology. It is typically measured indirectly, either behaviorally (e.g., as performance on a secondary task) or subjectively (e.g., as introspective self-assessment using calibrated psychometric scale). In most applied situations, subjective self-assessment is the only practical approach. While cognitive models have made great strides in replicating human performance and behavior, they have been much less successful in predicting or replicating human subjective processes, such as introspective assessment of workload. Such inabilities can be a major obstacle to more widespread applied use of cognitive models. By reinterpreting the workload construct in modeling terms, however, and making use of new cognitive model features such as metacognitive self-awareness, cognitive models can be made to produce reliable subjective self-assessments of workload.

Conceptualizing Workload in Cognitive (Modeling) Terms

The concept of workload has been used in confusing and sometimes conflicting ways in the literature, ranging from an aspect of the task (e.g., high-workload versus low-workload scenarios), to an internal state in the human (or model) that can affect task performance (e.g., workload-based strategies), to an output of the process (e.g., ratings produced by the model/person after task completion). Here, workload is viewed not as a state or a component, but rather as a relationship between a person (as information processing system) and the (complex) environment in which that person is working. More specifically, workload is viewed (and

modeled) as a product of interactions between the (external) problem/environmental dynamics, and the person's internal information processing system which contains both internal processing (i.e., cognitive) *mechanisms* and internal *expertise*. Each of these contributes to the relationship that can be called workload. For example, a person with expertise (i.e., more efficient and effective domain-knowledge and a broader range of experiences), will be able to perform a set of tasks with less cognitive processing than an individual with identical cognitive mechanisms but less expertise. A given work situation may involve much less processing for an individual with more expertise than for one with less. Thus, workload can not be, by itself, an input to the task, but is rather an attribute of how the cognitive system is being utilized in a specific work environment and given a specific body of expertise. The fact that people are able to adapt their processing strategy to this attribute suggests that there are mechanisms that provide some access, presumably symbolic access, to the momentary activity of the internal information processing mechanisms. This ability to access this information about internal cognition is here termed metacognitive self-awareness, is theorized as the basis not just for workload-based strategy adaptation, but also for introspective reporting or workload (see Zachary and Le Mentec, 2000). While the research reported here concerned modeling both of these activities, only the latter (modeling of introspective workload assessments) is discussed in this paper.

The Empirical Study

Modeling of workload self-reporting was undertaken in the context of a large comparative empirical study of cognitive modeling approaches (Tenney and Spector, 2001). The study involved a simplified air traffic control (ATC) simulation, in which human subjects had to control en-route traffic for series of problem scenarios involving varying difficulty (low, medium, or high density of aircraft tracks), and using two different human-computer interfaces (a 'baseline' interface and an 'aided' interface in which color coding was used to simplify the control process). An independent 'moderator' organization created the simulation, and collected a set of initial performance data from human subjects performing the task under all three difficulty conditions and using both interfaces (appropriately counterbalanced). Subjects were also asked to provide subjective workload self-assessments using the widely-used NASA Task Load Index (TLX) developed by Hart and Staveland (1988). Aggregate subject performance data, such as error rates, reaction time statistics, etc., as well as the workload ratings, were then provided to cognitive modeling teams (including the team represented by the authors), which used these data to develop and 'tune' air traffic controller cognitive models, with the goal of generating realistic human behavior, including the workload self-reports. Later, the models were each compared by the moderator to similar data from a second sample of subjects performing the same range of tasks, using different but equivalent problem scenarios. In the study, there were 8 subjects in the tuning data set, and 8 different ones in the comparison data set. The overall cognitive model development is discussed elsewhere (Zachary, Santarelli, Ryder, Stokes, and Scolaro, 2001). The main focus here is on the aspects of the modeling process (and comparison results) dealing with the generation of the workload ratings.

The overall approach to generating these introspective workload accounts involved four basic steps.

1) The specific subjective workload measures, and the introspective tasks they require, were analyzed and conceptually mapped into the internal architecture and principles of operation of the cognitive modeling architecture selected by the team, the COGNET architecture. COGNET was particularly appropriate because the necessary metacognitive processes and self-awareness instrumentation had recently been developed and integrated into it (Zachary, and LeMentec, 2000).

2) Each of the six measures comprising TLX was then operationalized in terms of specific aspects of metacognitive self-awareness, whether they existed or not within COGNET or its current software implementation.

3) Those metacognitive features identified in the second step which did not already exist in COGNET were then designed and implemented, and integrated with those that had previously been implemented to allow the self-reporting of the subjective workload assessments required. When integrated with the COGNET-based model of the expertise and knowledge needed to work in the ATC domain, this resulted in the ability of the model to introspect and create a report of its own subjective workload on the six measures involved, after completing a specific work task.

4) The scale of those measures resulting from the previous step was not necessarily the same as that used by the measurement instrument (i.e., the quasi-interval scales used by the human subjects when applying

TLX). In the fourth step, the measures generated by the model were calibrated to those specific measurement scales by a statistical regression process, using TLX data provided by the 'tuning' set of subjects.

Details of each of the four steps are provided below. No detailed overview of COGNET is provided here; instead the reader is referred to Zachary, Ryder & Hicinbothom (1998), and Zachary, Santarelli, Ryder, Stokes & Scolaro (2000).

Relating TLX Measures to COGNET Constructs

TLX elicits assessment of subjective workload on six separate scales:

- Physical demand – defined as "how physically demanding was the task"
- Mental demand – defined as "how mentally demanding was the task"
- Temporal demand – defined as "how hurried or rushed was the pace of the task"
- Performance self-estimate – defined as "how successful were you in accomplishing what you were asked to do"
- Effort estimate – defined as "how hard did you have to work to accomplish your level of performance"
- Frustration – defined as "how insecure, discouraged, irritated, and annoyed were you"

The respondent provides an estimate of each characteristic on a Likert-like scale divided into 10 intervals, and measured as 21 discrete values (integers 0-10 inclusive plus all intermediate half-values). Thus, the cognitive model would have to produce estimates of these same variables on this same scale. The general theoretical framework for this process was to relate each measure to the self-awareness of various aspects of the processing within the COGNET representation, as described above. The analysis of each measure in terms of COGNET constructs is given below.

Physical demand. This construct was based on self-awareness of the overall level of activity of the motor system. The Air Traffic Control model directed action to the motor system on different action channels (e.g., hands, voice, eyes) using different high-level operations. Each action duration was, in addition, given a duration by a specific micromodel (see Glenn, 1989). The awareness of physical workload is thus accomplished in two stages. First, the system had to be aware of (collect) the total time spent in each kind of action (e.g., move mouse, move eyes, give verbal message). Second, weights had to be assigned to discriminate low effort actions (e.g., eye-movements) from high-effort actions. The physical workload value could then be calculated as the weighted sum of the action times across all high-effort actions, normalized to the length of the scenario.

Mental demand. This construct was based on the self-awareness of the cognitive complexity of the various tasks being executed and their relative frequencies. Mental workload was estimated separately for each cognitive task in the model. (In COGNET, a cognitive task is a complex procedural chunk associated with a top-level work-domain goal). Because tasks can be carried out in many different ways, the average *complexity* of each task during the execution of a scenario is calculated as the average number of goals processed and lower-level methods invoked during task execution (including the number of goals and method invocations within the top-level methods invoked). The task complexity was then multiplied by the number of times the task was performed in the scenario. This weighted complexity was summed across all tasks and normalized to the length of the scenario.

Temporal demand. This is a difficult construct to relate to COGNET internal structure and dynamics. It was ultimately decided to do so in terms of a complementary construct, the sense of idleness or momentary sense of 'nothing to do now.' It was felt that the more frequently the model had such an awareness, the less time-pressure it would feel, and vice versa. This sense would occur, in model terms, when the model was aware that it had no 'queued' action or reasoning tasks but only was scanning the screen for new tracks needing attention, and finding none. Thus, a self-awareness capability for this 'nothing to do' state was needed, and its negative value was used to measure temporal workload, normalized to the length of the scenario. This use of negative value is analogous to the well-known use of 'regret' to measure (negative) utility in decision theory.

Performance. A similar regret-like approach was selected to relate performance to COGNET constructs. The model does not have any awareness of how well it is doing or how it is performing on a positive side, but it does have an awareness of when it makes errors of omission or commission, because it attempts to correct those errors when it becomes aware of them. Thus, the more errors the model is aware of, the worse its perceived performance would be, and when it is aware of no errors, its self-perception of its performance would be very high (whether it would be so empirically or not). The performance measure was ultimately assigned as the negative value of the count of perceived errors during a scenario, normalized to the length of the scenario.

Effort. Conceptually, the concept of effort as defined for the human subjects seems to refer to the total amount of time they spent 'working' in the air traffic scenario, possibly excluding or discounting the visual effort of scanning the display. (Why discount visual scanning? Although there is no data to confirm or disconfirm this position, it seems likely that a

scenario in which no tracks appeared would be said to have involved 'no effort', even though the eyes would still scan the screen, at least periodically.) In COGNET, there can be multiple threads of work going on in parallel at any time; for example, hands, voice, and eyes, all with different and potentially overlapping action start and end times. Because of this parallelism, it would be incorrect to simply sum all the work times, as many could be parallel. Alternatively, the total time in which some motor actions were occurring could be collected as the total amount of 'busy' time in the problem. Thus, the reporting of 'effort' required an awareness of the states when some activity was occurring on *any* motor channel. When divided by the total time of the scenario, it would yield a measure of the proportion of time spent working the problem, and thus was used to report the effort involved in the scenario.

Frustration. This is an extremely ill-defined concept, even to people (as evidenced by the range of emotional states that subjects were told to map into the term 'frustration', and by generally low inter-subject correlations on this scale). After considering a number of aspects of the model and execution architecture that could be related to one or more of the terms used in the elicitation frame (i.e., insecurity, discouragement, irritation, annoyance), it seemed that a simple approach was best. The approach selected is based on an awareness of the times that a cognitive task is interrupted by another cognitive task. While the nature of the stylized air traffic control task was such that interruption is minimized (i.e., because it's HCI provides limited ability to leave work elements in an interrupted state), there are still opportunities for this to occur, primarily with visual and/or purely interpretive tasks. Thus, frustration was simply reported as the number of cognitive task interruptions divided by the length of the scenario. (Some caveats on this approach are discussed in the conclusions.)

Operationalizing and Implementing TLX Measures in BATON

The preceding analysis translated the TLX workload constructs into terms consistent with our underlying conceptualization of subjective workload self-reporting. This analysis was next used to develop specific computational implementations of the measures within the BATON software that implements the COGNET cognitive architecture. In this operationalization process, effort was made to (re-)use various aspects of self-awareness that had already been implemented. When this was not possible, new features were defined as needed to provide explicit self-awareness of specific model states (such as awareness of having made an error). In some cases, it was also necessary to define additional instrumentation of BATON to create specific types of self-awareness of physical actions (either motor actions or deliberative perceptual actions).

The specific formula developed for producing each individual workload measure is provided in Table 1, where: the symbol TS in all cases refers to the length (in time) of the scenario, and the variables in italics represent new cognitive operators to measure individual events, such as awareness that an error has occurred, or new instrumentation inserted into BATON to quantify a specific aspect of the system's execution. In Table 1, several measures of self-awareness organic to BATON were used. These are:

DPC – a measure of the Dynamic Procedural Complexity of a task, it essentially counts the number of GOALs, and numerical/symbolic judgmental operations that are actually executed within a given problem-instance (i.e., scenario).

DTT – a measure of Dynamic Task frequency, it counts the number of times the task is actually executed in a given problem-instance.

DTI – a measure of Dynamic Task Interruption, it counts the number of times that a given task has been interrupted, while executing, by other tasks.

The integration of these measures made the information they collect part of the system's self-awareness in a portion of metacognitive memory. Two additional low-level cognitive operators also had to be created in BATON and retrofitted into the expertise model of the air traffic control task. These were:

'error-detected' – an operator that, when executed, places an awareness that the model has made an error of some sort into the metacognitive memory;

'nothing-to-do' – an operator that, when executed, places awareness into the metacognitive memory that the model has found nothing to do (other than scan).

Finally, two new types of instrumentation of the BATON mechanism had to be created:
'time spent in work' – an instrumentation of the scheduling mechanism that collects the total amount of time during which time was being consumed (via a Spend-Time operator), on any thread of activity within the system;
'action time' – an instrumentation of the motor action mechanism that collects, for a specific action type, the total amount of time during which time was spent performing that action via a Spend-Time operator.

Calibrating the Measures to Human Subject TLX Data

It should be clear that the formulae in Table 1, while arguably measuring the various self-perceptions collected by TLX, do not do so on the same Likert-like scale used by human subjects using TLX. They should be consistent with the TLX scales within a linear transformation, however. In addition, the values generated by the model were not inherently tuned to the relative differences in the judgements made by the human 'tuning-data' subjects. Thus, the final step in implementing the measures in Table 1 was a calibration process that dealt with these two issues.

Each subject in the initial tuning data set had provided an assessment on each of the six subjective factors for the six different scenarios (difficulty X HCI version). For each given factor and scenario i there was then a vector of j subject values x_{ij} on the scale for that factor, and a statistic X_i which represents the mean value of the x_{ij} for scenario j. For each of those same six scenarios, the model was able to produce a value y_i for the same factor, using the relevant measure from Table 1.

Table 1. BATON Operationalization of TLX Workload Measures

Measure	Computational Formula	Operationalization
Physical	$(S_{all\ i}\ k_i \cdot action\text{-}time_i)/T_S$	Where i is an action type, k_i is the weight of that action type, and $action\text{-}time_i$ is a function which collects total time spent taking that action during a scenario by instrumenting the action mechanism
Mental	$(S_{all\ i}\ DPC_i \cdot DTT_i)/T_S$	Where i is a cognitive task, and DPC_i and DTT_i are organic self-awareness measures (see text)
Temporal	$-(S_{all\ i}\ nothing\text{-}to\text{-}do_i)/T_S$	Where $nothing\text{-}to\text{-}do_i$ is a cognitive operator that returns a value of one iff the visual scan task has been completed and the model found nothing to do
Performance	$-(S_{all\ i}\ error\text{-}detected_i)/T_S$	Where $error\text{-}detected_i$ is a cognitive operator that returns a value of one iff a cognitive task found that the model had made an error and was about to try to correct it (if correctable)
Effort	$(S_{all\ i}\ time\text{-}spent\text{-}in\text{-}work_i)/T_S$	Where i is an increment in time, and $time\text{-}spent\text{-}in\text{-}work_i$ is a function measuring the time within that increment in which motor activity is occurring on any execution thread
Frustration	$(S_{all\ i}\ DTI_i)/T_S$	Where DTI_i is an organic self-awareness measure of the number of times cognitive task i was interrupted during the scenario (see text)

This yielded a set ordered pairs (X_i,y_i), representing the model's assessment and average subject assessment for that factor on scenario i. However, the y_i represent values on an open-ended ratio scale, while the X_i represent interval values on a closed-ended scale. To map the first into the second, a regression was done to calculate the X_i as a function of the y_i. This regression process yielded a linear function which then stated how the y_i could be transformed, once calculated, to yield a calibrated measure on the same scale used by the human subjects. If this function is written $F_i(Y)$, then the final value of the model's measure for factor i is defined as:

$F_i(Y)$ if in the interval [0,10],
0 if $F_i(Y) < 0$, and
10 if $F_i(Y) > 10$.

The resulting equations are:
PHYSICAL* = 9.1949*PHYSICAL + .7955
MENTAL* = 7.9385*MENTAL+ .5032
TEMPORAL* = -7.9865* TEMPORAL + 6.7737
PERFORM* = 380.8318*PERFORM + .7606
EFFORT* = 4.6704*EFFORT + 1.2269
FRUSTRATE* = .1703*FRUSTRATE - .7498

where the model-generated measure is named in capitals (e.g., EFFORT), and the calibrated measure is shown with an asterisk (e.g., EFFORT*).

Empirical Comparison of Model Subjective Assessments with Human Data

The modeling processes were followed by an experimental comparison of model behaviors, including the workload self-reporting, against data from a second group of human subjects (from the same population) using similar scenarios (i.e., rotated airspaces) to those used to collect the human 'tuning' data. Again, two ATC interfaces were used: a baseline human-computer interface, referred to as 'text-only' because it required more display text reading and manual/verbal interactions, and another called 'color' because it provided decision support information through the use of color coding of aircraft symbols. The COGNET cognitive model compared favorably to the human subjects in work performance. It was statistically indistinguishable from the human subjects on measures of reaction time, errors made, and overall performance (using an overall performance measure). Comparison details are found in Tenney & Spector (2000).

While cognitive models have been shown to be able to generate human-like *performance*, the ability to generate human-like subjective introspective assessments, such as subjective workload evaluations, is less evident. Thus, the comparison of the model's subjective assessments to the human data was a good test of the mechanism-based metacognitive approach to introspection described above. The comparisons with 'fly-off' subject data are shown below in Figure 1a – 1e. Each sub-figure shows a different TLX component measure, with the abcissa showing the six scenario combinations (low, medium, high track density X color or text-only HCI). In general, Figure 1 shows a good fit with the human data, increasing from low-load to high-load problems. The model appears to generally view the aided (i.e., color) condition as less demanding than the unaided (i.e., text-only) condition, but less so than the human subjects who often saw even the highest track-load scenario with the color condition as involving less workload than the lowest workload text condition. The expected divergence appeared with the frustration measure, as the model did not find the text condition as frustrating as the human subjects did. This was further complicated by the fact that the model, for some reason, found the intermediate track load problem more frustrating than the high-track-load problem for the unaided condition.

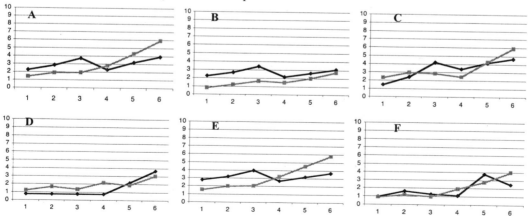

Figure 1. Model versus Human Subjects Means on TLX Measures

Discussion and Conclusions

The comparison to human subjects, while highly favorable, still reflects some limitations in the method used. One methodological remark is offered here concerning the calibration process. Due to the time schedule of the project, the calibration process was done in only two iterations. That is, an initial calibration was done, and then parameters in the workload prediction parts of the model (e.g., the weights of the action types in the physical demand measure) were revised. It is likely that given a few additional iterations a much tighter fit with the human subjects' assessments could have been obtained. At the same time, it is not clear that there would have been much value in doing so beyond the simple statistical exercise. The human subject data showed substantial inter-subject variability, and the two samples (tuning and final comparison) also showed substantial variability. Thus, the divergence that the COGNET model showed with reference to the aggregate human responses is probably indicative of the general variability that any individual would have shown when compared to group means.

The frustration measure seems to be the most problematical, for people as well as for the model. It is noted, for example, that human subjects overall found the text-based version of the interface more frustrating than the color version, although it is not clear (in terms of the cognitive model of the air traffic control process) why this was the case. Verbal protocol data collected from human subjects further showed that there was a strong sequence effect, in that subjects were much more frustrated with the text version after having first used the color version. However, since the design did not allow any knowledge of prior runs to be incorporated into this self-assessment process, this effect could not be used in producing the model's frustration self-report. Thus, it was expected that the form of self-reporting selected for this measure would under-report frustration for the text-only case, an expectation which was borne out by the empirical data (see below).

A major goal of this research is to create an organic capability for COGNET-based cognitive models to generate TLX workload assessments in any application context. A major application of cognitive models is design evaluation (see Kieras, 1992), and workload is a criterion often used in engineering psychology to evaluate interface designs. While cognitive models are showing increased ability to predict human performance from design/functional specifications only, it is important that the workload dimension of evaluation be added as well. This research demonstrates that it is now possible to do so.

At a more general level, there is broad interest in expanding cognitive modeling from an objective level (e.g., predicting performance) to a subjective level (e.g., predicting/modeling subjective states such as emotions, feelings, etc.) and to processes of evaluative introspection. This paper has argued that subjective workload assessment is an example of such a subjective state accessed through a subjective introspection process. While the scope of the prediction has been limited (to a specific method of assessing subjective workload), it is believed that the underlying approach could be of much broader use in achieving these general goals.

Acknowledgments

This research was supported by Contract F33615-99-C-6007 from the US Air Force.

References

Glenn, F. (1989). The Case for Micro-Models. In *Proceedings of Human Factors Society 33rd Annual Meeting*, Santa Monica, CA: HFES.

Hart, S. & Staveland, L. (1988). Development of NASA-TLX (Task Load Index): Results of empirical and theoretical research. In Hancock, P. & Meshkati, N., (Eds.),*Human Mental Workload*. Amsterdam: North-Holland.

Kieras, D. (1990). The role of cognitive simulation models in the development of advanced training and testing systems. In N. Frederiksen, R. Glaser, A. Lesgold, & M. Shafto (Eds.), *Diagnostic Monitoring of Skill & Knowledge Acquisition*. Hillsdale: Erlbaum.

Tenny, Y., & Spector, S. (2001). Comparison of HBR Models with Human-in-the-loop Performance in a Simplified Air Traffic Control Simulation with and without HLA Protocols: Task Simulation, Human Data, and Results. In *Proc. of the 10th Conf. on Computer Generated Forces and Behavioral Representation*. Orlando: Inst. for Sim. and Trng.

Zachary, W., & Le Mentec, J.-C. (2000). Incorporating Metacognitive Capabilities in Synthetic Cognition Systems, in *Proc. of the 9th Conference on Computer Generated Forces and Behavioral Representation*. Orlando: Institute for Simulation and Training.

Zachary, W., Ryder, J., & Hicinbothom, J. (1998). Cognitive Task Analysis and Modeling of Decision Making in Complex Environments, in J. A. Cannon-Bowers & Eduardo Salas, Eds., Making Decisions Under Stress. Wash, D. C.: Am. Psych. Assn.

Zachary, W., Santarelli, T., Ryder, J. M., Stokes, J., & Scolaro, D. (2001). Developing a Multi-tasking Cognitive Agent Using the COGNET/iGEN Integrative Architecture. In *Proc. of the 10th Conf. on Computer Generated Forces and Behavioral Representation*. Orlando: Inst. for Sim. and Trng.

Posters

A Closer Look at Exploratory Learning of Interactive Devices

Anna L Cox (a.cox@herts.ac.uk)
Richard M Young (r.m.young@herts.ac.uk)
Psychology Department, University of Hertfordshire
College Lane, Hatfield, AL10 9AB, United Kingdom

Abstract

This paper describes a new rational framework for modelling exploratory learning of interactive devices, first presented in Young & Cox (2000). The framework has been used as a basis for analysing a number of protocols taken from participants exploring a simulated central heating timer that provide examples supporting the framework. The results suggest that the framework can successfully explain episodes of the participants' behaviour during exploration and also what they learn from it. Finally, we describe the modeling work (in progress) in Soar (Newell, 1990) and COGENT (Cooper & Fox, 1998) implementing the framework.

The Framework. The framework described here provides a rational account of exploratory learning. Before describing how it works in practice, we outline the basic structure of the framework. It consists of an iterative cycle of three stages as shown in Figure 1. In the first stage all applicable possible things to do, or exploratory acts (EAs), are identified and their predicted efficiency calculated. Efficiency is defined as the ratio of the predicted increase in information that would be gained by carrying out the action, divided by its cost which is usually identified as the time taken to perform it. Secondly, the one with the highest efficiency is chosen and thirdly, it is executed. The cycle is then repeated until such time as the goal is met.

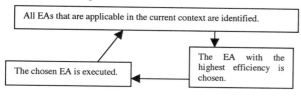

Figure 1: The Rational Framework for Modelling Exploratory Learning (EA = Exploratory Act)

As a starting point we concern ourselves with a user engaged in unstructured or free exploration of an interactive device. It is hypothesised that the user makes a decision between a number of EAs he can do, based on the cost of performing one of these changes and the expected gain. These EAs can be internal or external activities such as a) understanding something more about the layout, b) understanding something more about a component of the device, c) clicking a button, d) understanding a change that takes place on the display, e) forming a hypothesis (i.e. if I do X, Y will happen), and f) performing an experiment (to test a hypothesis).

Presuming the user has never encountered this device before, we can imagine that the EA he might choose to do is to understand something about the layout. This EA is likely to be chosen a number of times as the user looks at the layout of the various interface items and their relations to each other. A further number of internal EAs might follow as the user notices and considers the various labels on the interface items. At some point, simply looking and noticing things about the interface itself will not offer the same amount of information that one might expect in the first instance and so the user will choose to perform an action. The reason this action might be chosen could be as a result of a particular hypothesis that has been proposed that the user wishes to test, or alternatively, simply to see what happens. After each EA, the user chooses the next EA to perform depending on which EA offers the highest efficiency, or return for cost, in the current situation.

The Protocols. The protocols reported here were taken while participants explored a simulated central heating timer. In addition to the usual interface items one might expect there was a button called test. This button led to a screen where the participant could 'probe' each day and see what the behaviour of the device will be.

Case Study 1 – P1. Initially, P1 has a look around the display and then chooses to click on the test button. She mistakenly believes that this will give her some tasks to undertake. She quickly realises her mistake and goes back to the main screen of the device. She notices that the device is telling her that the heating is set to *off* and she says that she's going to click on the *24 hours* button. She follows this with a remark that she sees that the device is now indicating that the heating is on. This sequence illustrates how, from all the possible things she could try in the situation, she decides to click the *24 hours* button with a view to seeing what it does.

After this initial orientation phase, P1 sets herself the task of setting the heating to come on and go off on Monday. When she has achieved this, she tries to change the settings so that the heating comes on and goes off for some of the other days of the week. Throughout the exploration period she becomes more and more confused about how various aspects of the device work and is sometimes sidetracked into performing experiments to investigate what a particular button does or how it works.

Looking at this interlude in more detail, we see that the next episode begins with P1 clicking *Auto* and noticing that the event buttons are enabled. She then selects *ON1* and clicks the *day* button setting the event to Monday. Then, clicking on *Advance*, she remarks that "that's how I make the numbers change". She then generalises this knowledge to the *Back* button hypothesising that clicking it will make the time go backwards. She performs an experiment to check this hypothesis and clicks the *Back* button several times saying "....and how I make them go back". There are a number of similar episodes where P1 successfully learns how to use other parts of the device.

Case Study 2 – P2. Analysis of the protocol shows that P2 initially orients himself to the device and explores the basic button functions. He then tries to set up a pattern of on and off times for Monday and after an initial misinterpretation, learns to use the test screen to find out the behaviour of the heating system. The next task he tries to do is to set up an on and off pattern for Tuesday. While trying to achieve this goal, he discovers the cyclic nature of the day button and the groups of days that can be selected.

The protocol also shows that from about this time he starts to redundantly reselect an event after he has set the time and day for the event. This suggests that he is using the interface as a command composition interface and that he sees this reselection of the event button as a communication that *this* is the setting he wants, rather than seeing the interface as the state-setting interface that it really is.

One of the other errors P2 makes while using the device is to set up a pattern of on and off times, say for the weekend, on the same event buttons that have been used for a different pattern, say for Monday through Friday. When he came to probe the test screen to see the result of his programming, he was surprised to find that the original settings had been deleted. (This error has also been made by many of the participants using the device in other studies.) Our proposition that he believes that the interface communicates commands rather than sets states explains why he makes this error.

The Model. Models of exploratory learning are currently being built in COGENT (Cooper & Fox, 1998) and Soar (Newell, 1990). The aim of these models is not to replicate, button-press for button-press, the behaviour of the participants discussed in this paper, but to identify sequences of behaviour similar in nature to what has been observed. For example, given a free-exploration situation, we would expect the model initially to conduct device-oriented exploration and then to attempt self-imposed tasks such as mini-experiments to test hypotheses. These hypotheses regarding how the device works may have been built as a result of observing the feedback from a particular button press, or from generalising knowledge about the function of one button to another. Furthermore, analysis of the knowledge acquired by the model is expected to show that device-oriented knowledge is easily acquired but that an accurate understanding of task-oriented knowledge is less common. In addition, the framework predicts that there will be a difference in the knowledge acquired by those conducting free and focused exploration and it is expected that the implemented models will show this. This prediction is supported by evidence found by Trudel and Payne (1995) when they compared the performance of people who explored a digital watch under those two conditions.

Discussion & Conclusions. Previous research (Cox & Young, 2000; Draper & Barton, 1993; Trudel & Payne, 1995) has suggested that participants spend most of their time engrossed in device-oriented exploration and do not set themselves realistic tasks spontaneously. The protocols discussed here suggest that this distinction may not be so clear cut. P1 and P2 do seem to set themselves task-oriented goals but often become sidetracked into acquiring device-oriented knowledge when they are unable to complete their task-oriented goal. A number of episodes are explained in detail to illustrate that the protocols can be described using the framework and that using the framework as a basis for analysing the protocols is a useful tool in understanding both what people do during exploration and what they learn from it. This suggests that the framework will be successful as a basis for developing models of exploratory learning of interactive devices.

Acknowledgements. This research was supported by a post-graduate studentship to the first author by the Economic and Social Research Council and British Telecommunications Plc.

References

Cooper, R., & Fox, J. (1998). COGENT: A visual design environment for cognitive modeling. *Behaviour Research Methods, Instruments and Computers,* 30, 553-564.

Cox, A. L., & Young, R. M. (2000). Device-Oriented and Task-Oriented Exploratory Learning of Interactive Devices. *Proceedings of Third International Conference on Cognitive Modeling,* University of Groningen, Groningen, Netherlands.

Draper, S. W., & Barton, S. B. (1993). Learning by exploration, and affordance bugs. *Proceedings of Interchi '93.*

Newell, A. (1990). *Unified Theories of Cognition.* London: Harvard University Press.

Trudel, C.-I., & Payne, S. J. (1995). Reflection and Goal Management in Exploratory Learning. *International Journal of Human-Computer Studies,* 42, 307-339.

Young, R. M., & Cox, A. L. (2000). A New Rational Framework for Modelling Exploratory Device Learning ... but does it Fit with ACT-R? *Proceedings of 7th ACT-R Workshop,* Carnegie Mellon University.

Socionics: A New Challenge for Cognitive Modeling

Frank Detje (frank.detje@ppp.uni-bamberg.de)
Institute for Theoretical Psychology, University of Bamberg, Markusplatz 3
D-96047 Bamberg, Germany

Abstract

At the line of intersection between Distributed Artificial Intelligence, Multi-Agent-Based Modeling and Sociology a new research field has emerged: Socionics. Main aim of this new research discipline is to build and study artificial societies and to develop intelligent computer technologies by picking up sociological concepts. This paper attempts to show why Cognitive Modeling (CM) should also pick up this challenge.

1. Socionics

"Socionics" is a new research discipline. Like "bionics" it is a combination of two well established disciplines that forms a new interdisciplinary framework of research. Here the research fields of Sociology and Computer Science are brought together to benefit from each other in several ways. Sociologists want to compare, evaluate and validate their sociological concepts and theories by using existing computer technology and implementation strategies for simulation tools. Computer Science, especially in the field of Distributed Artificial Intelligence (DAI), looks for new techniques and concepts to satisfy the requirements demanded by the increasingly complex applications, e.g. Internet-Services. In the area of Social Simulation several sociological concepts are used to describe the interplay of artificial agents in a multi-agent world and to help in describing the architectures that have been built to model this kind of Distributed Artificial Intelligence. Terms like "society", "organization", "cooperation" or "conflict" are widely used but the image of an "socially" behaving "agent" is often misleading. Instead of merely pointing out these limitations that arise from such notions, Socionics starts to evaluate the power of using sociological concepts and theories for the development of computer technologies and implementation techniques. There are two main areas for which Socionics tries to develop new solutions to existing problems by exploiting sociological concepts: the first is Multi-Agent Systems (MAS) and the second is the growing area of Hybrid Systems (HS). From a sociological point of view "[m]odern society offers a rich reservoir of paradigms for modeling multi-agent systems, e.g. social role and cultural values, norms and conventions, social movements and institutions, power and dominance distribution. Computer Science might learn from the adaptability, robustness, scalability and reflexivity of social systems and use their building blocks to come up

with more powerful technologies" (Müller, Malsch & Schulz-Schaeffer 1998). But the benefit of an interdisciplinary approach like Socionics is bilateral. Sociology can profit from Computer Science by using DAI techniques as simulation tools for validating and extending their sociological concepts and theories. Thus, Socionics aims at generating answers in the context of (a) the emergence and dynamics of artificial social systems and (b) hybrid man-machine societies.

2. Cognitive Modeling and Socionics

Though strongly tied with sociology Socionics deals with agents, be it in hybrid or multi-agent systems. And these agents need to be modeled in a way acceptable for humans (in the case of hybrid systems) or restricted in their capacities and capabilities like humans (in the case of multi-agent based modeling) to exhibit patterns of behavior that can be labeled "social" in a sense that is more than just an illustrative metaphor.

Since cognitive models and architectures provide the "device for making it possible for something else to determine behavior, to wit the knowledge encoded in its memories" (Newell 1990, p.431), my claim here is that cognitive models and their underlying architectures can help in generating solutions to the problems Socionics faces. Cognitive Models offer a great variety of suggestions how to implement strategies of goal elaboration, decision making, learning and planing, perception, attention, memory, conflict resolution, pattern matching, and knowledge acquisition, just to mention the most important ones for Socionics. Social phenomena have not been in the focus of interest or in the scope of research for cognitive modeling until now. But "unified theories of cognition" (Newell 1990) always wanted to cover all of the regularities in human behavior. Therefore: "One important measure of success of a unified theory of cognition will be whether it extends into the social band and provides an improved base for the study of social psychology and other social sciences" (Newell 1990, p. 490).

3. Validation of the PSI-Approach

Our architectural proposal for a cognitive architecture is the implementation of the PSI-theory of human action regulation (Dörner 1999). This cognitive, emotional and motivated system is able to deal autonomously with complex environments, to care for its needs and to work on given tasks (e.g. Detje 2000b). Main goal of our current research project is to study the formation and change of social structures in groups of intelligent, multi-motivated and emotional agents.

The PSI-theory explains a wide range of psychological phenomena like perception, emotion, motivation, memory, planing, learning etc. on the basis of intention- and action-regulatory processes. The behavior of this implemented theory has been compared with human behavior with regard to many different aspects (Detje 2000a; Dörner 2000) and with regard to other cognitive architectures (Detje 1999). Recently we showed that PSI behaves similarly to humans that act in the same complex environment according to many behavioral and achievement indicators (Detje 2000a, Dörner 2000).

The sociological question arises whether this "artificial soul" (Dörner 1999) can serve as a basis for modeling social phenomena beyond individual psychological research questions. Central to our project is the question if and how the additional insertion of only one social motive into the existing PSI-framework has effects on the cooperation and the group structure of intelligent, multi-motivated and emotional agents.

The social motive that we add to PSI the need for affiliation, implemented as a need for signals of legitimacy (Boulding 1978). We want to investigate a) how interactions between agents develop from this additional need, b) if and how these interactions between agents lead to group structures, c) what kind of group structures can be observed and which develop spontaneously, d) how and under which conditions do groups with specific structures succeed in different environments, e) which conditions (variation of the environment, characteristics of the agent and resources) contribute to the stabilization or extinction of group structures, and f) to what extent can group specific phenomena like altruism or social conflict be observed (merely) by inserting such an additional motive.

For a first series of experiments we varied PSI in the following ways: 1) we only added to PSI a motive for affiliation, 2) then we also gave a new operator to PSI that allows to satisfy the need for affiliation, 3) we additionally inserted objects at one or 4) more places in PSI's environment that can satisfy PSI's need for affiliation if the new operator is successfully applied to one of these objects, and 5) as control group we observed a PSI group that did not have a need for affiliation, extended possibilities to act or new objects.

The data protocols created by the PSI-program consist of more then 50 different variables: the values of the need indicators, the actual behavior and the values of the parameters that indicate the internal state and that modulate PSI's behavior. We find many significant differences between the PSI-groups (1 to 5). A qualitative analysis of the indicator variables shows

differences between the PSI-groups, that can only be attributed to the "socionical" changes we have made (for details see Detje 2001)[1].

4. Concluding remarks

The Socionics' approach is more than merely providing technical solutions to questions that arise from Multi-Agent Based Modeling or from the creation of Hybrid Systems. Socionics also faces theoretical questions that stem from the reality of human societies. I think that it is time to seriously start with the extension of our models / architectures / theories into the social band and to model and explain social and sociological phenomena as well. Although it is impossible to foresee what will happen in detail if we extend our cognitive models to deal with a "social" environment or with a multitudes of models of the same or a different kind, we can expect an enhancement of our theoretical knowledge, experimental design knowledge and technical or implementation strategies. Thus, starting this adventure is worth taking the risk of not exactly knowing where it will lead us.

Acknowledgments

The German Research Foundation (DFG, Deutsche Forschungsgemeinschaft) established the special research program "Socionics: modeling artificial societies". Our project is supported by grants DO 200/20-1 and LE 525/7-1.

References

Boulding, K. E. (1978). *Ecodynamics*. Beverly Hills, CA: Sage.

Detje, F. (1999). Handeln erklären. Wiesbaden: DUV.

Detje, F. (2000a). Comparison of the PSI-theory with human behaviour in a complex task. *Proc. Third ICCM*, 86-93.

Detje, F. (2000b). *"Insel". Dokumentation – Versuche – Ergebnisse*. Bamberg: Institut für Theoretische Psychologie, Memorandum Nr. 39.

Detje, F. (2001). *PSI - Erste Schritte in Richtung sozialen Verhaltens*. Bamberg: Institut für Theoretische Psychologie, Memorandum Nr. 41.

Dörner, D. (1999). *Bauplan für eine Seele*. Reinbek: Rowohlt.

Dörner, D. (2000). The simulation of extreme forms of behaviour. *Proc. Third ICCM*, 94-99.

Müller, H. J., Malsch, T. & Schulz-Schaeffer, I. (1998). Socionics: introduction and potential. *Journal of Artificial Societies and Social Simulation, 1 (3)*.

Newell, A. (1990). *Unified theories of cognition*. Cambridge, Mass.: Harvard University Press.

---

[1] See also: http://www.uni-bamberg.de/ppp/insttheopsy/.

Strategies in a Complex Game and their Background

Dietrich Dörner (dietrich.doerner@ppp.uni-bamberg.de)
Institut für Theoretische Psychologie, Universität Bamberg,
Markusplatz 3, D-96045 Bamberg

Abstract

We tried to simulate the behaviour of 30 Ss in a complex
game situations. It turned out that the variance of human
Ss was much higher with respect to many behavioural
measures than the variance of simulated Ss. This is due
to the fact that human Ss use more different strategies
than the computer did and change strategies deliberately.
On the one hand the choice of a strategy seems to be
dependent on different "emotional" parameters of the Ss.
One important parameter is for instance the stability of
self-efficacy. Simulating emotional parameters yields an
increase of the strategic variety of the simulated Ss and
hence an increase of the similarity of human and
simulated behaviour. On the other hand phases of self-
reflection, which can be found with some Ss, can be the
reason for the choice and especially for the change of a
strategy.

The Island Game

We studied the behaviour of humans in a complex
game, the Island-game. The experimental subjects (Ss)
were given the task of "surviving" on an island. They
were required to control the behaviour of a robot-
vehicle, capable of moving and manipulating objects.
As the vehicle is powered by a steam-engine the
"navigators" have to provide for "food" (i.e. fuel in the
form of sunflower seeds or hazelnuts) and water. The
main task of the Ss is the collection of "nucleos" (a non-
dangerous form of fuel for nuclear power plants!).
Since "Island" is a general multiple-task environment;
Ss have to tackle a lot of different problems, such as the
following:

•   exploring the topology of the island, which is
unknown to them at the beginning.

•   learning what to do with unknown objects, e.g.
some plants might be edible, but some others poiso-
nous.

•   developing appropriate strategies to cope
simultaneously with different tasks. There is often a
conflict between the goal of obtaining fuel and water
and the goal of collecting nucleos. Similarly there is a
conflict between the necessity of exploration and the
goal of obtaining nucleos, fuel and water.

Theory and Simulation

We have developed a theory about the dynamics of
human action regulation in such complex, dynamic,
uncertain and polytelic (multiple goals) domains of
reality, the Psi–theory. This theory exists as a computer
model. It makes many assumptions about cognitive
processes and structures, and also about emotional and
motivational structures and processes. Fig. 1 exhibits a
very rough sketch of the theory.

There is a list of needs (for instance hunger, thirst,
uncertainty) which vary in strength as per consumption
or environment. Based on the experience with the given
environment, these needs are translated into goals. One
of the goals is selected as the "actual" one. Perception
of the situation is guided by the actual goal. According
to the actual goal and the situation at the given moment
a course of action is selected from memory or
constructed (planning) and then implemented. Memory
changes with new experiences. The number and the
strength of active needs trigger arousal as a part of
emotional modulations. Emotional modulations such as
arousal, resolution level, background control and
concentration are triggered by uncertainty, success and
failure. For example an emotion as "anxiety" roughly
consists of high arousal which is reflected in low
resolution level in planning, remembering and
perceiving and high degree of background control. (For
details of the theory see Dörner, 1999; Dörner & Hille,
1995).

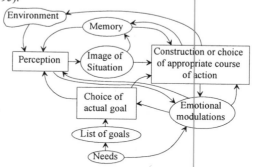

Fig. 1: A sketch of the Psi-Theory. See text.

We tried to simulate the behaviour of 30 Ss. This at
first glance was quite successful. The "behavioural
profiles" of the humans and the simulated Ss correlated
with an average coefficient of 0.91!. (These behavioural
profiles consisted of the values of 11 behavioural
measures, as for instance number of successful loco-
motions in a 1-hour gaming period, number of places

visited on the island, the frequency of breakdowns of the robot-vehicle, number of successful manipulations, the number of nucleos collected, the average level of need for fuel and other similar measures.) The correlation coefficient was calculated by transforming 900 correlations of the behavioural profiles of 30 human Ss with 30 artificial Ss into Fisher's Z and averaging the Z-scores.) This seems to be a quite satisfying result, indicating that the minds of our human Ss when attempting to survive on the island and the hypotheses of the Psi–theory have a great deal in common.

Strategies

On the other hand many differences exist between the human and the artificial-theoretical agents. Particularly the variance of the behavioural measures is much larger with the human than with the artificial Ss. This is due to the fact that human Ss use a broader variety of strategies as for instance:

Survival-strategy: Try to find as much water, hazel-nuts and sunflower seeds as you can.

Basis-Camp-strategy: Find a place where a lot of water and fuel exist. Use this place as a basis camp for expeditions to collect nucleos and turn back to this place when the vehicle begins to run out of water or fuel.

Nucleos first!-strategy: Don't care about the vehicle. You'll get a new one after each breakdown.

Action-strategy: Try to be as active as possible. Change whatever can be changed.

Carpe-diem-Strategy: Don't waste your time with long-term planning and strategy formation! Look for the opportunities of the moment.

Why do Ss adapt different strategies in this game? In our eyes this is due on the one hand to differences in the emotional parameters of the Ss and on the other hand to self-reflection.

In the Psi-computer model there is a variable "competence" which is dependent on the number of successes and failures and on the weights for the incremental or decremental effects of successes or failures. In Psi competence determines for instance whether a risky course of action is chosen or abandoned, it determines resolution level in planning and remembering and many other processes.

Competence in Psi is calculated in the following way:

(1) competence := competence + (Max − competence) $\times$ $weight_{success}$ $\times$ success;

(2) competence := competence − (competence − Min) $\times$ $weight_{failure}$ $\times$ failure;

(Here Max is the maximal value for competence and Min the minimal value.)

If in these commands $weight_{success}$ has a high value a high increase in competence will result, even with moderate success. If $weight_{success}$ has a low value competence will not increase considerably even with great successes. A low value in $weight_{failure}$ will result in a rather stable competence., Such a person will exhibit an unshakeable self-confidence, whereas a person with a high value of $weight_{failure}$ will exhibit a high tendency for anxiety, will be shy, not very active and will avoid exploration and other forms of risky behaviour.

It is possible to generate some of the above mentioned strategies by varying these weight-parameters.

A "person" (human or artificial) with a high $weight_{failure}$-value and a medium level of competence will avoid risks, will rank the existential – needs of the robot, namely the need for fuel and water high, will not explore very much (because the outcomes of explorative activities are always uncertain). A Survival – strategy will result.

A "person" with a high level of competence, a high value for $weight_{success}$ and a low value for $weight_{failure}$ will rank the existence – motives low ("there is no danger! Everything can be managed!"), the nucleo – motive hence will be relatively strong: We get a Nucleo-first! – strategy.

A "person" with a medium level of competence and a medium value for $weight_{failure}$ will try a lot to safeguard her always endangered competence, will exhibit a tendency for pointless actions just for the sake of a salient effect. We get an Action – strategy.

There is a second answer to the question why an individual adapts a certain strategy:

An individual adapts a strategy because he analyses the challenges and demands of the island – game, analyses his resources and capacities and finds a strategy as an appropriate fit between the external demands and his capacities. By this self-reflective meta-analysis the Basis-camp – Ss arrived at their strategy.

By varying the above mentioned parameters we were able to simulate certain forms of the adaptation of strategies. We are not yet able to simulate selfreflective activities.

References

Dörner, D. (1999): Bauplan für eine Seele (Blueprint for a Soul). Reinbek: Rowohlt.

Dörner, D. & Hille, K. (1995): Artificial Souls: Motivated Emotional Robots. IEEE International Conference, Vancouver.

Facial Expression Recognition with Modular Neural Networks

Leonardo Franco (lfranco@sissa.It)
Anna Montagnini (montagni@sissa.it)
Alessandro Treves (ale@sissa.it)
Cognitive Neuroscience Sector - SISSA; 2-4 Via Beirut,
Trieste, 34014 Italy

Abstract

We construct a modular neural network to perform facial expression recognition. The structure is a 4 layer feed-forward architecture consisting of two parts: first, a hidden layer with unsupervised learning is applied to the input images to obtain a reduced representation of the image; second, the network splits into modules ("experts") specialized in the different expressions, modules that are trained through the back-propagation algorithm. Using the Yale Face database for 14 subjects displaying 4 emotions each (neutral, happy, sad and surprise faces) we obtain a generalization rate of 78.6% on unseen faces using a hebbian unsupervised learning scheme compared to 70.8% when using random weights.

Introduction

Face perception is a very important component of human cognition. Faces are rich in information about individual identity, but also about mood and mental state, being accessible windows into the mechanisms governing our emotions. Facial expression interactions are relevant in social life, teacher-student interaction, credibility in different contexts, medicine, etc. Face expression recognition is also useful for designing new interactive devices offering the possibility of new ways for humans to interact with computer systems.

From a neurophysiological point of view face recognition appears to be very important. Experiments both in monkeys and humans show the existence of dedicated areas in the brain where neurons respond selectively to faces (Kanwisher, McDermott & Chun, 1997). Also it has been shown that complex visual processing related to discrimination of faces is a very rapid task that can be completed in approximately 100 msec suggesting the involvement of a feed-forward neural mechanism (Lehky, 2000).

In this work we construct a modular neural network consisting of two parts, trained in different ways: first, an unsupervised procedure is applied locally to reduce the dimensionality of the data, to be then classified by the specialized modules, sometimes called "experts", of the second part, trained with backpropagation.

Modularity appears to be a very effective solution to complicated tasks allowing better generalization properties, reducing the longer training times, and being also adaptive (Franco & Cannas, 2001; Haykin, 1995).

Different systems have been constructed to deal with facial expressions, see for instance Lisetti & Rumelhart, (1998) and references therein, but not many of them using a neural networks approach.

The Database of Images

We use a subset of the Yale Face Database (Belhumeur, P.N. & Kriegman, D.J., 1997) that consists of 14 subjects displaying 4 facial expressions: neutral face, happy, sad and surprised. The images were cropped to obtain input images 8 pixels width by 24 pixels height covering a portion of the face located on the left side. The images were centered taking the tip of the nose as reference and some slightly illumination correction was applied to a couple of images. Figure 1 shows a sample of the different expressions displayed by one of the subjects.

Figure 1: Sample subject showing the four full face expressions (neutral, happy, sad and surprised). The white rectangle inside the rightmost figure corresponds to the area cropped and used as input.

Network Structure

The network consists of a 4 layer modular neural structure composed of units computing a sigmoidal activation function. The input layer has 192 units corresponding to the 24x8 pixels of the area cropped from the original images. The first hidden layer, common to all modules, modifies with unsupervised learning. Four contiguous units of a row of the image are connected to one neuron in the first hidden layer, obtaining at this level a new reduced representation of the images, with 48 units, that preserves some topological aspects of the original input.

After this unsupervised compression the network splits into three modules corresponding to the expressions happy, sad and surprised. The structure of the modules could depend on the emotion they specialize in; in the case we consider here they have all the same type of architecture: one hidden layer fully connected with one output unit. There is a difference in the number of hidden neurons belonging to each modules since the recognition of happy and surprised faces is much easier than the recognition of sad ones; this fact is known from experiments both with humans and computers (Dailey, Cottrell & Adolphs, 2000). It was necessary to put 4 hidden neurons for sad faces while 3 neurons were enough for happy and surprised ones.

Table 1: Generalization error rates for the modules, specialized in happy, sad and surprise faces, and for the whole net using first layer hebbian, random and pixel average processing.

Expression Module	Error (Hebbian)	Error (Random)	Error (Average)
Happy	0.082	0.041	0.089
Sad	0.093	0.201	0.154
Surprise	0.039	0.050	0.071
Total	0.214	0.292	0.314

Training procedure

As the amount of data available for training and testing is limited (14 subjects, 56 images), we decided to use a cross-validation test.

The first layer of 192 weights, one for each input pixel, is trained with an unsupervised algorithm. For comparison, we use three different procedures: hebbian, random, and pixel average. The Hebbian rule used is Oja's rule, known to perform a principal component analysis of the input vector, converging to the largest eigenvector, while normalization is ensured (Oja, 1987).

The random processing consists in setting the weights to positive random values within the range [0 - 0.7]; no learning is performed on these weights. The random processing appears to be quite effective in some cases, being much better than taking the simple average of the input pixels (third case considered).

The rest of the weights, those belonging to the modules, were trained with the standard backpropagation algorithm (Haykin, 1995). To prevent overtraining and to permit a better generalization capacity we monitor the training error on each input image, to stop the training on this image when this error was lower than 0.20. All layers of weights were trained at the same time upon the presentation of an input image.

Results and Discussion

We explore the generalization ability of a modular neural system to classify facial expressions. Using a mixed learning scheme, unsupervised-supervised, we obtain a generalization ability with novel faces of 78.6 % (70.8 % when using a random processing and 69 % using pixel average). The generalization error rates produced by the different modules specialized in expressions are shown in table 1, where the values obtained using random, hebbian and pixel average, as unsupervised processing, are compared.

Hebbian learning, in our case applied locally, confirms to be an interesting procedure for compressing the images, making also the further backpropagation training faster than when using its random counterpart.

We are currently considering many possible extensions of this work, particularly in the unsupervised processing stage, trying to obtain some translational and illumination invariance properties.

Acknowledgments
We acknowledge partial support from the Human Frontiers Program Grant RG0110/1998-B.

References
Belhumeur, P.N. & Kriegman, D.J. (1997). *The Yale Face Database* URL: http://cvc.yale.edu/projects/yalefaces/yalefaces.html

Dailey, M.N., Cottrell, G.W., & Adolphs, R. (2000). A six-unit network is all you need to discover happiness. In Proceedings of the Twenty-Second Annual Conference of the Cognitive Science Society.

Franco, L. & Cannas, S.A. (2001). Generalization properties of modular networks implementing the parity function. *IEEE Transactions in Neural Networks*. In press.

Haykin, S. (1994). *Neural Networks: A Comprehensive Foundation*. Macmillan/IEEE Press.

Kanwisher, N., McDermott, J., & Chun, M.M. (1997). The fusiform face area: A module in human extrastriate cortex specialized for face perception. *Journal of Neuroscience*, 17, 4302–4311.

Lehky, S.R. (2000). Fine Discrimination of Faces can be Performed Rapidly. *Journal of Cognitive Neuroscience*, 12, (5), 848–855.

Lisetti, C.L. & Rumelhart, D. E. (1998). Facial Expression Recognition using a Neural Network. In Proceedings of the 11th International Florida Artificial Intelligence Research Society Conference (FLAIRS'98), Menlo Park, CA: AAAI Press.

Oja, E. (1989). Neural Networks, principal components, and subspaces. *International Journal of Neural Systems*, 1, 1, 61–68.

Human-Task Adaptations: The Next Step for Cognitive Modeling

Michael Freed, Michael Matessa, John Rehling, Roger Remington, and Alonso Vera
{mfreed, mmatessa, jrehling, rremington, avera}@arc.nasa.gov
NASA-Ames Research Center, Mailstop 262-4
Moffett Field, CA 94035-1000

Influences on behavior range in a continuum from task-specific (e.g. there are seven buttons on the interface) to architecture-specific (e.g., human working memory can span 7+/- 2 items). The study of this continuum has unfortunately been focused more on the ends than the center. Situated cognition approaches suggest that all behavior is specific to the situation in which it takes place. In contrast, traditional cognitive views suggest that there is a common set of architectural resources that underlie behavior consistently across situations. Somewhere between the implementation of a cognitive architecture and the analysis of a specific task, lies a set of psychological phenomena that determine how people actually perform in that task given a set of architectural constraints. These phenomena, which we will call *Human-Task Adaptations*, are consistent characteristics of the way the cognitive architecture shapes itself around and adapts to the specific characteristics and demands of a given task. Only by understanding this class of phenomena are we likely to make any serious progress in cognitive modeling.

There are ways in which humans multitask, plan reactively, use working memory, etc. that are relative, but not specific, to the kinds of tasks they are working on. That is, there are certain predictable ways in which people behave in given tasks and environments (e.g., air traffic control, flight deck, shuttle control, etc.) that are not specifically determined by the cognitive architecture nor uniquely determined by the specifics of the task. Computational cognitive modeling has demonstrated its value over the past decade but little progress has been made on the key issues that would allow us to predict error, cognitive load, resource allocation and so on. These phenomena, we argue, are a consequence of an interaction between the cognitive architecture and specific tasks.

If a task has frequent interruption, like ATC, then the behavior of experts might be expected to adapt to the patterns of interruptions in consistent ways. This may be achieved by evolving unit tasks with shallow goal stacks that allow for frequent checks of the environment for new information while maintaining a reasonable completion rate for ongoing unit-tasks. Nevertheless, performance on such tasks has typically been studied by cognitive scientists at the level of the architecture rather than relative to specific task domains. This is, of course, for good reason. There is little value in describing, in great detail, how the human architecture interacts with an interface such as that on a microwave oven. There is little to generalize from it with respect to the cognitive architecture.

Efforts to model human performance have traditionally focused on fundamental human characteristics such as limited attention and working memory. For brief tasks carried out in controlled environments, this focus is appropriate since performance often depends directly on fundamental capabilities. The issue is more complicated for more complex tasks that may be carried out in any of several ways. Since these may vary in important measures of performance (e.g. required time, likelihood of error), predicting performance depends on knowing how the task will be carried out. Experts will have learned how to minimize the constraints imposed by cognition and other potential sources of limitation. In some cases, native human limits will become largely irrelevant, influencing performance only indirectly by having shaped behavioral strategies.

A situated cognition perspective would prescribe that humans constantly undergo unique processes of adaptation to every aspect of new tasks, with little of the cognitive architecture affecting performance from one trial and one task to another. A strict cognitive architectural approach, on the other hand, might argue that the architecture should define every aspect of performance in any task. We have attempted to define a space between these two possibilities in which aspects of the architecture adapt to specific characteristics of tasks in ways that are consistent and predictable.

The key theoretical point behind *Human-Task Adaptations* is the argument that, although they are not directly determined by the cognitive architecture, they are nevertheless well-defined phenomena that are *generalizable* to tasks that impose similar demands on the architecture. We are not claiming that *Human-Task Adaptations* are learned explicitly and abstracted from situations in the way that using means-ends analysis or analogy might be considered to be. They are acquired implicitly and remain specific to the task from which they resulted. They are generalizable only in the sense that we, as scientist, can predict how an individual will adapt to the demands of a particular task.

HCI provides classes of problems that share relevant demand characteristics: Air-traffic control is similar to radar operation on AEGIS ships, shuttle operation, satellite operations, nuclear power-plant control, and so on. All of these tasks involve experts in dynamic, real-time, complex environments. Expertise makes their interactions with dynamically changing situations *routine*. Experts come to adapt their planning and decision-making in consistent ways with respect to the rapidly evolving characteristics of the situation. Specifically, their behavior adapts to variables like the patterns of interruption in the task, the number of tasks to be carried out in parallel and the amount of perceptual support provided by the interface to working memory. These are the human-task adaptations that must be understood and built into our computational cognitive models if we are to succeed in simulating complex human behavior. Complex HCI tasks provide an ideal test-bed for exploring psychological idioms exactly because they involve experts deploying routine behavior in rapidly changing environments.

Different kinds of tasks force the emphasis of an investigation into different points along a continuum. At one extreme (A), the kinds of tasks used in psychophysics experiments necessarily probe the fundamental abilities of the human cognitive architecture. At the other extreme (Z), a task like solving the missionaries-and-cannibals problem tells us very much about the task, quite independent of the cognitive architecture of the problem-solver; the constraints of the task ensure that a human, a martian, and Prolog would all produce the same solution. We argue that what is needed to elevate cognitive modeling to the next level is the development of a vocabulary of cognitive activities and the ways to model them, striving for a higher level of complexity than the findings (with a large corpus of them already

uncovered) at (A), but generalizable, unlike those at (Z). We observe that our ability to model many domains has little to gain from investigations focusing on either end of the continuum.

This is perhaps illustrated better by means of analogy to tasks that involve not only human cognition, but also human physiognomy. Consider that we were trying to enrich the field of human modeling with the goal in mind that future modelers might undertake modeling a task such as bear hunting. (We mean the task of hunting a bear without modern weaponry; people in pre-technological civilizations found a number of ways to go about this.) We argue that studies of tasks of this kind would uncover basic human strategies that would generalize to other tasks. For example, the use of several bowmen solve the problem in one way. The dead-fall trap, which uses bait to lure a bear underneath a log which can be released to break the bear's back, may be of use in other tasks in which human strength is a serious constraint. We observe that *no* amount of study of human abilities alone (A) is sufficient to generate the strategies of use in bear hunting. Likewise, studies with an excessive focus on the task (Z) will not generalize sufficiently. Even if a great deal is known about bears, that will not generalize to **hunting** bears (without taking human constraints into account, one will not focus on the importance of avoiding the use of sheer strength). In contrast, the study of a task that is very different from hunting and does not involve bears (such as how to split very large rocks) may generalize to bear hunting in useful ways - more than intensive and extensive fields of study dedicated to human capabilities, and to bears, respectively.

Similarly, studying a task such as Air Traffic Control, where genuine experts work on a complex, time-critical, highly interactive task, similarly sheds light on the unique ways in which the human architecture adapts its constraints to meet the demands of such tasks.

Modeling Cognitive versus Perceptual-Motor Tradeoffs using ACT-R/PM

Wai-Tat Fu (wfu@gmu.edu)
Wayne D. Gray (gray@gmu.edu)
Human Factors & Applied Cognition
George Mason University
Fairfax, VA 22030 USA

Abstract

Information stored *in-the-world* is retrieved from external memory via visual perception as rendered by the appropriate saccades and fixations. Recent research has suggested that when information in-the-world is readily accessible, internal storage is not needed. Perceptual-motor strategies will be deployed to reacquire information as needed. However, Fu & Gray (2000) found that when the cost of information access was increased from a simple key press to a one-second lockout time, the perceptual-motor strategy was replaced with a strategy that placed task-relevant information into working memory. This suggests that the decision to store information in-the-head versus in-the-world is sensitive to effort considerations. In this paper, we present our work-in-progress report on modeling the data using ACT-R/PM.

Introduction

If information in the external environment can be considered as an external memory store, the cost in searching for the relevant information in the external environment can be taken as the "memory" search cost. If the only cost associated with internal and external memory were a search cost, then we would expect that in most situations internal search would be faster than external search. However, for internal memory a significant additional cost is internal storage (encoding).

Compared to a memory strategy that includes encoding plus retrieval, a saccadic eye movement to a known location has a much lower time cost. However, when the cost of information access from the external environment is high enough, the expected utility of external memory would be lower than that of internal memory. In this case, one would expect a shift from external memory to internal memory. In other words, people would be more likely to adopt a memory strategy than a perceptual-motor strategy.

In this paper, we describe a ACT-R/PM model of this kind of cognitive versus perceptual-motor tradeoffs. Specifically we attempt to model the phenomenon that an increase in the perceptual-motor cost of information access will induce a shift from an external to an internal memory strategy.

The Task

The task is to copy a pattern of colored blocks shown in the *target* window to the *workspace* window, using the colored blocks in the *resource* window (for our version see Figure 1). All three windows were covered by gray boxes. Throughout the task only one of the windows could be uncovered at a time. The resource and workspace windows were uncovered by moving the mouse cursor into the window. They were covered again when the mouse cursor left the window. The effort required to uncover the target window varied between each of our three conditions.

To access the information in the target window participants could adopt either a predominately perceptual-motor or a predominately memory strategy. The predominately perceptual-motor strategy would entail one uncovering at the target window to obtain color information and another to obtain position information. In contrast, a predominately memory strategy would entail one uncovering at the target window to obtain both color and position.

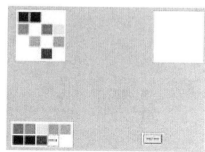

Figure 1. The blocks world task. In the actual task all windows are covered by gray boxes and at any time only one window can be uncovered. The window at the top left is the target window, at the bottom the resource window, and at the top right the workspace window.

Design and Procedure

The three conditions were designed to vary the cost of uncovering the target window. In the *low-cost* condition, participants had to press and hold down a function key. In the *control* condition, all three windows were uncovered when the mouse cursor entered the window. In the *high-cost* condition participants had to move the mouse cursor inside the target window and endure a one-second lockout before the target window was uncovered.

Empirical Results

An ANOVA on the number of times the target window was uncovered showed a significant main effect of condition ($F (2, 45) = 10.17$, $p = .0002$, $MSE = 159$). (See Figure 2). ANOVA on the time subjects spent looking at the model showed that there were significant main effects of conditions ($F (2, 45) = 20.6$, $p < .0001$, $MSE = 300$).

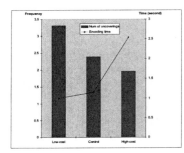

Figure 2. The mean total frequency of uncovering of the target window per trial and time uncovered of the target window.

The Model

The data were modeled using ACT-R/PM, a theory that combines the ACT-R theory of cognition (Anderson & Lebiére, 1998) with a modal theory of visual attention, and motor movement. In so doing, ACT-R/PM permits motor and visual attention processes to be executed in parallel with each other as well as with cognitive processes.

The main goal of the model is to capture the cognitive and perceptual-motor tradeoffs in the *control* and *high-cost* conditions. Perceptual-motor cost was represented by the movement time predicted by Fitts' law, and the one-second lockout time in the high-cost condition. Cognitive cost was represented by the time spent encoding information of the block(s) in the target window. In ACT-R, the total effort C associated with a production is represented by the sum of two parameters: a and b. ($C = a + b$) The a parameter represents the current effort in executing a particular production; the b parameter represents the downstream effort involved between the time after the current production is executed until the time when the current goal is accomplished (popped). The higher the sum of these values, the less likely the production will be executed. Since it is the sum of these two parameters that determines the result of the production selection, it is

possible that the model would choose a production rule that has a high current effort (a), but a low downstream effort (b).

The basic structure of the model is shown in Fig. 3. In the beginning of each trial, a strategy of encoding n blocks (n=1 to 8) is picked. The a parameter (current effort) associated with this production represents the encoding time, and therefore increases with n. The b parameter (downstream effort) decreases with n, since the more blocks one encodes per uncovering of the target window, the fewer number of times one needs to uncover the target window again. Therefore in general, when n is small, a is small but b is large; when n is large, a is large but b is small. Interestingly, when the cost of uncovering the target window increases, a remains unchanged, but the increase in b is much larger for small n than large n (since a strategy with small n entails more uncoverings of the target window). Therefore when the cost of uncovering the target window increases, the total cost ($C = a + b$) for strategies with small n will be higher than that with large n, producing the basic tradeoff effect as shown in Fig. 2.

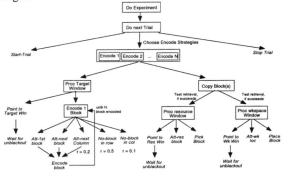

Figure 3. The basic structure of the model.

At this point, we are adjusting the effort parameters to obtain a good fit to the data. Our ultimate goal is to have the model learn the effort parameters and converge to an "optimal" encoding strategy that matches the empirical data in each condition. We believe that this will allow us to further understand the underlying mechanisms for these kind of cognitive versus perceptual-motor tradeoffs.

References

Anderson, J. R., & Lebiére, C. (Eds.). (1998). *Atomic components of thought*. Hillsdale, NJ: Erlbaum.

Fu & Gray (2000). Memory versus Perceptual-Motor Tradeoffs in a Blocks World Task. *Proceedings of the 22nd Annual Conference of the Cognitive Science Society* (pp. 154-159). Hillsdale, NJ: Erlbaum.

Failure to Learn from Negative Feedback in a Hierarchical Adaptive System

Andrew Corrigan-Halpern (ahalpe1@uic.edu)
Stellan Ohlsson (stellan@uic.edu)
Department of Psychology, (M/C 285), 1007 West Harrison St
The University of Illinois at Chicago, 60607-7137

Feedback and Hierarchy

Although consensus favors positive over negative feedback, adaptive systems must be able to learn from undesirable outcomes. In past work, we demonstrated that negative feedback is sufficient to learn cognitive skills of intermediate complexity (Ohlsson, 1996; Ohlsson & Rees, 1991; Ohlsson, Ernst & Rees, 1992) and that learning from errors can be more efficient than learning from successes (Ohlsson & Jewett, 1997a, 1997b) when the system's task representation consists of units that can be acquired independently.

However, adaptive systems tend towards hierarchical organization (Simon, 1969). Although the concepts of feedback and hierarchy are often invoked, the literature lacks a rigorous analysis of their relation. How should a hierarchical knowledge representation be revised in the face of feedback? We have already studied this question with respect to positive feedback (Ohlsson & Halpern, 1998); here we extend the work to negative feedback. Our main result is that there are conditions under which a hierarchical adaptive system does not learn even when it is given negative feedback after every wrong step.

Performance Module

We model a hierarchical task representation with an AND/OR tree in which goals are represented by OR nodes with links leading to the alternative methods, and methods are represented by AND nodes with links to the subgoals required to execute them. The model performs a task by traversing such a tree in a top-down manner. The terminal nodes in the tree represent executable and observable actions. The traversal of the tree generates a behavior in the form of a sequence of terminal nodes (actions). Behaviors differ depending on which method is selected in each OR node and in which order the subgoals are attempted.

A link L is associated with strength, s(L) that reflects past experience. At each OR node, the performance module retrieves all links leading to alternative methods and selects one for execution The probability that link L is selected is a function of s(L). At each AND node, the performance module retrieves all links leading to its subgoals and orders these in accordance with their strengths. The probability that link L_1 is ordered before link L_2 is a function of their strengths. Notice that decisions are made by comparing link strengths in both OR and AND nodes. Hence, both types of decisions are affected by strength adjustments.

Learning Mechanism

We designate an arbitrarily chosen sequence of terminal nodes as the performance to be learned. Initially, all links have strengths equal to unity. The models learns by adjusting the link strengths in such a way that the correct link is chosen in each OR node and the links are attempted in the correct order in each AND node. The choices are correct when the resulting sequence of terminal nodes coincides with an arbitrarily chosen target performance (sequence of terminal nodes).

During a simulation run, each terminal node is compared to the corresponding action in the target performance. If they do not match, the model receives negative feedback. In response, the model propagates a strength decrement upwards through the AND/OR tree. The strengths of all nodes above the unsuccessful terminal node are decremented. The key theoretical issue is how the strength decrement at level X in the goal-subgoal hierarchy relates to the strength decrement at level X+1. Cognitive models typically assume that a strength adjustment decreases in magnitude as it propagates through a network (e.g., Anderson & Lebiere, 1998). We refer to this as *dampened propagation*. The opposite hypothesis--that a strength adjustment increases in magnitude as it propagates--is seldom studied, because such *amplified propagation* is not possible in non-hierarchical networks. Amplified propagation can only work in a representation with a well-defined stopping point (the top goal). We define the *propagation parameter*, pp, as the proportion of the strength adjustment at level X that is applied to level X+1. If pp < 1, we have dampened propagation; if pp > 1, the propagation is amplified; if pp = 1, the strength adjustment is *sustained*, i.e., it has the same magnitude at each level of the hierarchy.

Strength adjustment in OR nodes is straightforward: The strength of the unsuccessful link is decreased by the amount specified by the propagation parameter. In AND nodes, the decrement of an unsuccessful subgoal is also a function of its position in the sequence of subgoals. A subgoal is weakened more if it fails as the first link selected in the relevant AND node than if it fails as, for example, the third link. Successive strength decrements thus orders the links in an AND node.

Results

The results reported here were achieved with an AND/OR tree with a branching factor of three and a height of six. One traversal of the tree is regarded as one training trial. The criterion for successful learning was three consecutive error-free trials. We systematically varied the propagation parameter, conducting 100 simulations for each value.

Figure 1 shows the main result. When the propagation is sustained or only slightly amplified, every simulation succeeds in learning the target skill. At a pp value of approximately 1.25, the probability of failing to learn increases sharply. When the propagation regimen is strongly amplified, pp ‡ 1.5, the probability that any run will fail to learn is close to 100%.

Discussion

Our results show that a hierarchical adaptive system can fail to learn even when it is provided with negative feedback after every incorrect step. Why? Feedback is propagated upwards, so correct links that are superordinate to incorrect links lower in the hierarchy receive negative feedback when the latter happen to be chosen.

Why do the strengths of correct and incorrect links decrease *at the same rate*? Intuition suggests that the incorrect link should be the recipient of more negative feedback than the correct link. However, if a subgoal is incorrect, this fact might be discovered quickly and that subgoal will be abandoned before it generates much negative feedback. On the other hand, if the subgoal is correct, the corresponding subtree will be explored more fully and so might generate more negative feedback, depending on how many errors the model happens to make during the exploration.

Why do the strengths of correct and incorrect links decrease *at the same rate*? Intuition suggests that the incorrect link should be the recipient of more negative feedback than the correct link. However, if a subgoal is incorrect, this fact might be discovered quickly and that subgoal will be abandoned before it generates much negative feedback. On the other hand, if the subgoal is correct, the corresponding subtree will be explored more fully and so might generate more negative

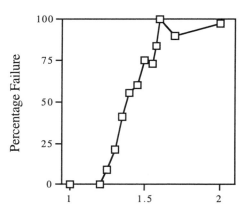

Figure 1. Percentage of instances of failure to learn from negative feedback.

feedback, depending on how many errors the model happens to make during the exploration.

When learning is rapid at the bottom of the tree and slow at the top, this problem does not arise. The general lesson is that errors and mistakes should be attributed to the lowest-level subgoals, not to the top goal.

References

Anderson, J. R., Lebiere, C. (1998). *The atomic components of thought*. Mahwah, NJ: Erlbaum.

Ohlsson, S. & Halpern, A. (1998). Strength adjustment in hierarchical learning. In M. A. Gernsbacher and S. J. Derry, (Eds.), *Proceedings of the Twentieth Annual Conference of the Cognitive Science Society* (pp. 782-787). Mahwah, NJ: Lawrence Erlbaum.

Ohlsson, S., & Jewett, J. (1997a). Simulation models and the power law of learning. In M. G. Shafto & P. Langley (Eds.), *Proceedings of the 19th Annual Conference of the Cognitive Science Society* (pp. 584-589). Mahwah, NJ: Erlbaum.

Ohlsson, S. (1996). Learning from performance errors. *Psychological Review, 103*, 241-262.

Ohlsson, S., Ernst, A., & Rees, E. (1992) The cognitive complexity of doing and learning arithmetic. *Journal for Research in Mathematics Education, 23*(5), 441-467.

Ohlsson, S., & Rees, E. (1991) The function of conceptual understanding in the learning of arithmetic procedures. *Cognition & Instruction, 8*(2), pp. 103-179.

Simon, H. A. (1969). *The sciences of the artificial*. Cambridge, MA: MIT Press.

The Strategic Use of Memory for Frequency and Recency in Search Control

Andrew Howes (HowesA@cardiff.ac.uk)
School of Psychology, Cardiff University, Cardiff, CF10 3YG, Wales, UK

Stephen J. Payne (PayneS@cardiff.ac.uk)
School of Psychology, Cardiff University, Cardiff, CF10 3YG, Wales, UK

Introduction

A requirement of an information processing account of human problem solving is that it includes a mechanism by which people remember which goals and operators have been evaluated and which still need to be evaluated. Whether the task is the Tower of Hanoii, a waterjugs problem, a world-wide web search problem or a spatial navigation task, a person engaged in search examines the consequences of applying an operator to a state by trying it out and perceiving to which state it, and subsequent operators, lead. At some point in the future, the person may, through backup, or because of loops, find themselves in a visited state. Recognition that the state has already been visited and/or that the operator has already been applied to this state, will in the long-term help prune the search space and thereby constrain the effort spent on attaining the goal. This constraint has been used in a number of models of human problem solving (Anderson, 1993; Howes, 1994). Atwood & Polson's (1996) model of human performance on the waterjugs problem, built up a representation of the 'familiarity' of states that was factored into the operator selection process. The more familiar an operator then the less likely it was to be selected.

One might expect that these are issues of such fundamental importance that they must have been solved or at least addressed by the two architectural accounts of cognition (ACT-R, Anderson, 1998; Soar, Newell, 1990), but in fact it is an issue that is glossed in both. In ACT-R the goal stack has privileged status. Items posted on the stack are not subject to the constraints of memory, i.e. they do not have decaying activation and cannot therefore be forgotten (though see Altman and Trafton, 1999).

Another resource for supporting decisions about which operator to apply is memory for previous attempts at a goal (either successful or failed). If a goal has been achieved prior to the current attempt then memories that indicate that an operator is familiar may be taken as evidence that it is more likely to lead to the goal than an unfamiliar operator (Payne, Richardson, Howes, 2000). However, an issue for the problem solver is how to determine the source of the familiarity. If the source is the current trial then the operator should be rejected, if it is a previous trial then perhaps it should be selected. Payne, Richardson, Howes (2000) investigated the role of familiarity in controlling interactive search. They tested the hypothesis that people help control search merely by recognising the actions that have been tried before (Howes, 1994) and found that the familiarity of items could affect decisions about which item to select. Moreover familiarity was used strategically. When participants had information indicating that familiarity would be more likely to indicate that an operator would lead to the goal, they were more likely to use familiarity to guide selection.

Again, one might expect that this issue would have been addressed in architectural theories of cognition. In ACT-R, each chunk stored in declarative memory has an activation that is used to determine probability of retrieval. This activation is made up of a base-level activation and an associative activation. Anderson and Lebiere (1998; page 123) state , "... base-level activation ... depends on the frequency and recency with which [the] chunk has been used." The frequency and recency components of base-level activation are not therefore independently inspectable by the production rules and it is not possible to write ACT-R production rules that make strategic use of frequency and recency information stored as components of chunk activations. It seems unlikely therefore that it is possible to write productions that, for example, prefer the most frequent operators at the expense of the most recent.

Model

To address the problems described above we have built a computational level model of how people search simple binary word-mazes. Participants in an experiment conducted by the authors, searched a number of mazes, each over a number of trials. Some participants used a systematic strategy on this first trial (e.g. always turning left in a garden maze) and others used a random strategy. On subsequent trials all participants used memory of previous trial to slowly eliminate unnecessary routes. Most achieved optimal performance after 4 or 5 trials.

The model of this data makes strategic use of frequency and recency information and demonstrates the cognitive plausibility of a search algorithm that is supported by a representation that delivers independent estimates of frequency and recency. The model was not based on assumptions about the structure of memory, rather it was based on assumptions about what information memory can deliver.

In order to simulate a lack of reliability in the information returned from memory, frequency and recency information decayed stochastically. Also false positives were randomly generated in answer to queries about whether operators had been applied on this trial. In Payne, Richardson, and Howes (2000) experiment, false positives occurred when participants were forced to make a decision about whether or not they had applied an operator before when in fact they may have only seen it and not applied it. The purpose of introducing the errors was not to capture some quantitative aspect of the data but instead to ensure that the search algorithm was robust given the return of incorrect information from memory.

Two models were constructed: One of the systematic participants and one of the random participants. These models made use of frequency and recency memory in four sets of heuristics: algorithm switches; random search heuristics; systematic search heuristics; memory-based heuristics. Both models used the memory-based heuristics after the first trial but switched back to random or systematic search if memory proved insufficient. Importantly the heuristics were able to distinguish whether memories were from the current trial or from previous trials and were thereby able to guide search appropriately.

We did not attempted to fit the model to the data, rather we explored the range of its behaviour. Importantly, the model did not perseverate. Regardless of errors made during search, it always recovered and eventually found the goal. Also, as the decay rate increased the model was still able to learn the task. A large number of errors in the first trial did not on average incapacitate the learning over subsequent trials.

An observed improvement in practice after the first trial was a result of a search algorithm that was guided by a combination for memory for previous trials and the current trial. If memory for previous trials proved inadequate then memory for the current trial ensured a reasonably efficient search.

Also, in accordance with the participants behaviour, the systematic algorithm produced more efficient and less varied searches on trial 1.

Discussion

The model briefly described here demonstrates that aspects of the way in which people search and learn paths through external problem spaces can be captured with heuristic rules that make strategic use of independent estimates of the frequency and recency of previously selected operators. Without access to this information it is impossible to write heuristics that distinguish an operator with high frequency with one that has high recency, and it is therefore a problem to determine whether key events occurred on the current trial or previous trials. The analysis of the model's behaviour under a range of memory decay and false-positive conditions reveals that it produces behaviour similar to human performance on a simple search task. Most notably, unlike previous activation-based models built by the authors, the model does not perseverate when receiving degraded information from memory. In addition, the mean performance of the model over ten trials consists of a practice curve similar to that of the participants.

However, further investigation revealed that, after the first trial, the model produced a much greater variance in behaviour than the participants in the experiment. This issue

is a matter for further investigation, and may well imply the need for some superordinate learning mechanism (perhaps rehearsal or impasse-driven learning).

A superordinate learning mechanism might involve the deliberate encodings of what the correct option is. This is an approach that was explored in Howes (1994), and while it deserves further attention, there are problems. One is that there is a dislocation in time between when the items are experienced and when a participant achieves the goal. In previous models the feedback of information about correctness produced recency effects in which lower levels of the tree were learnt first (Howes, 1994). These effects were not observed in our experiments.

It may be possible to construct algorithms in ACT-R designed to ensure that during search sufficient episodic information is stored in declarative chunks to enable the kinds of computations that are posited in the model report here. Altmann and Trafton (1999) have explored this possibility for encoding goal-stack information.

References

Altmann, E.M. & John, B.E. (1999). Episodic indexing: A model of memory for attention events. *Cognitive Science, 23*, 117-156.

Altmann, E. M. & Trafton, J. G. (1999). Memory for goals: An architectural perspective. *Proceedings of the twenty first annual conference of the Cognitive Science Society* (pp. 19-24). Hillsdale, NJ: Erlbaum.

Anderson, J. R. (1993). *Rules of the mind*. Hillsdale, NJ: Erlbaum.

Anderson, J. R. & Lebiere, C. (1998). *The Atomic Components of Thought*. NJ: Erlbaum.

Atwood, M. E. & Polson, P. G. (1976). A process model for water jug problems. *Cognitive Psychology, 8*, 191-216.

Howes, A. (1994). A model of the acquisition of menu knowledge by exploration. In B. Adelson, S. Dumais, J. Olson (Eds.) *Proceedings of Human Factors in Computing Systems CHI'94* (pp. 445-451), Boston, MA.: ACM Press.

Newell, A. (1990). *Unified Theories of Cognition*. Cambridge, MA: Harvard University Press.

Payne, S. J., Richardson, J. & Howes, A. (2000). Strategic use of familiarity in display-based problem solving. *Journal of Experimental Psychology-Learning Memory and Cognition, 2*, 1685-1701.

A connexionist model for category construction

Jean-Daniel Kant (Jean-Daniel.Kant@lip6.fr)
Laboratoire Informatique de Paris 6 ; Université Pierre et Marie Curie
Case 169; 4 place Jussieu ; 75252 Paris cedex 05, France

A cognitive model for categorization tasks

The cognitive model we started from comes from a psychological decision theory model, the Moving Basis Heuristics (MBH) (Barthélemy & Mullet, 1986). MBH is aimed to implement the bounded rationality of a Decision Maker (DM) as introduced by Simon (1969). It combines three basic principles. According to the *parsimony principle*, the DM extracts some subsets from a data set whose size is small enough to be compatible with human short-range abilities and with human computational abilities. The *reliability principle* states that the DM extracts from the data a subset large enough and composes values in such a way as to appear meaningful and to lead to reliable decisions. According to the *decidability principle*, the DM allows himself to change criterion if the current criterion does not lead to a decision (see (Barthélemy & Mullet, 1986) for details). We add a fourth principle to make our network achieve stable decisions: the *resonance principle* states that a decision made on an object is performed by a resonance between this object and an expectancy of what this decision should be. Here, resonance refers to of Grossberg 's Adaptive Resonance Theory (Carpenter & Grossberg, 1987).

To apply our model to categorization tasks, we add the following hypothesis, called Basic Categorization Hypothesis (BCH):
If a subject sorted an object O into a category C, then there exists a typical grouping of features G so that, on each attribute that composes G, O will take the same value as G. If we follow our cognitive model, this gives the structure of a categorization rule, which can be summarized by a polynomial (Barthélemy & Mullet, 1986) like for instance :

$$P(C) = R^2F^4 + D^3T^2 + R^3 \qquad (1)$$

which means that if an object has been sorted by a particular subject into category C, it is because it verifies R=2 and F=4 or D=3 and T=2 or R=3, where D, T, R et F are object features. Each of these monomials (R^2F^4, D^3T^2, R^3) represents a criterion to decide if an object belong to category C.

The Categ_ART neural network

The Categ_ART connexionist network, based on our cognitive model, implements a category construction process to account for categorizations made by a given subject.

Network architecture

The Categ_ART architecture is derived from the ART1 neural network (Carpenter & Grossberg, 1987) and is depicted in Figure 1. It is composed of two interconnected layers F_1 and F_2. The F_1 layer receives an object at the input of the network. The F_2 layer is composed of monomial cells j, that encode monomials. Connection w_{ij} between F_1 cell i and F_2 cell j encodes the value for monomial j on the ith feature, while connections z_{ji} encode thresholds in case of threshold decision rules. For our cognitive model all z_{ji} are permanently set to zero. The connections CM between monomial cells at the F_2 layer are used to group these cells and form the polynomial rules prescribed by our model.

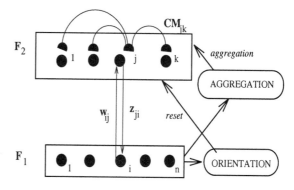

Figure 1: Categ_ART architecture

Network learning dynamics

The learning algorithm applies successively the three MBH principles we presented in the previous section.

The **first stage** is a direct application of the *parsimony principle*. Its aim is to form monomial cells as short as possible, that are composed of only one feature. At the beginning, there are no cells in the F_2 layer. Suppose for example we use 4 attributes - noted X_1, X_2, X_3 and X_4 - to describe the object and let $I = \{1, 2, 3, 4\}$ the index set for these attributes X_i. Now we have a first object - noted O - presented at the input layer F_1 of the network. O is encoded by the vector $[0, 1, 0, 3]$ of its four features (i.e four attribute values). The idea of the first stage is as follows : if our object O has been sorted into a particular category by the subject, it might be only because it has a value of 1 on attribute X_2 or because it has 3 on attribute X_4. So Categ_ART will create two one-feature monomial cells, X_2^1 and X_4^3, at the F_2 layer and each cell will be encoded using the w weights.

The **second stage** applies the *reliability principle*. A one feature monomial can generate categorization errors since two objects of two different categories may share the same feature. Therefore, for each F_2 created by the network we define an *error categorization rate* $TE(j)$ that measures the number of objects misclassified by a cell j. If $TE(j)$ falls below a predetermined threshold η the aggregation subsystem send a signal to j to start the aggregation process. Cell j is aggregated with one-feature cells k if they have no features in common and if they correspond to the same category. Then a new cell $j \oplus k$ is created to replace confusing cell j. This process is repeated until no F_2 cell exceeds error threshold η.

During the **third stage**, the network composes F_2 cells in a disjunctive way to get the complete categories, according to the *decidability* principle. The first step is to compute the CM connexion weights. All the objects are presented at the input of the network. Each presented object elicits a set of resonant F_2 cells. Each pair (j, k) of these resonant cells is examined. CM_{jk} weight evolves according to a differential equation such that at the convergence CM_{jk} measures what we call the *overlapping rate* between cell j and cell k : it is proportional to the number of objects that possess both the features encoded by cell j and cell k.

Once all CM connections have been computed, we can group F_2 into polynomials in order to perform *rule extraction*. A cell k will be added to a polynomial P if it shares the same category with the cells already put in P and if $TR(k, P) \leq \rho$ where ρ is a second network parameter and $TR(k, P)$ is the *redundancy rate* of cell k relatively to polynomial P: $TR(k, P) = max\{CM_{kl}$ where $l : l \in P\}$. Otherwise, if no current polynomial can be found for cell k, a new polynomial is created for this cell. The process ends when there is no more free cells to be examined.

Experimental results

We tested our model in a real situation, where 7 experts and 20 customers from a French bank had to categorize 180 savings schemes into 4 categories ranked by attractiveness. There were four features to describe the schemes: fiscality, availability, minimal warranty and expected yield. In this experiment, Categ_ART was able to account for all the categorization made by a subject and usually with parsimony (at most 20 monomials per subject). We used two types of simulation: the *validation* mode, where we want to account for the categorizations of the entire object set (180) for each subject. Therefore, all the 180 objects are used for learning. In this case, all the principles of our model were shown to account for the data. The other mode is the *generalization* one when for each subject, 90 objects are randomly chosen and used for learning; then, the 90 remaining objects are classified by the network and we compare these categorizations with the subject's ones. Here, Categ_ART shown classification performances at the same level of other competing machine learning systems (multi-layer perceptron, decision trees) but with a better parsimony (shorter and smaller rules).

Finally, an analysis of the network behavior and the rule produced for each subject enabled us to derive some predictions on the category construction process the subjects may have used. Let us take two examples. First, we have been able to measure the existence of *family-resemblance* structures (Rosch & Mervis, 1975). This occurred for 5 subjects out of 27 under validation mode, and for 13 subjects out of 27 under generalization mode, so family resemblance seems to play a important role to generalize prior categorizations to new object. Second, a deep analysis of the polynomial rules revealed a specific version of *anchoring and adjustment* heuristics (Lopes, 1982). The subjects seem to select one particular attribute and to sort all the objects only based the features of this particular attribute. Then, other attributes and features may be used to refine these categorizations. This heuristics we called the *main anchoring heuristics* was found to account for the results of 5 experts (out of 7 i.e. 71%) and 12 customers (out of 20 i.e. 60%).

References

Barthélemy, J.-P., & Mullet, E. (1986). *British Journal of Mathematical and Statistical Psychology, 43*, 106-124.

Carpenter, G., & Grossberg, S. (1987). *Computer Vision, Graphics and Image Processing, 37*, 54-115.

Lopes, L. (1982). *Toward a procedural theory of judgment* (Tech. Rep. No. 17). Madison: Human Information Processing Program.

Rosch, E., & Mervis, C. (1975). *Cognitive Psychology, 7*, 573-605.

Simon, H. (1969). *The sciences of the artificial.* Cambridge: MIT Press.

An ACT-R Model of Syllogistic Inference

José Augusto Leitão (**jleitao@ci.uc.pt**)
Instituto de Psicologia Cognitiva
Faculdade de Psicologia; R.do Colégio Novo
3000 Coimbra Portugal

Abstract

We describe SYLLOG, a model of syllogistic inference, built within the ACT-R framework. Its construction was guided by data obtained from 88 subjects performing the syllogistic inference task. The model's inference engine uses the PC inference rule Hypothetical Syllogism (HS) and a set of modal logic transformation rules either to create a representation of the premises that allows an appropriate use of HS, or to check the appropriateness of having already used HS to obtain a putative conclusion.

SYLLOG models the task of generating a necessarily true conclusion for the 64 pairs of categorical syllogistic premises (four "moods"[1] for the first premise x four "moods" for the second premise x 4 figures[2]). It can be described as comprising two stages. The initial one produces an interpretation of the input given to the model. This interpretative phase creates a declarative blueprint for building a production corresponding to each of the premises. This interpretation represents quantification over possible worlds instead of over objects. For instance, for "Some As are Bs", a procedural interpretation would, if the top goal were a represented object with property A, modify this goal chunk to represent that there would be a possible world or circumstance in which the corresponding object would have both property A and property B. The second stage is the inference engine of the system and it searches the problem space for a valid conclusion. In this stage, SYLLOG uses the information yielded at the last declarative level of the interpretation process of the premises[3]. These declarative structures contain the

necessary information to compile productions corresponding to each of the quantification "moods". This information can be notated as follows, using modal operators (M for the Possibility operator and L for the Necessity operator):

(1) $L_j (A(x_j) \supset B(x_j))$ (All As are Bs)
(2) $L_j (A(x_j) \supset M_j B(x_j))$ (Some As are Bs)
(3) $L_j (A(x_j) \supset \sim B(x_j))$ (No As are Bs)
(4) $L_j (A(x_j) \supset M_j \sim B(x_j))$ (Some As are not Bs)

Our use of modal operators is guided by the work of Venema & Marx (1999), on the modalization of first-order logic. The semantics for the modal formalism offers a far more interesting ground to explore from the psychological point of view than the standard model-theoretic construal of quantification in first order logic. Some of the subjects' verbalizations suggest that alternative states of affairs are being considered while interpreting a syllogistic problem, and it is common to encounter the use of expressions such as "can be" or "may be", as in "an A may be C", for which the model-theoretical approach in natural language semantics also proposes a rendering that uses modal logic. Our current approach yields a correlation coefficient $r=0.814$ among the predicted and empirical difficulty rankings of the 27 syllogistic problems that support valid conclusions.

From now on we will refer to (1) simply as $A \supset B$, and simplify (2)-(4) accordingly. We will assume that SYLLOG is dealing with a pair of premises of the figure AB-BC. We will consider the other figures under the heading "premise conversion".

Generating Putative Conclusions The task of producing a conclusion for a syllogistic problem is taken by SYLLOG as corresponding to building a blueprint for a production that integrates the condition of the interpreted first premise with the action of the interpreted second premise. The validity of such a conclusion depends on finding representations for the two premises corresponding to productions that will, in all circumstances, fire sequentially. Thus, SYLLOG attempts to transform the representations of the premises until they support an interpretation in which applying the instruction conveyed by the first premise always yields a chunk that always

---

[1] E.g. "all As are Bs" "Some As are Bs" "No As are B" and "Some As are not Bs".

[2] The "figure" of a syllogistic problem refers to the position of the terms in the pair of premises. If the terms were A, B and C, we would have the four figures AB-CB, BA-BC, AB-BC and BA-CB.

[3] SYLLOG does compile a production that instantiates the instruction conveyed by the premise: a Dependency is created, which, when popped, yields the corresponding production. Having a premise rendered as a Dependency signals that the interpretation is complete and prompts SYLLOG to continue to the next step in the process of solving the syllogistic problem. However, Only the declarative blueprint for the premise's interpretation is used

from this point on, because it is available for inspection and modifications, unlike the corresponding production.

requires the firing of the production that interprets the second premise. This amounts to transforming the representation of the premises until the use of the PC rule Hypothetical Syllogism is allowed. In fact, HS is the sole inference rule upon which SYLLOG's inference engine is based.

(5) $A \supset B$
     $B \supset C$
     $\overline{A \supset C}$

When dealing with the first premise while trying to generate a valid conclusion, SYLLOG may identify as obstacles to the use of HS the operators in the consequent of each of the three implications:

(6) $A \supset M_j B$
(7) $A \supset \sim B$
(8) $A \supset M_j \sim B$

For each of these, SYLLOG uses one of the following equivalences, namely (9) (valid) to deal with (6), either (10) (invalid[4]) or (11) (valid) to deal with (7), and any combination (9)/(10) or (9)/(11) to deal with (8).

(9) $(A \supset M_j B) \equiv M_j (A \supset B)$[5]
(10) $(A \supset \sim B) \equiv \sim (A \supset B)$
(11) $(A \supset \sim B) \equiv (A \supset (B \supset \sim (A \& B)))$

Rebutting Putative Conclusions SYLLOG's use of HS may be mislead. For instance, in the case of the pair "All of the As are Bs. Some of the Bs are Cs", the immediate use of HS upon $A \supset B$ and $B \supset M_j C$ to obtain $A \supset M_j C$ (Some of the As are Cs) doesn't provide a valid conclusion: in the set of circumstances compatible with the premises, the conclusion $A \supset M_j C$ is possible, but not necessarily true. It fails to be true if none of the Bs that are As is also C, which is a circumstance compatible with both premises. This contingency becomes apparent if the second premise is represented as an implication that holds only in some possible worlds, $M_j (B \supset C)$. The representation of the second premise may therefore be reconstructed in a way that blocks the use of HS, meaning that the production that interprets the second premise won't necessarily fire in sequence with the production that interprets the first premise. Negation may be treated in a similar manner: If $\sim (B \supset C)$ is obtained by using the invalid equivalence (10), the putative conclusion under scrutiny is also rejected, although erroneously. If (11) is used instead, disposal of the putative conclusion is considered, but eventually rejected. When used to check the validity of a putative conclusion, the productions that instantiate all of the above transformations have to compete with the productions that read off final conclusions. This makes them more unlikely to fire in this conclusion rebuttal stage then when they are used for creating a context for the use of HS, by transforming the representation of the first premise. This asymmetry follows closely the answer patterns found in the data set.

Premise Conversion The use of HS requires that the other three syllogistic figures besides AB-BC are dealt with by some premise conversion procedure that yields the AB-BC figure. SYLLOG most simple conversion procedure amounts to directly swapping the terms of the premise. This yields two invalid conversions, namely. "All of the As are Bs" being converted in "All of the Bs are As", and "Some of the As are not Bs" being converted in "Some of the Bs are not As"[6]. A subsequent, more sophisticated, conversion procedure may be applied. If reached, this stage involves "noticing" that the new structure is not true in all possible worlds, but only in those where the previous conditional had been true. To yield a valid outcome, SYLLOG has to signal this limitation. It does so by introducing a Possibility operator. This further procedure may then rectify the conversion of $A \supset B$ in $B \supset A$, which would now turn into $B \supset M_j A$. It also allows the detection of the impossibility of a valid conversion of $A \supset M_j \sim B$ and introduces a still valid, but weaker version of the previously valid conversion of $A \supset \sim B$, $B \supset M_j \sim A$. The stronger conversion $B \supset \sim A$ may still be recovered, if another production notices that the correction is not called for in this instance. Otherwise, the conclusions that SYLLOG will derive from the converted premise will reflect the loss introduced by the conversion.

References

Anderson, J. R., & Lebiere, C. (1998). *The atomic components of thought*. Hillsdale, NJ: Lawrence Erlbaum Associates.

Johnson-Laird, P. N., & Bucciarelli, M. (1999). Strategies in syllogistic reasoning. *Cognition*, *54*, 1-71.

Venema, Y., & Marx, M. (1999). A modal logic of relations. In E. Orlowska (Ed.), *Logic at work. Essays dedicated to the memory of Elena Rasiova*. Berlin: Springer Verlag.

---

[4] This invalid transformation allows SYLLOG to generate most of the invalid conclusions found in the data set for problems in which the first premise contains a negation.

[5] This equivalence is valid in the direction $M_j (A \supset B) \supset (A \supset M_j B)$, used for creating a structure from which SYLLOG can read a conclusion after applying HS, if a transformation in the opposite direction has previously taken place. This is always the case in SYLLOG.

---

[6] This is an example of the commonly found effect of interpreting a simple conditional as a bi-conditional. SYLLOG accommodates this effect particularly well, since it represents the implications under consideration using structures that would more accurately be notated as $A \supset (A \& B)$, which allows the bi-conditional reading. To keep this presentation brief, we have omitted a more detailed discussion of this particular aspect of SYLLOG.

Modeling an Opportunistic Strategy for Information Navigation

Craig S. Miller (cmiller@cs.depaul.edu)
School of Computer Science, DePaul University, 243 S. Wabash Ave.
Chicago, IL 60604 USA

Roger W. Remington (rremington@mail.arc.nasa.gov)
NASA Ames Research Center, MS 262-4
Moffet Field, CA 94036 USA

Abstract[1]

A computational model of a user navigating Web pages was used to identify factors that affect Web site usability. The model approximates a typical user searching for specified target information in architectures of varying menu depth. Link ambiguity was varied and model predictions were compared to human user data. A good fit to observed data was obtained for a model searching through a sufficiently ambiguous site and that opportunistically searched below threshold links on selected pages prior to returning to the parent page.

Introduction

Our effort focuses on understanding how a site's information architecture impacts a user's ability to effectively find content in a linked information structure such as a Web site. We develop our understanding through the construction and testing of a working computational model. The model simulates a user navigating through a site making choices about whether to select a given link or evaluate an alternate link on the same page. For this presentation, we build upon methods that we presented in an earlier paper (Miller & Remington, 2000), but we introduce a new navigation strategy and show how the model's aggregate behavior tightly fits results from an empirical comparison of different site architectures (Larson & Czerwinksi, 1998).

Modeling Information Navigation

Our model interacts with a simplified, abstract representation of a Web browser and a Web site. Each site has one root node (i.e. the top page) consisting of a list of labeled links, each leading to a separate child page. For a shallow, one-level site, child pages are terminal pages, one of which contains the target information that the user is seeking. For deeper, multi-level sites, a child page consists of a list of links, each leading to child pages at the next level. The bottom level of all our sites consists exclusively of terminal

pages, one of which is the target page. Our examples are balanced trees since we generally compare our results to studies that use balanced tree structures. However, our representation does not prevent us from running simulations on unbalanced trees, or even on structures involving multiple links to the same page and links back to parent pages.

When navigating through a site, a user must perceive link labels and gauge their relevance to the targeted information. For simplification, we fix a number for each link, which represents the user's immediately perceived likelihood that the target will be found by pursuing this link. This simplification allows us to easily investigate a range of numerical relationships between the link label and the target information.

Figure 1 shows an abstract representation of a site with ambiguous labels. For the top page, the most likely link has a perceived likelihood of only .7. In some cases, a user strategy that merely follows the most likely links would directly lead to the target. However, this figure shows a site where the user would find the target under what he or she perceives as a less plausible sequence of link selections (the target is under a likelihood value of 0.2 instead of the 0.5 value). In this way it is possible to represent sites that differ widely in strength of association between link label and target information.

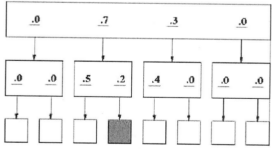

Figure 1 Site with ambiguous labels

Our model of Web navigation has three primitive actions:

- Selecting a link (and attending to and identifying a new page)

---
[1] An extended version of this paper appears in the proceedings of the 23rd Annual Conference of the Cognitive Science Society.

- Pressing the Back Button (and attending to and identifying a new page)
- Checking a link and evaluating its likelihood

Because of physical and cognitive limitations, only one of these actions can be performed at any one time. Fixed times are assigned to each action to account for its duration during a simulation. The model also simulates changing the color of a link when it is selected so that the modeled user can "perceive" whether the page under this link was previously visited.

Our model navigates a Web site by serially executing these three primitive actions, meaning that links are sequentially evaluated. Serial evaluation is motivated by evidence that the human user has a single unique focus of attention that must be directed at the link for this decision. The model presented here uses the **threshold** strategy: the user immediately selects and pursues any link whose probability of success exceeds a some specified threshold. With the appearance of a new page, the model's threshold strategy first attends to the page, which, if it is a terminal page, includes checking if it contains the target information. If it does not, the model sequentially scans the links on a page selecting any link whose likelihood is equal to or above a fixed threshold (0.5 in the simulations reported below). When a page appears by selecting a link, the process of checking and scanning the page is repeated.

Once the model detects no unselected links above the threshold value, it returns to the parent page by pressing the Back button and continues scanning links on the parent page starting at the last selected link. It does not scan links it has already evaluated. Determining the last link selected places no demands on memory since the last selected link is easily detected by its color, and many browsers return the user to the location of the last selected link.

Sometimes the targeted item lies behind ostensibly improbable links and, after some initial failures, human users must start selecting links even if the link labels indicate that they will probably not lead to the targeted item. One effective strategy opportunistically selects improbable links at a lower tier immediately after trying the more probable links and before returning to a higher tier in the site. We call this the **opportunistic** strategy.

We compared the model and results from hierarchical menu selection studies and obtained good fits with link evaluation costs set to 250 ms and link selection costs set to 500 ms. The use of time constants is well established (e.g., Card, Moran, & Newell, 1983) and these values are consistent with those previous estimates. We simulate various levels of label ambiguity by adding various amounts of gaussian noise to a representation with unambiguous labels (i.e. 1's and 0's).

Simulations

To further evaluate the model's design decisions, we compare its performance to the Web navigation results of Larson and Czerwinski (1998). They studied users navigating two-tiered (16x32 and 32x16) and three-tiered (8x8x8) site architectures that were otherwise comparable. Participants took significantly longer to find items in the three-tiered site (58 seconds on average) than the two-tiered sites (36 seconds for the 16x32 site and 46 seconds for the 32x16 site).

Using our model with the threshold strategy for link selection and the opportunistic strategy for backtracking, we ran simulations. For each site architecture (8x8x8, 16x32, and 32x16) 10,000 simulations were run using the following time costs: 250ms for evaluating a link, 500ms for selecting a link, and 500ms for return to the previous page (pressing the back button). Following Larson and Czerwinski (1998) any run lasting more than 300 seconds was terminated and assigned a duration of 300 seconds.

The 8x8x8 architecture produced faster times at low levels of noise but slower times at noise levels above 0.2. At these higher noise levels, the results are consistent with the human users. At noise levels of 0.4 and higher, simulated times were faster with the 16x32 architecture than the 32x16 architecture. This difference was also noted in the study with human users, albeit not reported as statistically significant. At a noise level of 0.4, the simulation results closely match the human results in absolute terms: 62s (compare to 58s for humans) for 8x8x8, 43s (compare to 46s) for 32x16, and 35s (compare to 36s).

We have also examined varying aspects of the model's design including memory limitations and time constants. In many case, varying these properties has not affected the model's qualitative comparisons as a function of site architecture. By experimenting with a range of strategies and site representations, we aim to over useful guidelines for effective Web site design.

References

Card, S. K., Moran, T. P., & Newell, A. (1983). *The Psychology of Human-Computer Interaction.* Hillsdale, NJ: Lawrence Erlbaum.

Larson, K. & Czerwinski, M. (1998). Web page design: Implications of memory, structure, and scent for information retrieval. *Proceedings of CHI'98 Human Factors in Computing Systems* (pp. 25-32). New York: ACM press.

Miller, C. S. & Remington, R. W. (2000). A computational model of Web navigation: Exploring interactions between hierarchical depth and link ambiguity. *Proceedings of the 6th Conference on Human Factors and the Web.* Retrieved February 5, 2001 from the World Wide Web: http://www.tri.sbc.com/hfweb/miller/article.html.

On the Normativity of Failing to Recall Valid Advice

David C. Noelle (NOELLE@CNBC.CMU.EDU)
Center for the Neural Basis of Cognition; Carnegie Mellon University
Pittsburgh, PA 15213 USA

In common learning environments, students attempting to learn a categorization skill are often directly instructed in the nature of a new category before being presented with specific examples thereof. They are frequently provided with definitional sentences and explicit rules prior to practice with illustrative instances. While the process of explicit instruction-following and the process of inductive learning from examples can cooperate to produce quick and robust learning, there are situations in which these two learning processes actually compete. Specifically, extensive experience with training examples can lead learners to categorize novel instances according to similarity to training items, rather than according to categorization rules communicated through explicit instruction. Thus, novel items which are highly similar to training examples from another category come to be misclassified as a result of practice.

This exemplar-based interference effect might be seen as the result of limitations of the cognitive system, such as imperfect working memory efficacy or difficulties recalling and applying verbal rules. There is an alternative view, however. It is possible that human learners neglect explicit instructions in favor of exemplar-similarity information because the latter form of information tends to be more reliable in a wide variety of learning contexts.

There are many aspects of common learning situations which may encourage students to rely more heavily on examples than on explicit rules. Consider, for example, how the instructions provided by teachers are frequently approximate and heuristic. Also, recalling past experiences with features similar to those of the current situation is often more useful than recalling dissimilar experiences. Thus, when faced with the task of categorizing a novel stimulus item, learners may be naturally inclined to recall other similar items rather than an explicit rule, which, due to its linguistic encoding, may bear little surface similarity to the situation at hand. Also, the recollection of experiences which are recent and frequently recurring is, on average, more useful than recalling rare experiences from one's distant past. Thus, when performing an instructed category learning task, it may be reasonable for a learner to selectively recall the training items which were recently and repeatedly studied in favor of briefly presented instructions. In short, we may conjecture that exemplar-based interference arises from a rational tendency to rely on similar, recent, and frequent past experiences when faced with a novel situation.

In order to evaluate this conjecture, we have modeled the exemplar-based interference results of Allen and Brooks (1991) using the normative, or "rational", account of memory formulated by Anderson (1990). The goal was to investigate the degree to which exemplar-based interference can be explained in terms of a Bayes optimal learning process, given some assumptions about the common demands placed on human memory.

Human Performance

In Experiment 1 of Allen and Brooks (1991), learners were asked to categorize illustrations of fictional animals into one of two categories. Each animal was composed of specific selections for five binary attributes, and each was depicted against one of four different backgrounds. From this space of $2^5 \times 4 = 128$ different possible stimuli, only 16 were actually used: 8 during an initial training phase and 8 during a subsequent testing phase. Each testing phase item had a "partner" in the training set — an item which differed from it only in one attribute.

Experimental participants were provided with explicit categorization rules, in which a target category was described as all animals with at least two of a list of three features. The rules were carefully chosen so that the 16 stimuli were equally split between the two categories. Also, exactly half of the testing set items had their training set "partner" items assigned to the opposite category.

After extensive training, with performance feedback, on categorizing the training set animals, the learners were asked to categorize the testing set items, without feedback. It was found that accuracy on the testing items whose "partners" were in the opposite category was much worse than on the other testing set items — around 55% correct as compared to 80%. This was a strong indication of exemplar-based interference.

Modeling Exemplar-Based Interference

Allen and Brooks argued that explicit memories for individual stimuli played an important role in the production of this effect. The presentation of a testing set stimulus was seen as provoking a recollection of that item's "partner" in the training set, with the category label of that training set item often being assigned to the new stimulus in lieu of a label based on explicit rule application. Following this intuition concerning the centrality of memory to this effect, we have attempted to model these data using a previous account of optimal memory performance: that of Anderson and Milson (1989).

From the perspective of this model, the central function of a memory system is to determine, for each memory trace, the normative probability that that trace would be useful in the current situation — its "need probability". Anderson and Milson (1989) provided a means to compute this value, conditioned on the current context and on the history of past retrievals of the given trace. They showed that their formulation of the need probability, along with the assertion that the traces with the highest need probabilities will be those which are retrieved, predicted a wide variety of human memory effects.

The instructed category learning task of Allen and Brooks (1991) can be viewed as a memory task. Initially, the learner must remember the explicit categorization rule, recalling it when it is needed to categorize a stimulus item. The rule need not always be recalled, however, as it will be sufficient in many cases to simply remember a previous presentation of the specific stimulus being viewed and its corresponding category label.

A computer program was written which simulated the performance of Anderson's rational memory on the experimental task examined by Allen and Brooks (1991).[1] Initial instruction involved the creation of a memory trace for the given categorization rule and the retrieval of that trace for ten consecutive time steps, representing a study period. After this instruction period, the training set items were presented to the optimal memory, one at a time. With each presentation, the need probability of each existing memory trace was estimated in the context of the current stimulus. The memory trace with the highest need probability, among those traces that contained a category label, was retrieved from the memory. The category label of the retrieved memory trace was taken to be the response provided to the current stimulus. The memory trace for the explicit rule was seen as containing the correct category label for every stimulus.

During the training phase, the solicitation of a categorization judgment from the memory was followed by the incorporation of performance feedback information. The memory system responded to feedback by immediately retrieving the memory trace corresponding to the current stimulus, marked with the given category label.

The protocol for memory trace retrieval during the testing phase was the same as during training, except that none of the newly generated memory traces contained category label information. Categorization errors made by the memory system during the testing phase were examined for signs of interference: relatively poor accuracy

---

[1] To calculate the need probabilities, the same parameters that were used by Anderson and Milson (1989) were used in this simulation: $b = 100$, $v = 2$, $\alpha = 2.5$, and $\beta = 0.04$. An associational strength over the 6 stimulus features (including background) was taken to be $P(x|i) = 0.65$. The Monte Carlo integration process consistently used $100,000$ samples in the calculation of each need probability estimate.

on those testing set stimuli whose "partner" items in the training set were in the opposing category.

Upon simulation, this model did *not* exhibit human-like patterns of responding. Depending on specific parameter values, one of two situations would arise. The model either failed to produce any exemplar-based interference, or it produced such interference but consistently ignored the given rule, even early in training.

Anderson experienced similar problems when he compared his model's performance to human behavior (Anderson, 1990). There were some aspects of human performance which could only be fit by the model with the help of an additional assumption: that the system would covertly rehearse recently retrieved traces. He added to the memory model a rehearsal buffer which contained the 4 most recently retrieved memory traces. On each time step, each trace in the rehearsal buffer had a 0.2 probability of being rehearsed on that time step. Rehearsal simply involved the retrieval of that trace from memory. Anderson demonstrated that this departure from normative processing was all that was required to capture a number of human memory phenomena. Following Anderson's lead, the optimal instructed category learning simulation was augmented with a rehearsal buffer, identical to that previously used.

With rehearsal, the optimal memory model came to qualitatively match human patterns of responding. The explicit rule maintained its perceived utility through much of the training phase, but was overcome by exemplar similarity by the time the testing items were presented. This produced consistent errors on those stimuli whose "partners" were in the opposite category. When traces were retrieved stochastically, in proportion to their need probabilities, the frequency of error on such items was 42%, comparing favorably with the 45% error exhibited by human learners. Thus, the rational memory model, when augmented with rehearsal, appears to be consistent with the observed exemplar-based interference effect in instructed category learning.

Acknowledgements

This work was supported, in part, by the NIMH via an NRSA (# 1 F32 MH11957-01). Thanks are extended to Garrison W. Cottrell for his helpful comments.

References

Allen, S. W. and Brooks, L. R. (1991). Specializing the operation of an explicit rule. *Journal of Experimental Psychology: General*, 120(1):3–19.

Anderson, J. R. (1990). *The Adaptive Character of Thought*. Studies in Cognition. Lawrence Erlbaum, Hillsdale, New Jersey.

Anderson, J. R. and Milson, R. (1989). Human memory: An adaptive perspective. *Psychological Review*, 96(4):703–719.

The Grain Size of Cognitive Models: How Low Should We Go?

John Rehling (jrehling@arc.nasa.gov)
Cognition Research Group
NASA-Ames Research Center, Mailstop 262-4
Moffett Field, CA 94035 USA

Abstract

There has been vigorous debate regarding the level at which it is appropriate and/or necessary to model human cognition (Smolensky, 1988). It is difficult to settle this issue because the many unknowns regarding human cognition confound efforts to attribute the success or failure of any particular modeling effort to one factor alone.

In order to study this matter without a large number of confounds, it is useful to consider how grain size affects the predictive power of computational models in physical domains that are simpler than cognition. For this purpose, a model of a physical system that is simple to describe but nonetheless has chaotic behavior has been used to isolate grain size as a variable that affects the behavior of the model in clear ways. While this does not settle the question of how grain size affects the accuracy of cognitive models, it does offer several possibilities for how grain size may, in principle affect the accuracy of a model. This has one advantage over debate that is concerned directly with the domain of primary interest (cognition) but cannot arrange any clean tests of its hypotheses.

Intuitions

In any computational model of human behavior, there is some set of real-world actions that map onto individual computer instructions. There is radical variation, from one modeling effort to another, in the grain size that is used to define the model s atomic actions. The events that are considered atomic may vary from the neural level to the life-decision level or to any level in between. There has been debate promoting one level or another as the appropriate choice for cognitive modeling (Smolensky, 1988), but the discussion has not settled the controversy. By considering modeling in different domains, one may find intuitions regarding how grain size may influence the predictive power of models of cognition.

Calculus: An obvious tradeoff?

Calculus is a means of quantitative analysis, rather than an inherently physical domain, but using numeric approximation to estimate the values of integrals has some things in common with modeling physical systems. Namely, there is an actual answer and the model will provide an approximation of the actual answer. Moreover, while it is very likely that some error will be introduced, one may hope that the error is small enough to be allowable.

Numerical methods of solving integrals make use of many, slender rectangles fitted under a curve to estimate the area bounded by the curve. While integral calculus reduces the error to zero, a numeric simulation is apt to have a certain degree of error due to the edges and corners of the rectangles not fitting the shape of the curve precisely. By using skinnier and skinnier rectangles, numeric models may estimate the actual area to any desired degree of accuracy. Of course, it requires greater computational resources to perform the calculation with skinnier rectangles because there will be more of them inside the area of interest. This suggests that models with smaller grain size are more demanding of resources, but yield in return more accurate results. Thus, effort versus accuracy is a basic tradeoff for numerical estimation of integrals.

Considering this domain suggests that smaller grain sizes should lead to more accurate cognitive models. This is perhaps a useful starting point for developing one s intuition about grain size in cognitive models. It seems reasonable that smaller grain sizes lead to greater accuracy, but this is not always true, as the next example will show.

Chaos: Diminishing (to zero) returns?

James Gleick s popular book <u>Chaos</u> opens with the tale of a crude computer model of the weather and how, in 1961, it led its creator, Edward Lorenz, to the idea of the Butterfly Effect. Lorenz noticed that very small differences between two starting conditions led to larger and larger discrepancies as time ran forward on each of the two worlds until the weather conditions on the two versions of the world, once very similar, bore no great resemblance to one another. This observation led to the formulation of the Butterfly Effect, which holds that a disturbance as small as the flapping of a butterfly s wings can eventually lead to large-scale (though unpredictable) alteration of the world s weather from what it otherwise would have been. Lorenz s model was a crude approximation of actual climatic events; however, the reality of the Butterfly Effect is reflected in the fact that meteorologists cannot accurately predict more than a few days in advance, due to a gradual drift that develops between models and reality.

If the chaotic nature of weather systems is taken as one s guide, then it seems that the effort of using small grain size is wasted because the actual behavior of a complex system cannot be captured, anyway.

Simulation

Gravitational systems

A physical domain that is easy to model numerically is that of dynamic systems of gravitationally bound objects. The simplicity of the domain allows for studies in which granularity is the only variable (and also the only important variable that separates the model from the physical system being modeled). Such a study offers some clean empirical data that may shed light on modeling in richer domains.

Poincar first noticed that the three-body problem (the behavior of a system of three bodies interacting only through gravitation) has no general closed-form solution. (This is distinct from the two-body problem, which always has a closed-form solution.) A three-body system is chaotic, and thus, can generate some interesting behavior over time (Poincar, 1892-9). Three-body systems can be chaotic even when the model is simplified a bit from practical real-world planetary systems by considering only two dimensions, treating the worlds as point masses, and ignoring any forces besides gravity that might be acting on the worlds.

The author ran a number of simulations of gravitational systems, using grain size as the only variable. Two-body systems and one three-body system were tested with a variety of grain sizes and the results are summarized below.

Two-body systems

Simulations of two-body systems (a smaller planet around a larger star) with a great variety of values for grain size (the amount of time in between steps in the model) and the masses and initial values of position and velocity of the two bodies showed the simulations are prone to deviate from reality in three basic ways: Elliptical orbits precess, orbits slowly decay inward, and close encounters between bodies produce unrealistic quantum jumps in velocity. Lowering the grain size of a simulation can reduce all these effects. While the counter-to-reality effects cannot be eliminated entirely, they can be minimized and kept unseen over long spans of simulation time. A follow-up simulation was used to model a chaotic three-body system and bring such effects to the forefront no matter how small of a grain size was used.

Three-body systems

The three-body simulation had one planet and a comet orbiting a star. The planet was much more massive than the comet and their orbits crossed, so that their intermittent close encounters led to the comet s orbit being perturbed. In a physical system of this kind, the inevitable consequence would be that the comet would either collide with another body (and thus be destroyed) or that the comet would be ejected from the system. In the simulation, the sizes of the bodies were made infinitesimal so that actual collisions were impossible. Thus, the fate of the comet would be ejection in all realistic simulations. The outcome of interest is how a simulated system evolves before cometary ejection. That can be expressed in terms of system parameters

such as the number of orbits the comet completed prior to its ejection and the direction in which it was ejected.

Many simulations were carried out with temporal grain size as the only variable. Intuition derived from the calculus domain suggests that smaller grain sizes would lead to a model whose behavior converges upon a correct answer. Intuition derived from Lorenz s chaotic weather model suggests that smaller grain sizes are of no avail, and that it is impossible to converge upon the correct behavior.

The three-body study showed that behavior did not converge as grain size got smaller, although it is impossible to extend the investigation to infinitely small grain sizes. System behavior varied wildly even between similar grain sizes differing by only 0.04% from one another. The chaotic results of the simulations make it difficult to say what the exact behavior of a physical system would have been. Malyshkin and Tremaine (1999) have concluded that modeling such systems can be done more efficiently (with acceptable accuracy) by assuming that all the changes in the orbit of the comet occur at a single point and are determined by nondeterministic calculations based upon a few parameters calculated once per orbit. A close look at the three-body study reported here led to the same conclusion, as the behavior of the system is only predictable within certain loose parameters.

While reducing grain size to small values did not converge upon any right answer, very **large** values of grain size did lead to clear flaws in the model (those described for crude two-body systems). With a sufficiently small value of grain size, it seems that one gets system behavior **typical** of what the behavior of a real system might be, although no such simulation can ever be said to predict exactly a real three-body system.

Conclusions

Clearly, gravitational systems with three bodies are too much simpler than, and generally different from, human cognition for anyone to claim that an effect seen in models of one will necessarily manifest itself in models of the other. It is only claimed that this work suggests that there is a level of grain size that will produce humanlike behavior, and that further reductions in grain size beyond that point will yield essentially no benefit.

References

Gleick, J. (1987). *Chaos*. New York: Penguin.

Malyshkin, L. and Tremaine, S. (1999). The Keplerian map for the planar-restricted three-body problem as a model of comet evolution. *Icarus*, 141:341—53.

Poincar, H. (1892-9). *Les m thodes nouvelles de la m canique c leste*. Paris: Gauthier-Villars.

Smolensky, P. (1988). On the proper treatment of connectionism. *Behavioral and Brain Sciences*, 11:1—23.

Human Performance in Transverse Patterning With A Hippocampal Model

Paul Rodriguez (pr9t@virginia.edu) and **William B. Levy (wbl@virginia.edu)**

Department of Neurosurgery
University of Virginia, Box 800420
Charlottesville, VA 22908 USA

Introduction The hippocampus is necessary in humans and rats for learning flexible/configural representations in which both elemental and conjunctive associations are formed. An example is the transverse patterning task: 3 stimuli, A,B, and C, in a pair-wise forced-choice paradigm. The correct/incorrect choices are: A+B-; B+C-; C+A-. This study applies a model of the CA3 region of the hippocampus to human data, extending a previous application to rat data (Wu, Tyrcha, & Levy, 1998). The model works with known biological constraints in CA3: low activity level, sparse connectivity, and uncorrelated background activity. Also, input is presented as a sequence, which better reflects experimental settings. The size of input is an important unconstrained factor. The main contribution is an analysis of how such biological constraints lead to neural codes that represent input items in spatio-temporal context.

Methods The model uses binary neurons, temporally asymmetric Hebbian learning, *k-winners-take-all* competitive mechanism, and is implemented as a discrete time recurrent network with synchronous updating. Each input vector is presented by clamping on a small portion of assigned neurons. The equations are:

$$y_j(t) = \sum_{i=1}^{N} c_{ij} w_{ij} z_i(t-1) \qquad (1)$$

$$z_j(t) = 1 \, if \, y_j(t) \geq \theta \, or \, x_j(t) = 1 \, else \, 0 \quad (2)$$

$$w_{ij}(t+1) = w_{ij}(t) + \eta \, z_j(t)(z_i(t-1) - w_{ij}(t)) (3)$$

where, $y_j(t)$ is net excitation for $j = 1...N$ neurons; $z_j(t)$ is the output; $w_{ij}(t)$ is the weight from neuron i to j; $c_{ij} \in \{0,1\}$ is the connection indicator ($i \neq j$), initialized prior to learning, $x_i \in \{0,1\}$ indicates externally activated neurons, θ is an activity dependent threshold, η is the learning rate constant.

Given $p = P(c_{i,j} = 1)$, then the number of connections from the active neurons, $\mathcal{A}$, to z_i, is binomially distributed, which is approximated by a normal distribution, $\mathcal{N}(\mu = \mathcal{A}p, \sigma^2 = \mathcal{A}p(1-p))$. Assuming all weights are equal, as they are prior to training, and no input, then expected activity is given by integrating the tail:

$$\mathcal{A}(t) = N * P[c_{\mathcal{A}}(t-1) > \theta/w]$$
$$= (N/2)(1 - Erf[(\theta/w - \mathcal{A}(t-1)p)/\sigma])(4)$$

where $c_{\mathcal{A}}$ are connections from $\mathcal{A}$, and Erf is the cumulative error function. The value of θ/w can be derived algebraically by setting Eq.4= k. From a random initial vector, $Z(0)$, the system wanders through phase space and $Z(t)$ appears as background activity, known to exist in hippocamus at low levels (e.g. 1-3%). During training activity becomes more dependent on the external input. The parameters used were $p = .02$, $N = 5000$, $\eta = .075$, all $w_{i,j} = .4$ initially, and a *k-winners-take-all* competitive mechanism, where $k = 250$ is a 5% activity level.

Training and Testing Each trial was composed of a sequence of input vectors: pairs (AB, BC, or CA), choice, (a, b, or c), and reward events (+ or -). Each item, A,B,C,a,b,c,+, and -, was assigned a unique set of neurons; A,B, and C had 1/2 that of the other items. There were 6 sequences, each of length 4: {AB,a,+,+}, {AB,b,-,-}, {BC,b,+,+}, {BC,c,-,-}, {CA,c,+,+}, {CA,a,-,-}. The reward was presented for an extra time step because input at time t has no effect on excitation until time $t+1$; hence, the the last time step was used for comparing sequences. Each trial was chosen by pattern completion test of partial sequence; e.g. the last state of {AB,a,-,-} and {AB,b,-,-} was the recalled neural code for the correct/incorrect choice respectively. The recalled code was compared by Hamming distance to +/- possible neural codes produced by full sequences, e.g. {AB,a,+,+}, {AB,a,-,-}, and {AB,b,+,+}, {AB,b,-,-}, to pick the choice that was more positive/less negative.Although neurons that code for reward-related events are underdetermined, cellular recordings do in fact show that such neurons depend on context. In this scheme, the hippocampus is primarily a sequence memory device.

Two training regimes used were *progressive and concurrent*: In progressive there are 3 phases: only AB trials; AB and BC; and then all types. In concurrent there is only 1 phase of all types. In both cases trials are alternated and training continues until a criterion of 13/15 correct is reached.

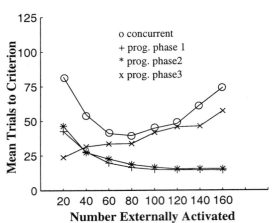

Figure 1: Performance curves averaged across 40 simulations.

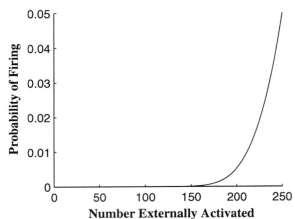

Figure 2: The probability of having enough connections to fire from a given number of input.

Results Early in training the choices are random, but as the network develops unique encodings for the different sequences it quickly learns to perform pattern completion for one or both of the positive and negative choices. As the demand for configural representations changes (e.g. as CAa- competes with ABa+), then the network learns some combination of pattern completion for both positive and negative choices. Figure 1 shows performance as a function of $|X| = \sum_{i=1}^{N} x_i$. Near $|X| = 80$ is the best balance of input and context; below, $|X|$ is too weak to quickly overcome the background activity; above it is too inflexible to learn all pairs. The network performance for $|X| = 80$ is similar human performance for both training regimes, see Table 1.

Table 1: Trials to Criterion.

	Human	Model $|X| = 80$
(Reed et al. 1999)	Progressive	37/40
phase 1	15.2	15.3(2.0)
phase 2	19.3	18.5(3.2)
phase 3	29	33.55(18)
(Astur et al. 1998)	Concurrent	38/40
Exp. 3,9/19	39.1(18.0)	40.2(20.1)

Analysis Using Eq. 4, a value of $\theta/w = 7.58$ was derived, meaning that at the beginning of training, or before weights change too much, a neuron needs ≥ 7.58 connections from the $k = 250$ active neurons to fire; and .05*N=250 neurons are expected to fire. Using $|X|$ substituted for $\mathcal{A}$ in Eq. 4., Figure 2 shows that for $|X| > 150$ there begins an exponential increase in the number of neurons that will fire solely from input connections, even though mean number of connections change linearly as $|X| * p$. Hence, for large $|X|$ the network can not develop

unique codes that depend on the context. In contrast, for $|X| = 80$ the neurons that fire must depend on connections from the previous time step to reach threshold. In other words, some neurons can only be activated for a particular conjunction of input, e.g. {a} in the context {AB} versus {a} the in context {CA}. Also, after weight changes, some neurons (not shown) will fire solely from stimuli, e.g. {a} in any context. This is the essential nature of configural representations in this model.

These results suggest that when biology limits the level of activity and external input competes with background activity, then configural learning depends upon recruiting neurons into an input-X-context representation. Conversely, it suggests that cortical learning is less flexible because neurons do not depend as much on context, and will more likely form attractors.

Acknowledgments NIH 1-F32-MH12762-01 to P.R., NIH MH48161 to W.B.L., and the Department of Neurosurgery.

References

[1] R.S. Astur and R. J. Sutherland. Configural learning in humans: The transverse patterning problem. *Psychobiology*, (3):176–182, 1998.

[2] J.M. Reed and L. R. Squire. Impaired transverse patterning in human amnesia is a special case of impaired memory for two-choice discrimination tasks. *Behavioral Neuroscience*, (1):3–9, 1999.

[3] X. B. Wu, J. Tyrcha, and W. B. Levy. A neural network solution to the transverse patterning problem depends on repetition of the input code. *Biological Cybernetics*, 6(79):203–213, 1998a.

Modeling Behavior in Complex and Dynamic Situations - The Example of Flying an Automated Aircraft

Wolfgang Schoppek, Robert W. Holt, Melanie S. Diez, & Deborah A. Boehm-Davis
University of Bayreuth, Germany and George Mason University, Fairfax, VA

In basic research, cognitive modeling has proven a valuable methodology for explicating theoretical assumptions, testing their dynamic interactions, and exploring the scope of theories. Cognitive architectures such as ACT-R or Soar provide a common basis for different models and enhance communication and exchange of solutions. In applied contexts too, modeling of real tasks and operators could further the understanding of human-machine systems; validated models could provide an objective guide to design and training decisions. However, as real tasks typically require more knowledge and are more complex than laboratory tasks, content independent cognitive architectures do not sufficiently constrain the modeling of these tasks. We argue that - despite this problem - models of behavior in real world tasks should also be developed within established architectures. In doing so, it is important to specify what parts of the model are derived directly from the architecture and for what parts new solutions had to be developed. Thus, models benefit from the broad empirical confirmation of the architecture, which in turn benefits from the identification of domains where it needs to be extended. As an example for this approach, we present an ACT-R (Anderson & Lebiere, 1998) model that simulates the interaction between airline pilots and the flight management system.

Characteristics of the task

The task we modeled is flying down a simulated Boeing 747-400 from the end of the cruise phase to the initial approach fix using the automation of the aircraft. This shall be accomplished under a variety of conditions, such as different ATC clearances or descent profiles. There are two basic modes of automation that can be used for that task: A fully automated mode - called VNAV - where the autopilot receives most of the reference values from a pre-programmed flight plan; in a semiautomatic mode the reference values must be provided by the pilot.

If there are no last minute changes in the flight plan, VNAV is the preferred mode, because it optimizes the flight profile. However, if ATC requires quick changes of the flight plan, the pilot can respond more flexibly using the semiautomatic mode. In both basic modes, the behavior of automation and aircraft must be monitored and reference values must be provided in a timely manner.

When we compare the characteristics of the flying task with those of more typical ACT-R tasks, such as memorizing lists of words (Anderson et al., 1998) or discriminating previously learned statements from distracters (Anderson & Reder, 1999), we find differences in many dimensions. The time scale for the flying task ranges from minutes to hours - much longer than the seconds to minutes of typical ACT-R tasks. Unlike these tasks, the flying task takes place in a dynamic environment that changes rapidly and autonomously. An environment like that often requires revision of plans due to changes in the situation, interrupting ongoing activities due to unexpected events, and deferring actions, because opportunities have to be awaited. There are also differences in the goal structure. Typical ACT-R tasks can be accomplished with a well defined goal hierarchy consisting of one main goal and subordinate goals related in a means-ends fashion. Flying, in contrast, involves heterogeneous goals that may compete for limited resources. For example, the goal of watching the plane pass a critical waypoint competes with the goal of encoding a new ATC clearance. Finally, much more previous knowledge must be brought to the flying task than to a typical ACT-R task.

All these differences require the modeler to find new solutions that are not obvious in the architecture and cannot be derived from existing models that successfully predict behavior in less complex tasks.

ACT-Fly model

The theoretical background of the model is a combination of GOMS (Card, Moran & Newell, 1983) and ACT-R. We developed ACT-R representations of GOMS elements and a way of translating GOMS analyses to ACT-R code. With earlier versions of the model, we found that relying entirely on methods, the model was too rigid to respond to unexpected events. Specifically, we found that the sequential structure of methods often did not match the less predictable order of events in the environment. Another problem with the method-only controlled version was the lack of situational awareness. The scope of a method is typically limited to local aspects of a task, and so there was no inherent need to create a "big picture". To achieve more flexibility and better situational awareness, we introduced an additional level to the control structure that operates in a non-sequential, knowledge based manner.

The activities demanded from the pilots range from situation specific decision making (e.g. deciding which mode to use for a specific leg) to the execution of standard procedures (e.g. entering an altitude restriction into the FMC). To account for the variety of actions, ACT-Fly's control structure is based on a goal stack limited to three levels with a clear division of responsibilities among the levels.

Level 1 can be characterized as the decision making level. At this level, rule based decisions are made as to what goals are pursued and what methods are selected to accomplished these goals. Also, level 1 serves as manager for level 2. Finally, level 1 contains some basic problem solving productions. The goal chunk (chunk is the ACT-R term for declarative memory element) representing this level stores molar information about the situation, such as the phase of flight, the position of the aircraft in the flight plan, or the status of ACT clearances.

Level 2 can be characterized as the method level. It is the level of operating described by frameworks like GOMS. Similar to GOMS, our methods consist of operators, sub-methods, and selection rules. Level 2 can execute hier-archical methods of virtually any depth on one level. This is possible, because subgoals are not stacked on top of each other, but rather, superordinate goals are released to memory and retrieved later on. This design has several advantages. First, the concept of a goal stack has been criticized for providing unrealistically perfect memory for goals (Altmann & Trafton, 1999). In ACT-Fly, goals do not simply appear on top of the goal stack once the previous goal has been popped, but must be retrieved from memory - a process that can fail and can predict certain types of errors. Second, as control is returned to level 1 after the execution of each submethod, the course of action can be corrected during the execution of a long and nested method. With a more traditional goal stack, the system would be "blocked" for the time such a method is executed. Thus, our solution makes the model more flexible and ready to handle interruptions.

The steps of most methods are represented as declarative chunks linked through associations. Thus, the retrieval of the next step is cued by the current method and the previous step, but is not constrained symbolically. That enables the model to simulate errors of omission and of commission in the execution of methods. Another advan-tage of the associative linking of steps is that methods are learned "by doing", using the associative learning mecha-nism of ACT-R. There is an Excel spreadsheet tool avail-able that allows easy translation of NGOMSL analyses to ACT-R code. Methods of ACT-Fly serve different funct-ions. There are methods that perform input operations to the automation, methods that do mental calculations with flight parameters to support decisions, and methods that return classifications of the current situation to maintain situational awareness.

Level 3 represents the interface between central cognition and peripheral systems. Since ACT-Fly does not model perceptual or motor processes, input-output operations are simulated on an abstract level. When the model requests information from the environment, a specialized chunk is pushed on level 3, completed with the requested infor-mation (through the TCP/IP-socket connection with the flight simulator), and the results are transferred to the goal chunk of level 2. Similar steps are performed for motor commands. After being popped, the I-O-chunks remain as episodic traces in memory.

The design process of ACT-Fly revealed a number of problems that appeared to be common, or even typical for complex tasks, but for which there are no standard solutions in extant ACT-R models:

Deferring actions: In dynamic systems, effects of actions often unfold slowly. In these cases, checking the success of an action must be deferred, while in the meantime other things are done. The problem for modeling is how the deferred intention is remembered on time. To simulate intention memory we use a mechanism that inhibits the representations of deferred actions for a certain time.

Expectations: One undesired type of event that can lead to errors is the "automation surprise" (Sarter & Woods, 1995). It occurs when the behavior of the automation does not match the pilots' expectation. We included two mech-anisms to model expectations. One involves the retrieval of a chunk that represents a situation-action-situation se-quence. The other models expectations implicitly through production rules that respond to "unexpected" outcomes.

Estimation of time: We identified several processes that rely on estimation of time: the resumption of intentions, the periodic repetition of monitoring behaviors, and the decision to try another method when one method fails after some repeated applications. We simulated time esti-mation by using the time function provided by ACT-R.

To summarize: Most aspects of the task for which ACT-R did not provide enough constraints followed from the task's dynamic and the requirement to interleave subtasks during long time intervals. Although our solutions to the identified problems are only crude approximations, they can be regarded as hints how the scope of ACT-R could be extended to reasoning and action in more complex and dynamic environments.

Acknowledgments

This research has been supported by grants NAG 2-1289 from the NASA and 99-G-010 from the FAA.

References

Altmann, E. & Trafton, J.G. (1999). Memory of goals: An architectural perspective. *Proceedings of the twenty first annual meeting of the Cognitive Science Society.* (pp. 19-24). Hillsdale, NJ: Erlbaum.

Anderson, J.R., & Lebiere, C. (1998). *Atomic components of thought.* Mahwah, NJ: Erlbaum.

Anderson, J.R., Bothell, D., Lebiere, C. & Matessa, M. (1998). An integrated theory of list memory. *Journal of Memory and Language, 38,* 341-380.

Anderson, J.R. & Reder, L.M. (1999). The fan effect: New Results and new theories. *Journal of Experimental Psychology: General, 128,* 186-197.

Card, S.K., Moran, T.P. & Newell, A. (1983). *The Psychology of Human - Computer Interaction.* Hillsdale, NJ: Erlbaum.

Sarter, N.B. & Woods, D.D. (1995). How in the world did we ever get into that mode? Mode error and awareness in supervisory control. *Human Factors, 37,* 5-19.

ACT-RS: A Neuropsychologically Inspired Module for Spatial Reasoning

Christian Schunn (schunn@gmu.edu)
Department of Psychology,
George Mason University
MSN 3F5, Fairfax, VA 22030-4444

Anthony Harrison (aharris8@gmu.edu)
Department of Psychology,
George Mason University
MSN 3F5, Fairfax, VA 22030-4444

Abstract

We present an extension to ACT-R, called ACT-RS, which adds a neurologically-inspired module for representing and interacting with space. The module includes four functionally different representations of external space that vary along dimensions of input modalities, tasks supported, format, resolution, extent, and features encoded.

Introduction

The current version of ACT-R (and indeed all current problem-solving architectures) encompasses a rather simple mechanism of vision and visual representation. An add-on to the modeling environment, ACT-R/PM, incorporates a more advanced theoretically-driven account of vision. However, it is still concerned entirely with representing what is viewed within a two dimensional space. The visual world of the model is bounded by the edges of the screen on which it is displayed. It is our aim to extend this theory to allow for complex reasoning with and about spatial objects.

Model Components

As a starting point for this model, we adopted Previc's neuropsychological theory of 3-D space (1998), which is based on a large amount of data from behavioral experiments, brain damage performance dissociations, and animal work. Previc's model is the most recent extension of such neuropsychological accounts (e.g. Rizzolatti & Camarda, 1987; Rizzolatti et al., 1985; Grusser, 1983; Cutting & Vishton, 1995). His model has four distinct regions of spatial processing, each with a separate form and function. The first region is called the perispersonal space. It extends about two meters beyond the individual through the central 60 degrees of the person's body and is used for reaching and grasping. The second region, extrapersonal focal, is retinotopic and is tied exclusively to foveation. The third region, extrapersonal action, spans a full 360 degrees around the individual, extending to the spatial bounds of the region that the person is occupying. Finally, there is the ambient extrapersonal space. This region only spans the frontmost 180 degrees of the spatial region and uses an exocentric representation.

Characteristics of Each Spatial Region

Each of the four spatial regions has distinctive functions and representations. In the design process, we considered the rational affordances of each of these regions while keeping their neurological distinctions in mind. These considerations produce a model that will permit computational efficiency in the face of rational necessity. The following sections deal more closely with these issues. The regions are present in order of increasing computational intensity.

Ambient (Extrapersonal) Space

Ambient space processing appears to emphasize the visual periphery extending to the most perceptually distant portion of the world, be it a windowed room or a row of bleachers in a football field (Dichgan & Brandt 1978; Leibowitz & Post, 1982; Previc & Neel, 1995). This information is used to ensure proper postural control and a locational reference within a given region. This system allows us to spatially orient our bodies in an earth-fixed manner without having to consciously attend to our position or motion (Leibowitz & Post, 1982). Surprisingly, the preconscious representation is often more veridical than the consciously registered representation (Loomis, et al., 1992; Proffit, Bhalla, Gossweiler, & Midget, 1995).

The core ambient space representation in our model is simply a geometric region that is determined by the bounds of the most perceptually distant borders. The agent's position and vertical orientation within this geometric region are automatically updated based on peripheral visual feedback as well as dead-reckoning of self-controlled locomotion. This representation of absolute position is then utilized by the other systems to interpret as well as to extrapolate the representations of other objects in the world.

Action (Extrapersonal) Space

The functional role of action space is to support navigation and target orientation with respect to a gaze-centered view. While the lateral limit of action space spans a full 360 degrees, there is a large compression effect outside the visible field of view (Beer, 1993). Additionally, while action space extends from around two meters almost to the limit of visual space, important distance cues begin to degrade after a certain radius limiting the actual functional range of action space to around 15 meters (Grusser, 1983; Fukusima, Loomis, & Da Silva, 1997).

In our model, action space representations contain just enough information to inform effective navigation and object avoidance. This representation includes three angle-range pairs. These angle-range pairs are all relative to the eye point of the agent and represent the relative position of the leftmost, rightmost and topmost (or bottommost for suspended objects) edges. The representations of objects that fall within the biased field of view (200 degrees, 2-15m, upper-field bias) are automatically updated with respect to the agent's head and body positions. Those that fall outside of this region are not updated and if queried, must be consciously re-encoded. This might produce many of the observed biases and distortions in dead reckoning and object localization tasks (e.g. Fukusima, Loomis, & Da Silva, 1997).

Focal (Extrapersonal) Space

Focal space is the region typically included in architectures of cognition (including ACT-R/PM). It is concerned with object recognition and attention to finer detail. This system is most closely regulated by conscious control and is influenced by top-down processing.

Object representations in the other spaces have no object recognition mechanism (i.e., objects are represented as blob objects rather than instances of particular categories). It is entirely up to the focal region to tag representations with their actual identity. To support this recognition process, we assume a recognition-by-components account in which object parts are represented by geons (Biederman, 1987). To facilitate object recognition with size and rotation invariance, we assume that the geons contain no metric information, and no real 3-dimensional extent.

Peripersonal Space

Finally there is the most three dimensional and metric of all the spaces, peripersonal space. This region is concerned with object manipulation. Once again, we assume a geon-based representation of object components, but this time the geons have detailed 3-dimensional metric information including surface texture information.

Computational Limitations

The previous descriptions paint a picture of four parallel systems that are almost boundless in their ability to automatically represent their particular piece of the picture. This is not accurate. Each of the regions has a series of limitations. The first of these is their uptake span. New objects are automatically encoded and updated within this angle span. Next, there is the wider maintenance span within which previously encoded representations are maintained and updated in memory. Anything outside of these regions must be consciously interpreted through indirect methods. Each of the regions also has biases towards specific parts of the visual field, representing a prioritization mechanism within the uptake and maintenance bounds. The finer details of this mechanism still have yet to be resolved.

Application and Testing

We are currently implementing the components of ACT-RS and expect to test the system in a 3-dimensional navigation tasks first. We then hope to apply the model to complex spatial problem-solving like the submarine sonar domain.

Acknowledgments

This work was funded by grant #N00014-01-1-0321 to the first author from the Office of Naval Research through Susan Chipman.

References

Biederman, I. (1987). Recognition-by-components: A theory of human image understanding. *Psychological Review, 94,* 115-147.

Beer, J.A. (1993). Perceiving scene layout through an aperture during visually simulated self-motion. *Journal of Experimental Psychology: Human Perception and Performance, 19,* 1066-1081.

Cutting, J.E. & Vishton, P. M. (1995). Perceiving layout and knowing distances: The integration, relative potency, and contextual use of different information about depth. In W. Epstein & S. Rogers (Eds.), *Handbook of perception and cognition, 5,* 69-117. San Diego, CA: Academic Press.

Dichgans, J. & Brandt, T. (1978). Visual-vestibular interaction: Effects on self-motion perception and postural control. In R. Held, H. Leibowitz, & H.-L. Teuber (Eds.), *Perception: Vol. . Handbook of sensory physiology,* 755-804. New York: Springer-Verlag.

Grusser, O.-J. (1983). Multimodal structure of extrapersonal space. In A. Hein & M. Jeannerod (Eds.), *Spatially oriented behavior,* 327-352. New York: Springer-Verlag.

Fukusima, S. S., Loomis, J. M., & Da Silva, J.A. (1997). Visual perception of egocentric distance as assessed by triangulation. *Journal of Experimental Psychology: Human Perception and Performance, 23,* 86-100.

Leibowitz, H. W. & Post, R. B. (1982). The two modes of processing concept and some implications. In J. Beck (Ed.), *Organization and representation in perception,* 343-363. Hillsdale, NJ: Erlbaum.

Loomis, J.M., Da Silva, J. A., Fujita, N. & Fukusima, S. S. (1992). Visual space perception and visually directed location. *Journal of Experimental Psychology, 18,* 906-921.

Previc, F. H. (1998). The neuropsychology of 3-D space. *Psychological Bulletin, 124,* 123-164.

Previc, F. H. & Neel, R. L. (1995). The effects of visual surround eccentricity and size of manual and postural control. *Journal of Vestibular Research, 5,* 399-404.

Proffitt, D. R., Bhalla, M., Gossweiler, R. & Midget, J. (1995). Perceiving geographical slant. *Psychonomic Bulletin and Review, 2,* 409-428.

Rizzolatti, G. & Camarda, R. (1987). Neural circuits for spatial attention and unilateral neglect. In M. Jeannerod (Ed.), *Neurophysiological and neuropsychological aspects of spatial neglect,* 289-313. Amsterdam: North-Holland.

Rizzolatti, G., Gentilucci, M., & Matelli, M. (1985). Selective spatial attention: One center, one circuit, or many circuits? In M. I. Posner, & O. S. M. Marin (Eds.), *Attention and performance 11,* 251-265. Hillsdale, NJ: Erlbaum.

Spatial Navigation Using Hierarchical Cognitive Maps

Horatiu Voicu (voicu@psych.duke.edu)

Nestor Schmajuk (nestor@duke.edu)
Department of Psychology, 9 Flowers Dr
Durham, NC 27708 USA

The present work describes a hierarchical cognitive system that is able to explore and navigate in large-scale environments. It is able to decompose the environment so that planning at higher spatial levels results in obstacle avoidance trajectories. Reaction time and memory requirements are improved.

The model contains an associative network (Kohonen, 1977) that stores associations between places and places, places and goals, regions and regions, regions and goals and region and places. The spatial information is structured on a two-level hierarchy. The environment (global level) is partitioned in regions and each region (local level) is divided in place fields. A graphic example of a spatial hierarchical structure is given in Figure 1. The model contains also an associative memory, depicted in Figure 2, that can retrieve only part of the information stored in the associative memory. The associative memory stores connections between adjacent places within a region or the connections between adjacent regions in the environment. It receives information about the current place and neighbors or the current region and neighboring regions and the current goal. The output of the associative working memory is stored in a short-term memory and is used in planning paths either at the global level or at the local level.

The agent is provided with the following a priori information. The space to be explored is divided in regions that are interconnected and preserve the continuity of space. Each region contains a partition of disjoint place fields that covers it completely.

If the agent is in place P_1 and P_2 is an adjacent place then the weight between the place unit representing place P_1 and the place unit representing place P_2 is updated using a Hebbian learning rule. For example, if place P_2 is unoccupied then the connection between P_1 and P_2 remains set to 1 and if place P_2 is occupied then the connection between P_1 and P_2 decreases to 0.

After the current region is explored, the agent activates the first place that has been visited and reinjects the activity a fixed number of times. If all places are active then, the agent proceeds to update the connection between regions. If at least one place is inactive then the current region is divided in two regions, one that contains all active places and one that contains all inactive places. Then, the agent proceeds to update the connection between the new current region and its neighbors and the new created region and its neighbors. Assuming R to be the new current region, the agent activates the first place visited in R and reinjects the activation a fixed number of times. The weights between the region representing R and the region activated by the spreading activation are strengthened using a Hebbian learning rule. The agent uses the same method for updating the connections of the new created region.

Figure 3 shows the environment before and after the exploration. The initial map has 9 (3X3) regions illustrated by the grid. Obstacles are represented by dark gray lines. The two areas shaded in gray in Figure 3B show the regions created during exploration. If the agent is surrounded by more than one unvisited place/region then the next place/region is selected according to a set of priorities. In our case, these are North, West, East, North-West, North-East, South, South-West, and South-East. Figure 4 shows the navigation paths used by the agent for traveling from one place in one region to a distant goal located in a non-adjacent region. In the path depicted in Figure 4A the agent uses only regions defined before exploration whereas Figure 4B shows the path between two places that belong to regions created during exploration.

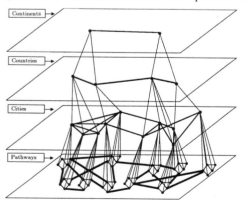

Figure 1. Spatial hierarchical structure.

Places, Regions   Goals

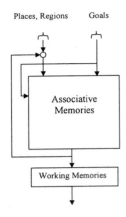

Figure 2. Cognitive System.

Many theories (Keirsey et. al., 1984; Klopf et. al., 1993; Tyrrell, 1993; (Digney, 1996; Mishkin et. al., 1999; Kuipers, 2000) and experiments (Rao and Fuentes, 1998) discuss the use of hierarchical structures as a means for improving behavioral performance. However, they use the concept of hierarchy in different contexts with different meanings. Fountain and Rowan (1995) use a hierarchical concept similar to the one presented in this work. They show that humans are able to abstract information and build hierarchical structures when they encounter highly organized serial patterns

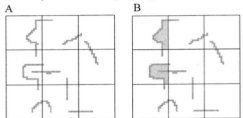

Figure 3. Large scale environment: A) before exploration, B) after exploration.

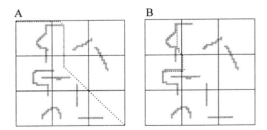

Figure 4. Navigation between regions: A) between already defined regions, B) newly created subregions.

and that rats are able to learn better hierarchical structures than linear ones.

The results presented in this work support the idea that hierarchical structures are an important factor in improving the performance of systems with limited working memories.

References

Digney, B.L. (1996). Emergent Hierarchical Control Structures: Learning Reactive/ Hierarchical Relationships in Reinforcement Environments. *From Animals to Animats 4*, MIT Press, 363-372.

Fountain, S. B. and Rowan, J.D. (1995). Coding for Hierarchical Versus Linear Pattern Structure in Rats and Humans. *Journal of Experimental Psychology: Animal B ehavior Processes*, 21, 187-202.

Keirsey, D.M., Mitchell, J.S.B., Payton, D.W., and Preyss, E.P. (1984). Multilevel Path Planning for Autonomous Vechicles. *Applications of Artificial Intelligence*, SPIE Proceedings, 485, 133-137.

Klopf, A.H.,Morgan, J. S., and Weaver S.E. (1993). Modeling Nervous System Function with a Hierarchical Network of Control Systems that Learn. *From Animals to Animats 2*, MIT Press, 254-261.

Kohonen, T. (1977). *Associative Memory*. Berlin: Springer Verlag.

Kuipers, B (2000). The Spatial Semantic Hierarchy. *Artificial Intelligence*, 119, 191–233.

Mishkin, M., Suzuki, W. A., Gadian D.G., and Vargha-Khadem, F. (1999). Hierarchical Organization of Cognitive Memory. *Hippocampal and Parietal Foundations of Spatial Cognition*, Oxford University Press, 290-304.

Rao, R. and Fuentes, O. (1998). Hierarchical Learning of Navigational Behaviors in an Autonomous Robot using Sparse Distributed Memory. *Machine Learning*, 31, 87-113.

Tyrrell, T. (1993). The use of Hierarchies for Action Selection. *Adaptive Behavior*, 1, 387-420.

Can Cognitive Modeling Improve Usability Testing and Rapid Prototyping?

Robert L. West (robert_west@carleton.ca)
Department of Psychology; Carleton University
Department of Cognitive Science, Carleton University
Ottawa, Canada

Bruno Emond (bruno_emond@uqah.uquebec.ca)
Department of Education; Université du Québec à Hull
Hull, Canada

Abstract

We argue that usability testing, as employed in the rapid prototyping cycle, could be improved by testing simulated users. We briefly review some of the benefits that this methodology could offer and discuss one approach to building a simulated user using ACT-R to embody a GOMS-like memory structure.

Rapid prototyping is frequently used to design interface systems for commercial software. The goal is to rapidly iterate a cycle of creating, evaluating, and redesigning, to produce an intuitive, easy to use interface. In this paper we discuss how usability testing, a popular means of evaluation for rapid prototyping, could be augmented by testing simulated users. The simulated user is not a new idea; it has its origins in GOMS modeling (Card, Moran, & Newell, 1983), and has also been explored using cognitive architectures (e.g., Gray, 2000; Howes & Young, 1996) such as ACT-R (Anderson & Lebiere, 1998) and SOAR (Newell, 1990). However, not much attention has been paid to integrating simulated users into rapid prototyping and usability testing.

Usability testing involves having users perform tasks on an interface prototype to see how well it works. The actual testing procedure is relatively quick and informal. Usually, four to seven subjects are asked to do a series of tasks using the interface prototype. While usability testing is effective, like any methodology, it is not without problems. There are a number of different ways that simulated users could improve usability testing but, due to space limitations, we will focus only on the problem of not enough subjects. Using lower numbers of subjects increases the chance of not finding a problem or of overestimating or underestimating the likelihood of a problem occurring in the user population (see the following for experimental evidence consistent with this claim: Spool & Schroeder 2001; Kessner, Wood, Dillon, & West, 2001; Molich, Thomsen, Karyukina, Schmid, Ede, van Oel, & Arcuri, 1999). Rapid prototyping does not allow enough time to test large numbers of subjects, so one solution is to use simulated subjects. However, in order to do this, simulated users need to be created and validated. Here we describe our initial attempts to do this.

The goal of this project is to develop a system that will improve the rapid prototyping process. However, developing a simulated user will not be much use if it is not accepted as a methodology within the usability domain. Related to this is the usability of the simulated user itself. In rapid prototyping there is a very strong emphasis on developing prototyping tools that are fast and relatively easy to use. Therefore the simulated user should be as easy as possible to program and understand. A good model for this, we believe, is keystroke level GOMS (Card, Moran, & Newell, 1983), which is designed to be easy to use, easy to understand, and good enough for describing typical interface designs. The type of system we would like to create would be similar in nature to keystroke level GOMS but capable of exploring and learning how to use a novel interface. Below we describe our initial attempts to create such a system using ACT-R.

For this type of system, issues concerning perception, attention, and action pose a problem. One solution would be to use an architecture designed to deal with these issues, such as ACT-RPM (Byrne & Anderson, 1998) or EPIC (Kieras & Meyer, 1997). However, in keeping with our goal of maintaining the simplicity of keystroke level GOMS, we assume that everything is accurately perceived so that the interface information can be coded (by LISP functions) into declarative memory as it becomes perceptually available. Perceptual, attentional, and motor operators are used only to estimate how long each action takes. Objects on graphical user interfaces tend to be fairly obvious and it is not commonly found that users fail to notice objects. However, the problem of not understanding the functionality of an object (e.g., not understanding what an icon symbolizes) is quite commonly found in usability testing. Unfortunately, it is problematic to model object recognition, even using ACT-RPM or EPIC. Therefore, object recognition would need to be assumed. Note though, that it can also be assumed that an object is not understood to simulate the effect of this.

GOMS models have been shown to be both effective at modeling interface use and relatively easy and intuitive to grasp (John, 1995). We hypothesize that the reason for this is that the GOMS structure actually reflects the way humans organize their knowledge of how to use interfaces. From this perspective, trying to figure out an interface can be understood as the user attempting to mentally construct something similar to a GOMS model. Based on this conceptualization, our approach has been to model the user as trying to construct a GOMS-like model of the task in their declarative memory system. The template for how this information is built-up and stored in memory is based on a hierarchical structure similar to that used in GOMS (i.e., goals, methods, operators).

Figure 1 illustrates the template structure. The rectangles represent goals, the boxes represent methods, and the circles represent operators. The gray shapes represent the elements related to completing the first goal, and the white shapes represent the elements related to completing the second goal. At each level, knowledge of the sequence of steps is represented by chunks describing each step, with each chunk containing a slot that identifies the next step. The model uses the ACT-R goal stack to move to lower levels by pushing subgoals that get popped when the sequence at that level is complete. For example, if the goal was to open a file, a subgoal for a method of opening a file would be pushed. The first step in the method (e.g., "open file menu") would then push a sub-subgoal to execute the operators necessary for this step. The operators would fire in sequence, pop the sub-subgoal, and the system would move on onto the next step in the method. This process would repeat until the goal of opening a file is completed. The system would then move onto the next goal by popping the method goal. Note, that there can be more than one method sequence per goal, and more than one operator sequence per method. Learning which to use would be based on the chunk activation system. This would mean that the user would tend toward a "winner take all" strategy, increasingly preferring the methods used most in the past.

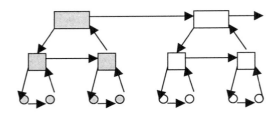

Figure 1. A template structure for storing interface operating knowledge

In a usability test, the trick is to provide the subject with enough information to understand the task, without revealing all of the steps involved. Thus, the subjects' task is to fill in the missing knowledge. In terms of the data structure described above this would be equivalent to a model of the task with some of the connecting chunks missing. In most cases these would be method chunks since the goal chunks would be needed to understand the task and the operator chunks would be based mainly on well known GUI objects (e.g., buttons, text fields, etc.). Based on this, we conceptualized the learning process as a search for missing method chunks. When the model reaches a gap in its knowledge it needs to search for chunks that it can link together to get to the next known step in the task. This process of building up chains of linked chunks to represent sequential actions is based on the scheme described by Lebiere & Wallach (1998) to account for sequence learning.

We plan to implement different strategies for searching for the missing chunks through production rules. As a starting point, we are considering four basic strategies. The first is choosing based on past associations from other interfaces. This would involve trying to achieve a goal by using methods that have been used successfully to achieve

the same goal on other interfaces. This creates a problem in that it is necessary to provide the simulated user with a fair amount of domain knowledge, but it is also beneficial as it explicitly addresses the role of existing knowledge. The second strategy is to try interface objects that are labeled to indicate to the user that they are related to the goal (it would need to be assumed that the user understands the label, see above). The third strategy is to try interface objects at random to see how they transform the problem space, and the fourth strategy is to attempt to use the "help" features of the interface. However, this is only a starting point for further development through comparisons with human data. In terms of development, in our opinion, the best way to proceed is by using the open source code concept. We believe that this would best facilitate the process of development as well as the use of simulated users for rapid prototyping.

References

Anderson, J. R., & Lebiere, C. (1998). *The atomic components of thought*. Mahwah, NJ: Lawrence Erlbaum Associates.

Byrne, M. D. & Anderson, J. R. (1998). Perception and action. In Anderson, J. R. & Lebiere, C. (Eds.), *The atomic components of thought*. Mahwah NJ: Lawrence Erlbaum.

Card, S. K., Moran, T. P., & Newell, A. (1983). *The psychology of human-computer interaction*. Hillsdale, NJ: Lawrence Erlbaum Associates.

Gray, W. D. (2000). The nature and processing of errors in interactive behavior. *Cognitive Science, 24(2)*, 205-248.

Howes, A., & Young, R. M. (1996). Learning consistent, interactive, and meaningful task-action mappings: A computational model. *Cognitive Science, 20*, 301-356.

John, B. E. (1995). Why GOMS? *Interactions. 2* (10), 80-89.

Kessner, M., Wood, J., Dillon, R. F., & West, R. L. (2001). On the reliability of usability testing. *Proceedings of CHI 2001*. ACM, Seatle.

Kieras, D. E., & Meyer D. E. (1997). An overview of the EPIC architecture for cognition and performance with application to human-computer interaction. Human-Computer Interaction, 12, 391-438.

Lebiere, C., & Wallach, D. (1998). Implicit does not imply procedural: A declarative theory of sequence learning. Paper presented at the *Forty First Conference of the German Psychological Society*, Dresden, Germany.

Molich, R., Thomsen, A. D., Karyukina, B., Schmid, L., Ede, M., van Oel, W., & Arcuri, M. Comparative evaluation of usability tests. *Human factors in computing systems CHI 99 Extended Abstracts*, 83-84, 1999.

Newell, A. (1990). *Unified theories of Cognition*. Cambridge, Mass: Harvard University Press.

Spool, J., & Schroeder, W. (2001). Testing web sites: Five users is nowhere near enough. *CHI 2001 Extended Abstracts*, 285-286.

Doctoral Consortium Posters

ICCM Doctoral Consortium

Deborah A. Boehm-Davis (dbdavis@gmu.edu)
HFAC Program/ARCH Lab, George Mason University
MSN 2E5, Fairfax, VA 22030-4444

Introduction

The Doctoral Consortium (DC) is a pre-conference event sponsored by ICCM. The DC is a closed session that provides an opportunity for doctoral students to explore their research interests in an interdisciplinary workshop under the guidance of a panel of established research faculty in a group setting. The participants receive feedback on their current research and guidance for future research directions. The consortium also aims toward the development of a supportive community of scholars while contributing to the conference goals through interaction with other researchers and participation in conference events.

Consortium participants were invited based on their dissertation proposals, and they reflected the wide range of disciplines within HCI research.

Consortium Format

The Doctoral Consortium opened with a dinner off site. This venue allowed us an opportunity to break the ice and start getting to know one another. Starting the next morning, each of the participants was given time for a presentation and discussion of their research plans, ideas, and outcomes.

The seven participants (4 men and 3 women) were each given an opportunity to present their research, followed by a discussion of the ideas presented. The research represented work being done in a number of different academic departments: Computer Science, Psychology, Cognitive Neuroscience, and Information Sciences.

The presentations provided an opportunity to comment on work at various levels of completion, from proposals that had just been approved to dissertations that had been recently defended.

The atmosphere was one of friendly and constructive criticism, focused primarily on design and interpretation issues, not on presentation style.

Some time in the afternoon was spent discussing applying for jobs, initial positions, and differences between positions in industry, academic, and government.

All of the DC participants also presented a poster describing their work during poster session held during the conference.

How to Find Us

Summaries of the dissertations presented are published following this overview. We invite you to peruse them and contact the authors if you have questions or comments on them.

If you are interested in information regarding the value of the experience in the DC, I would invite you to contact the students who participated this year.

If you, or someone you know, are trying to fill a position in academia or industry, I would encourage you to contact these bright and eager members of the modeling community.

ICCM Doctoral Consortium Participants and Topics

Roman Belavkin, "The Role of Emotion in Problem Solving"

Anna Cox, "What People Learn from Exploratory Device Learning"

Wai-Tat Fu, "The Influence of Experienced Effort on Learning and Choice of Solution Paths in a Simple Navigation Task"

Jenny Hayes, "Plural Morphology in Compounding is not Good Evidence to Support the Dual Mechanism Model"

Peter Moertl, "Computerized Modeling of Semantic Structure in Sequential Text"

Anna Montagnini, "Statistical Learning of Human Faces"

Carter Wendelken, "SHRUTI-agent: A Structured Connectionist Model of Decision-Making"

ICCM Doctoral Consortium Advisors (Faculty)

Deborah A. Boehm-Davis, George Mason University

Stellan Ohlsson, University of Illinois at Chicago

Randall C. O'Reilly, University of Colorado at Boulder

Modelling the Inverted-U Effect with ACT-R

Roman V. Belavkin (rvb@Cs.Nott.AC.UK)
School of Computer Science and Information Technology,
University of Nottingham
Jubilee Campus, Wollaton Road, Nottingham NG8 1BB, UK

Abstract

Properties of the ACT-R conflict resolution suggest the possibility of modelling a behaviour at different activation levels of the autonomic nervous system. A model of the classical Yerkes-Dodson experiment was built to test the predictions. The resulting model explains such psychological phenomena as the inverted-U curve, relating performance to arousal, within the mathematical representations of equations in ACT-R. Dynamical optimisation of the two crucial parameters, namely goal value and gain noise variance, may produce more optimal solution paths. We argue that subjects also perform such optimisation as including it into the models can produce a better match with the data. The dynamics corresponds to activational and motivational changes, related to experience of emotion during problem solving, which leads to interesting speculations about a role emotion in intelligence.

Introduction

Recent progress in cognitive modelling has allowed the testing of quite broad range of human psychology and cognition theories. A lot of experiments in psychology have been reproduced by cognitive scientists within theories such as SOAR or ACT. This produced new insights into understanding of some phenomena of human memory, learning, perception and reasoning. Yet there have been few attempts to understand emotion and affect within this framework.

It is known that emotion accompanies problem solving and it is closely related to cognitive processes such as learning, decision making and memory. It is becoming evident that cognitive models should take emotion into account (Belavkin, Ritter & Elliman 1999). A lot of these models simulate subjects solving various puzzles and problems, some models consider children, as in (Jones, Ritter & Wood 2000), whose emotions are easily observable. We believe that the cognitive science approach will help us to understand better what happens to the thinking process itself as a result of these emotions. What is the difference between assembling the tower of Hanoi in an angry or a happy mood?

Decision making in ACT-R

Many ideas in this work were inspired by the results of the Tower of Nottingham model (Jones et al. 2000), which was used to study cognitive development. In particular, the model with increased noise in conflict resolution, which produced a very good match with 7 y.o. children using just the noise variance parameter. This result pointed to the need for a closer investigation into the ACT-R conflict resolution mechanism.

In ACT-R a conflict between several production rules matching the goal is resolved by selecting a rule with the highest expected gain $E = PG - C + \xi(\tau)$, where P is expected probability of achieving the goal if the rule fires, G is the value of the current goal, C is expected cost of that rule, $\xi(\tau)$ is a random variable representing noisy, non-deterministic part of ACT-R, Here τ is the noise temperature related to the noise variance σ as $\tau = \sqrt{\sigma}/\pi$. In ACT-R P and C can be learned statistically, while G and τ are set through global parameters.

The probability of selecting a particular i-th rule out of n in the conflict set is given by the Boltzmann equation (see eq. 3.4 in Anderson & Lebiere, 1998). We looked at how this choice probability depends on Ps and Cs of rules at extreme values of G and τ. The resulting asymptotic properties can be summarised as follows:

i) $\tau \to 0$ (low noise). The choice is too deterministic: excessive reliance on the past experience, which may become obsolete in a changing environment.

ii) $\tau \to \infty$ (high noise). The choice is random and it does not depend on the learned expected probabilities P and costs C.

iii) $G \to 0$ (low motivation). The choice is completely determined by Cs and not by Ps.

iv) $G \to \infty$ (high motivation). Opposite to the previous, the choice does not depend on Cs, but is purely determined by Ps.

The ratio G/τ determines how much the choice depends on the learned statistics and it may represent confidence. It can be shown that even when the ratio remains constant, the costs are more important for low G and τ, while probabilities are more important for high values.

The Yerkes-Dodson experiment model

Asymptotic properties suggest that together the values of G and τ represent the activation or the "energy" of a cognitive process (*arousal* in activation theory of emotion). In order to illustrate different choice strategies at different activation levels, predicted by the properties, a model of the famous Yerkes-Dodson experiment (Yerkes & Dodson 1908) was built using ACT-R (Fig. 1). One of the objectives was to obtain the Inverted-U curve effect relating performance (speed of learning) and arousal.

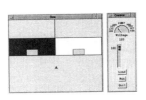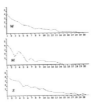

Figure 1: Left: user interface of the Yerkes-Dodson experiment simulation. Right: error curves for weak "W", medium "M" and strong "S" activation. The fastest decay is at medium ("M") stimulation.

The model uses both statistical and procedural learning (production compilation). High noise affects the use of the learned statistics resulting in performance degradation. In changing environment too little noise may result in repetitive errors (observed on the model). At low activation the model is unlikely to make decisions with high costs (as predicted by iii)), but the preference changes with the activation increase.

The model demonstrated that the Inverted-U curve effect can be observed: the fastest learning corresponds to a certain level of activation (values of G and τ) even when the ratio G/τ remains constant.

Optimal performance and emotion

The optimal activation level (G, τ values corresponding to the fastest learning) is task specific and it may not be known in advance. If G and τ remain constant during the simulation run (as they are by default in ACT-R), there is no chance to find their optimal values. The well known optimisation methods, such as simulated annealing, or search methods, such as best-first, suggest the following strategy for dynamic optimisation of G and τ: problem solving should begin with low goal value G and high noise τ (high temperature state; also low G results in breadth-first search behaviour); after some statistical information about the application of rules has

been learned, the increase of G and decay of τ will make the choice less random and rely more on the learned information (cooling the system down, or making the search deeper).

This optimisation strategy corresponds well to the behaviour of an emotional problem solver: on experiencing a success motivation and confidence increases (higher G and G/τ), as it is accompanied by positive emotions, such as joy. On failure the experienced negative emotion, such as frustration, results in decrease of motivation and confidence (G and G/τ), which corresponds to heating the system up from a glass state in simulated annealing.

Dynamic control over the goal value G and noise temperature τ may improve the match between in ACT-R models and data, which we demonstrate on the Tower of Nottingham and Yerkes-Dodson experiment models.

Conclusions

We showed how some effects of emotions on problem solving can be modelled in cognitive architectures with nondeterministic and statistical learning capabilities, like ACT-R. In such architectures, changes of motivation (maximum cost, or goal value G) and randomness (noise temperature τ) can produce noticeable effects on the behaviour of models. This can be used both for a better data matching and modelling the behaviour of subjects in highly active or passive emotional states. The demonstrated similarity between optimisation methods and emotional reactions during problem solving, suggests that emotion makes a positive contribution to intelligence, as it implements powerful heuristic methods already known and used elsewhere in AI.

Acknowledgements

This work is sponsored by EPSRC Credit and ORS Award Scheme.

References

Anderson, J. R. & Lebiere, C. (1998), *The atomic component of thought*, Lawrence Erlbaum Associates, Mahwah, NJ, London.

Belavkin, R. V., Ritter, F. E. & Elliman, D. G. (1999), Towards including simple emotions in a cognitive architecture in order to fit children's behaviour better, *in* N. Mahwah, ed., 'Proceedings of the 1999 Conference of the Cognitive Science Society', Lawrence Erlbaum, p. 784.

Jones, G., Ritter, F. E. & Wood, D. J. (2000), 'Using a cognitive architecture to examine what develops', *Psychological Science* **11**(2), 1–8.

Yerkes, R. M. & Dodson, J. D. (1908), 'The relation of strength of stimulus to rapidity of habit formation', *Journal of Comparative and Neurology and Psychology* **18**, 459–482.

What People Learn from Exploratory Device Learning

Anna L Cox (a.cox@herts.ac.uk) Psychology Department, University of Hertfordshire,
College Lane, Hatfield, AL10 9AB, United Kingdom

Abstract

The empirical investigations outlined in this paper are concerned with identifying what people do during exploratory learning and what they learn whilst they conduct it. The results have been used to develop a framework within which to model exploration. Implementation of the framework is proposed in order to test a number of predictions and to help explain and support findings from further empirical studies.

Keywords: Human-Computer Interaction, Exploratory Learning, COGENT, ACT-R

Introduction

Exploratory Learning. People often learn a novel device or software application by actually trying to use it, drawing on a combination of prior knowledge, information from the interface itself, and problem solving skills. We describe this phenomenon as exploratory learning. Rieman (1996) showed that in a real world situation, people prefer to learn by exploration in the context of a real task they need to perform, rather than taking time out to experiment with it or work through the documentation in a task-independent manner. Exploratory learning also occurs in situations when training or documentation is not available and in the case of walk-up-and-use devices.

Device and Task Oriented Knowledge. Before describing the work investigating exploratory learning, it is necessary to clarify the distinction between device-oriented and task-oriented knowledge. Device-oriented knowledge usually consists of a collection of facts about what the device as a whole (or parts of it) do. When a user is trying to learn about a new device, one of his goals, for example, will be to find out what each button does. Task-oriented knowledge, on the other hand, is knowledge about how to complete a task using a particular device. When learning about a novel device, a user may need to acquire both device knowledge and task knowledge, e.g., 'what does the button labelled on do?' and also 'how do I set this video-recorder to record my favourite programme while I'm out?'

Trudel & Payne 1995. Trudel & Payne (1995) carried out a series of investigations into reflection and goal management in exploratory learning. In their initial study, they compared the performance of three groups of participants on tests of declarative and procedural knowledge. They presented their participants with a simulation of a digital watch and asked them to explore it with a view to being tested afterwards. The participants either had 20 minutes in which to do this, or a limit of 250 keystrokes, or were given a list of 7 tasks to complete.

Their manipulations yielded dramatic results. They found that the keystroke-limited group did significantly better than the other two groups on the tests for declarative knowledge and procedural knowledge, despite actually spending less time exploring it. They concluded that the imposition of the keystroke limit had made the keystrokes a precious resource and had forced the participants to reflect more fully on each action.

Thesis Research Summary

Study 1 and Initial modeling in ACT-R. Following the work of Trudel & Payne, 1995, it was decided to conduct a partial replication of their first experiment using a different, less-moded device to ensure generalisability. Participants explored a simulated central heating timer in one of two conditions. Those in the unstructured exploration condition had 15 minutes in which to learn how to use the device while those in the mouseclick limited group had 100 mouseclicks or 15 minutes, which ever finished sooner.

The results suggested that the imposition of a mouseclick limit did not automatically improve performance. Two reasons for this non-replication were suggested. Firstly, that the central heating timer is a different kind of device from the digital watch. Unlike the users of the digital watch, in order to complete realistic tasks on the central heating timer, the user needs to know not just what each of the buttons does (device-oriented knowledge) but also how to use the device to perform tasks (task-oriented knowledge). The second reason put forward to explain these results was that participants in this study had prior knowledge of how this class of devices works, so once they had learnt what each of the buttons does they thought there was nothing else to learn. This over confidence resulted in them not setting themselves realistic tasks from which to learn how to use the device.

A simple initial model of exploratory learning of a pared down version of the device was built in ACT-R (Anderson & Lebiere, 1999). The model added support to the argument that in order to use the central heating timer successfully, participants need to acquire knowledge about the relationship between scenario situations and the actions on the device and that this can only be done by completing realistic tasks during training.

A more detailed account of this work can be found in (Cox & Young, 2000).

A Closer Look at Exploration. Concurrent verbal protocols were taken from participants while they carried out unstructured exploration of the central heating timer. These protocols provided evidence for a number of classes of different exploratory acts for example, pressing a button to see what effect it has, generalizing knowledge about the effect of one button to another, conducting an experiment to confirm a currently held belief, etc. Analysis of one of these protocols in particular resulted in predictions being made regarding the beliefs a participant held about how the central heating timer worked. These predictions were confirmed after inviting the participant back to answer a series of further questions.

A New Rational Framework and a Model in COGENT. The different exploratory acts that were identified as a result of the protocol analyses were used as the basis for a rational framework for modelling exploratory learning. Due to problems fitting this framework on to ACT-R's machinery that are outlined by Young & Cox, (2000), it was decided to try to implement the model in COGENT (Cooper & Fox, 1998). A more detailed account of the framework, protocols and model can be found in Cox & Young, (2001).

Although this model of exploratory learning is not expected to provide data that exactly matches any particular participant's record of interactions, it is predicted that it will provide keystroke records similar in nature to those of the human participants.

Furthermore, analysis of the knowledge acquired by the model is expected to show that device-oriented knowledge is easily acquired but that an accurate understanding of domain-oriented knowledge is less common.

In addition, the framework predicts that there will be a difference in the knowledge acquired by those conducting free exploration against those conducting focused exploration and this is expected to be shown by the implemented model. This prediction is supported by evidence found by Trudel and Payne (1995) when they compared the performance of people who explored a digital watch under those 2 conditions.

Study 2. A further study was conducted in order to test the prediction that realistic domain tasks must be completed during training for people to successfully use a device. This compared the post-exploration performance of those completing a period of free exploration against those completing two different kinds of focused exploration. Half of those completing focused exploration were given a list of device-oriented goals to try to achieve, which directed them to focus on identifying what each button did. The other half was given a list that directed them to try to use the device to complete real tasks.

The results showed that there was no difference between the groups regarding their performance on the questionnaire or online test. However, a significant difference was found in the performance of those with prior experience of other central heating timers, against those without. Although both groups performed at similar levels on the questionnaire, the group without prior experience outperformed those with prior experience on the online test. This suggests that the mental model of how this class of devices works that was gained from interactions with other central heating timers

only served to confuse participants when they interacted with this particular device.

Study 3. As one of the explanations for not replicating Trudel and Payne's findings with the CH timer was that it was a different class of device than the digital watch they had used, a study was conducted to investigate whether a replication of their result could be found using a more devicey-device. A simulated medical laser was identified as being an example of this class of device and two groups were tested following a period of free exploration with either a mouseclick limit or not.

It is expected that the results will confirm the hypothesis that improved levels of post-exploration performance will be found in the group who conduct their exploration with a limited amount of mouseclicks. This data will support the argument that increasing the cost of the interaction encourages reflection on the part of the user and discourages mindless clicking only when it is sufficient simply to learn what the function of each button on the device is.

Further Modeling. The empirical work above will be used to inform further developments of the model.

Acknowledgements
This research was supported by a post-graduate studentship by the Economic and Social Research Council and British Telecom.

References
Anderson, J. R., & Lebiere, C. (1999). The Atomic Components of Thought. Mahwah, New Jersey: Lawrence Erlbaum.

Cooper, R., & Fox, J. (1998). COGENT: A visual design environment for cognitive modeling. Behaviour Research Methods, Instruments and Computers, 30, 553-564.

Cox, A. L., & Young, R. M. (2000). Device-Oriented and Task-Oriented Exploratory Learning of Interactive Devices. Proceedings of Third International Conference on Cognitive Modeling, University of Groningen, Groningen, Netherlands.

Cox, A. L., & Young, R. M. (2001). A Closer Look at Exploratory Learning of Interactive Devices. Proceedings of Fourth International Conference on Cognitive Modeling, George Mason University, Fairfax, Virginia.

Rieman, J. (1996). A Field Study of Exploratory Learning Strategies. ACM Transactions on Computer-Human Interaction, 3(3), 189-218.

Trudel, C.-I., & Payne, S. J. (1995). Reflection and Goal Management in Exploratory Learning. International Journal of Human-Computer Studies, 42, 307-339.

Young, R. M., & Cox, A. L. (2000). A New Rational Framework for Modelling Exploratory Device Learning ... but does it Fit with ACT-R? Proceedings of 7th ACT-R Workshop, Carnegie Mellon University.

The influence of experienced effort on learning and choice of solution paths in a simple navigation task

Wai-Tat Fu (wfu@gmu.edu)
Human Factors & Applied Cognition
George Mason University
Fairfax, VA 22030 USA

Abstract

In my dissertation, I am going to study the influence of experienced effort on learning and problem-solving behavior. In a simple navigation task on a computer-simulated map, subjects have to acquire information on various levels of effort in different solution paths through experience. The experienced effort information allows subjects to improve their performance by finding faster solution paths on the map. I am planning to build ACT-R model to understand the underlying mechanisms. Specifically, I am interested in modeling the learning of the "current" effort and the "downstream" effort in ACT-R theory, and how each of them can influence problem-solving behavior in the task.

Introduction

For many problems, there are multiple solution paths that lead from the initial problem state to the goal state. Different paths may require different amount of time and effort. With experience, the problem-solver learns to choose solution paths that requires less time and effort, and as a result, performance improves. For example, if the problem is to drive to a particular destination in a city, numerous solution paths may exist. If the person is new to the city, very little knowledge is available to decide which paths to take. In this case, decisions on which paths to take may solely rely on simple heuristics, such as hill-climbing. Unless the city is extremely complex, simple heuristics are usually sufficient to lead the person to the destination. However, although simple heuristics are usually sufficient to provide a solution to the problem, there is no guarantee that the solution is good (or fast, in the current example). Fortunately, with experience, the person may be able to acquire information about the speeds for various routes in the city. With this kind of information, the person may be able to choose faster paths that lead to the destination. Although many cognitive mechanisms have been proposed to account for this kind of learning in problem solving (e.g. Anzai and Simon, 1979, Agre & Shrager, 1994, Lovett and Anderson, 1996), not many studies have directly addressed the effects of experienced effort in problem-solving, and how people learn to choose less effortful solution paths with experience. In my dissertation, I am going to design several experiments to understand how people acquire problem-specific information and how they use the information to improve their performance. Specifically, I will focus on how people learn the amount of effort involved in different solution paths, and how they improve performance by choosing the less effortful paths. I am planning to build cognitive models using ACT-R (Anderson & Lebiere, 1998) to understand the mechanisms behind this kind of learning. In this extended abstract, I will focus on describing the task and the model that I am planning to build.

The Task

I am going to use a simple navigation task in my experiments. In this task, subjects have to navigate from the starting point to the destination on a map, and multiple solution paths exist for all trials. Subjects are given maps as shown in Fig. 1, which shows the map of 3 transport systems, each represented by different colors (blue, green, and brown). Different transport systems have different speeds. Each circle in the map represents a station of one of the transport systems. To go from one transport system to the other, subjects have to use the transfers at the intersections of the transport systems. There are three different kinds of transfers (pink, orange, and black). Different transfers have different speeds.

In each trial, subjects are given a starting station (a blue circle) and a destination (a yellow circle), and the subjects are told that they have to go from the starting station to the destination. To do this, subjects have to click on the intermediate stations one by one until they reach the destination. When subjects click on an intermediate station, a little red line travels from the current station to the station just clicked on. The speeds of different transport systems are reflected by the speeds of the movement of the red line.

The subjects are instructed that different transport systems and transfers have different speeds, but are not told which one is faster and which one is slower. Since there are no numerical representations of the speeds, combining speeds of different transport systems is relatively inaccurate and difficult. This deters subjects from doing a complete mental look ahead from the starting station to the destination.

36 pairs of starting and end points are constructed so that simple hill-climbing will lead to suboptimal solutions. Since in the early trials, subjects do not have information about the speeds of different transport systems, the prediction is that simple hill-climbing strategy will be adopted – i.e. the most straightforward paths will be chosen. However, with experience, subjects will learn the relative speeds of different transport systems and transfer, and will be able to use this information to find faster paths that go from the starting point to the destination. Action, eyetracking, and verbal data are collected to understand how subjects make their decisions across trials.

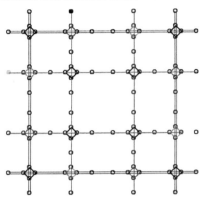

Fig. 1. The map used in the navigation task. There are three different transport systems, and three different transfers. Each of them has different speeds and represented by different colors.

The Model

I am planning to build an ACT-R model of the task. In ACT-R, procedural knowledge is represented as production rules. One of the central premises of the ACT-R theory is that the processes that act on the production rules reflect the statistical structure of the environment. For example, the process of selection among several production instantiations (conflict resolution) is based on the model's evaluation of their expected utility, and the one with the highest expected utility will be executed. The expected utility is calculated as the difference of the expected gain and the expected cost (PG-C) of executing the production. This conflict resolution mechanism allows for the influence of different levels of effort (cost) on the choice of solution paths. In my model, only effort will be taken in account. I believe this is a reasonable simplification, since eventually all paths lead to the destination, the probability of success does not play a significantly role in determining the choice of solution paths.

In ACT-R, the total effort C associated with a production is represented by the sum of two parameters:

a and b. ($C = a + b$) The a parameter represents the current effort in executing a particular production; the b parameter represents the downstream effort involved between the time after the current production is executed until the time when the current goal is accomplished (popped). The higher the sum of these values, the less likely the production will be executed. Since it is the sum of these two parameters that determine the result of the production selection, it is possible that the model would choose a production rule that has a high current effort (a), but a low downstream effort (b). Or in other words, the model would initially choose a slow path if the path chosen eventually would lead to a faster overall path.

In the beginning of the experiment, the values of the effort parameters for all productions will be the same. With experience, these parameters will be updated by the formula specified in ACT-R: $a^* = (z + \Sigma effort_i)/(\alpha + \beta + m + n)$, where z is the prior effort, $\Sigma effort_i$ is the total effort taken over all past uses of the production rule, α and β are the prior number of successes and failures, m and n are the experienced number of successes and failures. The formula for b^* is the same except that $\Sigma effort_i$ is the total amount of downstream effort taken over all past uses of the production rule.

Some interesting issues are whether subjects are equally sensitive to current and downstream effort, as implicitly assumed by the ACT-R theory. It is possible that people may weight the current effort more than downstream effort, especially when there is limited plan-ahead. If this is so, we may expect to see more localized improvement rather than gradual overall improvement in choosing better solution paths.

ACT-R therefore provides a theoretical basis for understanding the learning and use of experienced effort in problem-solving. By matching the data to the prediction made by the model, we should be able to have a better understanding of the underlying mechanisms for this kind of learning.

References

Agre, P. & Shrager, J. (1990). Routine evolution as the microgenetic basis of skill acquisition. *Twelfth Annual Conference of the Cognitive Science Society* (pp. 694-701), Hillsdale, NJ: Erlbaum.

Anderson, J. R., & Lebiére, C. (Eds.). (1998). *Atomic components of thought*. Hillsdale, NJ: Erlbaum.

Anzai, Y., & Simon, H. A. (1979). The theory of learning by doing. *Psychological Review*, 86 (2), 124-140.

Lovett, M. C. & Anderson, J. R. (1996). History of success and current context in problem solving. *Cognitive Psychology*, 31, 168-217.

Plural Morphology in Compounding is not Good Evidence to Support the Dual Mechanism model

Jenny Hayes (J.Hayes@Herts.ac.uk),
Psychology Department, University of Hertfordshire, College Lane, Hatfield, AL10 9AB, United Kingdom

Abstract

The compounding phenomena is considered to be good evidence to support the dual mechanism model of morphological processing (Pinker & Prince, 1992). However evidence from initial neural net modeling has shown that a single route associative memory based account might provide an equally, if not more valid explanation of the treatment of plurals in compounds. Further neural net modeling and empirical work is proposed to test this single route account.

Key words: Psycholinguistics, compounding, neural net modeling, connectionism

Introduction

The Compounding phenomenon Psycholinguistic research has shown that compound words with irregular plural nouns in non-head position (e.g. mice-eater) are produced far more frequently than compound words with regular plural nouns in non-head position (e.g. *rats-eater) (Gordon, 1985).

The Dual Mechanism Model's Explanation of Compounding It has been argued (Marcus, Brinkmann, Clahsen, Weise & Pinker, 1995) that the compounding phenomenon provides good evidence for the dual mechanism model of morphological processing (Pinker & Prince, 1992). The dual mechanism model proposes that irregular nouns and their plurals are stored as memorised pairs of words in the mental lexicon (e.g. mouse-mice) but that regular plurals are produced by the addition of the [−s] morpheme to the regular stem at a post lexical stage (e.g. rat + s = rats). Compounds are created in the lexicon by joining two stems together to form one word. Thus as irregular plurals are stored in the lexicon they are available to form compound words but as only the singular stems of regular nouns are stored in the lexicon the regular plural is never available to form compounds.

A Single Route Associative Memory Based Explanation of Compounding An explanation of the compounding phenomenon based on the frequency of occurrence of items in the linguistic input has not been considered to date. However an explanation of this sort may explain the treatment of both regular and irregular plurals in compounds (Murphy, 2000). The hypothesis has been put forward that children do not include the high type frequency regular [-s] plural morpheme in the middle of compounds because they

will always have heard it, and almost all other inflectional morphemes in English for that matter (Chandler, 1993), at the end of words (van Valin, personal communication). Thus, regular plurals are excluded from compounds due to an overwhelming input pattern in which the regular plural morpheme [-s] never occurs in the middle of words. Conversely, irregular plurals may appear in compounds as their usage is not guided by such a dominant input pattern. Irregular plurals have a much lower type frequency and while some irregulars are phonologically similar e.g. mouse-mice/ louse-lice; tooth-teeth/foot-feet/ goose-geese; man-men /woman-women there is no one dominant phonological pattern occurring in one particular place in the structure of English morphology.

An associative memory-based account of inflectional morphology has been investigated by numerous connectionist models. While the earliest connectionist model of inflectional morphology (Rumelhart & McClelland, 1986) was criticised for misrepresenting the input set available to children, subsequent models have successfully simulated the putative dissociation between regular and irregular inflection for both verbal morphology (Daugherty & Seidenberg, 1994) and plural morphology (Plunkett & Juola, 1999) using a single learning mechanism and no explicit rules. Thus it is entirely possible that a single route connectionist model could also simulate the behavioral dissociation between the treatment of regular and irregular plurals in compounds. Furthermore, as well as being able to learn mappings from input to output, connectionist models have also been able to learn sequential mappings (Elman 1990). Thus it is envisaged that a single route associative memory system could learn that the inclusion or omission of the regular plural morpheme [-s] is influenced by where that [-s] morpheme occurs in a sequence of language input.

Thesis Research Summary

Study 1: The Letter [-s] as a Predictor of Word Endedness An experiment has been carried out to test any role that [s] (either the letter or the morpheme) might play in indicating word endedness in a stream of concatenated letters. A neural network was trained on a concatenated stream of 200 sentences of child directed speech taken from the CHILDES (Child Language Data Exchange System) corpora (MacWhinney & Snow, 1985). The study was based on Elman (1990) who trained a simple recurrent network to discover word boundaries from a concatenated stream of letters. The network was required to predict the next letter it expected to occur given the letters it had seen previously. At the beginning of a word the error was high but as more letters were presented to the network the error decreased until it was at its lowest at the end of the word. It was hypothesised in that on a "next letter" prediction task of this kind, a neural network would learn that after the input [-s] there was a high probability that the next input would be a word ending marker i.e. that [-s] is a good predictor of word endedness.

The network's ability to learn that [–s] is a good predictor of word endedness was tested using 19 unseen words that ended in [-s] and 19 words that ended in other letters. The network was found to be more accurate (i.e. the error was lower) at predicting a word ending marker after an [-s] than after all other letters combined (t = -2.08, df =18, p= 0.05). The network's ability to learn that [-s] is a good predictor of word endedness was further tested by comparing the output for 5 unseen words that ended in [-s] with the output for 6 sets of 5 unseen words that ended in either [-d], [-e], [-g], [-l] [-r] and [-t] respectively. The difference between the mean error rate for a word ending marker after an [-s] was significantly lower than that recorded after [-l] (t = 5.63, df 4, p < 0.01) and [-r] (t=4.30, df 4, p = 0.01). However, while the mean error on predicting a word ending marker after [-s-] was also lower than the error rate for a word ending marker after [-d], [-e], [-g] and [-t] this difference was not significant.

As this model was intended to be a preliminary investigation of how the distribution of [-s] might influence its usage in compounds we can only draw tentative conclusions. However, it does seem that the presence of [-s] in the input is strongly associated with word endedness.

Study 2: Nouns never follow the plural [-s] morpheme
Frequency counts of child directed speech taken from the Wells corpus (1981), have shown that not only does the plural [-s] morpheme never occur in the middle of words it is also never followed by another noun. Thus further neural network modeling is planned in which it is hypothesised that on a syntactic class prediction task (Elman, 1990) that after the plural [-s] morpheme the error on predicting a noun will be much higher than the error on predicting any other syntactic class.

Further Neural net modeling In subsequent modeling the role that the possessive [-'s] morpheme may play in combination with the plural [-s] morpheme in predicting the next syntactic class will also be investigated. Several versions of the model are planned in which phonetic and semantic coding will be adopted.

Empirical Work Two empirical studies will also be carried out. The first study has examined whether presentation and response modality affect the rate at which plurals are included in compounds. The second empirical study will consider how word recognition might be impaired by the presence of inflectional morphology in the middle of words, as this is such an infrequent pattern in English.

Summary It is envisaged that it will be possible to show that a single route associative memory system can master the compounding phenomena. This will be achieved by demonstrating that the putative dissociation between regular and irregular plurals in compounds is due to learning that the regular plural [-s] morpheme is never present in the middle of a word and is never followed by a noun. If this is achieved, then an account, such as the dual mechanism model, which relies upon multiple forms of representation and learning mechanisms, is unwarranted.

References

Chandler, S. (1993). Are rules and modules necessary for explaining language? *Journal of Psycholinguistic Research, 22,* 593-606.

Daugherty, K. G. & Seidenberg, M. S. (1994). Beyond rules and exceptions. In S. D. Lima, R. L. Corrigan & G. K. Iverson (Eds.), *The reality of linguistic rules.* Amsterdam: John Benjamins.

Elman, J. L. (1990). Finding structure in time. *Cognitive Science, 14,* 179-211.

Gordon, P. (1985). Level-ordering in lexical development. *Cognition, 21 ,* 73-93.

MacWhinney, B. & Snow, C. E. (1985). The Child Language Data Exchange System. *Journal of Child Language, 12,* 271-296.

Marcus, G. F., Brinkmann, U., Clahsen, H., Weise, R. & Pinker, S. (1995). German inflection: The exception that proves the rule. *Cognitive Psychology, 29,* 189-256.

Murphy, V. A. (2000). Compounding and the representation of inflectional morphology. *Language Learning, 50,* 153-197.

Pinker, S. & Prince, A. (1992). Regular and irregular morphology and the psychological status of rules of grammar. In L. A. Sutton, C. Johnson, & R. Shields (Eds.), *Proceedings of the 17th Berkeley Linguistics Society* (pp.230-251).

Plunkett, K. & Juola, P. (1999). A connectionist model of English past tense and plural morphology. *Cognitive Science, 23,* 463-490.

Rumelhart D. E, & McClelland, J. L. (1986). On learning the past tense of English verbs. In J. L. McClelland, D. E. Rumelhart and the PDP Research Group (Eds.), *Parallel distributed processing: Explorations in the microstructure of cognition, Volume 2: Psychological and biological models.* Cambridge, MA: MIT Press.

Wells, C. G. (1981) *Learning through interaction: The study of language development.* Cambridge: Cambridge University Press.

Modeling User Knowledge and Semantic Structure for Information Extraction from Text

Peter M. Moertl (pmoertl@ou.edu)
University of Oklahoma
Department of Psychology, 455 West Lindsey Street
Norman, OK 73019 USA

Abstract

Latent Semantic Analysis (LSA, Landauer & Dumais, 1997) is used to represent user knowledge and to extract user relevant semantic structures from text. A model of user knowledge is created and empirically optimized. This model is then used to extract user relevant semantic structure from text. User model and quality of extracted semantic structure are empirically evaluated.

Information Extraction

Accessing large information spaces (e.g. the Internet) requires specific information retrieval tools in order to take advantage of such abundant resources. Information extraction concerns the exploration of information spaces: What information is contained in given texts?

Semantic structure of printed text is exhibited by tables of content, index terms, and book chapters that provide readers with fast access to content and organization of text. For the digital medium, semantic structure can be represented using hypertext links or graphical maps. These tools are based on the manual organization of human indexers.

Digital information sources, however, are often not thoroughly indexed but consist of "raw" text without explicit organization. Can semantic structure be extracted automatically? In order to make those information spaces available to users, automatic categorization tools have been developed (see e.g. Sanderson & Lawrie, 2000). Automatic categorization of text relies on information extraction mechanisms (see e.g. Lehnert 1997) that are able to relate extracted information to the knowledge of users.

Such information extraction and retrieval mechanisms however, usually do not make explicit assumptions about the specific knowledge of a user. Those algorithms often use word-document occurrence frequencies to estimate the likelihood of a match between query terms and retrieved information. Such algorithms allow the evaluation of information retrieval relevance only in comparison to query terms and are independent of the information seeker's knowledge. Relevance judgments of retrieved information, however, are complex processes along several variables (e.g. Mizzaro, 1997 proposes several "relevances"). One important variable is the specification of user knowledge which motivates approaches to model user knowledge (Billsus & Pazzani, 1999).

This project proposes a technique that integrates user knowledge representation with semantic structure extraction. A model of user knowledge is created and empirically optimized prior to the information extraction process. This model of user knowledge is then used to translate the semantic structure of sample texts into the terminology of the user.

Modeling Technique

LSA (Latent semantic analysis) has been proposed as a model and technique of knowledge representation (e.g. Landauer & Dumais, 1997). This model has been successful in matching human cognitive performance in tasks that involve semantic structure. LSA has been applied to assess textual coherence (Foltz, Kintsch, & Landauer, 1998), to retrieve documents (Derwester, Dumais, Furnas, Landauer & Harshman, 1990), to answer multiple-choice synonym questions, Landauer & Dumais, 1997), assess the quality of software interface labels (Soto 1998), and to aid the development of summarization skills (Kintsch, in press). Specifically, LSA has been shown to represent semantic structure of written essays and to match human judgments about essay quality by comparing it to prototypical essays (Foltz, Kintsch & Landauer, 1998).

LSA represents word meanings as vectors of principal components that are extracted from a word coocurrence matrix. The word-coocurrence matrix contains a count of occurrence of words in their context (e.g. a paragraph). Therefore, an LSA model of knowledge does not contain syntactic information but is solely based on word coocurrences. After initial transformations of this matrix (logarithmic weighting) a principal component analysis extracts components that are optimized to predict the initial matrix. These components are used to represent word meanings. The similarity between words is determined by the angle between the word vector. Landauer & Dumais (1997) for example found a very close match of LSA on selecting the correct synonym for a given word in a synonym test (Test of English as a foreign language, Educational Testing Service) with average test performance of foreign students. Moertl & Durso (2000) used LSA to represent knowledge contained in the FAA air traffic control manual (FAA 7110.65j) and measured representation quality using a multiple choice test on air traffic control. They report LSA performance of 45 % of correct answers (chance performance was 17 %).

Crucial for the LSA representation of knowledge is the optimal number of components. Optimal dimensionality is often tested empirically by, for example, comparing LSA-representations of answers to given question on a multiple choice test. The dimensionality that yields most correct responses is the optimal dimensionality of the representation.

Information Extraction Process

First a model of user knowledge is created from text that is representative for a given user population. The word-coocurrence structure of the text is analyzed and an LSA knowledge model is created. This model is empirically optimized by matching human performance on a test task. Having found the optimal dimensionality, the model of user knowledge is used to represent semantic structure of sample texts. Sample texts are translated into word representations of the user and the structure of word similarities is analyzed. Extracted semantic structure is empirically tested for quality and relevance to users using an information extraction task.

Keywords

Latent semantic analysis, knowledge extraction, information retrieval, information extraction, user modeling, knowledge representation.

References

Billsus, D. & Pazzani. M. J. (1999). A hybrid user model of an information retrieval system. UM99 User Modeling: Proceedings of the seventh international conference. 99-108. Springer, NewYork.

Derwester, S., Dumais, S. T., Furnas, G., W., Landauer, T. K. (1990). Indexing by Latent Semantic Analysis. Journal of the American Society for Information Science, 41(6), 391-407.

Federal Aviation Administration (1995), Air traffic control handbook (7110.65J). Washington DC.

Foltz, P. W., Kintsch, W. & Landauer, T. K. (1998). The measurement of textual coherence with latent semantic analysis. Discourse Processes, 25(2-3), 285-307.

Foltz, P. W., Laham, D. & Landauer, T. K. (1999). Automated Essay Scoring: Applications to Educational Technology. In proceedings of EdMedia '99.

Kintsch, E., Steinhart, D., Stahl, G. & LSA Research Group.(in press). Developing Summarization Skills through the Use of LSA-Based Feedback. Interactive Learning Environments.

Landauer, T., K. & Dumais, S., T. (1997). A Solution to Plato's Problem: The Latent Semantic Analysis Theory of Acquisition, Induction, and Representation of Knowledge. Psychological Review, 104(2), 211-240.

Lehnert, W. G. (1997). Information extraction: What have we learned? Discourse Processes, 23, 441-470.

Mizzaro, S. (1998). How many relevances in information retrieval? Interacting with Computers, 10(3), 303-320.

Moertl, P. M., Durso, F. T. (2000). Representing Knowledge in Air Traffic Control Using Latent Semantic Analysis. Presentation at the meeting of the Society for Applied Research in Memory and Cognition, Miami, June 7 – 8, 2000.

Sanderson, M., & Lawrie, D. (2000). Building, testing, and applying concept hierarchies. In W. B. Croft (Ed.).Advances in information retrieval, 235-262. Kluwer: Norwell, Massachussetts.

Soto, R. (1999). Learning and Performing by Exploration: Label Quality Measured by Latent Semantic Analysis. Proceedings of the Conference on Human Factors in Computing Systems, CHI '99, 418-425.

Statistical Learning of Human Faces

Anna Montagnini (montagni@sissa.it)
Cognitive Neuroscience Sector - SISSA; 2-4 Via Beirut,
Trieste, 34014 Italy

Abstract

We develop an approach to measure the statistical performance in *learning from noisy examples*, so as to draw a *learning curve*. Learning is quantified with a *distance-like* function, varying with the number of examples presented. Upper and lower benchmarks for the real learning curve can be considered, corresponding to an *ideal observer* and, to the other extreme, to a mere *random choice*. For the ideal observer, we consider some possible cognitive strategies for the identification of the stimuli, differing in the role of the features comprising the complex stimuli and in the amount of prior knowledge exploited. This theoretical framework can provide a tool for analysing experimental human performance in appropriate psychophysical tests.

Keywords: *Learning, Kullbach-Leibler divergence, complex stimuli, compositionality.*

Introduction

Real world objects come to our perception more as *noisy* examples of a certain set of complex stimuli, than as stable unchangeable entities. For example we can think at the set of human faces, on which we will mainly focus, or the set of popular songs, the set of food smells, etc. By *noisy examples* we mean all the slightly different forms in which an element of these sets can appear, producing a broad perceptual variability. The capability of correctly recognizing a given complex stimulus is therefore related to a sort of signal-to-noise discrimination ability. In other terms we have to *learn* the probability of appearance of the stimuli with some specific characteristics and this requires the observation of many different examples.

Interpretation of learning as "learning the underlying probability distribution" has been proposed at different levels of investigation, from language (Shannon, 1951) and to cognition (Anderson, 1991). Extensive numerical studies have been carried out with artificial neural networks and in general within the science of complexity (see for example Seung, Sompolinsky & Tishby (1992) and Bialek, Nemenman & Tishby (2000)).

The leading idea here is to produce a model cognitive task in which learning can be quantified, making it possible to compare the results of a psychophysical experiment with theoretical benchmarks. We are particularly interested in the role of the feature compositionality of stimuli in learning, therefore the degree of statistical complexity is an important parameter for our model cognitive task. We consider human faces as a suitable realization of the stimuli for this task.

Modeling a face identification test

The learning process is analysed with a numerical simulation reproducing a test: at each step n the module "partial stimulus presentation-subject completion (response)-correct completion" is simulated. The simulation has been thought and implemented as a theoretical template for a real psychophysical test on the identification of human faces, which we are at the moment carrying out with volunteers.

Our stimulus set contains p prototypes (we can imagine them as *identikit* images) and noisy versions of them (obtained with one or more of the N components modified). Examples for simultaneously training and testing the subjects are selected from the stimulus set following an *a priori* statistics, which simply sets the probability of modifying any component from its prototypical value. In the test the subject is shown with a partial cue (an incomplete face) and has to choose the missing elements (nose, mouth, eyes...) among different versions to complete the configuration. Following this subject response, the stimulus is completed anew according to the *prior* statistics. These complete configurations are stored in memory and they remain available for the following of the test.

Measuring learning

We assess learning as an approach to the hidden statistics of the set of stimuli, rather than as an increase in correct responses. After learning, an ideal student will respond according to the optimal strategy, i.e. filling the various response-states with a frequency distribution f_i which shadows the *a priori* probability distribution of complete stimuli p_i. Therefore a measure of learning can be related to the distance between these two distributions. We use the Kullbach-Leibler divergence $\Delta(n)$ (Cover & Thomas, 1991), which is a *quasi distance* (it is not symmetric) between f_i and p_i. Here the index i labels all the possible noisy configurations and n is the number of presentations.

Our learning curve reads, then

$$\Delta(n) = \sum_i f_i(n) \, \log_2 \left(\frac{f_i(n)}{p_i} \right). \qquad (0.1)$$

$\Delta(n)$ is always positive and it is expected to decrease with n, if learning occurs. Indeed, as f_i approaches p_i (perfect learning), $\Delta(n)$ vanishes.

Different individuals, different strategies

In our simulation we consider two limit type of subjects: an *ideal observer*, who knows the complete stimulus distribution already before the first example and responds accordingly and, on the other extreme, a subject who always responds at random, no matter how many examples have been presented. The Δ "learning" curves for these two subjects, neither of whom *really learns*, constitute theoretical benchmarks for real learning subjects, who should exhibit an intermediate behaviour.

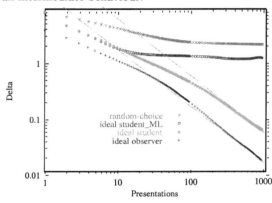

Figure 1: Examples of "learning" curves

A third type of individual can be simulated, the *ideal student*, who actually *does learn* the statistics from the examples with an optimal progression from ignorance to knowledge. This subject does not use any prior knowledge about stimuli; at any step he can access the memory deposit where the sequence of preceding configurations is stored and exploits the statistical information available therein for the response. An analytical evaluation of the asymptotic behaviour ($\sim \frac{1}{n}$) for the average Δ learning curve can be derived when perfect learning occurs and f_i converges to p_i.

Learning depends crucially also on the specific cognitive strategy used. In our simulated test a key

factor is whether the cooccurrence of face components is taken to be relevant in itself, or only in association to a specific prototype. We analysed therefore two possible strategies for the ideal observer and the ideal student, one of which is based on a *Maximum-Likelihood* estimate of the preferred face. Qualitative differences appear in the corresponding Δ curves.

In Figure 1, sample average "learning" curves for an ideal observer, for the random choice and for two ideal students are shown. The asymptotic $\frac{1}{n}$ behaviour is reached for both the ideal observer and one ideal student, as the straight lines in this log-log scale show. The *Maximum-Likelihood* strategy prevents the learning curve for the second ideal student (indicated as "ML") from decreasing to 0 and Δ converges to a finite value.

Discussion

The numerical simulation of a learning process for ideal subjects allowed us to establish the suitable range of parameters to design a psychophysical test for real subjects. A comparison with the simulation will be possible on the basis of the Δ learning curve, once the results of the test to human subjects will be complete. This will allow us to derive some indications about the cognitive strategy used in a face identification task in presence of noise.

It has been shown that processing of faces and other complex visual objects involves selective neural activity in a number of brain areas in the visual pathway of primates (Rolls, 1992 and Tanaka, 1993). We are planning now to use layered neural networks as an alternative benchmark system for the processing of complex stimuli. This might allow us to capture some features in the brain functions underlying this cognitive process.

References

Anderson J.R. (1991), Is human cognition adaptive? *Behavioral and Brain Sciences* **14**, 471–517.

Bialek W., Nemenman I. & Tishby N. (2000), Predictability, Complexity and Learning, available at *http://xxx.lanl.gov/abs/physics/0007070*.

Cover T. & Thomas J. (1991), *Elements of Information Theory*, Wiley.

Rolls E.T. (1992), Neurophysiological mechanisms underlying face processing within and beyond the temporal cortical visual areas, *Phil. Trans.R.Soc.Lond.B*, **335**, 11–21.

Seung H.S., Sompolinsky H. & Tishby T. (1992), Statistical mechanics of learning from examples, *Phys.Rev.A*, **45**, 6056–6091.

Shannon C.E. (1951), Prediction and entropy of printed English, *Bell Sys.Tech.J.*,**30**, 50–64.

Tanaka K. (1993), Neuronal mechanisms for object recognition, *Science*, **262**, 685–688.

SHRUTI-agent: a structured connectionist model of decision-making

Carter Wendelken (carterw@icsi.berkeley.edu)
International Computer Science Institute
1947 Center Street, Suite 600
Berkeley, CA 94704 USA

Abstract

A neurally plausible connectionist model of decision-making, based on the SHRUTI architecture, is being developed. Toward this end, issues of appropriate connectionist representations for belief and utility, necessary control mechanisms, and reinforcement-based learning are addressed.

Introduction

One particularly fascinating aspect of the mind/brain is the question of how it enables us to make decisions. I am approaching this question through the use of computational modeling. In particular, I am developing a neurally plausible connectionist model that is capable of assimilating information, making inferences, simulating and performing actions, seeking to fulfill goals, and learning useful behaviors. My immediate goal is to build a working system that is strongly constrained by the requirement of neural plausibility. Although I am not trying to model any particular set of psychological data per se, I do expect ultimately to produce a model that correctly predicts a good range of psychological data, and more importantly, one that also explains some of the brain circuitry behind it. The foundation of this connectionist model is SHRUTI [Shastri and Ajjanagadde, 1993], which demonstrates how a system of neuron-like elements can encode a large body of relational causal knowledge and provide a basis for rapid evidential inference. The overall aim of this project is to develop a decision-making system, SHRUTI-agent. Within this framework, there are several important questions that are being addressed: (1) How can the existing connectionist representation of belief and utility be extended to support decision-making? (2) What kinds of control mechanisms are needed, on top of the existing spreading activation model, in order to enable effective decision making, and how can these control mechanisms be implemented in a neurally plausible manner? (3) How can a SHRUTI-agent with a limited world model learn the right concepts and rules to make decision-making more efficient?

The SHRUTI model

At the core of the SHRUTI model is the idea of the focal cluster - a grouping of nodes of different types that participate in a common representation. Rules are encoded as connections between relational predicate focal clusters, and a type hierarchy is involves connections between entity and category focal clusters. Inference occurs as spreading activation over this representational substrate. Importantly, variable binding is accomplished by means of temporal synchrony, specifically synchronous firing of relational role nodes and the corresponding entity or category nodes. Long-term memory is encoded via temporal pattern matching circuits.

Recent developments with the SHRUTI model include: (1) extension to handle various forms of evidence combination [Shastri and Wendelken, 1999], (2) demonstration that approximately correct probabilistic reasoning can be acheived in this framework and that much of the model structure can be learned by means of an associative learning mechanism similar to Hebbian learning [Wendelken and Shastri, 2000], (3) development of mechanisms to support coherent interpretations of events [Shastri and Wendelken, 2000]

A representation of utility has been developed (initial work on this was done by Lokendra Shastri in collaboration with Bryan Thompson and Marvin Cohen). This consists primarily of a set of utility nodes associated with each predicate focal cluster, reward facts denoting reward and punishment, value facts denoting learned utility values, and probabilistically weighted utility-carrying connections between predicates. Some additional connectionist structures (e.g inhibitory links) support more complex utility inferences. Belief and utility representations in SHRUTI are tightly integrated, sharing much of the same structure, and are not separate modules in any conventional sense. Assertion of a particular goal, via activation of a utility node, leads in the simplest case to assertion of its potential causes as subgoals, via spreading activation backward along the causal chain. Belief in some predicate can lead to internal reward or punishment or recognition that such reward or punishment is likely.

Decision-Making and Control

With suitable representations of belief and utility in place, the ongoing task is development of neurally plausible connectionist mechanisms that enable effective decision-making. SHRUTI's causal model, integrated with utility, defines a sort of policy. The question to answer is how this can become the basis for a decision-

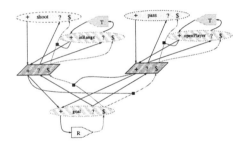

Figure 1: The connectionist structure for a simple soccer scenario, showing collector, enabler, and utility links.

making agent. Some decisions, involving selection of single actions or sequences of independent actions, can be made quite easily. Simple decisions often require only the spreading of activity from evidence nodes down to goals and from goal nodes back to relevant actions, without systematic consideration of alternatives. Complex decisions, which involve selecting sequences of interdependent actions, cannot be handled quite so simply. The spreading activation mechanisms of SHRUTI prove inadequate to the task of complex decision-making, and so something more is needed. One solution to this problem involves utilizing some form of control mechanism to overcome the limitations of spreading activation. In this context, any mechanism that functions substantially differently from the existing spreading activation model, but operates on it in some fashion, can be called a control mechanism. For example, a controller might test different action sequences in turn, posit certain predicates, attend preferentially to specific subgoals, and so forth. Importantly, there should be many simple control mechanisms, not some central homuncular controller. It is a major goal of this work to determine what sorts of control mechanisms are needed for effective decision-making and then to develop neurally plausible connectionist implementations of these proposed mechanisms.

MDPFC model   One control mechanism is being developed specifically as a model of mid-dorsolateral prefrontal cortex. The proposal here is that the specific role of MDPFC is to establish dynamic bindings between items maintained in working memory and different roles of spatial relations, for the purpose of organizing those working memory items [Wendelken, 2001]. This hypothesis is based on a considerable amount of evidence from lesion and imaging studies, as well as observations of regional connectivity. Clearly, the ability to organize actions in this manner would be useful for complex decision-making and planning.

Learning and Neural Reinforcement

The need for controlled processing associated with making some decisions can often be reduced or eliminated when the agent learns a better representation of the problem. This may involve learning new predicates, con-

juncts of existing predicates, or new rules. Ultimately, the mind/brain must choose what concepts to represent and also what relations between concepts to remember in a manner that supports effective decision-making. In order to do this, neural reinforcement is essential. In the SHRUTI-agent, the utility network, and in particular reward facts, provide the primary model of neural reinforcement. Global mechanisms, reflecting neuromodulation, may also play a role. I will explore with the SHRUTI-agent architecture several different mechanisms through which neural reinforcement enables a connectionist system to learn about the world and how to act therein.

Summary

The encoding of utility alongside belief as part of SHRUTI's connectionist architecture provides a neurally plausible mechanism for reasoning about preferences and a strong basis for creating a decision-making agent. Development of connectionist mechanisms for executive control of decision-making is ongoing. Once these are adequately developed and implemented, substantive experimentation on real decision-making tasks, and comparison to human performance, can begin. Concurrently, the SHRUTI-agent will be extended to incorporate reinforcement-based learning of elements of the model structure. It is expected that the resulting system will contribute significantly to an understanding of how decision-making can take place in the human mind/brain.

Acknowledgments   This work was partially funded by NSF grants SBR-9720398 and ECS-9970890.

References

[Shastri and Ajjanagadde, 1993] Shastri, L. and Ajjanagadde, V. (1993). From simple associations to systematic reasoning. *Behavioral and Brain Sciences*, 16(3):417–494.

[Shastri and Wendelken, 1999] Shastri, L. and Wendelken, C. (1999). Soft computing in shruti. In *Proceedings of the Third International Symposium on Soft Computing*, pages 741–747, Genova, Italy.

[Shastri and Wendelken, 2000] Shastri, L. and Wendelken, C. (2000). Seeking coherent explanations - a fusion of structured connectionism, temporal synchrony, and evidential reasoning. In *Proceedings of the Twenty-Second Conference of the Cognitive Science Society*, Philadelphia.

[Wendelken, 2001] Wendelken, C. (2001). The role of mid-dorsolateral prefrontal cortex in working memory: a connectionist model. In *submitted*.

[Wendelken and Shastri, 2000] Wendelken, C. and Shastri, L. (2000). Probabilistic inference and learning in a connectionist causal network. In *Proceedings of the Second International Symposium on Neural Computation*.

Author Index